OXFORD READINGS IN FEMINISM

Feminism, the Public and the Private

Edited by

Joan B. Landes

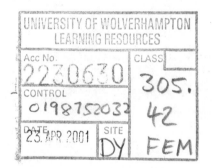

Oxford · New York

OXFORD UNIVERSITY PRESS

1998

Oxford University Press, Great Clarendon Street, Oxford OX2 6DP

Oxford New York
Athens Auckland Bangkok Bogota Bombay
Buenos Aires Calcutta Cape Town Dar es Salaam
Delhi Florence Hong Kong Istanbul Karachi
Kuala Lumpur Madras Madrid Melbourne
Mexico City Nairobi Paris Singapore
Taipei Tokyo Toronto Warsaw

and associated companies in
Berlin Ibadan

Oxford is a trade mark of Oxford University Press

Published in the United States
by Oxford University Press Inc., New York

Introduction and Selection © Oxford University Press 1998

British Library Cataloguing in Publication Data
Data available

Library of Congress Cataloging in Publication Data
Data available

ISBN 0–19–875203–2
ISBN 0–19–875202–4 (Pbk.)

Typeset by Graphicraft Typesetters Ltd., Hong Kong
Printed in Great Britain
on acid-free paper by
Bookcraft (Bath) Ltd
Midsomer Norton, Somerset

Contents

III. Gendered Sites in the Late Modern Public Sphere

IV. Public and Private Identity: Questions for a Feminist Public Sphere

Notes on Contributors

DAVID BELL teaches Cultural Studies at Staffordshire University.

SEYLA BENHABIB is Professor of Government at Harvard University and Senior Research Fellow at the Center for European Studies. She is the author of *Critique, Norm and Utopia: The Normative Foundations of Critical Theory* (Columbia University Press, 1987); *Situating the Self: Gender, Community and Postmodernism in Contemporary Ethics* (Routledge, 1992); *The Reluctant Modernism of Hannah Arendt* (Sage, 1996); and together with Judith Butler et al., *Feminist Contentions: A Philosophical Exchange* (Routledge, 1995).

LAUREN BERLANT teaches English at the University of Chicago. She is author of *The Anatomy of National Fantasy: Hawthorne, Utopia, and Everyday Life* (Chicago University Press, 1991) and *The Queen of America Goes to Washington City: Essays on Sex and Citizenship* (Duke University Press, 1997).

JON BINNIE teaches Human Geography and Criminal Justice at Liverpool John Moores University. His research and teaching interests include the sexual politics of consumption, migration, and nationhood, and he is currently writing a book on sexual citizenship with David Bell.

WENDY BROWN is Professor of Women's Studies and Legal Studies at University of California, Santa Cruz, and Visiting Professor of Political Science at University of California, Berkeley. Her most recent book is *States of Injury: Power and Freedom in Late Modernity* (Princeton University Press, 1995).

JULIA CREAM did a Ph.D. at University College London. She now works for Sense, the National Deafblind and Rubella Association, in London.

LEONORE DAVIDOFF is a Research Professor in Social History in the Sociology Department at the University of Essex. She is the Founding Editor of the journal *Gender and History* and co-author with Catherine Hall of *Family Fortunes: Men and Women of the English Middle Class 1780–1850* (Hutchinson and University of Chicago Press, 1987).

MARY G. DIETZ is Professor of Political Science at the University of Minnesota. She is the author of *Between the Human and the Divine: The*

Political Thought of Simone Weil (Rowman & Littlefield, 1988) and the editor of *Thomas Hobbes and Political Theory* (University Press of Kansas, 1990). Her essays have focused on Machiavelli, Arendt, and Habermas, as well as on feminism, citizenship, and the meaning of politics.

NANCY FRASER is Professor of Political Science in the Graduate Faculty of the New School for Social Research. She is the author of *Justice Interruptus: Rethinking Key Concepts of a 'Postsocialist' Age* (Routledge, 1997) and *Unruly Practices: Power, Discourse and Gender in Contemporary Social Theory* (University of Minnesota Press and Polity Press, 1989), the co-author of *Feminist Contentions: A Philosophical Exchange* (Routledge, 1994), and the co-editor of *Revaluing French Feminism: Critical Essays on Difference, Agency, and Culture* (Indiana University Press, 1992). Professor Fraser is also the co-editor of the journal *Constellations*.

BONNIE HONIG is Professor of Political Science at Northwestern University. She is the author of Political Theory and the Displacement of Politics (Cornell University Press, 1993), and editor of Feminist Interpretations of Hannah Arendt (Penn State University Press, 1995). Her latest book, *No Place Like Home: Democracy and the Politics of Foreignness* is forthcoming from Princeton University Press.

ERICA JONG, poet, novelist and essayist, is best known for her six best-selling novels and six award-winning collections of poetry. Her work has been translated into twenty-seven languages. Known for her commitment to women's rights, authors' rights, and free expression, Ms. Jong is a frequent lecturer in the U.S. and abroad. Her latest book, *Inventing Memory: A Novel of Mothers and Daughters*, published by HarperCollins in July, 1997, is a four-generational story told from the point of four women whose lives span the twentieth century.

BARBARA KRUGER is an artist who works in pictures and words.

MARILYN LAKE holds a Personal Chair in History at La Trobe University in Melbourne, Australia. Her recent books include *Creating a Nation: A Feminist History of Australia* (McPhee Gribble and Viking Penguin, 1994), co-authored with Patricia Grimshaw, Ann McGrath, and Marian Quartly. She is currently writing a history of feminist political thought in Australia.

JOAN B. LANDES is Professor of Women's Studies and History at The Pennsylvania State University, University Park. She is the author of

Women and the Public Sphere in the Age of the French Revolution (Cornell University Press, 1988).

W. J. T. MITCHELL teaches literature and art history at the University of Chicago, and is editor of *Critical Inquiry*. His most recent book, *Picture Theory*, won the College Art Association's Morey Prize for Art History in 1996, and the University of Chicago Press's Laing Prize in 1997.

SHERRY B. ORTNER is Professor of Anthropology at Columbia University. She has published extensively on feminist theory, social and cultural theory, and Sherpa ethnography.

CAROLE PATEMAN is Professor of Political Science, University of California, Los Angeles, and Adjunct Professor in the Research School of Social Sciences, Australian National University. Her books include *Participation and Democratic Theory* (Cambridge University Press, 1970) and *The Sexual Contract* (Stanford University Press and Polity Press, 1988).

ANNE PHILLIPS is Professor of Politics at London Guildhall University. Her books include *Engendering Democracy* (Pennsylvania State University Press, 1991), *Democracy and Difference* (Pennsylvania State University Press, 1993) and *The Politics of Presence* (Oxford University Press, 1995).

MARY P. RYAN is Professor of History and Women's Studies at the University of California, Berkeley. Her most recent book is entitled *Civic Wars: Democracy and Public Life in the American City during the Nineteenth Century* (University of California Press, June 1997).

GILL VALENTINE is a lecturer in Geography at the University of Sheffield. She is co-editor of *Mapping Desire: Geographies of Sexualities* (Routledge, 1995) and co-author of *Consuming Geographies* (Routledge, 1997).

JENNIFER WICKE is Professor of Comparative Literature at New York University. She has written extensively in the areas of nineteenth- and twentieth-century literature, critical thought, gender and feminist theory, and cultural studies.

PATRICIA J. WILLIAMS is a professor of law at Columbia University. She is a columnist for *The Nation* magazine and is the author of numerous publications, including the books, *The Rooster's Egg*, *The Alchemy of Race and Rights*, and *On Seeing a Colorblind Future*.

IRIS MARION YOUNG teaches Ethics and Political Theory in the Graduate School of Public and International Affairs at the University of Pittsburgh. Her most recent book is entitled *Intersecting Voices: Dilemmas of Gender, Political Philosophy, and Policy* (Princeton University Press, 1997).

Introduction

Joan B. Landes

Claiming that 'the personal is political', second-wave feminists boldly challenged the myths supporting conventional notions of the family and personal life.[1] Far from being a platform for personal fulfilment, in feminist writings the private sphere first figured as a site of sexual inequality, unremunerated work, and seething discontent. In Betty Friedan's evocative formulation, the housewife—the ideal woman of the post-Second World War years in the United States and other advanced industrial societies—suffered silently from a 'problem that has no name'.[2] Housewives, however, were only the tip of the iceberg. Students and civil rights activists, married and single women, heterosexuals and lesbians joined the ranks of a resurgent feminist movement which began to name the problems accompanying woman's multiple roles as wife, mother, sexual companion, worker, and political subject. Feminism offered women a public language for their private despair. Consciousness-raising groups and feminist organizations provided women with a route out of private isolation and into public activism. In the burgeoning field of feminist theory accompanying this new phase of activism, the problem of sexual subordination came to be linked closely to the division of public and private life. Breaking the silences of personal life, feminists sought the grounds for a more egalitarian private and public sphere. This last point bears repeating. Whereas it is commonly assumed that feminists, like women, are preoccupied with personal life, feminism's contribution to the theory and practice of a more robust, democratic public sphere is sometimes overlooked. As the slogan 'The Personal Is Political' attests, a feminist movement moves in two directions, placing the gendered organization of both public and private space at centre stage.

Feminists did not invent the vocabulary of public and private, which in ordinary language and political tradition have been intimately linked. The term 'public' suggests the opposite of 'private':

1

that which pertains to the people as a whole, the community, the common good, things open to sight, and those things that are accessible and shared by all. Conversely, 'the private' signifies something closed and exclusive, as in the admonition 'Private property—no trespassing'. The opposition between public and private is a distinguishing feature of both liberal and republican political argument, yet they offer practically opposing assessments of these two core terms. Liberals associate privacy with freedom: they value the private sphere and defend the individual's right to privacy against interference by other persons or the state. In contrast, republicans regard the private, which they associate with the body and its needs, as pertaining to those things that ought to be hidden from view. In turn, they associate the public with freedom, or acting in concert with others on behalf of the common good.

Feminism does not map comfortably onto either of these traditions, though, like republicans, feminists value public participation and, like liberals, they see the need to expand the contents of personal freedom. However, by focusing political attention on the private sphere feminists have challenged the effects of keeping the body and things sexual hidden from view; and they have denied that inherited views of freedom have applied equally to all people or to all aspects of the person. Does liberty, feminists ask, require that we sacrifice emotions to reason or domestic matters to public affairs? Feminism has therefore upset the firm divisions between public and private matters, which both liberals and republicans in their way maintain. Both theory and history have had a role to play in shaping new feminist understandings. Historians have exposed the changing, gendered contents of public and private life. By engaging with critical theory, structuralist, and post-structuralist arguments, theorists have explored the gendered construction of individual and social identity. In short, among modern oppositional movements, feminism is unrivalled in its contribution to a deepening understanding of the historical, symbolic, and practical effects of the organization of public and private life. The selections in this volume represent the exciting range of dialogue opened by feminist theorists on these topics. They are multi-disciplinary in scope, and they reflect the historical and cross-cultural orientations of feminist scholarship over the past several decades.

In comparison to the intense questioning of private life characteristic of the late 1960s and 1970s, repeated reference to the private in the public discourse of the 1990s might almost seem like the 'return of the repressed'. As before, critics and defenders of the body, the family, and the (gendered) person contest for public space. Yet across the political spectrum there is a heightened attention to privacy issues. This is not a simple case of the turning of the wheel. Indeed, many who protest vehemently on behalf of the individual are the first to advocate the use of state power to regulate the individual body and to restrict personal freedom. In this atmosphere, feminists have become ever more mindful of the need to safeguard personal identity and the body, while re-valuing the sphere of privacy. This has not meant an abandonment of the political in favour of the private or the forfeiture of a critical perspective on private life, the *sine qua non* of second-wave feminism. Rather, feminists have shown how the line between public and private is constantly being renegotiated. The most adamant defence of the private, Seyla Benhabib observes, necessarily involves bringing 'private matters' to public light. Calling attention to the mutual imbrication of public and private life, feminist theorists appreciate that lines between public and private life have been drawn and will continue to be drawn. However, the very act of description involves power. As Nancy Fraser points out, 'not everyone stands in the same relation to privacy and publicity; some have more power than others to draw and defend the line.'

Feminist theorists want to know whether the public/private distinction is universal, how it has emerged with singular force in certain times and places, and, not least, what accounts for the stability and instability of the boundaries that separate these regions of social life. A further complexity concerns the essentializing impulse of so much of what passes for a public discourse on public and private matters. As the readings in this volume attest, the public/private distinction provides a valuable lens through which to view issues of gender identity, on the one hand, and feminist politics, on the other.

I. THE PUBLIC/PRIVATE DISTINCTION IN FEMINIST THEORY

Feminists have always vacillated between optimism about the opportunities for social change and despair over the stubborn fact of female subordination. They have debated whether or not women's subordination is a universal feature of all human society or a product of specific historical circumstances. In her essay 'Is Female to Male as Nature Is to Culture?' Sherry Ortner puts the case for universal oppression in the starkest possible terms, but she locates its source not in biology but in the symbolic organization of human culture. Drawing upon Simone de Beauvoir and Claude Lévi-Strauss, Ortner posits that women are everywhere more associated with nature than culture, with activities that are more immanent, unmediated, and embedded in things. In contrast, men's relationships are more transcendent and transformative of persons and objects. Agreeing with Michelle Rosaldo and others who see a public/domestic split in all human societies, Ortner links women's association with the domestic context to their identification with a lower order of social and cultural organization.[3] Even women's equality in the institutions of public and private life will not resolve the problem of universal social devaluation, unless the ambivalent symbolic structures of gender are somehow dislodged.

Yet not all feminists were committed to a critique of the private sphere or to altering inherited gender patterns. By the early 1980s, 'pro-family' feminists began to defend women's role as mothers as the necessary basis for gender identity and feminist political consciousness. Pro-family feminists also sought to protect the private world of the family and personal life from all political intrusion, whether from meddlesome state policies or feminist politicization of the personal sphere. Focusing on the work of Jean Bethke Elshtain, Mary G. Dietz objects to such a maternalist vision of democratic political action or feminist political discourse. Dietz argues that democratic citizenship is constituted by the distinctive political bond between equal citizens, rather than by the exclusive and decidedly unequal relationship, even if benign or loving, between a mother and her child. Furthermore, Dietz charges maternalist feminists with committing the error of dividing the world 'naturally and abstractly into dual realms', with which they fault their liberal opponents. Thus, Elshtain posits a spurious choice between a virtuous private and an arrogant public existence. Dietz regards such notions as politically barren, and fruitless for interpreting the historical scope of women's public actions. It is not the superiority of one realm over the other but the nature of political action that decides the character of democratic politics. Even when women are motivated to act in public because of their position as mothers, what counts is how they act to transform their private concerns into public matters in concert with others.

Dietz calls for a feminist political theory that does not conflate democratic public life either with bureaucratic statist politics or with the values of intimacy. Her arguments set the stage for the continuing feminist engagement with the writings of Jürgen Habermas and Hannah Arendt, leading theorists of the public sphere, beginning in the 1980s down to the present day. Habermas's emphasis on accessibility, openness, democratic publicity, and equality seemed a congenial starting-point for an orientation to a non-state-dominated sphere of public life, as was Arendt's perspective on equality, freedom, and novelty in political life. In contrasting ways, both philosophers addressed the split between public and private life in modern society so central to feminist analysis. Neither, however, fully confronted the exclusion of women from public life, or queried the operations of gender difference. Yet there does exist now a lively appreciation of the category of the public sphere for feminist theory, and the latter has proved enormously productive for feminist investigations in and across numerous fields—including history, philosophy, literature, sociology, media and cultural studies. The contrasting selections by Benhabib and Honig foreground many of the arguments that animate the critical appropriation by feminists of liberal and democratic theories in later sections of this collection.

Seyla Benhabib compares the agonistic, legalistic, and discursive models of public space in the writings of Hannah Arendt, Jürgen Habermas, and the liberal tradition. Against liberal formalism, she upholds Arendt's view of both the agonistic and associational dimensions of political action. However, Benhabib objects to the rigid, gendered boundary established by Arendt between the public and the private, and to the masculinist and class implications of Arendt's version of agonistic public space. Similarly, she worries that oppositions between justice and the good life or public norms and private values in Habermas's model of discursive politics operate to reinstate the public/private boundary that has led to the exclusion of women and their point of view from moral theory. Benhabib argues that a theory of the public sphere (or universalist morality) must take account of difference—especially the differences in the experiences of male and female subjects in all domains of life. She finds the possibility of the democratization of the private as well as the public arena within a reconstructed, feminist version of Habermas's discourse model of publicity. In place of Habermas's universal public, Benhabib advocates alternative publics. She would bring the realm of moral emotions and

5

everyday moral interactions with concrete others into the domain of moral argument. While challenging traditionalist understandings of the public/private split, Benhabib still insists that a feminist project for the democratization of public and private does not obviate the need for some distinction between the private and the public. The discourse model is based upon a strong assumption of individual autonomy and consent.

Bonnie Honig is also concerned to enhance the possibilities for individuality, though she disputes any version of feminism that is based on a stable, expressive identity for women. She also turns to Arendt, but not from the perspective of discourse politics. Rather, Honig regards Arendt as a theorist of agonistic and performative action who offers feminists a way of engaging with 'entrenched distinctions between a public and a private realm'. Agonistic feminist politics struggles 'to achieve and enable individuation by interrupting conventional practices of sex/gender and decentring the would-be primacy of conventional sex/gender binaries'. From Honig's feminist/postmodernist perspective, 'nothing is ontologically protected from politicization'—neither the binary dichotomy separating political space into public and private zones nor even the prevailing constructions of sex and gender that similarly bind gender identities in binary form. In sum, the selections in Part I pose the question of what effect a feminist politics will have on the shape and content of gender identities, on the one hand, or public/private divisions, on the other. Furthermore, does feminism itself draw upon established female identities, or does it release women from the constraints of pre-existing definitions of woman? How in any case have such definitions of gender come to coexist with the shape and content of public and private life?

II. GENDER IN THE MODERN LIBERAL PUBLIC SPHERE

The gendered organization of public and private space is re-examined in an historical framework in the selections composing Part II. Drawing on examples from the eighteenth to the twentieth centuries, feminist scholars take up theoretical and political questions concerning the public sphere and female publicity, space and sexuality, identity and action, and gender and citizenship in France, Britain, the United States, and Australia. Although there is no one model of public space and public speech that has won feminist allegiance, feminists have devoted considerable attention to the category of the public sphere. As already suggested, Jürgen Habermas's theory of the public sphere has been an especially fruitful point of departure for many feminists. My own essay surveys many of the questions opened by a critical feminist engagement with his work, from the standpoint of the gendered development of public and private life in eighteenth-century France. I contend that Habermas's idealized model of the universal public fails to account for the ways in which a system of (Western) cultural representation eclipsed women's interests in the private domain and aligned femininity with particularity, interest, and partiality. Consequently, 'he misses the masquerade through which the (male) particular was able to posture behind the veil of the universal.' Therefore, I argue for a more robust and embodied concept of the subject, and suggest that Habermas's discourse model of politics be supplemented with accounts of non-verbal and non-textual forms of representation in a variety of (non-print) media. Similarly, Arendt's view of the public sphere as generating a 'space of appearances' may shed light on the way in which men achieved a new form of political embodiment through action within the French revolutionary public sphere. However, Arendt ignores the way in which women—and their bodies—were simultaneously excluded from public participation and rights. I conclude that a democratic and feminist reconstruction of public-sphere theory needs to take account of the gendered construction of embodied subjectivities within both public and private life.

Leonore Davidoff also addresses the association of masculine and feminine identities with the institutional development of separate spheres, while appreciating that the terms 'public' and 'private' simultaneously express a constantly shifting social and psychic world. Focusing broadly on nineteenth-century England, she proposes that gendered notions of public and private also interact with the institutions of private property and the market, as well as with notions of rational individualism. Davidoff charts the gendered creation of various public domains that had rational man at its centre and embodied woman at the periphery. Observing that the masculine domination of the public was never unproblematic, she calls attention to nineteenth-century British women's participation in the semi-public realm of 'the social' as charity workers or volunteers, and their role as feminist political activists.

Mary Ryan is also concerned with the gendered construction of citizenship and the distinctive experience of women citizens in the nineteenth century. Drawing on American rather than European materials, she offers a counter-narrative to Habermas's account of the rise and subsequent decline of the early liberal public sphere. Like Landes and Benhabib, she finds that in reality the democratic public sphere never achieved the unified, abstract, or wholly egalitarian form assumed by Habermas's model. Moreover, in the United States issues of race, ethnicity, class, and gender erupted in the multiple and cacophonous sites of public life. Ryan also points out that sometimes women citizens (like men) acted in abrasive or violent ways, nor were they exempt from the prejudices of race or class that characterized men's affairs. She speaks of 'imperfect publics' grounded in a historical construction and political articulation of separate identities and interests. Despite the barriers to equality in the nineteenth-century United States, she insists that the broadening access to public space was the vehicle for democratizing public discourse and public policy. She proposes that notions of interest and identity need not be antithetical to the public good. Likewise, she adds, 'because everyday politics falls short of standards of perfect rational discourse, a chimera even in the heyday of the bourgeois public sphere, the goal of publicness might best be allowed to navigate through wider and wilder territory.'

Marilyn Lake queries whether women's private and public identities have influenced feminist conceptions of citizenship. She examines the case of twentieth-century Australia, after the comparatively early granting of the vote and full political rights to white Australian women in 1902. The suffrage animated Australian women to engage in politics. They made claims on the state on behalf of women whom they saw as in the paradigmatic situation of the prostitute—'reduced to and defined by her sex, her degradation made possible by her economic dependence'. Lake points to an interesting contradiction between male and female views of citizenship, in that male citizens expected the state to facilitate their engagement in public life while resisting interference with their assumed authority in the private domain. The autonomy of wives—their independence and their inviolability—was a central goal of feminist citizens' activism, and this touched directly on the exercise of male conjugal rights. It also involved white women in efforts to achieve citizen status for Aboriginal women in order to rescue them from male sexual abuse by Aboriginal and non-Aboriginal men. Following Elizabeth Grosz, Lake concludes that ' "bodies matter", that subjectivities should be conceived of in terms of the primacy of corporeality'.[4] Yet Lake also points out that by subscribing to the same masculine view of sexuality that it critiqued, Australian feminist discourse helped to produced the very 'violable' bodies it sought to protect and govern.

Carole Pateman analyses women's citizenship in modern welfare states from the perspective of the patriarchal division between public and private life. She faults the leading theorists of democracy for ignoring the sexual division of labour, along with women's dependent status. 'They treat the public world of paid employment and citizenship', she remarks, 'as if it can be divorced from the private sphere.' Pateman discusses women's status as claimants, made ever more prominent by the growth of poverty among women in recent decades, and as public employees in the British, Australian, and American welfare systems. Although she regards the modern welfare state as a patriarchal institution, she sees some grounds for a challenge to patriarchal power in its recent development. It is only in the current wave of the organized feminist movement that 'the division between the private and public spheres of social life has become seen as a major political problem'. Since Mary Wollstonecraft's day, she observes, feminists have been caught on the horns of a dilemma over whether 'to become (like) men, and so full citizens; or to continue at women's work, which is of no value to citizenship'. A non-patriarchal definition of democratic citizenship that preserves women's autonomy would require the breaking down of the opposition between paid and unpaid work, public and private work, independence and dependence, and work and welfare—all of which are aspects of the gendered opposition between men and women in modern society.

Looking back over the last century or two in advanced industrial societies, several features of women's position stand out. Even as public and private life came to be powerfully gendered and divided into separate spheres, women's actions in the public sphere always threatened to exceed that sexual division. First, growing numbers of women joined the paid labour force, initially as industrial workers or domestic servants, later in the twentieth century as white-collar employees, especially in the public sector. Second, poverty and desperate working conditions led many urban working women to a life of prostitution. As a result, urban life was often associated in the public mind with unlicensed female sexuality. Third, women who joined organized feminist movements were also charged with violating the boundaries of respectable domesticity. In addition, the feminist struggles to reform the family, democratize the workplace, and exercise the vote provoked a heightened level of antagonism between women and the state.[5] As the articles discussed above allege, even at the height of the period of Victorian separate-spheres ideology, the boundaries between public and private were constantly being tested and redrawn—and in the process issues of public and private became ever more pronounced.

III. GENDERED SITES IN THE LATE MODERN PUBLIC SPHERE

The selections in Part III exemplify the intersections between art, media, commerce, and publicity in the contemporary or 'late modern' public sphere. These essays problematize the representation of feminism in the media-saturated public sphere, by introducing feminist perspectives on representation—of bodies, sexuality, and feminism. They pose the question of where, how, by whom, and with what effects boundaries of public and private are continually being drawn. The intimate connections between culture and politics set forth in Part II are re-explored from the standpoint of sexuality, race, gender, and citizenship. The connection between politics and style leads to an inquiry into the potentialities of political performance and gesture in public life.

Lauren Berlant addresses some meanings of privacy as a category of law and a condition of property that constitute a boundary between proper and improper bodies. She examines how the public sphere is anchored in a concept of privacy as straight sex, which in turn supports the fantasy of national citizenship in the United States: 'citizens aspire to dead identities, abstract constitutional notions of personhood and reproductive heterosexuality in the zone of privacy.' Berlant examines recent public controversies over continued congressional funding of the arts, efforts by feminists and political conservatives to expand obscenity laws, and campaigns to restrict the sexual and violent content of the media. In each arena, an appeal is made to protect an innocent youth— typically, a little girl—from the knowledge of illicit or live sex acts. In the sentimental logic of anti-pornography arguments or censorship arguments, infantilized women and children are linked to the nation in ways that 'kill' identity by limiting its expression to the deadening kind of straight sex authorized by national culture. Furthermore, 'rights' are construed as parents' rights 'to control what they and their children encounter as a model for national political agency itself'. Berlant proposes that 'the scandal of sexual subculture in the contemporary American context derives in part from its assertion of a non-infantilized political counterpublic that refuses to tie itself to a dead identity'. Against 'dead citizenship', she calls for 'a radical social theory of sexual citizenship'.

The artist Barbara Kruger also challenges the appeal to innocence, as in the notion of an innocent spectator who is seduced. Similarly, she rejects Habermas's notion of the oppositional public sphere as one uncontaminated by commerce, primarily a culture-debating rather than an image-consuming public. Kruger insists, 'I live and speak through a body which is constructed by moments which are formed by the velocity of power and money. So I don't see this division between what is commercial and what is not commercial.' Producing work that belongs as much to the sphere of advertising as to the gallery and museum, Kruger challenges the idea of privileged sites of publicity. She acknowledges that certain pictures are better suited for intimate gallery spaces than billboards, just as certain works speak more to certain people: 'in order for these images and words to do their work they have to catch the eye of the spectator.' Kruger focuses on the inflections of gender difference in cultural objects, seeking to re-embody cultural stereotypes that women and men confront on a daily basis.

Nancy Fraser reconsiders the issue of democratic publicity in light of the 1991 Senate Judiciary Committee's hearings concerning Anita Hill's accusations of sexual harassment by Clarence Thomas, who was subsequently appointed to the Supreme Court of the United States. Starting from what first looked like a 'text-book example of the [Habermasian] public sphere in action', she asks whether women and men are positioned differently with respect to privacy and publicity and, further, how issues of class and race are played out in the public sphere. Diagnosing these hearings from the standpoint of an overlapping struggle over gender, race, and class, Fraser concludes: 'we need to revise the standard liberal view of the public sphere, which takes the categories of public and private as self-evident.' Giving the example of sexual harassment, she points out that not all understandings of these categories promote democracy, especially when it amounts to enforcing 'men's privacy rights to harass women with impunity in part by smearing in public any women who dares to protest'. For Fraser, 'the feminist project aims in part to overcome the gender hierarchy that gives men more power than women to draw the line between public and private'. Yet the legacy of American slavery and racism means that 'black women [have been denied] even the minimal protections from abuse that white women have occasionally managed to claim'. Fraser insists that publicity is 'always and unambiguously an instrument of empowerment and emancipation. For members of subordinate groups, it will always be a matter of balancing the potential political uses of publicity against the dangers of loss of privacy.'

Blending personal, historical, and cultural observations, Patricia J. Williams asks what it means to be constituted as 'the object of property'. Williams reflects on the contradictory meanings of self that she, an Afro-American women, is possessed by and possesses. She reconsiders the effects of slavery, contrasting the definitions of blacks in slave and market law. She looks at the practice of sterilization, from the standpoint of poor black women. As a professor of law, she turns her professional attention to the subject of contract law and surrogacy contracts. She proposes that the making and maintenance of rights in our society necessarily involve the power to make and manipulate images, visual or linguistic. Williams believes that only by acknowledging the complex level of meanings that surround the topic of rights can rights discourse be advanced.

In 'All Hyped Up and No Place to Go', the sexual dimension of normative public space is explored from the standpoint of notions of transgression and parody in recent queer theory, particularly the work of Judith Butler. Complementing Berlant's examination of the heterosexual construction of private space, this article scrutinizes the performance of sexual identities in public space. The authors examine the effects of two dissident sexual identities of the 1990s—the hypermasculine 'gay skinhead' and the hyperfeminine 'lipstick lesbian'. As we have seen with race and class, issues of sexuality also present questions for democratic publicity. Rather than taking sex or gender identity for granted—as defining a stable, private identity—the authors emphasize how identity is constructed, that is, produced and reproduced through ongoing performances that are enacted in public space.

Jennifer Wicke asks what happens when feminism goes public. In the absence of movement feminism, how does feminism fare in the sphere of celebrity culture? Wicke names Camille Paglia, Carol Gilligan, Naomi Wolf, Catherine MacKinnon, as well as the decidedly non-academic Susan Powter, as examples of celebrity feminists; but she mentions other likely candidates—including Hillary Clinton, who is the subject of the contribution by Erica

Jong—along with academic celebrities like Judith Butler. She proposes that 'the celebrity zone is the public sphere where feminism is negotiated, where it is now in most active cultural play'. Not unlike Kruger, Wicke cautions against repudiating celebrity culture as 'a realm of ideological ruin', pointing out that 'the energies of the celebrity imaginary are fuelling feminist discourse and political activity as never before'. Wicke wholly endorses the non-essentialist feminist 'struggle against the multiple forms in which the category "women" is constructed in subordination'.[6] She nevertheless maintains that these struggles are 'now largely waged symbolically rather than in the type of political engagement summoned up by the word "struggle"'.

Wicke's analysis is complemented by Erica Jong's consideration of Hillary Rodham Clinton on the occasion of her husband's re-election to the Presidency in 1996. As in the case of Anita Hill analysed by Nancy Fraser, Jong demonstrates that Hillary has had far less control over the demands of democratic publicity than Bill Clinton. The perilous borders of public and private are revisited from the standpoint of the nation's premier public woman. Jong's observation about Hillary resonates with the discussion of identity in many articles throughout this collection, except that here a woman is struggling to resist the representations of her over which she has so little control. Not the 'hollow woman' she appears to be but 'a seething mass of contradictions', Hillary 'dares let none of her feelings show—She seems to be holding herself together with hairspray.' According to Jong, the sacrifice of a woman to her husband's ambitions and the deformation of her personality compose a disturbingly familiar portrait of the political wife. 'You might almost say she is taking the punishment for him, and for all the women who step outside the lines prescribed for paper-doll political wives—in fact, for all contemporary women.'

IV. PUBLIC AND PRIVATE IDENTITY: QUESTIONS FOR A FEMINIST PUBLIC SPHERE

Part IV revisits many of the questions concerning the cultural and political prospects for a democratic public sphere raised throughout the volume, in light of the rise in the 1980s and 1990s of identity or difference politics within feminism. The three selections relate the demand for the representation of gender, race, ethnicity, and sexuality in the cultural/symbolic sphere to the problem of political representation. They ask how the feminist demand for the representation of matters consigned to private life may offer political opportunities as well as risks for the further development of democratic politics. In response to those who suggest that feminism is now primarily a cultural rather than a political movement, these authors insist on the need for an explicitly political resolution of the problems raised by feminist demands.

Iris Marion Young proposes that an emancipatory ethics must develop a normative conception of reason that does not oppose reason to desire and affectivity. Similarly, by promoting heterogeneity in public in place of a unified universality, an emancipatory conception of public life would best ensure the inclusion of all persons and groups. Despite its promise, Young argues that Habermas's theory of communicative action does not meet the requirements she sets forth for an emancipatory ethical/political theory. Moreover, she worries that the distinction between public and private in modern political theory 'expresses a will for homogeneity that necessitates the exclusion of many persons and groups, particularly women and racialized groups culturally identified with the body, wildness and irrationality'. Rather than following Habermas's invitation to recover suppressed Enlightenment ideals, Young looks to feminist, gay, and other new social movements of recent decades for an alternative conception of democratic public life that would neither exclude nor sacrifice personal or private matters. She interprets the feminist slogan 'The Personal Is Political' to mean, 'No persons, actions or attributes of persons should be excluded from public discussion and decision-making, although the self-determination of privacy must nevertheless remain.'

Wendy Brown pursues these questions in light of the current configuration of oppositional politics, the phenomenon of identity politics.[7] She asks how a radical democratic politics fares once the very differences that are suppressed under the rubrics of liberal neutrality and humanist inclusion are instead embraced by marginal groups and persons in late-modern democracies. 'Just when polite liberal (not to mention, correct leftist) discourse ceased speaking of us as dykes, faggots, coloured girls or natives, we began speaking of ourselves this way.' Noting such groups' investments in their own history of suffering, Brown suspects that 'identity's desire for recognition may sometimes breed a politics of recrimination and rancour, of culturally dispersed paralysis and suffering, a tendency to reproach power rather than to aspire to it, to disdain freedom rather than practise it?' If such politicized definitions of identity are fuelled by claims to injury and exclusion that rein-scribe and dramatize this pain in politics within an unproductive cycle of repetition, Brown counsels the virtues of 'forgetting' in Nietzsche's sense or giving up on these same investments. She upholds political against therapeutic discourse, and would sup-plant the language of 'I am' with the language of 'I want'. Thus, she points to the role played by language and political conscious-ness in making personal demands public.

Anne Phillips complements Brown's discussion by looking at the specific political challenges posed by identity politics to the actual workings of democratic institutions. Whereas liberal demo-cracies have traditionally relied on the practice of tolerance to accommodate difference, this no longer seems sufficient. Propon-ents of what Phillips calls the 'new politics of presence' demand equal public worth, not just permission for private deviation. As Phillips notes, 'toleration is a poor substitute for recognition. We only tolerate what we do not like or approve of (otherwise there is no need for toleration), and yet where difference is bound up with identity, this is hard for the tolerated to accept.' Identity politics has the potential to affirm publicly aspects of our private selves, to rescue identity from being ignored as a merely 'pri-vate' feature of our selves. However, recourse to 'non-negotia ble identities' may just as likely fuel resentment and essentialize the identities of race, gender, sexuality, or ethnicity. To avert this danger, Phillips considers different mechanisms by which contem-porary democracies may address the problem of representation in a heterogeneous society. She asks how different political mech-anisms have sought to resolve the problem of political exclusion by granting recognition as well as toleration: caucuses and quota systems, the redrawing of boundaries around black-majority con-stituencies in the United States, or power-sharing practices in con-sociational democracies. She suggests that the more satisfactory ways of redressing group exclusions may be those which are less group-specific. Such developments acknowledge the danger in pre-emptive classifications of people's political identities, without resorting to the more traditional treatments of diversity as merely the toleration of contested ideas.

Second-wave feminism has traversed a wide intellectual and political territory. Having discovered that the 'personal is polit-ical', feminists then asserted the importance of the gendered divi-sion of public and private life, and debated whether this division was a universal feature of human culture or the product of history. They explored the historical underpinnings of the public/private split and addressed its implications for cultural and social politics in the present. Feminist interest in the category of the public sphere was occasioned by several impulses, both theoretical and practical. First, a growing dissatisfaction among feminists with the conventional way of mapping social reality as dichotomous—a division which derives, at least in Western thought, from the categories of Roman law and Greek philosophy. Not only does such an approach risk smuggling in false universal assumptions, but also it occludes an understanding of non-state forms of political and cultural association. Second, as the expression of just such a social movement, feminism itself exceeds a dualistic model. Moreover, by focusing on questions of public and private life, feminism calls attention to the ways in which public and private divisions have been drawn in the past and continue to be drawn today. Third, feminist practice has revitalized democratic theory. Increasingly, questions of recognition and representation, culture and interest, equality and justice are discussed in terms of the gendered organization of public and private life.

As this collection demonstrates, feminists are not united in their evaluation of the public/private split, or in their approach to its study. On the other hand, it serves no good purpose to exaggerate the differences among feminists. To do so would only risk freezing, perhaps 'essentializing' the positions within feminist theory that have generated an ongoing conversation about the contours of public and private life. Rather, it is hoped that these readings will inspire further investigation into how the territories they inhabit shape men's and women's public and private selves, and in turn affect the prospects for democratizing the intimate and civic spheres.

Notes

1. By the 'second wave' I mean the feminist movements emerging in the 1960s, down to the present day. For a useful overview of the different stages of feminism, see Jo Freeman, 'From Suffrage to Women's Liberation: Feminism in Twentieth-Century America', in Jo Freeman (ed.), *Women: A Feminist Perspective*, 5th edn. (Mountain View, Calif.: Mayfield, 1995).
2. Betty Friedan, *The Feminine Mystique* (New York: W. W. Norton, 1963), ch. 1. Susan J. Douglas notes: 'in 1964, while teenagers were

discovering the Beatles, older women made *The Feminine Mystique* the number one best-selling paperback in the country'; *Where the Girls Are: Growing Up Female with the Mass Media* (New York: Random House, 1994), 125.

3. Lively debates ensued between those who attributed the public/private split to capitalism and the modern organization of society and those, like Sherry Ortner and Michelle Zimbalist Rosaldo, who saw the division as a feature of all human societies. See Michelle Zimbalist Rosaldo, 'Woman, Culture and Society: A Theoretical Overview', in Michelle Zimbalist Rosaldo and Louise Lamphere (eds.), *Woman, Culture and Society* (Stanford, Calif.: Stanford University Press, 1974). Marxist feminist contributions from the 1970s offer a contrasting point of view: see Sheila Rowbotham, *Woman's Consciousness, Man's World* (Harmondsworth: Penguin, 1973), *Hidden from History: Rediscovering Women in History from the Seventeenth Century to the Present* (New York: Pantheon, 1974); Juliet Mitchell, *Woman's Estate* (New York: Pantheon, 1972); Zillah Eisenstein (ed.), *Capitalist Patriarchy and the Case for Socialist Feminism* (New York: Monthly Review, 1979).

4. Lake draws on Elizabeth Grosz, *Volatile Bodies: Toward a Corporeal Feminism* (Sydney: Allen & Unwin, 1994).

5. Such conflicts culminated in the early 20th century in the arrest, imprisonment, and force-feeding of radical suffragettes in England and America. Earlier in France and elsewhere on the Continent, women's initiatives were defeated during the revolutions of 1830 and 1848, and the Paris Commune of 1870.

6. Wicke cites Chantal Mouffe, 'Feminism, Citizenship, and Radical Democratic Politics', in Judith Butler and Joan Wallach Scott (eds.), *Feminists Theorize the Political* (New York: Routledge, 1992), 384.

7. See Sneja Gunew and Anna Yeatman (eds.), *Feminism and the Politics of Difference* (Boulder, Colo.: Westview Press, 1993).

Part I. The Public/Private Distinction in Feminist Theory

1   Is Female to Male as Nature Is to Culture?

Sherry B. Ortner

Much of the creativity of anthropology derives from the tension between two sets of demands: that we explain human universals, and that we explain cultural particulars. Given this tension, woman provides us with one of the more challenging problems to be dealt with. The secondary status of woman in society is one of the true universals, a pan-cultural fact. Yet within that universal fact, the specific cultural conceptions and symbolizations of woman are extraordinarily diverse and even mutually contradictory. Further, the actual treatment of women and their relative power and contribution vary enormously from culture to culture, and over different periods in the history of particular cultural traditions. Both of these points—the universal fact and the cultural variation— constitute problems to be explained.

My interest in the problem is of course more than academic: I wish to see genuine change come about, the emergence of a social and cultural order in which as much of the range of human potential is open to women as is open to men. The universality of female

From Michelle Zimbalist Rosaldo and Louise Lamphere (eds.), *Woman, Culture and Society* (Stanford University Press, 1974), 67–87. Copyright © 1974 by the Board of Trustees of the Leland Stanford Junior University. Reprinted by permission. The first version of this paper was presented in October 1972 as a lecture in the course 'Women: Myth and Reality' at Sarah Lawrence College. I received helpful comments from the students and from my co-teachers in the course: Joan Kelly Gadol, Eva Kollisch, and Gerda Lerner. A short account was delivered at the American Anthropological Association meetings in Toronto, November 1972. Meanwhile, I received excellent critical comments from Karen Blu, Robert Paul, Michelle Rosaldo, David Schneider, and Terence Turner, and the present version of the paper, in which the thrust of the argument has been rather significantly changed, was written in response to those comments. I, of course, retain responsibility for its final form. The paper is dedicated to Simone de Beauvoir, whose book *The Second Sex* (1953), first published in French in 1949, remains in my opinion the best single comprehensive understanding of 'the woman problem'.

subordination, the fact that it exists within every type of social and economic arrangement and in societies of every degree of complexity, indicates to me that we are up against something very profound, very stubborn, something we cannot rout out simply by rearranging a few tasks and roles in the social system, or even by reordering the whole economic structure. In this paper I try to expose the underlying logic of cultural thinking that assumes the inferiority of women; I try to show the highly persuasive nature of the logic, for if it were not so persuasive, people would not keep subscribing to it. But I also try to show the social and cultural sources of that logic, to indicate wherein lies the potential for change.

It is important to sort out the levels of the problem. The confusion can be staggering. For example, depending on which aspect of Chinese culture we look at, we might extrapolate any of several entirely different guesses concerning the status of women in China. In the ideology of Taoism, *yin*, the female principle, and *yang*, the male principle, are given equal weight; 'the opposition, alternation, and interaction of these two forces give rise to all phenomena in the universe' (Siu, 1968: 2). Hence we might guess that maleness and femaleness are equally valued in the general ideology of Chinese culture.[1] Looking at the social structure, however, we see the strongly emphasized patrilineal descent principle, the importance of sons, and the absolute authority of the father in the family. Thus we might conclude that China is the archetypal patriarchal society. Next, looking at the actual roles played, power and influence wielded, and material contributions made by women in Chinese society—all of which are, upon observation, quite substantial—we would have to say that women are allotted a great deal of (unspoken) status in the system. Or again, we might focus on the fact that a goddess, Kuan Yin, is the central (most worshipped, most depicted) deity in Chinese Buddhism, and we might be tempted to say, as many have tried to say about goddess-worshipping cultures in prehistoric and early historical societies, that China is actually a sort of matriarchy. In short, we must be absolutely clear about *what* we are trying to explain before explaining it.

We may differentiate three levels of the problem:

1. The universal fact of culturally attributed second-class status of woman in every society. Two questions are important here. First, what do we mean by this; what is our evidence that this is

a universal fact? And second, how are we to explain this fact, once having established it?

2. Specific ideologies, symbolizations, and socio-structural arrangements pertaining to women that vary widely from culture to culture. The problem at this level is to account for any particular cultural complex in terms of factors specific to that group—the standard level of anthropological analysis.

3. Observable on-the-ground details of women's activities, contributions, powers, influence, etc., often at variance with cultural ideology (although always constrained within the assumption that women may never be officially preeminent in the total system). This is the level of direct observation, often adopted now by feminist-oriented anthropologists.

This paper is primarily concerned with the first of these levels, the problem of the universal devaluation of women. The analysis thus depends not upon specific cultural data but rather upon an analysis of 'culture' taken generically as a special sort of process in the world. A discussion of the second level, the problem of cross-cultural variation in conceptions and relative valuations of women, will entail a great deal of cross-cultural research and must be postponed to another time. As for the third level, it will be obvious from my approach that I would consider it a misguided endeavour to focus only upon women's actual though culturally unrecognized and unvalued powers in any given society, without first understanding the overarching ideology and deeper assumptions of the culture that render such powers trivial.

THE UNIVERSALITY OF FEMALE SUBORDINATION

What do I mean when I say that everywhere, in every known culture, women are considered in some degree inferior to men? First of all, I must stress that I am talking about *cultural* evaluations; I am saying that each culture, in its own way and on its own terms, makes this evaluation. But what would constitute evidence that a particular culture considers women inferior?

Three types of data would suffice: (1) elements of cultural ideology and informants' statements that *explicitly* devalue women, according them, their roles, their tasks, their products, and their social milieux less prestige than are accorded men and the male correlates; (2) symbolic devices, such as the attribution of defilement, which may be interpreted as *implicitly* making a statement of inferior valuation; and (3) social-structural arrangements that exclude women from participation in or contact with some realm in which the highest powers of the society are felt to reside.[2] These three types of data may all of course be interrelated in any particular system, though they need not necessarily be. Further, any one of them will usually be sufficient to make the point of female inferiority in a given culture. Certainly, female exclusion from the most sacred rite or the highest political council is sufficient evidence. Certainly, explicit cultural ideology devaluing women (and their tasks, roles, products, etc.) is sufficient evidence. Symbolic indicators such as defilement are usually sufficient, although in a few cases in which, say, men and women are equally polluting to one another, a further indicator is required—and is, as far as my investigations have ascertained, always available.

On any or all of these counts, then, I would flatly assert that we find women subordinated to men in every known society. The search for a genuinely egalitarian, let alone matriarchal, culture has proved fruitless. An example from one society that has traditionally been on the credit side of this ledger will suffice. Among the matrilineal Crow, as Lowie (1956) points out, 'Women . . . had highly honorific offices in the Sun Dance; they could become directors of the Tobacco Ceremony and played, if anything, a more conspicuous part in it than the men; they sometimes played the hostess in the Cooked Meat Festival; they were not debarred from sweating or doctoring or from seeking a vision' (p. 61). None the less, 'Women [during menstruation] formerly rode inferior horses and evidently this loomed as a source of contamination, for they were not allowed to approach either a wounded man or men starting on a war party. A taboo still lingers against their coming near sacred objects at these times' (p. 44). Further, just before enumerating women's rights of participation in the various rituals noted above, Lowie mentions one particular Sun Dance Doll bundle that was not supposed to be unwrapped by a woman (p. 60). Pursuing this trail we find: 'According to all Lodge Grass informants and most others, the doll owned by Wrinkled-face took precedence not only of other dolls but of all other Crow medicines whatsoever. . . . This particular doll was not supposed to be handled by a woman' (p. 229).[3]

In sum, the Crow are probably a fairly typical case. Yes, women have certain powers and rights, in this case some that place them in fairly high positions. Yet ultimately the line is drawn: menstruation is a threat to warfare, one of the most valued institutions of the tribe, one that is central to their self-definition; and the most sacred object of the tribe is taboo to the direct sight and touch of women.

Similar examples could be multiplied ad infinitum, but I think the onus is no longer upon us to demonstrate that female subordination is a cultural universal; it is up to those who would argue against the point to bring forth counterexamples. I shall take the universal secondary status of women as a given, and proceed from there.

NATURE AND CULTURE[4]

How are we to explain the universal devaluation of women? We could of course rest the case on biological determinism. There is something genetically inherent in the male of the species, so the biological determinists would argue, that makes them the naturally dominant sex; that 'something' is lacking in females, and as a result women are not only naturally subordinate but in general quite satisfied with their position, since it affords them protection and the opportunity to maximize maternal pleasures, which to them are the most satisfying experiences of life. Without going into a detailed refutation of this position, I think it fair to say that it has failed to be established to the satisfaction of almost anyone in academic anthropology. This is to say, not that biological facts are irrelevant, or that men and women are not different, but that these facts and differences only take on significance of superior/inferior within the framework of culturally defined value systems.

If we are unwilling to rest the case on genetic determinism, it seems to me that we have only one way to proceed. We must attempt to interpret female subordination in light of other universals, factors built into the structure of the most generalized situation in which all human beings, in whatever culture, find themselves. For example, every human being has a physical body and a sense of nonphysical mind, is part of a society of other individuals and an inheritor of a cultural tradition, and must engage in some relationship, however mediated, with 'nature', or the nonhuman realm, in order to survive. Every human being is born (to

25

a mother) and ultimately dies, all are assumed to have an interest in personal survival, and society/culture has its own interest in (or at least momentum toward) continuity and survival, which transcends the lives and deaths of particular individuals. And so forth. It is in the realm of such universals of the human condition that we must seek an explanation for the universal fact of female devaluation.

I translate the problem, in other words, into the following simple question. What could there be in the generalized structure and conditions of existence, common to every culture, that would lead every culture to place a lower value upon women? Specifically, my thesis is that woman is being identified with—or, if you will, seems to be a symbol of—something that every culture devalues, something that every culture defines as being of a lower order of existence than itself. Now it seems that there is only one thing that would fit that description, and that is 'nature' in the most generalized sense. Every culture, or, generically, 'culture', is engaged in the process of generating and sustaining systems of meaningful forms (symbols, artefacts, etc.) by means of which humanity transcends the givens of natural existence, bends them to its purposes, controls them in its interest. We may thus broadly equate culture with the notion of human consciousness, or with the products of human consciousness (i.e. systems of thought and technology), by means of which humanity attempts to assert control over nature.

Now the categories of 'nature' and 'culture' are of course conceptual categories—one can find no boundary out in the actual world between the two states or realms of being. And there is no question that some cultures articulate a much stronger opposition between the two categories than others—it has even been argued that primitive peoples (some or all) do not see or intuit any distinction between the human cultural state and the state of nature at all. Yet I would maintain that the universality of ritual betokens an assertion in all human cultures of the specifically human ability to act upon and regulate, rather than passively move with and be moved by, the givens of natural existence. In ritual, the purposive manipulation of given forms toward regulating and sustaining order, every culture asserts that proper relations between human existence and natural forces depend upon culture's employing its special powers to regulate the overall processes of the world and life.

One realm of cultural thought in which these points are often articulated is that of concepts of purity and pollution. Virtually every culture has some such beliefs, which seem in large part (though not, of course, entirely) to be concerned with the relationship between culture and nature (see Ortner, 1973; n.d.). A well-known aspect of purity/pollution beliefs cross-culturally is that of the natural 'contagion' of pollution; left to its own devices, pollution (for these purposes grossly equated with the unregulated operation of natural energies) spreads and overpowers all that it comes in contact with. Thus a puzzle—if pollution is so strong, how can anything be purified? Why is the purifying agent not itself polluted? The answer, in keeping with the present line of argument, is that purification is effected in a ritual context; purification ritual, as a purposive activity that pits self-conscious (symbolic) action against natural energies, is more powerful than those energies.

In any case, my point is simply that every culture implicitly recognizes and asserts a distinction between the operation of nature and the operation of culture (human consciousness and its products); and further, that the distinctiveness of culture rests precisely on the fact that it can under most circumstances transcend natural conditions and turn them to its purposes. Thus culture (i.e. every culture) at some level of awareness asserts itself to be not only distinct from but superior to nature, and that sense of distinctiveness and superiority rests precisely on the ability to transform—to 'socialize' and 'culturalize'—nature.

Returning now to the issue of women, their pan-cultural second-class status could be accounted for, quite simply, by postulating that women are being identified or symbolically associated with nature, as opposed to men, who are identified with culture. Since it is always culture's project to subsume and transcend nature, if women were considered part of nature, then culture would find it 'natural' to subordinate, not to say oppress, them. Yet although this argument can be shown to have considerable force, it seems to oversimplify the case. The formulation I would like to defend and elaborate on in the following section, then, is that women are seen 'merely' as being *closer* to nature than men. That is, culture (still equated relatively unambiguously with men) recognizes that women are active participants in its special processes, but at the same time sees them as being more rooted in, or having more direct affinity with, nature.

The revision may seem minor or even trivial, but I think it is a more accurate rendering of cultural assumptions. Further, the argument cast in these terms has several analytic advantages over the simpler formulation; I shall discuss these later. It might simply

27

be stressed here that the revised argument would still account for the pan-cultural devaluation of women, for even if women are not equated with nature, they are nonetheless seen as representing a lower order of being, as being less transcendental of nature than men are. The next task of the paper, then, is to consider why they might be viewed in that way.

WHY IS WOMAN SEEN AS CLOSER TO NATURE?

It all begins of course with the body and the natural procreative functions specific to women alone. We can sort out for discussion three levels at which this absolute physiological fact has significance: (1) woman's *body and its functions*, more involved more of the time with 'species life', seem to place her closer to nature, in contrast to man's physiology, which frees him more completely to take up the projects of culture; (2) woman's body and its functions place her in *social roles* that in turn are considered to be at a lower order of the cultural process than man's; and (3) woman's traditional social roles, imposed because of her body and its functions, in turn give her a different *psychic structure*, which, like her physiological nature and her social roles, is seen as being closer to nature. I shall discuss each of these points in turn, showing first how in each instance certain factors strongly tend to align woman with nature, then indicating other factors that demonstrate her full alignment with culture, the combined factors thus placing her in a problematic intermediate position. It will become clear in the course of the discussion why men seem by contrast less intermediate, more purely 'cultural' than women. And I reiterate that I am dealing only at the level of cultural and human universals. These arguments are intended to apply to generalized humanity; they grow out of the human condition, as humanity has experienced and confronted it up to the present day.

Woman's Physiology Seen as Closer to Nature

This part of my argument has been anticipated, with subtlety, cogency, and a great deal of hard data, by de Beauvoir (1953). De Beauvoir reviews the physiological structure, development, and functions of the human female and concludes that 'the female, to a greater extent than the male, is the prey of the species' (p. 60). She points out that many major areas and processes of the woman's body serve no apparent function for the health and stability of the individual; on the contrary, as they perform their specific organic functions, they are often sources of discomfort, pain, and danger. The breasts are irrelevant to personal health; they may be excised at any time of a woman's life. 'Many of the ovarian secretions function for the benefit of the egg, promoting its maturation and adapting the uterus to its requirements; in respect to the organism as a whole, they make for disequilibrium rather than for regulation—the woman is adapted to the needs of the egg rather than to her own requirements' (p. 24). Menstruation is often uncomfortable, sometimes painful; it frequently has negative emotional correlates and in any case involves bothersome tasks of cleansing and waste disposal; and—a point that de Beauvoir does not mention—in many cultures it interrupts a woman's routine, putting her in a stigmatized state involving various restrictions on her activities and social contacts. In pregnancy many of the woman's vitamin and mineral resources are channelled into nourishing the foetus, depleting her own strength and energies. And finally, childbirth itself is painful and dangerous (pp. 24–7). In sum, de Beauvoir concludes that the female 'is more enslaved to the species than the male, her animality is more manifest' (p. 239).

While de Beauvoir's book is ideological, her survey of woman's physiological situation seems fair and accurate. It is simply a fact that proportionately more of woman's body space, for a greater percentage of her lifetime, and at some—sometimes great—cost to her personal health, strength, and general stability, is taken up with the natural processes surrounding the reproduction of the species.

De Beauvoir goes on to discuss the negative implications of woman's 'enslavement to the species' in relation to the projects in which humans engage, projects through which culture is generated and defined. She arrives thus at the crux of her argument (pp. 58–9):

Here we have the key to the whole mystery. On the biological level a species is maintained only by creating itself anew; but this creation results only in repeating the same Life in more individuals. But man assures the repetition of Life while transcending Life through Existence [i.e. goal-oriented, meaningful action]; by this transcendence he creates values that deprive pure repetition of all value. In the animal, the freedom and variety of male activities are vain because no project is involved. Except for his services to the species, what he does is immaterial. Whereas in serving the species, the human male also remodels the face of the earth, he creates new instruments, he invents, he shapes the future.

In other words, woman's body seems to doom her to mere reproduction of life; the male, in contrast, lacking natural creative functions, must (or has the opportunity to) assert his creativity externally, 'artificially', through the medium of technology and symbols. In so doing, he creates relatively lasting, eternal, transcendent objects, while the woman creates only perishables—human beings.

This formulation opens up a number of important insights. It speaks, for example, to the great puzzle of why male activities involving the destruction of life (hunting and warfare) are often given more prestige than the female's ability to give birth, to create life. Within de Beauvoir's framework, we realize it is not the killing that is the relevant and valued aspect of hunting and warfare; rather, it is the transcendental (social, cultural) nature of these activities, as opposed to the naturalness of the process of birth: 'For it is not in giving life but in risking life that man is raised above the animal; that is why superiority has been accorded in humanity not to the sex that brings forth but to that which kills' (p. 59).

Thus if male is, as I am suggesting, everywhere (unconsciously) associated with culture and female seems closer to nature, the rationale for these associations is not very difficult to grasp, merely from considering the implications of the physiological contrast between male and female. At the same time, however, woman cannot be consigned fully to the category of nature, for it is perfectly obvious that she is a full-fledged human being endowed with human consciousness just as a man is; she is half of the human race, without whose cooperation the whole enterprise would collapse. She may seem more in the possession of nature than man, but having consciousness, she thinks and speaks; she generates, communicates, and manipulates symbols, categories, and values. She participates in human dialogues not only with other women but also with men. As Lévi-Strauss says, 'Woman could never become just a sign and nothing more, since even in a man's world she is still a person, and since insofar as she is defined as a sign she must [still] be recognized as a generator of signs' (1969a: 496).

Indeed, the fact of woman's full human consciousness, her full involvement in and commitment to culture's project of transcendence over nature, may ironically explain another of the great puzzles of 'the woman problem'—woman's nearly universal unquestioning acceptance of her own devaluation. For it would seem that, as a conscious human and member of culture, she has followed out the logic of culture's arguments and has reached culture's conclusions along with the men. As de Beauvoir puts it (p. 59):

For she, too, is an existent, she feels the urge to surpass, and her project is not mere repetition but transcendence towards a different future —in her heart of hearts she finds confirmation of the masculine pretensions. She joins the men in the festivals that celebrate the successes and victories of the males. Her misfortune is to have been biologically destined for the repetition of Life, when even in her own view Life does not carry within itself its reasons for being, reasons that are more important than life itself.

In other words, woman's consciousness—her membership, as it were, in culture—is evidenced in part by the very fact that she accepts her own devaluation and takes culture's point of view.

I have tried here to show one part of the logic of that view, the part that grows directly from the physiological differences between men and women. Because of woman's greater bodily involvement with the natural functions surrounding reproduction, she is seen as more a part of nature than man is. Yet in part because of her consciousness and participation in human social dialogue, she is recognized as a participant in culture. Thus she appears as something intermediate between culture and nature, lower on the scale of transcendence than man.

Woman's Social Role Seen as Closer to Nature

Woman's physiological functions, I have just argued, may tend in themselves to motivate[5] a view of woman as closer to nature, a view she herself, as an observer of herself and the world, would tend to agree with. Woman creates naturally from within her own being, whereas man is free to, or forced to, create artificially, that is, through cultural means, and in such a way as to sustain culture. In addition, I now wish to show how woman's physiological functions have tended universally to limit her social movement, and to confine her universally to certain social contexts which *in turn* are seen as closer to nature. That is, not only her bodily processes but the social situation in which her bodily processes locate her may carry this significance. And insofar as she is permanently associated (in the eyes of culture) with these social milieux, they add weight (perhaps the decisive part of the burden) to the view of woman as closer to nature. I refer here of course to woman's confinement to the domestic family context, a confinement motivated, no doubt, by her lactation processes.

Woman's body, like that of all female mammals, generates milk during and after pregnancy for the feeding of the newborn baby. The baby cannot survive without breast milk or some similar formula at this stage of life. Since the mother's body goes through its lactation processes in direct relation to a pregnancy with a particular child, the relationship of nursing between mother and child is seen as a natural bond, other feeding arrangements being seen in most cases as unnatural and makeshift. Mothers and their children, according to cultural reasoning, belong together. Further, children beyond infancy are not strong enough to engage in major work, yet are mobile and unruly and not capable of understanding various dangers; they thus require supervision and constant care. Mother is the obvious person for this task, as an extension of her natural nursing bond with the children, or because she has a new infant and is already involved with child-oriented activities. Her own activities are thus circumscribed by the limitations and low levels of her children's strengths and skills:[6] she is confined to the domestic family group; 'woman's place is in the home.'

Woman's association with the domestic circle would contribute to the view of her as closer to nature in several ways. In the first place, the sheer fact of constant association with children plays a role in the issue; one can easily see how infants and children might themselves be considered part of nature. Infants are barely human and utterly unsocialized; like animals they are unable to walk upright, they excrete without control, they do not speak. Even slightly older children are clearly not yet fully under the sway of culture. They do not yet understand social duties, responsibilities, and morals; their vocabulary and their range of learned skills are small. One finds implicit recognition of an association between children and nature in many cultural practices. For example, most cultures have initiation rites for adolescents (primarily for boys; I shall return to this point below), the point of which is to move the child ritually from a less than fully human state into full participation in society and culture; many cultures do not hold funeral rites for children who die at early ages, explicitly because they are not yet fully social beings. Thus children are likely to be categorized with nature, and woman's close association with children may compound her potential for being seen as closer to nature herself. It is ironic that the rationale for boys' initiation rites in many cultures is that the boys must be purged of the defilement accrued from being around mother and other women so much of the time, when in fact much of the woman's defilement may derive from her being around children so much of the time.

The second major problematic implication of women's close association with the domestic context derives from certain structural conflicts between the family and society at large in any social system. The implications of the 'domestic/public opposition' in relation to the position of women have been cogently developed by Rosaldo (1974), and I simply wish to show its relevance to the present argument. The notion that the domestic unit—the biological family charged with reproducing and socializing new members of the society—is opposed to the public entity—the superimposed network of alliances and relationships that *is* the society—is also the basis of Lévi-Strauss's argument in *The Elementary Structures of Kinship* (1969a). Lévi-Strauss argues not only that this opposition is present in every social system, but further that it has the significance of the opposition between nature and culture. The universal incest prohibition[7] and its ally, the rule of exogamy (marriage outside the group), ensure that:

the risk of seeing a biological family become established as a closed system is definitely eliminated; the biological group can no longer stand apart, and the bond of alliance with another family ensures the dominance of the social over the biological, and of the cultural over the natural. (p. 479)

And although not every culture articulates a radical opposition between the domestic and the public as such, it is hardly contestable that the domestic is always subsumed by the public; domestic units are allied with one another through the enactment of rules that are logically at a higher level than the units themselves; this creates an emergent unit—society—that is logically at a higher level than the domestic units of which it is composed.

Now, since women are associated with, and indeed are more or less confined to, the domestic context, they are identified with this lower order of social/cultural organization. What are the implications of this for the way they are viewed? First, if the specifically biological (reproductive) function of the family is stressed, as in Lévi-Strauss's formulation, then the family (and hence woman) is identified with nature pure and simple, as opposed to culture.

But this is obviously too simple; the point seems more adequately formulated as follows: the family (and hence woman) represents lower-level, socially fragmenting, particularistic sort of concerns, as opposed to interfamilial relations representing higher-level, integrative, universalistic sorts of concerns. Since men lack a 'natural' basis (nursing, generalized to child care) for a familial orientation, their sphere of activity is defined at the level of interfamilial relations. And hence, so the cultural reasoning seems to go, men are the 'natural' proprietors of religion, ritual, politics, and other realms of cultural thought and action in which universalistic statements of spiritual and social synthesis are made. Thus men are identified not only with culture, in the sense of all human creativity, as opposed to nature; they are identified in particular with culture in the old-fashioned sense of the finer and higher aspects of human thought—art, religion, law, etc.

Here again, the logic of cultural reasoning aligning woman with a lower order of culture than man is clear and, on the surface, quite compelling. At the same time, woman cannot be fully consigned to nature, for there are aspects of her situation, even within the domestic context, that undeniably demonstrate her participation in the cultural process. It goes without saying, of course, that except for nursing newborn infants (and artificial nursing devices can cut even this biological tie), there is no reason why it has to be mother—as opposed to father, or anyone else—who remains identified with child care. But even assuming that other practical and emotional reasons conspire to keep woman in this sphere, it is possible to show that her activities in the domestic context could as logically put her squarely in the category of culture.

In the first place, one must point out that woman not only feeds and cleans up after children in a simple caretaker operation; she in fact is the primary agent of their early socialization. It is she who transforms newborn infants from mere organisms into cultured humans, teaching them manners and the proper ways to behave in order to become full-fledged members of the culture. On the basis of her socializing functions alone, she could not be more a representative of culture. Yet in virtually every society there is a point at which the socialization of boys is transferred to the hands of men. The boys are considered, in one set of terms or another, not yet 'really' socialized; their entrée into the realm of fully human (social, cultural) status can be accomplished only by men. We still see this in our own schools, where there is a gradual inversion in the proportion of female to male teachers up through the grades: most kindergarten teachers are female; most university professors are male.[8]

Or again, take cooking. In the overwhelming majority of societies cooking is the woman's work. No doubt this stems from practical considerations—since the woman has to stay home with the baby, it is convenient for her to perform the chores centred in the home. But if it is true, as Lévi-Strauss has argued (1969b), that transforming the raw into the cooked may represent, in many systems of thought, the transition from nature to culture, then here we have woman aligned with this important culturalizing process, which could easily place her in the category of culture, triumphing over nature. Yet it is also interesting to note that when a culture (e.g. France or China) develops a tradition of *haute cuisine*—'real' cooking, as opposed to trivial, ordinary domestic cooking—the high chefs are almost always men. Thus the pattern replicates that in the area of socialization—women perform lower-level conversions from nature to culture, but when the culture distinguishes a higher level of the same functions, the higher level is restricted to men.

In short, we see once again some sources of woman's appearing more intermediate than man with respect to the nature/culture dichotomy. Her 'natural' association with the domestic context (motivated by her natural lactation functions) tends to compound her potential for being viewed as closer to nature, because of the animal-like nature of children, and because of the infrasocial connotation of the domestic group as against the rest of society. Yet at the same time her socializing and cooking functions within the domestic context show her to be a powerful agent of the cultural process, constantly transforming raw natural resources into cultural products. Belonging to culture, yet appearing to have stronger and more direct connections with nature, she is once again seen as situated between the two realms.

Woman's Psyche Seen as Closer to Nature

The suggestion that woman has not only a different body and a different social locus from man but also a different psychic structure is most controversial. I will argue that she probably *does* have a different psychic structure, but I will draw heavily on Chodorow (1974) to establish first that her psychic structure need not be assumed to be innate; it can be accounted for, as Chodorow convincingly shows, by the facts of the probably universal female socialization experience. None the less, if we grant the empirical near universality of a 'feminine psyche' with certain specific characteristics, these characteristics would add weight to the cultural view of woman as closer to nature.

It is important to specify what we see as the dominant and universal aspects of the feminine psyche. If we postulate emotionality or irrationality, we are confronted with those traditions in various parts of the world in which women functionally are, and are seen as, more practical, pragmatic, and this-worldly than men. One relevant dimension that does seem pan-culturally applicable is that of relative concreteness vs. relative abstractness: the feminine personality tends to be involved with concrete feelings, things, and people, rather than with abstract entities; it tends toward personalism and particularism. A second, closely related, dimension seems to be that of relative subjectivity vs. relative objectivity: Chodorow cites Carlson's study (1971: 270), which concludes that 'males represent experiences of self, others, space, and time in individualistic, objective, and distant ways, while females represent experiences in relatively interpersonal, subjective, immediate ways'. Although this and other studies were done in Western societies, Chodorow sees their findings on the differences between male and female personality—roughly, that men are more objective and inclined to relate in terms of relatively abstract categories, women more subjective and inclined to relate in terms of relatively concrete phenomena—as 'general and nearly universal differences' (p. 43).

But the thrust of Chodorow's elegantly argued paper is that these differences are not innate or genetically programmed; they arise from nearly universal features of family structure, namely that 'women, universally, are largely responsible for early child care and for (at least) later female socialization' (p. 43) and that 'the structural situation of child rearing, reinforced by female and male role training, produces these differences, which are replicated and reproduced in the sexual sociology of adult life' (p. 44). Chodorow argues that, because mother is the early socializer of both boys and girls, both develop 'personal identification' with her, i.e. diffuse identification with her general personality, behaviour traits, values, and attitudes (p. 51). A son, however, must ultimately shift to a masculine role identity, which involves building an identification with the father. Since father is almost always more remote than mother (he is rarely involved in child care, and perhaps works away from home much of the day), building an identification with father involves a 'positional identification', i.e. identification with father's male role as a collection of abstract elements, rather than a personal identification with father as a real individual (p. 49). Further, as the boy enters the larger social world, he finds it in fact organized around more abstract and universalistic criteria (see Rosaldo, 1974: 28–9; Chodorow, 1974: 58), as I have indicated in the previous section; thus his earlier socialization prepares him for, and is reinforced by, the type of adult social experience he will have.

For a young girl, in contrast, the personal identification with mother, which was created in early infancy, can persist into the process of learning female role identity. Because mother is immediate and present when the daughter is learning role identity, learning to be a woman involves the continuity and development of a girl's relationship to her mother, and sustains the identification with her as an individual; it does not involve the learning of externally defined role characteristics (Chodorow, 1974: 51). This pattern prepares the girl for, and is fully reinforced by, her social situation in later life; she will become involved in the world of women, which is characterized by few formal role differences (Rosaldo, 1974: 29), and which involves again, in motherhood, 'personal identification' with *her* children. And so the cycle begins anew.

Chodorow demonstrates to my satisfaction at least that the feminine personality, characterized by personalism and particularism, can be explained as having been generated by social-structural arrangements rather than by innate biological factors. The point need not be belaboured further. But insofar as the 'feminine personality' has been a nearly universal fact, it can be argued that its characteristics may have contributed further to the view of women as being somehow less cultural than men. That is, women would tend to enter into relationships with the world that culture might see as being more 'like nature'—immanent and embedded in things as given—than 'like culture'—transcending and transforming things through the superimposition of abstract categories and transpersonal values. Woman's relationships tend to be, like nature, relatively unmediated, more direct, whereas man not only tends to relate in a more mediated way, but in fact ultimately often relates more consistently and strongly to the mediating categories and forms than to the persons or objects themselves.

It is thus not difficult to see how the feminine personality would lend weight to a view of women as being 'closer to nature'. Yet at the same time, the modes of relating characteristic of women undeniably play a powerful and important role in the cultural process. For just as relatively unmediated relating is in some sense at the lower end of the spectrum of human spiritual functions, embedded and particularizing rather than transcending and synthesizing, yet that mode of relating also stands at the upper end of that spectrum. Consider the mother–child relationship. Mothers tend to be committed to their children as individuals, regardless of sex, age, beauty, clan affiliation, or other categories in which the child might participate. Now any relationship with this quality—not just mother and child but any sort of highly personal, relatively unmediated commitment—may be seen as a challenge to culture and society 'from below', insofar as it represents the fragmentary potential of individual loyalties *vis-à-vis* the solidarity of the group. But it may also be seen as embodying the synthesizing agent for culture and society ('from above', in that it represents generalized human values above and beyond loyalties to particular social categories. Every society must have social categories that transcend personal loyalties, but every society must also generate a sense of ultimate moral unity for all its members above and beyond those social categories. Thus that psychic mode seemingly typical of women, which tends to disregard categories and to seek 'communion' (Chodorow, 1974: 55, following Bakan, 1966) directly and personally with others, although it may appear infracultural from one point of view, is at the same time associated with the highest levels of the cultural process.

THE IMPLICATIONS OF INTERMEDIACY

My primary purpose in this paper has been to attempt to explain the universal secondary status of women. Intellectually and personally, I felt strongly challenged by this problem; I felt compelled to deal with it before undertaking an analysis of woman's position in any particular society. Local variables of economy, ecology, history, political and social structure, values, and world view—these could explain variations within this universal, but they could not explain the universal itself. And if we were not to accept the ideology of biological determinism, then explanation, it seemed to me, could only proceed by reference to other universals of the human cultural situation. Thus the general outlines of the approach

—although not of course the particular solution offered—were determined by the problem itself, and not by any predilection on my part for global abstract structural analysis.

I argued that the universal devaluation of women could be explained by postulating that women are seen as closer to nature than men, men being seen as more unequivocally occupying the high ground of culture. The culture/nature distinction is itself a product of culture, culture being minimally defined as the transcendence, by means of systems of thought and technology, of the natural givens of existence. This of course is an analytic definition, but I argued that at some level every culture incorporates this notion in one form or other, if only through the performance of ritual as an assertion of the human ability to manipulate those givens. In any case, the core of the paper was concerned with showing why women might tend to be assumed, over and over, in the most diverse sorts of world views and in cultures of every degree of complexity, to be closer to nature than men. Woman's physiology, more involved more of the time with 'species of life'; woman's association with the structurally subordinate domestic context, charged with the crucial function of transforming animal-like infants into cultured beings; 'woman's psyche', appropriately moulded to mothering functions by her own socialization and tending toward greater personalism and less mediated modes of relating—all these factors make woman appear to be rooted more directly and deeply in nature. At the same time, however, her 'membership' and fully necessary participation in culture are recognized by culture and cannot be denied. Thus she is seen to occupy an intermediate position between culture and nature.

This intermediacy has several implications for analysis, depending upon how it is interpreted. First, of course, it answers my primary question of why woman is everywhere seen as lower than man, for even if she is not seen as nature pure and simple, she is still seen as achieving less transcendence of nature than man. Here, 'intermediate' simply means 'middle status' on a hierarchy of being from culture to nature.

Second, intermediate may have the significance of 'mediating', i.e. performing some sort of synthesizing or converting function between nature and culture, here seen (by culture) not as two ends of a continuum but as two radically different sorts of processes in the world. The domestic unit—and hence woman, who in virtually every case appears as its primary representative—is one of culture's crucial agencies for the conversion of nature into culture, especially with reference to the socialization of children. Any culture's continued viability depends upon properly socialized individuals who will see the world in that culture's terms and adhere more or less unquestioningly to its moral precepts. The functions of the domestic unit must be closely controlled in order to ensure this outcome; the stability of the domestic unit as an institution must be placed as far as possible beyond question. (We see some aspects of the protection of the integrity and stability of the domestic group in the powerful taboos against incest, matricide, patricide, and fratricide.[9]) Insofar as woman is universally the primary agent of early socialization and is seen as virtually the embodiment of the functions of the domestic group, she will tend to come under the heavier restrictions and circumscriptions surrounding that unit. Her (culturally defined) intermediate position between nature and culture, here having the significance of her *mediation* (i.e. performing conversion functions) between nature and culture, would thus account not only for her lower status but for the greater restrictions placed upon her activities. In virtually every culture her permissible sexual activities are more closely circumscribed than man's, she is offered a much smaller range of role choices, and she is afforded direct access to a far more limited range of its social institutions. Further, she is almost universally socialized to have a narrower and generally more conservative set of attitudes and views than man, and the limited social contexts of her adult life reinforce this situation. This socially engendered conservatism and traditionalism of woman's thinking is another— perhaps the worst, certainly the most insidious—mode of social restriction, and would clearly be related to her traditional function of producing well-socialized members of the group.

Finally, woman's intermediate position may have the implication of greater symbolic ambiguity (see also Rosaldo, 1974). Shifting our image of the culture/nature relationship once again, we may envision culture in this case as a small clearing within the forest of the larger natural system. From this point of view, that which is intermediate between culture and nature is located on the continuous periphery of culture's clearing; and though it may thus appear to stand both above and below (and beside) culture, it is simply outside and around it. We can begin to understand then how a single system of cultural thought can often assign to woman completely polarized and apparently contradictory meanings, since extremes, as we say, meet. That she often represents both life and death is only the simplest example one could mention.

For another perspective on the same point, it will be recalled that the psychic mode associated with women seems to stand at both the bottom and the top of the scale of human modes of relating. The tendency in that mode is to get involved more directly with people as individuals and not as representatives of one social category or another; this mode can be seen as either 'ignoring' (and thus subverting) or 'transcending' (and thus achieving a higher synthesis of) those social categories, depending upon the cultural view for any given purpose. Thus we can account easily for both the subversive feminine symbols (witches, evil eye, menstrual pollution, castrating mothers) and the feminine symbols of transcendence (mother goddesses, merciful dispensers of salvation, female symbols of justice, and the strong presence of feminine symbolism in the realms of art, religion, ritual, and law). Feminine symbolism, far more often than masculine symbolism, manifests this propensity toward polarized ambiguity—sometimes utterly exalted, sometimes utterly debased, rarely within the normal range of human possibilities.

If woman's (culturally viewed) intermediacy between culture and nature has this implication of generalized ambiguity of meaning characteristic of marginal phenomena, then we are also in a better position to account for those cultural and historical 'inversions' in which women are in some way or other symbolically aligned with culture and men with nature. A number of cases come to mind: the Sirionó of Brazil, among whom, according to Ingham (1971: 1098), 'nature, the raw, and maleness' are opposed to 'culture, the cooked, and femaleness';[10] Nazi Germany, in which women were said to be the guardians of culture and morals; European courtly love, in which man considered himself the beast and woman the pristine exalted object—a pattern of thinking that persists, for example, among modern Spanish peasants (see Pitt-Rivers, 1961; Rosaldo, 1974). And there are no doubt other cases of this sort, including some aspects of our own culture's view of women. Each such instance of an alignment of women with culture rather than nature requires detailed analysis of specific historical and ethnographic data. But in indicating how nature in general, and the feminine mode of interpersonal relations in particular, can appear from certain points of view to stand both under and over (but really simply outside of) the sphere of culture's hegemony, we have at least laid the groundwork for such analyses.

In short, the postulate that woman is viewed as closer to nature than man has several implications for further analysis, and can be interpreted in several different ways. If it is viewed simply as a *middle* position on a scale from culture down to nature, then it is still seen as lower than culture and thus accounts for the pan-cultural assumption that woman is lower than man in the order of things. If it is read as a *mediating* element in the culture–nature relationship, then it may account in part for the cultural tendency not merely to devalue woman but to circumscribe and restrict her functions, since culture must maintain control over its (pragmatic and symbolic) mechanisms for the conversion of nature into culture. And if it is read as an *ambiguous* status between culture and nature, it may help account for the fact that, in specific cultural ideologies and symbolizations, woman can occasionally be aligned with culture, and in any event is often assigned polarized and contradictory meanings within a single symbolic system. Middle status, mediating functions, ambiguous meaning—all are different readings, for different contextual purposes, of woman's being seen as intermediate between nature and culture.

CONCLUSIONS

Ultimately, it must be stressed again that the whole scheme is a construct of culture rather than a fact of nature. Woman is not 'in reality' any closer to (or further from) nature than man—both have consciousness, both are mortal. But there are certainly reasons why she appears that way, which is what I have tried to show in this paper. The result is a (sadly) efficient feedback system: various aspects of woman's situation (physical, social, psychological) contribute to her being seen as closer to nature, while the view of her as closer to nature is in turn embodied in institutional forms that reproduce her situation. The implications for social change are similarly circular: a different cultural view can only grow out of a different social actuality; a different social actuality can only grow out of a different cultural view.

It is clear, then, that the situation must be attacked from both sides. Efforts directed solely at changing the social institutions—through setting quotas on hiring, for example, or through passing equal-pay-for-equal-work laws—cannot have far-reaching effects if cultural language and imagery continue to purvey a relatively devalued view of women. But at the same time efforts directed solely at changing cultural assumptions—through male and female consciousness-raising groups, for example, or through revision of educational materials and mass-media imagery—cannot be successful unless the institutional base of the society is changed to support and reinforce the changed cultural view. Ultimately, both men and women can and must be equally involved in projects of creativity and transcendence. Only then will women be seen as aligned with culture, in culture's ongoing dialectic with nature.

Notes

1. It is true of course that *yin*, the female principle, has a negative valence. None the less, there is an absolute complementarity of *yin* and *yang* in Taoism, a recognition that the world requires the equal operation and interaction of both principles for its survival.
2. Some anthropologists might consider this type of evidence (social-structural arrangements that exclude women, explicitly or de facto, from certain groups, roles, or statuses) to be a subtype of the second type of evidence (symbolic formulations of inferiority). I would not disagree with this view, although most social anthropologists would probably separate the two types.
3. While we are on the subject of injustices of various kinds, we might note that Lowie secretly bought this doll, the most sacred object in the tribal repertoire, from its custodian, the widow of Wrinkled-face. She asked $400 for it, but this price was 'far beyond [Lowie's] means', and he finally got it for $80 (p. 300).
4. With all due respect to Lévi-Strauss (1969a; 1969b; and *passim*).
5. Semantic theory uses the concept of motivation of meaning, which encompasses various ways in which a meaning may be assigned to a symbol because of certain objective properties of that symbol, rather than by arbitrary association. In a sense, this entire paper is an inquiry into the motivation of the meaning of woman as a symbol, asking why woman may be unconsciously assigned the significance of being closer to nature. For a concise statement on the various types of motivation of meaning, see Ullman (1963).
6. A situation that often serves to make her more childlike herself.
7. David M. Schneider (pers. comm.) is prepared to argue that the incest taboo is not universal, on the basis of material from Oceania. Let us say at this point, then, that it is virtually universal.
8. I remember having my first male teacher in the fifth grade, and I remember being excited about that—it was somehow more grown-up.
9. Nobody seems to care much about sororicide—a point that ought to be investigated.

SHERRY B. ORTNER

10. Ingham's discussion is rather ambiguous itself, since women are also associated with animals: 'The contrasts man/animal and man/woman are evidently similar ... hunting is the means of acquiring women as well as animals' (p. 1095). A careful reading of the data suggests that both women and animals are mediators between nature and culture in this tradition.

References

Bakan, David (1966), *The Duality of Human Existence*. Boston.
Carlson, Rae (1971), 'Sex Differences in Ego Functioning: Exploratory Studies of Agency and Communion', *Journal of Consulting and Clinical Psychology*, 37: 267–77.
Chodorov, Nancy (1974), 'Family Structure and Feminine Personality', in Michelle Zimbalist Rosaldo and Louise Lamphere, eds., *Woman, Culture and Society*. Stanford, Calif.
de Beauvoir, Simone (1953), *The Second Sex*. New York. Originally published in French in 1949.
Ingham, John M (1971), 'Are the Sirionó Raw or Cooked?' *American Anthropologist*, 73: 1092–9.
Lévi-Strauss, Claude (1969a), *The Elementary Structures of Kinship*. Trans. J. H. Bell and J. R. von Sturmer; ed. R. Needham. Boston.
—— (1969b), *The Raw and the Cooked*. Trans. J. and D. Weightman. New York.
Lowie, Robert (1956), *The Crow Indians*. New York. Originally published in 1935.
Ortner, Sherry B (1973), 'Sherpa Purity', *American Anthropologist*, 75: 49–63.
—— (n.d.), 'Purification Beliefs and Practices', *Encyclopaedia Britannica*, forthcoming.
Pitt-Rivers, Julian (1961), *People of the Sierra*. Chicago.
Rosaldo, Michelle Zimbalist, 'Women, Culture, and Society: A Theoretical Overview', in Rosaldo and Louise Lamphere, eds., *Woman, Culture and Society*. Stanford, Calif.
Siu, R. G. H. (1968), *The Man of Many Qualities*. Cambridge, Mass.
Ullman, Stephen (1963), 'Semantic Universals', in Joseph H. Greenberg, ed., *Universals of Language*. Cambridge, Mass.

Citizenship with a Feminist Face: The Problem with Maternal Thinking

Mary G. Dietz

In the past twenty years, perhaps no other theoretical issue has created as much controversy within the feminist movement as the role of women in the family. First-wave feminists as varied as Kate Millett, Betty Friedan, Juliet Mitchell, and Shulamith Firestone all shared at least one common task: to desanctify the family and demystify motherhood.[1] These first-wave thinkers considered the bureaucratic state, capitalism, and the patriarchal family to be three sides of an iron triangle of women's oppression. By the mid-1970s, later feminists were deepening first-wave criticism by further examining the relations between capitalism and patriarchy, the family and the capitalist mode of production, housework and surplus labour, motherhood and oppression.[2] Needless to say, the family did not fare well under this withering criticism. Far from being an idyllic haven in a heartless world, the family appeared to reproduce capitalism at home and to subordinate and oppress women on a daily basis.

But the family soon came to have its feminist defenders, and now a battle is brewing between those feminists who stand by the earlier critiques of the family and those who argue that we must reconsider the value of the family and motherhood for feminist consciousness. The 'pro-family' feminists' aim is both a practical and a theoretical one: practical insofar as they seek to wrest the defence of the family from the New Right (which they correctly perceive as having distorted and mystified the role of women as mothers and wives); and theoretical insofar as they intend to reclaim mothering as a dimension of women's experience and defend it as

Reprinted by permission from *Political Theory*, 13/1 (Feb. 1985): 19–37. Copyright © 1985 Sage Publications, Inc. An earlier version of this article was presented at the Western Political Science Association meeting in Seattle, WA., March 24–26, 1983. I would like to thank Terence Ball, Amy Gutmann, Hanna Pitkin, Joan Tronto, and especially James Farr for their many helpful comments and suggestions on various drafts of this article.

necessary for both gender identity and feminist political consciousness. Among these 'pro-family' feminists, two are particularly important: Sara Ruddick and Jean Bethke Elshtain. Seizing upon the 'social practice of mothering' and its attendant virtues and 'metaphysical attitudes', Sara Ruddick has sought to promote 'maternal thinking' as an antidote to a male-dominated culture and as an alternative vision of a 'way to be' in the world.[3] Jean Bethke Elshtain challenges what she takes to be the matriphobia of the feminist movement by bringing out the political implications of maternal thinking, and by attempting to restructure political consciousness on the basis of what she calls 'social feminism'.[4]

In this essay, I want to argue against 'social feminism' because it harbours some serious problems for feminist political discourse and democratic political action. Despite the best of sentiments in attempting to find something unique in women's identity as (potential) mothers, social feminism distorts the meaning of politics and political action largely by reinforcing a one-dimensional view of women as creatures of the family. But women are not uniquely identified by maternal thinking, nor does maternal thinking necessarily promote the kind of democratic politics social feminism purports to foster. Accordingly, I contend that feminism can only succeed in its political mission by encouraging democratic practices and by nurturing the reality of women as, in large part, citizens. Thus my general intention is to set one possible course for future feminist political thought. Its first movements are presented here by way of critique.

My critique proceeds as follows. In the first section I briefly reconstruct Elshtain's argument with an eye to its political implications. In the second section I counter Elshtain's view of the relationship between the public and private realms, by way of considering her interpretations of Aristotle and *Antigone*. The result of these interpretative excursions in the history of political thought is developed in the final section, where I argue that maternal thinking and social feminism cannot deliver on the kind of politics or feminist political consciousness they claim to underwrite.

I

The hallmark of Elshtain's 'social feminism' is her attempt to 'make a case for family ties' and the practice of mothering.[5] Her case proceeds both historically (by reconsidering episodes in the history of political thought from the standpoint of the treatment of women) and programmatically (by criticizing current feminist theories and by offering her own 'reconstructive ideal of public and private').[6] Elshtain wants to show that the family is neither the reactionary and repressive institution of feminist and leftist critics nor the perfectly harmonious world of Filmerian patriarchs and the New Right. In the face of these critics and apologists, both Left and Right, Elshtain insists that 'the family remains the locus of the deepest and most resonant human ties, the most enduring hopes, the most intractable conflicts, the most poignant tragedies and the sweetest triumphs human life affords'.[7]

Making short work of the Right, Elshtain levels criticism mainly at past feminist thought. In her view, previous feminism threatens to demean or destroy women's most powerful experiences, perhaps their very identities. What survives the demeaning or the destruction are some unacceptable alternatives: the distortion of identity and the obliteration of the private (the way radical feminists see women as 'hags' and 'witches'); the juridical levelling of identity and the elevation of the 'social' (the way liberal feminists see women and men merely as equal legal entities); or the reduction of identity and instrumentalization of the private (the way Marxist feminists see women as reproducers).

Social feminism is expressly designed to overcome these liabilities and to supplant these other feminist alternatives. For the sake of new feminist politics, it seeks to foster the identity of 'women-as-mothers' and to establish the moral primacy of the family, and so the private realm of human life. For Elshtain, the family is existentially paramount because humans are 'first and foremost not political or economic man, but family men and women'. Moreover, because the family has a 'trans-historical' existence, it 'constitutes our common humanity' and so is the 'universal basis for human culture'.[8] This is not just existentially significant, but morally as well. For it is in the family that human beings experience the most ennobling dimensions of existence: long-term ties with specific others, the need for roots, obligation to kin, intimacy, love, and attentiveness. Thus the family makes a morality of responsibility possible. So Elshtain hardly dissembles when she openly declares: 'the feminism I seek is not reducible to a clever strategic move; it is, instead, the affirmation of moral imperatives and their insertion into the heart of feminist politics.'[9]

For social feminism, then, the family is the most elevated and primary realm of human life. It has existential priority, and moral superiority, over the public realm of politics. To dramatize the radicalness of this position, Elshtain contrasts social feminism with the entire 2,500-year tradition of political thought.

Aristotle and all the other political theorists down through the centuries who asserted the primacy of politics and viewed man (the male, at any rate, if not generic humanity) as pre-eminently a political animal even as they downgraded or simply took for granted the private sphere, were guilty of a serious distortion.[10]

To remedy this Aristotelian distortion, social feminists not only must reject the political priority of men over women; they must also reverse the existential priority of the public realm over the private realm.

At least in light of its attempted reversal of the tradition of political thought, social feminism is not far removed from true conservatism. Both emphasize the family, traditional bonds of kinship, the web of relationships that emerge from a respect for and remembrance of past generations, and a sense of rootedness. All of these values are 'conservative' in their attempt to conserve or preserve the moral fabric of the family and its cherished privacy, and as such are in sharp contrast to the rational, competitive, atomized world of liberals and so-called 'conservatives'.

Nevertheless, social feminism does not purport to be a conservative case against liberalism, but rather a feminist one. And what makes Elshtain's argument expressly feminist is her claim that women's experience in the private realm, as mothers, provides the only grounds, indeed the 'moral imperative', for countering the prevailing liberal-individualist world view.[11] Elshtain explicitly rejects the notion that mothering is simply one 'role' among many. Rather, mothering is 'a complicated, rich, ambivalent, vexing, joyous, activity' that 'carries profoundly resonant emotional and sexual imperatives'.[12] Women as mothers, on Elshtain's account, are the preservers of 'vulnerable human life', and the attitude that distinguishes maternal thinking upholds the principle that 'the reality of a single human child [must] be kept before the mind's eye'.[13] Accordingly, what counts as failure within the maternal perspective is 'the death, injury or damage of a child through carelessness or neglect or the stunting or shaming of a child through over-control and domination.'[14]

With the reality of a single human child before its eye, maternal thinking entails some striking political implications. In contrast to the kind of bureaucratic-administrative abstractionism that is fathered by the liberal order, the social practice of mothering generates a mentality that emphasizes attentiveness toward others and is personal, empathic, and loving. The tragedy of the contemporary world is that concrete human lives are in jeopardy. A 'technocratic public order', a 'socially irresponsible corporate structure', an 'unjust economic system that denies families a living', 'bureaucratic statism', all militate against the recognition of the 'concrete specificity' of human beings and 'the needs of children'.[15] Thus 'seizure', 'control', and the 'judgment by impersonal standards'— the hallmarks of these supra-human entities—must be rejected. The political point of the criticism is clearly-stated: 'Were maternal thinking to be taken as the base for feminist consciousness, a wedge for examining an increasingly overcontrolled public world would open immediately.'[16] In this way, maternal thinking can 'chasten arrogant public power'.[17]

Social feminism, guided by maternal thinking, also chastens what Elshtain calls the 'article of faith' of the contemporary feminist movement: 'The personal is the political.'[18] She reads this credo as a theoretical justification to politicize, criticize, and manipulate the private world of the family and personal life. Social feminism would seek to protect the private sphere from this sort of desecration. By preserving and protecting its 'moral imperatives', social feminism would purge feminism's soul of its antifamilial and matriphobic spectre and restore an authentic and unique identity to women.

From such an identity would emerge a vital public-moral consciousness and a renewed vision of citizenship. This is the more constructive—or rather, reconstructive—vision of social feminism. Drawing upon the 'private virtues' and the 'humanizing imperative' that emerge from the social practice of mothering, social feminism promotes a 'politics of compassion' and seeks to create an 'ethical polity'.[19] Although this reconstructive politics is not (yet) fully elaborated, it would appear that an 'ethical polity' would embody or forward: (1) privacy and the protection of the private realm from politicization; (2) individual freedom ('from some all encompassing public imperative'); (3) equality (because all individuals are 'irreplaceable beings and immortal souls'); (4) pluralism (of 'diverse spheres and competing ideals'); (5) non-violence; (6) civic virtue (based on a 'devotion to public, moral responsibilities and ends'); and (7) an active citizenry (in which 'men and women alike partake of the public sphere on an equal basis for participatory dignity and equality').[20]

This, in a word, is democracy by social feminist means. Social feminism promises a great deal, then, from the restoration of women's identities as (potential) mothers to the creation of a democratic and ethical polity. We must now, in the interest of feminist political consciousness, assess the strengths of these promises.

II

Social feminism is open to a number of criticisms, most of which cannot be developed here, and some of which can only be mentioned.[21] Many of these criticisms seize upon the incompleteness of Elshtain's accounts of the family, of the social practice of mothering, or of maternal thinking. There is, for example, the definitional problem of just what sorts of relationship count as a 'family'. With some justification, perhaps, Elshtain does not want 'to throw the honourable mantle "family" over every ad hoc collection of persons who happen to be under one roof at the same time'.[22] But where legitimately to throw the mantle is not clear. This is especially troubling, given the great diversity of what have been and continue to be taken in different cultures and eras as families. Contemporary feminists and women generally may rightly wonder whether an extended non-nuclear family, a kibbutz, an ashram, a cooperative, or a lesbian household display (or do not display) the right sort of 'genuine commitment of family men and women who retained their commitments to and for one another'.[23]

Women with empirical and sociological sensibilities may also call attention to the lack of caring and love often displayed in modern families (however defined). Such lack may range from professional or upper-class families in which children are not in fact 'kept before the mind's eye', though they are otherwise well treated, to those tragic cases of families with battered wives and abused children. Should not actual families be investigated before we place women's and feminists' ideals and hopes on the material basis of the family and the social practice of mothering? Some critics might contend that the family is still generally the scene of women's housework, unpaid labour, or of their second shift. First-wave and socialist—not social—feminists were not, I think, so wide of the mark that these features of family life do not impinge upon what it is to engage in 'maternal thinking'. Even setting aside the family as an institution, women and feminists may also wonder upon what basis we are 'maternal thinkers'. Are we that as mothers, as potential future mothers, as women generally, even if, individually, some of us cannot or choose not to have children?

These may or may not prove insuperable problems, but until they are addressed and overcome we must judge the case for social feminism as incomplete, at the least. But there are more serious problems with social feminism, problems that threaten to undermine the political relevance of maternal thinking and so Elshtain's hopes for a new feminist political consciousness. Social feminism reinforces an abstract split between the public and private realms that cannot or should not be maintained; and no theoretical connection is provided for linking maternal thinking and the social practice of mothering with the kind of 'ethical polity' Elshtain envisions, namely one informed by democratic thinking and the political practices of citizenship.

I want to begin my criticism of social feminism indirectly by considering what might seem to be two unlikely figures—Aristotle and (Sophocles') Antigone. I begin here because Elshtain herself considers Aristotle and Antigone to be important episodes in a reconstructed history of feminist political thought. Her interpretations of them—in *Public Man, Private Woman*, and in 'Antigone's Daughters'—are illustrative of social feminism: its critical powers in the case of Aristotle; its praise and prescriptions in the case of Antigone. I think both interpretations are misguided, however, and symptomatic of the general difficulties of social feminism, difficulties I will turn to more directly in the following section.

Aristotle can be approached in two very different ways, one we might call 'deprecative', the other 'generous'. According to the former approach, one that Elshtain endorses, Aristotle consigns the private realm to insignificance. He leaves no doubt as to who occupies the private realm, where 'mere life' is preserved, and who acts in the public realm in pursuit of the 'good life'. Preserving 'mere life' is the task of women, slaves, and certain kinds of labourers. Children also exist in this realm, though young males are liberated from it when they come of age. The private realm is mute: 'a modest silence is a woman's crown.' It is functional in that it serves to satisfy primary needs: 'First house, and wife, and ox to draw the plough.' And it is hierarchic by nature: 'the relation of male to female is naturally that of the superior to the inferior— of the ruling to the ruled.'[24] Aristotle allows that rule of this familial sort is of a higher nature than, say, rule over an animal, but the fact that in his view women or slaves rank only slightly above oxen is not particularly comforting. Conversely, women and slaves cannot partake or participate in the 'good life' of the polis where Greek males, 'naturally fitter to command', bask in heroic admiration of themselves and each other and 'aim at being equal' as public citizens.[25]

In Elshtain's reading, Aristotle is elitist because women are privatized, slaves oppressed, and aliens condemned as barbarians. Here she rightly calls attention to the oppressive institutions that Aristotle accepts and ardently justifies as 'given' by nature. But Elshtain's criticisms go deeper still, to Aristotle's theoretical foundations. It is the split between the public and the private realms, and Aristotle's glorification of the former, to which she objects. 'It is important to remember', Elshtain argues, 'that most of the debates in the "public space" had little to do with great or noble ends, and much to do with jockeying for position and pelf, raising money by any means necessary.'[26] The 'public space', in short, is a deceptive notion, a relic of a distant past, and a way of demeaning the private and familial concerns of everyday life. Conversely, the social feminist response to Aristotelian elitism is to resurrect the family, establish it as the primary realm of human life, and declare that the private virtues of love and humility, for example, are the bases for public consciousness. And when Elshtain accuses Aristotle of distorted thinking and seeks to reclaim the 'family man and woman' as primary over 'political and economic man', she plainly wants us to reject Aristotle's mute, functional, and hierarchic view of the family and of women, and his adulation and mystification of the polis and of men. In effect, social feminism stands Aristotle on his head. The virtues of private woman are lauded over the vices of public man, but social feminism remains locked in the same public/private perspective that it espies in Aristotelianism.

The consequences of standing Aristotle on his head are clear. The private realm of the family takes on an aura of holiness—a social feminist holiness—that radiates from loving and attentive mothers who personify specific 'moral imperatives'. The public realm becomes a dark and ominous antithesis to the virtuous private. Indeed, all that is public, in Elshtain's view, is statist, cold, brutal, uncompromisingly arrogant, eminently in need of maternal chastening. The political conclusion is obvious: feminists must embrace 'the perspective that flows from their experiences' (that is, family life and mothering) and resist 'the imperious demands and overweening claims of state power' and a public life 'created by men'.[27]

Nowhere is the impact of Elshtain's commitment to this public/private metaphor revealed more graphically than when she mobilizes a particular interpretation of *Antigone*. Antigone, Elshtain tells us, is the exemplar of the private realm in all its robust strength and familial attentiveness. There is no question as to which of her alternatives Elshtain thinks Antigone chooses. This is the drama of a woman pitted against 'the arrogant insistencies of statecraft', a defender of the 'domain of women' and 'primordial family morality'. Antigone defies the abstract obligations of the state and rejects public life as represented by Creon, the king. Not surprisingly, Elshtain offers Sophocles' heroine as an archetype for 'female identity' and a 'feminist perspective'.[28]

It may seem to some that using Antigone—a literary character from a classical Greek tragedy—as an archetype for feminists of the 1980s is odd or anachronistic. But assuming that this use is legitimate, it is not clear that Elshtain has interpreted the meaning of *Antigone* correctly. To appreciate this, let us first consider a more generous interpretation of Aristotle. Aristotle, on this generous reading is arguing that politics is not an endeavour tied to a particular 'realm'. Rather, it is a special kind of human activity, an activity that is primary to all other human activities, be they public or private. Aristotle thinks this for two reasons. First, he argues that human existence must be viewed as a complex of diverse practices and 'associations' that have distinct natures and ends, but that are integrally connected and aim toward some good. These practices include the provision of necessities of life, procreation, the care of children, the acquisition and exchange of goods, the production of artefacts and institutions, the making of culture—in short, all those things that distinguish human societies. But Aristotle goes on to illuminate one activity or association as existentially primary because it surveys all other particular activities from a more general point of view and determines which will be 'private' and which 'public'. This primary activity is politics, which Aristotle calls 'the most sovereign and inclusive' of all associations.[29] By this he means to suggest that politics is an integrative experience; all other human acts and occupations are examined in its light and made its subject-matter.[30] Thus it was the case in Aristotle's time, and is no less true in ours, that family life and privacy, as well as social practices and economic issues, are matters of political decision-making. Family practices, control over family property, the rights of children, the nature of schooling and child labour laws, benefits for single mothers, the regulation of birth control—all of those things, whether we like it or not, are potentially open to political control and may be politically determined. Even the decision to allow them to remain 'private'—that is, left in the hands of mothers, fathers, and individual citizens —is ultimately political. The forms for reaching these decisions have varied from era to era, polity to polity. They have been made by kings, oligarchs, dictators, politburos, parliaments, and faceless bureaucrats. But my point about Aristotle is this: the questions of who we are allowed to be and what rights we are allowed to exercise, even in the supposed sanctity of the family, have always been and will continue to be governed by political determinations. This governance stretches across the whole range of our lives and sets the conditions for what we consider to be 'private' and what we deem to be 'public' pursuits. And this is why, according to Aristotle, politics is existentially prior to all other human activities and practices.[31]

There is a second and more moral way in which politics is primary. In this activity, human beings can collectively and inclusively relate to one another not as strong over weak, fast over slow, master over apprentice, or mother over child, but as equals who render judgements on matters of shared importance, deliberate over issues of common concern, and act in concert with one another. As Aristotle puts it, 'the members of a political association aim by their very nature at being equal and differing in nothing.'[32] Aristotle's shorthand for this activity is 'citizenship'. He calls the experience of citizenship, of simultaneously ruling and being ruled, the good life.[33] For it is when human beings act as citizens that they, and not a king or a parliament or a phalanx of faceless bureaucrats, have the power to determine the conditions of their 'mere' lives. Aristotle's point is not that citizens are the warrior-heroes of some fixed public realm, but rather that citizenship is a qualitatively distinct form of activity in which individuals collectively and perpetually determine the forever shifting boundaries of what is private and public. This endless collective self-determination is what it means to be free. Without question, Aristotle was wrong to restrict women to the household and render them eternally subject to natural and familial inequalities. But this forms no necessary part of his argument concerning politics and citizenship. Surely his vision of the good life, as one in which citizens relate to one another as equals, collectively determine their lives, and strive to be free, remains a compelling one. When compared to fascist terror, communist collectivizations, and liberal interest-group politics, it is a noble vision and one for which democracy still strives.[34]

What I am suggesting, in short, is that we learn different lessons from Aristotle about the political—not those based on an abstract split between the public and private realms, nor on the necessary consignment of women to the household. These different lessons will help us better understand the nature of a feminist political consciousness than will the deprecatory reading.

Related lessons follow if we read *Antigone* differently and more carefully. Rather than viewing the tension in the drama, as Elshtain does, as one of public (male) versus private (female), as one between the vices of public power and the virtues of private familial love, we might read *Antigone* as illustrative of two opposing *political* viewpoints. One is of Creon, who represents the state and centralized power, and the other is of Antigone, who represents the customs and traditions of a collective civil life, an entire political ethos, which Creon's mandate and he himself threaten. If we interpret *Antigone* this way, the character of the heroine deepens immensely, for she emerges not simply as a 'sister' whose familial loyalties pit her against a king, but as a citizen of Thebes whose defence of her brother is rooted in a devotion to the gods and to the ways and laws of her city. Likewise, Creon is not simply a man —a king of the public realm who besmirches a family's honour and trivializes private loyalties. He is the manifestation of a particular kind of politics, authoritarian rulership, to which Antigone, as citizen, is in opposition.

For Elshtain to read Antigone's loyalty as 'private' or 'familial' is not only anachronistic (for the defence of the 'private' against the 'state' is a later, liberal construct), but also unpolitical, for she misses the very thing that makes Antigone such a strikingly unusual Greek character (and Sophocles, despite his views on women's silence, such a visionary tragedian). She is a political person (that is, neither a 'private woman' nor a 'public man'). Antigone transcends the public/private split because she embodies the personal made political. Through her speech and her action, she transforms a matter of private concern into a public issue. In the Aristotelian idiom, Antigone realizes her human and distinctively political potentiality when she refuses to maintain a 'modest silence'. Indeed, if anyone in the drama symbolizes the sort of commitment to the private that Elshtain would have feminists adopt, it is Ismene, who shares Antigone's horror of the treatment of Polynices, but nevertheless begs her sister not to challenge Creon, to stay at home and remain silent. Of the two sisters surely Ismene is by far the more fierce defender of *oikos* [the household], for she tries her utmost to preserve the household and family peace between her sister and their uncle. She wants to save her sister from destruction. It is Antigone who insults and then deserts Ismene.

The reason why Antigone is a heroine and Ismene is not has nothing to do with 'private' or 'familial' virtues, for both sisters loved their brother. The difference between them has to do with political consciousness. Antigone understands that Creon's refusal to allow Polynices' burial is not just a singular personal insult but a collective political threat. The former may be countered with a 'modest silence' or supplication; the latter demands decisive political action. Antigone takes such action; Ismene does not.

There is more here than mere interpretative disputes in the history of political ideas. Feminist political consciousness, not just Aristotle or Antigone, are at issue. Because Elshtain envisions a world divided naturally and abstractly into dual realms, and human beings as either virtuous private or arrogant public creatures, feminist political consciousness is perilously close to becoming politically barren. To understand more precisely why this is so, we must recall the values of the private realm—intimacy, love, and attentiveness—and the defining aim of social feminism—'the preservation of life'—and determine why these are inadequate bases for feminist political consciousness.

III

Without question, the protection of life is a necessary prerequisite for any political order. Who would not argue that the growth and preservation of children are vital social imperatives, or that the protection of vulnerable human life is important? But surely a movement or a political consciousness committed simply to caring for 'vulnerable human existence', as Elshtain's social feminism is, offers no standards—indeed, it can only echo the silence of Ismene—when it comes to judging between political alternatives or establishing political values that are worthy of feminist support. An enlightened despotism, a welfare state, and a democratic republic may all protect children's lives or show compassion for the poor. But what standards for judging further among these political orders can social feminism offer us? Its moral imperative —the preservation and growth of children—has been fulfilled. This should be a matter of considerable concern for social feminists because, as we have seen, Elshtain intimates that social feminists are indeed committed to a particular kind of political order—namely, a democratic community. And in a generous acknowledgement, she applauds 'those aspects of Aristotelian thought that turn on the imperative that acting in common together with others to agreed upon ends is a worthy form of human life'.[35] But Elshtain fails to provide a theoretical argument which links maternal thinking and the social practice of mothering *to* democratic values and a democratic politics.

In order to link these successfully, she would have to show that maternal virtues are conceptually connected to, or that the social practice of mothering causally brings about, democratic values— particularly active citizenship, self-government, egalitarianism, and the exercise of freedom. But this Elshtain cannot do. Maternal virtues cannot be political in the required sense because, as Elshtain herself acknowledges, they are connected to and emerge out of an activity that is special, distinctive, unlike any other. We must conclude, then, that this activity is unlike the activity of citizenship; the two cannot be viewed as somehow encompassing the same attributes, abilities, and ways of knowing. Thus, to be a mother is not in itself to have the requisite capacity for citizenship. (Good) mothers may also be (good) citizens, but their being (good) mothers does not make them (good) citizens. The two descriptions of women are not interchangeable.

We must press this point further by considering the actual relationship between a mother and her child. It is not analogous to the relationship among citizens even when (and that is, as yet, empirically undetermined) it displays the ideal virtues Elshtain praises. The mother and the child are in radically different positions in terms of power and control. The child is subordinate to the mother, and the need relations are highly differentiated as well. The infant's is absolute; the mother's relative. A mother experiences her infant as continuous with self, not separate.[36] In other words, the special and distinctive aspects of mothering emerge out of a decidedly unequal relationship, even if benign or loving, in which one person is responsible for a given period of time for the care and preservation of another. This is an intimate, exclusive, and particular activity, and mothers preserve their children, not mothering itself. Following Elshtain, we might call this the condition of attentive love.

Democratic citizenship, on the other hand, is collective, inclusive, and generalized. Because it is a condition in which individuals aim at being equal, the mother–child relationship is a particularly inappropriate model. For citizenship is an active condition, in which many persons share the responsibility of ruling and concern themselves not only with matters of general public policy but also with perpetuating the very activity of citizenship itself. Following Aristotle, we might call this the condition of freedom.

Furthermore, the bond among citizens is not like the love between a mother and child, for citizens are, not intimately, but politically involved with each other. Looked at in this way, social feminism commits a version of one of the ideological extravagances of the French Revolution, namely, the demand that democratic citizenship reflect the 'brotherhood of man'. But citizens do not, because they cannot, relate to one another as brother does to brother, or mother does to child. We look in the wrong place for a model of democratic citizenship if we look to the family (even when we have carefully defined the family).[37] We would do better to look at friendship in Aristotle's sense, or, better still, at mutual respect in Hannah Arendt's sense, for a model of the kind of bond we might expect from, or hope to nurture in, democratic citizens.

To argue, then, that the virtues that arise in the social practice of mothering must be or give rise to the values that inform the political practice of citizenship misperceives the meaning of political life and miscontrues the 'metaphysical attitudes' that mothers are said to experience. Intimacy, love, and attentiveness are precious things in part because they are exclusive and so cannot be experienced just anywhere or by just anyone with just any other. That is why love and intimacy, if they are to remain pure and sustain women's identities in the way Elshtain wants, must not be made the basis of political action and discourse, for intimacy loses its meaning, and love its 'concrete specificity', when they are applied to a people as a whole or marshalled for political ends. The outside world can only taint or break, it cannot share, these bonds.

When Elshtain reminds us of the fragility and the resilience of family life and the special knowledge of women-as-mothers, she seems to admit all this. But when she urges us to make maternal thinking a 'wedge' for examining the public world and to see it as a way of 'diffusing' attentive love throughout society, she is undermining precisely what is most valuable about maternalness and love—their deeply personal and intensely intimate natures.[38] Perhaps this is why Elshtain's language always sounds so strained when she attempts to make maternal virtues the basis for political discourse and action. The very impossibility of such a task reveals itself in a rhetoric of sharp-edged words like 'wedge' or 'insert', or words of craftlike instrumentality like 'template', or words that expose the diminution of the intensity of maternal thinking, as when it gets 'diffused' over the members of political society as a whole. The rhetoric belies the argument.

Thus, in her determination to revive the family and maternalize feminist consciousness, Elshtain strains a distinctive social practice—that of mothering—to its breaking-point. In the end, all women-as-mothers can do is to chasten arrogant public power; they cannot democratize it. Women who do not venture beyond the family or participate in practices beyond mothering cannot attain an adequate understanding of the way politics determines their own lives. Nor can they—as mothers or creatures of the family—help transform a politics that stands in conflict with maternal values. The only consciousness that can serve as a basis for this transformation and so for the sort of active citizenry that Elshtain wishes to promote is a distinctly political consciousness steeped in a commitment to democratic values, participatory citizenship, and egalitarianism. Likewise, the only practice that can generate and reinforce such a consciousness is not mothering, but the practice of acting politically, of engaging with other citizens in determining and pursuing individual and common interests in relation to the public good. In sum, the political practice of citizenship must not be forsaken for the social practice of mothering, if feminism is to succeed.

Women, of course, may be motivated in the first instance to enter politics because of special interests they have as mothers or potential mothers. The examples we now have are plentiful and important (for example, Mothers Against Drunk Drivers, Mothers of Love Canal, mothers who protest against nuclear war or the instalment of missiles). But we must not mistake the nature of these enterprises either in the context of contemporary politics or in the context of Elshtain's own argument. Elshtain is not just promoting 'women's issues' or counselling women-as-mothers to organize as pressure groups in the political arena of the liberal capitalist state. Quite the contrary. Her vision vehemently opposes this conception of politics, and all its competitiveness and marketeering. Women or mothers may, of course, in instances like those above, be awakened to the necessity of becoming active citizens because of the particular interests they have as women and mothers. But, as I have been arguing, being a citizen is not (the same as) being a mother, nor vice versa. These different social descriptions of women entail different virtues and ideals, and are founded on different material practices. If we are to have the kind of democratic—and ethical—polity Elshtain desires, then women who become motivated to enter politics in their role as mothers must remain in politics as citizens, and act with and toward other citizens as citizens do—and not as a mother does toward her child. And if women retreat to their homes after a periodic—and rare— victory, they will never contribute to a democratic and ethical polity, and—worse still—they will recapitulate the worst features of political participants in the liberal-capitalist state.

The matter hinges, then, not on the 'victory' of one 'realm' of human life over the other, but on the nature of human action and the meaning of 'politicization'. Indeed, to press the issue, to establish maternal thinking as the basis for feminist political consciousness, is to get matters precisely backwards; for it is only when mothers become politicized and, in particular, when they act collectively as feminists that they can secure public policies that, among other things, protect children. In the process, they begin to realize that they are not just mothers, but women who share a common political situation with other women, some of whom are mothers, some of whom are not. Accordingly, the values that they must defend are not as such maternal (the growth and preservation of children) but political (freedom, equality, community power). For it is only once these political values have been realized that specific issues, including maternal ones, can be pursued with determination and imagination.[39] Generously, that is why Aristotle said that the polis was prior to all other associations and activities, not that 'the public' was a superior realm of male virtues. And that is why the goal of feminism must be to politicize consciousness, not to maternalize it.

This goal is programmatic in the face of the future. But it is not without its historical roots. Feminist historians have begun to recover and reclaim women's experiences long ignored by generations of male historians. The reclamation has revealed not only women's private lives, but also their political lives. Their politicalness has most assuredly not been of the sort Elshtain describes as 'embracing a public life . . . created by men'.[40] Rather, it has often been in opposition to injustice, oppression, and institutionalized systems of power. Feminist historians have discovered that women develop distinctive organizational styles and generate reform movements, act collectively and in distinctively democratic ways, agitate for social change and challenge political corruption.[41] One of the most interesting aspects of current studies in American women's history concerns the politicalization of women's social and community associations. We are discovering that women have been and remain eminently capable of politicizing themselves without losing their souls. Thus if we are to locate a dimension of women's experience that is unique to us as women, we would do well to look to our history, our organizational styles, and our distinctive modes of political discourse—but not to our role as (potential) mothers.[42] The latter collapses our identity into a single dimension, however nurturing and loving that may be in some possible world.

The need to challenge 'arrogant public power' and an 'amoral political order'—to use Elshtain's words—remains a crucial feminist task. But the only effective challenge to a corrupt or unjust state is one that is itself expressly political. Not the language of love and compassion, but only the language of freedom and equality, citizenship and justice, will challenge non-democratic and oppressive political institutions. Accordingly, what feminist political consciousness must draw upon is the potentiality of women-as-citizens and their historical reality as a collective and democratic power, not upon the 'robust' demands of motherhood. In practice, we might expect such consciousness to take shape not in the silent procession of empty baby strollers, nor in acquiescence to interest-group and party politics, but in public speeches and debates, organized movements with expressly political goals, and democratic activities in which feminist citizens challenge the 'givens' and seek to revitalize democratic values with a view toward the generations of citizens to come.

Notes

1. See Kate Millett, *Sexual Politics* (New York: Ballantine Books, 1969); Betty Friedan, *The Feminine Mystique* (New York: Dell, 1963); Juliet Mitchell, *Woman's Estate* (New York: Vintage Books, 1971); and Shulamith Firestone, *The Dialectic of Sex* (New York: Bantam Books, 1970).
2. See e.g. Sheila Rowbotham, *Women, Resistance and Revolution: A History of Women and Revolution in the Modern World* (New York:

Random House, 1972); Zillah Eisenstein, *Capitalist Patriarchy and the Case for Socialist Feminism* (New York: Monthly Review Press, 1979); Mariarosa Della Cosa and Selma James, *The Power of Women and the Subversion of Community* (Bristol: Falling Water Press, 1973); and Wendy Edmond and Suzi Fleming, eds., *All Work and No Pay: Women, Housework and the Wages Due* (Bristol: Falling Water Press, 1975).

3. Sara Ruddick, 'Maternal Thinking', *Feminist Studies*, 6/2 (Summer 1980): 342–67; 'Pacifying the Forces: Drafting Women in the Interests of Peace', *Signs*, 8/3 (Spring 1983): 471–89; and 'Preservative Love and Military Destruction: Reflections on Mothering and Peace', in Joyce Treblicot (ed.), *Mothering: Essays on Feminist Theory* (Totowa, NJ: Littlefield Adams, 1983).

4. Jean Bethke Elshtain, *Public Man, Private Woman* (Princeton, NJ: Princeton University Press, 1981); 'Feminists Against the Family', *The Nation* (Nov. 1979): 497–500; 'Feminism, Family and Community', *Dissent*, 29/4 (Fall 1982): 442–9; 'Feminist Discourse and Its Discontents: Language, Power and Meaning', *Signs*, 7/3 (Spring 1982): 603–21; 'Antigone's Daughters', *Democracy*, 2/2 (Apr. 1982): 46–59; 'On Feminism, Family and Community' (response to Ehrenreich), *Dissent*, 30/1 (1983): 103–9; 'On "the Family Crisis"', *Democracy*, 3/1 (Winter 1983): 137–9; and 'On Beautiful Souls, Just Warriors, and Feminist Consciousness', *Women's Studies International Forum*, 5/3–4 (Winter 1982): 341–8.

5. Elshtain, 'Feminism, Family and Community', 447.

6. Elshtain, *Public Man, Private Woman*, 337, 343.

7. Elshtain, 'On "the Family Crisis"', 183.

8. Elshtain, 'Antigone's Daughters', 56; *Public Man, Private Woman*, 327.

9. Elshtain, 'Feminism, Family and Community', 447.

10. Elshtain, *Public Man, Private Woman*, 327.

11. Ibid. 326–7.

12. Ibid. 243.

13. Elshtain, 'Antigone's Daughters', 55.

14. Elshtain, 'On Beautiful Souls, Just Warriors and Feminist Consciousness', 346.

15. Elshtain, 'Feminism, Family and Community', 448.

16. Elshtain, 'Antigone's Daughters', 49.

17. Ibid.

18. Elshtain, 'Feminists Against the Family', 1.

19. This may account for Elshtain's extremely curious statement in *Public Man, Private Woman*: 'I shall spend somewhat less time discussing a reconstructive notion of the public because it stands in less need of a defense and reaffirmation within feminist political discourse than our besieged sphere of the private' (p. 337). This is surprising

for at least three reasons: first, because we have been led to believe that one of Elshtain's major goals is the reconstruction of the public; second, because she has argued that previous feminist discourse has been woefully inadequate in its attempt to formulate a political (public) consciousness; and third (and most important), it reconfirms that Elshtain thinks the 'public' and 'private' are distinct entities that can be split apart and examined separately—as if changing or 'reconstructing' one has nothing to do with the other.

20. This is a reconstruction of Elshtain's very brief sketch in the final chapter of *Public Man, Private Women*, esp. pp. 349–53.

21. See esp. Barbara Ehrenreich's comments in *Dissent*, 30/1 (Winter 1983); and Marshall Berman, 'Feminism, Community, Freedom', *Dissent*, 30/2 (Spring 1983).

22. Elshtain, *Public Man, Private Woman*, 448, 322 n. 30, where Elshtain acknowledges, but does not pursue, the problem of defining 'family'. For an analysis that captures the conceptual and material complexities of the family, see Philippe Ariès, *Centuries of Childhood: A Social History of Family Life* (New York: Vintage Books, 1962).

23. Elshtain, *Public Man, Private Woman*, 441.

24. Aristotle, *Politics*, ed. E. Barker (New York: Oxford University Press, 1962), I. xiii, p. 36; I. ii, p. 4; I. xiii, pp. 34–6.

25. Ibid. I. xii, p. 32. See discussion in Elshtain, *Public Man, Private Woman*, 346.

26. Ibid.

27. Elshtain, 'Antigone's Daughters', 56; 'Feminism, Family, and Community', 447.

28. Elshtain, 'Antigone's Daughters', 55.

29. Aristotle, *Politics*, I. i, p. 1.

30. See Aristotle's remarks on the *essential* difference between the *politikos* and other persons in other associations, *Politics*, I. i, p. 2.

31. Ibid. I. ii, p. 6.

32. Ibid. I. xii, p. 32.

33. Ibid. I. ii, pp. 4–5; and III. vi, pp. 110–13.

34. For a 'generous' view of the *vita activa* that has none of the sexist characteristics of Aristotelian thought, see Hannah Arendt, *The Human Condition* (Chicago: University of Chicago Press, 1958).

35. Elshtain, *Public Man, Private Woman*, 351.

36. For a more detailed analysis of the mother–child relationship, see Nancy Chodorow, *The Reproduction of Mothering: Psychoanalysis and the Sociology of Gender* (Berkeley: University of California Press, 1978). For analysis of mother–child relations that acknowledges the problems of maternal authority, see Dorothy Dinnerstein, *The Mermaid and the Minotaur* (New York: Harper Colophon, 1977). Dinnerstein's conclusion implies that we should be concerned not with 'familizing' the polity, but with democratizing the family. Hence

she argues for 'dual parenting', a subject neither Ruddick nor Elshtain addresses. Nor do they consider, as does Dinnerstein, the possibilities and meaning of 'fathering'.

37. Though this issue cannot be discussed here in the detail it deserves, familial metaphors are inappropriate for understanding political arrangements. Those who are tempted to think otherwise would do well to return to Locke's arguments against Filmer's *Patriarcha*. For a modern view, see Martha Acklesberg, ' "Sisters" or "Comrades"? The Politics of Friends and Families', in Irene Diamond (ed.), *Families, Politics, and Public Policy: A Feminist Dialogue on Women and the State* (New York: Longman, 1983), 339–56.

38. For a discussion of why love, goodness, and intimacy (and the Christian virtues in general) are 'anti-political', see Arendt, *The Human Condition*, 51–6, 75–8. Arendt would agree with Elshtain's premise that love is a 'private' thing, but emphatically object to Elshtain's attempt to make it 'public'.

39. I do not think feminists pursue these expressly political goals forcefully enough in theory, though they certainly do in practice. Despite its cogent exposure of patriarchal power, feminist theory has yet to develop its own political theory in opposition of forms of political power it finds objectionable. Feminist theorists need to do more by way of integrating feminist goals with specific political values. I am suggesting only one possible set of such values here—those that constitute democratic citizenship.

40. Elshtain, 'Feminism, Family, and Community', 447.

41. See e.g. Sara Evans and Harry C. Boyte, 'Schools for Action', *Democracy*, 2/4 (Fall 1982): 55–65, for a view of 'women's historical social identity' that, unlike Elshtain's, is not a privatized one. See also Sara Evans, *Personal Politics: The Roots of Women's Liberation in the Civil Rights Movement and the New Left* (New York: Vintage Books, 1980); Louise Tilly, 'Paths of Proletarianization: Organization of Production, Sexual Division of Labor, and Women's Collective Action', *Signs*, 7/2 (Winter 1981): 400–17, for a discussion of women's collective action outside 'formalized' political structures.

42. See e.g. Carol Gilligan, *In a Different Voice: Psychological Theory and Women's Development* (Cambridge, Mass.: Harvard University Press, 1982).

Models of Public Space: Hannah Arendt, the Liberal Tradition, and Jürgen Habermas

Seyla Benhabib

The art of making distinctions is always a difficult and risky undertaking. Distinctions can enlighten as well as cloud an issue. One is always also vulnerable to objections concerning the correct classification of the thought of certain thinkers. This chapter will sidestep questions of historical interpretation and classification in order to delineate three different conceptions of 'public space' that correspond to three main currents of Western political thought. The view of public space common to the 'republican virtue' or 'civic virtue' tradition is described as the 'agonistic' one, and the thought of Hannah Arendt will be the main point of reference. The second conception is provided by the liberal tradition, and particularly by those liberals who, beginning with Kant, make the problem of a 'just and stable public order' the centre of their political thinking. This will be named the 'legalistic' model of public space. The final model of public space is the one implicit in Jürgen Habermas's work. This model, which envisages a democratic-socialist restructuring of late-capitalist societies, will be named 'discursive public space'.

By situating the concept of 'public space' in this context, the discussion is restricted from the outset to normative political theory. The larger sense of the term *Öffentlichkeit*, which would include a literary, artistic and scientific public, will not be of concern here; for whatever other applications and resonances they might have,

Chapter 3 in Seyla Benhabib, *Situating the Self: Gender, Community and Postmodernism in Contemporary Ethics* (Routledge, 1992), 89–120. Reprinted by permission of Blackwell Publishers Ltd and Routledge Inc. This paper was first delivered at the conference on Habermas and the Public Sphere at the University of North Carolina at Chapel Hill, which took place in September 1989, and published in *Habermas and the Public Sphere*, ed. Craig Calhoun (Cambridge, Mass.: MIT Press, 1992), 73–98.

the terms 'public', 'public space', 'res publica' will never lose their intimate rootedness in the domain of political life. This approach will help highlight certain very significant differences among political theories all of which on the surface appear to accord central place to 'public space' or 'publicity' in political life. Not only are there important differences among these three conceptions of public space, but two of these views are severely limited in their usefulness for analysing and evaluating political discourse and legitimation problems in advanced capitalist, and possibly even in what is now being referred to as 'soviet style' societies.[1] When compared with the Arendtian and liberal conceptions, the strength of the Habermasian model is that questions of democratic legitimacy in advanced capitalist societies are central to it. Nevertheless, whether this model is resourceful enough to help us think through the transformation of politics in our kinds of societies is an open question. Taking the women's movement and the feminist critique of the public/private distinction as a point of reference, the final sections of this chapter will probe the discourse model of public space from this point of view.

HANNAH ARENDT AND THE AGONISTIC CONCEPT OF PUBLIC SPACE

Hannah Arendt is the central political thinker of this century whose work has reminded us with great poignancy of the 'lost treasures' of our tradition of political thought, and specifically of the 'loss' of public space, of *der öffentliche Raum*, under conditions of modernity. Arendt's major theoretical work, *The Human Condition*, is usually, and not altogether unjustifiably, treated as an anti-modernist political work. By 'the rise of the social' in this work, Arendt means the institutional differentiation of modern societies into the narrowly political realm on the one hand and the economic market and the family on the other. As a result of these transformations, economic processes which had hitherto been confined to the 'shadowy realm of the household' emancipate themselves and become public matters. The same historical process which brought forth the modern constitutional state also brings forth 'society', that realm of social interaction which interposes itself between the 'household' on the one hand and the political state on the other.[2] A century ago, Hegel had described this process as the development in the midst of ethical life of a 'system of needs' (*System der Bedürfnisse*), of a domain of economic activity governed by commodity exchange and the pursuit of economic self-interest. The expansion of this sphere meant the disappearance of the 'universal', of the common concern for the political association, for the *res publica*, from the hearts and minds of men.[3] Arendt sees in this process the occluding of the political by the 'social' and the transformation of the public space of politics into a pseudospace of interaction in which individuals no longer 'act' but 'merely behave' as economic producers, consumers and urban city dwellers.

This relentlessly negative account of the 'rise of the social' and the decline of the public realm has been identified as the core of Arendt's political 'anti-modernism'.[4] Indeed, at one level Arendt's text is a panegyric to the agonistic political space of the Greek polis. What disturbs the contemporary reader is perhaps less the high-minded and highly idealized picture of Greek political life which Arendt draws but more her neglect of the following constellation of issues. The agonistic political space of the polis was only possible because large groups of human beings like women, slaves, labourers, non-citizen residents, and all non-Greeks were excluded from it, and made possible through their 'labor' for the daily necessities of life that 'leisure for politics' which the few enjoyed; by contrast, the rise of the social was accompanied by the emancipation of these groups from the 'shadowy interior of the household' and by their entry into public life; is Arendt's critique of this process also a critique of political universalism as such? Is the 'recovery of the public space' under conditions of modernity necessarily an elitist and anti-democratic project which can hardly be reconciled with the demand for universal political emancipation and the universal extension of citizenship rights that have accompanied modernity since the American and French revolutions?[5]

Yet it is greatly misleading to read Hannah Arendt primarily as a nostalgic thinker. She devoted as much space in her work to analysing the dilemmas and prospects of politics under conditions of modernity as she did to the decline of public space in modernity. If we are not to read her account of the disappearance of the public realm as a *Verfallsgeschichte* (a history of decline) then, how are we to interpret it? The key here is Arendt's odd methodology which conceives of political thought as 'storytelling'. Viewed in this light, her 'story' of the transformation of public space is an 'exercise' of thought. Such thought exercises dig under the rubble of history in order to recover those 'pearls' of past experience, with their sedimented and hidden layers of meaning, such as to cull from them a story that can orient the mind in the future.[6] The vocation of the theorist as 'storyteller' is the unifying thread of Arendt's political and philosophical analyses from the origins of totalitarianism to her reflections on the French and American revolutions to her theory of public space and to her final words to the first volume of *The Life of the Mind* on 'Thinking'.

I have clearly joined the ranks of those who for some time now have been attempting to dismantle metaphysics, and philosophy with all its categories, as we have known them from their beginning in Greece until today. Such dismantling is possible only on the assumption that the thread of tradition is broken and we shall not be able to renew it. Historically speaking, what actually has broken down is the Roman trinity that for thousands of years united religion, authority, and tradition. The loss of this trinity does not destroy the past . . .

What has been lost is the continuity of the past . . . What you then are left with is still the past, but a *fragmented* past, which has lost its certainty of evaluation.[7]

Read in this light, Arendt's account of the 'rise of the social' and the decline of public space under conditions of modernity can be viewed not as a nostalgic *Verfallsgeschichte* but as the attempt to think through the human history sedimented in layers of language. We must learn to identify those moments of rupture, displacement, and dislocation in history. At such moments language is the witness to the more profound transformations taking place in human life. Such a *Begriffsgeschichte* is a remembering, in the sense of a creative act of 're-membering', that is, of putting together the 'members' of a whole, of a rethinking which sets free the lost potentials of the past. 'The history of revolutions . . . could be told in a parable form as the tale of an age-old treasure which, under the most varied circumstances, appears abruptly, unexpectedly, and disappears again, under different mysterious conditions, as though it were a *fata morgana*.'[8]

Nonetheless, Arendt's thought is not free of assumptions deriving from an *Ursprungsphilosophie* which posits an original state or temporal point as the privileged source to which one must trace back the phenomena such as to capture their 'true' meaning. As opposed to rupture, displacement, and dislocation, this view emphasizes the continuity between the past origin and the present condition, and seeks to uncover at the origin the lost and concealed essence of the phenomena. There are really two strains in Hannah Arendt's thought, one corresponding to the method of fragmentary historiography, and inspired by Walter Benjamin,[9] the other inspired by the phenomenology of Husserl and Heidegger, and according to which memory is the mimetic recollection of the lost origins of phenomena as contained in some fundamental human experience. In accordance with this latter approach, reminders abound in *The Human Condition* of 'the original meaning of politics' or of the 'lost' distinction between the 'private' and the 'public'.[10] The concept that perhaps best illustrates Arendt's equivocation between fragmentary history and *Ursprungsphilosophie* is that of 'public space'. This topographical figure of speech is suggested early on in her work, at the end of *The Origins of Totalitarianism*, to compare various forms of political rule. Constitutional government is likened to moving within a space where the law is like the hedges erected between the buildings and one orients oneself upon known territory. Tyranny is like a desert; under conditions of tyranny one moves in an unknown, vast, open space, where the will of the tyrant occasionally befalls one like the sandstorm overtaking the desert traveller. Totalitarianism has no spatial topology: it is like an iron band, compressing people increasingly together until they are formed into one.[11]

Indeed, if one locates Arendt's concept of 'public space' in the context of her theory of totalitarianism, it acquires a rather different focus from the one dominant in *The Human Condition*. The terms 'agonistic' and 'associational' can capture this contrast. According to the 'agonistic' view, the public realm represents that space of appearances in which moral and political greatness, heroism and preeminence are revealed, displayed, shared with others. This is a competitive space, in which one competes for recognition, precedence and acclaim; ultimately it is the space in which one seeks a guarantee against the futility and the passage of all things human: 'For the *polis* was for the Greeks, as the *res publica* was for the Romans, first of all their guarantee against the futility of individual life, the space protected against this futility and reserved for the relative permanence, if not immortality, of mortals.'[12]

By contrast, the 'associational' view of public space suggests that such a space emerges whenever and wherever, in Arendt's words, 'men act together in concert'.[13] On this model, public space is the space 'where freedom can appear'.[14] It is not a space in any topographical or institutional sense: a town hall or a city square where people do not 'act in concert' is not a public space in this

Arendtian sense. But a private dining room in which people gather to hear a *Samizdat* or in which dissidents meet with foreigners becomes a public space; just as a field or a forest can also become public space if they are the object and the location of an 'action in concert', of a demonstration to stop the construction of a highway or a military airbase, for example. These diverse topographical locations become public spaces in that they become the 'sites' of power, of common action coordinated through speech and persuasion. Violence can occur in private and in public, but its language is essentially private because it is the language of pain. Force, like violence, can be located in both realms. In a way, it has no language, and nature remains its quintessential source. It moves without having to persuade or to hurt. Power, however, is the only force that emanates from action, and it comes from the mutual action of a group of human beings: once in action, one can make things happen, thus becoming a source of a different kind of 'force'.

The distinction between the 'agonal' and the 'associational' models corresponds to the Greek as opposed to the modern experience of politics. The agonal space of the polis was made possible by a morally homogeneous and politically egalitarian, but exclusive community, in which action could also be a revelation of the self to others. Under conditions of moral and political homogeneity and lack of anonymity, the 'agonal' dimension, the vying for excellence among peers, could take place. But for the moderns public space is essentially porous; neither access to it nor its agenda of debate can be predefined by criteria of moral and political homogeneity. With the entry of every new group into the public space of politics after the French and American revolutions, the scope of the public gets extended. The emancipation of workers made property relations into a public-political issue; the emancipation of women has meant that the family and the so-called private sphere become political issues; the attainment of rights by non-white and non-Christian peoples has put cultural questions of collective self- and other-representations on the 'public' agenda. Not only is it the 'lost treasure' of revolutions that eventually all can partake in them, but equally, when freedom emerges from action in concert, there can be no agenda to *predefine* the topic of public conversation. The struggle over what gets included in the public agenda is itself a struggle for justice and freedom. The distinction between the 'social' and the 'political' makes no sense in the modern world, not because all politics has become administration and because the economy has become the quintessential 'public', as Arendt thought, but primarily because the struggle to make something public is a struggle for justice.

Perhaps the episode which best illustrates this blind spot in Arendt's thought is that of school desegregation in Little Rock, Arkansas. Arendt likened the demands of the black parents, upheld by the US Supreme Court, to have their children admitted into previously all-white schools to the desire of the social parvenue to gain recognition in a society that did not care to admit her. This time around Arendt failed to make the 'fine distinction' and confused an issue of public justice—equality of educational access—with an issue of social preference—who my friends are or whom I invite to dinner. It is to her credit, however, that after the intervention of the black novelist Ralph Ellison she had the grace to reverse her position.[15]

At the root of Arendt's vacillations on this issue lies a more important problem, namely her phenomenological essentialism. In accordance with essentialist assumptions, 'public space' is defined either as that space in which only a certain *type of activity*, namely action as opposed to work or labour, takes place or it is delimited from other 'social' spheres with reference to the *substantive content* of the public dialogue. Both strategies lead to dead ends. Let us note that the differentiation of action types into labour, work, and action, and the principle of public space operate on different levels. Different action types, like work and labour, can become the locus of 'public space' if they are reflexively challenged and placed into question from the standpoint of the asymmetrical power relations governing them. To give a few examples: obviously 'productivity quotas' in the factory workshop, how many chips per hour a worker should produce, can become matters of 'public concern', if the legitimacy of those setting the quotas, their right to do so, their reasons for doing so are challenged. Likewise, as recent experience has shown us, even the most intricate questions of nuclear strategy, like the number of nuclear warheads on a missile and the time required to diffuse them, can be 'reclaimed' by a public under conditions of democratic legitimacy and become part of what our *res publica* is about. Arendt, by contrast, relegated certain types of activity like work and labour, and by extension most, if not all, issues of economics and technology, to the 'private' realm alone, ignoring that these activities and relations, insofar as they are based on power relations, could become matters of public dispute as well.

Likewise, the attempt to define 'public space' by specifying the agenda of the public conversation is futile. Even in Arendtian terms, the effect of collective action in concert will be to put ever new and unexpected items on the agenda of public debate. Arendt herself in the 'associational' model developed not a substantive but a *procedural* concept of public space, which is in fact compatible with this view. What is important here is not so much what public discourse is about as the way in which this discourse takes place: force and violence destroy the specificity of public discourse by introducing the 'dumb' language of physical superiority and constraint and by silencing the voice of persuasion and conviction. Power alone is generated by public discourse and is sustained by it. From the standpoint of this procedural model, neither the distinction between the social and the political nor the distinction between work, labour, or action are that relevant. At stake is the reflexive questioning of issues by all those affected by their foreseeable consequences and the recognition of their right to do so.

When compared to Hannah Arendt's reflections, the advantage of the liberal concept of public space is that the link between power, legitimacy, and public discourse is made most explicit by it. Yet this model is also more sterile than the Arendtian one in that it conceives of politics too closely along the analogy of juridical relations, thereby losing that emphasis on spontaneity, imagination, participation, and empowerment which Arendt saw to be the mark of authentic politics whenever and wherever it occurred.

THE LIBERAL MODEL OF PUBLIC SPACE AS 'PUBLIC DIALOGUE'

With his model of 'liberal dialogue', Bruce Ackerman expresses a fundamental tenet of contemporary liberalism: liberalism is a form of political culture in which the question of legitimacy is paramount.[16] Liberalism is a way of talking about and publicly justifying power, a political culture of *public dialogue* based on certain kinds of *conversational constraints*. The most significant conversational constraint in liberalism is *neutrality*, which rules that no reason advanced within a discourse of legitimation can be a good reason if it requires the power holder to assert two claims: (a) that his conception of the good is better than that asserted by his fellow citizens; or (b) that regardless of his conception of the good, he is intrinsically superior to one or more of his fellow citizens.[17]

Bruce Ackerman bases his case for public dialogue 'not on some general feature of the moral life, but upon the distinctive way liberalism conceives of the problem of public order'.[18] His question is how different primary groups, about whom we only know that they do not share the same conception of the good, can 'resolve the problem of coexistence in a *reasonable* way'.[19] Ackerman believes that citizens in a liberal state must be guided by a Supreme Pragmatic Imperative (SPI) which states that they must be willing to participate in an ongoing dialogue about their conception of the good with others who are not members of their primary group.

Ackerman is concerned to find a justification of this imperative that will not fall into the three traps which traditionally affect moral philosophies of liberalism. One must find a justification of the SPI that is not based on trumping, that is, already asserting as supreme one moral view over others. Furthermore, one cannot assume, as utilitarians do, that there is a translation manual neutral enough in its language and in terms of which all our various moral commitments can be stated. According to Ackerman, such a translation manual would violate the sense of the good of one of the parties. Finally, one cannot ask the parties to assume a 'transcendental perspective' as the precondition for entering into dialogue. Such a transcendental perspective, let us say the point of view of the 'original position' or that of the 'ideal speech situation', abstracts so radically from the condition of existing differences that it forces the parties to the public dialogue to assent to moral truths which they do not hold.

The way out is the path of 'conversational restraint'.

When you and I learn that we disagree about one or another dimension of the moral truth, we should not search for some common value that will trump this disagreement; nor should we try to translate our moral disagreement into some putatively neutral framework; nor should we seek to transcend our disagreement by talking about how some hypothetical creature would resolve it. We should simply say *nothing at all* about this disagreement and try to solve our problem by invoking premises that we *do* agree upon. In restraining ourselves in this way, we need *not* lose the chance to talk to one another about our deepest, moral disagreements in countless other, *more private, contexts*. Having constrained the conversation in this way, we may instead use dialogue for pragmatically productive purposes: to identify normative premises all political participants find reasonable or, at least, not unreasonable.[20]

The pragmatic justification of 'conversational restraint' is not morally neutral; this justification trumps certain conceptions of the good life in that it privatizes them and pushes them out of the agenda of public debate in the liberal state.[21] Not only members of certain religious groups, who may still seek to convert others to their faith, but also all groups working for the radical change of the social structure would then have to withdraw from the public arena of the liberal state into other more 'private' contexts. The difference between my defence of a communicative ethic which also trumps certain conventional views of morality and Bruce Ackerman's defence of conversational restraints is that on the model of practical discourse following from communicative ethics, no issues of debate and no conceptions of the good life are precluded from being voiced in the public arena of the liberal state. Ackerman and I agree that conventional views of morality are not likely to be impartial and comprehensive enough to allow the public coexistence of differing and competing conceptions of the good life. Thus they cannot serve as the moral foundations of a liberal-democratic state. Yet they should be allowed to exist in such a state as partial conceptions of the good which enjoy an equal public forum with other, more comprehensive views.[22]

The pragmatic justification not only trumps but also 'transcends', for it asks the parties to the conversation to agree to 'say nothing at all about' fundamental disagreements. It is unclear why this agreement *not to talk* about fundamental disagreements in public is any less loaded or controversial an assumption than the idea of a 'veil of ignorance' which asks us to feign ignorance about our conception of the good. If I am deeply committed to the belief that prevalent conceptions of sexual division of labour in our societies are morally wrong because they oppress women and hinder their full expression of themselves as human beings, why should I agree not to do the best I can to make this a public issue and to convince others of my point of view? Or suppose I am a member of the Israeli opposition to the occupation of the West Bank and Gaza territories. I consider this occupation wrong not on pragmatic grounds but on moral grounds, because I believe that the occupation is corrupting the ethical values of the Jewish people. I may well be aware that under current conditions, public opinion is so divided that I stand no chance of winning assent; nevertheless is it unreasonable of me to seek the widest possible forum of public discussion and participation to air my views, rather than to agree with you, as Ackerman advocates, not to talk about what is of most concern to me. Either Ackerman's justification of the

SPI is based on stronger moral grounds than he admits to or it cannot claim the supreme status it is supposed to enjoy.[23]

But is the path of conversational restraint indeed so arbitrary? Why not regard it as one of those procedural constraints on dialogue that we all have to agree to on reasonable, moral grounds, even if not wholly pragmatic ones? The idea of conversational restraint, as it has been presented so far, presupposes a questionable moral epistemology which implicitly justifies a separation between the public and the private that is oppressive to the concerns of certain groups. On these grounds as well its moral persuasiveness is limited.

By the 'moral epistemology' of the conversational restraint model I mean the following. The liberal theorist of conversational restraint presupposes that the primary groups to the conversation already know what their deepest disagreements are even before they have engaged in the conversation. These groups already seem convinced that a particular problem is a moral, religious, or aesthetic issue as opposed to an issue of distributive justice or public policy. While we can legitimately discuss the second, says the liberal theorist, let us abstract from the first. Take, however, issues like abortion, pornography, and domestic violence. What kinds of issues are they? Are they questions of 'justice' or of the 'good life'? The moral or political theorist is in possession of no moral dictionary or moral geometry in this matter such as would allow her to classify these issues as being matters of 'justice' or of the 'good life'. In part it is the unconstrained public dialogue that will help us define the nature of the issues we are debating. Certainly, as citizens and as theorists we enter the public fray with a set of more or less articulated, more or less preformed opinions, principles, and values. As democratic citizens and theorists we are participants in a debate, but we should not seek to define the agenda of the debate. We may, on the basis of more or less well-supported principles and values, wish to maintain that abortion should be considered a matter of individual choice for the women involved; but it is not a (nonexistent) consensus about the kind of issue this is that leads us to this position. Rather, principles of moral autonomy and moral choice, the right of women to self-realization, and some sensitivity to the often tragic and irreconcilable aspects of our value commitments inform our views. Indeed, citizens must feel free to introduce, in Bruce Ackerman's words, 'any and all moral arguments into the conversational field'. For it is only after the dialogue has been opened in this radical fashion that we can be sure that we have come to agree upon a mutually acceptable definition of the problem rather than reaching some compromise consensus.

The issue of pornography illustrates my point well. This question has been so divisive and has created such strange and unholy alliances—between Andrea Dworkin and Jerry Falwell, for example —that it is the paradigm example of the kind of moral disagreement that the *modus vivendi* liberal may urge us to agree not to publicly disagree about. This, however, is precisely what we should not do at this stage of the debate. Whether pornography is to be defined as a question of the reasonable limitations to be imposed upon the First Amendment right of free speech; whether pornography is to be thought of as a private, moral issue concerning matters of sexual taste and style; whether pornography is to be thought of as a matter of aesthetic-cultural sensibility and as a question of artistic fantasy—we simply cannot know before the process of unconstrained public dialogue has run its course. I no more want to live in a society which cannot distinguish between *Hustler* magazine and Salinger's *Catcher in the Rye* than Ackerman does, or in a society that would place Henry Miller and D. H. Lawrence in the company of *Deep Throat*. As sensitive as one may be to the traditional liberal fear that unlimited public conversation might erode those few constitutional guarantees we can rely upon, the reprivatization of issues that have become public only generates conceptual confusion, political resentment, and moral outrage. I consider limitations upon the content and scope of public dialogue, other than constitutional guarantees of free speech, to be unnecessary. A normative theory of such conversational constraints fails to become a critical model of legitimation.

An additional limitation of the liberal model of public space is that it conceives of political relations all too often narrowly along the model of juridical ones. The chief concern expressed by the idea of 'dialogic neutrality' is that of the rightful coexistence of different groups, each subscribing to a different conception of the good, in a pluralistic society. The just in modern societies, it is said, should be neutral *vis-à-vis* fundamental assumptions concerning the good life. Neutrality is indeed one of the fundamental cornerstones of the modern legal system: modern, promulgated law, unlike ancient and customary law, should not 'ethically' mould character but should provide the space within which autonomous individuals can pursue and develop various conceptions of the good life. Even under conditions of a modern, pluralist, democratic society, however, politics is about something other than 'neutrality'. Democratic politics challenges, redefines, and renegotiates the divisions between the good and the just, the moral and the legal, the private and the public. For these distinctions, as they have been established by modern states at the end of social and historical struggles, contain within them the result of historical power compromises.

To illustrate. Before the emergence of strong working-class movements and the eventual establishment of social-welfare-type measures in European countries and North America, questions relating to the health of workers in the workplace, problems of accidents on the job, and, in our days, the harmful side-effects of certain chemicals, were frequently construed by employers as issues of 'trade secrets' and 'business privacy'. As a result of political struggles, the definition of these issues was transformed from trade secrets and private business practices to major issues of 'public concern'. The principle of liberal neutrality is not helpful in guiding our thoughts on such matters. All it says is that once this redefinition and political renegotiation of the right and the good has occurred, then the law should be neutral; that is, the OSHA (Office of Safety and Health Administration) should be neutral in applying this legislation to Chinese laundromats, Italian restaurants, or the Lockheed corporation. But public dialogue is not about what all the Chinese laundromats, Italian restaurants, and the Lockheed corporation know they agree to, even before they have entered the public fray; rather, public dialogue means challenging and redefining the collective good, and one's sense of justice as a result of the public fray. The liberal principle of dialogic neutrality, while it expresses one of the main principles of the modern legal system, is too restrictive and frozen in application to the dynamics of power struggles in actual political processes. A public life, conducted according to the principle of liberal dialogic neutrality, would not only lack the agonistic dimension of politics, in Arendtian terms, but, perhaps more severely, would restrict the scope of the public conversation in a way which would be inimical to the interests of oppressed groups. All struggles against oppression in the modern world begin by redefining what had previously been considered 'private', non-public, and non-political issues as matters of public concern, as issues of justice, as sites of power which need discursive legitimation. In this respect, the women's movement, the peace movement, the ecology movements, and new ethnic identity movements follow a similar logic. There is little room in the liberal

77

model of neutrality for thinking about the logic of such struggles and social movements. In Arendtian language, liberalism ignores the 'agonistic' dimension of public-political life.

Given the historical concerns out of which political liberalism has emerged and to which it has sought an answer, like the limits of absolutist state power and the problems of religious tolerance, this is hardly surprising. The search for a just, stable, and tolerant political order has been the distinguishing mark of liberal political theory. This search has also led to an excessive focus in contemporary liberalism upon the limits and justification of state power and other public agencies, to the neglect of other dimensions of political life such as life in political associations, movements, citizens' groups, town meetings, and public fora. In Benjamin Barber's perspicacious words, among the cognitive requirements of contemporary liberalism appears to be 'an antipathy to democracy and its sustaining institutional structures (participation, civic education, political activism) and a preference for "thin" rather than strong versions of political life in which citizens are spectators and clients while politicians are professionals who do the actual governing'.[24] Certainly, this is no place to settle the old conflict between liberalism and democracy. Benjamin Barber's observation is quite to the point insofar as it might help us see why the concept of 'public space', as a space of political deliberation, action, and exchange, plays such a minimal role in contemporary liberalism. It is as if once the 'constitutional assembly' in which we select principles of a just political association is over, the citizens of the liberal state retire into their private abodes and quit the democratic arena of political give and take.

The contrast between democratic deliberation, of the sort envisaged by Arendt and Barber, and the liberal conception of public dialogue can be well captured when juxtaposed to John Rawls's idea of 'free public reason'.

Just as a political conception of justice needs certain principles of justice for the basic structure to specify its content, it also needs certain guidelines of enquiry and publicly recognized rules of assessing evidence to govern its application. Otherwise, there is no agreed way for determining whether these principles are satisfied, and for settling what they require of particular institutions, or in particular situations. . . . And given the fact of pluralism, there is, I think, no better practical alternative than to limit ourselves to the shared methods of, and the public knowledge available to common sense, and the procedures and conclusions of science when these are not controversial.[25]

Rawls adds the very important observation: 'The maxim that just-ice must not only be done, but be seen to be done, holds good not only in law but in free public reason.'[26]

The idea that the justice of institutions be 'in the public's eye', so to speak, for the public to scrutinize, examine, and reflect upon is fundamental. That it recognizes the legitimation of power or the examination of the justice of institutions to be a public pro-cess, open to all citizens to partake in, is one of the central tenets of liberalism and one which has its roots in the political primacy of consent in social contract theories. From the standpoint of a discourse model of legitimacy as well, this is crucial. Note, how-ever, that for Rawls 'free public reason' does not describe the kind of reasoning used by citizens and their representatives in the polity. Undoubtedly, Rawls would like them to exercise their 'free public reason' in this way. But as the idea of free public reason has been formulated, it applies less to a process of democratic discussion or parliamentary debate than to the reasoning of a parliamentary investigative body, or the kind of investigation a federal agency may conduct when determining whether a hospital which has received public funds has also complied with affirmative action regulations. In Rawls's view, free public reason is the manner in which public associations account for their doings and conduct their affairs in a polity.[27]

While there is little doubt that this principle of free public rea-son expresses a governing normative rule for the public account-ability of the major institutions of a liberal-democratic society, consider also what is missing from it. All contestatory, rhetorical, affective, impassioned elements of public discourse, with all their excesses and virtues, are absent from this view. Free public reason is not freely wielded public reasoning, with all the infuriating ideo-logical and rhetorical mess that this may involve. Again in his com-ment on Ackerman, Benjamin Barber captures this point well.

It is neutrality that destroys dialogue, for the power of political talk lies in its creativity, its variety, its openness and flexibility, its inventiveness, its capacity for discovery, its subtlety and complexity, its potential for empathetic and affective expression—in other words, in its deeply para-doxical, some would say, dialectical, character.[28]

Certainly, one cannot only focus on the speeches of Abraham Lincoln, Adlai Stevenson, and Jesse Jackson to the exclusion of the less ennobling outbursts of a Richard Nixon, Fidel Castro, or Nikita Khrushchev. What Barber's observation captures none the less is the open-ended, contestatory, affective dimension of the political through which free public reason can assume the character of 'shared reasoning'.

To this conception of contestatory public speech[29] or shared reasoning, the liberal theorist will respond that, lofty and ennobling as its vision may be, the agonistic view of the political leaves the floodgates open for the whim of majoritarian decisions. What if less than noble majorities challenge the principles of neutrality and the lines between the right and the good in such ways as to lead to religious fanaticism, persecution of unpopular minorities, intrusion of the state into the domain of private life, or even the political condoning of surveillance by children of parents, by spouses of each other, all in the name of some shared good? In response to such concerns Rawls suggests that certain matters be taken off the political agenda of the liberal state insofar as 'They are part of the public charter of a constitutional regime and not a suitable topic for on-going public debate and legislation, as if they can be changed at any time, one way or the other'.[30] The rejection of slavery and serfdom and the guarantee for all religions of equal liberty of conscience are among the topics which should be taken off the political agenda of the liberal state for Rawls. He adds: 'Of course, that certain matters are taken off the political agenda does not mean that a political conception of justice should not explain why this is done. Indeed, as I note above, a political conception should do precisely this.'[31]

This standard liberal concern about the corrosive effect of unbridled majoritarian politics upon civil and political liberties is, I believe, incontrovertible. Agonistic visions of the political are often inattentive to the institutional preconditions which must be fulfilled for such a politics to unfold. But for complex, democratic societies the contrast between the 'agonistic' and the 'legalistic' conceptions of public space may be overly simplistic, to the extent that a liberal, legal-constitutional framework guaranteeing equal civil and political rights as well as rights of conscience is a precondition for universal citizenship participation. In her reflections on Kant's concept of judgement, Hannah Arendt confronted the question of what the liberal theorist would name fundamental rights and liberties, and what I name the normative foundations of the political. She was unable to offer a satisfactory resolution to this problem, and the question of the normative presuppositions of the political runs through her work like a red thread from her melancholy reflections on 'the right to have rights' in *The*

Origins of Totalitarianism to her ruminations on constitutions in *On Revolution*.[32]

If both the agonistic and the legalistic models of public space are insufficiently complex to deal with the realities of highly differentiated and pluralistic modern societies, and must be viewed as complementing rather than excluding one another, then it is plausible to assume that a more adequate conception of the public space should combine both dimensions. Although it has not been often presented in this way, the Habermasian principle of *Öffentlichkeit* can fulfil this requirement. The discursive public space is the essential sociological correlate of the discourse concept of legitimacy. It is in such discursive spaces that such dialogues of legitimacy expire. In the next section, I will explore these features of Habermas's concept of *Öffentlichkeit*, but I also would like to show how the contestatory dimension of public discourse gets overridden in this model by Habermas's rigid distinctions between 'justice' and 'the good life', 'needs' and 'interests', 'values' and 'norms'.

THE DISCURSIVE MODEL OF PUBLIC SPACE

Since *The Structural Transformation of the Public Sphere*, Habermas has analysed the development of modern societies in light of the extension of the sphere of public participation.[33] Along with social differentiation and the creation of independent value spheres, modernity brings with it a threefold possibility.[34] In the realm of institutions, the consensual generation of general norms of action through practical discourses moves to the fore. In the realm of personality formation, the development of individual identities becomes increasingly more dependent on the reflexive and critical attitudes of individuals in weaving together a coherent life story beyond conventional role and gender definitions. Self-definitions —who one is—become increasingly autonomous *vis-à-vis* established social practices, and fluid when compared to rigid role understandings. Likewise the appropriation of cultural tradition becomes more dependent upon the creative hermeneutic of contemporary interpreters. Tradition in the modern world loses its legitimacy of simply being valid because it is the way of the past. The legitimacy of tradition rests now with resourceful and creative

81

appropriations of it in view of the problems of meaning in the present. Viewed in this threefold fashion, the principle of participation, far from being antithetical to modernity, is one of its chief prerequisites. In each realm—society, personality, and culture —in the functioning of institutional life, the formation of stable personalities over time, and the continuity of cultural tradition, the reflective effort and contribution of individuals becomes crucial.

Placed in this broader sociological context, the meaning of participation is altered. The exclusive focus on 'political' participation is shifted toward a much more inclusive concept of 'discursive will formation'. Participation is not seen as an activity that is only and most truly possible in a narrowly defined political realm, but as an activity that can be realized in the social and cultural spheres as well. Participating in a citizens' initiative to clean up a polluted harbour is no less political than debating in cultural journals the pejorative presentation of certain groups in terms of stereotypical images (combating sexism and racism in the media). This conception of participation, which emphasizes the determination of norms of action through the practical debate of all affected by them, has the distinctive advantage over the republican or civic virtue conception in that it articulates a vision of the political true to the realities of complex modern societies.

This modernist understanding of participation yields a novel conception of public space. Public space is not understood *agonistically*, as a space of competition for acclaim and immortality among a political elite; it is viewed democratically, as the creation of procedures whereby those affected by general social norms and by collective political decisions can have a say in their formulation, stipulation, and adoption. This conception of the public is also different from the liberal one; for although Habermas and liberal thinkers believe that legitimation in a democratic society can only result from a public dialogue, in the Habermasian model this dialogue does not stand under the constraint of neutrality, but is judged according to the criteria represented by the idea of a 'practical discourse'. The public sphere comes into existence whenever and wherever all affected by general social and political norms of action engage in a practical discourse, evaluating their validity. In effect, there may be as many publics as there are controversial general debates about the validity of norms. Democratization in contemporary societies can be viewed as the increase and growth of autonomous public spheres among participants. As Jean Cohen has astutely observed:

Both the complexity and the diversity within contemporary civil societies call for the posing of the issue of democratization in terms of a variety of differentiated processes, forms, and *loci* depending on the axis of division considered. Indeed, there is an elective affinity between the discourse ethic and modern civil society as the terrain on which an institutionalized plurality of democracies can emerge.[35]

Now this model of a plurality of public spaces emerging in modern societies around contested issues of general concern transcends the dichotomy of majoritarian politics versus constitutional guarantees of civil liberties discussed in the previous section. The discourse model of legitimacy and the discursive view of public space are radically proceduralist. They present normative dialogue as a conversation of justification taking place under the constraints of an 'ideal speech situation'. The normative constraints of the ideal speech situation or of practical discourses have been specified as the conditions of *universal moral respect* and *egalitarian reciprocity*. The presence of these constraints avoids the dilemmas of simple majoritarian political outcomes. Kenneth Baynes has explained this issue well:

If there are no substantive constraints on what can be introduced into a practical discourse, what is to prevent the outcome from conflicting with some of our most deeply held moral convictions? What is to prevent the participants agreeing to anything, or perhaps, more plausibly, never reaching any general agreement at all?[36]

Baynes suggests that the imposition of certain constraints on discourses is the only way to avoid this dilemma. Yet he also stresses, quite in line with a suggestion made above, that the 'constraints imposed on discourse are subject to discursive vindication',[37] themselves, and he adds:

At a less fundamental level, many other constraints may well be imposed on discourses in view of the issues or tasks at hand. It is reasonable to assume, for example, that the basic rights and liberties specified in Rawls's first principle and contained in the U.S. Constitution would serve as constraints on most public debates, *removing topics from the agenda because of their deeply personal nature or close connection with recognized spheres of privacy. However, discussion about the nature and scope of these rights is always something that can become the subject of public debate.* As arguments about rights become more closely tied to specific interpretations of social goods, what counts as a good argument will no doubt depend more heavily on the shared meanings and practices that make up the everyday life-world . . .[38]

As the above quote reveals, there is a tension for most communicative or discourse theorists between the desire for unconstrained dialogue not to be subject to traditional liberal constraints on the one hand and not to have majoritarian decision procedures corrode civil liberties and rights on the other. I concur with Baynes that formulating the 'normative constraints of discourses', as constraints whose fairness and appropriateness can themselves become topics of debate, is plausible. The normative constraints of practical discourses would occupy the same place in discourse theories of legitimacy and public space as the Rawlsian basic liberties and rights specified under the first principle of justice occupy in his theory.[39]

Where I would differ both from Rawls's formulation about keeping certain topics 'off limits' and Baynes's desire to remove them from the agenda of discourse is in the matter of procedure. Basic human, civil, and political rights, as guaranteed by the Bill of Rights to the US Constitution and as embodied in the constitutions of most democratic governments, are never 'off the agenda' of public discussion and debate. They are simply constitutive and regulative institutional norms of debate in democratic societies which cannot be transformed and abrogated by simple majority decisions. The language of keeping these rights off the agenda mischaracterizes the nature of democratic debate in our kinds of societies: although we cannot change these rights without extremely elaborate political and juridical procedures, we are always disputing their meaning, their extent, and their jurisdiction. Democratic debate is like a ball game where there is no umpire to definitively interpret the rules of the game and their application. Rather, in the game of democracy the rules of the game, no less than their interpretation and even the position of the umpire, are essentially contestable. But contestation means neither the complete abrogation of these rules nor silence about them. When basic rights and liberties are violated, the game of democracy is suspended and becomes either martial rule, civil war, or dictatorship; when democratic politics is in full session the debate about the meaning of these rights, what they do or do not entitle us to, their scope and enforcement, is what politics is all about. In communicative ethics and in democratic politics we assume critical and reflexive distance precisely toward those rules and practices which we also cannot but uphold. One cannot challenge the specific interpretation of basic rights and liberties in a democracy without taking these also absolutely seriously; likewise, one cannot question the texture and nature of our everyday moral commitments in communicative ethics without permanent and continuous embroilment in them on a day-to-day level.

The discourse theory of legitimacy and public space then transcends the traditional opposition of majoritarian politics versus liberal guarantees of basic rights and liberties, to the extent that the normative conditions of discourses are, like basic rights and liberties, rules of the game which can be contested within the game but only insofar as one first accepts to abide by them and play the game at all. This formulation seems to me to correspond to the reality of democratic debate and public speech in real democracies much more than the liberal model of constitutional conventions. In democratic politics nothing is really off the agenda of public debate; but there are fundamental rules of discourse which are both constitutive and regulatory in such a manner that, although what they mean for democratic give and take is itself always contested, the rules themselves cannot be suspended or abrogated by simple majoritarian procedures.

Having argued that the discourse model of legitimacy and the discourse model of public space capture the role of democratic debate more successfully than the Arendtian and the liberal versions, I would now like to turn to an issue which will allow me to explore some of the limitations of the discourse model more specifically.

FEMINIST CRITIQUES OF THE PUBLIC/PRIVATE DISTINCTION

Any theory of publicness, public space, and public dialogue must presuppose some distinction between the private and the public. In the tradition of Western political thought down to our own days, the way in which the distinction between the public and the private spheres has been drawn has served to confine women, and typically female spheres of activity like housework, reproduction, nurturance, and care of the young, the sick, and the elderly, to the 'private' domain, and to keep them off the public agenda in the liberal state. These issues have often been considered matters of the good life, of values, of non-generalizable interests. Along with their relegation, in Arendt's terms, to the 'shadowy interior of the household', they have been treated, until recently, as 'natural' and 'immutable' aspects of human relations. They have remained pre-reflexive and inaccessible to discursive analysis. Much of our tradition, when it considers the autonomous individual or the moral point of view, implicitly defines this as the standpoint of the *homo politicus* or the *homo economicus* but hardly ever as the female self.[40] Challenging the distinction of contemporary moral and political discourse, to the extent that they privatize these issues, is central to women's struggles which intend to make these issues 'public'.

'Privacy', 'privacy rights', and the 'private sphere', as invoked by the modern tradition of political thought, have included at least three distinct dimensions: first and foremost, privacy has been understood as the sphere of moral and religious conscience. As a result of the historical separation of church and state in Western European and North American countries, and as a consequence of developments in modern philosophy and science, matters of ultimate faith concerning the meaning of life, of the highest good, of the most binding principles in accordance with which we should conduct our lives, come to be viewed as rationally 'irresolvable', and as issues about which individuals themselves should decide according to the dictates of their own consciences and world-views.

In the emergence of Western modernity, a second set of privacy rights accompany the eventual establishment of the liberal separation of the church and state. These are privacy rights pertaining to *economic liberties*. The development of commodity relations in the market-place and of capitalism does not only mean 'the rise of the social', in Arendtian terms. Along with the socialization of the economy, that is along with the decline of subsistence-type household economies and the eventual emergence of national markets, a parallel development establishing the 'privacy' of economic markets takes place. In this context 'privacy' means first and foremost non-interference by the political state in the free flow of commodity relations, and in particular non-intervention in the free market of labour-power.

The final meaning of 'privacy' and 'privacy rights' is that of the 'intimate sphere'. This is the domain of the household, of meeting the daily needs of life, of sexuality, and reproduction, of care for the young, the sick, and the elderly. As Lawrence Stone's path-breaking study on the origins and transformations of the early bourgeois family shows,[41] from the beginning there were tensions between the continuing patriarchal authority of the father in the bourgeois family and developing conceptions of equality and consent in the political world. As the male bourgeois citizen was battling for his rights to autonomy in the religious and economic spheres against the absolutist state, his relations in the household were defined by non-consensual, non-egalitarian assumptions. Questions of justice were from the beginning restricted to the 'public sphere', whereas the private sphere was considered outside the realm of justice.

To be sure, with the emergence of autonomous women's movements in the nineteenth and twentieth centuries, with women's massive entry into the labour force in this century, and their gain of the right to vote, this picture has been transformed. Contemporary moral and political theory, however, continues to neglect these issues, and ignores the transformations of the private sphere resulting from massive changes in women's and men's lives. While conceptually matters of justice and those of the good life are distinct from the sociological distinction between the public and private spheres, the frequent conflation of religious and economic freedoms with the freedom of intimacy, under the one title of 'privacy' or of 'private questions of the good life', has had two consequences: first, contemporary normative moral and political theory, Habermas's discourse ethics not excluded, has been 'gender-blind', that is, these theories have ignored the issue of 'difference', the difference in the experiences of male versus female subjects in all domains of life. Second, power relations in the 'intimate sphere' have been treated as though they did not even exist. The idealizing lens of concepts like 'intimacy' does not allow one to see that women's work in the private sphere, like care for the young and the running of the household, has been unremunerated. Consequently, the rules governing the sexual division of labour in the family have been placed beyond the scope of justice. As with any modern liberation movement, the contemporary women's movement is making what were hitherto considered 'private' matters of the good life into 'public' issues of justice by thematizing the asymmetrical power relations on which the sexual division of labour between the genders has rested. In this process, the line between the private and the public, between issues of justice and matters of the good life, is being renegotiated.

Certainly a normative theory, and in particular a critical social theory, cannot take the aspirations of any social actors at face value and fit its critical criteria to meet the demands of a particular social movement. Commitment to social transformation, and yet a certain critical distance, even from the demands of those with

87

whom one identifies, are essential to the vocation of the theorist as social critic. For this reason, the purpose of these final considerations is not to criticize the critical theory of Habermas simply by confronting it with the demands of the women's movement. Rather, my goal is to point to an area of conceptual unclarity as well as political contestation in contemporary debates. Any theory of the public, the public sphere, and publicity presupposes a distinction between the public and the private. These are the terms of a binary opposition. What the women's movement and feminist theorists in the last two decades have shown is that traditional modes of drawing this distinction have been part of a discourse of domination which legitimizes women's oppression and exploitation in the private realm. But the discourse model, precisely because it proceeds from a fundamental norm of egalitarian reciprocity and precisely because it projects the democratization of all social norms, cannot preclude the democratization of familial norms and of norms governing the gender division of labour in the family as well.[42] If in discourses the agenda of the conversation is radically open, if participants can bring any and all matters under critical scrutiny and questioning, then there is no way to predefine the nature of the issues discussed as being public ones of justice versus private ones of the good life. Distinctions such as those between justice and the good life, norms and values, interests and needs are 'subsequent' and not prior to the process of discursive will formation. As long as these distinctions are renegotiated, reinterpreted, and rearticulated as a result of a radically open and procedurally fair discourse, they can be drawn in any of a number of ways. Thus there is both an 'elective affinity' and a certain tension between the demands of social movements like the women's movement and the discourse ethic. Let me explain:

The 'elective affinity', to use Max Weber's felicitous phrase, between discourse ethics and social movements like the women's movement derives from the fact that both project the extension of a postconventional and egalitarian morality into spheres of life which were hitherto controlled by tradition, custom, rigid role expectations, and outright inegalitarian exploitation of women and their work. Discourse ethics, like the women's movement, has argued that only relations of egalitarian reciprocity, based upon the mutual respect and sharing of the parties involved, can be fair from a moral point of view. Conventional relations and role expectations as between the 'wife' and the 'husband', the 'parents' and the 'children' are thus opened to questioning, renegotiation and redefinition. There is also an elective affinity between the commitment to an ethics of dialogue and feminist ideals. In many ways, the contemporary women's movement is the culmination of the logic of modernity which projects the discursive negotiation of societal norms, the flexible appropriation of tradition, and the formation of fluid and reflexive self-identities and life histories.

The tension between discourse ethics and the models of legitimacy and public space deriving from it on the one hand and the claims of the women's movement on the other rests primarily[43] upon the overly rigid boundaries which Habermas has attempted to establish between matters of justice and those of the good life, public interests versus private needs, privately held values and publicly shared norms. But, as I suggested above, it is only the unconstrained process of discourse and not some moral calculus which will allow us to re-establish these boundaries once their traditional meaning has been contested.

Faced with this claim, Habermas as well as the liberal political theorist might respond that this position invites the corrosion of rights of privacy and the total intrusion of the state into the domain of the individual. The issue, they will argue, is not that these distinctions must be reconceptualized but of where the line between the private and the public will be situated as a result of this discursive reconceptualization. Put in more familiar terms, does discourse theory allow for a theory of individual rights guaranteeing privacy, or is it simply a theory of democratic participation which does not respect the legal boundaries of individual liberty? The tension between democratic politics and liberal guarantees of constitutional rights, which I have claimed discourse theory to have solved, returns once more. Let me suggest, and ironically against Habermas himself, why the kind of discourse about the family and the gender division of labour initiated by the women's movement is an instance both of the democratization of the public sphere and of why the discourse model can accommodate such challenges to the public/private distinction.

In principle, the discourse model is based upon a strong assumption of individual autonomy and consent; thus even in discourses which renegotiate the boundaries between the private and the public, the respect for the individuals' consent and the necessity of their voluntarily gained insight into the validity of general norms guarantees that this distinction cannot be redrawn in ways that jeopardize, damage, and restrict this autonomy of choice and insight.

Although in this case, too, processes of discursive will formation decide the boundary between the private and the public, they cannot entirely abolish the private. Indeed, the meta-norms of discourse themselves provide for the autonomy of the individual moral conscience. If all those affected must have an equal chance to assume dialogue roles, if the dialogue must be free and unconstrained, and if each individual can shift the level of the discourse, then practical discourse presupposes autonomous individuals with the capacity to challenge any given consensus from a *principled* standpoint. The very rules which underlie argument and the cooperative search for consensus predicate the distinction between morality and legality. By articulating the meta-norms of the principle of democratic legitimacy and rights, the discourse ethic provides the justification for the autonomy of morality, grounding, as it were, its own self-limitation.[44]

I concur with Cohen that the very logic of discourses permits us to challenge the traditionalist understandings of the public/private split but that the very resources of the discourse model of publicity also prohibit the drawing of these distinctions in ways which jeopardize the autonomy and insight of individuals involved. Having argued this far, one has suggested why the discourse model can serve as a norm of democratic legitimacy and public speech in societies like ours, where the line between the private and the public is being hotly contested. But it is not only discourse theory which must be confronted with the claims of feminists; feminist theory itself sorely needs a model of public space and public speech which returns it to the politics of empowerment. The feminist critique of Habermas's model of the public sphere must be complemented by the appropriation by feminists of a critical theory of the public sphere.

Undoubtedly, our societies are undergoing tremendous transformations at the present. In Western democracies, under the impact of corporatization, the mass media, and the growth of business-style political associations like PACs (Political Action Committees) and other lobbying groups, the public sphere of democratic legitimacy has shrunk. In the US presidential campaign of 1988, the level of public discourse and debate, both in terms of substance and style, had sunk so low that major networks like CBS and ABC felt compelled to run sessions of self-reflexive analysis on their own contributions as the electronic media to the decline of public discourse. The autonomous citizen, whose reasoned judgement and participation was the *sine qua non* of the public sphere, has been transformed into the 'citizen consumer' of packaged images and messages, or the 'electronic mail target' of large lobbying groups and organizations.⁴⁵ This impoverishment of public life has been accompanied by the growth of the society of surveillance and voyeurism on the one hand (Foucault) and the 'colonization of the lifeworld' on the other (Habermas). Not only has public life been transformed, private life as well has undergone tremendous changes, only some of which can be welcome for furthering the values of democratic legitimacy and discursive will formation.

As the sociologist Helga Maria Hernes has remarked, in some ways welfare state societies are ones in which 'reproduction' has gone public.⁴⁶ When, however, issues like child-rearing, care of the sick, the young, and the elderly, reproductive freedoms, domestic violence, child abuse, and the constitution of sexual identities go 'public' in our societies, more often than not a 'patriarchal-capitalist-disciplinary bureaucracy' has resulted.⁴⁷ These bureaucracies have frequently disempowered women and have set the agenda for public debate and participation. In reflecting about these issues as feminists we have lacked a *critical model of public space and public discourse.* Here is where, as feminists, we should not only criticize Habermas's social theory but enter into a dialectical alliance with it. A critical model of public space is necessary to enable us to draw the line between 'juridification', *Verrechtlichung* in Habermas's terms, on the one hand, and making 'public', in the sense of making accessible to debate, reflection, action, and moral-political transformation on the other. To make issues of common concern public in this second sense means making them increasingly accessible to discursive will formation; it means to democratize them; it means bringing them to the standards of moral reflection compatible with autonomous, post-conventional identities. As feminists, we have lacked a critical model which could distinguish between the bureaucratic administration of needs and collective democratic empowerment over them. More often than not, debates among feminists have been blocked by the alternatives of a legalistic liberal reformism—the NOW (National Organization for Women) agenda; ACLU (American Civil Liberties Union) positions—and a radical feminism which can hardly conceal its own political and moral authoritarianism.⁴⁸

For reasons which I have already explored, some of the models of public space discussed in this essay are severely limited to help us cope with this task. Arendt's agonistic model is at odds with the sociological reality of modernity, as well as with modern political struggles for justice. The liberal model of public space transforms the political dialogue of empowerment far too quickly into a juridical discourse about basic rights and liberties. The discourse model is the only one which is compatible both with the general social trends of our societies and with the emancipatory aspirations of new social movements like the women's movement. The radical proceduralism of this model is a powerful criterion for demystifying discourses of power and their implicit agendas. In a society where 'reproduction' is going public, practical discourse will have to be 'feminized'. Such feminization of practical discourse will mean first and foremost challenging unexamined normative dualisms as between justice and the good life, norms and values, interests and needs, from the standpoint of their gender context and subtext.

Notes

1. See Andrew Arato, 'Civil Society Against the State: Poland 1980–81', *Telos*, 47 (1981): 23–47, and 'Empire vs. Civil Society: Poland 1981–82', *Telos*, 50 (1981–2): 19–48; Andrew Arato and Jean Cohen, *Civil Society and Political Theory* (Cambridge, Mass.: MIT Press, 1992); John Keane (ed.), *Civil Society and the State: New European Perspectives* and *Democracy and Civil Society* (both London: Verso, 1988).

2. H. Arendt, *The Human Condition*, 8th edn. (Chicago: University of Chicago Press, 1973), 38–49.

3. See G. W. F. Hegel, *Rechtsphilosophie* (1821), 189 ff.; trans. T. M. Knox as *Hegel's Philosophy of Right* (Oxford: Clarendon Press, 1973), 126 ff.

4. Cf. Christopher Lasch's introduction to the special Hannah Arendt issue of *Salmagundi*, 60 (1983): pp. v ff.; Jürgen Habermas, 'Hannah Arendt's Communications Concept of Power', *Social Research, Hannah Arendt Memorial Issue*, 44 (1977): 3–24.

5. For a sympathetic critique of Arendt along these lines, see Hannah Pitkin, 'Justice: On Relating Public and Private', *Political Theory*, 9/3 (1981): 327–52.

6. See Hannah Arendt, *Men in Dark Times* (New York: Harcourt, Brace & Jovanovich, 1968), 22; 'Preface', in *Between Past and Future: Six Exercises in Political Thought* (Cleveland: Meridian, 1961), 14. An excellent essay by David Luban is one of the few discussions in the literature dealing with Hannah Arendt's methodology of storytelling; 'Explaining Dark Times: Hannah Arendt's Theory of Theory', *Social Research*, 5/1: 215–47; see also E. Young-Bruehl, 'Hannah Arendt als Geschichtenerzaehlerin', in *Hannah Arendt: Materialien zu Ihrem Werk* (Munich: Europaverlag, 1979), 319–27.

7. H. Arendt, *The Life of the Mind*, i: *Thinking* (New York: Harcourt, Brace & Jovanovich, 1977), 212.

8. Arendt, 'Preface', in *Between Past and Future*, 5.

9. Cf. Arendt's statement with Note A appended to the English edition of Benjamin's 'Theses on the Philosophy of History' (which Arendt edited in English): 'Historicism contents itself with establishing a causal connection between various moments in history. But no fact that is cause is for that very reason historical. It became historical posthumously, as it were, through the events that may be separated from it by thousands of years. A historian who takes this as his point of departure stops telling the sequence of events like the beads of a rosary. Instead, he grasps the constellation which his own era has formed with a definite earlier one. Thus he establishes a conception of the present as the "time of the now" which is shot through with chips of Messianic time.' In Walter Benjamin, *Illuminations*, ed. and introd. H. Arendt (New York: Schocken, 1969).

10. Arendt, *The Human Condition*, 23, 31 ff.

11. Arendt, *The Origins of Totalitarianism* (New York: Harcourt, Brace & Jovanovich, 1968), ch. 13, p. 466.

12. Arendt, *The Human Condition*, 56.

13. Hannah Arendt's persistent denial of the 'women's issue', and her inability to link together the exclusion of women from politics and this agonistic and male-dominated conception of public space, is astounding. The 'absence' of women as collective political actors in Arendt's theory—individuals like Rosa Luxemburg are present— is a difficult question, but to begin thinking about this means first challenging the private/public split in her thought as this corresponds to the traditional separation of spheres between the sexes (men = public life; women = private sphere). I explore this issue more extensively in *The Reluctant Modernism of Hannah Arendt* (Calif.: Sage, 1996).

14. Arendt, 'Preface', in *Between Past and Future*, 4.

15. See Hannah Arendt, 'Reflections on Little Rock', *Dissent*, 6/1 (Winter 1959): 45–56; Ralph Ellison in *Who Speaks for the Negro?*, ed. R. P. Warren (New York: Random House, 1965), 342–4; and Arendt to Ralph Ellison in a letter of 29 July 1965, as cited by Young-Breuhl, *Hannah Arendt: For Love of the World* (New Haven, Conn.: Yale University Press, 1982), 316.

16. Bruce Ackerman, *Social Justice in the Liberal State* (New Haven, Conn.: Yale University Press, 1980), 4.

17. Ibid. 11.

18. 'Why Dialogue?' *Journal of Philosophy*, 86 (Jan. 1989): 8.

19. Ibid. 9.

20. Ibid. 16–17 (emphasis added). Ackerman is unclear if by the principle of 'conversational restraint' and 'neutrality' he means the

version stated in this more recent article, which actually *removes* controversial moral conceptions from the public agenda of debate in the liberal state, or if he means the version advocated in *Social Justice in the Liberal State*, which *constrains* the kinds of grounds one can put forward in justifying one's conception of the good without, however, excluding such conceptions from being aired in public; see *Social Justice in the Liberal State*, 11. I have no difficulties in accepting the latter argument, for reasons pertaining to the logic of moral argumentations. It is his most recent version which I find indefensible. Ackerman's reply to his critics, 'What is Neutral About Neutrality?', does not clarify the matter further either; see *Ethics*, 93 (Jan. 1983): 372–90.

21. I have modified this paragraph in this version of this article. My original argument, which maintained that Ackerman's position 'trumped' the views of those primary groups who did not regard 'public peace and order' as the supreme good, was not quite to the point. Since all of us, the communicative ethicist no less than the liberal theorist, are concerned with peaceful and civil coexistence in complex, modern societies, the views of groups who reject such principles of coexistence clearly present a limit case in our considerations. Their views, however, can hardly be considered the representative case from which to proceed in deliberating about such matters. The issue of political, cultural, and moral marginalization is an extremely difficult one to solve in societies which are increasingly multinational, multiracial, and multicultural. My assumption is that the radically open and egalitarian model of public space which I am advocating has more of a chance to give the marginals access to the agenda of the public dialogue, thus eliminating some of the causes of their marginality.

22. Part of the difficulty in Ackerman's position derives from a lack of precision as to what constitutes the 'agenda of the liberal state'. Does Ackerman mean by this phrase the constitution and debates at the Supreme Court level, or does he mean the electronic and the printed media, or other public fora like mailings or, open meetings? The same constraints of neutrality may not automatically hold for all public fora in our societies; this is why conflicts between the constitutional right of free speech and the actual practice of associations and citizens are likely to be such a recurrent feature of a liberal-democratic society. For example, should racism in the media be allowed? Does artistic freedom allow us to stage plays some may consider 'anti-semitic'? I wholeheartedly agree with Ackerman that certain forms of conversational constraints may be wholly appropriate and desirable for the legal system in modern societies. As I have argued elsewhere, in this context what is meant by the term 'neutrality' is that the norms embodied in the legal and public institu-

tions of our societies should be so abstract and general as to permit the flourishing of many different ways of life and many different conceptions of the good. It is plurality, tolerance, and diversity in culture, religion, lifestyles, aesthetic taste, and personal expression which are to be encouraged. In a situation of conflict among diverse conceptions of the good, appeal must be made to the principles embodied in the constitutions of liberal democracies like basic civil and political rights. The modern legal system mediates among the conflicting claims of various life-forms, lifestyles, and visions of the good. In cases of a conflict between the principles of right which make coexistence possible among adherents of divergent conceptions of the good and principles of other more partial conceptions of the good, of which we know that they cannot be generalized beyond their specific adherents, the right trumps over that particular conception of the good. This seems to me to be the only defensible conception of 'neutrality' in the liberal state; but the model of conversational restraints which Ackerman has in view does not only limit the *forms of justification* to be used by the major public institutions in our societies, like the Supreme Court, the Congress and the like; instead it limits the *range of debate* in the liberal state which may very well involve divergent, incompatible, and even hostile conceptions of the good. As long as this agonistic conversation does not lead to the imposition of one understanding of the good upon all others as the officially sanctioned way of life, there is no reason why these partial conceptions of the good cannot be out there, competing and arguing with each other, in the public space of the liberal state.

23. It is not inconceivable that there will be situations when restraining public dialogue in a polity may be a morally desirable option. The most frequently cited instances are national security considerations or what the tradition used to describe as 'raison d'état'. I must admit that I am extremely skeptical even about such prima facie morally plausible cases which would lead to the imposition of 'gag rules' in a society. Take the case of the suppression by the State Department and some officials of the media of the news of the extermination of the Jews and the building of concentration camps in Europe during World War II. In order not to exacerbate public pressure for the United States to enter the war, the government temporarily censored this news. Is it so clear, however, which is the better argument in such an instance? Were the national security considerations of the US at that point in time so clearly superior to the moral claims of the European Jews to demand help and an end to their extermination from any source? And may it not have been desirable on moral grounds for the American public to be informed right away and as fully as possible of these circumstances rather than under conditions of a carefully orchestrated war effort? (Cf. David S. Wyman, *The*

Abandonment of the Jews, New York: Pantheon, 1984.) Ironically, as these lines are being written the military command of the Allied forces in the Persian Gulf and the news media are struggling over the justification for and the extent of the military censorship on coverage of events in the Gulf. No party to this controversy challenges the principle that in a situation of war, in order not to violate the safety of troops or reveal information about logistics, transportation and sensitive equipment certain restraints should be respected. Beyond these self-imposed rules of journalistic restraint, the exercise of military censorship violates the public's right to know and to form an opinion on a matter as crucial as war and peace. The situation in the Persian Gulf shows once more the incompatibility of democracy and 'gag rules' in a society. I believe that the moral burden of proof in cases when such restrictions on free speech and the free flow of information are imposed is almost always on the shoulders of the advocates of 'gag rules'. None the less, every polity in which political discourse is an institution respects certain constraints of the use of free speech; furthermore, individuals and associations may be guided by a certain sense of what is appropriate 'public speech'. A philosophical and moral theory of public dialogue, which views this as a procedure for moral legitimation, accepts constitutional guarantees to free speech as well as suggesting some norms of public dialogue. But insofar as it is also critical of existing relations such a view may challenge both existing legal practices and cultural codes of speech from the standpoint of a moral norm.

24. Benjamin Barber, *The Conquest of Politics: Liberal Philosophy in Democratic Times* (Princeton, NJ: Princeton University Press, 1988), 18.
25. John Rawls, 'The Idea of an Overlapping Consensus', *Oxford Journal of Legal Studies*, 7/1 (1987): 8.
26. Ibid. 21.
27. This connection between the model of reasoning appropriate for corporate bodies and the idea of free public reason is more clear in John Rawls, 'On the Idea of Free Public Reason', lecture delivered at the conference on Liberalism and the Moral Life at the City University of New York in April 1988.
28. Barber, *The Conquest of Politics*, 151.
29. I owe this phrase to Nancy Fraser, who introduces it in the context of her discussion of discourses in the welfare state; see *Unruly Practices: Power, Discourse and Gender in Contemporary Social Theory* (Cambridge: Polity, 1989), 144 ff.
30. Rawls, 'The Idea of an Overlapping Consensus', 14, n. 22.
31. Ibid.
32. See Arendt, *The Origins of Totalitarianism*, pt. 2, ch. 5, and *On Revolution* (New York: Viking, 1969), 147 ff.

33. J. Habermas, *Structural Transformation of the Public Sphere*, trans. Thomas Burger (Boston: MIT Press, 1989); originally published as *Strukturwandel der Öffentlichkeit* (Darmstadt: Luchterland, 1962).

34. The following is a condensed summary of the argument of the second volume of *The Theory of Communicative Action*, and in particular of the chapter on the 'Dialectics of Rationalization' (Boston: Beacon, 1985).

35. Jean Cohen, 'Discourse Ethics and Civil Society', *Philosophy and Social Criticism*, 14/3–4 (1988): 328.

36. Kenneth Baynes, 'The Liberal/Communitarian Controversy and Communicative Ethics', *Philosophy and Social Criticism*, 14/3–4 (1988): 304.

37. Ibid.

38. Ibid. 305 (emphasis added).

39. The step leading from the norms of 'universal moral respect' and 'egalitarian reciprocity' to basic rights and liberties is not a very big one, but one which will not be undertaken in this essay. Suffice it to say that a discourse theory of basic rights and liberties needs to be developed.

40. See Benhabib, 'The Generalized and the Concrete Other: The Kohlberg–Gilligan Controversy and Moral Theory', in: *Situating the Self. Gender, Community and Postmodernism in Contemporary Ethics* (New York & London: Routledge & Polity, 1994).

41. L. Stone, *The Family, Sex and Marriage in England*, abridged edn. (New York: Harper & Row, 1979).

42. Nancy Fraser has raised these considerations pointedly in her 'What's Critical about Critical Theory? The Case of Habermas and Gender', in Seyla Benhabib and Drucilla Cornell (eds.), *Feminism as Critique* (Minneapolis: University of Minnesota Press, 1987), 31–56.

43. Nancy Fraser has argued that Habermas's model of public space is also incompatible with feminist aspirations insofar as it is unitary as opposed to being multiple, dispersed, and plural; is overly rationalistic and privileges rational speech over more evocative and rhetorical modes of public speech; and is prudish in that it minimizes the role of the body and the carnivalesque elements in public self-presentation. I agree with Fraser about the last two criticisms, although in my opinion these do not affect the *principle* of the public sphere itself, that is the necessity of discursive justification of democratic politics; these observations only highlight the need to give a less rationalistic formulation of this principle than Habermas himself has done. As far as the charge of monism versus plurality of public spaces is concerned, I believe that Fraser here misreads Habermas, and that in principle there can be as many publics as there are discourses concerning controversial norms. Thus there is today in the USA a 'public' on the pornography debate in which

lawmakers, the art community, the various religious institutions, the women's movement with its theorists and activists are participants. The 'public sphere' of the pornography debate is not necessarily coextensive with the public sphere of the foreign policy debate in which all of us as citizens are more or less involved. I see no evidence, textual or otherwise, that Habermas's concept of the public sphere must be monistic. See Nancy Fraser, 'Rethinking the Public Sphere: A Contribution to the Critique of Actually Existing Democracy', in Calhoun, *Habermas and the Public Sphere*, 109–42; for Habermas's recent formulations on the issue, see the statement: 'The idea of people's sovereignty is dematerialized [*entsubstantialisiert*] in this process. Even the suggestion that a network of associations can assume the place of the now displaced body of the people remains too concretistic. Sovereignty which is now completely dispersed does not even embody itself in the minds of the associated members [of the polity—S.B.], rather—if we can still use the term embodiment at all—it is in those subjectless forms of communication that regulate the flow of discursive opinion and will-formation that such sovereignty finds its place. The regulation of opinion and will-formation through such subjectless networks of communication gives rise to fallibilistic conclusions which we can presume to incorporate practical reason. When popular sovereignty becomes subjectless and anonymous and is dissolved into processes of intersubjectivity, it limits itself to democratic procedures and to the ambitious communicative presuppositions of their implementation.' J. Habermas, 'Ist der Herzschlag der Revolution zum Stillstand gekommen? Volkssouveränität als Verfahren. Ein normativer Begriff der Öffentlichkeit?' in *Die Ideen von 1789 in der deutschen Rezeption*, ed. Forum für Philosophie Bad Homburg (Frankfurt a.M.: Suhrkamp, 1989), 30–1.

44. Cohen, 'Discourse Ethics and Civil Society', 321. Cf. also Cohen's suggestion: 'In point of fact, however, discourse ethics logically presupposes *both* classes of rights. By basing rights not on an individualistic ontology, as classical liberals have done, but on the theory of communicative interaction, we have strong reason to emphasize the cluster of rights of communication. . . . The rights of privacy would be affirmed because of the need to reproduce autonomous personalities without which rational discourse would be impossible. . . . From this point of view, the rights of communication point us to the legitimate domain for formulating and defending rights. The rights of the personality identify the subjects who have the rights to have rights' (ibid. 327). See also Baynes, 'The Liberal/Communitarian Controversy and Communicative Ethics', 304 ff.

45. Kiku Adatto has provided an impressive empirical study on the transformations of the television coverage of presidential elections by the three major evening newscasts of ABC, CBS, and NBC from

1968 to 1988. Two empirical findings stand out most saliently and indicate why 'the democratic public space' is increasingly less a reality in American political life. Adatto reports: 'The average "sound bite", or block of uninterrupted speech, fell from 42.3 seconds for presidential candidates in 1968 to only 9.8 seconds in 1988. In 1968, almost half of all sound bites were 40 seconds or more, compared to less than one percent in 1988.... In 1968, most of the time we saw the candidates on the evening news, we also heard them speaking. In 1988 the reverse was true; most of the time we saw the candidates, someone else, usually a reporter, was doing the talking.' Adatto observes that in this process 'television displaced politics as the focus of coverage ... the images that once formed the background of political events—the setting and the stagecraft—now occupied the foreground.' See Kiku Adatto, 'Sound Bite Democracy: Network Evening News Presidential Campaign Coverage', Research Paper R-2, Joan Shorenstein Barone Center on Press, Politics and Public Policy (June 1990), 4–5.

46. Helga Maria Hernes, *Welfare State and Woman Power: Essays in State Feminism* (London: Norwegian University Press, 1987).
47. Cf. Fraser, *Unruly Practices*, ch. 7, 'Women, Welfare, and the Politics of Need Interpretation'.
48. For a very good example of the first trend, see Rosemarie Tong, *Women, Sex and the Law* (Totowa, NJ: Rowman & Littlefield, 1984); for the second trend see Catharine MacKinnon's work, and the amazing 'return of the repressed' Marxist orthodoxy of the state and the law in her writings, e.g. her early article, 'Feminism, Marxism, Method and the State: An Agenda for Theory', *Signs*, 7/3 (Spring 1982): 514 ff.; 'Feminism, Marxism, Method and the State: Towards a Feminist Jurisprudence', *Signs*, 8 (Summer 1983): 645 ff.; and the more recent *Feminism Unmodified: Discourses on Life and Law* (Cambridge, Mass.: Harvard University Press, 1987).

Toward an Agonistic Feminism: Hannah Arendt and the Politics of Identity

Bonnie Honig

Hannah Arendt is an odd, even awkward figure to turn to if one is seeking to enrich the resources of a feminist politics. Notorious for her rigid public/private distinction, Arendt protects the *sui generis* character of her politics and the purity of her public realm by prohibiting the politicization of issues of social justice and gender. These sorts of occupation belong not to politics but to the traditional realm of the household as Aristotle theorized it. In short, the 'Woman Problem', as she called it, was not one that Arendt thought it appropriate to pose, politically.[1]

Why turn to Arendt, then? I turn to her not as a theorist of gender, nor as a woman, but as a theorist of an agonistic and performative politics that might stand a feminist politics in good stead. I turn to Arendt because of what she does include in her vision of politics, and also because (not in spite) of what she excludes from it. The terms of that exclusion are instructive for a feminist politics that engages entrenched distinctions between a public and a private realm. In spite of Arendt's insistent reliance on her public/private distinction, the resources for its politicization are present within her account of politics and action. A reading of Arendt that grounds itself in the agonistic and performative impulse of her politics must, for the sake of that politics, resist the a priori determination of a public/private distinction that is beyond augmentation and amendment. This resistance (for the sake of perpetuating the possibility of augmentation and amendment) is itself an important and component part of Arendt's account of politics and political action.

Chapter 6 in Bonnie Honig (ed.), *Feminist Interpretations of Hannah Arendt* (Pennsylvania State University Press, 1995), 135–66. First published in Judith Butler and Joan Wallach Scott (eds.), *Feminists Theorize the Political* (Routledge, 1992). Copyright © Routledge Inc. (1992) Reprinted by permission.

I begin by arguing that resistibility (not necessarily resistance) is a *sine qua non* of Arendt's politics. Next, I briefly examine the terms of her exclusion of the body from the realm of politics, focusing first on the univocal, despotic, and irresistible character of the body, as Arendt theorizes it, and then on the multiplicity of the acting self whose performative speech acts win for it the politically achieved identity that Arendt valorizes. On Arendt's account, identity is the performative production, not the expressive condition or essence of action. This feature of Arendt's work, combined with the public/private distinction upon which it is mapped, have led feminist critics of Arendt to fault her for theorizing a politics that is inhospitable to women and women's issues.[2] In my view, however, it is precisely in Arendt's rejection of an expressive, identity-based politics that her value to a feminist politics lies. The problem is that Arendt grounds that rejection in a refusal to treat private-realm identities, like gender, as potential sites of politicization. I note, however, that Arendt's famous engagement with Gershom Scholem over the terms of her Jewish identity and its responsibilities illustrates her failure in practice to contain (so-called) private identities to a 'prepolitical' realm, and suggests the need for alternative strategies of resistance and resignification that are more empowering because more directly engaged with the politics of identity.

I conclude that Arendt's politics is a promising model for those brands of feminism that seek to contest (performatively and agonistically) the prevailing construction of sex and gender into binary and binding categories of identity, as well as the prevailing binary division of political space into a public and private realm. Arendt herself would undoubtedly have been hostile to this radicalization of her work, but I believe that, as an amendment of her (founding) texts, it is very much in keeping with her politics.

POLITICAL ACTION AND RESISTIBILITY

Arendt's briefest and most pointed discussion of her vision of politics and action comes to us by way of her reading of the American Declaration of Independence. Here we have all the basic elements of Arendt's account. The Declaration is a political act, an act of power, because it founds a new set of institutions and constitutes a new political community; it 'brings something into being which did not exist before', it 'establishes new relations and creates new realities'.[3] It is a 'perfect' instance of political action because it consists 'not so much in its being "an argument in support of an action"' as in its being an action that appears in words.[4] It is a performative utterance, a speech act, performed among and before equals in the public realm.

Focusing on the famous phrase 'We hold these truths to be self-evident', Arendt argues that the new regime's power, and ultimately its authority, derive from the performative 'we hold' and not from the constative reference to self-evident truths.[5] Both dramatic and non-referential, the performative brings a new political community into being; it *constitutes* a 'we'. This speech act, like all action, gives birth, as it were, to the actors in the moment(s) of its utterance (and repetition).

In contrast to the performative 'we hold', the constative reference to self-evident truths expresses not a free coming together but an isolated acquiescence to compulsion and necessity. A self-evident truth 'needs no agreement'; it 'compels without argumentative demonstration or political persuasion'; it is 'in a sense no less compelling than "despotic power"'. Constatives are 'irresistible'; they 'are not held by us, but we are held by them' (*OR* 192–93). For the sake of free political action, Arendt cleanses the Declaration and the founding of their violent, constative moments, of the irresistible anchors of God, self-evident truth, and natural law. There is to be no 'being' behind this doing. The doing, the performance, is everything.[6]

In Arendt's account the real source of the authority of the newly founded republic was the performative, not the constative moment, the action in concert, not the isolated acquiescence, the 'we hold', not the self-evident truth.[7] And the real source of authority in the republic, henceforth, would be the style of its maintenance, its openness to refounding and reconstitution: 'Thus, the amendments to the Constitution augment and increase the original foundations of the American republic; needless to say, *the very authority of the American Constitution resides in its inherent capacity to be amended and augmented*' (*OR* 202; emphasis added). A regime so favourably disposed to constitutional amendment and augmentation, to refounding, must reject the foundational anchors of God, natural law, and self-evident truth because it knows that God defies augmentation, that God is what does not need to be augmented. God, natural law, self-evident truth are, all three, irresistible and complete. These devices petrify power. Their reification of performativity into constation closes the spaces of politics and de-authorizes a regime by diminishing its possibilities of refounding and augmentation. Resistibility, openness, creativity, and incompleteness are the sine qua non of this politics. And this is why Arendt insists on the inadmissibility of the body, and its needs, to the public realm.

THE SINGLE, UNIVOCAL BODY

The human body is, for Arendt, a master signifier of necessity, irresistibility, imitability, and the determination of pure process:

The most powerful necessity of which we are aware in self-introspection is the life process which permeates our bodies and keeps them in a constant state of a change whose movements are automatic, independent of our own activities, and *irresistible*—i.e., of an overwhelming urgency. The less we are doing ourselves, the less active we are, the more forcefully will this biological process assert itself, impose its inherent necessity upon us, and overawe us with the fateful automatism of sheer happening that underlies all human history. (*OR* 59; emphasis added)

One of the reasons for action in the public realm, then, is to escape the pure process that afflicts labouring, working, and (most of all) impoverished beings in the private realm. At least this is what Arendt says in *On Revolution*, where she documents the horrific failures of the French Revolution and attributes them to the fact that 'the poor, driven by the needs of their bodies, burst onto the scene' and effectively closed the spaces of politics by making the 'social question' the centre of political attention (*OR* 59). When demands are made publicly on behalf of the hungry or poor body, then the one individuating and activating capacity that humans possess is silenced. There can be no speech, no action, unless and until the violently pressing, indeed irresistible, needs of the body are satisfied.

Elsewhere, in *The Human Condition*, Arendt's emphasis is different. Here her hostility to the political consideration of the 'social' is unabated, but the 'rise of the social' is theorized in terms of the usurpation of political space by behaviourism, mass society, and the administration of 'housekeeping' concerns that are no less obtrusive than the body's urgency but that seem to be less urgently irresistible. Here, the social *rises*, it does not *burst*, onto the scene.

In contrast to *On Revolution, The Human Condition* tends not to discuss the body directly. And when things of the body are addressed, the emphasis is less on the body's irresistibility than on its imitability.[8] For example, Arendt says that in the political speech and action that distinguish him, man 'communicate[s] himself and not merely something—thirst or hunger, affection or hostility or fear' (*HC* 176). Thirst or hunger are 'merely something' because they are common, shared features of our biological existence and as such are incapable of distinguishing us from each other in any significant way. This commonality is exaggerated in modernity as the social develops into a strongly conformist set of arrangements that 'by imposing innumerable and various rules, . . . tend to "normalize" its members, to make them behave, to exclude spontaneous action or outstanding achievement' (*HC* 40). Here, the reason to act is not situated in a need to escape the body and be freed, episodically, from its urgency; instead, Arendt focuses on the need to escape or contain the normalizing impulse of the social through the antidotal but also *sui generis* goods of politics and action. The reason to act is situated in action's unique, individuating power, and in the self's agonal passion for distinction, individuation, and outstanding achievement.

When they act, Arendt's actors are reborn (*HC* 176). Through innovative action and speech, they 'show who they are, reveal actively their unique personal identities and thus make their appearance in the human world' (*HC* 179). Their momentary engagement in action in the public realm engenders identities that are lodged forever in the stories told of their heroic performances by the spectators who witness them. Prior to or apart from action, this self has no identity; it is fragmented, discontinuous, indistinct, and most certainly uninteresting. A life-sustaining, psychologically determined, trivial, and imitable biological creature in the private realm, this self attains identity—becomes a 'who'—by acting. For the sake of 'who' it might become, it risks the dangers of the radically contingent public realm where anything can happen, where the consequences of action are 'boundless' and unpredictable, where 'not life but the world is at stake.'[9] In so doing, it forsakes the comforting security of 'what' it is, the roles and features that define (and even determine) it in the private realm, the 'qualities, gifts, talents and shortcomings, which [it] may display or hide', and the intentions, motives, and goals that characterize its agency.[10] Thus, Arendt's actors are never self-sovereign. Driven by the despotism of their bodies (and their psychologies) in the private realm, they are never really in control of what they do in the public realm, either. This is why, as actors, they must be courageous. Action is spontaneous, it springs up *ex nihilo* and, most disturbing, it is self-surprising: '[I]t is more than likely that the "who" which appears so clearly and unmistakably to others, remains hidden from the person himself.'[11]

There is nothing interesting nor distinct about 'what' we are, nothing remarkable about the psychological and biological self. The features of the private self are, like our inner organs, 'never unique' (*HC* 206). Arendt says of the biological self: 'If this inside were to appear, we would all look alike.'[12] Here the silence that is opposed to the performative speech acts valorized by Arendt is not the muteness provoked by violently urgent bodily need, but rather a kind of silent communication, a constative speaking that is strictly communicative and narrowly referential, so narrowly referential that it need not even be spoken. Here, 'speech plays a subordinate role, as a means of communication or as a mere accompaniment to something that could also be achieved in silence' (*HC* 179; emphasis added). Since the point of language in the private realm is 'to communicate immediate identical needs and wants' (of the body), this can be done mimetically. The single, univocal body is capable of handling this task without the aid of speech: 'signs and sounds', Arendt says, 'would be enough' (*HC* 176).

THE MULTIPLE, ACTING SELF

By contrast with the single, univocal body, the acting self is multiple. This bifurcated self maps onto the bifurcated constative and performative structure of the Declaration of Independence. Constatives and bodies are both despotic, irresistible, univocal, and uncreative. Both are disruptive, always threatening to rise, or burst, onto the scene and close the spaces of politics. Because of this ever-present threat, we must be vigilant and guard the public realm, the space of performativity, against the intrusion of the bodily or constative compulsion.

The acting self is like the performative moments of the Declaration: free, (self-)creative, transformative, and inimitable. Arendt's performatives postulate plurality and her actors postulate multiplicity. The power of the performative 'we hold' is actualized by distinct and diverse individuals with little in common prior to action except a care for the world and an agonal passion for distinction (*OR* 118). Likewise, Arendt's actors do not act because of what they already are, their actions do not express a prior, stable identity; they presuppose an unstable, multiple self that seeks its (at best) episodic self-realization in action and in the identity that is its reward.

This multiple self is characterized by Arendt as the site of a struggle that is quieted, temporarily, each time the self acts and achieves an identity that is a performative production. The struggle is between the private and the public self, the risk-averse stay-at-home and the courageous, even rash actor in the contingent public realm. This bifurcation between its private and public impulses marks the self but does not exhaust its fragmentation. In the private realm alone, this self is also animated and conflicted by three distinct, rival, and incompatible mental faculties—thinking, willing, and judging—each of which is also internally riven, 'reflexive', recoiling 'back upon itself'. Always, Arendt says, 'there remains this inner resistance'.[13] This is why she insists that autonomy is an impositional construction. It imposes a univocity on a self that is fragmented and multiple; it involves 'a mastery which relies on domination of one's self and rule over others'; it is a formation to which the self, on Arendt's account, is resistant (*HC* 244). This self is not, ever, one. It is itself the site of an agonistic struggle that Arendt (sometimes) calls politics.[14] And she approves of this because, like Nietzsche, she sees this inner multiplicity of the self as a source of its power and energy, as one of the conditions of creative performative action.[15]

These bifurcations, between the univocal body and the multiple self, are presented as attributes of individual selves; but they actually operate to distinguish some selves from others in the ancient Greece that is Arendt's beloved model. Here the experience of action is available only to the very few. The routine and the urgency of the body are implicitly identified in *The Human Condition*, as they were explicitly in ancient Greece, with women and slaves (but also with children, labourers, and all non-Greek residents of the polis), the labouring subjects who tend to the body and its needs in the private realm where 'bodily functions and material concerns should be hidden'.[16] These inhabitants of the private realm are passively subject to the demands that their bodies and nature make upon them, and to the orders dictated to them by the master of the household to which they belong as property. As victims of both the tiresomely predictable, repetitious, and cyclical processes of nature and the despotism of the household, they are determined incapable of the freedom that Arendt identifies with action in the public realm. Free citizens, by contrast, could tend to their private needs in the private realm (or, more likely, have them tended to), but they could then leave these necessitarian, life-sustaining concerns behind to enter the public realm of freedom, speech, and action. Indeed, their ability to leave these concerns behind is the mark of their capacity to act. In politics, after all, 'not life but the world is at stake'.

This passage, made periodically by free citizens from the private to the public realm, indicates that the chasm between the two realms is not non-negotiable (*HC* 24). But this is true only for citizens, only for those who are not essentially identified with their condition of embodiment, for those who can be other than only, and passively, embodied beings. This is, in effect, the criterion for their citizenship. For 'others', whose very nature prevents them from ever becoming citizens because their identity *is* their embodiment (and this is the criterion for their barbarism), there is no negotiating the public/private impasse.

This problematic feature of political action is certainly one that Arendt attributes to the polis, but is it right to attribute it to Arendt herself?[17] Arendt does often speak as if her private realm and its activities of labour and work were to be identified with particular classes of people, or bodies, or women in particular. But, as Hanna Pitkin points out, at other times the private realm and its activities of labour and work seem to represent not a particular class or gender but 'particular *attitude[s]* against which the public realm must be guarded'.[18] Labour, for example, 'the activity which corresponds to the biological process of the human body', is a mode in which the necessitarian qualities of life and the instrumental character of a certain kind of rationality dominate us so thoroughly that the freedom of politics and its brand of generative performativity cannot surface (*HC* 7). Since Arendt's real worry about labour and work is that they require and engender particular sensibilities that hinder or destroy action, Pitkin suggests that 'Perhaps a "laborer" is to be identified not by his manner of producing nor by his poverty but by his "process" oriented outlook; perhaps he is driven by necessity not objectively, but because he regards himself as driven, incapable of action.'[19]

Or, better, perhaps it is the labouring sensibility that is excluded from political action, a sensibility that is taken to be characteristic

of labouring as an activity but which may or may not be characteristic of the thinking of any particular labourer, a sensibility that
is certainly not taken to signal a labouring nature or essence that
is expressed when the labourer labours. There is no 'being' behind
this doing. The same analysis applies to work. In this account, there
is no determinate class of persons that is excluded from political
action. Instead, politics is protected from a variety of sensibilities,
attitudes, dispositions, and approaches all of which constitute *all*
selves and subjects to some extent, all of which engage in a struggle
for dominion over the self, and all of which are incompatible with
the understanding(s) of action that Arendt valorizes. In short,
the construal of labour, work, and action as sensibilities could de-
essentialize or denaturalize them. Each would be understood as
itself a performative production, not the expression of the authentic essence of a class, or a gender, but always the (sedimented)
product of the actions, behaviours, norms, and institutional structures of individuals, societies, and political cultures.[20]

This reading of labour, work, and action as (rival) sensibilities
is compatible with Arendt's view of the self as multiplicity. And it
might point the way to a gentle subversion of Arendt's treatment
of the body as a master signifier of irresistibility, imitability, and
the closure of constation. Labour is, after all, a bodily function
in Arendt's account, as well as being the mode in which the body
is tended to, the mode that is preoccupied with things that are
'needed for the life process itself' (*HC* 96). If labour (that determining sensibility by which all are sometimes driven) can be a
performative production, why not the body itself? Why not allow
this reading of labour, work, and action as sensibilities to push us
to de-essentialize and denaturalize the body, perhaps pluralize it,
maybe even see *it* as a performative production, a possible site of
action, in Arendt's sense?

DISTINGUISHING PUBLIC AND PRIVATE

If there is one thing in the way of this radicalization of Arendt's
account, it is her reliance on that series of distinctions that I
have grouped together under the heading of performative versus
constative. Arendt treats these distinctions as binary oppositions,
non-negotiable and without overlap, and she maps them onto a

(historically invidious) public/private distinction that lies at the (shifting) centre of her work. Indeed, as it turns out, there is more than one thing in the way since Arendt secures her public/private distinction with a multi-layered edifice. The distinction spawns numerous binaries, each one a new layer of protective coating on the last, each one meant to secure, that much more firmly, the distinction that resists the ontologizing function that Arendt assigns to it. Performative versus constative, 'we hold' versus 'self-evident truth', multiple self versus univocal body, male versus female, resistible versus irresistible, courageous versus risk-averse, speech versus mute silence, active versus passive, open versus closed, power versus violence, freedom versus necessity, action versus behaviour, extraordinary versus ordinary, inimitable versus imitable, disruption versus repetition, light versus dark, in short: public versus private.

Why so many? In the very drawing of the distinction, where the drawing is an extraordinary act in Arendt's sense (it has the power to create new relations and new realities), Arendt is caught in a cycle of anxious repetition. Binary distinctions and adjectival pairs are heaped, one upon another, in a heroic effort to resist the erosion of a distinction that is tenuous enough to need all of this. Tenuous, indeed. There are, in Arendt's account, numerous instances of the permeation of these distinctions. She is quite straightforward about the fact that the public realm is all too easily colonized by the private and turned into the social (it is to this problem that she responds in *The Human Condition* and in *On Revolution*). Her candour tempts us to think that these distinctions are, above all else, drawn to protect the public from the private realm's imperialism. But the converse is also true. It is equally important to Arendt to protect the private realm's reliability, univocality, and ordinariness from the disruptions of action and politics.[21] In short, she domesticates not only behaviour but also action itself. She gives action a place to call home and she tells it to stay there, where it belongs. But, of course, it refuses.

Here is the real risk of action: in this refusal. The self-surprising quality of action is not limited to the fact that action does not always turn out as we would have intended it to; nor even to the fact that we, as actors, are never quite sure 'who' it is that we have turned out to be. Action is self-surprising in another sense as well, in the sense that it happens to us. We do not decide to perform, then enter the public realm, and submit our performance to the contingency that characterizes that realm. Often, political action comes to us; it involves us in ways that are not deliberate, wilful, or intended. Action produces its actors; episodically, temporarily, we are its agonistic achievement. In Arendt's account, the American Revolution happened to the American revolutionaries: 'But the movement which led to the revolution was not revolutionary except by inadvertence' (*OR* 44). And, sometimes, particularly in her account of willing, action happens to the private self, initially in the *private* realm.

Arendt treats willing as an antecedent of action, but it is a funny kind of antecedent because it actually defers action. Caught in a reflexive, internal, and potentially eternal dynamic of willing and nilling, a dynamic it is incapable of arresting, the will awaits redemption. And when that redemption comes, it comes in the form of action itself. *Action* liberates the self from the will's paralysing 'disquiet and worry' by disrupting the compulsive repetitions of the will. Action comes in, as it were, to the private realm; it happens to the as yet unready and not quite willing (because still also nilling) subject in the private realm. Like a coup d'état, action 'interrupts the conflict between *velle* and *nolle*', and redeems the will. 'In other words,' Arendt adds, 'the Will is redeemed by ceasing to will and starting to act and *the cessation cannot originate in an act of the will-not-to-will* because this would be but another volition.'[22]

Examples of public/private realm cross-fertilizations abound; they are as manifold as the distinctions that are supposed to account for their impossibility, their perversion, their monstrosity. What is to prevent us, then, from applying 'performativity to the body itself', as one feminist theorist of sex/gender performance does?[23] What prohibits the *attenuation* of the public/private distinction? What would be the punishment for unmasking the private realm's constative identities as really the (sedimented) products of the actions, behaviours, and institutional structures and norms of individuals, societies, and political cultures? What is at stake?

At stake for Arendt is the loss of action itself, the loss of a realm in which the actionable is vouchsafed. This is a real cause of concern, especially given the astonishing and disturbing success of the 'innumerable and various rules' of the social in producing normal, well-behaved subjects. But in order to vouchsafe it, Arendt empties the public realm of almost all content. Things possessed of content are constatives, after all, sites of closure in Arendt's theorization, irresistible obstacles to performativity. Hence Hanna

Pitkin's puzzled wonderment at what those citizens 'talk about together in that endless palaver of the *agora*'.[24] Arendt's effective formalization of action, her attempts to safeguard action with a non-negotiable public/private distinction, may contribute more to the loss or occlusion of action than any rise of the social, than any bursting forth of ostensibly irresistible bodies.

The permeability, inexactness, and ambiguity of the distinction between public and private, however, are not reasons to give it up. Instead, they suggest the possibility of attenuation. What if we took Arendt's own irresistibly lodged public/private distinction to be a line drawn in the sand, itself an illicit constative, a constituting mark or text, calling out agonistically to be contested, augmented, and amended? And what if we began by dispensing with the geographical and proprietary metaphors of public and private? What if we treated Arendt's notion of the public realm not as a specific topos, like the ancient Greek agon, but as a metaphor for a variety of (agonistic) spaces, both topographical and conceptual, that might occasion action? We might be left with a notion of action as an event, an agonistic disruption of the ordinary sequence of things that makes way for novelty and distinction, a site of resistance of the irresistible, a challenge to the normalizing rules that seek to constitute, govern, and control various behaviours. And we might then be in a position to identify sites of political action in a much broader array of constations, ranging from the self-evident truths of God, nature, technology, and capital to those of identity, of gender, race, and ethnicity. We might then be in a position to *act*—in the private realm.

Arendt would no doubt be concerned that these amendments of her account politicize too much, that (as Nancy Fraser puts it on her behalf) 'when everything is political, the sense and specificity of the political recedes'.[25] For Fraser, Arendt's theorization of politics highlights a paradox: if politics is everywhere then it is nowhere. But not everything is political in this (amended) account; it is simply the case that nothing is ontologically protected from politicization, that nothing is necessarily or naturally or ontologically *not* political. The distinction between public and private is seen as the performative product of political struggle, hard-won and always temporary. Indeed, the paradox is reversible. The impulse to secure, foundationally, the division between the political and the non-political is articulated as a concern for the preservation of the political but is itself an antipolitical impulse. Arendt knew this: it was the basis of her critique of the constative, foundational ground of the Declaration of Independence. This is what motivated her to apply performativity to the self-evidence of the Declaration. And the same impulse can motivate the application of performativity to Arendt's public/private distinction itself.

This dispersal of the agon is also authorized by another, somewhat different moment in Arendt's theorization of politics. Arendt understood that there were times in which the exigencies of a situation forced politics to go underground. She looks to the underground politics of occupied France, and valorizes its proliferation of sites of resistance, its network of subversive political action.[26] Occupation might not be a bad term for what Arendt describes as the 'rise of the social' and the displacement of politics by routinized, bureaucratic, and administrative regimes. In the absence of institutional sites, a feminist politics might well go underground, looking to locate itself in the rifts and fractures of identities, both personal and institutional, and doing so performatively, agonistically, and creatively, with the hope of establishing new relations and realities.

ACTING IN THE PRIVATE REALM

This notion of an agonistic politics of performativity situated in the self-evidences of the private realm is explored by Judith Butler, who focuses in particular on the construction and constitution of sex and gender. Butler unmasks the private realm's constations—described by Arendt as the mindless, tiresome, perfect, and oppressive repetitions of the cycles of nature—and redescribes them as performativities that daily (re-)produce sex/gender identities. These performances, Butler argues, are the enforced products of a regulative practice of binary gender constitution centred on and by a 'heterosexual contract'. But these acts are 'internally discontinuous'; the identities they produce are not 'seamless'. The 'multiplicity and discontinuity of the referent [the self] mocks and rebels against the univocity of the sign [sex/gender]'. There are 'possibilities of gender transformation' in these spaces of mockery and rebellion, 'in the arbitrary relation between such acts, in the possibility of a different sort of repeating'.[27] A subversive repetition might performatively produce alternative sex/gender identities that would proliferate and would, in their proliferation (and strategic deployment), contest and resist the reified binaries that now regulate and seek to constitute, exhaustively, the identities of sex/gender.

The strategy, then, is to unmask identities that aspire to successful constation, to de-authorize and redescribe them as performative productions by identifying spaces that escape or resist identitarian administration, regulation, and expression. In Arendtian terms, this strategy depends upon the belief that the sex/gender identities that 'we hold' can be amended and augmented in various ways through action. Political theory's task is to aid and enable that practice of (re-)founding by widening the spaces (of tension, undecidability, and arbitrariness) that might be hospitable to new beginnings.[28] These are spaces of politics, spaces (potentially) of performative freedom. Here action is possible in the private realm because the social and its mechanisms of normalization consistently fail to achieve the perfect closures that Arendt attributes to them too readily. This failure of the social to realize its ambitions means that it is possible to subvert the concretized, petrified, reified, and naturalized identities and foundations that paralyse politics and to broaden the realm of the actionable, to resist the sedimentation of performative acts into constative truths, and to stand by the conviction that in matters of politics and in matters of identity, it is not possible to get it right, over and done with. This impossibility structures the needs and the repressions of Arendt's public and private realms. And it provides good reasons to resist and to problematize any politics of identity.

Hanna Pitkin energetically criticizes Arendt's refusal to theorize politics as a practice or venue of the representation of interests, and of shared material needs and concerns.[29] She rightly worries that Arendt's politics is so formal as to be left without import or content. But Pitkin fails to appreciate the promise in Arendt's vision. There is promise in Arendt's unwillingness to allow political action to be a site of the re-presentation of 'what' we are, of our reified private-realm identities. In Arendt's view, a politics of representation projects a false commonality of identity and interests that is impositional, and ill-fitting. Further, it obstructs an important alternative: a performative politics that, instead of reproducing and re-presenting 'what' we are, agonistically generates 'who' we are by episodically producing new identities, identities whose 'newness' becomes 'the beginning of a new story, started—though unwittingly—by acting [wo]men [and] to be enacted further, to be augmented and spun out by their posterity'.[30]

IDENTITY POLITICS

The centrality of performativity to Arendt's theory of action stems from Arendt's opposition to attempts to conceive of politics as expressive of shared (community) identities such as gender, race, ethnicity, or nationality. Performativity and agonism are not coincidentally connected in Arendt's account. Arendt's politics is always agonistic because it resists the attractions of expressivism for the sake of her view of the self as a complex site of multiplicity whose identities are always performatively produced. This agonism eschews the complacent familiarities of the what-ness of subjectivity and it rejects the seductive comforts of the social for the sake of action and its exhilarating capacity to generate new relations and new realities.

From Arendt's perspective, a political community that constitutes itself on the basis of a prior, shared, and stable identity threatens to close the spaces of politics, to homogenize or repress the plurality and multiplicity that political action postulates. Attempts to overcome that plurality or multiplicity, Arendt warns, must result in 'the abolition of the public realm itself' and the 'arbitrary domination of all others', or in 'the exchange of the real world for an imaginary one where these others would simply not exist' (*HC* 220, 234). The only way to prevent such an exchange is by protecting the spaces of politics in the non-identity and heterogeneity of political communities, and also in the resistances of the self to the normalizing constructions of subjectivity and the imposition of autonomy (and perhaps also to the formation of sex/gender identities into binary categories of male and female, masculine and feminine). The self's agonistic ill-fittedness to the social, psychological, and juridical categories that seek to define it is a source of the generation of power, a signal that there are sites from which to generate (alternative) performativity(ies).

It is this care for difference and plurality as conditions of politics and action that accounts for Arendt's hostility to the nation-state, whose repugnant 'decisive principle' is its 'homogeneity of past and origin' (*OR* 174). And it might also account for her silence on the subject of a feminist politics: Arendt would have been quite wary of any proclamation of homogeneity in 'women's experience', or in 'women's ways of knowing'. She would have been critical of any feminist politics that relies on a category of woman that aspires to or implies a universality that belies (or prohibits, punishes, or silences) significant differences and pluralities within —and even resistances to—the bounds of that (so-called) identity.

These remarks are speculative, because Arendt did not address the issues of feminism or a feminist politics in her theoretical work. I myself have been reluctant to pose gender questions to her directly because those questions tend to be posed by her feminist critics in a moralistic mode. The assumption is that, as a woman, Arendt had a responsibility to pose the 'woman question' or at least to theorize a politics that showed that she had women in mind. Her failure to do so marks her as a collaborator. The charge is made most bluntly and forcefully by Adrienne Rich, who describes *The Human Condition* as a 'lofty and crippled book', exemplary of the 'tragedy of a female mind nourished on male ideology'.[31] I am less certain about the responsibilities assumed here and so I seek to pose these questions, but not in that mode; that is, without assigning or even implying that responsibility. In fact, I feel a certain respect for Arendt's refusal to be a joiner, for her wariness of identity politics and of membership in identity communities, for the startling perversity that led her to say of Rosa Luxemburg (but also, I think, of herself) that 'her distaste for the women's emancipation movement, to which all other women of her generation and political convictions were irresistibly drawn, was significant. In the face of suffragette equality, she might have been tempted to reply, "*Vive la petite différence.*" '[32]

An odd remark; certainly unfair to the suffragists whose political dedication is dismissed as a product of an 'irresistible' identification with a 'movement', not a politics; but an intriguing remark nonetheless. What is this *petite différence* that Arendt imagines Luxemburg celebrating? It is not sexual difference—that is *la différence*, nothing petite about it. *La petite différence* is an intra-sex /gender difference (albeit one that is itself gendered by Arendt's significant choice of phrasing). It is the difference that sets Luxemburg apart from these other women. Arendt admires in Luxemburg a quality that she herself strove for: the refusal of membership, the choice of difference or distinction over a certain kind of equality.[33] The 'suffragette equality' to which she refers in this passage is not the civic equality with male voters for which these women were still striving; it is the equality among the suffragettes, their devotion to a common cause in the name of which (Arendt alleges) differences among them are effaced. Arendt constructs and celebrates a Rosa Luxemburg who was 'an outsider', a 'Polish Jew in a country she disliked', a member of a political 'party she came soon to despise', and 'a woman', the sort of excellent woman who resisted the 'irresistible' allure of a women's movement, called other contests her own, and won for herself, thereby, an identity of distinction, not homogeneity (*MDT* 45).

The same sentiments, the same distancing techniques and distaste for identity politics are evident in Arendt's exchange with Gershom Scholem, an exchange that professed to be about Arendt's controversial book on Eichmann but that was really or also a contestation of the terms of her (would-be private-realm) identity as a Jew.[34] This short exchange is an instructive and provocative study in identity politics. Scholem's letter to Arendt is an exercise in identification and politicization. He tells Arendt that her book has little in it of the 'certainty of the believer', that it manifests 'weakness' and 'wretchedness, and power-lust', that it leaves '*one* with a sense of bitterness and shame . . . for the compiler', that he has a 'deep respect' for her and that that is why he must call to her attention the 'heartless' and 'almost sneering and malicious tone' of her book. He can find 'little trace' in her ('dear Hannah') of any '*Ahabath Israel*: "Love of the Jewish People"', and this absence is typical of 'so many intellectuals who came from the German Left'. What licenses Scholem to say all of these things, and to mark them as moral failings? The fact that he regards Arendt 'wholly as a daughter of our people and in no other way'.[35]

Arendt responds with two strategic refusals. First, she contests Scholem's claim that she is 'wholly' Jewish and is neither riven nor constituted by differences or other identities. Second, she contests Scholem's assumption that Jewish identity is expressive, that it has public effects and carries with it certain clear responsibilities. She resists the claim that particular sorts of action, utterance, and sentiment ought necessarily to follow from the fact that she is Jewish. Throughout, however, she assumes, as does Scholem, that Jewish identity is an 'indisputable', univocal, and constative 'fact' (like the other facts of her multiple but private identity), 'not open to controversy' nor to 'dispute'. Thus she can say that many of Scholem's statements about her 'are simply false' and she can correct them. For example, she is not 'one of the "intellectuals who come from the German Left"'; if Arendt 'can be said to "have come from anywhere"', it is from the tradition of German philosophy'.

To Scholem's 'I regard you wholly as a daughter of our people, and in no other way', Arendt responds cryptically: 'The truth is I have never pretended to be anything else or to be in any other way than I am and I have never even felt tempted in that direction.'

The point is not that she has not pretended to be anything other than 'a daughter' of the Jewish people; she has simply not pretended to be anything other than what she is. But Arendt never says what she is, she never identifies herself affirmatively. All she says is that to pretend 'to be anything...other than I am... would have been like saying that I was a man and not a woman —that is to say, kind of insane'. Again, there is no affirmative identification of herself, in this case as a woman, just the claim that to assert its contrary would be 'insane'. (What would it be to assert it affirmatively?)[36]

Where Scholem regards her '*wholly* as a daughter of our people and in no other way', Arendt has 'always regarded' her own 'Jewishness as *one of* the indisputable factual data of my life'. She does not regard it as the 'wholly' constitutive identity that Scholem projects it to be. Arendt is constituted by other 'facts', as well, two of which she mentions here—sex/gender, and her schooling in German philosophy.[37] Thus, Arendt says, Scholem's depiction of her as 'wholly' a 'daughter of our people' is a 'label' that he 'wish[es] to stick' on her, but it has 'never fitted in the past and does not fit now'.[38] The label is a label, ill-fitting and stuck on, because Arendt's Jewishness is a fragment of a complex and conflicted identity.

For Arendt, nothing follows from the fact of her Jewishness as she understands that fact. Her Jewishness is a private matter; because it is a fact, it is not at all actionable. And for that, for its facticity, she is grateful: 'There is such a thing as a basic gratitude for everything that is as it is; for what has been given and was not, could not be, made; for things that are *physei* and not *nomoi*', for things that are 'beyond dispute or argument'. This insistence on her ethnic, religious, cultural identity as a given, private fact, not to be made or acted upon, is structurally figured in her letter to Scholem. Arendt begins the letter with a discussion of the facts of her private identity, presented as a series of corrections aimed at what she treats as factual errors. These matters of fact are uninteresting, 'not open to controversy'. Arendt sets this part of the letter up as a pre-political preamble, separate from the political debate that follows. Only the latter treats 'matters which merit discussion' and speech. She underscores this distinction by beginning the paragraph that marks the end of the identity-centred preliminaries and the start of the political debate with the phrase: 'To come to the point'.

But the very thing for which Arendt expresses her gratitude in this letter is the one thing that Scholem will not grant her in this encounter. Scholem will not treat her Jewish identity as a private affair. For Scholem, certain identifiable and incontestable public responsibilities and implications follow from the indisputable and univocal fact of Arendt's Jewishness. This is why Arendt resists Scholem's inclusions, this is why she resists his writing of her 'wholly as a daughter' of the Jewish people. She treasures difference, even a *petite différence*, over and above the equality or sameness that Scholem ascribes to and demands from Jews. She sees in his identity politics insidious resources for the homogenizing control of behaviour and the silencing of independent criticism. And that is why she resists. Her resistance, however, is not all it could be.

Instead of insisting on the privacy of Jewish identity, a privacy that is already problematized by Scholem's charges and by this very public, highly politicized identity debate, Arendt would have done better to contest the terms of Scholem's construal of Jewishness as identity. This strategy was not available to Arendt, however, because she agrees with Scholem on the most important point. Both she and Scholem treat Jewish identity as a univocal, constative fact. They disagree on whether it is a public or a private fact,[39] on whether any prescriptions or requirements for action follow from it, but both agree that Jewishness is a fact that 'could not be made', nor indeed unmade; it is unaffected by what the actor does. This is why Scholem can regard Arendt, in spite of all the things that she has written, in spite of her apparently total lack of any *Ahabath-Israel*, as 'wholly' a 'daughter of our people'. Arendt could not deny or subvert her authentic identity as a Jew no matter what she did. With this Arendt is in perfect agreement. Her defence strategy mimes the basic premiss of Scholem's accusations: nothing she does can call into question or subvert the indisputable, constative fact of her Jewishness.

In treating Jewish identity as constative, Arendt relinquishes the opportunity to engage or even subvert Jewish identity performatively, to explore its historicity and heterogeneity, to dislodge and disappoint its aspirations to univocity, to proliferate its differentiated possibilities. This leaves her without any resources with which to respond critically to Scholem's portrayal of Jewishness as a homogeneous, univocal identity that implies certain incontestable responsibilities and claims certain loyalties. Scholem's constative criterion for distinguishing good Jews from bad is left intact. The same would be true of Adrienne Rich's strategy for distinguishing healthy from crippled women, loyal women from those who are treasonous. After all, Rich's approach mirrors Scholem's: it is because she regards Arendt 'wholly as a [woman] and in no other way' that she can treat Arendt's other constituting identities (like her schooling in German philosophy) as betrayals of Arendt's authentic and univocal identity—as a woman.

The more powerful and empowering defence against Scholem or Rich or, indeed, against any identity politics is to resist the irresistible, not by privatizing it but by unmasking the would-be irresistible, homogeneous, constative, and univocal identity in question as a performative production, fractured, fragmented, ill-fitting, and incomplete, the sedimented and not at all seamless product of a multitude of performances and behaviours, the natur-alized product of innumerable repetitions and enforcements. This is Arendt's strategy for empowering the 'we hold' of the Declara-tion against the coercive violence of that document's 'self-evident truths'. Why not usurp this strategy of empowerment to unmask, engage, subvert, or resist the violent closures of univocity and self-evidence assumed by some Jewish and feminist politics of identity?

The strategy here is to interrupt established identities, to the-orize and to practise a Jewishness that is not homogenizing and a feminism that does not efface difference for the sake of an equal-ity of sameness. The strategy here is to proliferate and explore differences rather than reify them, and the result might be the empowering discovery or insistence that there are many ways to do one's Jewishness, many ways to do one's gender.[40] The homo-genizing effects of some (so-called) private-realm identities would be weakened, and that would allow for greater differentiation and contestability with*in* the frame of the 'identities' themselves.

This strategy of interruption constitutes an important alternat-ive to the notions of a pariah, and a pariah perspective, so celeb-rated by Arendt.[41] Arendt treats the conscious pariah's position of outsider (personified by Rosa Luxemburg as well as by others whom Arendt admired) as a privileged site from which one can secure the distance necessary for independent critique, action, and judge-ment. But Arendt's location of the pariah position is fuelled by her problematic assumption that there is no critical leverage to be had from inside formed identities. Arendt celebrates the pariah's outsider status because she believes that identities succeed, that they do attain seamlessness and closure, that they are necessar-ily homogenizing. The agonistic politics of performativity that I extend and explore here assumes instead that identities are never seamless, that there are sites of critical leverage within the ruptures, inadequacies, and ill-fittednesses of existing identities. It assumes, therefore, that the position of the pariah is itself unstable, that the pariah is never really an outsider, and that its sites are multiple. These multiple sites decentre the privileged public space of Arendtian politics, and proliferate the sites of action beyond the single public realm to explore a broader range of spaces of potential power and resistance.[42]

This agonistic feminism also departs from the implied individualism of Arendt's pariah by postulating agonism as a kind of action in concert.[43] The identities engaged by agonistic feminists are shared, public practices, not merely markers of individual personalities. While any particular agonistic action may be performed by one or many actors, the point of the action is to offset the normalizing effects of the social by opening up and founding new spaces of politics and individuation for others to explore, augment, and amend in their turn. This feminist politics presupposes, not an already known and unifying identity of 'woman', but agonistic, differentiated, multiple non-identified beings that are always becoming, always calling out for augmentation and amendment. Agonistic (resistant but always also responsive to the expressive aspirations of any identity) and performative, this politics seeks to create new relations and establish new realities, as well as to amend and augment old ones . . . even in the private realm.

AFTERWORD: AGONISM VERSUS ASSOCIATIONISM?[44]

Political theorists and feminists, in particular, have long criticized Arendt for the agonistic dimensions of her politics, charging that agonism is a masculinist, heroic, violent, competitive, (merely) aesthetic, or necessarily individualistic practice.[45] For these theorists, the notion of an agonistic feminism would be at best a contradiction in terms and at worst a muddled and perhaps dangerous idea. Their perspective is effectively endorsed by Seyla Benhabib, who, in a recent series of powerful essays, tries to rescue Arendt for feminism by excising agonism from her thought.[46] Juxtaposing agonism to 'associationism', Benhabib argues that these are two alternative 'models of public space'[47] and that, of the two, the associative model is to be preferred because it is 'the more modernist conception of politics' and a better model for feminism as well. Rather than reassess the meaning of agonism and its possibilities for feminism, Benhabib accepts and even expands upon earlier feminist genderings of agonism as the provenance of male action. Privileging the associative model of individuals acting with each other in concert, she deprives feminism of a much-needed appreciation of the necessarily agonistic dimension of all action in concert, in which politically engaged individuals act *and* struggle both with *and* against each other.

In 'Feminist Theory and Hannah Arendt's Concept of Public Space', Benhabib constructs agonism and associationism as perfect, mirror opposites. In contrast to the agon, which presupposes a 'morally homogeneous and politically egalitarian, but exclusive community', the modern public space is heterogeneous: 'neither access to it nor its agenda of debate can be predefined by criteria of moral and political homogeneity.' While the agon locates freedom in a stable public space, the associative model treats freedom as a practice, not a space: it 'emerges from action in concert' wherever and whenever that occurs. 'The agonal space is based on competition rather than collaboration', focused on 'greatness, heroism, and pre-eminence' not on action in concert. It 'individuates those who participate in it and sets them apart from others', rather than binding them together.[48]

This rejection of agonism in favour of its supposed opposite, associationism, depends upon a problematic series of contestable definitions and elisions. First, agonism is defined strictly in classical terms, while associationism is revised and updated for modernity. This depiction of the Arendtian agon as essentially and necessarily a site of classical heroic individualism flies in the face of Arendt's own resignification of agonism as a practice of concerted action. (Arendt makes it quite clear that, on her account, action —even in its most agonal forms—is always, always in concert.)[49] Benhabib then moves on to revise and update Arendtian associationism in order to produce the more modern conception of the public sphere she wants to endorse. Pointing out that Arendt 'limit[s] her concept of public space in ways which are not compatible with her own associative model', Benhabib eases the incompatibility by amending Arendt's associationism to include concerns that Arendt rejected as antipolitical (no such amendment is forwarded for agonism) and to identify associationism, again *contra* Arendt's own account, with 'not a substantive but a procedural' model of public discourse.[50]

The problem is not that Benhabib amends Arendt's account. She quite clearly positions her own project as one that proceeds by 'thinking with Arendt against Arendt'.[51] The problem lies in her bifurcation of Arendt's complex vision of political action into two distinct, separable, and mutually exclusive types of public space, in her insistence that we must choose between them, in her loading of that choice with her asymmetric treatment of the pair, and in her (at this point unsurprising) conclusion that associationism is the better, because more modernist, notion of the two.

In another essay, 'Hannah Arendt and the Redemptive Power of Narrative', the agon is again devalued, this time by contrast with discursive (associative) public space. Once again proceeding asymmetrically, Benhabib metaphorizes the discursive moment in Arendtian action but leaves its agonistic other behind, arguing that agonistic public space is a 'topographical or institutional' *place*, while insisting that discursive public space, Arendt's more 'modernist' notion, 'emerges whenever and wherever men act together in concert.'[52] This limitation of the metaphorization is arbitrary, however. There is nothing in Arendt's account of the various more and less agonistic and associative public spaces to suggest that the latter are any more amenable than the former to the dispersal sought by Benhabib. If we are to say, 'with Arendt against Arendt', that associative public space emerges whenever people act together in concert, why may we not also say that agonistic public space emerges whenever people act and struggle with and against each other in concert?

In a more recent essay, 'The Pariah and Her Shadow: Hannah Arendt's Biography of Rahel Varnhagen', Benhabib further genders the agonism/associationism binary, juxtaposing male agonistic space to a now explicitly feminized associationism, here modelled by the salon. Drawing boldly on *Rahel Varnhagen*, Arendt's early biography of a Romantic-era Jewish German salon hostess, Benhabib champions the salon as an associative, female-dominated semi-public space that enables association, intimacy, conversation, friendship, and female agency. Agonal space, by contrast, is said to exclude women and to generate struggle and competition.[53]

But the salon is less supportive of Benhabib's feminized associationism than it is of efforts (like my own) to attenuate the oppositions that Benhabib seeks to secure, such as those between agonism and associationism or male- and female-friendly models of public space. Women did have more power in the salons than in other public spheres, but their power depended upon public and private patriarchal power. The salons hosted by women were owned by temporarily absent fathers and husbands. The brief success of

Rahel's salons derived partly from the fortuitous and temporary absence of any competing, male, cultural centres like a university, parliament, or royal court.[54] Moreover, the salons were famous for generating not only friendship, communication, and intimacy but also gossip, intrigue, competition, and struggle; one is even tempted to say . . . agonism.

Benhabib concedes all of this, but argues that these imperfections in the salons' representation of her associative ideal do not pose a problem because she is not interested in recuperating the salons as such, but in treating them as 'precursors' of associationism, as 'past carriers of some of its future potentials'.[55] Fair enough. But might not the salons' imperfections as models of a feminized associationism raise questions none the less about Benhabib's deployment of the salon as a figure through which to gender the agonism/associationism binary?[56] The salons' complicated combination of agonistic and associative dimensions might unsettle (rather than support) the mutually exclusive opposition that Benhabib seeks to ground in the salons' example.

The brand of agonism explored in this essay is not the agonism rejected by Benhabib. It models a kind of action in concert that resists or exceeds her binary. Neither a heroic individualism nor a consensus-based associationism, this agonism models an action in concert that is also always a site of struggle, a concerted feminist effort that is always with *and* against one's peers because it takes place in a world marked and riven by difference and plurality. This agonism takes as its point of departure Arendt's resignified agonism, not the classical polis experience. It does not map neatly onto any male/female oppositions; it takes those conventional oppositions as its adversaries. And it is centred, not on excellence and theatrical self-display, but on the quest for individuation and distinction against backgrounds of homogenization and normalization. Benhabib sees agonism as a practice in which actors compete 'for distinction and excellence'.[57] She is not wrong. But her immediate identification of agonism's distinction-awarding effects with a craving for fame and excellence forecloses an alternative reading of 'distinction' that is no less true to classical agonism but that may also have more (post-)modern dimensions. The agonal passion for distinction, which so moved Arendt's theoretical account, may also be read as a struggle for individuation, for emergence as a distinct self: in Arendt's terms, a 'who' rather than a 'what', a self possessed not of fame *per se* but of individuality, a self that is never exhausted by the (sociological, psychological, and juridical) categories that seek to define and fix it.

What makes this passion an *agonal* passion once it is no longer tethered to the fame and excellence that only the classical agon could award? The feminist practices endorsed here are agonistic because they are tied to struggle; specifically, to a political struggle to (re-)found, augment, and amend governing practices of sex/ gender. Just as the combatants in the agon individuated themselves in a publicly supported relation of struggle with and against an Other, so too agonistic feminists support the struggles of their peers to individuate and position themselves with and against various feminisms, dominant practices, and identities of sex/gender, and those others who practise and enforce them.[58] Agonistic feminists achieve and enable individuation and distinction by interrupting conventional practices of sex/gender and decentring the would-be primacy of conventional sex/gender binaries.[59] This process of individuation is not *for* an audience, though any set of actions or performances may be witnessed by one. It is for the self who in concert with others like herself gains individuation, and for others who are enabled to do the same by way of these shared, if also always conflicted, practices of support and struggle. Agonistic individuation need not be the goal of political or feminist action. As Arendt well knew, individuation tends, rather, to be one of the by-products of political engagement. Through the acid test of political action in concert, Arendtian actors find out who they are. This self-discovery or transformation need not be shunned as mere boyish posturing; it may just as well be taken to signal the development of character and individuality in worldly settings.

The emphasis of agonistic feminism on the development of individuality as an effect of participation in concerted political action restores Arendt's original partnering of agonism and associationism.[60] The restoration is important for contemporary feminisms at this time, because our recent focus on difference and plurality in response to the deployment by some feminisms of the homogenizing and disciplinary category of 'woman' has led some to wonder how, in the absence of a unifying identity, cause, or ground, any future feminism might motivate concerted action. Arendt helps us to answer the question (albeit not for feminism in particular) by theorizing an agonistic action in concert that postulates difference and plurality, not identity, at its base. By insisting that action not take the what-ness of subjectivity as its point of departure, she (unwittingly but none the less valuably) provides a model for those feminisms that seek to put 'woman' into question rather than take that figure to signify an identity that is always already known. By theorizing an action in concert that is riven by differences (both within and among the agents of action), Arendt invites us to think of concerted action as a practice of (re-)founding, augmentation, and amendment that involves us in relations not only 'with' but also always simultaneously 'against' others. In short, once we stop thinking of agonism and associationism as mutually exclusive alternatives, we are empowered to develop, 'with Arendt against Arendt', an (augmented and amended) vision of agonistic, feminist political action that is well positioned to engage rather than simply redeploy the dominant sex/gender binaries that feminists have always sought to decentre, resist, or transcend.[61]

Notes

1. *Rahel Varnhagen: The Life of a Jewish Woman*, rev. edn., trans. Richard and Clara Winston (New York: Harcourt Brace Jovanovich, 1974), p. xviii.
2. The most hostile charges are in Adrienne Rich's *On Lies, Secrets and Silence: Selected Prose, 1966–1978* (New York: Norton, 1979) and Mary O'Brien's *The Politics of Reproduction* (Boston: Routledge & Kegan Paul, 1981). I discuss Rich's charges briefly below, and take up the issues surrounding feminist rejections of agonism in the final section of this essay.
3. *The Human Condition* (Chicago: University of Chicago Press, 1958), 155, 200; hereafter cited as *HC*.
4. *On Revolution* (New York: Penguin Books, 1963), 130; hereafter cited as *OR*.
5. Henceforth, I allow J. L. Austin's terms 'performative' and 'constative' to play an integral role in my reading of Arendt. As I have argued elsewhere, Austin's distinction usefully and aptly adumbrates arguments that Arendt herself makes about the illicit tension between two moments in the founding document: the 'we hold' versus the 'self-evident truths'. That tension, which is ultimately ineliminable (in spite of Arendt's effort to resolve it in favour of the performative 'we hold') makes it impossible for institutions to legitimate themselves 'all the way down'. Arendt effectively affirms that impossibility when she responds to it by brilliantly theorizing authority as a nonfoundational, *political* practice of augmentation and amendment. I argue here that that practice also covers the engagements and interruptions of identity that I identify with an agonistic feminism.

   My use of Austin's distinction is not, as Seyla Benhabib argues, an attempt to use a 'linguistic' distinction to settle the problem of legitimacy, nor does it amount to a defence of 'Derrida's thesis of the ultimate arbitrariness of all power' (this is not, in any case, his thesis). If it looks that way to Benhabib, that is because she assumes that the problem of political legitimacy must be solvable within the domain of theory. From that perspective, it is no surprise that my own project should appear either as a failed attempt to solve the problem of legitimacy or as a theoretical claim that the problem of legitimacy is unsolvable (or, as in this case, somehow both). But Benhabib's perspective and her project are different from mine. The lesson I draw from Arendt's reading of the Declaration, with help from Austin and Derrida, is that the resolution of the problem of legitimacy is itself an ongoing, never-ending project of political work, a perpetual practice of democratic augmentation and amendment, not a philosophical problem to be solved. The attempt to solve the problem of legitimacy at a philosophical level (or the belief that it is susceptible to philosophical resolution) is distinctively un-Arendtian in spirit and symptomatic of political theory's generally problematic tendency to displace politics. More to the point, her assumption that legitimacy is a philosophical rather than a political problem unhelpfully limits Benhabib's diagnostic options to only two: that of total legitimacy versus total arbitrariness. In my view, one of the main attractions of Arendt's theorization of authority as a political practice of augmentation is that it escapes and unsettles this binary. See Seyla Benhabib, 'Democracy and Difference: Reflections on the Metapolitics of Lyotard and Derrida', *Journal of Political Philosophy*, 2 (1994): 11 n. 24; and Bonnie Honig, 'Declarations of Independence: Arendt and Derrida on the Problem of Founding a Republic', *American Political Science Review*, 85 (1991): 97–113. On political theory's tendency to displace politics, see my *Political Theory and the Displacement of Politics* (Ithaca, NY: Cornell University Press, 1993).

6. I am paraphrasing Nietzsche, to whom Arendt is greatly, albeit ambivalently, indebted here. See Friedrich Nietzsche, *On the Genealogy of Morals*, ed. Walter Kaufmann, trans. Walter Kaufmann and R. J. Hollingdale (1887; New York: Vintage Books, 1969), 1, xiii.

7. I criticize and amend this essentialist component of Arendt's reading of the Declaration in 'Declarations of Independence' and argue, following Jacques Derrida, that the success of the Declaration actually depends not on its really performative character but on its structural undecidability, on the fact that we cannot tell for sure whether this founding speech act is a performative or a constative utterance. My argument here, that agonistic feminism should proceed by redescribing would-be constative identities as performatives, does not suggest that all identities are up for grabs and available for easy reenactments. Instead, the point is to recapture the undecidability

(between constative and performative) that touches all regimes, identities, and foundings but that is then hidden and disguised as pure
constation (of nature, the body, or God). That structural undecidability is a space of augmentation and amendment. It enables not a free-
floating set of performances but a series of political engagements and
struggles with the estimable forces of constation and naturalization.

8. Hanna Pitkin notes this difference, too; see her 'Justice: On Relating Public and Private', *Political Theory* 9 (1981): 303–26. However,
she reads it differently, arguing that *On Revolution* is 'franker', presumably a more genuine expression of Arendt's real views on the
body and the social (334). But this conclusion is unwarranted: it
implies that *The Human Condition* is reticent in a way that is unchar-
acteristic of any of Arendt's texts. Moreover, Pitkin's treatment of
one of Arendt's accounts of the body as a thin veil for the other
obscures the fact that Arendt *layers* distinct characterizations of the
body, one on top of the other. In a more recent essay, 'Conformism, Housekeeping, and the Attack of the Blob: The Origins of
Hannah Arendt's Concept of the Social' (in Bonnie Honig (ed.),
Feminist Interpretations of Hannah Arendt (University Park, Penn.:
Pennsylvania State University Press, 1995)), Pitkin adopts a less
essentialist approach, seeking to denaturalize Hannah Arendt's concept of the social by tracing its complex transformations through
several of Arendt's texts.

9. Hannah Arendt, 'What Is Freedom?' in *Between Past and Future*,
enlarged edn. (New York: Penguin, 1977), 156.

10. Arendt, *HC*, 179; 'What is Freedom?', 151–2. Arendt reads these
attributes of agency behaviourally, as *causes* of action that compromise its freedom.

11. Arendt, *HC*, 179. I borrow the term 'self-surprising' from George
Kateb's treatment of Arendt, *Hannah Arendt: Politics, Conscience,
Evil* (Totowa, NJ: Rowman & Allanheld, 1984).

12. Hannah Arendt, *Thinking*, vol. i of *The Life of the Mind*, ed. Mary
McCarthy (New York: Harcourt Brace Jovanovich, 1978), 29. This
claim is clearly false. Arendt may have meant not that all 'insides'
look identical but that biological differences are not interesting or
significant: as bodies we are all alike.

13. Hannah Arendt, *Willing*, vol. ii of *The Life of the Mind*, 69. Arendt
makes this claim specifically with reference to willing, but it is characteristic of a recoiling that affects all three of the mental faculties.

14. I mean to say that Arendt terms 'political' the phenomenon of agonistic struggle, not that she herself would use the term 'political' to
describe these internal struggles. She would not.

15. Elisabeth Young-Bruehl is the only reader of Arendt to note the multiplicity of Arendt's self, but she does not pursue the connections
between this view of the self as multiplicity and Arendt's treatment

of action as performative, not expressive. Nor does Young-Bruehl see this multiple self as a site of agonistic struggle. On the contrary, she refers to the 'checks and balances existing within an individual', implying an overarching unity that is inapt in this context. See *Mind and the Body Politic* (New York: Routledge, 1989), 23.

16. Arendt, *HC*, 73. Arendt describes 'the laborers who "with their bodies minister to the bodily needs of life" [here quoting Aristotle's *Politics* 1254b25] and the women who with their bodies guarantee the physical survival of the species' (72).

17. Arendt often fails to distinguish clearly her (admittedly admiring) descriptions of the practice of agonal politics in the polis from her own vision of politics; and her critics often mistake the first for the second. For example, Pitkin notes that Arendt's account of action is 'individualistic', but the citation upon which Pitkin relies (from *HC*, 41) is one in which Arendt describes the agon of the polis. Where Arendt describes her own view of action, even in the early, some say too agonal, *Human Condition*, she says that it is always, always 'in concert'.

18. Pitkin, 'Justice', 342.

19. Ibid. I borrow the term 'sensibilities' from Shiraz Dossa, who makes a case quite similar to Pitkin's. Both he and Pitkin, however, stop short of arguing that, as sensibilities, labour, work, and action are characteristic of *all* selves. See *The Public Realm and the Public Self: The Political Theory of Hannah Arendt* (Waterloo: Wilfred Laurier University Press, 1989), ch. 3; and my review of Dossa in *Political Theory*, 18 (1990): 322.

20. This call to denaturalize labour, work, and action so as to see their effects as the products of our own doings parallels the position that informs Pitkin's 'Conformism'. Pitkin puzzles over the incredible power that Arendt assigns to the social: 'Coming from a thinker whose main effort was to teach us our powers—that we are the source of our troubles and should stop doing as we do—the science-fiction vision of the social as Blob ['intent on taking us over, gobbling up our freedom and our politics'] is truly astonishing' (53).

21. Arendt insists that the 'whole sphere of' politics be 'limited', that it not 'encompass the whole of man's and the world's existence' ('What is Freedom?', 264).

22. Arendt, *Willing*, 37–8, 101–2 (emphasis added). I have argued elsewhere that, on Arendt's account, the will is both self-generating *and* capable of bringing its own activity to an end; see 'Arendt, Identity, and Difference', *Political Theory*, 16 (Feb. 1988): 81. However, the phrase highlighted in the text here has persuaded me that Arendt did not attribute the latter feature to the will, but to action.

23. Judith Butler, 'Performative Acts and Gender Constitution: An Essay in Phenomenology and Feminist Theory', in Sue-Ellen Case (ed.),

Performing Feminisms (Baltimore: Johns Hopkins University Press, 1990), 273.

24. Pitkin, 'Justice', 336.

25. Nancy Fraser, *Unruly Practices: Power, Discourse, and Gender in Contemporary Social Theory* (Minneapolis: University of Minnesota Press, 1989), 76.

26. Arendt, 'Preface', in *Between Past and Future*, 3–4.

27. Butler, 'Performative Acts', 276, 271, 280, 271.

28. See n. 5 for my defence of this view of political theory's task against the view that the proper mission of theory is to provide a comprehensive justification of political institutions.

29. Pitkin, 'Justice', 336.

30. Arendt, *OR*, 47. Cf. Butler, 'Performative Acts', 274.

31. Rich, *On Lies, Secrets and Silence*, 211–12. Arendt's readers have been recirculating this citation for some time. Less often noted is that Rich's essay 'On the Conditions of Work' also opens with a citation from Arendt's *The Human Condition*, which is, after all, a 'lofty' even if also a 'crippled' book.

32. Hannah Arendt, *Men in Dark Times* (New York: Harcourt Brace Jovanovich, 1968), 44; hereafter cited as *MDT*. Arendt never considers the possibility that politically active women were drawn to suffragist activities because the suffragist movement was one of the few available opportunities for political action open to women at the time.

33. The story is probably apocryphal, but Arendt is reported to have refused to appear at an American Political Science Association Women's Caucus panel devoted to her work, saying 'I do not think of myself as a woman'.

34. The controversy surrounding the publication of Arendt's *Eichmann in Jerusalem* is well documented in Dagmar Barnouw's *Visible Spaces: Hannah Arendt and the German-Jewish Experience* (Baltimore: Johns Hopkins University Press, 1990).

35. Gershom Scholem, ' "Eichmann in Jerusalem": An Exchange of Letters between Gershom Scholem and Hannah Arendt', *Encounter* (Jan. 1964): 51–2 (emphasis added). All citations from Scholem henceforth are from pp. 51–2; all citations from Arendt in this section are from pp. 53–4.

36. Even when she identifies herself with 'the tradition of German philosophy', the identification is conditional: '*If* I can be said to have come from anywhere, it is from the tradition of German philosophy.' More broadly, the phrasing suggests that Arendt would have preferred that the question of her origins simply not be a subject for speech, i.e. that she not be '*said* to have come from anywhere' (emphasis added).

37. And so is Scholem, of course, constituted by differences and identities other than his Judaism and Zionism. Arendt reminds him of

this—and retaliates in kind for his projections of her identity—by addressing her letter to 'Dear Gerhard' even though Scholem signs his letter to her with his Hebrew name, 'Gershom Scholem'.

38. Emphasis added. I treat Scholem's use of the term 'daughter' in this context less as a recognition that Arendt is distinctly constituted by sex/gender difference than as a means of invoking a sense of obligation to the paternal figure, 'our people'. In short, the term 'daughter' in Scholem's phrase seeks to assimilate Arendt's sex/gender *unproblematically* into her Jewish identity.

39. Arendt's claim that identity is a fact is unchanging. Her claim that it is a *private* fact does change, however, depending on the context. There are times, she says, when one has to defend oneself 'in terms of the identity that is under attack'. At other times, though, positioning oneself in terms of one's identity can be no more than a pose. Given the strategy's context-dependence, one has always to diagnose the situation and decide whether to accede to the (for Arendt, unfortunate) relevance of identity in the space of action or to insist on its privacy or irrelevance. (This diagnostic debate is one that feminism regularly confronts.) My argument is that, in the case of her exchange with Scholem, Arendt misdiagnosed the situation. She should have responded in terms of the identity that was under attack, her own way of being Jewish. I suspect that her failure to do so stemmed partly from her identitarian assumption that since she and Scholem were both Jews, her Jewish identity could not be the one that was under attack and so neither could it be a ground from which to respond.

40. I borrow the notion of 'doing one's gender' from Butler, 'Performative Acts', 276.

41. Hannah Arendt, *The Jew as Pariah*, ed. Ron H. Feldman (New York: Grove, 1978).

42. I track the multiple sites of political space in Arendt's account in *Political Theory and the Displacement of Politics*, 116–17.

43. In fact, the implied individualism of Arendt's pariah perspective contributes to the weakening of her position in relation to Scholem's. Scholem repeatedly invokes the communal figure of the Jewish people to which he aims to restore Arendt, whom he figures as a renegade. Arendt accepts these terms and responds from within their frame. But she need not have done so. She could have forged coalitions with others (past or present) who might have been sympathetic with her views, and she might have positioned herself *vis-à-vis* the Jewish community as part of an alternative Judaic history of intra-Jewish criticism. Arendt uses this last strategy in her Lessing Address when she reclaims Lessing from the German Enlightenment tradition and positions him as part of an alternative intellectual genealogy to which she herself is heir.

44. My thanks to Linda Zerilli and Morris Kaplan for their comments on earlier drafts of this section.
45. Hanna Pitkin, for example, accuses Arendt's political actors of 'boyish posturing' and of membership in a 'romanticized' and 'agonistic male warriors'' club ('Justice'). See also Patricia Springborg, 'Hannah Arendt and the Classical Republican Tradition', in *Thinking, Judging, Freedom*, ed. G. T. Kaplan and C. S. Kessler (Sydney: Allen & Unwin, 1989); and Wendy Brown, *Manhood and Politics* (Totowa, NJ: Rowman & Littlefield, 1988).
46. In short, Benhabib effectively reprises the 1970s and early 1980s debates, which charged Arendt with being either a phallocentric (agonistic) or a gynocentric (associative) thinker. Benhabib's innovation inheres in her refusal to identify Arendt exclusively with either one of these dimensions of her thought, in her acknowledgment of the presence of both in the Arendtian schema. But like those earlier feminists, she goes on to position these two dimensions oppositionally and hierarchically and to insist that we must choose between them. (For more detailed discussions of these early feminist receptions of Arendt, see my 'The Arendt Question in Feminism', and Mary Dietz's 'Feminist Receptions of Hannah Arendt', chs. 1 and 2 of Honig, *Feminist Interpretations of Hannah Arendt*.)
47. Seyla Benhabib, 'Feminist Theory and Hannah Arendt's Concept of Public Space', *History of the Human Sciences*, 6 (1993): 97–114.
48. Ibid. 103–4, 102.
49. See n. 18. Benhabib ignores Arendt's resignification of agonism in this context only. Elsewhere she clearly attends to one dimension of it, arguing that Arendt 'subdues and, yes, "domesticates" the Homeric *warrior-hero* to yield the Aristotelian *deliberative citizen*' (ibid. 103; emphasis original).
50. Ibid. 104, 105.
51. Ibid. 100.
52. Seyla Benhabib, 'Hannah Arendt, and the Redemptive Power of Narrative', *Social Research*, 57 (1990): 193–4.
53. 'The Pariah and Her Shadow', in Honig, *Feminist Interpretations of Hannah Arendt*, 94–5, 97–100.
54. Ibid. 87–8, 93, 97. The very temporary success of Varnhagen's salon and its dependence upon this fortuitous and temporary vacuum in patriarchal institutional power suggest that the real lesson of this example is that those who would champion associationism must also learn and affirm agonism if they are going to preserve their valued alternative spaces of action against the hegemonic aspirations of the state and/or the patriarchal public realm.
55. Ibid. 104 n. 23.
56. In short, my goal here is not to debate the merits of the salon as a model of associative or feminist public space but briefly to note the

role of the salons in Benhabib's larger effort to position—and to gender—agonism and associationism as binary opposites in order to develop a feminism and an Arendt capable of meeting on the common ground of a discourse and consensus model of politics.

57. 'Feminist Theory and Hannah Arendt's Concept of Public Space', 103.

58. For an account of the agon as a site of both concerted action and struggle, see my 'The Politics of Agonism', *Political Theory*, 21 (Aug. 1993): 528–33.

59. For some examples of this (shifting coalitional) practice, see Melissa Orlie's essay, 'Forgiving Trespasses, Promising Futures', in Honig, *Feminist Interpretations of Hannah Arendt*, 337–56. Orlie valuably highlights the ways in which a politics of sex/gender is also always imbricated in a politics of race, class, and sexuality.

60. Insofar as this agonism departs from Arendt's to broaden her realm of the actionable and include so-called social concerns and so-called constative facts, it ought not to be taken to treat identity as its necessarily *central* concern. It does so merely in this essay. If this agonism is always to some extent interested in the politics of identity, that is because it knows that identity—specifically, the formation and production of subjectivity under the (juridical or social) law—is always *an* effect or instrument of social-political-juridical orders and, therefore, *an* indispensable site of political engagement.

61. Notably, this phrase, 'with and against', is the one that Benhabib uses to describe her own relation to Arendt as a reader ('Feminist Theory and Hannah Arendt's Concept of Public Space', 100). In so doing, she describes an *agonistic* relation and this is apt; her reading of Arendt is a concerted action that simultaneously individuates Benhabib's own position. It should also be noted that Benhabib herself seems to recognize, if only momentarily, that agonism and her variety of associationism are not really mutually exclusive: 'While all genuine politics and power relations involve an agonistic dimension, in the sense of vying for distinction and excellence, agonal politics also entails an associative dimension based on the power of persuasion and consensus. In this sense the sharp differentiation between these two models needs to be softened' (103). Having said this, however, Benhabib goes on further to specify the terms of the opposition and does nothing to soften it.

Part II. Gender in the Modern Liberal Public Sphere

5

The Public and the Private Sphere:
A Feminist Reconsideration

Joan B. Landes

After a quarter-century delay, Jürgen Habermas's *Strukturwandel der Öffentlichkeit* appeared finally in English translation in the MIT Press series 'Studies in Contemporary German Social Thought', edited by Thomas McCarthy. Habermas's philosophical-historical critique of the concept and function of the public sphere in England, France, and Germany (with some parting glances at the United States) from the Renaissance to the twentieth century served as a direct inspiration for the German New Left and opened up new lines of scholarship and political debate in Germany and Western Europe. The 1989 translation coincided with a series of events (radical transformations in Eastern Europe, the bloody suppression of the democracy movement in China, and the bicentennial celebrations of the French Revolution) which once again pointed to the pertinence of Habermas's diagnosis of civil society for democratic theory and practice. Originally submitted to the Philosophical Faculty at Marburg as the author's *Habilitationsschrift*, the book deserves to be celebrated as a classic: It has stood the test of time, surviving the fortunes of mercurial literary tastes and changing intellectual seasons; its new translation has markedly widened the author's circle of readers. Nowadays, one is just as apt to hear 'Habermas talk' at humanities or legal studies meetings as among social scientists, philosophers, media critics, or feminist theorists.

In the spirit of dialogue, I approach *The Structural Transformation of the Public Sphere* from the interrelated standpoints of critical theory, political thought, and intellectual history, with a special interest in questions of gender. I will review the model

Chapter 3 in Johanna Meehan (ed.), *Feminists Read Habermas: Gendering the Subject of Discourse* (Routledge, 1995), 91–116. Reprinted by permission of Routledge Inc., New York.

of the public sphere that Habermas derives from eighteenth-century philosophy and society, as well as his account of the rise of democratic social institutions, 'universalistic' cultural practices, and the structures of 'bourgeois representation' during the age of Enlightenment and Revolution. I lay particular stress on recent scholarship concerning eighteenth-century France. In place of a language-centred model of representation, I will emphasize the multiplicity of representation in human communication. Likewise, I will ask whether Habermas's normative subject is sufficiently multi-dimensional, embodied, or gendered to account for the organization of power in different cultural settings. None the less, in my estimation Habermas's text sets a high standard for the kind of political communication research that can help to bridge present divisions between literature, political theory, and philosophy on the one hand and history on the other. By isolating the public sphere as a structure within civil society, Habermas established a new field of research on the political, distinguishable both from a narrower definition of the state and from a more broadly conceived 'political system'. By focusing on the 'structural transformations' of the public sphere, Habermas invited concrete investigations of specific forms of political and cultural life, the benefits of which continue to be realized.[1]

Ironically, this gifted historical-sociological account was produced by an author whose later works earned him a reputation for rigorous, abstract, 'rationalistic' scholarship. In this context, an analogy with the recovery of Marx's 'early writings' may be instructive. Marx had been dead for over half a century when the rediscovery of these writings prompted a fundamental philosophical reappraisal of his science. To be sure, *Strukturwandel der Öffentlichkeit* is among Habermas's most influential and widely translated books into languages other than English. Still, as Thomas McCarthy acknowledges, a more timely translation of Habermas's book 'would likely have facilitated the reception of his thought among Anglo-American scholars by showing how the more abstract and theoretical concerns of his later work arose out of the concrete issues raised in this study'.[2] While McCarthy's observations are to the point, the problematic of *Strukturwandel* can also be appreciated on its own terms, or at least somewhat independently of the trajectory taken in Habermas's later writings. The path taken by the independent European reception of the book leads towards feminist and critical theorists who are reconstructing the original model of the public sphere, and to those scholars who are charting the possibilities for what is variously called the 'new historicism' or the 'new cultural and intellectual history'. In this regard, we might consider whether Habermas has set forth a programme for what might yet become a 'new historicism' in political or socio-logical theory.[3]

THE PUBLIC SPHERE AS A CATEGORY OF BOURGEOIS SOCIETY: DEFENCE OF MODERNITY?

Construed as a narrative of modernity, *Strukturwandel* reads as a tale of the rise of the public sphere (against great political obs-tacles posed by censorship and other forms of political despotism practised by the absolutist state); its triumph (in the vibrant insti-tutions of a free press, clubs, philosophical societies, and the cul-tural life of early liberal society, and through the revolutionary establishment of parliamentary and democratic regimes); and its fateful decline (under the pressures of a late capitalist economy and state). In short, a sorrowful voyage from reason to mediatized consumption.[4] Are we then in the company of another 'dialectic of Enlightenment'? Has the once autonomous and rational sub-ject ended life as a candidate for Foucault's disciplinary society of total surveillance? Is this an early anticipation of Habermas's plaint against the 'colonization of the lifeworld'; a Marxist protest against capitalist economic and state organization; or perhaps a civic repub-lican defence of virtue against the evils of commerce?

Surely, Habermas shares with others a dark outlook on mod-ern public culture. Those who would characterize him as a blind and bland proponent of modernity therefore risk misunderstand-ing the complexity of his vision and the novelty of his attempt to sketch a historically saturated discourse theory of society.[5] Nor is language in some abstracted sense Habermas's sole object of con-cern. Rather, he proposes to investigate the political effects of a specific discourse on society, along with the institutional (that is, social and cultural) preconditions for this discourse to have come into existence in the first place. By beginning with an ety-mology of the terms public and private, Habermas signals from the outset the inherited ideological weight of these categories. He observes how the vocabulary of Greek political categories stamped by Roman law characteristic of the Renaissance civic republican tradition continues to structure political scholarship on the topic of public life even in the late twentieth century.[6] Inviting his readers to examine their own unacknowledged premises about public and private matters, Habermas proceeds to a critical reconstruction of the category of the modern bourgeois public sphere by way of its immediate historical antecedents.

Just as feudal authority could not be made to fit the Roman law contrast between private dominion (*dominium*) and public autonomy (*imperium*), so too, according to Habermas, medieval 'lordship was something publicly represented. This *publicness* (or *publicity*) *of representation* in late medieval society was not constituted as a social realm, that is, as a public sphere; rather, it was something like a status attribute.' Hence, the lord 'displayed himself, presented himself as an embodiment of some sort of "higher" power'.[7] Habermas calls attention to the features of visibility, display, and embodiment; that is, the 'aura' that surrounded and endowed the lord's concrete existence. Habermas observes that something of this legacy is preserved in recent constitutional doctrine, where representation is deemed to be a public, never a 'private' matter. Moreover, these medieval features of staged publicity are fundamental to the 're-presentative' public sphere of absolutist society within early modern territorial nation-states. The 're-presentative' public sphere was not a sphere of political communication, nor did it require any permanent location. Rather, it was marked by the staged performance of authority, displayed before an audience, and embodied in the royal subject. After the Renaissance, aristocratic society also came less to represent its own lordliness (its manorial authority) and to serve more as a vehicle for the representation of the monarch. Thus the grand spectacle of absolutism required a repeated reenactment of the sources and conditions of public power through festivals, balls, banquets, coronations, and entry ceremonies in which the visual aspects of theatre were in command.

Habermas relates the genesis of the bourgeois public sphere to changes in the social organization and communication networks of early modern territorial states: the growth of urbanism, capitalist commerce and stock markets, new systems for news and the mail, and, finally, state administrations for taxation and 'policing' subject populations. Consequently, civil society came into existence 'as the corollary of a depersonalized state authority'.[8] To a well-worn view of the privatization of economic production, Habermas adds a strong appreciation for the role performed by a new set of cultural institutions that flourished in urban centres: coffee-houses, clubs, reading and language societies, lending libraries, concert halls, opera houses, theatres, publishing companies, lecture halls, salons, and, above all, journals and the commercial press. He charts the way in which state authorities first made use of the press as a vehicle for addressing its promulgations to the public, and he identifies the crucial position of a new stratum of the bourgeoisie within the educated, literate public of late seventeenth- and eighteenth-century society. Thus, Habermas marks the emergence of a critical public within Old Regime society:

Because, on the one hand, the society now confronting the state clearly separated a private domain from public authority and because, on the other hand, it turned the reproduction of life into something transcending the confines of private domestic authority and becoming a subject of public interest, that zone of continuous administrative contact became 'critical' also in the sense that it provoked the critical judgment of a public making use of its reason. The public could take on this challenge all the better as it required merely a change in the function of the instrument with whose help the state administration had already turned society into a public affair in a specific sense—the press.⁹

The bourgeois public sphere is conceived to be a sphere of private people coming together as a public through the 'historically unprecedented' public use of their reason. This informal association of private persons mediated between, on the one hand, civil society (the economy or sphere of commodity exchange and social labour) and the family, and, on the other hand, the state (the realm of the police or state administration and the court). The bourgeois public sphere consists of both a literary/cultural and political public sphere. Habermas addresses the process whereby culture was constituted as an object for discussion and packaged for purchase. At the same time, he insists that the literary public sphere functioned as a precursor to the public sphere operative in the political domain. 'It provided the training ground for a critical public reflection still preoccupied with itself—a process of self-clarification of private people focusing on the genuine experiences of their novel privateness.'¹⁰ Nor could this have occurred without the emergence of a new form of the private sphere—the patriarchal conjugal family's intimate domain—and the intensification of processes of (psychological) individualism. As a result, an audience-oriented subjectivity on the part of private individuals promoted the commodification of culture and served the polemical functions of the political public sphere.

Anticipating what Stephen Greenblatt has termed 'self-fashioning', Habermas describes the interplay between the codes of intimacy characteristic of fiction (the novel), the forms of subjectivity that were fitted to print, and the appeal of literature to a widening public of readers.[11] Likewise, by appropriating aspects of the Frankfurt School's account of 'authority and the family', Habermas concludes that the experiential complex of audience-oriented privacy affected the political realm's public sphere. He thereby undermines Hannah Arendt's despairing survey of the emergence of the categories of the social and the private.[12] Accordingly, Habermas rejects the Greek model of a citizenry acting in common to administer the law and to ensure the community's military survival. Instead he locates the *specificity* of the modern public sphere in the civic task of a society engaged in critical public debate to protect a commercial economy. In contrast to the older *res publica*, he deems the bourgeois public sphere to be the site for the political regulation of civil society, and credits it with a willingness to challenge the established authority of the monarch. Such a public sphere was from the outset both private and polemical. Neither trait was characteristic of the Greek model of the public sphere:

for the private status of the master of the household, upon which depended his political status as citizen, rested on domination without any illusion of freedom evoked by human intimacy. The conduct of the citizen was agonistic merely in the sportive competition with each other that was a mock war against the external enemy and not in dispute with his own government.[13]

In this manner Habermas critically reconstructs the specific contours of the modern public sphere. He provides nuanced descriptions of the distinctive institutions of eighteenth-century French, British, and German society: e.g. *salons*, coffee-houses, and *Tischgesellschaften*. Acknowledging their differences, he none the less identifies a series of common institutional criteria that they shared. First, the ideal of equality was institutionalized and stated as an objective claim, insofar as a kind of social intercourse occurred irrespective of social status so that the authority of the better argument could assert itself against that of social hierarchy. Second, cultural communities, stripped of their former 'aura' and freed from their ties to the church's and court's re-presentative forms of publicity, established new meanings and new domains of common concern based on rational, verbal communication among private people. Third, no matter how inclusive the newly constituted public may have been in practice, the issues discussed became general in their significance and in their accessibility. In principle, everyone had to *be able to participate.*

On the basis of these social criteria, Habermas claims that the 'liberal fiction of the discursive formation of the public will' was created.[14] In addition, political objections to the secret dictates of absolute sovereignty encouraged appeals to general, abstract, objective, and permanent norms—e.g. to constitutional law, wherein 'a rationality in which what is right converges with what is just; the exercise of power is to be demoted to a mere executor of the norm'.[15] Against secrecy and will, the new rationality— anchored in the principle of critical public debate among private people—held out the goals of publicity and universality.

But Habermas also grants the practical limitations of the bourgeois model of the public sphere. From the outset, a tension arose between the formal criteria of abstract moral reason and the goals of substantive rationality. Ambivalences in the principle of privacy derived from the system of private property and from a family caught up in the requirements of the market. In addition, conflicts arose in the identity of the privatized individuals who occupied the public sphere, insofar as their status derived either from a position as property-owners rather than from their basic humanity; e.g. a conflict between Rousseau's *bourgeois* and *citoyen.* Hence, class and its accoutrements (property, income, literacy, and cultural background) were major barriers to full participation in the bourgeois public sphere.[16] The bourgeois public sphere was for the most part a restricted male preserve, except for salon society, which was shaped by women 'like that of the rococo in general'.[17] Still, Habermas suggests that the exclusion of women from English coffee-houses may have been an advantage insofar as 'critical debate ignited by works of literature and art was soon extended to include economic and political disputes, without any guarantee (such as was given in the *salons*) that such discussions would be inconsequential, at least in the immediate context'.[18] On the other hand, he distinguishes between the literary and the political sphere, observing that, whereas women and dependents were factually and legally excluded from the political public sphere, 'female readers as well as apprentices and servants often took a more active part in the literary public sphere than the owners of private property and family heads themselves'.[19]

ONE PUBLIC OR MANY? WHERE ARE THE WOMEN?

By Habermas's own account, then, the oppositional bourgeois public sphere only partially achieved its stated goals of equality and participation. But he sees this as a limitation of actually existing society, not of the model of a universal public according to which pre-existing social inequalities are bracketed. Within the region of social discourse, he believes, a public body is created wherein the differential rights of private individuals cease to matter. Yet there were stringent requirements for admission to this club, as to any other. Even if property did not become a topic for discourse, it remained the precondition for participation in the bourgeois public sphere. Furthermore, because the public sphere and the conditions for publicity presupposed a distinction between public and private matters, it was ill equipped to consider in public fashion the political dimension of relations in the intimate sphere. Equally disabling was the expectation that all those who engaged in public discourse would learn to master the rules of disinterested discourse. Under ideal conditions, then, the members of a theoretical public were to behave according to the bourgeois liberal principle of abstract equality. Just as the laws of market assumed a certain forgetfulness concerning the real existence of property, so too the laws of the public sphere were predicated on the principle of disinterestedness and on the observance of the norms of reason not power, rationality not domination, and truth not authority. Still, Habermas never asks whether certain subjects in bourgeois society are better suited than others to perform the discursive role of participants in a theoretical public.

In my study *Women and the Public Sphere in the Age of the French Revolution*, however, I argued that Habermas's formulation effaces the way in which the bourgeois public sphere from the outset worked to rule out all interests that would not or could not lay claim to their own universality.[20] The notion of an enlightened, theoretical public reduced to 'mere opinion' (cultural assumptions, normative attitudes, collective prejudices, and values) a whole range of interests associated with those actors who would not or could not master the discourse of the universal. Moreover, the structural division between the public sphere on the one hand and the market and the family on the other meant that a whole range of concerns came to be labelled as private and treated as improper subjects for public debate. Habermas overlooks the strong association of women's discourse and their interests with 'particularity', and conversely the alignment of masculine speech with truth, objectivity, and reason. Thus he misses the masquerade through which the (male) particular was able to posture behind the veil of the universal.

In any event, none of this was the accidental consequence of the lesser status of women in pre-liberal society, to be amended in a more democratic order. Rather, the resistance of enlightened liberal and democratic discourse to femininity was rooted in a symbolization of nature that promised to reverse the spoiled civilization of le monde where stylish women held sway, and to return to men the sovereign rights usurped by an absolutist monarch. Furthermore, when women during the French Revolution and the nineteenth century attempted to organize in public on the basis of their interests, they risked violating the constitutive principles of the bourgeois public sphere: in place of one, they substituted the many; in place of disinterestedness, they revealed themselves to have an interest. Worse yet, women risked disrupting the gendered organization of nature, truth, and opinion that assigned them to a place in the private, domestic but not the public realm. Thus an idealization of the universal public conceals the way in which women's (legal and constitutional) exclusion from the public sphere was a constitutive, not a marginal or accidental feature of the bourgeois public from the start.

From parallel vantage-points, other feminist scholars have also challenged the presuppositions of an abstract, universal model of the public sphere. Mary Ryan queries whether 'the olympian notion of a sphere of rational deliberation may be incompatible with genuine publicness, with being open and accessible to all'.[21] She traces women's entrance into public spaces in nineteenth-century America despite the strong barriers confronting them in the officially sanctioned public sphere. Yet the pressures of social diversity meant that the public sphere was subject to powerful gender, race, class and regional cleavages. Anna Yeatman challenges the one-sided model of individuality on which universal citizenship in the natural rights tradition has been grounded.[22] Nancy Fraser draws a lesson from several historical investigations of the public sphere, observing that because Habermas failed to examine examples of non-liberal, non-bourgeois, or competing public spheres, 'he ends up idealizing the liberal public sphere'. Fraser observes that 'virtually from the beginning, counterpublics contested the exclusionary norms of the bourgeois public, elaborating alternative styles of political behavior and alternative norms of public speech'[23] that bourgeois publics in turn attempted to block. She concludes that in both stratified and egalitarian societies a multiplicity of publics is preferable to a single public sphere; and that an adequate conception of the public sphere would countenance the inclusion, not the exclusion, of interests and issues 'that bourgeois masculinist ideology labels "private" and treats as inadmissible'.[24]

A question arises as to whether a universalistic discourse model can satisfy conditions of genuine equality. I have suggested that the virtues of universality and reason are offset by the role they play within a system of Western cultural representation that has eclipsed women's interests in the private domain and aligned femininity with particularity, interest, and partiality. In this context, the goals of generalizability and appeals to the common good may conceal rather than expose forms of domination, suppress rather than release concrete differences among persons or groups. Moreover, by banishing the language of particularity, the liberal public sphere has jeopardized its own bases of legitimation in the principles of accessibility, participation, and equality. Last, I have argued that style and decorum are not incidental traits but constitutive features of the way in which embodied, speaking subjects establish the claims of the universal in politics.[25]

In complementary fashion, Seyla Benhabib argues that a range of distinctions in the Western philosophical tradition—between justice and the good life, norms and values, interests and needs —have operated to confine women and typically female spheres of activity like housework, reproduction, nurturance and care for the young, the sick, and the elderly to the 'private' domain. 'These issues have often been considered matters of the good life, of values, of non-generalizable interests . . . and treated, until recently, as "natural" and "immutable" aspects of human relations. They have remained pre-reflexive and inaccessible to discursive analysis.'[26] Iris Young also protests that 'the Enlightenment ideal of the civil public where citizens meet in terms of equality and mutual respect is too rounded and tame an ideal of public. This idea of equal citizenship attains unity because it excludes bodily and affective particularity, as well as the concrete histories of individuals that make groups unable to understand one another.'[27] In this light, we might consider whether Habermas's ideal representation of the public sphere or his normative description of the subject are perhaps too tame to accommodate the dilemmas raised by feminist critics.

SUBJECTS, ACTORS, AND SPECTATORS

According to Habermas, the modern bourgeois public sphere came into existence when private persons joined together to exercise their reason in a public fashion. Public opinion is the end product of all the dialogues between discoursing individuals, each one of whom is capable of reflexive self-questioning and successful at internalizing the rules of rational discourse. In contrast, Hannah Arendt conceives of the political realm of the polis as rising directly out of acting together, the 'sharing of words and deeds' that in turn generates a 'space of appearances'.[28] Both Habermas and Arendt agree on the potential of words or discourse to generate power, and they set this potential of the public sphere apart from violence or force. But Arendt locates power not merely in the associational space but also in the competition for excellence that occurs among actors who are by definition moral and political equals.[29] She deems action to be the only sphere in which individuals may distinguish themselves, even to the point of 'greatness'; they do so through word and deed when they narrate the distinctive story of their own lives.[30] Through storytelling, then, men 'create their own remembrance'.[31] Indeed, the polis is 'a kind of organized remembrance'.[32]

Now, Habermas has distanced himself justifiably from Arendt's anti-modernistic perspective; her seeming indifference to the emancipation of women, workers, and minorities; her uncritical attitude toward property relations in the polis; and her agonistic view of the public sphere. He grasps that Arendt's individuals are a rather narrow slice of the human population: in Athens, the propertied, free, slave-holding men who inhabited the world of the *polis*, in contrast to women and slaves who belonged to the *oikos*, the sphere of biological reproduction and property. Still, Habermas has learned a great deal from Arendt's discussion of the public sphere, and the two theorists share a strong appreciation of the political implications of speech and language.[33] But Habermas's individuals participate in the public sphere as speakers and readers (of novels and the press). By contrast, in Arendt's public sphere individuals perform deeds and narrate stories; they are not just talking heads but embodied, suffering subjects who move in the world in relation to others. Such a world is a 'web of relationships' constituted by 'enacted stories'. It is neither labour (the metabolic interaction with nature) nor work (the making of products), but action which

145

produces relationships that bind people together. Action discloses the agent in the act; otherwise it loses its specific character. So, Arendt believes, it is in performing rather than writing the story that each actor reveals his individuality. She even submits that actors are not the authors of their own stories:

Although everybody started his life by inserting himself into the human world through action and speech, nobody is the author or producer of his life story. In other words, the stories, the results of action and speech, reveal an agent, but this agent is not an author or producer. Somebody began it and is its subject in the twofold sense of the word, namely, its actor and sufferer, but nobody is its author.[34]

Thus Arendt appreciates several dimensions of the public sphere absent from Habermas's discursive model. Although she is nowhere concerned either with women or with the gendered construction of subjectivity, certain aspects of her discussion are worthy of feminists' attention. Arendt addresses the performative dimension of human action and human speech. She implies that insofar as persons display themselves in public, they do so as storytellers, revealing aspects of their selves by acting in and through their bodies. Perhaps most radically, Arendt suggests that the subject is displaced within a wider communication network. Still, let us not confuse her metaphors of the stage with a post-structuralist abandonment of the subject. Her foremost objective is to describe and exalt exemplary moral actions. In that respect, she sees the theatre as the political art *par excellence*, the site where the political sphere of human life is transposed into art. And she holds out a privileged role for historians who reconstitute stories already told and for political theorists who narrate exemplary stories about the political.[35]

A radically different perspective on the intimate relationship between theatre and politics—and politics as theatre—is offered in Marie-Hélène Huet's *Rehearsing the Revolution: The Staging of Marat's Death, 1793–1797*. In a sense, Huet picks up where both Arendt and Habermas leave off. In place of 'the message', on the one hand, or the endless circuit of opinion, on the other, Huet investigates the spectatorial function of the always already theatricalized public sphere. Drawing on Diderot's remarks in *Jacques le fataliste*, she discovers some striking parallels between the spectator of a judicial action and of an aesthetic work. First, Huet asserts it is not the message that interests the spectator: 'What interests the spectator is the spectacle per se. His position as a receiver is established, constituted, made use of, independently of the significance of the message received. There is not one public thirsting for blood and tortures and another public eager for entertainments and pleasures; a public is formed the moment there is a spectacle.' Second, like Diderot, Huet appreciates the possibility of a transmutation from the role of spectator-receiver to that of actor; for in retelling every spectator has the potential to act: 'Diderot is . . . describing the formation of a *mise en scène*, a "rehearsal" properly speaking, in which the spectator ultimately finds his justification: to have become an actor.'[36]

In place of a retrospective ideological analysis of public participation, Huet pursues a semiotic approach. She underscores the implicit reversibility, as well as the incompleteness and alienation, that constitutes the role of the spectator/receiver:

Inherent in the notion of the spectator is that of the future actor; part of the pleasure of the spectacle lies in anticipation of another spectacle in which the spectator will finally be actor. To appeal to an audience is to appeal to this possibility of a spectator-actor exchange, and an audience that does not achieve this exchange, this cycle, this transformation, is a mutilated audience.[37]

Now, Huet is concerned specifically with the production of the French revolutionary public, which she sees as being 'inscribed in a tradition that consists in repressing by means of the spectacle'.[38] She observes how the legislation freeing the theatres was accompanied by new regulations, constant surveillance of audiences and plays, a Rousseauian preference for open-air festivals and an accompanying suspicion of the closed theatrical chamber—emblem, it was believed, of counter-revolutionary designs. Although Huet cautions against conflating the revolutionary dynamic with political liberalism, her argument adds immeasurably to a general understanding of the performative dimensions of the bourgeois public sphere. Likewise, she challenges us to consider the alienated and mutilating features of the open spaces of public speech which Habermas and Arendt otherwise celebrate. In contrast to the latter, Huet focuses attention not only on the actors but on the shared forms of representation between theatre and politics. In very different terms from those employed by Habermas, Huet describes the communication network of a theoretical public—that public which acts as both spectator and judge and presumes that its judgement will always be right.[39] She concludes that during the Revolution this theoretical public was composed of the people who were invited by the legislators to the deliberations of the juries as a guarantor of justice and a protection of the innocent. Yet, she cautions, 'they were carefully separated from the spectacle to which they were exposed, they were subjected to a rule of silence, and they were constantly held to the passive role of spectators'.[40]

In a provocative essay, *The Body and the French Revolution*, Dorinda Outram adds a heightened concern with physicality and gender to structural accounts of political culture conceived solely in verbal terms. By way of a phenomenology of embodiment, Outram resituates many of the features of Huet's theatrical politics, Arendt's public sphere and its public actors, and Habermas's public opinion.[41] She argues that the construction and use of dignified bodies—in Arendt's terms, their 'enacted stories'—became a source of authority in both the private and public realm. However, the other side of this new political culture of the body involved the sanctioning of physical violence in the revolutionary process and the planting of seeds of self-destructiveness in the individual. In place of an abstracted classicism or a celebration of agonistic relations for their own sake, then, Outram discerns that stoicism and other classical motifs were reworked by a new revolutionary class that faced the task of 'creating a new political embodiment for the individuals concerned and a new audience for their politics'.[42]

The Revolution's most essential feature may not have been the production of a new state, but rather the production of new public spaces dominated by the authoritative public bodies of individuals. Men created models of heroic masculinity through dignity, self-containment, and suicide. Not surprisingly, many historians have observed that the political culture of the Revolution aimed 'to redistribute various attributes of the king's body throughout the new body politic'. As Outram explains,

The public space of France before 1789 had also focused on an image of heroic public dignity almost exclusively applied to monarchy and aristocracy: it was such images that the middle class had to re-create. The new public bodies which they created and filled with attributes of heroic dignity were in turn inconceivable without, and were created for, the audiences that mass politics made possible. They possessed the power, which the competing linguistic discourses obviously did not, to focus dignity and legitimacy in incontestable, because non-verbal, ways on the bodies of known individuals who acted as personifications of value systems.[43]

For Outram, the body is not an undifferentiated object and behaviour is not indifferent. She argues that the victory of *homo clausus*, 'the male type validated by his separation of affect from instinct, by body-separation from other individual human beings', was achieved over and against traits associated with the feminine and popular behaviour encapsulated in the carnavalesque.[44] She views the Revolution as a contest between male and female, resulting in the validation of only male political participation, supported by images of heroic masculinity. In social and philosophical terms,

Homo clausus legitimated himself by his superiority to the somatic relations enjoyed by other classes—aristocracy, peasants, and workers—and by the other gender. In other words, what he possessed was a body which was also a non-body, which, rather than projecting itself, retained itself. In doing so, it became the location of abstract value-systems, such as rationality and objectivity. As Pierre Bourdieu has remarked such a move is integral to the production of middle-class systems of cultural hegemony, which privilege over-arching *languages*, such as the language of objectivity and rationality, rather than privileging energy or displays of integration between body and personality: display is characterized as aristocratic, emotionality and subjectivity as feminine, physical energy as plebian.[45]

Unlike Habermas, then, Outram unequivocally links the production of new public spaces to a new gender division in bourgeois public culture. In contrast to Arendt's vision of the polis as a sphere of organized remembrance and her celebration of agonistic action, Outram underscores the fragility of the poses of heroic dignity: 'unlike fully sacralized bodies which exist *above* time, desacralized ones exist *in* time. They can only really find validation through death—not through re-creation.'[46] She proposes that personal autonomy has been purchased at the price of exclusion (of women and the lower classes); that the subject's 'self image of rationality, reflexivity, universalism, autonomy, individuation, and emancipation always [contain] the potential for transposition into its direct opposite'.[47] Thus, to Habermas's version of the modern subject, Outram holds up the mirror of Horkheimer and Adorno's 'dialectic of Enlightenment'; and it is by no means inconsequential that in that mirror she finds the faces of women and workers.

WHOSE OPINION?

Revisionist historians of the Revolution have sketched an equally disturbing portrait of how revolutionary politics strove toward absolute consensus, monitoring and expelling all instances of division within the revolutionary public. Rather than a contest over interests, revolutionary politics became the site of symbolic legitimations.[48] Benjamin Nathans aptly relates the challenge that recent historiography poses to Habermas's model of the public sphere:

One finds here a stunning reversal of Habemas's principle of general accessibility: rather than adjusting the public sphere (as embodied by the various clubs) to accommodate society, society was radically tailored by a series of brutal excisions and exclusions in order to fit the mold of a fictitious public of abstract individuals. The exclusion of 'enemies,' in fact, took the place of critical discussion as the mechanisms for establishing the 'general good.' Behind the fiction of a unified, authoritative public opinion, an anonymous oligarchy thus 'prefabricated consensus' in the form of an ideology that acted as a substitute for the nonexistent public competition of ideas.[49]

In fact, Habermas has observed that the discursively organized public under the terms of bourgeois representation claimed not to equate itself with *the* public 'but at most claimed to act as its mouthpiece, in its name, perhaps even as its educator'.[50] Yet, he holds out the possibility that a distance can be maintained between *the* public and its representative (the one who claims to speak in its name). In direct contrast, François Furet presents the problem posed by popular sovereignty as that of eccentricity: the centre is always vacant. Revolutionary politics is inherently unstable: because the source of sovereignty resides everywhere and nowhere, there is a perpetual slippage between the public and its representatives. As he states, 'the Revolution replaced the conflict of interests for power with a competition of discourses for the appropriation of legitimacy.'[51] Furthermore, in their respective investigations of the art public and the revolutionary festival, Mona Ozouf and Thomas Crow exhibit the repressive potential of the didactic or educative role that Habermas assigns to the public's representative.[52] In addition, Sarah Maza reveals the way in which late Old Regime lawyers used the device of the *mémoires judiciaires* to publish their (otherwise censurable) views and to influence the outcome of a given trial. Thus, by appealing to public opinion, they exploited the capacity of the public to serve as a tribunal for the nation.[53] These and other empirical studies construct a much more complex picture of the workings of the oppositional public sphere than Habermas allows. Indeed, Keith Baker and Mona Ozouf have even challenged the notion that the new public sphere offered a straightforward alternative to the traditional system. They demonstrate that the monarchy was forced to compete for the judgement of public opinion, so that contestatory politics also shaped the regime's evolution.[54]

Yet Habermas is not unaware of the conceptual and political problems posed by a concept of public opinion as transcendent reason. In an immensely rewarding chapter titled 'The Bourgeois Public Sphere: Idea and Ideology', he charts the most conspicuous philosophical contributions to the concept of public opinion, beginning with Hobbes, Locke, and Bayle, proceeding through the English and European thinkers of the eighteenth century (the physiocrats, Rousseau, Forster, Kant, and Hegel) and concluding with the critical reflections of Marx, Tocqueville, and Mill on a range of difficulties such as the role of property interest, class restrictions on the free circulation of opinion, the distorting functions of propaganda, the problems of majority rule, the issue of tolerance, and the compulsion toward conformity. His final appraisal, however, is that neither the liberal nor the socialist model was adequate for a diagnosis of the breakdown of the public sphere, especially in its loss of critical publicity deriving from both too much and too little publicity. As he remarks, 'The *principle* of the public sphere, that is, critical publicity, seemed to lose its strength in the measure that it expanded as a *sphere* and even undermined the private realm.'[55]

Analytically, this assessment only makes sense against the backdrop of the eighteenth-century model. There, Habermas locates a crucial tension between the principle of critical publicity on the one hand and a legislative model of opinion on the other. In France, the former is associated with the physiocrats and the latter with Rousseau. Thus, he observes, 'only when the physiocrats ascribed it to the *public éclairé* itself did *opinion publique* receive the strict meaning of an opinion purified through critical discussion in the public sphere to constitute a true opinion.'[56] In contrast to their British contemporaries, who understood the public spirit to be an authority that could compel lawmakers to legitimize themselves, the physiocrats still acceded to absolutism. Yet conceptually they achieved a novel fusion of the older contradiction between *opinion* and *critique*.[57] On the other hand, Habermas argues that 'Rousseau projected the unbourgeois idea of an intrusively political society in which the autonomous private sphere, that is, civil society emancipated from the state, had no place'.[58] He situates the undemocratic foundations of 'Rousseau's democracy of unpublic opinion' in the manipulative exercise of power:[59]

The general will was always right, the notorious passage stated, but the judgment that guided it was not always enlightened. . . . A direct democracy required that the sovereign be actually present. The *volonté générale* as the *corpus mysticum* was bound up with the *corpus physicum* of the people as a consensual assembly. The idea of a plebiscite in permanence presented itself to Rousseau in the image of the Greek *polis*. There the people were assembled in the square without interruption; thus in Rousseau's view, the *place publique* became the foundation of the constitution. *Opinion publique* derived its attribute from it, that is, from the citizens assembled for acclamation and not from the rational-critical public debate of a *public éclairé*.[60]

We have seen that Habermas's neat analytical distinction between the publicity function of opinion and its tendency to absolutize itself has been challenged in recent studies of eighteenth-century political culture. While rejecting Rousseau's democracy of 'unpublic opinion' and registering the limits of opinion in a class-bound society, Habermas still adheres to a physiocratic concept of publicity, notwithstanding its appeal to a transcendent concept of reason. He most favours Kant's cosmopolitan version of enlightenment—stripped perhaps of some of its 'moral' wrapping—predicated on free and open communication between rational beings, each of whom possesses knowledge of the world ('humanity'). These citizens, Kant tells us and Habermas concurs, are engaged in rational-critical discussions concerning the affairs of the commonwealth. They are citizens of a 'republican constitution' who enjoy a sphere of private autonomy, the safeguarding of personal liberties, equality before the law, and legislation that conforms to the popular will. Notably, they are not storytellers but rather critical disputants who know how to use their reason on behalf of the common good. In Kant's estimation, 'if we attend to the course of conversation in mixed companies consisting not merely of scholars and subtle reasoners but also of business people or women, we notice that besides storytelling and jesting they have another entertainment, namely, arguing.'[61]

PRINT AND OTHER MEDIA: ON THE MULTIPLE FORMS OF REPRESENTATION

Kant's model of free publicity is a direct antecedent of Habermas's interest in communicative action: different versions of a language-based model of human communication.[62] Yet in the last instance we are dealing not only with a prejudice toward 'linguisticality', but with a compelling account of the historical emergence of textuality as the dominant form of representation in the modern bourgeois public sphere, in contrast to visuality or theatricality in the 're-presentative' public sphere of the Old Regime. Now, there is much to commend this position. It calls attention to a dramatic shift in the organization of the system of representation which I likened to a shift from icon to text in my own study of the gendered public sphere. However, further consideration suggests that a singular emphasis on language may be misleading from both a methodological and an empirical perspective.

The privilege that Habermas accords to the institutions of the press and literature has been only partially sustained in subsequent examinations of the eighteenth-century public sphere. On the one hand, research on the French language press before and during the Revolution has augmented Habermas's appreciation for the central contribution played by the print media in the rise of public opinion.[63] Investigations of the workings of provincial academies, freemasonry, and salon society, as well as the role of literary and art criticism, have more than repaid Habermas's invitation for a text-centred criticism, and sustained his insight that reading practices are best understood not merely as a personal habit but as a new kind of institution.[64] Indeed, even those who view the Revolution as a 'return to the oral' acknowledge that the culture of the spoken word 'always rests on writing or printing'.[65]

On the other hand, studies of the print media and political discourse have introduced complexities not originally entertained by Habermas. Robert Darnton's portrait of critical journalism in late Old Regime France—hack writers in the cafes of Grub Street—subverts any representation of the literary profession restricted to its most successful, enlightened publicists. By implication, Darnton also challenges Habermas's effort to link literary subjectivity and political criticism by presenting the *libelle*, not the confession, as the characteristic genre of the period.[66] Likewise, Bernadette Fort finds in the parodic art criticism of Darnton's Grub Street an appropriation of figures, forms, and strategies from popular theatre and from carnival.[67] Contributors to Lynn Hunt's recent collection *Eroticism and the Body Politic* explore the intimate connections among political, sexual, and gender themes in printed and graphic political pornography within Old Regime and revolutionary France. Together, then, these studies offer a perspective

153

on political representation that diverges in good measure from Habermas's explication of rational and introspective forms of political opinion.[68] In addition, other scholars point to the restrictiveness of a narrowly defined print model. The selections in *Revolution in Print* demonstrate the extent to which political messages were communicated through a range of media that employed mechanically reproduced words or images.[69] And studies of the revolutionary graphic arts explore how political communication is manifested through visual as well as textual means.[70] In short, even in a period which saw the incontestable triumph of the print media, the production of complex representations also involved the creative intermixing of media. Political arguments, we may want to allow, may be communicated in discursive and non-discursive forms, and the two may interact in unanticipated ways.

Furthermore, Habermas has noted but hardly accounted for the symbolic structure of bourgeois representation; that is, the ability of one to stand in for, substitute for, or otherwise represent an absent other who remains the only legitimate source of authority for that representative. To speak in the people's name, to act on its behalf, and to claim to do so on behalf of the universal or general good, all bespeak a fundamental alienation in the source and nature of power. As Michael Warner observes, the transition from what Habermas would term the 'oppositional' bourgeois public sphere to the national state was grounded in a cultural formation of print discourse, and not just in the legitimacy of the people or the rule of law:

It required assumptions between individual subjects and general sovereignty. These assumptions derived not just from any popular group, but from a model of a reading public. Through the new constitutionalism, the metapolitics of print discourse became entrenched as an ideology of legitimate power. If this is a way of saying that the modern state commits a kind of fraud in claiming to represent the people and the law, it is no simple fraud. For the fraud is only the pretense that representational democracy derives its legitimacy from the people and their law, when in fact it performs what it claims to describe. A way of representing the people constructs the people.[71]

In practice, democratic discourse has exhibited an unfortunate potential for substituting its own universal for the real competition of interests. Likewise, appeals to the universal have concealed the gendered division of space and power; and, the creation of open spaces for public speech has fostered a conception of a transcendent, theoretical public which sanctioned the silent participation of spectators. In any event, I have observed that not all speech acts or styles of talking are necessarily equal. More generally, by privileging speech acts Habermas distorts the performative dimension of human action and interaction. In the specific context of the bourgeois Revolution, for example, an analysis of the iconography of power in the new republic might want to describe the theatrics and arguments of the Assembly as well as its published laws and proclamations; and further, to explore the graphic arts as well as acoustic media—speech, song, and music—alongside printed and verbal discourse. Habermas may be right to assume that certain representations are privileged for the representation of power in a given regime—hence textual representations under the early bourgeois regime. On the other hand, a theory of 'public representations' needs to account for the culturally variant ways that humans produce and make use of multiple representations. Pragmatics, the formal use of language in interaction, is best accompanied by a theory and observation of (stylized and informal) bodily gestures and postures. As Dorinda Outram insists, 'words do not give up their full meaning without an account of the physical behaviour which accompanies them'. We are in agreement, then, on the need to examine 'both verbal and physical behaviour and both verbal and physical symbolism', while recalling that 'physicality [is] always mediated, for individuals, by words'.[72]

PROSPECTS FOR A DEMOCRATIC PUBLIC SPHERE

Of all Habermas's feminist critics, Benhabib is perhaps most optimistic that

the discourse model, precisely because it proceeds from a fundamental norm of egalitarian reciprocity and precisely because it projects the democratization of all social norms, cannot preclude the democratization of familial norms and of norms governing the gender division of labor. Once this is granted, the distinction between matters of justice and those of the good life, between generalizable interests and culturally interpreted needs, can be reconceptualized.[73]

Benhabib is confident that once practical discourse is 'feminized', the emancipatory aspirations of new social movements such as the women's movement can be best served by the radical proceduralism of the discourse model. In a more critical vein but with many of the same objectives in mind, Fraser exhorts us to adopt 'a post-bourgeois conception that can permit us to envision a greater role for (at least some) public spheres than mere autonomous opinion formation removed from authoritative decision-making'.[74]

By problematizing Habermas's initial conception of enlightened opinion and public space, I have sought to underscore just how radical the revisions proposed by Benhabib and Fraser would have to be in order to arrive at a process of deliberation and opinion formation from which no subject or person is barred. On the other hand, my intention is not to discount but rather to join in their efforts to democratize and feminize the public sphere. For Benhabib's discursive conditions to obtain, the constraints placed on opinion formation by the authoritative structures of a non-egalitarian polity and economy would need not only to be bracketed but to be eliminated entirely. Nor could the gendered construction of an embodied subjectivity and the body politic remain an unexamined premiss. Likewise, we would have to allow for the intersecting and multiple media of representation in any given setting.

These are utopian but not impossible goals. There is ample evidence, despite the barriers posed by the hegemonic order, that a democratic politics in the present would have been from the outset a politics of the public sphere, not of the state. Habermas's alertness to a zone of democratic participation—neither state, economy, nor family—is as pertinent to today's circumstances as to those of the late eighteenth century. Paradoxically, we seem to be once again in a period where iconic relations on the model of the older 're-presentative' public sphere count for more, stylistically and substantively, than the symbolic, predominantly textual relations promoted by the early bourgeois public sphere. Yet our task is surely not to resort to texts in place of images, but instead to comprehend and deploy all means of representation in a counter-hegemonic strategy against established power wherever it resides.

Notes

1. For an investigation of the public sphere under welfare state conditions and a consideration of the role of mediatized publics under late capitalism, see 'The Phantom Public Sphere', special issue of *Social Text*, 25–6 (1990); and the Craig Calhoum (ed.), *Habermas and the Public Sphere* (Cambridge, Mass.: MIT Press, 1991). For an

excellent appraisal, by a French historian, see Benjamin Nathans, 'Habermas's "Public Sphere" in the Era of the French Revolution', *French Historical Studies*, 16(3) (Spring 1990): 620–44.

2. Jürgen Habermas, *The Structural Transformation of the Public Sphere: An Inquiry into a Category of Bourgeois Society* [original German publication 1962], trans. Thomas Burger with the assistance of Frederick Lawrence (Cambridge, Mass.: MIT Press, 1989), p. xi.

3. See H. Aram Veeser (ed.), *The New Historicism* (New York: Routledge, 1989); Hans Kellner, *Language and Historical Representation: Getting the Story Crooked* (Madison: University of Wisconsin Press, 1989); Dominick LaCapra, *Rethinking Intellectual History: Texts, Contexts, Language* (Ithaca, NY: Cornell University Press, 1983); idem, *History and Criticism* (Ithaca, NY: Cornell University Press, 1985); Dominick LaCapra and Steven L. Kaplan, *Modern European Intellectual History: Reappraisals and New Perspectives* (Ithaca, NY: Cornell University Press, 1982); Keith Michael Baker, *Inventing the French Revolution* (Cambridge: Cambridge University Press, 1990).

4. Habermas has been charged by some new-style media critics with a one-sided dismissal of media structured by advertising and the capitalist profit motive. Pushing the argument further, a group of cultural analysts attempt to reappraise the relationship between performance and audience in light of what they see as a present-day crisis in the spectacle form itself. See e.g. Paolo Carpignano et al., 'Chatter in the Age of Electronic Reproduction', *Social Text*, 25–6 (1990): 33–55.

5. See Jürgen Habermas, 'Modernity: An Incomplete Project', in *The Anti-Aesthetic: Essays on Postmodern Culture*, ed. and intro. Hal Foster (Port Townsend, Wash.: Bay Press, 1983).

6. Since *Strukturwandel's* publication, a rich literature on the topic of civic republicanism has been produced, spurred on by J. G. A. Pocock's seminal study *The Machiavellian Moment: Florentine Political Thought and the Atlantic Republican Tradition* (Princeton, NJ: Princeton University Press, 1975). Unfortunately, Habermas does not clarify well enough the role of republicanism. Some readers have perhaps mistaken some of what he says about civic republicanism for an argument on liberalism.

7. Habermas, *The Structural Transformation of the Public Sphere*, 7.

8. Ibid. 19.

9. Ibid. 24. Or, as Habermas also states, 'The *publicum* developed into the public, the *subjectum* into the [reasoning] subject, the receiver of regulations from above into the ruling authorities' adversary'; ibid. 26.

10. Ibid. 29.

11. Stephen Greenblatt, *Renaissance Self-Fashioning: From More to Shakespeare* (Chicago: University of Chicago Press, 1980).

12. Against intimacy, or what she regards as the modern world's flight into the inner subjectivity of the individual, and the tendency for wealth to take over the public realm, Arendt contrasts the ancients' practice of hiding the body—hence labour and reproduction, women and slaves—as well as property within the sphere of the household (*oikos*). See *The Human Condition* (Chicago: University of Chicago Press, 1958).

13. Habermas, *The Structural Transformation of the Public Sphere*, 52.

14. Jürgen Habermas, *Theory and Practice*, trans. John Viertel (Boston: Beacon Press, 1973), 4.

15. Habermas, *The Structural Transformation of the Public Sphere*, 53.

16. Habermas does cite one instance of a more broadly popular sphere, the English coffee-house, where the poor artisan, craftsman, and shop-keeper mingled with their betters; ibid. 32–3. For another appraisal, see Terry Eagleton, *The Function of Criticism: From 'The Spectator' to Post-Structuralism* (London: Verso/NLB, 1984).

17. Habermas, *The Structural Transformation of the Public Sphere*, 33.

18. Ibid.

19. Ibid. 56.

20. Joan B. Landes, *Women and the Public Sphere in the Age of the French Revolution* (Ithaca, NY: Cornell University Press, 1988).

21. Mary Ryan, *Women in Public: Between Banners and Ballots, 1825– 1880* (Baltimore: Johns Hopkins University Press, 1990), 13.

22. Anna Yeatman, 'Beyond Natural Right: The Conditions for Universal Citizenship', *Social Concept*, 4(2) (June 1988): 3–32.

23. Nancy Fraser, 'Rethinking the Public Sphere', *Social Text*, 25–6 (1990): 61.

24. Ibid. 77.

25. In another context, Jane Mansbridge has observed how styles of deliberation may serve as masks for domination and render mute the claims of members of disadvantaged groups. See her 'Feminism and Democracy', *American Prospect*, 1 (Spring 1990), and discussion of Mansbridge by Fraser, 'Rethinking the Public Sphere', 64.

26. Seyla Benhabib, 'Models of Public Space: Hannah Arendt, the Liberal Tradition and Jürgen Habermas', Chapter 3, pp. 85–6. Benhabib goes on to mention Habermas's defence against these charges. She agrees with him that in principle the distinction between 'justice' and 'the good life' in moral theory and the categories of 'public' and 'private' in sociological theory need not overlap, but she argues that they have done so in the modern social contract tradition from Locke to Rawls to which Habermas is indebted partly in his discourse theory of ethics. Cf. Benhabib, 'The Generalized and the Concrete Other: The Kohlberg–Gilligan Controversy and Feminist Theory', in *Feminism as Critique: On the Politics of Gender*, ed. and intro. Seyla Benhabib and Drucilla Cornell (Minneapolis: University of

Minnesota Press, 1987); and Nancy Fraser, 'What's Critical about Critical Theory? The Case of Habermas and Gender', in *Feminism as Critique*.

27. Iris Marion Young, 'Impartiality and the Civic Public: Some Implications of Feminist Critiques of Moral and Political Theory', in *Feminism as Critique*, 76.

28. Arendt, *The Human Condition*, 198.

29. Arendt seems to take for granted the conditions of slavery, labour, and gender division of labour which are the basis for the equality between free propertied male subjects in the sphere of the polis. On Arendt's anti-modernism, see Hanna Pitkin, 'Justice: On Relating Public and Private', *Political Theory*, 9(3) (1981): 327–52; Seyla Benhabib's *The Reluctant Modernism of Hannah Arendt* (Thousand Oaks: Sage, 1996); George Kateb, *Hannah Arendt: Politics, Conscience, Evil* (Totowa, NJ: Rowman & Allanheld, 1983).

30. 'Action can be judged only by the criterion of greatness because it is in its nature to break through the commonly accepted and reach into the extraordinary, where whatever is true in common and everyday life no longer applies because everything that exists is unique and sui generis'; Arendt, *The Human Condition*, 205.

31. Ibid. 208. On storytelling, see Melvyn A. Hill, 'The Fictions of Mankind and the Stories of Men', in Melvyn A. Hill (ed.), *Hannah Arendt: The Recovery of the Public World* (New York: St. Martin's, 1979); Elizabeth Young Bruehl, 'Hannah Arendt's Storytelling', *Social Research*, 44(1) (Spring 1977): 183–90; Benhabib, 'Models of Public Space: Hannah Arendt, the Liberal Tradition and Jürgen Habermas', Ch. 3 of this volume.

32. Arendt, *The Human Condition*, 198. 'It assures the mortal actor that his passing existence will never lack the reality that comes from being seen, being heard, and, generally, appearing before an audience of fellow men, who outside the *polis* could attend only the short duration of the performance and therefore needed Homer and "others of his craft" in order to be presented to those who were not there.'

33. Cf. Jürgen Habermas, 'Hannah Arendt's Communications Concept of Power', *Social Research*, 44(1) (Spring 1977): 3–24.

34. Arendt, *The Human Condition*, 184.

35. 'Action reveals itself fully only to the storyteller, that is, to the backward glance of the historian, who indeed always knows better what it was all about than the participants' (ibid. 192).

36. Marie-Hélène Huet, *Rehearsing the Revolution: The Staging of Marat's Death, 1793–1797* (Berkeley: University of California Press, 1982), 33.

37. Ibid. 34.

38. Ibid. 35.

39. Dolf Sternberger observes that Arendt had in mind a model of the citizen in the polis performing a dual role of actor and spectator,

though she draws none of the disturbing conclusions from this relationship that I have seen in Huet. In any event, Sternberger reproduces an important passage from the German edition of *The Human Condition* omitted in the English text. There, Arendt speaks of the citizen 'in an auditorium in which everyone is watching and performing at the same time'. Cited in Dolf Sternberger, 'The Sunken City: Hannah Arendt's Idea of Politics', *Social Research*, 44(1) (Spring 1977): 134–5. It is interesting to consider Arendt's remarks here in light of Rousseau's estimation of the festival as a moment of pure transparency where there is no division between the roles of spectator and actor. On this theme, see Jean Starobinski, *Jean-Jacques Rousseau: Transparency and Obstruction*, trans. Arthur Goldhammer, intro. Robert J. Morrissey (Chicago: University of Chicago Press, 1988).

40. Huet, *Rehearsing the Revolution*, 37.
41. For an explicit and related critique of Habermas's theory of communicative competence, see Theodore Mills Norton, 'Language, Communication, and Society: Jürgen Habermas, Karl-Otto Apel, and the Ideal of a Universal Pragmatics' (Ph.D., New York University, 1981).
42. Dorinda Outram, *The Body and the French Revolution* (New Haven, CT: Yale University Press, 1989), 69.
43. Ibid. 4.
44. Ibid. 16, 158.
45. Ibid. 158.
46. Ibid. 160.
47. Ibid. 164.
48. See François Furet, *Interpreting the French Revolution*, trans. Elborg Forster (Cambridge: Cambridge University Press, 1981); Lynn Hunt, *Politics, Culture and Class in the French Revolution* (Berkeley: University of California Press, 1984); Patrice Higonnet, ' "Aristocrate", "Aristocratie": Language and Politics in the French Revolution', in *The French Revolution 1789–1989: Two Hundred Years of Rethinking*, a special issue of *The Eighteenth Century: Theory and Interpretation* (Lubbock: Texas Tech University Press, 1989); Keith Michael Baker (ed.), *The Political Culture of the Old Regime* (Oxford: Pergamon Press, 1987).
49. Nathans, 'Habermas's "Public Sphere" in the Era of the French Revolution', 643–4.
50. Habermas, *The Structural Transformation of the Public Sphere*, 37.
51. Furet, *Interpreting the French Revolution*, 49. Cf. François Furet and Mona Ozouf (eds.), *A Critical Dictionary of the French Revolution*, trans. Arthur Goldhammer (Cambridge, Mass.: Belknap Press of Harvard University Press, 1989).
52. Mona Ozouf, *Festivals and the French Revolution*, trans. Alan Sheridan (Cambridge, Mass.: Harvard University Press, 1988); Thomas Crow,

Painters and Public Life in Eighteenth-Century Paris (New Haven, CT: Yale University Press, 1985).

53. Sarah Maza, 'Le Tribunal de la nation: les mémoires judiciaires et l'opinion publique à la fin de l'ancien régime', *Annales: Economies, Société, Civilisations*, 42(1) (Jan.–Feb. 1987): 73–90. Cf. Sarah Maza, 'The Rose-Girl of Salency: Representations of Virtue in Prerevolutionary France', *Eighteenth-Century Studies* (Spring 1989): 395–412. Mona Ozouf notices that the key word in late old regime evocations of public opinion was 'tribunal', implying that all must appear before this infallible judge. This anonymous, impersonal tribunal was to be visible to all: ' "Public Opinion" at the End of the Old Regime', *Journal of Modern History*, 60, supplement (Sept. 1988): S1–S21.

54. Baker, *Inventing the French Revolution*; idem, 'Politics and Public Opinion under the Old Regime: Some Reflections', in Jack R. Censer and Jeremy D. Popkin (eds.), *Press and Politics in Pre-Revolutionary France* (Berkeley: University of California Press, 1987); Ozouf, ' "Public Opinion" at the End of the Old Regime', 58 and *passim*.

55. Habermas, *The Structural Transformation of the Public Sphere*, 140.

56. Ibid. 95.

57. Whereas Ozouf agrees with Habermas's attribution of a key place to the physiocrats, she places more emphasis than he on the absolutist or coercive strain in their thinking, deriving from their appeal to a transcendent Reason. See her ' "Public Opinion" at the End of the Old Regime'; and 'Public Spirit', in *A Critical Dictionary of the French Revolution*.

58. Habermas, *The Structural Transformation of the Public Sphere*, 97.

59. Thus Habermas distances himself from a dominant Rousseauist strain in so many versions of Marxist, anarchist, and radical political thought and practice.

60. Habermas, *The Structural Transformation of the Public Sphere*, 98–9.

61. Kant, *Critique of Practical Reason*, cited in Habermas, *The Structural Transformation of the Public Sphere*, 106.

62. Habermas distinguishes 'discourse ethics' from Kant's ethics in 'Morality and Ethical Life: Does Hegel's Critique of Kant Apply to Discourse Ethics?' See this and other contributions to *Moral Consciousness and Communicative Action*, trans. Christian Lenhardt and Shierry Weber Nicolsen, intro. Thomas McCarthy (Cambridge, Mass.: MIT Press, 1990).

63. For two excellent overviews, see Jeremy Popkin, 'The Press and the French Revolution after Two Hundred Years', *French Historical Studies* 16(3) (Spring 1990): 664–83; idem, 'The French Revolutionary Press: New Findings and New Perspectives', *Eighteenth-Century Life*, 5 (1979): 90–104. I also appraise these developments in a review essay on print culture during the French Revolution, *Eighteenth-Century Studies* 25:1 (Fall 1991). Notable studies include:

Robert Darnton and Daniel Roche (eds.), *Revolution in Print: The Press in France 1775–1800* (Berkeley: University of California Press, 1989); Jack R. Censer, *Prelude to Power* (Baltimore: Johns Hopkins University Press, 1976); Jeremy D. Popkin, *The Right-Wing Press in France, 1792–1800* (Chapel Hill, NC: University of North Carolina Press, 1980); idem, *News and Politics in the Age of Revolution: Jean Luzac's Gazette de Leyde* (Ithaca, NY: Cornell University Press, 1989); idem, *Revolutionary News: The Press in France, 1789–1799* (Durhan, NC: Duke University Press, 1990); Jack R. Censer and Jeremy Popkin (eds.), *Press and Politics in Pre-Revolutionary France* (Berkeley: University of California Press, 1987); Claude Labrosse and Pierre Retat, *Naissance du journal révolutionnaire 1789* (Lyon: Presses Universitaires de Lyon, 1989); Pierre Retat (ed.), *La Révolution du journal, 1788–1794* (Paris: CNRS, 1989); Klaus Herding and Rolf Reichardt, *Die Bildpublizistik der Französischen Revolution* (Frankfurt a.M.: Suhrkamp, 1989).

64. Daniel Roche, *Le Siècle des Lumières en Province: académies et académiciens provinciaux, 1660–1783* (2 vols., Paris: Mouton, 1978); Maurice Agulhon, *Pénitents et francs: maçons de l'ancienne Provence* (Paris: Fayard, 1968); Anthony Vidler, *The Writing of the Walls: Architectural Theory in the Late Enlightenment* (New York: Princeton Architectural Press, 1987); Thomas Crow, *Painters and Public Life in Eighteenth-Century Paris* (New Haven, CT: Yale University Press, 1985); Dena Goodman, 'Enlightenment Salons: The Convergence of Female and Philosophic Ambitions', *Eighteenth-Century Studies*, 22(3) (Spring 1989): 329–50; Robert Darnton, *The Business of Enlightenment: A Publishing History of the Encyclopédie, 1775–1800* (Cambridge, Mass.: Harvard University Press, 1979); outside France, see esp. Elizabeth L. Eisenstein, *The Printing Press as an Agent of Change: Communications and Cultural Transformations in Early-Modern Europe*, i and ii (Cambridge: Cambridge University Press, 1979); Peter Uwe Hohendahl, *The Institution of Criticism* (Ithaca, NY: Cornell University Press, 1982); Michael Warner, *The Letters of the Republic: Publication and the Public Sphere in Eighteenth-Century America* (Cambridge, Mass.: Harvard University Press, 1990); Anna Lena Lindberg, *Konstpedagogikens dilemma: historiska rötter och moderna strategier* (Lund: Studentlitteratur, 1991).

65. Roger Chartier, cited in Popkin, 'The Press and the French Revolution', 682. Cf. Roger Chartier, *The Cultural Uses of Print in Early Modern France*, trans. Lydia G. Cochrane (Princeton, NJ: Princeton University Press, 1987); Roger Chartier (ed.), *The Print: Culture of Power and the Uses of Print in Early Modern Europe*, trans. Lydia G. Cochrane (Princeton, NJ: Princeton University Press, 1989); Roger Chartier and Henri-Jean Martin (eds.), *Histoire de l'édition française: le livre triomphant, 1660–1830* (Paris: Fayard/Promodis, 1990).

66. Robert Darnton, *The Literary Underground of the Old Regime* (Cambridge, Mass.: Harvard University Press, 1982).
67. Bernadette Fort, 'Voice of the Public: The Carnivalization of Salon Art in Prerevolutionary France', *Eighteenth-Century Studies*, 22(3) (Spring 1989): 368–95.
68. Lynn Hunt (ed.), *Eroticism and the Body Politic* (Baltimore: Johns Hopkins University Press, 1991).
69. Darnton and Roche, *Revolution in Print.*
70. See *French Caricature and the French Revolution, 1789–1799* (Los Angeles, Grunwald Center for the Graphic Arts, 1988); Antoine de Baecque, *La Caricature révolutionnaire*, preface Michel Vovelle (Paris: CNRS, 1988); Claude Langlois, *La Caricature contre-révolutionnaire* (Paris: CNRS, 1988); Michel Vovelle (ed.), *Les Images de la révolution française* (Paris: Publications de la Sorbonne, 1988); Joan B. Landes and Sura Levine (eds.), *Representing Revolution: French and British Images, 1789–1804* (Amherst, Mass.: Mead Art Museum, Amherst College, 1989).
71. Warner, *The Letters of the Republic*, xiv.
72. Outram, *The Body and the French Revolution*, 34, 151.
73. Benhabib, 'Models of Public Space', 34. [This quotation does not appear in full in the revised version of this paper which is included as Chapter 3 of the present volume.]
74. Fraser, 'Rethinking the Public Sphere', 76.

6

Regarding Some 'Old Husbands' Tales': Public and Private in Feminist History

Leonore Davidoff

There is no easy passage from 'women' to 'humanity'
(Denise Riley, 1988)

Prologue

A central platform of feminist critique and attempted revision of mainstream thought has focused on the construction and boundaries of classifications: of femininity and masculinity, women and men, woman and man. These classifications have in turn been linked to the construction of other highly significant categories, the complicated—and slippery—notions of *public* and *private*.

The everyday usage of a public and private distinction has led to much confusion. When feminists, mainly anthropologists, first

Excerpts from Chapter 8 in Leonore Davidoff, *Worlds Between: Historical Perspectives on Gender and Class* (Polity Press, 1995). Copyright Blackwell Publishers Ltd (1995). Reprinted by permission. The main arguments in this essay were first presented to the interdisciplinary symposium, 'The Construction of Sex/Gender: What is a Feminist Perspective?', Swedish Council for Research in the Humanities and Social Sciences, Stockholm, 1990. The thoughtful discussions around subsequent presentations in Britain, Norway, the USA, and Australia offered many useful new insights. A brief version was published in *Passato e Presente*, 27 (Sept.–Dec. 1991), and *L'Homme: Zeitschrift für feministische Geschichtswissenschaft* (1993). The present version incorporates many of the ideas published in my article, 'Adam Spoke First and Named the Orders of the World: Masculine and Feminine Domains in History and Sociology', in Helen Corr and Lynn Jamieson (eds.), *The Politics of Everyday Life: Continuity and Change in Work and Family* (London: Macmillan, 1990).

I am grateful for advice and suggestions about these ideas from discussion with Carole Adams, Monika Bernold, Barbara Caine, Delfina Dolza, Christe Hammerle, Alice Kessler-Harris, Catherine Hall, David Lee, Jane Lewis, Susan Margarey, Jill Matthews, Jane Rendall, Sonya Rose, Alison Scott, Eleni Varikas, Ulla Wikander, and especially to my colleague Ludmilla Jordanova for her critical but always supportive suggestions. Diana Gittins provided invaluable editorial critique. Finally, my thanks to Citlali Rouirusa, who provided the title.

focused on the distinction, there was an apparent universal sexual asymmetry that fitted neatly into a public/private dimension. This was then used, often implicitly, to *explain* women's powerlessness.[1] However, the obvious objection to the automatic connection of women with the private (or the 'natural') is the nonsensical logic which would then make men 'naturally' cultural or 'naturally' rational.[2]

This convention, indeed, has continued to be part of the problem, for the public/private divide has played a dual role as both an *explanation* of women's subordinate position and as an *ideology* that constructed that position. As Ludmilla Jordanova has argued, 'The distinction itself has to be treated as an artefact whose long life history requires careful examination.'[3] Furthermore, like gender itself, public and private have been used as a rich source of metaphor.

For feminist historians, the *public/private* distinction has been linked to the notion of *separate spheres*, one of the most powerful concepts within women's history since its recrudescence in the 1960s. Such binary distinctions have come under attack from a range of theoretical positions, including powerful feminist solvents which stress multiplicity, plurality, and the blurring of boundaries. Yet there continues to be fascination with the seeming separation of private and public life in our own later twentieth-century situation as we juggle the multi-layered psychic structures of femininity as well as confronting feminine roles of daughter, wife, and mother with professional identity and/or political activism. In Ann Snitow's memorable phrase: 'Modern women experience moments of free fall. How is it for you, there, out in space near me? Different I know. Yet we share—some with more pleasure, some with more pain—this uncertainty.'[4]

Nevertheless, out of the confusion a consensus is emerging that public and private are not (and never have been) 'conceptual absolutes', but a minefield of 'huge rhetorical potential'.[5] Despite their instability and mutability, public and private are concepts which also have had powerful material and experiential consequences in terms of formal institutions, organizational forms, financial systems, familial and kinship patterns, as well as in language. In short, they have become a basic part of the way our whole social and psychic worlds are ordered, but an order that is constantly shifting, being made and remade.

Historians grappling with this complicated web of structures, meanings, and behaviours have had to work on a number of different levels. Should these dichotomous categories be treated only in terms of languages, or of attitudes and values. Or should they be described in terms of the organization of space, time, the location of people? Are they, and were they, ideologies imposed, cultures created, or simply a set of given boundaries to be observed? If the 'separate spheres' of home and work, to take one derivation, was 'a trope which hid its instrumentality even from those who employed it',[6] then how can we retrieve more than the most partial picture 100 or 200 years later?

Part of the problem is the form in which historians of women have entered the debate. For example, in a discussion of the eighteenth century, the claim has been made that:

At bottom, the separation of the home and workplace, the rise of the new domestic woman, the separation of the spheres, and the construction of the public and private all describe the same phenomenon in different words.[7]

This may, indeed, be the way these ideas have come to be used, but it is a profound misunderstanding to think that they are either analytically or descriptively the same thing. For example, while conceptual dichotomies such as public and private are constructed with a drive to fix boundaries between at least two *different* constructs which can be separated and contrasted, the concept of *domesticity* and its concomitant, *domestic ideology*, seems historically to have no other 'half'. (The literal opposite of domesticity would be the wild or untamed or, alternatively, foreign or strange, as in domestic goods versus foreign imports.)

Until recently, debates about the public and private have taken the domestic for granted as well as being unaware of a gender dimension. The most common distinction has focused on the state as representative of the public in contrast with private organizations such as the church, voluntary societies, and, particularly, privately owned business or professional enterprises. At times this private sector has been conflated into 'civil society', regarded as 'above all else, the sphere of private interest, private enterprise and private individuals'.[8] In this formulation, civil society would include a notion of 'private life', the family, and sexuality,[9] especially in discussions of totalitarian as opposed to democratic regimes.

There has been unease, however, about the place of morality within these distinctions, for neither the modern state nor the private enterprise was conceived in moral terms.[10] In England, this was re-echoed in late nineteenth-century legal debates about the relationship of the individual to the state at the time of increased separation of law and legal forms from ethical concerns.[11] The distinction between justice and morality (the good life) subsumes a gendered notion of public versus private spheres which runs like a thread through social-contract tradition from John Locke to John Rawls, and which contains 'a fundamental ambiguity governing the term *privacy*'.[12]

This uncertainty has continuously resurfaced. Its latest manifestation is explicitly linked to gender issues as seen in debates over the work of writers such as Carol Gilligan and Catharine MacKinnon.[13] But these discussions make little reference to the terms 'public' and 'private'. In the nineteenth century, on the other hand, debates about these terms could be at a level which had no feminine component at all. Given that men were the 'unmarked' and therefore invisible category, the gendered nature of these assumptions has not until very recently been part of the debate. At the same time, the whole edifice was predicated on an unspoken assumption about a shadow world of reproduction, sexuality, and at least parts of the morality which had come to be jettisoned from the public realm as the constructs developed through the nineteenth century. Domestic, personal life, regarded as embedded in the biological, universal, and pre-social, remained outside the terms of debate, an exclusion which has been used to restrict the universe of *legitimate* public, and hence political, contestation.

Thus the institutions of family, kinship, marriage, and parenthood, which should have been central to debates on the public and private, have been either neglected or taken for granted.[14] And within feminist history, while aspects of these institutions and their cultures have been extensively researched, the categories have rarely been interrogated. Meanwhile, family history and demographic history have proceeded, for the most part, as quite distinct from women's history, much less a feminist approach. But the family and household remain the primary 'mediating institutions' in gender systems. They are the crucible within which individuals, both psychologically and symbolically, learn to speak a gendered language as well as the languages of their many other identities, ethnic, racial, national, sexual.

It is within the family—however that has been constituted— that formation of both body and psyche, literally and symbolically, first takes place. By laying most emphasis on understanding gender distinctions at the social level, particularly within the sexual division of labour, feminist research has at times, paradoxically, fallen back on some biological constants, especially those related to birth and breast-feeding. The body thus becomes too much the bearer of the timeless and static. Only by refocusing on the body can feminist research apply the logic of change and, therefore, redeem a site of some of our deepest conceptual sources of gender construction,[15] including the imbrication of masculinity and femininity with the public and private.

In applying conceptual understandings to such a range of levels, in floundering through such a conceptual and linguistic minefield, feminist historians have to be clear about what they are trying to do. As with most human institutions and cultural forms, *public* and *private* have a long history; they represent both continuity and change. Among many groups and in many cultures they do not even appear as relevant concepts.[16]

My focus will be on the public and private as they were understood through the 'long nineteenth century' (*c.*1780–1914) in England. For the practising historian, in particular, it is vital to locate concepts in use at the time as well as those we have inherited. In what follows, I examine the consequences of the gendered nature of such root concepts as *rationality*, the *individual, property*, and the *market*. In particular, I explore the way in which these ideas and the relationships, organization, and distribution of power associated with them have structured the particular English public and private domains. Specific areas covered include the gendered nature of class relations; the relation of men to the putative private sphere; and, especially, the relation of women to the public sphere.

AS YE SOW, SO SHALL YE REAP: CONCEPTS AND THEIR CONSEQUENCES

Gender, Class, and Status

The gendered substructure under discussion has had massive impact on Western political and social institutions and systems of thought, as well as on people's lives. The concept of the rational individual and his domain, the category of public sociality became not only an idealization of nineteenth-century society in general but also the primary orientation of social scientific inquiry. Indeed, the extension of the idea of science to social science has been seen as a key moment in the creation of a liberal public sphere.[17]

The fledgeling discipline of sociology was moulded during the volatile decades of the early nineteenth century, conterminous with, and contributing to, the struggles for dominance of these basic concepts. The keystone of the sociological edifice, the concept of *class*, was based on the premiss of a totally separate productive order. In this formulation, family and kinship were taken as necessary but natural corollaries and were constructed around a similar concept of the individual self.[18]

The category 'woman' was explicitly located within the construct of family and kinship, just as 'man' was assumed within the economy, polity, and the realms of knowledge. Sociologists (and historians influenced by them) have assumed the family to be secondary and peripheral, always responsive to changes in the public sphere, although some latter-day social historians have begun to argue that, in special cases, lines of influence might have run the other way. But both assumptions rest on the original gendered dualisms already explored. The proliferation of 'hyphen solutions', such as Marxist-feminism, to bind together the separate spheres has not proved adequate. It is increasingly evident that the most valiant attempts to extend concepts of rationality or universalism to women, and thus to embrace them within the class system, are bound to founder on the fact that, as Joan Scott reminds us, these 'languages' are already dualistic and already gendered.[19]

For in classical Marxist and Weberian as well as more modern formulations class is based on assumptions about an economic sphere derived from neo-classical economic theory.[20] The implied abstract notion of a *mode of production*, as separated from consumption and other social tasks, assumes a separate productive order which embraces the fiction of disembodied actors with capacity to sell labour away from the person (the body) of the labourer. But since women were defined by their familial relationships, they potentially lacked both the ability and the legitimacy to sell their labour *freely*. Implicit in this disability was the idea that women were inevitably embodied beings, trailing their sexuality always with them, while men were somehow abstracted from their own material substance.

The 'domino effect' of such a model can be readily appreciated. The basis of class analysis rests on the relationship of individuals and groups to the economic structure of society. It follows, then, that if women as a category (and married women in particular) were outside the basic capitalist system centred on production, they could never become—at least directly—part of the class structure and, *pari passu*, take part in class action. Indeed, within the middle class, women were often viewed as trivial, non-political creatures, while within the working class, women, with their constant carping about domestic concerns, might be regarded as a dead weight pulling down the political aspirations of the the rational working man.

While sociologists have wrestled with these issues particularly in relation to class identity and voting behaviour, most historians have been rather more unsophisticated, often using a rule-of-thumb descriptive notion of class. In so doing, they unconsciously betray their lack of understanding of the way gender has structured that concept. Witness, for example, such phrases as 'the working classes with their wives and families'.[21] In her critique of E. P. Thompson, Joan Scott notes that 'the organization of the story and the master codes that structure the narrative are gendered in such a way as to confirm rather than challenge the masculine representations of class'.[22]

Feminist historians should keep in mind that such conceptual limitations go back to the underlying concept of a market economy, which informally also excludes paupers, servants, children (and in the USA, blacks or in the UK, the Irish) from class analysis. These groups are thus precluded a place within class action, an exclusion which would be extended in colonial situations, carried as part of the cultural baggage of an expanding empire. Ultimately, male, adult, ethnic superiority has had the power to impose the original definitions from which our models are derived.

Class, which plays such a powerful role in modern British culture, is, however, more complicated than such models, both in the experience of everyday life and in the hands of social investigators. A working definition of class usually employs some non-economic, even symbolic, indicators of boundaries beyond the question of ownership of the means of production. As the sociologist Rosemary Crompton has recently admitted, in practice it is exceptionally difficult to separate *theoretically* as well as empirically the 'economic' from the social or 'cultural'.[23]

The traditionally invoked sociological division between *manual* and *non-manual* occupations emphasizes other, more relational aspects of class. These 'status considerations', or claims to social honour, must ultimately depend on having the wealth and resources to maintain them. It is generally recognized, however, that social honour is never exactly synonymous with material and financial power, as, for example, in the case of the nouveau riche entrepreneur on the one hand or the impecunious gentry on the other. Wealth or force do not translate easily into high status, for usually lifestyle intervenes, and that lifestyle may take more than one generation to inculcate. The escalating difficulties of class analysis raised by the expansion of the salariat, developments of later twentieth-century technologies, and a large, mainly feminized service sector indicate that the standard (and ungendered) version of class analysis may need to become more complicated and nuanced.[24]

As illustration, let us consider the early nineteenth century, the period when classical social scientific thought was being formed. At that time the growth of more specialized functions, larger-scale operations, and market contacts beyond the local area meant that men with resources in property or skill became more responsible for the external affairs of buying and selling. The small manufacturer no longer donned an apron to handle his goods physically, but remained closeted in his counting house or dealt with customers, while the farmer of larger acreage spent much of his time at market, only riding out to the fields to give orders from on high to labourers on foot.

The deep-seated derogation of *manual* work, the preoccupation with clean, unblemished 'non-working' hands, was built into class relations at a deep, even subconscious level; early factory workers were, for instance, referred to simply as (genderless) 'hands'. For men, however, while markers such as clean, soft hands might establish a higher position in the class hierarchy, too great a preoccupation with dress and with cleanliness, and finicky attention to personal appearance, might border on the effeminate. Commercial and professional occupations which exhibited such features, particularly those under the authority of an employer or master such as clerical and salaried workers, as well as the despised male domestic servant, had an even less positive masculine image. By contrast, the rugged independent craftsman, despite his dirty apron and calloused, blackened hands, was clearly a *man*. Both class and gender components were thus part of identity but in complicated and sometimes contradictory ways.

Middle-class women, or at least those whose menfolk were owners of some wealth-producing enterprises or had sufficient income from fees or salaries, also took part in this delicate restructuring of the meaning of work during the nineteenth century. They

171

had no more taste for grinding toil than their men, who preferred the ledger and pen to the plough, anvil, or loom. Younger and lower-status women (and sometimes men) had for centuries carried out the most toilsome, noisome tasks such as heavy lifting, fetching water, and dealing with garbage and the contents of slop-pails and chamber-pots. But in the nineteenth-century middle-class home, the wife, daughters, and sisters were doing less manual work and were increasingly hiring lower-class recruits to take over the drudgery of the 'housework' and childcare. The women of the household were still busy with the myriad tasks to be done, but the amount of housework had escalated with divided living and working space as well as a novel, complicated variety of furnishings, carpets, curtains, crockery, clothing—a much higher material and social standard of living.

Yet middle-class women's relationship to manual work was, and still is, not as clear-cut as men's. How much of childcare, for example, should be turned over to others when the physical care of children was so intermingled with their intellectual, moral, and spiritual development? What of food provision, cooking, and meal preparation, when women's role as nurturer and caretaker was central to feminine identity? Through the nineteenth and well into the twentieth century, the mark of genteel womanhood was white, unblemished hands. Women's dress, with tight waist, billowing crinoline, or great bunched bustle and trailing skirts, was designed to make strenuous physical work difficult, if not impossible. Women carried middle-class status on their bodies, yet their tasks were never as clearly differentiated as for men.

As subordinates themselves, women did not so clearly exercise the power of authority. But in addition, they were more intimately bound up with the *relational* aspects of class. In their social rounds, in philanthropic activities and dispensing charity, they were cultivating, smoothing, and negotiating the relationships created and sustained by the productive sphere. In a word, they were deeply implicated in the marking of class boundaries. In particular, they were concerned with the other side of the circle, that is, *consumption*. Since men were so closely associated with generating income through 'work', women came to be increasingly associated with correctly consuming the products of that work, an activity increasingly located in the differentiated private sphere of the 'Home'.[25]

Despite recent attempts at delineating class groups as based on lifestyle where taste comes to be a resource deployed by groups in the social hierarchy,[26] consumption cannot be understood outside relations of production, but needs to be seen as part of it. The desire for goods and services created the demand for goods and services, but was also implicated in the workings of productive activity. For example, in the early nineteenth century, when banks and other financial institutions were rudimentary, a middle-class man's 'worth' was judged not only by his own appearance and behaviour, his contributions to charity, membership of voluntary societies, his house(s), and his carriage, but also by the standard of demeanour and lifestyle of his whole household, particularly the sexual honour of his womenfolk.

Partly because of prescriptive statements of the time, partly because of our own perceived separation of production/public from consumption/private, interaction between these spheres has been constantly overlooked. Yet recent feminist historical studies of institutions such as the department store show the intimate connection between 'shopping' as a mainly feminine activity and the commercialization of consumption which drew women into the wage-labour market.[27] The recent work of such feminist historians as Alice Kessler-Harris and Joy Parr demonstrates how widening the boundaries of the economic to include household affairs has decentred workplace history and reforged the analysis of politics as well as class: the household is no longer construed as a private domain; rather it is the source of conciousness that generates public activity.[28]

It is also too often forgotten that cross-class interaction took place not only between employer and workman but also between mistress and servant, who between them were responsible for organizing and displaying the family lifestyle in the home. In fact, the line between those servants working for the productive enterprise and for the home was not rigidly made until well into the nineteenth century. When more service activities were later drawn into the cash nexus, many of the features of personal service were carried over in the form of secretaries, shop assistants, and nurses —not, coincidentally, posts largely staffed by women.

These myriad connections point to the need for a reconceptualization of societal hierarchies to incorporate more than the narrowly based class model. The nuances of relational status have to be recognized as a crucial site of group interaction which, in some cases, can cross traditional 'class' lines. Within the nineteenth-century working class, for example, the division between *rough* and *respectable* was not unlike the *genteel/ungenteel* divisions within the middle class; both rested on judgements of worth, partly material and partly moral.[29]

The core of nineteenth-century femininity had been constructed as outside the amoral market. Thus the feminine, always regarded within a familial context, became an idealized carrier of morality. With the late nineteenth-century decline of both formal religious belief and commonly held 'people's wisdom', the 'Home' and 'Motherhood' became even more powerful spiritual and emotional icons.[30] Women, putatively placed in the private sphere and commanding a central role in representing the family in face-to-face relationships, were often the controlling force in local status systems which relied on moral regulation, from the 'old wives' of villages and small towns to the 'queen bees' of the urban slum court and the dowager matrons of London's West End.

Middle-class women were harnessed to the 'moral enterprise' of building status and reputation for the family, which had been especially important in creating commercial and professional probity in an era before limited liability freed family assets from the devastation of business failure. It is striking how the nineteenth-century uplift literature for such women likens their duties to the *business* of creating and maintaining the ethical fabric of society. Yet when women attempted to impose a set of moral values upon men of their own status group, as in late nineteenth-century moral reform or social purity campaigns, these men became uncomfortable and restive, accusing women of being prudes or killjoys—in other words defending their claims to men's privileges as males.

This contradictory situation draws attention to the importance of rethinking the categories *men* and *women* as part of what might be called in Weberian terms a status system. For it is status—attributions which give people certain group identities and preclude them from others—which, in the last analysis, determines the life-chances of individuals and groups. One of the main purposes of a status order is to protect the privileged by providing them with a resource not easily acquired by others[31]—in this case masculinity. The way status operates is most clearly seen in the way certain groups, such as 'women' or 'blacks', have been denied inclusion into civil society as well as full citizenship rights. And it is status allocation which gives—or withholds—opportunities to manipulate marketable skills, since these skills depend on estimations of social worth.

But 'woman' was defined by being outside the realm of legitimate marketable skill; and in terms of her own status *qua* woman she was systematically disadvantaged, although these disadvantages took different forms at different class levels. Instead, most women used their role as status markers and enhancers in the interests of wider class, religious, and kinship groups, families, and the individual men to whom their own fortunes were attached. When women did operate on their own account, it was through the alternative realm of possible opportunities given by their embodied definition—the marriage market or its equivalent, a commercialized sexuality through a range of relationships from prostitution to cohabitation. The only women exempt from selling or bartering their sexuality for support were aristocratic or other wealthy heiresses.

In this context, it may be significant that sexuality was a commodity seldom 'sold' by adult, white English men—precisely those groups whose identity has been most clearly included in analysis of the *class* system. Class, like 'the economy' or rational discourse to which it is so closely related, is thus a conceptual system which through its inherent nineteenth-century masculinity is cleansed of identification with human reproduction or desire.

What, then, of considering women and men as *separate* status groups in terms of their interests, access to monopolies of power, knowledge, and material resources? Certainly, if status is determined by the proximity to the creative and charismatic centres of society,[32] then women *as a group*—not in their capacity as kin to men—were, and still are, on the periphery. The higher reaches and inner circles of such centres—the churches, political parties, armed services, universities, law courts, business corporations, trade unions—remain adamantly masculine if not wholly male.

Unlike any other status groups, however, for example those based on ethnicity, racial category, nationality, religion, or language, men's and women's ability to close ranks *against each other* is complicated. Men could, and did, use their privileged position to create all-male organizations and spaces. Yet, obviously, the usual strategies of endogamy, accompanied by exclusive commensality, which, along with linguistic barriers, are such potent creators of group identification, would be extremely difficult to maintain completely between men and women (after all, 49 per cent of children are boys and, in their early years at least, usually cared for by women). As banal a truism as it may be and science fiction notwithstanding, even if somehow total permanent segregation of the sexes were possible, the most likely result would be the dying out of populations.

In pressing for an inclusive analysis of difference, the fact may be overlooked that class position and identity, like those of race, ethnicity, and religious affiliation, are always built on the assumption of physical and cultural reproduction. When all is said and done, that reproduction *must* include diverse, but always present, gender orders.

Multiple Publics, the 'Social' Semi-Public, and the Private Sphere

So far the discussion has focused on the creation of political and economic 'public' domains and indicated how gender was basic to their formation. The way these constructions constrained beliefs and behaviours in nineteenth- and early twentieth-century English society has been further explored. From the seventeenth century onwards, however, there had emerged a range of other public spheres. Indeed, as we have seen, the creation of different and specialized public arenas was in itself part of masculine identification in contrast to the resolutely generalized, private, and domesticated world of women.

Among the most influential of differentiated publics, the area of science and medicine has begun to attract attention from feminist historians. As long as scientific practice was linked to household production, female relatives of scientific practitioners could take part in and were sometimes the unacknowledged driving force of the enterprise. Female aristocratic patrons, in both fact and imagery, mediated for bourgeois scientific men.[33] But when scientific knowledge began to be conceptualized as rational and abstract, women were cooled out. By the later nineteenth century, practising scientists came to be equated with the detached, distinguished male expert focusing his gaze on, revealing and conquering, the feminized subject: 'Nature'.[34] 'Woman' (and thus sexuality) represented the irrationality of superstitious 'old wives' tales', in opposition to progressive rational scientific procedure.

The worlds of art and cultural production have a similar history, although complicated by the early nineteenth-century Romantic movement which took the male protagonist outside society altogether into a No Man's (*sic*) Land of individuality and genius. The extra-mundane performance of such men, however, took place in a remarkably public arena and, like all the other publics, remained dependent on the unacknowledged contributions of excluded, mainly female supporters.[35] To take part in this public, in the world of the studio culture as protagonist rather than muse or model, in Griselda Pollock's words, women had to choose between being human and being a woman.[36]

A variety of public organizations developed as part of a growing working-class culture, the trade unions being the most obvious. As oppositional to the dominant culture some, such as the Cooperative Movement, had more space to incorporate feminine interests, if not women themselves. The most incisive analyses of gender relations, as well as a few attempts at practical rearrangements, had been put forward by Owenite socialists early in the century.[37] Working-class movements themselves faced exclusion from participation in civil society and the state. Anna Clark has argued that during the period of Chartist debate, middle-class commentators had used gendered notions of virtue, expressed in the discourses of civic humanism, separate spheres, Malthusianism, and political economy to create and maintain this general exclusion. It was contested whether working-class men qualified for the masculinity of traditional citizenship.

Therefore, in addition to claiming property in skill and labour, working men turned to arguing that reason, rather than property itself, should be the basis for political participation. In so doing, they created a possible space for women who, it could be maintained, had reason too. It was also argued that the 'People' should have rights beyond property—the right of humanity for survival. The problem came in defining who were the People; if they included women, did these women exhibit reason? The inclusion of women in the rubric of radical politics varied, with textile communities where many women were employed in mills and were members of trade unions, not surprisingly, being more receptive to their contribution.[38] Nevertheless, by the 1850s it was clear that it had fallen to the men to speak to the outside world.[39]

By the late nineteenth century, the growth of state organization, voluntary societies' concern with working-class life, and shifts in patterns of employment within an expanding urban culture emphasized a version of working-class respectability more squarely based on marriage and a species of domesticity.[40] The 'residuum' was at least partially defined by deviance from expected gender behaviour.[41] The twentieth-century labour movement retained an underlying conception based on the gendered worlds derived from the triumph of political economy's fundamental categories, despite these variations and the inherent difficulty in maintaining

177

expected gender distinctions based on a male breadwinner and dependent wife and children.

Each one of these segmented public worlds had rational man at its centre and embodied woman at the periphery. Nevertheless, such masculine domination of publics was by no means unproblematic. From around the third quarter of the nineteenth century, the emergence of a separate semi-public realm of 'the social', as distinct from the economic and political, began to take shape. This was in part a result of negotiation and protest from politically active women seeking to gain entry into the public arena through engagement with local issues and philanthropy, seen as extension of familial concerns.[42] But the conception of a separate social sphere also remained a source of constraint, limiting what became known as 'women's issues'—the family, children, health, and welfare—thus minimizing feminine influence in the 'real' business of politics and the economy.

At the same time as an acknowledged realm of social life was claiming the attention of charity workers and nascent civil servants, there also existed an informal world of high politics linked to 'Society', the intermingling of political influence with entertainment based on kinship and a common upper-class culture. But by the 1880s this was gradually giving way to more professional party politics, a shift signalled by measures such as the secret ballot, the creation of party agents, and the reform of local government.[43] Nevertheless, middle-class domesticity had never been unconditionally adopted by the gentry and aristocracy, where men ran their estates or entered politics using the manor house as a base while women attended to the public functions of entertaining and social functions which were the hallmark of their station. The wife and daughters of the church dignitary, the diplomat, the headmaster, the admiral had as clear a position as the woman who had 'married a country house'; ideally, none of them would have spent much time in the nursery or any at all in the kitchen except, possibly, to give orders.

Many upper-class women were already active in a semi-public social sphere. Their middle-class counterparts, however, tended to be the backbone of those organizations and movements making up the feminized and depoliticized domain of welfare action aimed at those lower down the social scale. Together with an emerging feminist movement, several aspects of family and sexual relations began to enter into public discourse, the best known being the Anti-Contagious Diseases Campaign.

But in the 1860s and 1870s there were other, less obvious issues which raised passionate public reactions, suggesting that the tensions generated by gender relations could surface under the increasing pressure of proto-feminist reactions. One such was the furore over the practice of leaving infants with paid caretakers (wet-nursing and 'baby-farming'); another was the bitter controversy over definitions of permitted power over—and violence towards—wives. A sense of unease colours discussions of such practices, which in many cases had gone unnoticed for decades.[44]

Such debates indicate that the definition of what was public did not remain static, but shifted over time. One might ask, for example, whether the political and salon hostesses who continued to operate as important but informal power-brokers were in a public or private sphere. Because of the particular structure of gender relations, the vaunted Victorian 'women's influence' was not without a tinge of reality: the power of 'pillow talk' should not be underestimated. And towards the end of the nineteenth century, women were finding a more genuinely public voice in writing, editing, and publishing as well as providing an influential readership. Of course women had been engaging in all these activities as soon as literacy touched lower than a narrow elite band. The difference in the late nineteenth century was that they were able to do so more frequently in their own voice and through a wider range of more sympathetic outlets.[45] Yet it must be kept in mind that all these activities were still conducted in the semi-privacy of bedroom, parlour, or study. Genteel women, at any rate, were seldom to be found roaming freely around the environs of Grub Street, not at least without a male sponsor or protector.

Variation, change, blurred boundaries—all left spaces for re-grouping the gender components of these cornerstones of modern English society. Even in those public preserves most intensely masculine in character, the category 'woman' was always part of the definition, if in no other way as the shadow without which there can be no image projected. Fantasized 'others' never can be totally evaded, either conceived in the form of those who are *not* like the group with power to define or as those in whose supposed interests the powerful legitimate the actions that they take. Emphasis on *difference* could be conveyed as misogyny or chivalry, two sides of the same coin.

There can be no doubt, then, that an understanding of 'the public sphere(s)' is central to feminist history. Once this is accepted, it follows that key questions about the creation of *identity* have to be extended beyond family, home, and childhood. The ragged frontiers between public and private must be recognized as a site where identity—of race, ethnicity and class, and sexual orientation as well as gender—is formed.

In this respect, it may be unfortunate that feminists' rightful preoccupation with questions of identity has often privileged, rather than simply recognized, the psychic level. Psychoanalytic perspectives, in particular, may be used in a manner which inevitably draws attention away from the public or deals with it crudely as a *deus ex machina*. But there is no inherent opposition between recognizing the power of the public and giving equal weight to the dynamic place of psychic structures in gender identities, behaviour, and symbolism. Happily, there have been some recent encouraging signs that feminist historians are using psychological concepts, but carefully placed within specific historical situations.[46]

With these developments, in a sense, feminist history has come full circle. Recognition that identity for women as well as men is forged both by individual life situations and by the construction of the idea of the public confirms the original point that the private has to be taken not only as problematic but also as a social construction. In revising these conceptions of the public, we can appreciate that a simple equation of the private with home and family has obfuscated important assumptions about gender. For example, historians of the family have taken it for granted that men, who were seen to be prime actors in the public, were somehow not constituted in the family, at least not beyond childhood. In this they followed the nineteenth-century convention that the attainment of manhood was achieved by leaving childish—that is, familial—identity behind. To quote John Demos's classic study of family life in colonial America: 'The family, in particular, stands quite apart from most other aspects of life. We have come to assume that whenever a man leaves his home "to go out into the world" he crosses a very critical boundary.'[47] Furthermore, many men, who spent so much of their time in the public world of waged work and a selection of formal organizations, also had access to a 'private' life spent in non-domesticated (public?) spaces such as theatres, racecourses, boxing rings, clubs, the market square. Even their most private, 'sexual' activities came to be shared between the home and the public arenas of café, pub, saloon, inn, and brothel.[48] It could be argued that these strongly masculine spaces, quite as much as the domestic hearth, were seen to provide a haven against the harsh world of the market, but within a culture of masculinity where paternalistic and fraternal relationships flourished unimpeded by claims from dependent and/or demanding womenfolk.[49]

The category 'women', on the other hand (and married women in particular), even those who may have spent much time in public places, was defined by a limited kind of all-embracing privacy: 'the easy divorce of public and private had no real meaning for them.'[50]

Women in Public and Feminism

Understanding the complicated and shifting relations between public and private—politics, work (science, art, religion, philanthropy, warfare) and home, men and women—could help to unravel the tangles which have plagued recent efforts to study the history of women in public as well as the history of feminism, overlapping *but by no means synonymous* topics. It could also aid efforts to grapple with the notoriously tricky issues of *equality* and *difference*, for both classifications are predicated on a gender-neutral public realm into which women can/should or cannot/should not be fitted.[51]

Analyses of nineteenth-century British politics have concentrated on class and class action; given the previous explication, this means that women may have conceived, and responded to, such action differently from men. For example, a recent Australian study shows how the struggle between a nascent urban 'gentry' and the existing commercial leadership in a provincial city was experienced as political conflict of interests by men, but as a struggle for social (status) relations among women from the same strata and even the same families.[52] Or take the story of women's place in the history of British Chartist politics: not only the issues raised but the *form* of organizations adopted had an unacknowledged but heavily gendered dimension.[53]

What is defined as 'political action' may have been, at least in part, what was defined as masculine, but recent feminist questions have pushed out the boundaries of 'political' to encompass other arenas of conflict. Such redefinition shifts the boundaries of the private as well as the public. It has, for example, come to light that throughout the modern period some women apparently chose not to marry (although they often remained part of kinship and family groups). Could this and the 'silent strike' involved in the deliberate limitation on births from the third quarter of the nineteenth century represent a type of women's politics within the private realm?[54]

Women were also entering the public arena more openly; some from middle-class backgrounds literally transferred their private life into public institutions—settlement houses, schools, hospitals, colleges. In such cases, living away from a familial home itself was a public action where women expected to be involved in business, labour, welfare, and charity as workers (whether or not they were actually financially self-supporting). In this they followed a tradition of working-class women who had acted as Poor Law workhouse matrons and similar less glorified positions.[55] Such women, however, tended to be exceptional. More often, those who did become politically active usually had to do so through an already male-defined domain with male-structured institutions and rituals, for example pressure groups, political parties, or trade unions. This was largely a result of women's location in the family, which gave a particular cast to the relational aspects of class, sections of classes, interest groups, religious affiliations, and ethnic groups.[56]

Those women who began to identify their interests as coinciding with other women rather than, or as well as, with men of their own strata, were in a particularly stressful position. Their loyalties stretched between family and class on the one hand and a status identity as *women* on the other. During the period of the suffrage campaign, specific issues such as complete sexual equality in voting rights, as opposed to working-class representation in Parliament through a male-only working-class franchise, affected women from all strata of society, since most suffragists brought to their campaigning pre-existing class and party loyalties.[57] Women within traditional party auxiliaries such as the Women's Liberal Party Federation experienced a classic conflict between feminism and party loyalty raised in various disputes—over the employment of barmaids, for example, when their interests as women lay with supporting temperance. This stance opposed official Liberal Party policy, backed by the liquor trade, which cynically used feminist arguments to support 'equal employment opportunities'.[58] Simultaneous affirmation and denial of 'women' as a particular grouping was endemic among Labour Party members through to the inter-war period.[59]

Too often historians have seen such conflicts either as instances of the equality/difference divide or as personal conflicts between the demands of a woman's immediate family on the one hand,

and devotion to the 'first women's movement' on the other. But because women were so deeply implicated in relational aspects of the social hierarchy, their disloyalties were often interpreted as much wider than the simple disregard of familial duty—although that was serious enough. Such women were also 'letting the side down', disengaging from their special role in moral—and thus social—boundary maintenance of their particular group, whether that be of a social stratum or even of the English 'race'.[60]

What few could face up to was that campaigns which used liberal principles of individual autonomy and equality, or even those claims which were made on the basis of women's place within the family, would ultimately unleash the radical contradictions of the public/private divide, including the rational individual man and the feminized, dependent woman.[61] In some ways anti-feminist rhetoric was more aware of this potential than others were, or have been since.

Family loyalties mediated women's public commitment in complicated ways. Working-class women in areas where waged work was customary and available, such as in textiles or shoemaking, were often torn between a virtuous independence, which renegotiated their womanliness in terms of supporting their families by their waged work, and the more remote bonds which brought together all women: married and unmarried, housewives, outworkers, workshop and factory women. Such cases highlight the tension between consciousness of identity as workers and as women.[62]

But even when 'going public', many women did so (and do so now) to protect and further their position within the bounds of the category 'women' as it has been constructed within the home and family. From the early nineteenth-century involvement in the anti-slavery movement, many women entered political campaigns around issues generally designated as domestic and private.[63] Claims of equality within the male-defined public sphere, on the other hand, could be seen as a double threat, first to the 'foundation of personal identity, social stability, and the moral order' but also contributing to the destruction of feminine culture. That culture crucially included claims on men for support and protection, so that the exposure of women as autonomous individuals 'devoid of nurturing, affiliative virtues' seemed to weaken that position.[64] In the face of such powerful 'secondary gains', equal-rights feminist issues have often been difficult to keep on the agenda. In summing up the complexities of these positions, the concept of 'cooperative or pacific conflict' has sometimes been employed, although such notions tend to glide over the power differentials embedded in many nineteenth-century gender relationships.[65]

Women acting *as a group in their own interests* have been met with particular virulence. The reaction points to the outrage felt at the putative disloyalty perceived in those women who sought individual autonomy, as if there was something almost obscene in the feminine guardians of morality and status boundaries presuming to take part in the political domain as individuals. The nineteenth-century epithets 'strong-minded', 'unsexed', 'spayed' applied to such women entering the public arena in their own right betray a fear of embodied sexuality bursting asunder the abstraction of that sphere.

The nineteenth-century embargo on women speaking and writing in public, from the pulpit as well as the political platform, was an integral part of this process (although, as we now know, ironically, thousands of women did write, if not speak, 'in public' places). How could it be otherwise if the category of 'women' came to be understood as conditional, dependent on a relationship to 'their' men? And masculinity, full manhood, was at least partly defined as the ability 'to speak' for others. All types of masculine interest, parties and groups as well as individual men, have consistently used female symbolism, the protection of 'their' women, as central to masculine dignity and power, including power over other men[66]—the all-male dining or drinking ritual gathering rounding off the evening with the toast: 'To the ladies, God bless them'.

It is thus understandable that the call to women to move beyond family, class, or other group and identify with their fellow (*sic*) sisters as women, which was sent out by the nineteenth-century women's movement, invoked similarly passionate devotion from its followers. Martha Vicinus's original and illuminating discussion of the spiritual as well as embodied character of the British militant suffrage campaign emphasizes how the peculiar construction of 'women' both as a category and as a group energized and moulded that movement,[67] for feminism, like women, grew from an idea of self which was embodied.

The same forces which constructed women as the key figures of the moral order, however, as we have seen, deprived them of access to major institutions and the means of generating group resources in time, energy, money, organization, buildings and training. Their efforts at group action were often ridiculed, their attempts to create rituals or traditions of their own were written off as trivial and tawdry. Women's public appearances were always open to sexual innuendo because the category 'woman' had been defined as embracing the sexual, from which the category 'man' had been exempt.

For many women, the courage necessary to act in formal public arenas was formidable, and it is encouraging that such efforts are being sought out and recorded. Yet feminist historians, in their enthusiasm for finding 'women in public', have tended to overlook the distinctions between women acting as familial, class, or other group members rather than as (or in addition to) 'women'. As Joan Landes has written, the women's movement could not take possession of a public sphere that had been enduringly constituted along masculinist lines.[68] In practice, the way nineteenth- and early twentieth-century individual women experienced these divisions in their excursions into the public domain may not have been so clear-cut, but in terms of the effectiveness of women's group action they were vital. Recent historical inquiry into such varied groups as the Women's Cooperative Guild, the Mothers' Union, the Women's Institutes, and the Townswomen's Guilds, as well as the women's auxiliaries of the major political parties, shows the extent of activity compared to purely feminist organizations.[69]

The varied, detailed historical studies of women in public, as well as of feminist organization and action, carried out over the last decade have demonstrated beyond doubt the variety of versions of public life. Somehow, we have to give full play to that lively and fluid vision while recognizing problems created by the categories with which we do our historical work. How far did the masculinity of public institutions, language, and imagery affect women's view of themselves, including the transgressive behaviour and, later into the twentieth century, definitions of lesbianism? Were there ways in which women used the male language of the public to their own advantage and as disruptive of public discourse? What were the long-term effects of such disruption?

To answer such questions we have to listen carefully to the use of 'public' and 'private' in the language of historical actors themselves.[70] How to acknowledge that exclusion from political thought, economic and social theory, and tradition might, under certain circumstances, have actually left women free to grasp the initiative? Where and under what circumstances were some women in some places able to shift the terms of debate, including the definition of what was political, what was economic, what was social— indeed, what was public and what was private?

Epilogue

Given the structure of gender categories and their centrality to the nineteenth-century concept of the family, with its attendant male breadwinner, female housewife, non-working child roles, as well as the language of femininity and masculinity, it is not difficult to understand why women in public life posed such a threat to identity—for both men and women. In a period of such rapid technological change, geographical and social mobility, together with the later nineteenth-century loss of religious faith among the middle and upper classes, a sense of self, of identity, was crucial to psychic as well as to material survival. And in the twentieth century that sense of self turned increasingly inward towards a private and ultimately sexual self.

As the whole edifice of rational individualism and the public/private division has come to be taken for granted, and is solidly established within state, educational, and economic bureaucracies, it is the concept of 'sexuality' which has come to 'hold the key to the hermeneutics of the self'.[71] The same dichotomies that produced languages of equal rights and, by implication, posited sexual difference also shaped the erotic realm, 'exaggerating divisions between carnality and love, desire and reason, excitement and companionship which profoundly scarred men as well as women'.[72] The novelty of such a world-view is evinced in the case studies, mainly of lesbian and gay identity, which have begun to investigate how sexuality and sexual orientation as a core part of Western identity grew as part of the differentiation of the public and private. Homosexual identity as we know it could not exist unless sexuality as part of a private realm had not already been carved away from a putatively public sphere.[73]

'Sexuality', the desires and fantasies it accompanies, as well as the physical reproduction it implies, cannot be cut away from the rest of human life with impunity. The Cartesian schema, in its defiant gesture of masculine independence from physicality and thus from what was defined as the feminine, was a claim which was also a compensation for a profound loss.[74] We are beginning to recognize through a variety of empirical studies that often independence was elevated and loss denied by categorizing women (and with them 'effeminate' Jews, blacks, or native, inferior others) as mired in their biology. These groups represented potentially disruptive procreative forces which male individuality had to subdue

—the particularistic, familial ties that civic man must rise above and that some men would attempt to educate/rescue women from.[75]
While women had the potential to give birth to babies and thus renew populations, inevitably these frail and mortal human lives must, in their turn, end. It was within the abstract masculine realm that the power of infinite and indestructible generativity would lie. In the seventeenth and eighteenth centuries it was men, through the social contract, who give birth to civil society.[76] It was early nineteenth-century engineers and entrepreneurs, through their 'all but miraculous creations', the machines, who appeared to give birth by immaculate conception, and in the process endow machine-based industrial production with women's life-creating function.[77] In the later nineteenth century it was only men, it seemed, who 'could give birth to the political entity, the imperishable community of the nation'.[78] Such appropriations of reproduction and gestures towards immortality were built upon, as they served to maintain, the division between the public and the private.

We, in the late twentieth century, are the inheritors of a world structured by these categories and these conceptions. They continue to operate subtextually and informally to the disadvantage of women (and other subordinate groups) long after explicit formal restrictions on women's entry into the public realm have been lifted.[79] As in every human society, constructing such categories represents our culture's way of coming to terms with the mysteries of creation and of mortality. The difference from all previous cultures is that nineteenth-century England, through its empire and the diffusion of its economic and military dominance, through its values, technologies, and language, had the power—certainly never uncontested but nevertheless always present—to shape not only our destiny but potentially that of a goodly portion of our planet.

Notes

1. Olivia Harris, 'Households as Natural Units', in Kate Young, Carol Wolkowitz, and Roslyn McCullagh (eds.), *Of Marriage and the Market: Women's Subordination in International Perspective* (London: CSE Books, 1981).
2. There was an extended debate on this topic in the 1970s, starting with Michelle Rosaldo, joined by Edward Ardener and Sherry Ortner. See in particular Sherry Ortner, 'Is Female to Male as Nature Is to Culture?' (1974), included as Ch. 1 in this volume. This was answered

by Nicole-Claude Mathieu, 'Man–Culture and Woman–Nature?', *Women's Studies International Quarterly*, 1(1) (1978).

3. Ludmilla Jordanova, 'Women's Testimonies on "Public" and "Private" in Eighteenth-Century England', paper delivered at the conference on the public and private spheres in early modern Europe, University of Exeter, Mar. 1993, by permission of the author.

4. Ann Snitow, 'A Gender Diary', in Marianne Hirsch and Evelyn Fox-Keller (eds.), *Conflicts in Feminism* (London: Routledge, 1990), 137; see also Nancy Hewitt's elegant plea for a concept of 'compound identities', studying elements both in isolation and as a whole. 'Compounding Differences', *Feminist Studies*, 18(2) (1992): 318.

5. Jordanova, 'Women's Testimonies', 6.

6. Linda Kerber, 'Separate Spheres, Female Worlds, Women's Place: The Rhetoric of Women's History', *Journal of American History*, 75(1) (1988): 30.

7. Amanda Vickery, 'Golden Age to Separate Spheres? A Review of the Categories and Chronology of English Women's History', *Historical Journal*, 36(2) (1993): 412.

8. Carole Pateman, 'Feminist Critiques of the Public/Private Dichotomy', in *The Disorder of Women: Democracy, Feminism and Political Theory* (Cambridge: Polity Press, 1989), 122.

9. Nancy Fraser, 'Rethinking the Public Sphere: A Contribution to the Critique of Actually-Existing Democracy', in Craig Calhoun (ed.), *Habermas and the Public Sphere* (Cambridge, Mass.: MIT Press, 1992).

10. Geoff Eley, 'Nations, Publics and Political Cultures: Placing Habermas in the Nineteenth Century', in Calhoun, *Habermas and the Public Sphere*.

11. G. R. Rubin and David Sugarman, 'Changing Views of Credit, Economy and the Law', in *Law, Economy and Society 1750–1914: Essays in the History of English Law* (Abingdon: Professional Books, 1984).

12. Seyla Benhabib, 'Models of Public Space: Hannah Arendt, the Liberal Tradition and Jürgen Habermas', in Calhoun, *Habermas and the Public Sphere*, 90. [This quotation does not appear in the revised version of this paper which is included as Chapter 3 of the present volume.]

13. See Drucilla Cornell, *Beyond Accommodation: Ethical Feminism, Deconstruction and the Law* (London: Routledge, 1991).

14. Pateman, *The Disorder of Women*. Feminist sociologists seem to have been more aware of the centrality of family and kinship than some historians. See e.g. Carol Smart, *The Ties That Bind: Law, Marriage and the Reproduction of Patriarchal Relations* (London: Routledge & Kegan Paul, 1984).

15. Eva Lundgren, 'The Hand That Strikes and Comforts: Gender Construction in the Field of Tension Encompassing Body and Symbol, Stability and Change', in Maud Edwards et al. (eds.), *Rethinking*

Change: Current Swedish Feminist Research (Uppsala: Swedish Science Press, 1992); see also the discussion of motherhood, the embodied connection, and their relationship to the category of 'person', in Susan Bordo, *Unbearable Weight: Feminism, Western Culture and the Body* (Berkeley: University of California Press, 1993).

16. Chandra Mohanty, Ann Russo, and Lourdes Torres (eds.), *Third World Women and the Politics of Feminism* (Bloomington: Indiana University Press, 1991).

17. Calhoun, *Habermas and the Public Sphere*, 37; see also Anna Yeatman, 'Gender Differentiation of Social Life in Public and Domestic Domains', *Social Analysis: Journal of Cultural and Social Practice*, 15 (Aug. 1984).

18. Jane Collier and S. Yanagisakdo (eds.), *Gender and Kinship: Essays Toward Unified Analysis* (Stanford, Calif.: Stanford University Press, 1987), introd.

19. Joan Scott, 'A Reply to Criticism', *International Labour and Working-Class History*, 32 (Fall 1987).

20. Acker, 'Making Gender Visible'; R. E. Bologh, *Love or Greatness: Max Weber and Masculine Thinking—A Feminist Enquiry* (London: Unwin Hyman, 1990).

21. Quoted in R. J. Morris, *Class, Sect and Party: The Making of the British Middle Class; Leeds 1820–1850* (Manchester: Manchester University Press, 1990), 196. E. P. Thompson has a similar formulation for the 'common people': he denies that they 'married wives and begat children in order to exploit them'—presumably women are not part of the common people. See 'Happy Families', *Radical History Review*, 20 (1979): 48.

22. Joan Scott, 'Women in *The Making of the English Middle Class*', in *Gender and the Politics of Class* (New York: Columbia University Press, 1988), 72.

23. Rosemary Crompton, *Class and Stratification: An Introduction to Current Debates* (Cambridge: Polity Press, 1993), 207.

24. D. Lockwood, *The Blackcoated Worker: A Study in Class Consciousness* (Oxford: Clarendon Press, 1989), postscript.

25. This does not mean that men took no part in consumption. On the contrary, they spent a great deal of time and thought on buying and fitting goods for the home, although there tended to be some differentiation between masculine goods—wine, carpets, carriages, horses, large items of furniture—and feminine—smaller items, curtains, kitchenware, tableware, decorative materials. For a general discussion, see Neil McKendrick, John Brewer, and J. H. Plumb (eds.), *The Birth of a Consumer Society: The Commercialization of Eighteenth-Century England* (London: Europa, 1982).

26. This issue of consumption, taste, and taken-for-granted behaviours in the construction of classification has been explored in detail in

Pierre Bourdieu, *Distinction: A Social Critique of the Judgement of Taste* (London: Routledge, 1986).

27. Susan Benson, *Counter Cultures: Saleswomen, Managers and Customers in American Department Stores 1890–1940* (Urbana: University of Illinois Press, 1988); Gail Reekie, *Temptations: Sex, Selling and the Department Store* (St Leonards, NSW: Allen & Unwin, 1993); fears about the role of female shopping activities as blurring the distinction between market and home are explored in Erika Rappaport, 'A Husband and his Wife's Dresses: Consumer Credit and the Debtor Family in England 1864–1914', in Victoria de Grazia, with Ellen Furlough (eds.), *The Sex of Things: Gender and Consumption in Historical Perspective* (Berkeley: University of California Press, 1996).

28. Alice Kessler-Harris, 'Treating the Male as "Other": Redefining Parameters of Labor History', *Labor History*, 34 (Spring/Summer 1993); Joy Parr, 'Keynsianism, Consumerism and Gender Politics in Canada and Sweden 1943–56', paper delivered to 'New Directions in Women's History', Schlesinger Library, Radcliffe College, Mar. 1994.

29. On the relation between status, honour, official power, and wealth see Max Weber, 'Class, Status and Party', in H. Gerth and C. W. Mills (eds.), *From Max Weber: Essays in Sociology* (New York: Oxford University Press, 1948).

30. This has been particularly ignored for the working class. But for an analysis of the idealization of 'Our Mam' as the centre of family life, see Ellen Ross, *Love and Toil: Motherhood in Outcast London 1870–1918* (New York: Oxford University Press, 1994).

31. Murray J. Milner, *Status and Sacredness: A General Theory of Status Relations and an Analysis of Indian Culture* (New York: Oxford University Press, 1994), 32.

32. Edward Shils, *Centre and Periphery: Essays in Macrosociology* (Chicago: University of Chicago Press, 1982).

33. Londa Schiebinger, *The Mind Has No Sex? Women in the Origins of Modern Science* (Cambridge, Mass.: Harvard University Press, 1989).

34. L. Jordanova, *Sexual Visions: Images of Gender in Science and Medicine Between the Eighteenth and Twentieth Centuries* (Hemel Hempstead: Harvester Wheatsheaf, 1989).

35. C. Battersby, *Gender and Genius: Towards a Feminist Aesthetics* (London: Women's Press, 1989).

36. Griselda Pollock, 'Painting, Feminism and History', in Michèle Barrett and Ann Phillips (eds.), *Destabilizing Theory: Contemporary Feminist Debates* (Cambridge: Polity Press, 1992), 56.

37. Taylor, *Eve and the New Jerusalem*.

38. This section owes much to the analysis in Anna Clark, *The Struggle for the Breeches: Gender and the Making of the British Working Class* (Berkeley: University of California Press, 1995); see also Jutta

Schwarzkopf, *Women in the Chartist Movement* (London: Macmillan, 1991).

39. Sally Alexander, 'Women, Class and Sexual Differences in the 1830s and 1840s: Some Reflections on the Writing of Feminist History', *History Workshop Journal*, 17 (1984).

40. See John Gillis, *For Better, For Worse: British Marriages from 1600 to the Present* (Oxford: Oxford University Press, 1986).

41. Jane Lewis on Helen Bosanquet and Fabian Women's understanding of the difficulties, in her *Women and Social Action in Victorian and Edwardian England* (Aldershot: Edward Elgar, 1991); Ross, *Love and Toil.*

42. Denise Riley, *'Am I That Name?' Feminism and the Category of 'Women' in History* (London: Macmillan, 1988); Jane Lewis, *Women and Social Action in Victorian and Edwardian England* (Aldershot: Edward Elgar, 1991).

43. Leonore Davidoff, *The Best Circles: Society, Etiquette and the Season* (London: Century Hutchinson, 1986).

44. Margaret Arnot, 'Infant Death, Child Care and the Law: "Baby-Farming" and the First Infant Life Protective Legislation of 1872', *Continuity and Change*, 9(4) (Aug. 1994); James Hammerton, *Cruelty and Companionship: Conflict in Nineteenth-Century Married Life* (London: Routledge, 1992).

45. There is a vast literature on women as writers and readers. The standard work tracing some of these changes over the nineteenth century, however, remains Elaine Showalter, *A Literature of Their Own* (Princeton, NJ: Princeton University Press, 1977).

46. Alex Owen, *The Darkened Room: Women, Power, and Spiritualism in Late Victorian England* (London: Virago, 1989); for a more problematic example, see Lyndal Roper, 'Witchcraft and Fantasy', *History Workshop Journal*, 32 (Autumn 1991).

47. John Demos, *A Little Commonwealth: Family Life in a Plymouth Colony* (New York: Oxford University Press, 1974), 186; but see also a more recent example: James Casey, 'The Individual: His Wife and Family', in *The History of the Family* (Oxford: Blackwell, 1989), 15.

48. Peter Bailey analyses the shifts in place and form of some of these activities at the end of the nineteenth century in 'Parasexuality and Glamour: The Victorian Barmaid as Cultural Prototype', *Gender and History*, 2(2) (1990).

49. Mary Ann Clawson, *Constructing Brotherhood: Class Gender and Fraternalism* (NJ: Princeton University Press, Princeton, 1989); Marilyn Lake, 'The Politics of Respectability: Identifying the Masculinist Context', *Historical Studies*, 22 (Apr. 1986).

50. Phillipa Levine, ' "So Few Prizes and So Many Blanks": Marriage and Feminism in Later Nineteenth-Century England', *Journal of British Studies*, 28(2) (Apr. 1989): 151.

51. Jane Rendall (ed.), *Equal or Different: Women's Politics 1800–1914* (Oxford: Blackwell, 1987), introd.; Joan Scott, 'Deconstructing Equality-versus-Difference; or The Uses of Post-Structuralist Theory for Feminism', *Feminist Studies*, 14(4) (Spring 1988).

52. Penelope Russell, *A Wish of Distinction: Colonial Gentility and Femininity* (Melbourne: Melbourne University Press, 1994).

53. Clark, *The Struggle of the Breeches*; see also Dorothy Thompson, 'Women, Work and Politics in Nineteenth-Century England: The Problem of Authority', in Rendall, *Equal or Different*.

54. The notion of 'domestic feminism' in connection with the fall in the middle-class birth rate was first put forward in the 1970s, by Daniel Scott Smith among others, but these ideas have resurfaced in more sophisticated form. See e.g. the concept of the 'silent strike' in Lucy Bland, 'Marriage Laid Bare: Middle-Class Women and Marital Sex 1880–1914', in Jane Lewis (ed.), *Labour of Love: Women's Experience of Home and Family 1850–1940* (Oxford: Blackwell, 1986), 138; Kerreen Reiger, *The Disenchantment of the Home: Modernizing the Australian Family 1880–1940* (Oxford: Oxford University Press, 1985).

55. Martha Vicinus, *Independent Women: Work and Community for Single Women, 1850–1920* (Chicago: University of Chicago Press, 1985); Sarah Deutsch, 'Reconceiving the City: Women, Space and Power in Boston 1870–1910', *Gender and History*, 6(2) (1994).

56. Recent interest in the relationship of gender to national identity has raised similar issues in a variety of contexts. See Catherine Hall, Jane Lewis, Keith McClelland, and Jane Rendall (eds.), 'Gender and National Identity', special issue, *Gender and History*, 5(2) (1993).

57. Sandra Stanley Holton, *Feminism and Democracy: Women's Suffrage and Reform Politics in Britain 1900–1918* (Cambridge: Cambridge University Press, 1986), 5.

58. Claire Hirschfield, 'A Fractured Faith: Liberal Party Women and the Suffrage Issue in Britain 1892–1914', *Gender and History*, 2(2) (1990): 190.

59. Claire Collins, 'Women and Labour Politics in Britain 1893–1932', University of London Ph.D. thesis, 1990; Pat Thane, 'Visions of Gender in the Making of the British Welfare State: The Case of Women in the British Labour Party and Social Policy, 1906–1945', in Gisela Bock and Pat Thane (eds.), *Maternity and Gender Policies: Women and the Rise of the European Welfare State* (London: Routledge, 1991).

60. Lockwood, 'Class, Status and Gender', 233.

61. Mary Lyndon Shanley, *Feminism, Marriage and the Law in Victorian England 1850–1895* (Princeton, NJ: Princeton University Press, 1989), 20.

62. Clare Evans, 'The Separation of Work and Home? The Case of the Lancashire Textiles 1825–1865', University of Manchester Ph.D. thesis, 1991; Mary Blewett, *Men, Women and Work: Class, Gender,*

Protest in the New England Shoe Industry 1780–1910 (Urbana: University of Illinois Press, 1988); Alice Kessler-Harris, 'Gender Ideology in Historical Reconstructions: A Case Study from the 1930s', *Gender and History*, 1(1) (1989).

63. Claire Midgeley, 'Anti-Slavery and Feminism in Nineteenth-Century Britain', *Gender and History*, 5(3) (1993).

64. Jane Sherron DeHart, 'Gender and the Right: Meanings Behind the Existential Scream', in 'Gender and the Right', ed. Nancy Hewitt, special issue, *Gender and History*, 3(3) (1991): 248. See also Susan Kingsley Kent, 'The Politics of Sexual Difference: World War I and the Demise of British Feminism', *Journal of British Studies*, 27 (1988). Such a position takes seriously the 'secondary gains' which some women could hold through marriage (or as dutiful sisters or daughters) in terms of men's attention and support. For the power, as well as the costs, of this position, particularly in its psychic dimension, see Jean Baker Miller, *Toward a New Psychology of Women* (Boston, Mass.: Beacon Press, 1976).

65. Amartya Sen, 'Gender and Cooperative Conflicts', in Irene Tinker (ed.), *Persistent Inequalities: Women and Third World Development* (Oxford: Oxford University Press, 1990); see also Emily Grosholz, 'Women, History and Practical Deliberation', in Mary Gergen (ed.), *Feminist Thought and the Structure of Knowledge* (New York: New York University Press, 1988).

66. Mary Ryan, 'Gender and Public Access: Women's Politics in Nineteenth-Century America', in Calhoun, *Habermas and the Public Sphere*.

67. Martha Vicinus, 'Male Space and Women's Bodies: The Suffragette Movement', in her *Independent Women*.

68. Joan B. Landes, *Women and the Public Sphere* (Ithaca, N.Y.: Cornell University Press, 1988) 202.

69. Kate Beaumont 'Women and Citizenship in England 1928–1950', unpublished paper, cited by permission of the author; Jean Gaffin and Jarid Thomas, *Caring and Sharing: The Centenary History of The Cooperative Women's Guild* (Manchester: Holyoake Books, 1983).

70. Jane Rendall, 'Nineteenth-Century Feminism and the Separation of Spheres: Reflections on the Public/Private Dichotomy', in T. Andreasen et al. (eds.), *Moving On: New Perspectives on the Women's Movement* (Aarhus: Aarhus University Press, 1990).

71. Robert A. Padgug, 'Sexual Matters: On Conceptualizing Sexuality in History', in K. Peiss and C. Simmons (eds.), *Passion and Power: Sexuality in History* (Philadelphia: Temple University Press, 1989); David M. Halperin, 'Is There a History of Sexuality?', *History and Theory*, 28 (1989): 271.

72. Dina Copelman, 'Liberal Ideology, Sexual Difference and the Lives of Women: Recent Works in British History', *Journal of Modern History*, 62(2) (June 1990): 325.

73. Jeffrey Weeks, *Sex, Politics and Society: The Regulation of Sexuality since 1800* (London: Longmans, 1981).
74. Susan Bordo, 'The Cartesian Masculinization of "Thought"', *Signs*, 11(3) (Spring 1986), 451.
75. Laura Englestein, *The Keys to Happiness: Sex and the Search for Modernity in Fin-de-siècle Russia* (Ithaca, NY: Cornell University Press, 1992), 302. Public discussions of sexual behaviour and the nature of sexuality reached a crescendo in England in the early decades of the twentieth century. For a particularly illuminating case study of attempts to link public and private life through sexuality, see Jane Lewis, 'Intimate Relations between Men and Women: The Case of H. G. Wells and Amber Pember Reeves', *History Workshop Journal*, 37 (1994).
76. Pateman, *The Disorder of Women*, 45.
77. Judith Newton, 'Sex and Political Economy in *The Edinburgh Review*', in *Starting Over: Feminism and the Politics of Cultural Critique* (Ann Arbor: University of Michigan Press, 1994).
78. Marilyn Lake, 'Mission Impossible: How Men Gave Birth to the Australian Nation: Nationalism, Gender and Other Seminal Acts', *Gender and History*, 4(3) (1992): 307.
79. Fraser, 'Rethinking the Public Sphere', 32. For an original view of many of these issues in the Norwegian context, see Tordis Borchgrevink and Øystein Gullvåg Hotter (eds.), *Labour of Love: Exploring Gender, Work and Family Interaction* (Aldershot: Avebury, forthcoming).

7

Gender and Public Access: Women's Politics in Nineteenth-Century America

Mary P. Ryan

In the twenty-five years since *The Structural Transformation of the Public Sphere* was written, public life has shifted, convulsed, and been transformed anew. With those changes the political and intellectual project that the book inaugurated has become more crucial than ever. The word 'public' has long served as the place-marker for the political ideal of open, inclusive, and effective deliberation about matters of common and critical concern. Early in the 1960s such a public discourse was hardly audible in the United States amid the manipulative communications of consumer culture and consensus politics. Before that decade ended, however, the staid surfaces of welfare-state mass democracy had been fractured. The civil rights and anti-war movements disturbed the equanimity and passivity of public discourse, shattered consensus, and revitalized a conception of politics based on participatory democracy. Those movements and student activism around the globe opened a narrow wedge in entrenched political structures and permitted their participants to experience, however briefly, a more commodious public space.

In that same historical moment, a rekindled feminism ignited the consciousness of that sex whose relationship to the public had been most tenuous and ever problematic. The illumination that the women's movement cast over public life exposed the gendered limits on participation in the public sphere and at the same time gave new urgency to the ideals that the term encapsulated. The strictures of gender were quickly discerned as among the tightest, oldest, most categorical restrictions on public access. Women were patently excluded from the bourgeois public sphere, that ideal historical type that Habermas traced to the eighteenth century, and

Chapter 11 in Craig Calhoun (ed.), *Habermas and the Public Sphere* (MIT Press, 1992), 259–88. © The MIT Press (1992) Reprinted by permission.

were even read out of the fiction of the public by virtue of their ideological consignment to a separate realm called the private. The subsequent historical transformation of the public did little to accommodate women, who were constrained just as tightly within mass welfare-state democracy. Their sex was the special target of consumer culture, yet they were poorly represented among those who wielded power in both the state and the capitalist sectors. Accordingly, the appropriate feminist stance toward the public seemed deceptively simple: to position women and their political concerns for a direct assault upon that hallowed sphere to which they had been so long denied access. Public access held many promises for women: escape from manipulative media of consumerism (called the 'feminine mystique' by Betty Friedan), recognition of the unwaged, unrewarded labours of social reproduction for Marxist-feminists, some taste of efficacy and power to those like the members of the National Organization for Women intent on entering the 'mainstream' of American public life. The new feminists were not simply demanding admission to the public; they also placed a multitude of specific issues, often drawn from their 'private' experience, on the public agenda. Finally, as feminists made haste to construct theoretical guidelines for their political activism, they located the structural underpinnings of gender inequality along the private–public axis. Michelle Rosaldo's hypothesis that neither biology nor reproductive functions but the denial of access to the public realm was the basic underpinning of women's secondary status became a classic postulate of feminist theory.[1]

Through the first decade of the new feminism the significance of the public was assumed more than articulated or examined. The first task of feminist scholars and activists was to dredge through their personal lives and women's everyday experience for those issues that required publicity. Having found the substance of women's politics in the family, sexuality, and the relations of reproduction, feminists took their grievances directly into the public arena through any pragmatic avenue available, be it an arm of the state (courts and legislative bodies) or any media of communication (from street demonstrations to scholarly journals to TV talk shows). To this day much of feminist theory is still occupied on the private side of this political project, debating the notion of gender identity as it takes form in the private spaces of the psyche, infant development, and the family. Two decades of feminist practice, however, has left a well-marked trail through the public sphere itself, a record of women in public that feminist theorists have begun to address forthrightly.[2]

Locating women in the theory of the public is not a simple task, especially for American feminists. The intellectual guardians of that sphere have not provided a very legible map of this august territory. Certainly the mountains of voting studies and administrative analyses compiled by political scientists are not of ready use to feminist theorists. Even a political philosopher like Hannah Arendt, who characterized the public in more compelling terms, constructed that realm along its classic boundary with household concerns and thereby seemed to banish women. In this theoretical void, Habermas's 'The Public Sphere: An Encyclopedia Article' began to circulate among feminist scholars, and its compact and yet capacious outline of the concept became a key text in a search for women in public.[3]

Habermas's construction of the public sphere had a singular advantage for feminists; it freed politics from the iron grasp of the state which, by virtue of the long denial of the franchise to women and their rare status as public officials, effectively defined the public in masculine terms. The concept of the public sphere was suffused with a spirit of openness that feminists found inviting. (The second sentence of the encyclopedia article read, 'Access is guaranteed to all citizens.') The public for Habermas, writing in 1964, was centred in a wide, diffuse, open field: 'Citizens behave as a public body when they confer in an unrestricted fashion—that is, with the guarantee of freedom of assembly and association and the freedom to express and publish their opinions—about matters of general interest.' Not only could women find access to a sphere so constructed, but once there, they seemed to be promised a hearing, whatever their concerns. In other words, Habermas's enunciation of the public sphere, as I first read it, was formulated in such a magnanimous way that female subjects and their opinions were a legitimate part of the common good.

When in 1989 English-speaking feminists turned to *The Structural Transformation of the Public Sphere* for a more elaborate blueprint of this inviting territory, their vision was refracted through theoretical developments that long postdate its German publication. It is not surprising to find that Habermas was not so clairvoyant as to foresee the full agenda of feminist concerns that accumulated in the twenty-five years after its writing. Nor could he anticipate the fundamental critiques that feminism, in combination with postmodernism, would level against key elements in his model and his history, especially his confidence in abstract rationality and his tendency to construe the conjugal family as a natural reservoir of pure subjectivity. At the same time, to the extent to which the reader of the 1990s can place herself back in the intellectual climate of the early 1960s, she might be impressed by Habermas's cognizance of the historical malleability of the border between private and public, as well as his recognition of the patriarchal caste of the bourgeois family.

AN AMERICAN SETTING FOR THE PUBLIC SPHERE

I do not intend to enter the discussion on this theoretical plane, however, and will leave it to others to identify the gendered assumptions that underwrite public philosophy from Aristotle through Habermas.[4] Rather, I will engage the subject of women and the public sphere on the ground of history. From the vantage point of a historian of the United States, I will sketch a counter-narrative to Habermas's depiction of the chronological decline from an idealized bourgeois public sphere. Starting at approximately the same time and place where Habermas commences his story of the eviscerating transformation of the public sphere (Western republics in the eighteenth and nineteenth centuries), feminist historians plot out the ascension of women into politics. This discrepancy cannot be ironically dismissed with the painful observation that when women finally won the franchise and official access to the public, they found themselves the conquerers of a hollow fortress. Although female suffrage did not swiftly lead to gender equality, it did remove a major constitutional impediment to public access and in the process undermined a gender division that had both hamstrung women as political subjects and blemished the whole doctrine of the public sphere. Moreover, in a critical slice of history that postdates the writing of *Structural Transformation*, the new women's movement injected considerable feminist substance into public discourse, articulating concerns once buried in the privacy of one sex as vital matters of public interest. Even the barest outlines of women's political history are sufficient to call into question a characterization of the last century as a blanket, undifferentiated decline of public life. I propose to outline in a very sketchy and condensed way how this feminist-inspired history of the public deviates from Habermas's account. From a woman's perspective this history starts out from different premises, evolves through a different and more problematic relationship to the public sphere, and presents a distinctive projectory into the future.

The geographical location and temporal parameters of my abbreviated history, the United States between 1825 and 1880, introduce additional contrasts with Habermas's model, based largely in Western Europe. The public as built on American soil in the nineteenth century was structured around different political possibilities and challenges. The relatively painless and rapid expansion of suffrage to adult white males circumvented the intense, abrasive encounter between the bourgeois public sphere and French revolutionaries or English Chartists. Subsequently the American polity was divided more fractiously by ethnic, racial, and sectional differences than on the Continent. These divisions, along with more mottled class differences, were organized swiftly and in a bipolar fashion into two mass political parties. Perhaps most decisive of all, the American Republic, stepchild of the parliament of Great Britain, was not born in a ferocious struggle against absolutism, nor in close conjunction with a strong mercantilist state. The limited government of confederated states endured through the Civil War. As Stephen Showronek has recently pointed out and as Tocqueville observed long ago, antebellum public life was intensely focused at the local and municipal level. It is at this historical site that I (drawing evidence especially from New York, New Orleans, and San Francisco) have based my search for women in public.[5]

Since I share Habermas's premiss that no prototype of the public sphere can be 'abstracted to any number of historical situations that represent formally similar constellations', my search for an American public spotlights different times, institutions, forms, and locations as the markings of the public. First of all, from my historical vantage-point the most robust expressions of American publicness date from the 1820s and 1830s, not the eighteenth century. Second, this public spirit flourished in distinctive spaces, not primarily in literary and political clubs and in the culture of print but in outdoor assemblages, in open, urban spaces, along the avenues, on street corners, and in public squares. Third, American citizens enacted publicness in an active, raucous, contentious, and unbounded style of debate that defied literary standards of rational and critical discourse. Fourth, the practice of publicness in nineteenth-century America took shape in a distinctive class and social context. Although elite merchants dominated local public offices, convened their own public meetings, set up their own literary clubs, and were treated deferentially in the public press, this American garden variety of the bourgeoisie was not the major staging ground of public politics. Nor could the most exuberant public formations of Jacksonian America be characterized as plebian. Rather, this urban public found its social base in amorphous groupings of citizens aggregated according to ethnicity, class, race, pet cause, and party affiliation. These widespread, diverse, and intersecting political conventions were a popular enactment of the principle of open access to public debate on matters of general interest. Not the ideal bourgeois public sphere but this variegated, decentred, and democratic array of public spaces will be the setting of my story and serve as my historical standard of publicness.

Although this pivot of my history is quite remote from the starting-point of Habermas's chronology, it provides the best American approximation of the optimal function of the public sphere as he presents it: 'a process in which the exercise of social power and political domination is effectively subjected to the mandate of democratic publicity'. Moreover, these social, political, and cultural practices of the American public resemble Western European publicness in critical ways. On both sides of the Atlantic publicness is premissed on and propelled by a normative allegiance to open discussion of matters of general concern, and yet every Western republic was founded on the exclusion of the female sex and the elision of gender difference. So in chronicling the American history that proceeded from these premisses, I will be detouring away from Habermas's text in two ways: by simultaneously presenting a different historical construction of the public sphere and a distinct experience, that of women citizens.

THE REPUBLICAN PUBLIC CIRCA 1825

My history starts early in the nineteenth century, when citizens walked the compact spaces of the small port cities of New York and New Orleans with the proud demeanour of republicans. They did not, however, exercise very public modes of politics. Most American municipalities were private corporations, vesting in the officers of the city corporation the privileges of collecting a few taxes and adjudicating the disputes brought by individual petitioners. Election days brought little popular excitement, and elevated elite merchants to a position of public stewardship. Political clubs like New York's Tammany Hall added faction and fervour to this representative politics but seldom challenged the social hierarchy, which deferentially linked voters to elite officials. Given the limited public business, there was little local conflict capable of disturbing the republican premiss that virtuous public-spirited citizens could oversee a transcendent common good. Maintaining public consensus did require, however, something akin to that display of reputation calculated to elicit popular acclamation of authority that Habermas found in both absolutist and modern democratic states. The elite officers of the city corporation demonstrated their superior civic stature by giving public dinners, leading processions through the streets, and organizing public festivals.[6]

Women, largely absent from all the institutional sites of the public—from polling places, city councils, public offices, the newspaper rooms, and political clubs—were an extreme case of the social exclusions of early American republicanism. Unlike those barred from citizenship on the basis of age, lack of property, or colour of skin, however, some women had a particularly honoured place in the ceremonial representations of the public. The 'ladies' were toasted at public dinners and honored at civic celebrations, like those that marked the completion of the Erie Canal in New York harbour and the visit of Lafayette to New Orleans in 1825. Female symbols, like the goddess of liberty and Columbia, were favoured emblems of civic virtue carried in procession by merchants, artisans, and students alike. As a symbol or goddess, as a consort of the elite on ceremonial days, or as a sexual pariah in public houses, women bore the mark of either ornament or outcast in public life. This negative relationship between women and the ruling political circles of the early nineteenth-century city betokens the severe social limits of the bourgeois public sphere. It indicates as well that it was not beneath the dignity of the bourgeois custodians of the commonweal to make use of provocative yet seemingly superfluous symbols, in particular gratuitous references to femininity, to ornament their public identities.

But women constituted far more than just a quiescent population awaiting the structural changes or liberal reforms that would bring them directly into public life. The same stroke that inscribed gender differences on the public as a principle of exclusion placed a mark of selective social identity on citizenship in general. Republican ideology held that the female sex embodied those uncurbed human passions that inevitably subverted the self-control and rationality required of citizens. This rationale for gender boundaries on the public sphere inspired toasts to the ladies at public dinners, such as this pithy philosophy of gender heard in New Orleans in 1825: 'The fair sex—Excluded by necessity from participation in our labours: we profess equality, the presence of woman would make us slaves, and convert the temple of wisdom into that of love.' The converse gender logic made 'manliness' the standard of republican character and 'effeminacy' the most debilitating political malady. As historians of the early republic and feminist political theorists have amply demonstrated, the universal citizen was not genderless but a male. As such he carried a constricted notion of the general interest into public discourse. He, no less than a twentieth-century lobbyist, was the representative of a private interest group.[7]

From the first the American public sphere was constructed in the shadow of both gender restrictions and an emerging private sector of social life. This relationship was expressed in the eighteenth-century notion of the republican mother. This now familar prescription that women's stake in the polity was the private nurturance of infant citizens was more than a rationalization of misogynist politics. It invested the social practices of bourgeois wives and mothers with public significance. Sequestered from the developing market economy and barred from public politics, wives of merchants and professionals took up the practice of socializing children with alacrity, devising methods of moral education that placed particular stock in maintaining a buffer of privacy between future (male) citizens and the corrupting influence of the city. In other words, the same structural transformation that gave definition to a public realm designated women a second species of citizens and marked out around them a social space called the private. The public sphere of bourgeois America was moored in a private and gendered social geography, built, that is, on a fragile foundation.

TOWARD A DEMOCRATIC PUBLIC, 1830–1860

The mantle of publicness in American cities none the less provided ample room for expanding the public jurisdiction beyond its vanguard class of commercial elites. The steady expansion of the franchise and rapid growth of the urban population had significantly enlarged and diversified the American citizenry by the second quarter of the nineteenth century. This process agitated everyday public life with particular force in the 1830s, when a popular penny press attuned for the first time to local political issues broadcast calls for public assemblies with head-spinning regularity. By the 1840s the dailies labelled densely packed columns of newsprint with the words 'Public Meetings'. These public notices invited citizens to assemble to discuss a wide range of special issues, like the public school, relief during a severe winter, erecting a public building, providing a public service, or organizing a public celebration. The political parties were a mainstay of public culture; working men and nativists, as well as Whigs and Jacksonians, met weekly. ['Nativists' promoted an American-centred ideology, which opposed immigration and the rights of the foreign-born, especially of Catholics.] Sometimes these proliferating public groupings met at merchants' exchanges, mechanics' halls, grand hotels, or neighbourhood saloons. Often the meeting spilled out into the streets. Just as often, the designated spot for assembly was a public thoroughfare, street corner, or town square. Wherever their location, these invitations to popular assemblies were steeped in a language of publicness. The notices read 'Great Public Meeting', 'Mass Meeting of the Citizens', 'Great Meeting of the People', 'Great Democratic Republican Meeting'. When in 1849 a collection of goldminers and fortune hunters gathered along San Francisco Bay, determined to constitute themselves a public, they simply issued a notice in the local press inviting every inhabitant to assemble in the central square to draw up blueprints for self-government. San Francisco used the public living-room of Portsmouth Plaza again a few years later to select delegates to the constitutional convention of the State of California. Those delegates were instructed that 'all political power is inherent in the people', whose inalienable rights included that of 'public assembly'.[8]

These homespun democratic theorists were also careful to prescribe the procedures for maintaining public sovereignty. Invitations to public assemblies were regularly rescinded when it was discovered that a private, vested interest had contrived them. One such meeting was aborted in New Orleans in 1837 on the grounds that it was not based on 'an understanding among the citizens generally'. One of the most conspicuous political events in Jacksonian America, the creation of the Locofoco Party in New York in 1835 (which established the radical and anti-bank platform of the

Democrats), erupted into being when party leaders were found tampering with the democratic procedures for convening the meeting and choosing its officers. The public meetings held to a rough-hewn standard of parliamentary procedure, raised upwards of 3,000 hands to vote on scores of resolutions, and employed the device of literally 'dividing the hall'—yeahs to the front and nays to the rear—to resolve their disputes. This is not to say that the meticulous efforts to ensure open, democratic expression made for a contemplative and sedate style of public discourse. Public meetings were rowdy (erupting in shouting matches and fist fights), festive (spiced with drink and riddled with laughter), and fiercely partisan (sometimes culminating in an assault on the polling place of the opposition).

This cacophonous style of politics might appear as a symptom of the descent of the public sphere from the height of logical-critical discourse. The Jacksonians were more rambunctious than rational in style of debate, and militantly asserted the identities and interests of specific sectors of the population. But the same evidence can also be read as an effective means of fulfilling the public promise openly to challenge political domination. Once public access had been translated into popular ideology, harnessed to a machinery of public communication, and regularly practised in the open spaces of the city, a larger citizenry could contribute to the historical construction of the public good. Furthermore, in such democratized public spaces with citizens mobilized on so many fronts, the pretence of one indivisible and transcendent common good lost credibility. No incident exposed this bourgeois fiction more dramatically than the action of the vigilance committee of San Francisco in the 1850s. When the Vigilantes hanged two unsavoury citizens without benefit of trial in 1856, they posed as 'the people in their sovereign capacity'. In fact, the 'people' were merchants, Protestants, and Republicans defying a local government with an Irish, Catholic, Democratic, and plebeian composition.[9] This clash of interests was one unseemly manifestation of a muscular democratic public. This unruly incident and many others like it were set in a political climate of vigorous publicity and broad, active citizenship, which might be read as a moment of democratic possibility that coincided with the relative decline of bourgeois political hegemony.

The proliferation of publics—convened around concrete, localized, and sometimes 'special' interests—also opened up new political possibilities for women. In the 1830s women first joined in the public meetings convened by men and then gathered publicly among themselves. The first order of going public was the least likely to insert female interests in the public good. The failure of this strategy was dramatically demonstrated by the public appearances of Fanny Wright in New York City. Wright's radical opinions, as well as her gender, provoked catcalls, sexual epithets, and stink-bombs and led to her prompt exile from the major public halls of the city. The prominence of women among abolitionists led to similar conclusions: riotous attacks on promiscuous anti-slavery meetings and a shift in anti-slavery tactics to focusing on the masculine method of electoral politics. Women's participation in the meetings of working men also led only so far: to the incorporation of women's interests into appeals for a family wage, paid, of course, to husbands, fathers, or sons. The sorry story of a Madam Ranke, who addressed a meeting of unemployed men camped in New York City's Tompkins Square in 1857, records this stalemated attempt to desegregate the male public. When Madam Ranke took the public podium, she was greeted by cries like 'Don't listen to a woman', or alternatively, 'Damn it, don't interrupt a woman.' The female voice was neither easily blended nor distinctly heard in the embattled sectors of the male public sphere, and Madam Ranke was escorted from the square under a protective escort of women.[10]

This did not mean, of course, that male-dominated public spaces were gender-blind. They were riddled with gender distinctions: masculine definitions of a legitimate public actor and a profusion of newly feminized symbols of political identity. The democratic constituents of the Jacksonian public were perhaps more inveterately masculine than ever. They organized primarily around male roles: the voter, the worker, the militiaman. It was around these same male roles that democrats performed their own ritual representation of the political order, the all-American parade. Formed into units of the chamber of commerce, craftsmen, labourers, Democrats, and Whigs, citizens took manly strides through the streets on 4 July and a score of annual anniversaries, giving a masculine embodiment to the diverse components of the polity. The putative universality of the public now inhered less in the civic virtue of the bourgeoisie and more in the gender characteristics of males. This more plebeian and democratic era seemed no more receptive to women than its bourgeois, republican predecessor.[11]

This new configuration of the public did draw on the female and private sphere, not for members or issues, but for a symbolic reinforcement of the legitimacy of different segments of the male public. In the 1840s the mass parties took the lead in deploying these cultural cues of political status, inviting 'the ladies' to the rallies that ratified party nominees and posing their feminine supporters as badges of their respectability. Ethnic brotherhoods were quick to employ the same tactic, mounting Goddesses of Liberty and Maids of Erin on their banners, thereby pointedly demonstrating that ethnic identity was rooted in kinship bonds and imbricated both sexes. Temperance associations, yet another segment of the urban public activated in the 1840s, were steeped in the feminized symbols that linked politics to the private sphere of sobriety and domestic tranquillity. Local political squabbles also dredged up issues from the usually private domain of sexuality. The vitriol of nativist fights in the 1850s was often churned up by images of the sexual licence of the foreign-born, which tarnished civic reputation and defiled true womanhood. Campaigns to control prostitution, which figured prominently in the rhetoric of local politics during the 1850s, were largely a smokescreen for economic interests and partisan differences. However much the Know-Nothings of New Orleans or the Vigilantes of San Francisco posed as the protectors of female purity or the bane of prostitutes, they failed to represent the interests of women citizens and declined to invite females to participate in open public debate. The increasingly elaborate feminine symbols of antebellum politics lured women closer to the public sphere, but along duplicitous, dependent, and manipulative avenues, and then only to a centre of discourse still dominated by men.[12]

At the same time the democratic expansion of publicness in the decades before the Civil War also created space in which women could politically organize in their own behalf. The first conventions of an embryonic women's rights movement date from this era but remained scattered, ad hoc, and ill-attended public affairs. Another public convention of women had earlier origins, more forceful impact on the local political scene, and more sustained organization. Female Moral Reform Societies, which garnered full publicity in north-eastern cities in the 1830s, demonstrate the possibilities and the limitations of opening a female space in a democratic public. First activated by male evangelicals who were outraged by the ugly blemishes of sexual immorality on the civic countenance, moral reform brought women flocking to public meetings early in the 1830s. Soon women took over the campaign for sexual reform, transposed its political agenda into a woman's crusade, and even succeeded in changing the law as well as public opinion. Construing sexual immorality as acts of male seduction, New York's Female Moral Reform Society pushed through a state statute that inflicted stiff fines or jail sentences on men guilty of these private transgressions.[13]

Despite this success in the heart of the public sector, female moral reform was buffeted by a contrary political wind, wafting in the direction of privacy. Before 1850 female moral reformers had left the public stage to practise their campaign of purification in more secluded domains. They worked away from the spotlight of newspaper publicity and public meetings in the quieter female vistas of the church and family visits, and in their own private institutions for the rehabilitation of prostitutes. Most crucially, they came to rest their hopes for moral regeneration not on public action but in the ministrations of women to their children and husbands in the privacy of their homes. Soon the organ of their movement was converted into a general mothers' magazine, trafficking in advice on how to rear sons to more exacting standards of sexual purity.

The retreat of female reformers was typical of the more secluded channels favoured by women social activists during the antebellum period. While menfolk flocked to public meetings, American women, especially of the urban middle classes, worked just as frantically to infuse the home with social functions, giving new definition to the border between public and private life. In the antebellum years, republican motherhood became inflated into what one writer called the 'empire of the mother'. The maternal role of socializing citizens was codified into an exacting profession, accorded its own literary channel of communication in women's magazines, and touted as an extensive sphere of female influence. By popularizing the notion of a separate female sphere of discourse and social practice, the antebellum cult of domesticity distanced vital civic concerns, as well as issues of specific interest to women, from the world of open public debate.[14]

Antebellum middle-class privacy was more than the residue of the public; it expanded and engendered a realm that bourgeois political theory regarded as the uncontaminated wellspring of civic virtue. The centrifugal force that an expanded private domain exerted on the public sphere was powerful enough by mid-century to generate platitudinous formulations of the relation between the public and private, to wit, the assertion that private virtue is the fountainhead of public order. One newspaper editor declared that the family was 'the foundation of public morality and intelligence'. Another wrote, 'If all is right in the private domain, we need not be concerned for the public.' Yet another editor cast the symbiotic relationship between public and private in liberal economistic terms by defining the public as an 'aggregation of our personal obligations'. As the ideal of the public good dissolved into these popular platitudes, the middle-class residents of the city were observed retreating from public spaces, vacating the streets, squares, and public halls for their homes and offices.[15]

The democratic public space of antebellum America was situated in a complicated and shifting civic geography. Even as the open spaces of the city were populated by a more diverse and active constituency, an equally robust private sphere grew up and exerted a gravitational pull away from the public. The force of that pull did not stem just from the splintering of the public into specialized interest groups but also grew up along an axis of gender. It was women—excluded, silenced, or shouted down in the public, democratic, and male-dominated spaces—who carved out another space in which to invest psychic, social, and political energies. If social life was divided between male and female, public and private, the history enacted on each side of that shifting border was deeply politicized and intricately interrelated. Indeed, as early as the midpoint of the last century the elaboration of private space had begun to eat away at the commonweal.

CIVIL WAR AND THE MODERN STATE

This pattern of public life had been set in place at a time when the American state was relatively weak and functioned in the unobtrusive ways of the courts and local governments. All this was to change in the 1860s, as signified by the Civil War, which recast civil society into two militarized sections. During the war the municipality of New York witnessed the power of the state with especial force. Resistance to military conscription brought the Union Army into the streets firing on civilians and mounting howitzers on public buildings. In the southern city of New Orleans the power of the state intruded into everyday life when the Union Army marched into the municipality and set up a government, which would endure for over a decade. The victorious Yankees legislated everything from public health to public assembly. The growing size of urban populations throughout the nation (New York surpassed the million mark) necessitated the expansion of public services and the recourse to more bureaucratic methods of public administration. The city manuals of the late nineteenth century ran on for pages, listing the departments and commissions of municipal government along with their appointed, rather than elected, officers. Cities also increasingly lost local autonomy—a process typified by the creation of metropolitan police districts whose commissioners were selected by the governor rather than the mayor or city council.

The transformation of government procedures transpired within a shifting economic context. The expanding industrial sector was now the largest employer in most cities, and it was organized on a national scale of finance, production, and distribution. In the 1870s the railroads became the staging-ground for the most tumultuous display of the new class configurations of industrial America. The rash of strikes by railroad workers in 1877 converted the public life of American cities into a violent clash between capital and labour. At this point Habermas's concept of welfare-state mass democracy begins to bear some resemblance to American historical development. The major interests, labour and capital, squared off against each other against a background of mass political parties, which, by the late nineteenth century, had perfected rituals of popular acclamation, had diluted the politics of substantive issues, and continued to generate a huge popular vote. The zenith of national electoral politics was not a convention of the public sphere but a 'monster mass meeting' on the eve of the election.[16]

The monster mass meeting was but one linguistic marker of the new modes of convening the public under industrial capitalism. Calls to 'Mass Union Meetings', 'Monster Torchlight Parades', 'Spontaneous Congregations of the Working Class', 'People's Mass Meetings', 'Public Political Demonstrations', and 'Citizens' Mass Meetings' all evoked the rising scale and impersonality of mass politics. Behind these wide-open invitations to political rallies and the gargantuan size of outdoor meetings (with audiences of up to 50,000) stood more bureaucratic methods of convening the public. The biggest rallies were 'Ratification Meetings', called to rubber-stamp the nominee chosen by committees or conventions. As befitting this less public, more bureaucratic style of politics, the term 'committee' became ubiquitous in the language of politics. Californians were invited to assemble under the instructions of the 'executive committee of the people' or the 'popular nominating committee of one hundred'.

None the less, a crazy quilt of social groups continued to make their way around and through mass politics and into public prominence and public space. The parties were cross-hatched by motley lines of class and ethnicity; merchants and workers alike paraded as the public; and alternate and selective groups mobilized around specific issues, pretending to represent the 'sovereign will of the people'. The demographic overlay of public space assumed a slightly different shape during and after the Civil War. Newspapers recorded how the lower classes commandeered a larger, more aggressive, and self-conscious place in open public spaces. Tompkins Square in New York became a congregating point for the unemployed and the trade unions, while the streets of the East Side were regularly filled with parades of striking workers. In San Francisco through the 1860s and 1870s the Workingmen's Party of California had a constant and vocal public presence, meeting thousands-strong outside city halls, organizing major public processions, and taking up reams of newspaper headlines. In occupied New Orleans, workers found public access to even the military government. For example, 5,000 marched to the headquarters of General Banks to oppose restrictions on the rights of the foreign-born among them. An estimated 200 coloured citizens were counted in this particular crowd. Civil War and Reconstruction opened up the possibility that this marginalized, recently enslaved racial group could make political use of public space. Under the sponsorship of Radical Republicans, African-Americans of New Orleans swiftly and energetically claimed their right of public assembly. The *Louisiana Tribune*, a radical reconstruction paper, enjoined African-Americans to use the streets and squares as schools of citizenship and bask in public legitimacy by displaying their hard-won political status before their former masters. They responded by congregating in public meetings, conventions, and street parades.

These public assemblies only rarely galvanized the whole of the people. The largest public gatherings were called to display sectional solidarity during the heights of wartime patriotism. Yet even the great Union and Confederate rallies staged during the war and based on this lowest common denominator of civic loyalty soon lost their lustre. The prolonged and bloody conflict led disgruntled New Yorkers to mount peace rallies, while the Union occupation of New Orleans drove rebels into a sullen retirement from public life. Only when radical reconstruction was about to end did the public life of white New Orleans rejuvenate. In 1874, claiming that 'public opinion would no longer support military rule', the former rebels reclaimed the rights of public assembly, along with the constitutional privilege of bearing arms. Thousands of white men marched on military headquarters and temporarily took the reins of local government. As the Union army finally prepared to leave the city in January 1877, New Orleanians were called to a 'Citizens' Mass Meeting' at Lafayette Square, there to 'represent the Sovereign will'. An estimated 20,000 people assembled in response to this public appeal, and stayed to celebrate the restoration of political authority to unregenerate Confederates. In this instance, like many before and after, the invocation of popular sovereignty poorly disguised the special, private, and racial interests at work; the public that gathered in Lafayette Square in 1877 was restoring white men to their customary position of dominance in civic life.[17]

Those social groups that dominated cultural and industrial production late in the nineteenth century seldom presented such a clear and public display of their power. Be it public ceremony or public meetings, parades or party rallies, the professional, financial, and industrial elites had retreated from public view after mid-century. This disappearance of the upper echelons of the public was registered by newspaper editors as the decline of public spirit among 'the best men', who were said to have ceded the commonweal to corrupt professional politicians, city bosses, and their foreign-born henchmen. In the 1870s the 'better class' became more visible in the public sphere, but on terms that diluted the former meaning of the concept. Organized for the purpose of reforming corrupt municipal government, these groups of businessmen directly challenged the political principle of openness and democracy and even called for restrictions on the franchise. While those who joined forces against the Tweed Ring in New York City called their movement a 'glorious resurrection of public virtue', they aimed to reserve public office for the 'wisest and best citizens'. [William Marcy Tweed (1823–1878), known as 'Boss' Tweed, was an American politician who headed Tammany Hall. He and the Tweed Ring of politicians became the symbols of urban political corruption.] Significantly, municipal reformers often rejected citizenship as the ground for public participation, instead issuing invitations to public meetings only to 'taxpayers', 'property holders', the 'most respectable citizens', or even 'capitalists'. The economic interest of the affluent but parsimonious taxpayer was now the measure of public virtue.[18] This vitiation of the notion of publicness was not necessarily a corruption of the bourgeois public sphere but rather a recognition of the social restrictions that had applied to this domain from the outset. The political formations of the late nineteenth century seemed only to reverse the spatial ordering, if not the power relations, of public life: the lower classes claimed open public places as the sites of political resistance, while their social superiors retreated into private recesses to exert power behind the scenes, in reform associations or bureaucratic channels.

On this reordered plane of late nineteenth-century public life, women continued to locate and exploit the political possibilities for their sex. In many ways women's public presence remained veiled and distorted by the manipulation of gender symbolism dating from antebellum political culture, which was now used to garnish the increasingly stark racial and class partitions of the public. During the war women were an honoured presence, and female symbols were prolifically displayed amid the pageantry of sectional solidarity. When white dominance was restored in the South, it was portrayed as an act of public purification, a defence of the honour of the ladies. Meanwhile, antiwar Democrats in the North raised cheers to white ladies. Both labour and capital draped their interests in female symbols. The parades of the Workingmen's Party of California mounted wives and daughters in carriages as testimony to the respectability of their membership, support of their demand for a family wage, and a countersymbol to Chinese immigration, which they pictured as a flood of bachelors and prostitutes. According to this gender logic, immigration from Asia robbed working-class women of jobs as domestic servants and bred Chinese prostitution, which was especially offensive to ladies. The upper-class opponents of the Tweed Ring in New York characterized the rapacious city politicians as simian featured Irishmen preying on a demure Miss Liberty. The stock of gender symbols had not been exhausted by the late nineteenth century, and still provided ample images with which to drape the multifarious interests that competed with one another in the male-dominated political domain.

At the same time, women could still be found congregating on their own turf and in convocations which, like those of their menfolk, were enlarged to a massive scale. Mobilization for the Civil War brought women into service provisioning Union troops. The press labelled meetings called to recruit women's sewing skills and culinary abilities as part of the war effort 'mass meetings of the ladies' and 'another mass ladies' movement'. The national organization that coordinated these efforts, the Sanitary Commission, was a well-oiled machine, producing, collecting, and distributing vital war supplies. Excused by the exigency of wartime and disguised as feminine charity, these efforts demonstrated that women could be highly effective administrators of public services.[19]

The unobtrusive but critically important public work of the Sanitary Commission was but one example of women's increasing assumption of public functions—a practice that began well before the war and flourished thereafter. Even in the days when municipalities were private corporations with tiny budgets, women had taken on themselves the responsibility of caring for dependent and impoverished classes. First founding orphan asylums and societies to care for widows, then organizing a variety of relief and charitable associations, and ultimately creating institutions that provided education, vocational training, and moral guidance to the poor, women volunteers constructed a private system of public welfare. This female sector of the urban political economy generally abided by *laissez-faire* principles and financed their benevolent operations through the proceeds of bazaars and bake sales. At the same time, female charities were less reluctant than most male politicians to seek state funding for social welfare. From early in the century and with increasing persistence and success after the Civil War, women went directly to the city council and to state legislatures, soliciting appropriations for these projects. Civic leaders and newspaper editors chivalrously acknowledged the beneficent public consequences of women's charitable work. As one San Francisco editor put it, women's unremunerated labours revealed that beneath the masculine mind of the city there beat a 'mother's heart'.

Beyond this flimsy scrim of privacy, women met a public need, saved public funds, and behaved as shrewd politicians. Their parlours and churches were the perfume-filled backrooms of gender politics where women established policy concerning the practice of social welfare without being subject to public scrutiny. Their method of ministering to the needy was never subjected to open discussion, and as a consequence flowed through class and ethnic hierarchies as a condescending, restrictive, and niggardly distribution of alms and advice. Rather than operating in a spirit of open, public largesse, female charities were a closed welfare system

213

extending only from middle-class, usually Protestant matrons to those they deemed the 'worthy poor'. Like the welfare state of the twentieth century, this extensive sphere of female municipal service was bureaucratically organized, lobbied to garner state funds for its selective purposes, and carved out a sphere of hierarchical relations with a dependent class. Once again, behind a veil of privacy and femininity, women navigated a political history deeply imbricated in the transformation of the public sphere.[20]

Although women's charitable and reform associations were especially solicitous about the welfare of their own sex, their efforts were as much an outgrowth of the class position they shared with their husbands, as an extension of their gender roles. Before 1880, moreover, their activities seldom generated a challenge to sexual inequality itself. Other, smaller bands of women activists did position themselves in or near public spaces, where their own gender interests and identity became more visible. One such strategic location was an early confrontation with a particularly aggressive arm of the welfare state bureaucracy, the board of public health. After the Civil War, members of the medical profession flexed their political muscles to create public health agencies at the municipal, state, and national levels. One of their earliest routes toward public power was by way of gender politics through the regulation of prostitution. In the 1860s and 1870s, public health officials across the country hoped to stem the growth of venereal disease by subjecting prostitutes to compulsory medical examinations and hospitalization.[21]

This offensive of the bureaucratic state was promptly squelched by a group of women who entered the public sector to defend these least reputable members of their sex. The female politicians who opposed the regulation of prostitution in New York and San Francisco used every political force they could muster to resist this legislation, which, as they saw it, legitimated the traffic in women, institutionalized the double standard, and constituted state intrusion into the private lives of the second sex. The techniques they deployed were various, ingenious, and indicative of the many ways in which some intrepid women found access to the public affairs of industrial capitalism. Occasionally they held public meetings calculated to influence public opinion on the subject. At other times they directly petitioned the state legislature and appeared at city council meetings, arguing their position. In other circumstances they chose to use the private techniques of lobbying legislatures and capitalizing on their personal contacts among public officials.

They even opened an office in Washington to monitor developments in the nation's capital. Nor were these wily politicians above deploying the established codes of gender politics to their own ends. They alternately used the threat of publicity and the mantle of female privacy to affect public opinion. The most notable leader of the campaign against prostitution regulation, Susan B. Anthony, reputedly blackmailed a New York official by threatening to open the whole unseemly question of sexuality to public scrutiny, should New York legislators permit this practice. In keeping with the Victorian moral code, female sex reformers of the 1870s used the stereotype of pure womanhood as a point of personal privilege in the matter of prostitution legislation. In the 1870s, even as public politics began to corrode into state bureaucracy, the private sex found an arsenal of weapons and an array of avenues through which to influence public policy.[22]

FEMINISM IN THE PUBLIC SPHERE

Such public access put women in a position to ponder their own political identity and to formulate the claims of their sex on the public good. In political skirmishes like the campaign against prostitution legislation, some women even forged an ad hoc gender identity that bridged class divisions. Still, the politics of prostitution, like female moral reform, was but one rather prickly way to generate gender identity. It placed the woman citizen in a defensive position and identified her by her sexual and reproductive biology. To contemporary feminists, this is an invitation to essentialism and a narrow base on which to mount gender politics. Fortunately, at the time of the anti-prostitution campaign, women were also assembling in the public sphere on an altogether broader and more radical principle, that of women's rights. The women's rights conventions first convened in 1848 and meeting irregularly through the next decade did not cohere as a national and sustained organization until the Civil War. The National Loyal Women's League and subsequently the Equal Rights Association, both headquartered in New York and presided over by Elizabeth Cady Stanton, were the crucible of an independent women's movement that would appropriate the ideal of the public sphere for the second sex.

The Loyal Women's League was founded as an appendage of the anti-slavery movement with the specific goal of pushing the Lincoln administration toward emancipating the slaves. Its postwar, post-emancipation sequel, the Equal Rights Association, championed the civil and political liberties of African-Americans. At the very first meeting of the LWL, however, Stanton and her partner in feminism, Susan B. Anthony, placed women's public interest on the same agenda, forcing through a resolution in favour of women's suffrage. In a now familiar story, the alliance between African-Americans and women was broken when the 'negro first' policy of Radical Republicans secured suffrage and the privileges of citizenship for African-American men and simultaneously wrote a gender restriction into the Constitution. Stanton and Anthony promptly founded a national association for the single and explicit purpose of securing the rights of women. Stanton, Anthony, and their colleagues across the country decided forthwith to form a women's suffrage association and to build their politics on the solid, independent base of their own gender position. As this autonomous public, the women's rights movement proceeded to identify a broad agenda of gender issues for black and white women, not just suffrage but also marriage reform, equal pay, sexual freedom, and reproductive rights.[23]

For veteran politicians like Stanton, the time had come to purge the public sphere of gender distinctions. She turned to the Republican tradition, 'the birth right of the revolution', and 'the rights of man' to legitimate women's direct assault on the public sphere. But Stanton had learned through more than thirty years' experience in every sector of politics open to her sex that to win rights for those who occupied the social position of women required the explicit acknowledgement of gender difference. Only by taking up a political position explicitly as feminists, rather than trusting in formal commitments to abstract principles of public discourse, could women escape from the obfuscation, occlusion, and manipulation that had hitherto characterized their place in American public life. From this position Stanton slightly but critically revised the concept of the public handed down by her forefathers. Her goal was that 'government may be republican in fact as well as form; a government by the people, and the whole people; for the people and the whole people'. To Stanton, the whole was made up of separate parts, and especially excluded populations like African-Americans and women. Stanton was still a lonely voice in the American public, still likely to be ridiculed in the public press, and

scarcely heard in the citadels of power. But at a time when public ideology and deep-rooted social structures sentenced women
to privacy, she had taken a critical step toward the longest yet
incomplete revolution.[24]

Even at a time when the public was supposedly in decline and
as avenues to power seemed to narrow, women like Stanton laid
claim to a public space for their sex. Late in the nineteenth century, in the face of a more powerful state apparatus and amid the
cacophony of mass politics, women had found multiple points of
access to the public. They won state funds for their private welfare
schemes, lobbied for their sex-specific interests, and prohibited
state bureaucracies from trampling on the liberties of their sex.
By occupying these scattered public places, nineteenth-century
women worked out their own political identities, opened up the
public to a vast new constituency, and enlarged the range of issues
that weighed into the 'general interest'.

These peregrinations through gender politics are but one illustration of the transformation of American public life that progressed outside the bourgeois public sphere during the nineteenth
century. Much of this critical history was located in democratic
public spaces, at proliferating points of access to political discussion where established authority could be challenged. Whether the
occupants of these dispersed public spaces were working men,
immigrants, African-Americans, or women, each fought their way
into the public from a distinctive position in civil society, usually
a place of political marginality and social injustice. Like the bourgeoisie before them, these social groups gave definition to their
own particular stakes in the public interest as they expanded the
domain of the public. The imperfect public they constituted was
grounded in a historical construction and political articulation of
diverse, malleable, and separate identities and interests. In a complex and far from egalitarian society like the nineteenth-century
United States, this method of broadening access to public space
proved to be the vehicle for democratizing public discourse and
public policy.

Women's politics is a powerful example of this democratizing process and a critical index of publicness. Gender restrictions
patently contradicted public ideology and had built exclusion into
the very foundation of the public sphere. Denied public, formal,
and direct legitimacy, gender issues found their way into politics
in corrupted forms, like the cloying feminine symbols used in electoral campaigns or the periodic, partisan-inspired crackdowns on

217

prostitution. Denied admission to the public sphere directly and in their own right, women found circuitous routes to public influence. The ways women manoeuvred around the gender restrictions of the public are stocked with meaning for those who cherish the public. As sex reformers, for example, women exposed the fictions of privacy on which the segregation of gender and politics was supposedly based, while female-run charities built up a private system of meeting public needs that presaged the welfare state and some of its more anti-democratic features. Before 1880 it was only a small group of women's rights advocates who saw through all the obfuscations and contradictions of this largely clandestine gender politics and made their claim for full citizenship in the public sphere. Yet the tenacious efforts of women to subvert these restrictions and to be heard in public testify to the power of public ideals, that persistent impulse to have a voice in some space open and accessible to all where they could be counted in the general interest.

Each of the many ways whereby nineteenth-century women became political tells us something important about that privileged space called the public sphere. I will suggest just a few implications we might draw from the experience of our foremothers. First, the public as read through women's history spotlights the simple colloquial meaning of 'public', that of open access to the political sphere. The women's politics of the last century warns against a spatial or conceptual closure that constrains the ideal of the public to a bounded sphere with a priori rules about appropriate behaviour therein. Feminists and female citizens played for high stakes in a real world of politics, and would find far more comfort in a plural and decentred concept of the public.

Second, women's assiduous efforts to win and exercise the right of public access is an example of the practical ways in which the public ideal has maintained its resilience over time, that is, through a progressive incorporation of once-marginalized groups into the public sphere. As long as the distributive issues of justice remain unachieved civic goals, this proliferation of publics is a particularly significant measure of the public wellbeing. Furthermore, as Andrew Arato and Jean Cohen have pointed out, demands for public access by once marginalized groups or insurgent social movements serve over time to accumulate and expand the rights of all citizens.[25]

Third, the history of women in and on the way to the public sphere suggests that the notions of interest and identity need not be antithetical to the public good. From the vantage-point of women's history, the identification of a political interest of one's own was not a fall from public virtue but a step toward empowerment. Because the second sex, like many marginalized populations, was socially dependent on their politically dominant superiors, their empowerment necessitated the construction of a separate identity and the assertion of self-interest. In practice, inclusive representation, open confrontation, and full articulation of social and historical differences are as essential to the public as is a standard of rational and disinterested discourse.

Finally, the history of women in public challenges us to listen carefully and respectfully for the voices of those who have long been banished from the formal public sphere and polite public discourse. Those most remote from public authorities and governmental institutions and least versed in their language sometimes resort to shrill tones, civil disobedience, and even violent acts in order to make themselves heard. Therefore, my chronicle would not be complete without reference to those women least likely to find a voice in the formal public sphere and those most likely, therefore, to express their interests in loud, coarse, and, yes, abrasive ways. These women citizens are represented by the participants in the New York Draft Riots of 1863. The women rioters, mostly poor Irish-Americans, were found looting businesses, physically assaulting policemen, helping to set the Colored Orphan Asylum afire, and committing ugly, violent acts on the corpses of their adversaries. There was no civility, virtue, or logic in their political acts, yet their grievances against a draft policy that exacted an excessive cost of war from their class and sex were both just and reasoned, if tragically misdirected. However we draw the normative or procedural boundaries of the public sphere, they must be permeable to even distorted voices of people like these, many of whom still remain outside its reach.

These stray morals of my story might be drawn together in a simple public sentiment. Because everyday politics inevitably falls short of standards of perfect rational discourse, a chimera even in the heyday of the bourgeois public sphere, the goal of publicness might best be allowed to navigate through wider and wilder territory. That is, public life can be cultivated in many democratic spaces where obstinate differences in power, material status, and hence interest can find expression. The proliferation of democratic publics that posed a major counter-force to the escalating dominance of the state and capitalism in the nineteenth-century United

States is carried forward in our own time by feminist movements. The movement of women into the public is a quantum leap in our public life; it both expands membership in the public and articulates vital aspects of the general interest that have hitherto been buried in gender restrictions and disguised as privacy. In the late twentieth century, women's historically problematic relationship to the public has become transformed into a public asset, both a practical and theoretical boon to the utopian aspirations that Jürgen Habermas set before us twenty-five years ago.

Notes

1. Michelle Zimbalist Rosaldo, 'Women, Culture, and Society: A Theoretical Overview', in Rosaldo and Louise Lamphere (eds.), *Women, Culture and Society* (Stanford, 1974), 17–42.
2. For recent examples, see Carole Pateman, *The Sexual Contract* (Stanford, 1988); Susan Moller Okin, *Justice, Gender, and the Family* (New York, 1989); Nancy Fraser, *Unruly Practices* (Minneapolis, 1989).
3. Joan B. Landes, *Women and the Public Sphere in the Age of the French Revolution* (Ithaca, NY, 1988); Anna Yeatman, 'Gender and the Differentiation of Social Life into Public and Domestic Domains', *Social Analysis: Journal of Cultural and Social Practices*, 15 (1984): 32–49; Leonore Davidoff and Catherine Hall, *Family Fortunes* (Chicago, 1987), ch. 10.
4. See e.g. Nancy Fraser, 'What's Critical about Critical Theory? The Case of Habermas and Gender', *New German Critique* (1985): 97–133; Iris Marion Young, 'Impartiality and the Civic Public: Some Implications of Feminist Critiques of Moral and Political Theory', in Seyla Benhabib and Drucilla Cornell (eds.), *Feminism as Critique* (Minneapolis, 1987); Pateman, *The Sexual Contract*.
5. Stephen Skowronek, *Building a New American State* (Cambridge, 1982).
6. See Mary P. Ryan, *Women in Public: Between Banners and Ballots* (Baltimore, 1990); Hendrik Hartog, *Public Property and Private Power: The Corporation of the City of New York in American Law, 1730–1870* (Chapel Hill, NC, 1983); Jon C. Teaborg, *The Municipal Revolution in America: Origins of Urban Government, 1650–1825* (Chicago, 1975).
7. Hanna Fenichel Pitkin, *Fortune Is a Woman: Gender and Politics in the Thought of Niccolo Machiavelli* (Berkeley, Calif., 1984); Ruth Bloch, 'Gender and the Meaning of Virtue in Revolutionary America', *Signs*, 13/1 (Aug. 1987): 37–58.

8. For examples of public meetings, see *New York Evening Post*, 2 July 1827, 28 Mar., 5 Apr. 1834; *New Orleans Daily Picayune*, 22, 27 Nov. 1837; *Daily Alta California*, 15 Feb. 1849.

9. R. A. Burchell, *The San Francisco Irish, 1848–1880* (Berkeley, Calif., 1980), 117–32; *Daily Alta California*, 24 May 1855.

10. Celia Morris Eckhardt, *Fanny Wright, Rebel in America* (Cambridge, 1984), 258–67; Leonard Richards, *Gentlemen of Property and Standing* (New York, 1970), 110–35; *New York Tribune*, 11 Nov. 1857.

11. Mary P. Ryan, 'The American Parade: Representations of the Nineteenth Century Social Order', in Lynn Hunt (ed.), *The New Cultural History* (Berkeley, Calif., 1988), 131–53.

12. Richard Tansey, 'Prostitution and Politics in Antebellum New Orleans', *Southern Studies*, 18 (1979): 449–79; James F. Richardson, 'Fernando Wood and the New York Police Force, 1855–57', *New York History*, 1 (1965): 5–54; Jacqueline Baker Barnhart, *The Fair but Frail: Prostitution in San Francisco, 1849–1900* (Reno, Nev., 1986).

13. Carroll Smith-Rosenberg, *Disorderly Conduct: Visions of Gender in Victorian America* (New York, 1985); Barbara Meil Hobson, *Uneasy Virtue: The Politics of Prostitution and the American Reform Tradition* (New York, 1987).

14. Anne Douglas, *The Feminization of American Culture* (New York, 1979); Gillian Brown, *Domestic Individualism* (Berkeley, Calif., 1991); Mary P. Ryan, *The Empire of the Mother* (New York, 1981).

15. *New York Tribune*, 25 Dec. 1844; Edward Crapsey, *The Netherside of New York* (Montclair, NJ, 1969, repr. of 1872 edn.), preface, pp. 9, 120; Revd E. H. Chapin, *Humanity in the City* (New York, 1854), 11–45.

16. Michael McGerr, *The Decline of Popular Politics* (New York, 1986).

17. *New Orleans Picayune*, 6 Apr. 1877.

18. *New York Herald*, 29 Oct. 1875; Crapsey, *The Netherside of New York*; *New Orleans Picayune*, Mar. 1877; *San Francisco Examiner*, 21 Oct. 1875.

19. *New York Herald*, 30 Apr. 1861; *New York Times*, 1 May 1861.

20. Suzanne Lebsock, *The Free Women of Petersberg: Status and Culture in a Southern Town, 1784–1860* (New York, 1984), ch. 7; Nancy Hewitt, *Women, Activism and Social Change: Rochester, 1822–1872* (Ithaca, NY, 1984); Mary P. Ryan, *Cradle of the Middle Class: The Family in Oneida County, New York, 1790–1865* (Cambridge, 1981), 210–18; Michael Katz, *The Undeserving Poor: From the War on Poverty to the War on Welfare* (New York, 1989); Paula Baker, 'The Domestication of Politics: Women and American Political Society, 1780–1920', *American Historical Review*, 89 (1984): 620–47.

21. John Duffy, *A History of Public Health in New York City, 1625–1866* (New York, 1968); David Pivar, *Purity Crusade: Sexual Morality and Social Control, 1868–1900* (West port, Conn., 1873).

22. See Mary P. Ryan, *Women in Public: Between Banners and Ballots, 1825–1880* (Baltimore, 1990), 122–7.
23. Ellen Carol DuBois, *Feminism and Suffrage: The Emergence of an Independent Women's Movement in America, 1848–1869* (Ithaca, NY, 1978).
24. Stanton, quoted in Nanette Paul, *The Great Woman Statesman* (New York, 1925), 63–4.
25. Andrew Arato and Jean Cohen, 'Civil Society and Social Theory', *Thesis Eleven*, 21 (1988): 40–64.

The Inviolable Woman: Feminist Conceptions of Citizenship in Australia, 1900–1945

Marilyn Lake

The meaning of citizenship is currently attracting renewed attention around the world. At the same time that people are identifying new democratic possibilities in a revitalized citizenship, however, feminists have been pointing both to the masculinist terms in which citizenship has been conceptualized and to women's effective exclusion, in practice, from the basic citizen's right of self-government in Western democracies.[1] These theoretical and practical issues are, of course, related. The assumed autonomy of the citizen, for example, rested on the understanding that someone else was responsible for domestic work and the maintenance of everyday life.[2] To participate fully as active citizens in public life, women have had to emulate men's condition of freedom from private constraints and domestic responsibilities. Comparatively few have been willing and able to do so, and one result is that women everywhere are dramatically under-represented in political institutions. Both the discourse and practice of citizenship, feminist scholars have concluded, are profoundly gendered activities.

Women have in past times, nevertheless, placed great faith in the emancipatory possibilities of the status of citizen. Although there has been much work by feminists on masculine definitions of citizenship, there has been little investigation of the ways in which feminist citizens in past times have conceptualized this status. This article explores the promise of citizenship as it was identified and conceptualized by the first women citizens in the world to be granted full political rights, that is, the right to vote and stand for election to their national parliament. White Australian women were granted these entitlements in 1902, just one year after the inauguration of the Commonwealth of Australia as a nation-state.

Reprinted by permission from *Gender and History*, 8/2 (August 1996), 197–211. Copyright © Blackwell Publishers Ltd (1996).

Australian feminists entered into prolonged debate in the post-suffrage decades about the meaning and possibilities of citizenship for women. They took their citizenship seriously, and formed numerous feminist organizations specifically to pursue a 'real' equality of status, reward and opportunity.

In many ways the post-suffrage decades were, in Australia, a golden age of feminist citizenship. The popular (US-derived) idea of 'two waves' of feminist activity, punctuated by a long lull in between, is distinctly misleading here. In the post-suffrage decades women's rights and reform organizations proliferated, and the feminist as amateur politician or activist citizen came into her own. Women's modes of doing politics usually involved an espousal of the non-party ideal in organizations such as the Women's Political Educational League (WPEL), the Women's Political Association (WPA), the Feminist Club, the Woman's Christian Temperance Union (WCTU), the Women's Service Guild (WSG), the Australian Federation of Women Voters (AFWV), the Victorian Women's Citizens' Movement, the Women's Non-Party Association of South Australia, and the United Associations of Women (UAW). Feminists were often supported in their campaigns by women in the trade union and labour movement who decried the oppression of women but were wary of sporting the feminist label. Feminist activists elaborated distinctively feminist theories of citizenship which are still relevant to the task of developing 'woman-friendly' versions of citizenship today. As in neighbouring New Zealand, as Barbara Brooks has written, 'for the activists in the women's movement, the franchise was a beginning rather than an end. The vote was a first step in a wider feminist agenda, which sought to bring equality between the sexes by challenging male prerogatives, one of which was male access to women's bodies.'[3]

The significance and difference of the feminist post-suffrage contribution to the theorization of citizenship has not yet been given recognition in historical scholarship. In explicating the Australian contribution, I wish to suggest that it is important to recognize that conceptions of citizenship have not only been gendered but profoundly embodied articulations, grounded in historically and sexually specific social experience. This is an article about bodies and politics. It shares the feminist assumption that for a revitalized citizenship to be meaningful to women we need to give renewed attention to the body in the body politic, to the ways in which citizens act as sexed embodied subjects.[4] I first elaborate the ways in which these pioneering women citizens conceptualized the promise of citizenship as self-possession and self-government, a realization of the vision of women as 'mistresses of themselves'.[5] In the second section, I argue for the importance of a theoretical perspective that grounds political subjectivities and thus political history in experiences of sexed embodiment.

For these feminist citizens the paradigmatic woman was still the prostitute, reduced to and defined by her sex, her degradation made possible by her economic dependence. The woman citizen's 'use of [the] vote', Rose Scott, president of the WPEL, wrote to her friend, the novelist Miles Franklin, would work to elevate 'our deeply degraded sex'. Long ago, Scott added, 'I learned that to most men women are women, not human beings—women of their use and pleasure'.[6] The situation of the wife was understood in terms of her similarity to the prostitute; hence the preoccupation amongst post-suffrage feminists with achieving the 'economic independence of the married woman'. In a 1903 lecture on this subject to the newly formed New South Wales post-suffrage organization, the Women's Political Educational League, Scott observed that 'many women submitted to the most degrading and tyrannical conditions, because they and their children were economically dependent upon their husbands, being compelled thereby to sacrifice very much of their self-respect'.[7]

Post-suffrage feminism was animated by a vision of the woman citizen's inviolability. Hence the crusade against vice, the central demand of raising the age of consent, the alarms about white slavery, the insistence that women be appointed to all public offices charged with the welfare of women and girls, campaigns to censor films, the opposition to the regulation of prostitution and venereal disease, claims for the rights and sovereignty of mothers, the campaign to achieve the economic independence of all women, the efforts to rescue Aboriginal women and girls from the routine sexual abuse perpetrated by men, both black and white. And hence, too, Rose Scott's opposition to mixed bathing. In 1912 she resigned her presidency of the New South Wales' Amateur Swimming Association because of its decision to admit men as spectators at women's carnivals. For Scott, the invitation to men to 'stare' at women, the positioning of women as spectacles, represented a further violation of women's bodily integrity.[8] Most of these concerns and objectives represented a continuation of nineteenth-century feminist preoccupations, with the important difference that the advent of citizenship and Australian feminists' close identification with the new nation-state encouraged them to formulate their claims as claims on the State, as the rights now owed to women in their identity as citizens, in their new relationship as individuals with the State.

Male theorists of citizenship have tended to define its rights and duties in terms that assume an engagement with society by active, masculine, able-bodied subjects, who take for granted a certain self-possession, independence, physical mastery, and self-determination. In Australia, male citizens were expected to be available to serve in industry at home and the military abroad. 'The three basic duties of a citizen', declared the nationalist journal *Lone Hand* in 1920, 'are to contribute to the population, the defence and the finances of his country.'[9] The latter two occupations were assumed to be masculine responsibilities; the former feminine obligation, the paper argued, needed further government support. Masculine conceptions of citizenship assume the capacity of mobile individuals to act in and on the world. Their charters demand freedom from constraint and from arbitrary arrest, for example. As Hilary Charlesworth has written, 'the primacy traditionally given to civil and political rights by western international lawyers and philosophers is directed towards protection for men in public life, their relationship with government. But these are not the harms from which women most need protection.'[10] Social democrats have posited social and civil rights, such as unemployment benefits, to substantiate their political rights.[11] Male citizens have expected the state to facilitate men's engagement in public life (by instituting payment of Members of Parliament, for example), while resisting interference with their assumed authority in the private domain, an interference seen in feminist demands that men be forced to share their wages with their wives. A contradiction emerged in these decades between men's citizen rights (which included conjugal rights) and women's rights as citizens which were understood to guarantee inviolability and individuality.

Women citizens, in the post-suffrage decades in Australia, demanded that the state make good its promise of individuality, interpreted as personal and bodily integrity. Women's dependent status had rendered them 'sex slaves', subject to male control and bodily violation, whether in the streets or at home, in prostitution or marriage. Bodily violation also rendered women vulnerable to disease and unwanted pregnancies. The independence promised by citizenship would eliminate, so they hoped, the need of women to sell their sex, 'in marriage or out of it'.[12] At a special conference convened in 1936 by the national citizens' organization, the Australian Federation of Women Voters, to discuss the 'Equal Moral Standard', it was resolved that 'in view of the relationship to the question of prostitution, every effort be made to render every woman economically independent'.[13] As economic dependents, wives also lacked self-possession and self-government. They were utterly dependent on men's generosity. In a radio talk on behalf of the United Association of Women entitled 'The Fruit of Her Hands', Muriel Cheyne announced: 'A man who controls a woman's purse controls her actions and consequently her essential freedom as a citizen.' She added: 'To know that the average housewife has such a sword of Damocles hanging over her lessens the effect of those who preach so fervently of the Liberty of the Individual.'[14] Feminists believed that the rights of citizenship were incompatible with women's status as wives.

In a letter to Prime Minister John Curtin in 1941, the UAW observed: 'women's organisations the world over for the last hundred years have been working for the legal recognition of the individual and independent status of women.'[15] In women's new relationship with the nation-state as individuals, then, post-suffrage feminists identified a vehicle of escape from their old status as appendage, chattel, sex slave, and wife. In the post-suffrage years they looked to the state to give substance to their new civic status. The mother of a family had 'a status in her own home', said Mary Perry of the Housewives' Association of New South Wales, but 'she had no status with the state; the state does not give her any consideration for bearing a family.'[16] The state was called upon to recognize her status as an individual citizen by paying her for (maternal) services rendered, just as it paid men for military service. Thus did Labor women welcome the introduction of the Maternity Allowance in 1912, for which they had lobbied, as an 'instalment of the mothers' maternal rights'.[17]

As citizens, feminists stressed the sanctity of their persons in arguments that led them to interrogate the position of the wife and the institution of marriage. In addressing the prevalence of venereal disease in 1914, Vida Goldstein of the WPA, writing in the significantly named *Women Voter*, took issue with the medical profession's support of 'early marriage' as a preventative measure. 'Boiled down to bald conclusions it means that women are still to be regarded primarily as sex creatures: they are to be on hand in numbers . . . to be chosen by men as sex mates . . . as outlets for the sexual impulses and alleged needs of men'.[18] In feminist discourse the citizen stood in opposition to the slave, specifically the 'sex slave'. In a world of individual self-possessing citizens the married women was an anomalous figure. 'The economic dependence of woman on man is sex slavery—the only slavery that exists today,' affirmed the Communist activist, Nelle Rickie, in 1924.[19] And twenty years later Mrs R. R. Doyle, in a radio broadcast on behalf of the non-party feminist organization, the UAW, repeated that the 'only legal bondage' evident in modern democracies was the 'bond of marriage'.[20] The wife's continuing condition of bondage was rendered inescapable by her continuing condition of economic dependence. Her status as citizen was invoked to justify feminist claims on the state for both the economic independence of the married woman and recognition of women's bodily integrity. The autonomy of wives was a central goal of feminist citizens' activism.

Married women in Australia had been granted rights to own property in the decades preceding their enfranchisement, but they did not have equivalent rights over their bodies. Even though enjoying the status of individual citizens, wives were still subject to their husbands' exercise of 'conjugal rights'. Not until the 1980s did 'rape in marriage' legislation, enacted in Australia on a state-by-state basis, finally end the legal obligation of wives to surrender their bodies to their husbands. In earlier post-suffrage decades men could and did go to court to have their rights of access to their fellow citizens' bodies enforced. Refusal of sexual intercourse was grounds for divorce. In one extraordinary case in Tasmania in the 1940s, a woman challenged conventional understanding of the marriage contract by agreeing to return to her husband only on certain written terms, which included that she not be 'required to live with her husband as his wife'. Her husband persisted with his requests for sexual intercourse, his wife refused, and in 1946 the frustrated husband filed a petition in the Hobart Supreme Court for the dissolution of his marriage on the ground that from the month of October 1942, his wife wilfully and unjustifiably refused to permit him to have sexual intercourse. At the trial, evidence was given that his wife was very resentful of her second pregnancy and even more so of her third. After the third child was born about March 1941, she told her husband he would have to go without sexual intercourse for eighteen months as a punishment for causing her to become pregnant. Intercourse then stopped and was not resumed until July 1942. Thereafter, it continued until October when the wife refused to permit it further. It had been refused since, notwithstanding repeated requests by her husband. The petition for divorce was dismissed because of the husband's consent to the new contract.[21]

In the same year Jessie Street, a leading New South Wales feminist and founding member of the UAW, received a letter from Lilian Watson, a married woman living in Hunters Hill, who sought Street's support in her effort to retain household savings being claimed by her estranged husband. The letter contained an account of her brief wedded life. She had only been married a short time when her husband had been called up for military service and sent to New Guinea. When he left, she moved in with her parents. On his return twenty months later, she attempted to fulfil her conjugal obligations:

I was prepared to and did give him all the love and understanding as a wife should. I became pregnant during September 1944 and many a time I was made so distressed and unhappy by his conduct . . . I was forced by his attitude to ask him to remain in camp until our baby was born. When he saw me after our baby's birth . . . I asked him to remain away a little longer until I regained my strength. Our baby was born on 21st June 1945. A few weeks after, I got a terrible shock having served on me a petition for restitution of conjugal rights, claiming in the petition that I had withdrawn from him and ceased to cohabit with him . . . I did not defend the suit, nor comply with the Court's order to 'return' to him and I am not being maintained by him.

In detailing her plight to Street, she implored, 'surely there is a woman's movement for the protection of wives'.[22]

In her letter, Lilian Watson made clear the connection between the two factors that conventionally defined the meaning of marriage for a woman: that in return for a husband's maintenance, a wife made herself available for sexual intercourse. It was this exchange that was so offensive to feminists, who argued relentlessly in the post-suffrage decades that the state should make provision for married women's right to economic independence as a basis for their personal independence and freedom. As Lilian Watson did not respond to her husband's claim for the 'restitution of conjugal rights', he was able to obtain a quick divorce. Moves to have the Married Women's Property Act reformed to allow wives ownership of domestic savings were resisted by Labor men, who thought the government should 'keep out of the domestic life of citizens'.[23] But it was precisely the domestic life of citizens that was feminists' concern.

Feminists believed that women's rights of citizenship were incompatible with their treatment as 'creatures of sex' and that, so long as men assumed a right of access to women's bodies, women could never enjoy an equal political status. In Australian feminist discourse prior to the 1960s, sexuality was 'licensed or unlicensed vice', associated with disease, immorality, and women's degradation. Thus the feminist organizations formed in this period to achieve full citizenship status for women and a 'real' equality of opportunities, such as the Australian Federation of Women Voters, the United Associations of Women, and the London-based British Commonwealth League (BCL), proclaimed 'an equal moral standard for men and women' as a key objective. The three articles of policy adopted by the AFWV were that the Federation be non-party and non-sectarian, that it promote equality of opportunity, status, and reward, and that it uphold an 'equal moral standard for men and women'. In 1936, the Federation reiterated its resolve that 'the same high moral standard based on respect for human personality . . . be established for both sexes'.[24]

'Self-control' and 'purity' in sexual relations were thus considered to constitute the very preconditions of equal citizenship. As Rose Scott insisted, 'we cannot have too much modesty, refinement and delicacy in relations between men and women'.[25] The problem was that in modern society the 'sex passion' seemed to be intensifying. Everywhere women were confronted with the 'vices of the over-sexed males of today', but the contagion was also spreading to women.[26] 'I am not suggesting for one moment that anything like a large percentage of women are sharing in promiscuous or illicit relations,' a BCL delegate told the conference on equal citizenship in 1925, 'but everybody knows that there is that tendency beginning in society.'[27] The real challenge, then, to feminist citizens was 'how to make men and women moral', or how to de-sexualize relations between men and women.[28] In this they were going against the tide, for by the early decades of the twentieth century it was clear that 'the story of men and women today [was] the story of their sex experience'.[29]

Education was necessary to achieve 'good morals and good citizenship', and these aims were inextricably linked.[30] 'In education,' feminist lawyer Marie Tiernan wrote in a 1925 essay, 'feminists place their hope for a brighter future for both men and women,' especially through co-education. 'Certain it is that the segregation of the sexes which exists in many civilised countries today is undesirable resulting as it does in the over-emphasis of sex.'[31] The feminist reform of the abolition of the double standard, 'mention of which could scarcely be omitted in any paper on feminism', would lead men and women to a common espousal of higher ideals. Women could not be simultaneously sexual subjects and equal citizens; sex and citizenship were profoundly at odds. Thus the labour activist, Jean Daley, decried the self-conscious 'preening of sex' as antithetical to the citizen's sense of public duty, undermining the capacity to identify with 'one's fellows' which was 'the greatest thing in life'. Like Rose Scott, Daley also believed that economic dependence bred a spirit of servility in women inimical to the exercise of independent citizenship; the dependent woman 'moulded herself to man's desire'.[32] In this Australian discourse on women's citizenship, sexual freedom could not be imagined as a feminist goal. Premarital continence and postmarital monogamy or chastity were the ideals. Freedom was 'freedom from promiscuous intercourse'.[33] Contraceptive birth control was not advocated as a feminist policy in these decades; many explicitly condemned these 'revolting' practices as giving freer rein to the sex instinct, though recognizing that they provided a 'protection' for 'the average wife from the average husband'.[34] Feminist citizenship defined itself in antipathy to sexual freedom. Feminism was not riven by conflict over these issues as happened in the US and Britain during the same years.

The feminist vision of the inviolability and self-possession of the woman citizen inspired three quite distinctive policy engagements in the post-suffrage decades, which I shall elaborate in turn: first, a concentration on reforms that would curb men's sexual access to women and desexualize relations between men and women; second, a multifaceted campaign to win all women's economic independence; and third, campaigns to achieve citizen status for Aboriginal women and to rescue them from male sexual abuse. The history of feminism has in recent times tended to be discussed in terms of a conceptual framework of sameness/difference, but this is not useful in illuminating the nature of Australian feminist discourse and strategy on citizenship during these decades.[35] It was taken for granted that men and women were both different and the same at the same time. This was not the issue; rather, it was how to secure all women's independence and thus their inviolability.

Feminist organizations before and after the achievement of suffrage had persistently lobbied for the appointment of women to all public offices charged with the welfare of women and girls. Determined that women need never fall into men's hands, feminists successfully argued for the appointment of female doctors, factory inspectors, gaol warders, magistrates, welfare officers, and police. They regarded these appointments as major achievements. They opposed occupations which sexualized women, such as that of barmaid. They opposed developments in leisure and technology that sexualized relations between men and women, such as moving pictures. They opposed legislation that allowed for the regulation and surveillance of prostitutes and women thought to be suffering from venereal disease. They advocated raising the age of consent (the Women's Political Association advocated 21 for both sexes) so that young people could not 'consent' to their own degradation. This 'protection' legislation, as it was often called, saw the age raised to 16 in most Australian states. They supported sex education to promote respect for purity and restraint, especially among boys. 'Sex hygiene', said Adela Pankhurst, should be taught to 'adolescent boys' to impress on them the importance of self-control.[36] They called for inquiries into the white slave traffic and distributed advice on how young women might elude the traffickers. Such reforms were often aimed at 'unprotected' women and girls who found themselves beyond the safety of home, but it was also recognized that the dependence of women in the home made them, too, vulnerable to masculine tyrannies.

By 1920, it was evident that unmarried women and even married women without children might win a measure of economic independence by entering the labour market. Women had become a 'permanency in industry'.[37] These new opportunities simply highlighted the problematic position of mothers, burdened with the awesome and time-consuming work of rearing children but, as dependants themselves, entirely at the mercy of their husbands. 'The truly equal and happy marriage', said Jean Daley, 'is often the one in which both the husband and wife are wage-earners and share the household income in proportion to their income. When children come, however, they complicate the situation.'[38] From early in the century, labour women activists led the way in lobbying for motherhood endowment as a state income to be paid in recognition of the mother's service to the community and to secure her right of independence. The framework of citizen rights enabled activists to demand motherhood endowment as a reward for service to the state and as the basic right of the citizen to be treated as an individual.[39] As Lena Lynch of the New South Wales branch of the Labor party explained to the Royal Commission on Child Endowment in 1928, the payment of a breadwinner's wage to the husband 'did not recognise women and children as individuals at all—they were just appendages to men . . . endowment would recognise the women citizens and the child.'[40] Labor women were wary of being seen as desirous of tampering with working men's income; they preferred to argue for the state endowment of motherhood and childhood in addition to the basic wage, rather than for legislation requiring men to share their income with their wives. Non-party organizations such as the UAW promoted both policies, variously arguing that marriage should be reconstituted as a legal, economic partnership and that the state should remunerate mothers for services rendered.

From the late 1930s the UAW issued a series of propaganda pamphlets. The first, called 'Income for Wives How It Can be Managed or the Economic Independence of Married Women', attacked the 'deeply rooted' idea that 'women exist for the service and convenience of men' and argued that legislation should entitle women to half their husband's earnings.[41] Other pamphlets put the case for the right of homemakers to an independent income from the state in recognition that as mothers they performed 'the most indispensable and important work done anywhere by anyone' and for the payment of Child Endowment: 'It should be recognised that the work a mother does is of more fundamental importance to the state than any other performed, for without it, the state could not continue and yet in spite of its value it is entirely without remuneration.'[42] Another pamphlet attacked legislation which had been introduced by the NSW government during the Depression banning the employment of married women teachers and lectures. Such legislation infringed 'the democratic rights and liberties of the individual'.[43]

All feminist citizen organizations as well as labour movement women campaigned to defend and extend all women's right to paid labour and equal pay for the sexes. A minimum income for every adult was 'an individual right' and rates of pay, it was argued, should be fixed according to the occupation and not the sex of the worker. Feminists were especially alarmed at political developments during the 1930s that threatened women's right to work. Many Labor organizations and trade unions resolved that increasing unemployment necessitated reserving all jobs for men. For example, while the AFWV was meeting in Adelaide in 1936, the local branch of the Labor party passed a motion criticizing the employment of women whose husbands or fathers were also employed. The Federation condemned the move, affirming in turn that the right to earn was the 'inalienable right of the individual whether man or woman'.[44] A questionnaire to political candidates in 1940 asked whether they favoured the federal government paying an endowment 'in recognition of the value to the state of the work performed by mothers', and whether they would adopt the principle of equal pay and equal opportunity in the public service and render illegal all restrictions on women's right to work.[45]

Feminist citizens' focus on women's right to bodily possession and economic independence led them to extend their reform efforts to encompass the condition of Aboriginal women and girls. Their sexual use by Aboriginal and non-Aboriginal men was seen to represent women's degradation at its most blatant. The geographical proximity of white men's abuse of native women led them to emphasize anew 'the right of women to the sanctity of the person'; this was the 'most fundamental reform of all'.[46] Leading Western Australian activist Mary Montgomery Bennett deplored the 'white slave traffic in black women' and campaigned for recognition of the rights of their 'unfortunate sisters' to citizenship, land rights, and self-possession.[47] If a 'woman whether white or black has not the control of her body she is a slave', confirmed fellow activist Edith Jones.[48] Feminists attributed the appalling plight of Aboriginal women to white men's unbridled lusts, and for many Australian feminists it was the behaviour of 'average white men . . . not of the mean whites but of the overwhelming majority of white men' enjoying the 'freedom' of the frontier that confirmed them in their view of the inherently degrading nature of free sexual relations.[49] They were convinced that if Aboriginal women were granted economic and physical independence they could become 'the most magnificent citizens that any country could desire'.[50] Aboriginal women themselves petitioned for their freedom from official 'protection' and the right to self-government: 'we ask for our freedom, so that when the chance comes along we can rule our lives and make ourselves true and good citizens.'[51]

During the first decades of the twentieth century, Australian feminists were actively engaged in numerous organizations and campaigns to realize the full potential of women's status as citizens: to render women inviolable and independent political subjects. This meant in effect that they shaped a protectionist welfare state for women and children; and they counted reforms such as raising the age of consent, the establishment of children's courts, the appointment of women to a range of public offices, the establishment of women's hospitals and infant and welfare clinics, the censorship of films, and restrictions on alcohol among their most important achievements. They were less successful in securing the income for women which would secure their inviolability, winning only small measures such as the 1912 maternity allowance, boarding-out allowances (or mothers' pensions), and childhood (not motherhood) endowment in New South Wales in 1927 and federally from 1941. The principle of equal pay was not formally recognized by the centralized Commonwealth Arbitration Court until 1972. Equal political representation still proves elusive, as it does everywhere, but it should be noted that, precisely because feminist reform campaigns concentrated on changing the condition of women as a whole, the achievement of parliamentary office by a few was not the priority that it has become in more recent times.[52]

The conceptions of citizenship formulated by post-suffrage feminists in Australia were profoundly embodied articulations. They came from, and spoke to, the historical experience of women for whom heterosexuality was equated with violation and degradation. Their distinctive interpretations of the promise of citizenship suggest the importance of recognizing sexed embodiment as the ground of our experience, our knowledge of the world, and our political mobilizations. They point to the ways in which people come to experience power, or the lack of it, through our bodies. This is *not* to say that the meaning of sexed embodiment is fixed, but precisely that it is constructed in political and other discourses, such as that on women's citizenship, which speak to and in turn shape women's distinctive social and historical experience.

Much recent feminist scholarship has been concerned to establish that 'bodies matter', that subjectivities should be conceived of in terms of the primacy of corporeality.[53] The body that matters is the 'ally of sexual difference', as Elizabeth Grosz puts it, helping to problematize the universalistic and universalizing assumptions that underpin masculinist knowledge and power. Our conceptions of reality, knowledge, truth, politics, ethics, and aesthetics are all effects of sexually specific, usually male, bodies. But as Grosz insists, bodies are *not* pre-given natural objects which may be differently represented; rather, it is representations and cultural inscriptions that quite literally constitute bodies and produce them as such,[54] as effective instruments or as weak and defenceless. The body's materiality can thus be rethought as 'power's most productive effect'.[55]

What was most material to feminists about citizen women's bodies was their violability and vulnerability. Feminist discourses on citizenship incorporated a psychical representation of the subject's lived body which in many ways matches the account provided by

Iris Marion Young in 'Throwing Like a Girl'.[56] In a study of feminine comportment and motility, Young suggests that what distinguishes feminine existence is that the body is frequently both subject and object for itself at the same time, and that women's subjectification, their assuming a position as moving or speaking subjects, incorporates their lived experience of objectification. 'The modalities of feminine bodily existence have their root in the fact that feminine existence experiences the body as a mere thing—a fragile thing, which must be picked up and coaxed into movement, a thing that exists as looked at and acted upon.'[57] Unlike masculine subjects, she says, we are not 'open and unambiguous transcendences that move out to master a world that belongs to us'.[58] Experiencing herself as an object-thing rather than as a capable subject, a woman constantly lives the threat of bodily invasion. Iris Young is interested in women's embodied subjectivity for the effects on comportment and task orientation; but she concludes by raising the possibility of developing a theoretical account of the bodily existence of women and other aspects of our experience. In my exploration of the feminist theorization of citizenship in the post-suffrage decades in Australia, I have suggested the important relationship between sexed embodiment and people's identities as political subjects or citizens.

The irony of the feminist account of women's violability was its faithful echoing of the masculine view of sexuality that it critiqued. Both assumed that in heterosexual relations women were the objects of men's practice, the ground on which men's subject status was erected. Thus, in many ways, feminist interventions ironically served to endorse the masculinist definition of men as sexual subjects and women as passive objects. Thus did feminist discourse play its part in producing the 'violable' bodies it also sought to protect and govern. The violability of women justified and authorized a politics of 'protection'. Thus was sexual difference materialized as an effect of power, of men's power, but also of women's.

Ninety years after white Australian women assumed the political rights of citizenship, feminist politics must still address women's experience of violability, the threat of rape, sexual harassment, and pornography. There has been an interesting shift in orientation: now it is the rape victim rather than the prostitute who is represented as the paradigmatic oppressed woman. Whereas, for the first feminist citizens, the prostitute suffered the degrading effects of her lack of economic independence, the rape victim today is rendered helpless in the face of men's aggression. Some current feminist strategies emphasize empowering women through self-defence, but other feminist responses echo earlier positions and arguably exacerbate the problem by exaggerating men's power and women's helplessness. Current debates about women's citizenship are still concerned with devising ways to secure women's physical and economic independence as a precondition for equal citizenship. The challenge is to establish the conditions in which women can take their rightful place in the world as active, political subjects, enabled by bodies that empower rather than disqualify us for public life.

Notes

1. There is an expanding literature on this subject. See e.g. Carole Pateman, 'The Patriarchal Welfare State', Chapter 9 pp. 241–274 in this book; Kathleen B. Jones, 'Citizenship in a Woman-Friendly Polity', *Signs*, 15 (1990): 781–912; Anne Phillips, *Engendering Democracy* (Cambridge: Polity Press, 1991); Gisela Bock and Susan James (eds.), *Beyond Equality and Difference: Citizenship, Feminist Politics, Female Subjectivity* (London: Routledge, 1992).
2. Anne Phillips, *Democracy and Difference* (Cambridge: Polity Press, 1993), 111.
3. Barbara Brooks, 'A Weakness for Strong Subjects: The Women's Movement and Sexuality', *New Zealand Journal of History*, 27 (1993): 140.
4. Jones, 'Citizenship in a Woman-Friendly Polity'.
5. Woman's Christian Temperance Union, 'Warning to the Girls of Australia', in *Woman Voter* (13 May 1913), repr. in Marilyn Lake and Katie Holmes (eds.), *Freedom Bound 2: Documents on Women in Modern Australia* (Sydney: Allen & Unwin, 1995), 16–17.
6. Quoted in Judith Allen, *Rose Scott: Vision and Revision in Feminism* (Melbourne: Oxford University Press, 1994), 187.
7. Rose Scott, 'The Economic Independence of the Married Woman', 1903; Scott Family Papers, Mitchell Library, Sydney, 38/39.
8. Allen, *Rose Scott*, 211.
9. *Lone Hand* (2 Mar. 1920), quoted in Lake and Holmes, *Freedom Bound 2*, 37.
10. Hilary Charlesworth, 'What Are Women's International Rights?', in Rebecca J. Cook (ed.), *Human Rights of Women: National and International Perspectives* (Philadelphia: University of Pennsylvania Press, 1994), 71.
11. See e.g. David Held, 'Between State and Civil Society', and Raymond Plant, 'Social Rights and the Reconstruction of Welfare', both in Geoff Andrews (ed.), *Citizenship* (London: Lawrence & Wishart, 1981), 19–25, 50–64; Pateman, 'The Patriarchal Welfare State'; Ann Orloff, 'Gender and the Social Rights of Citizenship: The

Comparative Analysis of Gender Relations and the Welfare States', *American Sociological Review*, 58 (1993): 303–28; Nick O'Neill and Robin Handley, *Retreat from Injustice: Human Rights in Australian Law* (Sydney: Federation Press, 1994).

12. Angela Booth, *The Payment of Women's Work* (Melbourne, 1919), 9.
13. AFWV Conference on the Equal Moral Standard, 12 June 1936; UAW Papers, Mitchell Library, MS 2160/Y789.
14. Muriel Cheyne, 'The Fruit of her Hands', radio talk, Station 2 GB; UAW Papers, MS 2160/Y791.
15. UAW letter to Prime Minister Curtin, 20 Nov. 1941; UAW Papers, MS 2160/Y791.
16. Royal Commission on Childhood Endowment or Family Allowances, *Commonwealth Parliamentary Papers*, 1929, Minutes of Evidence, p. 132.
17. *Age*, 6 Sept. 1912.
18. Vida Goldstein, 'Venereal Disease, A Woman's Question', *Woman Voter* (10 Mar. 1914), 2.
19. Nelle Rickie to editor, *Labor Call* (6 May 1924), in Lake and Holmes, *Freedom Bound 2*, 45.
20. Mrs R. R. Doyle, radio broadcast, Radio 2 GB, Apr. 1943; UAW Papers, MS 2160/Y791.
21. *The State Reports, Tasmania: Cases Determined in the Supreme Court of Tasmania*, 1946, 1–7.
22. Letter from Lilian Watson (pseud.) to Jessie Street, 1 June 1946; UAW papers, MS 2160/Y791.
23. Newsclipping, *Sun* (9 Oct. 1947); UAW papers, MS 2160/Y791.
24. AFWV, 5th Triennial Conference, Adelaide, 1936, Report of Proceedings; UAW Papers, MS2160/Y789.
25. Allen, *Rose Scott*, 83.
26. Goldstein, 'Venereal Disease'.
27. Alison Neilans, quoted in British Commonwealth League Conference Report on the Citizen Rights of Women within the British Empire, 9 and 10 July 1925, *Conference Reports*, p. 40.
28. Neilans, in *Conference Reports*, p. 40.
29. Adela Pankhurst Walsh, 'The Home and the Labor Movement' No. 2, *Labor Call* (28 May 1925).
30. Neilans, in *Conference Reports*, p. 40.
31. Marie Tiernan, 'Feminism', *Labor Call* (29 Jan. 1925).
32. Jean Daley, 'Woman's Voice', *Woman's Clarion* (Dec. 1924): 7; (Jan. 1925): 6.
33. Adela Pankhurst Walsh, 'The Home and the Labor Movement' No. 1, *Labor Call* (10 Mar. 1925).
34. Vida Goldstein, 'Race Suicide', *Woman Voter* (11 Mar. 1912): 2. See also Ann Curthoys, 'Eugenics, Feminism and Birth Control: The Case of Marion Piddington', *Hecate*, 15 (1989): 73–89.

35. See e.g. Carol Lee Bacchi, *Same Difference: Feminism and Sexual Difference* (Sydney: Allen & Unwin, 1990).
36. Adela Pankhurst Walsh, 'Assaults on Children', *Labor Call* (28 June 1923).
37. See e.g. Nelle Rickie in Lake and Homes, *Freedom Bound 2*, 45.
38. Jean Daley, 'Independence', *Woman's Clarion* (Feb. 1925), in Lake and Holmes, *Freedom Bound 2*, 50.
39. Marilyn Lake, 'A Revolution in the Family: The Challenge and Contradiction of Maternal Citizenship', in Seth Koven and Sonya Michel (eds.), *Mothers of a New World* (New York: Routledge, 1993); Marilyn Lake, 'The Independence of Women and the Brotherhood of Man', *Labour History*, 63 (1992): 1–24.
40. Royal Commission on Childhood Endowment, Minutes of Evidence, p. 923.
41. UAW Pamphlet No. 1, 'Income for Wives: How It Can Be Managed or the Economic Dependence of Married Women'; UAW Papers, MS 2160/Y4481.
42. Jessie Street, 'Woman as a Homemaker'; UAW Pamphlet, 'Child Endowment', Pamphlet No. 12; UAW Papers, MS 2160/Y4481.
43. Jessie Street, circular letter to Members of Parliament, 23 Apr. 1940; UAW Papers, MS 2160/Y789.
44. AFWV 5th Triennial Conference, Adelaide, 1936, Report of Proceedings; UAW Papers, MS 2160/Y789.
45. UAW letter to election candidates, 9 Sept. 1940; UAW Papers, MS 2160/Y789.
46. 'A Call to the Women of Australia to Demand an Honourable Native Policy'; Rischbieth Papers, National Library of Australia (NLA), MS 2004/12/197.
47. Newsclipping, *West Australian* (9 May 1932); Rischbieth Papers, NLA, MS 2004/12/35.
48. Edith Jones, Conference of representatives of Missions, etc., Report of Proceedings; Rischbieth Papers, NLA, MS 2004/12/506.
49. Bennett, in *West Australian* (9 May 1932); Rischbieth papers, NLA, MS 2004/12/35.
50. Mary Bennett to Bessie Rischbieth, 16 Nov. 1934; Rischbieth Papers, NLA, MS 2004/12/64.
51. Petition to Royal Commission from the 'Half-castes of Broome', in Lake and Holmes, *Freedom Bound 2*, 64.
52. Marilyn Lake, 'Feminist History as National History: Writing the Political History of Women', *Australian Historical Studies*, 106 special issue (April 1996).
53. See esp. Judith Butler, *Bodies That Matter: On the Discursive Limits of Sex* (New York: Routledge, 1993), and Elizabeth Grosz, *Volatile Bodies: Toward a Corporeal Feminism* (Sydney: Allen & Unwin, 1994).

54. Grosz, *Volatile Bodies*, p. x.
55. Butler, *Bodies That Matter*, 2.
56. Iris Marion Young, *Throwing Like a Girl and Other Essays in Feminist Philosophy and Social Theory* (Bloomington: Indiana University Press, 1990).
57. Young, *Throwing Like a Girl*, 150.
58. Ibid. 153.

9   The Patriarchal Welfare State

Carole Pateman

According to Raymond Williams's *Keywords*, 'the Welfare State, in distinction from the Warfare State, was first named in 1939'.[1] The welfare state was set apart from the fascist warfare state, defeated in the Second World War, and so the welfare state was identified with democracy at the christening. In the 1980s most Western welfare states are also warfare states, but this is not ordinarily seen as compromising their democratic character. Rather, the extent of democracy is usually taken to hinge on the *class* structure. Welfare provides a social wage for the working class, and the positive, social democratic view is that the welfare state gives social meaning and equal worth to the formal juridical and political rights of all citizens. A less positive view of the welfare state is that it provides governments with new means of exercising power over and controlling working-class citizens. But proponents of both views usually fail to acknowledge the sexually divided way in which the welfare state has been constructed. Nor do most democratic theorists recognize the *patriarchal* structure of the welfare state; the very different way that women and men have been incorporated as citizens is rarely seen to be of significance for democracy.[2] Even the fact that the earliest developments of the welfare state took place when women were still denied, or had only just won, citizenship in the national state is usually overlooked.[3]

I do not want do dispute the crucial importance of class in understanding the welfare state and democracy. To write about the welfare state is, in large part, to write about the working class. However, my discussion treats class in a manner unfamiliar to most democratic theorists, who usually assume that the welfare state, democracy and class can be discussed theoretically without any attention to the character of the relation between the sexes. I shall suggest some reasons why and how the patriarchal structure of

Chapter 10 in Gutmann Amy (ed.), *Democracy and the Welfare State* 231–60. Copyright © 1988 by Princeton University Press. Reprinted by permission of Princeton University Press.

the welfare state has been repressed from theoretical consciousness. I shall also consider the connection between employment and citizenship in the patriarchal welfare state, the manner in which 'women' have been opposed to the 'worker' and the 'citizen', and a central paradox surrounding women, welfare and citizenship. By 'the welfare state' here, I refer to the states of Britain (from which I shall draw a number of my empirical and historical examples), Australia and the United States. In the more developed welfare states of Scandinavia, women have moved nearer to, but have not yet achieved, full citizenship.[4]

For the past century, many welfare policies have been concerned with what are now called 'women's issues'. Moreover, much of the controversy about the welfare state has revolved and continues to revolve around the question of the respective social places and tasks of women and men, the structure of marriage and the power relationship between husband and wife. So it is not surprising that the Reagan administration's attack on the welfare state was seen as prompted by a desire to shore up the patriarchal structure of the state; the Reagan budgets, 'in essence, ... try to restabilize patriarchy ... as much as they try to fight inflation and stabilize capitalism'.[5] The difficulties of understanding the welfare state and citizenship today without taking the position of women into account are not hard to illustrate, because contemporary feminists have produced a large body of evidence and argument that reveals the importance of women in the welfare state and the importance of the welfare state for women.

Women are now the majority of recipients of many welfare benefits. In 1980 in the United States, for example, 64.8 per cent of the recipients of Medicare were women, while 70 per cent of housing subsidies went to women, either living alone or heading households;[6] and by 1979, 80 per cent of the families receiving Aid to Families with Dependent Children (AFDC) were headed by women (the number of such families having grown fourfold between 1961 and 1979).[7] A major reason why women are so prominent as welfare recipients is that women are more likely than men to be poor (a fact that has come to be known as 'the feminization of poverty'). In the United States, between 1969 and 1979, there was a decline in the proportion of families headed by men that fell below the official poverty line while the proportion headed by women grew rapidly.[8] By 1982 about one-fifth of families with minor children were headed by women, but they constituted 53 per cent of all poor families,[9] and female heads were over three times as likely as male heads to have incomes below the poverty line.[10] By 1980 two out of every three adults whose incomes were below the poverty line were women. The National Advisory Council on Economic Opportunity reported in 1980 that, if these trends continued, the entire population of the poor in the United States would be composed of women and children by the year 2000.[11] In Australia women are also likely to be poor. A survey for the Commission of Inquiry into Poverty in 1973 found that, of the groups with 'disabilities', fatherless families were poorest; 30 per cent of such families were below the poverty line, and another 20 per cent only marginally above it.[12] Nor had the situation improved by 1978–9: 41 per cent of women who were single parents were then below the poverty line.[13]

The welfare state is now a major source of employment for women. For instance, in Britain the National Health Service is the biggest single employer of women in the country; about three-quarters of NHS employees, and 90 per cent of NHS nurses, are women.[14] In 1981 there were more than five million jobs in the public health, education and welfare sector in Britain (an increase of two million from 1961) and three-fifths of these jobs were held by women.[15] In the United States in 1980 women occupied 70 per cent of the jobs at all levels of government concerned with social services, which was a quarter of all female employment and about half of all professional jobs occupied by women. Employment is provided largely at state and local levels in the United States. The federal government subsidizes the warfare state where there are few jobs for women; only 0.5 per cent of the female workforce is employed on military contracts. One estimate is that, for each billion dollar increase in the military budget, 9,500 jobs are lost to women in social welfare or the private sector.[16]

Women are also involved in the welfare state in less obvious ways. Negotiations (and confrontations) with welfare state officials on a day-to-day basis are usually conducted by women; and it is mothers, not fathers, who typically pay the rent, deal with social workers, take children to welfare clinics, and so forth. Women are also frequently in the forefront of political campaigns and actions to improve welfare services or the treatment of welfare claimants. The services and benefits provided by the welfare state are far from comprehensive and, in the absence of public provision, much of the work involved, for example, in caring for the aged in all three countries is undertaken by women in their homes (something to which I shall return).

Finally, to put the previous points into perspective, there is one area of the welfare state from which women have been largely excluded. The legislation, policy-making and higher-level administration of the welfare state have been and remain predominantly in men's hands. Some progress has been made: in Australia the Office of the Status of Women within the (Commonwealth) Department of Prime Minister and Cabinet monitors cabinet submissions, and the Women's Budget Program requires all departments to make a detailed assessment of the impact of their policies on women.

HEGEL'S TWO DILEMMAS

To gain some insight into why the welfare state can still be discussed without taking account of these factors, it is useful to begin by looking at Donald Moon's account[17] of the welfare state as a response to 'Hegel's dilemma'. Hegel was the first political theorist to set out the moral dilemma that arises when citizenship is undermined by the operation of the capitalist market. The market leaves some citizens bereft of the resources for social participation and so, as Moon states, as 'undeserved exiles from society'. Citizens thrown into poverty lack both the means for self-respect and the means to be recognized by fellow citizens as of equal worth to themselves, a recognition basic to democracy. Poverty-stricken individuals are not and—unless the outcome of participation in the market is offset in some way, cannot be—full citizens. The moral basis of the welfare state lies in the provision of resources for what T. H. Marshall called the 'social rights' of democratic citizenship. For Moon, then, Hegel's dilemma is concerned with the manner in which the participation of some individuals as workers in the capitalist economy (or, in Hegel's terminology, in the sphere of civil society) can make a mockery of their formal status as equal citizens. In contemporary terms, it is a problem of class or, more exactly, now that mass unemployment could well be a permanent feature of capitalist economies, a problem of an underclass of unemployed social exiles. There is no doubt that this is an important problem, but Moon's reading of Hegel focuses on only *part* of the dilemma with which Hegel was faced.

In addition to the category of citizens who become social exiles through the accident that they can find no one to buy their labour-power at a living wage, Hegel also had to deal with a category of beings who are exiles because they are *incapable* of being incorporated into civil society and citizenship. According to Hegel—and to almost all the modern theorists who are admitted to the 'tradition of Western political philosophy'—women naturally lack the attributes and capacities of the 'individuals' who can enter civil society, sell their labour power and become citizens.[18] Women, Hegel held, are natural social exiles. Hegel therefore had to find an answer to *two* dilemmas, and his theory gives a moral basis to both class division and sexual division. The welfare state could not provide a solution to the problem of women. Hegel's response was simultaneously to reaffirm the necessity of women's exile and to incorporate them into the state. Women are not incorporated as citizens like men, but as members of the family, a sphere separate from (or in social exile from) civil society and the state. The family is essential to civil society and the state, but it is constituted on a different basis from the rest of conventional social life, having its own ascriptive principles of association.

Women have now won the formal status of citizens, and their contemporary social position may seem a long way removed from that prescribed by Hegel. But Hegel's theory is still very relevant to the problem of patriarchy and the welfare state, although most contemporary political theorists usually look only at the relation between civil society and the state, or the intervention that the public power (state) may make in the private sphere (economy or class system). This view of 'public' and 'private' assumes that two of Hegel's categories (civil society and state) can be understood in the absence of the third (family). Yet Hegel's theory presupposes that family/civil society/state are comprehensible only in *relation* to each other—and then civil society and the state become 'public' in contrast to the 'private' family.

Hegel's social order contains a double separation of the private and public: the *class* division between civil society and the state (between economic man and citizen, between private enterprise and the public power); and the *patriarchal* separation between the private family and the public world of civil society/state. Moreover, the public character of the sphere of civil society/state is constructed and gains its meaning through what it excludes—the private association of the family. The patriarchal division between public and private *is also a sexual division*. Women, naturally lacking the capacities for public participation, remain within an association constituted by love, ties of blood, natural subjection and

245

particularity, and in which they are governed by men. The public world of universal citizenship is an association of free and equal individuals, a sphere of property, rights and contract—and of men, who interact as formally equal citizens.

The widely held belief that the basic structure of our society rests on the separation of the private, familial sphere from the public world of the state and its policies is both true and false. It is true that the private sphere has been seen as women's proper place. Women have never in reality been completely excluded from the public world, but the policies of the welfare state have helped ensure that women's day-to-day experience confirms the separation of private and public existence. The belief is false in that, since the early twentieth century, welfare policies have reached across from public to private and helped uphold a patriarchal structure of familial life. Moreover, the two spheres are linked because men have always had a legitimate place in both. Men have been seen both as heads of families—and as husbands and fathers they have had socially and legally sanctioned power over their wives and children—and as participants in public life. Indeed, the 'natural' masculine capacities that enable them, but not their wives, to be heads of families are the same capacities that enable them, but not their wives, to take their place in civil life.

Moon's interpretation of Hegel illustrates the continuing strength of Hegel's patriarchal construction of citizenship, which is assumed to be universal or democratic citizenship. The exiles from society who need the welfare state to give moral worth to their citizenship are male workers. Hegel showed deep insight here. Paid employment has become the key to citizenship, and the recognition of an individual as a citizen of equal worth to other citizens is lacking when a worker is unemployed. The history of the welfare state and citizenship (and the manner in which they have been theorized) is bound up with the history of the development of 'employment societies'.[19] In the early part of the nineteenth century, most workers were still not fully incorporated into the labour market; they typically worked at a variety of occupations, worked on a seasonal basis, gained part of their subsistence outside the capitalist market and enjoyed 'Saint Monday'. By the 1880s full employment had become an ideal, unemployment a major social issue, and loud demands were heard for state-supported social reform (and arguments were made against state action to promote welfare).[20] But who was included under the banner of 'full employment'? What was the status of those 'natural' social exiles seen as properly having no part in the employment society? Despite many changes in the social standing of women, we are not so far as we might like to think from Hegel's statement that the husband, as head, 'has the prerogative to go out and work for [the family's] living, to attend to its needs, and to control and administer its capital'.[21]

The political significance of the sexual division of labour is ignored by most democratic theorists. They treat the public world of paid employment and citizenship as if it can be divorced from its connection with the private sphere, and so the masculine character of the public sphere has been repressed. For example, T. H. Marshall first presented his influential account of citizenship in 1949, at the height of the optimism in Britain about the contribution of the new welfare state policies to social change—but also at the time (as I shall show) when women were being confirmed as lesser citizens in the welfare state. Marshall states that 'citizenship is a status bestowed on those who are full members of a community',[22] and most contemporary academic discussions of citizenship do not question this statement. But, as shown graphically and brutally by the history of blacks in the United States, this is not the case. The formal status of citizen can be bestowed on, or won by, a category of people who are still denied full social membership.

Marshall noted that the Factory Acts in the nineteenth century 'protected' women workers, and he attributes the protection to their lack of citizenship. But he does not consider 'protection'—the polite way to refer to subordination—of women in the private sphere or ask how it is related to the sexual division of labour in the capitalist economy and citizenship. Nor does the 'in some important respects peculiar' civil status of married women in the nineteenth century inhibit his confidence in maintaining, despite the limited franchise, 'that in the nineteenth century citizenship in the form of civil rights was universal', and that, in economic life, 'the basic civil right is the right to work'. Marshall sees the aim of the 'social rights' of the welfare state as 'class-abatement': this is 'no longer merely an attempt to abate the obvious nuisance of destitution in the lowest ranks of society. . . . It is no longer content to raise the floor-level in the basement of the social edifice, . . . it has begun to remodel the whole building.'[23] But the question that has to be asked is, are women in the building or in a separate annex?

CITIZENSHIP AND EMPLOYMENT

Theoretically and historically, the central criterion for citizenship has been 'independence', and the elements encompassed under the heading of independence have been based on masculine attributes and abilities. Men, but not women, have been seen as possessing the capacities required of 'individuals', 'workers' and 'citizens'. As a corollary, the meaning of 'dependence' is associated with all that is womanly—and women's citizenship in the welfare state is full of paradoxes and contradictions. To use Marshall's metaphor, women are identified as trespassers into the public edifice of civil society and the state. Three elements of 'independence' are particularly important for present purposes, all related to the masculine capacity for self-protection: the capacity to bear arms, the capacity to own property and the capacity for self-government.

First, women are held to lack the capacity for self-protection; they have been 'unilaterally disarmed'.[24] The protection of women is undertaken by men, but physical safety is a fundamental aspect of women's welfare that has been sadly neglected in the welfare state. From the nineteenth century, feminists (including J. S. Mill) have drawn attention to the impunity with which husbands could use physical force against their wives,[25] but women/wives still find it hard to obtain proper social and legal protection against violence from their male 'protectors'. Defence of the state (or the ability to protect your protection, as Hobbes put it), the ultimate test of citizenship, is also a masculine prerogative. The antisuffragists in both America and Britain made a great deal of the alleged inability and unwillingness of women to use armed force, and the issue of women and combat duties in the military forces of the warfare state was also prominent in the recent campaign against the Equal Rights Amendment in the United States. Although women are now admitted into the armed force and so into training useful for later civilian employment, they are prohibited from combat duties in Britain, Australia and the United States. Moreover, past exclusion of women from the warfare state has meant that welfare provision for veterans has also benefited men. In Australia and the United States, because of their special 'contribution' as citizens, veterans have had their own, separately administered welfare state, which has ranged from preference in university education (the GI bills in the United States) to their own medical benefits and hospital services, and (in Australia) preferential employment in the public service.

In the 'democratic' welfare state, however, employment rather than military service is the key to citizenship. The masculine 'protective' capacity now enters into citizenship primarily through the second and third dimensions of independence. Men, but not women, have also been seen as property-owners. Only some men own material property, but as 'individuals', all men own (and can protect) the property they possess in their persons. Their status as 'workers' depends on their capacity to contract out the property they own in their labour-power. Women are still not fully recognized socially as such property-owners. To be sure, our position has improved dramatically from the mid-nineteenth century when women as wives had a very 'peculiar' position as the legal property of their husbands, and feminists compared wives to slaves. But today, a wife's person is still the property of her husband in one vital respect. Despite recent legal reform, in Britain and in some of the states of the United States and Australia, rape is still deemed legally impossible within marriage, and thus a wife's consent has no meaning. Yet women are now formally citizens in states held to be based on the necessary consent of self-governing individuals.[26] The profound contradiction about women's consent is rarely if ever noticed and so is not seen as related to a sexually divided citizenship or as detracting from the claim of the welfare state to be democratic.

The third dimension of 'independence' is self-government. Men have been constituted as the beings who can govern (or protect) themselves, and if a man can govern himself, then he also has the requisite capacity to govern others. Only a few men govern others in public life—but all men govern in private as husbands and heads of households. As the governor of a family, a man is also a 'breadwinner'. He has the capacity to sell his labour power as a worker, or to buy labour power with his capital, and provide for his wife and family. His wife is thus 'protected'. The category of 'breadwinner' presupposes that wives are constituted as economic dependents or 'housewives', which places them in a subordinate position. The dichotomy breadwinner/housewife, and the masculine meaning of independence, were established in Britain by the middle of the last century; in the earlier period of capitalist development, women (and children) were wage-labourers. A 'worker' became a man who has an economically dependent wife to take care of his daily needs and look after his home and children. Moreover, 'class', too, is constructed as a patriarchal category. 'The working class' is the class of working *men*, who are also full citizens in the welfare state.

This observation brings me back to Marshall's statement about the universal, civil right to 'work', that is, to paid employment. The democratic implications of the right to work cannot be understood without attention to the connections between the public world of 'work' and citizenship and the private world of conjugal relations. What it means to be a 'worker' depends in part on men's status and power as husbands, and on their standing as citizens in the welfare state. The construction of the male worker as 'breadwinner' and his wife as his 'dependant' was expressed officially in the Census classifications in Britain and Australia. In the British Census of 1851, women engaged in unpaid domestic work were 'placed . . . in one of the productive classes along with paid work of a similar kind'.[27] This classification changed after 1871, and by 1911 unpaid housewives had been completely removed from the economically active population. In Australia an initial conflict over the categories of classification was resolved in 1890 when the scheme devised in New South Wales was adopted. The Australians divided up the population more decisively than the British, and the 1891 Census was based on the two categories of 'breadwinner' and 'dependant'. Unless explicitly stated otherwise, women's occupation was classified as domestic, and domestic workers were put in the dependant category.

The position of men as breadwinner-workers has been built into the welfare state. The sexual divisions in the welfare state have received much less attention than the persistence of the old dichotomy between the deserving and undeserving poor, which pre-dates the welfare state. This is particularly clear in the United States, where a sharp separation is maintained between 'social security', or welfare-state policies directed at 'deserving workers who have paid for them through "contributions" over their working lifetimes', and 'welfare'—seen as public 'handouts' to 'barely deserving poor people'.[28] Although 'welfare' does not have this stark meaning in Britain or Australia, where the welfare state encompasses much more than most Americans seem able to envisage, the old distinction between the deserving and undeserving poor is still alive and kicking, illustrated by the popular bogey-figures of the 'scrounger' (Britain) and the 'dole-bludger' (Australia). However, although the dichotomy of deserving/undeserving poor overlaps with the divisions between husband/wife and worker/housewife to some extent, it also obscures the patriarchal structure of the welfare state.

Feminist analyses have shown how many welfare provisions have been established within a two-tier system. First, there are the benefits available to individuals as 'public' persons by virtue of their participation, and accidents of fortune, in the capitalist market. Benefits in this tier of the system are usually claimed by men. Second, benefits are available to the 'dependants' of individuals in the first category, or to 'private' persons, usually women. In the United States, for example, men are the majority of 'deserving' workers who receive benefits through the insurance system to which they have 'contributed' out of their earnings. On the other hand, the majority of claimants in means-tested programmes are women—women who are usually making their claims as wives or mothers. This is clearly the case with AFDC, where women are aided because they are mothers supporting children on their own, but the same is also true in other programmes: '46 per cent of the women receiving Social Security benefits make their claims as wives.' In contrast: 'men, even poor men, rarely make claims for benefits solely as husbands or fathers.'[29] In Australia the division is perhaps even more sharply defined. In 1980–1, in the primary tier of the system, in which benefits are employment-related and claimed by those who are expected to be economically independent but are not earning an income because of unemployment or illness, women formed only 31.3 per cent of claimants. In contrast, in the 'dependants group', 73.3 per cent of claimants were women, who were eligible for benefits because 'they are dependent on a man who could not support them, . . . [or] should have had a man support them if he had not died, divorced or deserted them'.[30]

Such evidence of lack of 'protection' raises an important question about *women's* standard of living in the welfare state. As dependants, married women should derive their subsistence from their husbands, so that wives are placed in the position of all dependent people before the establishment of the welfare state; they are reliant on the benevolence of another for their livelihood. The assumption is generally made that all husbands are benevolent. Wives are assumed to share equally in the standard of living of their husbands. The distribution of income *within* households has not usually been a subject of interest to economists, political theorists, or protagonists in arguments about class and the welfare state—even though William Thompson drew attention to its importance as long ago as 1825[31]—but past and present evidence indicates that the belief that all husbands are benevolent is mistaken.[32] Nevertheless, women are likely to be better off married than if their marriage fails. One reason why women figure so prominently among the poor is that after divorce, as recent evidence from the United States reveals, a woman's standard of living can fall by nearly 75 per cent, whereas a man's can rise by nearly half.[33]

The conventional understanding of the 'wage' also suggests that there is no need to investigate women's standard of living independently from men's. The concept of the wage has expressed and encapsulated the patriarchal separation and integration of the public world of employment and the private sphere of conjugal relations. In arguments about the welfare state and the social wage, the wage is usually treated as a return for the sale of *individuals'* labour power. However, once the opposition breadwinner/housewife was consolidated, a 'wage' had to provide subsistence for several people. The struggle between capital and labour and the controversy about the welfare state have been about the *family wage*. A 'living wage' has been defined as what is required for a worker as breadwinner to support a wife and family, rather than what is needed to support himself; the wage is not what is sufficient to reproduce the worker's own labour power, but what is sufficient, in combination with the unpaid work of the housewife, to reproduce the labour power of the present and future labour force.

The designer of the Australian Census classification system, T. A. Coghlan, discussed women's employment in his *Report* on the 1891 Census, and he argued that married women in the paid labour market depressed men's wages and thus lowered the general standard of living.[34] His line of argument about women's employment has been used by the trade union movement for the past century in support of bargaining to secure a family wage. In 1909 motions were put to the conferences of the Labour Party and Trades Union Congress in Britain to ban the employment of wives altogether, and as recently as 1982 a defence of the family wage was published arguing that it strengthens unions in wage negotiation.[35] In 1907 the family wage was enshrined in law in Australia in the famous Harvester judgement in the Commonwealth Arbitration Court. Justice Higgins ruled in favour of a legally guaranteed minimum wage—and laid down that a living wage should be sufficient to keep an unskilled worker, his (dependent) wife, and three children in reasonable comfort.

Of course, a great deal has changed since 1907. Structural changes in capitalism have made it possible for large numbers of married women to enter paid employment, and equal-pay legislation in the 1970s, which in principle recognizes the wage as payment to an individual, may make it seem that the family wage has had its day. And it was always a myth for many, perhaps most, working-class families.[36] Despite the strength of the social ideal of the dependent wife, many working-class wives have always been engaged in paid work out of necessity. The family could not survive on the husband's wage, and the wife had to earn money, too, whether as a wage-worker, or at home doing outwork, or taking in laundry or lodgers or participating in other ways in the 'informal' economy. In 1976 in Britain the wages and salaries of 'heads of household' (not all of whom are men) formed only 51 per cent of household income.[37] The decline of manufacturing and the expansion of the service sector of capitalist economies since the Second World War have created jobs seen as 'suitable' for women. Between 1970 and 1980 in the United States over thirteen million women entered the paid labour force.[38] In Britain, if present trends in male and female employment continue, women employees will outnumber men in less than ten years.[39] Nevertheless, even these dramatic shifts have not been sufficient to make women full members of the employment society. The civil right to 'work' is still only half-heartedly acknowledged for women. Women in the workplace are still perceived primarily as wives and mothers, not workers.[40] The view is also widespread that women's wages are a 'supplement' to those of the breadwinner. Women, it is held, do not need wages in the same way that men do—so they may legitimately be paid less than men.

When the Commonwealth Arbitration Court legislated for the family wage, 45 per cent of the male workforce in Australia were single.[41] Yet in 1912 (in a case involving fruit pickers) Justice Higgins ruled that a job normally done by women could be paid at less than a man's rate because women were not responsible for dependants. On the contrary, while many men received a family wage and had no families, and breadwinners were given the power to determine whether their dependants should share in their standard of living, many women were struggling to provide for dependants on a 'dependant's' wage. Eleanor Rathbone estimated that before and just after the Great War in Britain a third of women in paid employment were wholly or partially responsible for supporting dependants.[42] About the same proportion of women breadwinners was found in a survey of Victorian manufacturing industries in Australia in 1928.[43] Nevertheless, the classification of women as men's dependants was the basis for a living wage for women, granted in New South Wales in 1918; lower wages for women were enshrined in law and (until a national minimum wage for both sexes was granted in 1974) were set at 50–54 per cent of the male rate. Again in Britain, in the late 1960s and 1970s, the National Board for Prices and Incomes investigated low pay and argued that, as part-time workers, women did not depend on their own wage to support themselves.[44] In the United States, as recently as 1985, it was stated that 'women have generally been paid less [than men] because they would work for lower wages, since they had no urgent need for more money. Either they were married, or single and living at home, or doubling up with friends.'[45]

Women are prominent as welfare claimants because, today, it is usually women who are poor—and perhaps the major reason why women are poor is that it is very hard for most women to find a job that will pay a living wage. Equal-pay legislation cannot overcome the barrier of a sexually segregated occupational structure. Capitalist economies are patriarchal, divided into men's and women's occupations; the sexes do not usually work together, nor are they paid at the same rates for similar work. For example, in the United States 80 per cent of women's jobs are located in only 20 of the 420 occupations listed by the Department of Labor.[46] More than half of employed women work in occupations that are 75 per cent female, and over 20 per cent work in occupations that are 95 per cent female.[47] In Australia in 1986, 59.5 per cent of women employees worked in the occupational categories 'clerical, sales and services'. In only 69 out of 267 occupational categories did the proportion of women reach a third or more.[48] The segregation is very stable; in Britain, for example, 84 per cent of women worked in occupations dominated by women in 1971, the same percentage as in 1951, and in 1901 the figure was 88 per cent.[49]

The economy is also vertically segregated. Most women's jobs are unskilled[50] and of low status; even in the professions women are clustered at the lower end of the occupational hierarchy. The British National Health Service provides a useful illustration. About one-third of employees are at the lowest level as ancillary workers, of whom around three-quarters are women. Their work is sex-segregated, so that the women workers perform catering and domestic tasks. As I noted previously, 90 per cent of NHS nurses are female but about one-quarter of senior nursing posts are held by men. At the prestigious levels, only about 10 per cent of consultants are female and they are segregated into certain specialities, notably those relating to children (in 1977, 32.7 per cent women).[51]

Many women also work part-time, either because of the requirements of their other (unpaid) work, or because they cannot find a full-time job. In Australia in 1986, 57.4 per cent of all part-time employees were married women.[52] In Britain two out of every five women in the workforce are employed for thirty hours or less. However, the hourly rate for full-time women workers was only 75.1 per cent of men's in 1982 (and it is men who are likely to work overtime).[53] In 1980 women constituted 64 per cent of the employees in the six lowest paid occupations.[54] During the 1970s women's earnings edged slightly upward compared with men's in most countries, but not in the United States. In 1984 the median of women's earnings as full-time workers over a full year was $14,479, while men earned $23,218.[55] The growth in the service sector in the United States has largely been growth in part-time work; in 1980 almost a quarter of all jobs in the private sector were part-time. Almost all the new jobs appearing between 1970 and 1980 were in areas that paid less than average wages; in 1980 '51 per cent [of women] held jobs paying less than 66 per cent of a craft worker's wages'.[56]

WOMEN'S WORK AND WELFARE

Although so many women, including married women, are now in paid employment, women's standing as 'workers' is still of precarious legitimacy. So, therefore, is their standing as democratic citizens. If an individual can gain recognition from other citizens as an equally worthy citizen only through participation in the capitalist market, if self-respect and respect as a citizen are 'achieved' in the public world of the employment society, then women still lack the means to be recognized as worthy citizens. Nor have the policies of the welfare state provided women with many of the resources to gain respect as citizens. Marshall's social rights of citizenship in the welfare state could be extended to men without difficulty. As participants in the market, men could be seen as making a public contribution, and were in a position to be levied by the state to make a contribution more directly, that *entitled* them to the benefits of the welfare state. But how could women, dependants of men, whose legitimate 'work' is held to be located in the private sphere, be citizens of the welfare state? What could, or did, women contribute? The paradoxical answer is that women contributed—welfare.

The development of the welfare state has presupposed that certain aspects of welfare could and should continue to be provided by women (wives) in the home, and not primarily through public provision. The 'work' of a housewife can include the care of an invalid husband and elderly, perhaps infirm, relatives. Welfare-state policies have ensured in various ways that wives/women provide welfare services gratis, disguised as part of their responsibility for the private sphere. A good deal has been written about the fiscal crisis of the welfare state, but it would have been more acute if certain areas of welfare had not been seen as a private, women's matter. It is not surprising that the attack on public spending in the welfare state by the Thatcher and Reagan governments goes hand-in-hand with praise for loving care within families, that is, with an attempt to obtain ever more unpaid welfare from (house) wives. The Invalid Care Allowance in Britain has been a particularly blatant example of the way in which the welfare state ensures that wives provide private welfare. The allowance was introduced in 1975—when the Sex Discrimination Act was also passed—and it was paid to men or to single women who relinquished paid employment to look after a sick, disabled or elderly person (not necessarily a relative). Married women (or those cohabiting) were ineligible for the allowance.

The evidence indicates that it is likely to be married women who provide such care. In 1976 in Britain it was estimated that two million women were caring for adult relatives, and one survey in the north of England found that there were more people caring for adult relatives than mothers looking after children under 16.[57] A corollary of the assumption that women, but not men, care for others is that women must also care for themselves. Investigations show that women living by themselves in Britain have to be more infirm than men to obtain the services of home helps, and a study of an old people's home found that frail, elderly women admitted with their husbands faced hostility from the staff because they had failed in their job.[58] Again, women's citizenship is full of contradictions and paradoxes. Women must provide welfare, and care for themselves, and so must be assumed to have the capacities necessary for these tasks. Yet the development of the welfare state has also presupposed that women necessarily are in need of protection by and are dependent on men.

The welfare state has reinforced women's identity as men's dependants both directly and indirectly, and so confirmed rather than ameliorated our social exile. For example, in Britain and

Australia the cohabitation rule explicitly expresses the presumption that women necessarily must be economically dependent on men if they live with them as sexual partners. If cohabitation is ruled to take place, the woman loses her entitlement to welfare benefits. The consequence of the cohabitation rule is not only sexually divided control of citizens, but an exacerbation of the poverty and other problems that the welfare state is designed to alleviate. In Britain today

when a man lives in, a woman's independence—her own name on the weekly giro [welfare cheque] is automatically surrendered. The men become the claimants and the women their dependents. They lose control over both the revenue and the expenditure, often with catastrophic results: rent not paid, fuel bills missed, arrears mounting.[59]

It is important to ask what counts as part of the welfare state. In Australia and Britain the taxation system and transfer payments together form a tax-transfer system in the welfare state. In Australia a tax rebate is available for a dependent spouse (usually, of course, a wife), and in Britain the taxation system has always treated a wife's income as her husband's for taxation purposes. It is only relatively recently that it ceased to be the husband's prerogative to correspond with the Inland Revenue about his wife's earnings, or that he ceased to receive rebates due on her tax payments. Married men can still claim a tax allowance, based on the assumption that they support a dependent wife. Women's dependence is also enforced through the extremely limited public provision of child-care facilities in Australia, Britain and the United States, which creates a severe obstacle to women's full participation in the employment society. In all three countries, unlike Scandinavia, child care outside the home is a very controversial issue.

Welfare-state legislation has also been framed on the assumption that women make their 'contribution' by providing private welfare, and, from the beginning, women were denied full citizenship in the welfare state. In America 'originally the purpose of ADC (now AFDC) was to keep mothers out of the paid labor force. . . . In contrast, the Social Security retirement program was consciously structured to respond to the needs of white male workers.'[60] In Britain the first national insurance, or contributory, scheme was set up in 1911, and one of its chief architects wrote later that women should have been completely excluded because 'they want insurance for others, not themselves'. Two years before the scheme was introduced William Beveridge, the father of the contemporary British welfare state, stated in a book on unemployment that the 'ideal [social] unit is the household of man, wife and children maintained by the earnings of the first alone. ... Reasonable security of employment for the breadwinner is the basis of all private duties and all sound social action.'[61] Nor had Beveridge changed his mind on this matter by the Second World War; his report, *Social Insurance and Allied Services*, appeared in 1942 and laid a major part of the foundation for the great reforms of the 1940s. In a passage now (in)famous among feminists, Beveridge wrote that 'the great majority of married women must be regarded as occupied on work which is vital though unpaid, without which their husbands could not do their paid work and without which the nation could not continue.'[62] In the National Insurance Act of 1946 wives were separated from their husbands for insurance purposes. (The significance of this procedure, along with Beveridge's statement, clearly was lost on T. H. Marshall when he was writing his essay on citizenship and the welfare state.) Under the act, married women paid lesser contributions for reduced benefits, but they could also opt out of the scheme, and so from sickness, unemployment, and maternity benefits, and they also lost entitlement to an old-age pension in their own right, being eligible only as their husband's dependant. By the time the legislation was amended in 1975, about three-quarters of married women workers had opted out.[63]

A different standard for men and women has also been applied in the operation of the insurance scheme. In 1911 some married women were insured in their own right. The scheme provided benefits in case of 'incapacity to work', but, given that wives had already been identified as 'incapacitated' for the 'work' in question, for paid employment, problems over the criteria for entitlement to sickness benefits were almost inevitable. In 1913 an inquiry was held to discover why married women were claiming benefits at a much greater rate than expected. One obvious reason was that the health of many working-class women was extremely poor. The extent of their ill health was revealed in 1915 when letters written by working women in 1913–14 to the Women's Cooperative Guild were published.[64] The national insurance scheme meant that for the first time women could afford to take time off work when ill—but from which 'work'? Could they take time off from housework? What were the implications for the embryonic welfare state if they ceased to provide free welfare? From 1913 a dual standard of eligibility for benefits was established. For men the criterion was fitness for work. But the committee of inquiry decided that, if a woman could do her housework, she was not ill. So the criterion for eligibility for women was also fitness for work—but unpaid work in the private home, not paid work in the public market that was the basis for the contributory scheme under which the women were insured! This criterion for women was still being laid down in instructions issued by the Department of Health and Social Security in the 1970s.[65] The dual standard was further reinforced in 1975 when a non-contributory invalidity pension was introduced for those incapable of work but not qualified for the contributory scheme. Men and single women were entitled to the pension if they could not engage in paid employment; the criterion for married women was ability to perform 'normal household duties'.[66]

WOLLSTONECRAFT'S DILEMMA

So far I have looked at the patriarchal structure of the welfare state, but this is only part of the picture; the development of the welfare state has also brought challenges to patriarchal power and helped provide a basis for women's autonomous citizenship. Women have seen the welfare state as one of their major means of support. Well before women won formal citizenship, they campaigned for the state to make provision for welfare, especially for the welfare of women and their children; and women's organizations and women activists have continued their political activities around welfare issues, not least in opposition to their status as 'dependents'. In 1953 the British feminist Vera Brittain wrote of the welfare state established through the legislation of the 1940s that 'in it women have become ends in themselves and not merely means to the ends of men', and their 'unique value as women was recognised'.[67] In hindsight, Brittain was clearly over-optimistic in her assessment, but perhaps the opportunity now exists to begin to dismantle the patriarchal structure of the welfare state. In the 1980s the large changes in women's social position, technological and structural transformations within capitalism, and mass unemployment mean that much of the basis for the breadwinner/dependant dichotomy and for the employment society itself is being eroded (although both are still widely seen as social ideals). The social context of Hegel's two dilemmas is disappearing. As the current concern about the 'feminization of poverty' reveals, there is now a very visible underclass of women who are directly connected to the state as claimants, rather than indirectly as men's dependants. Their social exile is as apparent as that of poor male workers was to Hegel. Social change has now made it much harder to gloss over the paradoxes and contradictions of women's status as citizens.

However, the question of how women might become full citizens of a democratic welfare state is more complex than may appear at first sight, because it is only in the current wave of the organized feminist movement that the division between the private and public spheres of social life has become seen as a major *political* problem. From the 1860s to the 1960s women were active in the public sphere: women fought not only for welfare measures and for measures to secure the private and public safety of women and girls, but for the vote and civil equality; middle-class women fought for entry into higher education, and the professions and women trade unionists fought for decent working conditions and wages and maternity leave. But the contemporary liberal-feminist view, particularly prominent in the United States, that what is required above all is 'gender-neutral' laws and policies, was not widely shared.[68] In general, until the 1960s the focus of attention in the welfare state was on measures to ensure that women had proper social support, and hence proper social respect, in carrying out their responsibilities in the private sphere. The problem is whether and how such measures could assist women in their fight for full citizenship. In 1942 in Britain, for example, many women welcomed the passage in the Beveridge Report that I have cited because, it was argued, it gave official recognition to the value of women's unpaid work. However, an official nod of recognition to women's work as 'vital' to 'the nation' is easily given; *in practice*, the value of the work in bringing women into full membership in the welfare state was negligible. The equal worth of citizenship and the respect of fellow citizens still depended on participation as paid employees. 'Citizenship' and 'work' stood then and still stand opposed to 'women'.

The extremely difficult problem faced by women in their attempt to win full citizenship I shall call 'Wollstonecraft's dilemma'. The dilemma is that the two routes toward citizenship that women have pursed are mutually incompatible within the confines of the patriarchal welfare state, and, within that context, they are impossible to achieve. For three centuries, since universal citizenship first appeared as a political ideal, women have continued to challenge their alleged natural subordination within private life. From at least the 1790s they have also struggled with the task of trying to become citizens within an ideal and practice that have gained universal meaning through their exclusion. Women's response has been complex. On the one hand, they have demanded that the ideal of citizenship be extended to them,[69] and the liberal-feminist agenda for a 'gender-neutral' social world is the logical conclusion of one form of this demand. On the other hand, women have also insisted, often simultaneously, as did Mary Wollstonecraft, that *as women* they have specific capacities, talents, needs and concerns, so that the expression of their citizenship will be differentiated from that of men. Their unpaid work providing welfare could be seen, as Wollstonecraft saw women's tasks as mothers, as women's work *as citizens*, just as their husbands' paid work is central to men's citizenship.[70]

The patriarchal understanding of citizenship means that the two demands are incompatible because it allows two alternatives only: either women become (like) men, and so full citizens; or they continue at women's work, which is of no value for citizenship. Moreover, within a patriarchal welfare state neither demand can be met. To demand that citizenship, as it now exists, should be fully extended to women accepts the patriarchal meaning of 'citizen', which is constructed from men's attributes, capacities, and activities. Women cannot be full citizens in the present meaning of the term; at best, citizenship can be extended to women only as lesser men. At the same time, within the patriarchal welfare stare, to demand proper social recognition and support for women's responsibilities is to condemn women to less than full citizenship and to continued incorporation into public life as 'women', that is, as members of another sphere who cannot, therefore, earn the respect of fellow (male) citizens.

The example of child endowments on family allowances in Australia and Britain is instructive as a practical illustration of Wollstonecraft's dilemma. It reveals the great difficulties in trying to implement a policy that both aids women in their work and challenges patriarchal power while enhancing women's citizenship. In both countries there was opposition from the right and from *laissez-faire* economists on the ground that family allowances would undermine the father's obligation to support his children and undermine his 'incentive' to sell his labour-power in the market. The feminist advocates of family allowances in the 1920s, most notably Eleanor Rathbone in Britain, saw the alleviation of poverty in families where the breadwinner's wage was inadequate to meet the family's basic needs as only one argument for this form of state provision. They were also greatly concerned with the questions of the wife's economic dependence and equal pay for men and women workers. If the upkeep of children (or a substantial contribution toward it) was met by the state outside of wage bargaining in the market, then there was no reason why men and women doing the same work should not receive the same pay. Rathbone wrote in 1924 that 'nothing can justify the subordination of one group of producers—the mothers—to the rest and their deprivation of a share of their own in the wealth of a community.'[71] She argued that family allowances would, 'once and for all, cut away the maintenance of children and the reproduction of the race from the question of wages'.[72]

But not all the advocates of child endowment were feminists —so that the policy could very easily be divorced from the public issue of wages and dependence and be seen only as a return for and recognition of women's private contributions. Supporters included the eugenicists and pronatalists, and family allowances appealed to capital and the state as a means of keeping wages down. Family allowances had many opponents in the British union movement, fearful that the consequence, were the measure introduced, would be to undermine the power of unions in wage bargaining. The opponents included women trade unionists who were suspicious of a policy that could be used to try to persuade women to leave paid employment. Some unionists also argued that social services, such as housing, education and health, should be developed first, and the TUC adopted this view in 1930. But were the men concerned, too, with their private, patriarchal privileges? Rathbone claimed that 'the leaders of working men are themselves subconsciously biased by prejudice of sex. . . . Are they not influenced by a secret reluctance to see their wives and children recognised as separate personalities?'[73]

By 1941 the supporters of family allowances in the union movement had won the day, and family allowances were introduced in 1946, as part of the government's wartime plans for post-war reconstruction. The legislation proposed that the allowance would be paid to the father as 'normal household head', but after lobbying by women's organizations, this was overturned in a free vote, and the allowance was paid directly to mothers. In Australia the union movement accepted child endowment in the 1920s (child endowment was introduced in New South Wales in 1927, and at the federal level in 1941). But union support there was based on wider redistributive policies, and the endowment was seen as a supplement to, not a way of breaking down, the family wage.[74] In the 1970s, in both countries, women's organizations again had to defend family allowances and the principle of redistribution from 'the wallet to the purse'.

The hope of Eleanor Rathbone and other feminists that family allowances would form part of a democratic restructuring of the wage system was not realized. Nevertheless, family allowances are paid to women as a benefit in their own right; in that sense they are an important (albeit financially very small) mark of recognition of married women as independent members of the welfare state. Yet the allowance is paid to women as *mothers*, and the key question is thus whether the payment to a mother—a private person—negates her standing as an independent citizen of the welfare state. More generally, the question is whether there can be a welfare policy that gives substantial assistance to women in their daily lives *and* helps create the conditions for a genuine democracy in which women are autonomous citizens, in which we can act *as women* and not as 'woman' (protected/dependent/subordinate) constructed as the opposite to all that is meant by 'man'. That is to say, a resolution of Wollstonecraft's dilemma is necessary and, perhaps, possible.

The structure of the welfare state presupposes that women are men's dependents, but the benefits help to make it possible for women to be economically independent of men. In the countries with which I am concerned, women reliant on state benefits live poorly, but it is no longer so essential as it once was to marry or to cohabit with a man. A considerable moral panic has developed in recent years around 'welfare mothers', a panic that obscures significant features of their position, not least the extent to which the social basis for the ideal of breadwinner/dependent has crumbled. Large numbers of young working-class women have little or no hope of finding employment (or of finding a young man who is employed). But there is a source of social identity available to them that is out of the reach of their male counterparts. The socially secure and acknowledged identity for women is still that of a mother, and for many young women, motherhood, supported by state benefits, provides 'an alternative to aimless adolescence on the dole' and 'gives the appearance of self-determination.' The price of independence and 'a rebellious motherhood that is not an uncritical retreat into femininity'[75] is high, however; the welfare state provides a minimal income and perhaps housing (often sub-standard), but child care services and other support are lacking, so that the young women are often isolated, with no way out of their social exile. Moreover, even if welfare state policies in Britain, Australia and the United States were reformed so that generous benefits, adequate housing, health care, child care, and other services were available to mothers, reliance on the state could reinforce women's lesser citizenship in a new way.

Some feminists have enthusiastically endorsed the welfare state as 'the main recourse of women' and as the generator of 'political resources which, it seems fair to say, are mainly women's resources.'[76] They can point, in Australia for example, to 'the creation over the decade [1975–85] of a range of women's policy machinery and government subsidized women's services (delivered by women for women) which is unrivalled elsewhere'.[77] However, the enthusiasm is met with the rejoinder from other feminists that for women to look to the welfare state is merely to exchange dependence on individual men for dependence on the state. The power and capriciousness of husbands is being replaced by the arbitrariness, bureaucracy and power of the state, the very state that has upheld patriarchal power. The objection is cogent: to make women directly dependent on the state will not in itself do anything to challenge patriarchal power relations. The direct dependence of male workers on the welfare state and their indirect dependence when their standard of living is derived from the vast system of state regulation of and subsidy to capitalism—and in Australia a national arbitration court—have done little to undermine class power. However, the objection also misses an important point. There is one crucial difference between the construction of women as men's dependents and dependence on the welfare state. In the former case, each woman lives with the man on whose benevolence she depends; each woman is (in J. S. Mill's extraordinarily apt phrase) in a 'chronic state of bribery and intimidation combined'.[78] In the welfare state, each woman receives what is hers by right, and she can, potentially, combine with other citizens to enforce her rightful claim. The state has enormous powers of intimidation, but political action takes place collectively in the public terrain and not behind the closed door of the home, where each woman has to rely on her own strength and resources.

Another new factor is that women are now involved in the welfare state on a large scale as employees, so that new possibilities for political action by women also exist. Women have been criticizing the welfare state in recent years not just as academics, as activists, or as beneficiaries and users of welfare services, but as the people on whom the daily operation of the welfare state to a large extent depends. The criticisms range from its patriarchal structure (and, on occasions, especially in health care, misogynist practices), to its bureaucratic and undemocratic policy-making processes and administration, to social work practices and education policy. Small beginnings have been made on changing the welfare state from within; for example, women have succeeded in establishing Well Women Clinics within the NHS in Britain and special units to deal with rape victims in public hospitals in Australia. Furthermore, the potential is now there for united action by women employees, women claimants and women citizens already politically active in the welfare state—not just to protect services against government cuts and efforts at 'privatization' (which has absorbed much energy recently), but to transform the welfare state. Still, it is hard to see how women alone could succeed in the attempt. One necessary condition for the creation of a genuine democracy in which the welfare of *all* citizens is served is an alliance between a labour movement that acknowledges the problem of patriarchal power and an autonomous women's movement that recognizes the problem of class power. Whether such an alliance can be forged is an open question.

Despite the debates and the rethinking brought about by mass unemployment and attack on the union movement and welfare state by the Reagan and Thatcher governments, there are many barriers to be overcome. In Britain and Australia, with stronger welfare states, the women's movement has had a much closer relationship with working-class movements than in the United States, where the individualism of the predominant liberal feminism is an inhibiting factor, and where only about 17 per cent of the workforce is now unionized. The major locus of criticism of authoritarian, hierarchical, undemocratic forms of organization for the last twenty years has been the women's movement. The practical example of democratic, decentralized organization provided by the women's movement has been largely ignored by the labour movement, as well as in academic discussions of democracy. After Marx defeated Bakunin in the First International, the prevailing form of organization in the labour movement, the nationalized industries in Britain and in the left sects has mimicked the hierarchy of the state—both the welfare and the warfare state. To be sure, there is a movement for industrial democracy and workers' control, but it has, by and large, accepted that the 'worker' is a masculine figure and failed to question the separation of (public) industry and economic production from private life. The women's movement has rescued and put into practice the long-submerged idea that movements for, and experiments in, social change must 'prefigure' the future form of social organization.[79]

If prefigurative forms of organization, such as the 'alternative' women's welfare services set up by the women's movement, are not to remain isolated examples, or if attempts to set them up on a wider scale are not to be defeated, as in the past, very many accepted conceptions and practices have to be questioned. Recent debates over left alternatives to Thatcherite economics policies in Britain, and over the Accord between the state, capital and labour in Australia, suggest that the arguments and demands of the women's movement are still often unrecognized by labour's political spokesmen. For instance, one response to unemployment from male workers is to argue for a shorter working week and more leisure, or more time but the same money. However, in women's lives, time and money are not interchangeable in the same way.[80] Women, unlike men, do not have leisure after 'work', but do unpaid work. Many women are arguing, rather, for a shorter working day. The point of the argument is to challenge the separation of part- and full-time paid employment and paid and unpaid 'work'. But the conception of citizenship needs thorough questioning, too, if Wollstonecraft's dilemma is to be resolved; neither the labour movement nor the women's movement (nor democratic theorists) has paid much attention to this. The patriarchal opposition between the private and public, women and citizen, dependent and breadwinner is less firmly based that it once was, and feminists have named it as a political problem. The ideal of full employment so central to the welfare state is also crumbling, so that some of the main props of the patriarchal understanding of citizenship are being undermined. The ideal of full employment appeared to have been achieved in the 1960s only because half the citizen body (and black men?) was denied legitimate membership in the employment society. Now that millions of men are excluded from the ideal (and the exclusion seems permanent), one possibility is that the ideal of universal citizenship will be abandoned, too, and full citizenship become the prerogative of capitalist, employed and armed men. Or can a genuine democracy be created?

The perception of democracy as a class problem and the influence of liberal feminism have combined to keep alive Engels' old solution to 'the woman question'—to 'bring the whole female sex back into public industry'.[81] But the economy has a patriarchal structure. The Marxist hope that capitalism would create a labour force where ascriptive characteristics were irrelevant, and the liberal-feminist hope that anti-discrimination legislation will create a 'gender-neutral' workforce, look utopian even without the collapse of the ideal of full employment. Engel's solution is out of reach—and so, too, is the generalization of masculine citizenship to women. In turn, the argument that the equal worth of citizenship, and the self-respect and mutual respect of citizens, depend upon sale of labour-power in the market and the provisions of the patriarchal welfare state is also undercut. The way is opening up for the formulation of conceptions of respect and equal worth adequate for democratic citizenship. Women could not 'earn' respect or gain the self-respect that men obtain as workers; but what kind of respect do men 'achieve' by selling their labour power and becoming wage-slaves? Here the movement for workplace democracy and the feminist movement could join hands, but only if the conventional understanding of 'work' is rethought. If women as well as men are to be full citizens, the separation of the welfare state and employment from the free welfare work contributed by women has to be broken down and new meanings and practices of 'independence', 'work' and 'welfare' created.

For example, consider the implications were a broad, popular political movement to press for welfare policy to include a guaranteed social income to all adults, which would provide adequately for subsistence and also participation in social life.[82] For such a demand to be made, the old dichotomies must already have started to break down—the opposition between paid and unpaid work (for the first time all individuals could have a genuine choice whether to engage in paid work), between full- and part-time work, between public and private work, between independence and dependence, between work and welfare—which is to say, between men and women. If implemented, such a policy would at last recognize women as equal members of the welfare state, although it would not in itself ensure women's full citizenship. If a genuine democracy is to be created, the problem of the content and value of women's contribution as citizens and the meaning of citizenship has to be confronted.

To analyse the welfare state through the lens of Hegel's dilemma is to rule out such problems. But the history of the past 150 years and the contemporary record show that the welfare of all members

of society cannot be represented by men, whether workers or capitalists. Welfare is, after all, the welfare of all living generations of
citizens and their children. If the welfare state is seen as a response
to Hegel's dilemma, the appropriate question about women's citizenship is: how can women become workers and citizens like men,
and so members of the welfare state like men? If, instead, the
starting-point is Wollstonecraft's dilemma, then the question might
run: what form must democratic citizenship take if a primary task
of all citizens is to ensure that the welfare of each living generation of citizens is secured?

The welfare state has been fought for and supported by the
labour movement and the women's movement because only public or collective provision can maintain a proper standard of living
and the means for meaningful social participation for all citizens
in a democracy. The implication of this claim is that democratic
citizens are both autonomous and interdependent; they are autonomous in that each enjoys the means to be an active citizen,
but they are interdependent in that the welfare of each is the collective responsibility of all citizens. Critics of the class structure
of the welfare state have often counterposed the fraternal interdependence (solidarity) signified by the welfare state to the bleak
independence of isolated individuals in the market, but they have
rarely noticed that both have been predicated upon the dependence (subordination) of women. In the patriarchal welfare state,
independence has been constructed as a masculine prerogative.
Men's 'independence' as workers and citizens is their freedom from
responsibility for welfare (except insofar as they 'contribute' to the
welfare state). Women have been seen as responsible for (private)
welfare work, for relationships of dependence and interdependence.
The paradox that welfare relies so largely on women, on dependents and social exiles whose 'contribution' is not politically relevant to their citizenship in the welfare state, is heightened now
that women's paid employment is also vital to the operation of
the welfare state itself.

If women's knowledge of and expertise in welfare are to become
part of their contribution as citizens, as women have demanded
during the twentieth century, the opposition between men's independence and women's dependence has to be broken down, and
a new understanding and practice of citizenship developed. The
patriarchal dichotomy between women and independence–work–
citizenship is under political challenge, and the social basis for
the ideal of the full (male) employment society is crumbling. An

opportunity has become visible to create a genuine democracy, to move from the welfare state to a welfare society without involuntary social exiles, in which women as well as men enjoy full social membership. Whether the opportunity can be realized is not easy to tell now that the warfare state is overshadowing the welfare state.

Notes

1. R. Williams, *Keywords: A Vocabulary of Culture and Society*, rev. ed. (New York: Oxford University Press, 1985), 333.
2. I have presented a theoretical elaboration of a modern conception of 'patriarchy' as the systematic exercise by men of power over women in *The Sexual Contract* (Cambridge: Polity Press, 1988).
3. Women were formally enfranchised as citizens in 1902 in Australia, 1920 in the USA, and 1928 in Britain (womanhood franchise in 1918 was limited to women over 30 years old).
4. On Scandinavia see e.g. H. Holter (ed.), *Patriarchy in a Welfare Society* (Oslo: Universitetsforlaget, 1984), esp. H. Hernes, 'Women and the Welfare State: The Transition from Private to Public Dependence'; and E. Haavio-Mannila et al. (eds.), *Unfinished Democracy: Women in Nordic Politics* (Oxford: Pergamon, 1985).
5. Z. Eisenstein, *Feminism and Sexual Equality* (New York: Monthly Review Press, New York, 1984), 125.
6. B. Nelson, 'Women's Poverty and Women's Citizenship: Some Political Consequences of Economic Marginality', *Signs*, 10/2 (1984), 221.
7. S. Erie, M. Rein, and B. Wiget, 'Women and the Reagan Revolution: Thermidor for the Social Welfare Economy', in I. Diamond (ed.), *Families, Politics and Public Policy: A Feminist Dialogue on Women and the State* (New York: Longman, 1983), 96.
8. Ibid. 100.
9. S. Kamerman, 'Women, Children and Poverty: Public Policies and Female-Headed Families in Industrialized Countries', *Signs*, 10/2 (1984), 250.
10. J. Smith, 'The Paradox of Women's Poverty: Wage-Earning Women and Economic Transformation', *Signs*, 10/2 (1984), 291.
11. B. Ehrenreich and F. Fox Piven, 'The Feminization of Poverty', *Dissent* (Spring 1984), 162.
12. L. Bryson, 'Women as Welfare Recipients: Women, Poverty and the State', in C. Baldock and B. Cass (eds.) *Women, Social Welfare and the State*, (Sydney: Allen & Unwin, 1983), 135.
13. B. Cass, 'Rewards for Women's Work', in J. Goodnow and C. Pateman (eds.), *Women, Social Science and Public Policy* (Sydney: Allen & Unwin, 1985), 92. Cass also notes that women and their children were overrepresented among the poor making claims on

colonial and post-colonial charities in Australia (p. 70). Similarly, in Britain, from 1834 during the whole period of the New Poor Law, the majority of recipients of relief were women, and they were especially prominent among the very poor; see D. Groves, 'Members and Survivors: Women and Retirement Pensions Legislation', in J. Lewis (ed.), *Women's Welfare Women's Rights* (London: Croom Helm, 1983), 40.

14. L. Doyal, 'Women and the National Health Service: The Carers and the Careless', in E. Lewin and V. Olesen (eds.), *Women, Health and Healing* (London: Tavistock, 1985), 237, 253.

15. H. Land, 'Beggars Can't Be Choosers', *New Statesman* (17 May 1985), 8.

16. Ehrenreich and Fox Piven, 'The Feminization of Poverty', 165; also Erie et al., 'Women and the Reagan Revolution', 100–3.

17. D. Moon, 'The Moral Basis of the Democratic Welfare State', in Amy Gutmann (ed.), *Democracy and the Welfare State* (Princeton, NJ: Princeton University Press, 1988).

18. For examples see T. Brennan and C. Pateman, ' "Mere Auxiliaries to the Commonwealth": Women and the Origins of Liberalism', *Political Studies*, 27 (1979), 183–200.

19. I have taken the term from J. Keane and J. Owens, *After Full Employment* (London: Hutchinson, 1986), 11.

20. Ibid. 15–18, 89–90.

21. G. W. F. Hegel, *Philosophy of Right*, trans. T. M. Knox (Oxford: Clarendon Press, 1952), §171.

22. T. H. Marshall, 'Citizenship and Social Class', repr. in D. Held et al. (eds.), *States and Societies* (New York: New York University Press, 1983), 253.

23. Ibid. 250–1, 257.

24. The graphic phrase is Judith Stiehm's, in 'Myths Necessary to the Pursuit of War' (unpublished paper), 11.

25. See esp. F. Cobbe, 'Wife Torture in England', *Contemporary Review*, 32 (1878), 55–87. Also Mill's remarks when introducing the amendment to enfranchise women in the House of Commons in 1867, repr. in S. Bell and K. Offen (eds.), *Women, the Family and Freedom: The Debate in Documents* (Stanford, Calif.: Stanford University Press, 1983), 487.

26. For more detail, see my 'Women and Consent', *Political Theory*, 8 (1980), 149–68.

27. D. Deacon, 'Political Arithmetic: The Nineteenth-Century Australian Census and the Construction of the Dependent Woman', *Signs*, 11/1 (1985), 31 (my discussion draws on Deacon); also H. Land, 'The Family Wage', *Feminist Review*, 6 (1980), 60.

28. T. Skocpol, 'The Limits of the New Deal System and the Roots of Contemporary Welfare Dilemmas', in M. Weir, A. Orloff, and

T. Skocpol (eds.), *The Politics of Social Policy in the United States* (Princeton, NJ: Princeton University Press, 1988).

29. Nelson, 'Women's Poverty and Women's Citizenship', 222–3.
30. M. Owen, 'Women: A Wastefully Exploited Resource', *Search*, 15 (1984), 271–2.
31. Thompson was a utilitarian, but also a feminist, cooperative socialist, so that he took his individualism more seriously than most utilitarians. In *Appeal of One Half the Human Race, Women, against the Pretensions of the Other Half, Men, to Retain Them in Political, and then in Civil and Domestic Slavery* (New York: Source Book Press, 1970 [first published 1825]), Thompson, writing of the importance of looking at the distribution of interests, or 'the means of happiness', argues that the 'division of interests' must proceed 'until it is brought home to every *individual* of every family'. Instead, under the despotism of husbands and fathers, 'the interest of each of them is promoted, in as far only as it is coincident with, or subservient to, the master's interest' (pp. 46–7, 49).
32. As Beatrix Campbell has reminded us, 'we protect men from the shame of their participation in women's poverty by keeping the secret. Family budgets are seen to be a *private* settlement of accounts between men and women, men's unequal distribution of working-class incomes within their households is a right they fought for within the working-class movement and it is not yet susceptible to *public* political pressure within the movement' (*Wigan Pier Revisited: Poverty and Politics in the 80s*, London: Virago, 1984, 57). Wives are usually responsible for making sure that the children are fed, the rent paid, and so on, but this does not mean that they always decide how much money is allocated to take care of these basic needs. Moreover, in times of economic hardship women are often short of food as well as money; wives will make sure that the 'breadwinner' and the children are fed before they are.
33. L. J. Weitzman, *The Divorce Revolution* (New York: Free Press, 1985), ch. 10, esp. pp. 337–40.
34. Deacon, 'Political Arithmetic', 39.
35. Cited in A. Phillips, *Hidden Hands: Women and Economic Policies* (London: Pluto, 1983), 76.
36. See M. Barrett and M. McIntosh, 'The "Family Wage": Some Problems for Socialists and Feminists', *Capital and Class*, 11 (1980), 56–9.
37. Ibid. 58.
38. Smith, 'The Paradox of Women's Poverty', 300.
39. Phillips, *Hidden Hands*, 21.
40. The perception is common to both women and men. (I would argue that women's perception of themselves is not, as is often suggested, a consequence of 'socialization', but a realistic appraisal of their

structural position at home and in the workplace.) For empirical evidence on this view of women workers, see e.g. A. Pollert, *Girls, Wives, Factory Lives* (London: Macmillan, 1981); J. Wacjman, *Women in Control: Dilemmas of a Workers' Cooperative* (New York: St Martin's Press, 1983).

41. C. Baldock, 'Public Policies and the Paid Work of Women', in Baldock and Cass, *Women, Social Welfare and the State*, 34, 40.
42. Land, 'The Family Wage', 62.
43. B. Cass, 'Redistribution to Children and to Mothers: A History of Child Endowment and Family Allowances', in Baldock and Cass, *Women, Social Welfare and the State*, 62.
44. Campbell, *Wigan Pier Revisited*, 130–1.
45. A. Hacker, ' "Welfare": The Future of an Illusion', *New York Review of Books* (28 Feb. 1985). 41.
46. Ehrenreich and Fox Piven, 'The Feminization of Poverty', 163.
47. S. Hewlett, *A Lesser life: The Myth of Women's Liberation in America* (New York: William Morrow, 1986), 76.
48. Women's Bureau, Department of Employment and Industrial Relations, *Women At Work* (Apr. 1986).
49. I. Bruegel, 'Women's Employment, Legislation and the Labour Market', in Lewis, *Women's Welfare*, 133 and table 7.4.
50. 'Skill' is another patriarchal category; it is men's work that counts as 'skilled'. See the discussion in C. Cockburn, *Brothers: Male Dominance and Technological Change* (London: Pluto, 1983), 112–22.
51. Doyle, 'Women and the National Health Service', 250–4; and A. Oakley, 'Women and Health Policy', in Lewis, *Women's Welfare*, 120 and table 6.3.
52. *Women at Work* (Apr. 1986).
53. Phillips, *Hidden Hands*, 15.
54. Bruegel, 'Women's Employment', 135.
55. Hewlett, *A Lesser Life*, 72.
56. Smith, 'The Paradox of Women's Poverty', 304, 307; quotation, 306.
57. J. Dale and P. Foster, *Feminists and the Welfare State* (London: Routledge & Kegan Paul, 1986), 112.
58. H. Land, 'Who Cares for the Family?', *Journal of Social Policy*, 7/3 (1978), 268–9. Land notes that even under the old Poor Law twice as many women as men received outdoor relief, and there were many more old men than women in the workhouse wards for the ill or infirm; the women were deemed fit for the wards for the able-bodied.
59. Campbell, *Wigan Pier Revisited*, 76.
60. Nelson, 'Woman's Poverty and Women's Citizenship', 229–30.
61. Both quotations are taken from Land, 'The Family Wage', 72.
62. Cited in Dale and Foster, *Feminists and the Welfare State*, 17.
63. H. Land, 'Who Still Cares for the Family?', in Lewis, *Women's Welfare*, 70.

64. M. Davis, *Maternity: Letters from Working Women* (New York: Norton, 1978) (first published 1915).

65. Information taken from Land, 'Who Cares for the Family?', 263–4.

66. Land, 'Who Still Cares for the Family?', 73.

67. Cited in Dale and Foster, *Feminists and the Welfare State*, 3.

68. There was considerable controversy within the women's movement between the wars over the question of protective legislation for women in industry. Did equal citizenship require the removal of such protection, so that women worked under the same conditions as men; or did the legislation benefit women, and the real issue become proper health and safety protection for both men and women workers?

69. I have discussed the earlier arguments in more detail in 'Women and Democratic Citizenship', Jefferson Memorial Lectures, University of California, Berkeley, 1985, Lecture I.

70. For example, Wollstonecraft writes, 'speaking of women at large, their first duty is to themselves as rational creatures, and the next, in point of importance, as citizens, is that, which includes so many, of a mother.' She hopes that a time will come when a 'man must necessarily fulfil the duties of a citizen, or be despised, and that while he was employed in any of the departments of civil life, his wife, also an active citizen, should be equally intent to manage her family, educate her children, and assist her neighbours'. *A Vindication of the Rights of Woman* (New York: Norton, 1975), 145, 146.

71. Cited in Land, 'The Family Wage', 63.

72. Cited in Cass, 'Redistribution to Children and to Mothers', 57. My discussion draws on Land and Cass. In the USA during the same period, feminists supported the movement for mothers' pensions. Unlike mothers eligible for family allowances, mothers eligible for pensions were without male breadwinners. The complexities of mothers' pensions are discussed by W. Sarvesy, 'The Contradictory Legacy of the Feminist Welfare State Founders', paper presented to the annual meeting of the American Political Science Association, Washington, DC, 1986.

73. Cited in Cass, 'Redistribution', 59.

74. Ibid. 60–1.

75. Campbell, *Wigan Pier Revisited*, 66, 78, 71.

76. F. Fox Piven, 'Women and the State: Ideology, Power, and the Welfare State', *Socialist Review*, 14/2 (1984), 14, 17.

77. M. Sawer, 'The Long March through the Institutions: Women's Affairs under Fraser and Hawke', paper presented to the annual meeting of the Australasian Political studies Association, Brisbane, 1986, 1.

78. J. S. Mill, 'The Subjection of Women', in *Essays on Sex Equality*, ed. A. Rossi (Chicago: University of Chicago Press, 1970), 137.

79. See S. Rowbotham, L. Segal, and H. Wainright, *Beyond the Fragments: Feminism and the Making of Socialism* (London: Merlin, 1979), a book that was instrumental in opening debate on the left and in the labour movement in Britain on this question.

80. See H. Hernes, *Welfare State and Woman Power: Essays in State Feminism* (Oslo: Norwegian University Press, 1987), ch. 5, for a discussion of the political implications of the different time-frames of men's and women's lives.

81. F. Engels, *The Origin of the Family, Private Property and the State* (New York: International Publishers, 1942), 66.

82. See also the discussion in Keane and Owens, *After Full Employment,* 175–7.

Part III. Gendered Sites in the Late Modern Public Sphere

10 Live Sex Acts (Parental Advisory: Explicit Material)

Lauren Berlant

> I am a citizen of the United States, and in this country where I live, every year millions of pictures are being made of women with our legs spread. We are called beaver, we are called pussy, our genitals are tied up, they are pasted, makeup is put on them to make them pop out of a page at a male viewer. . . . I live in a country where if you film any act of humiliation or torture, and if the victim is a woman, the film is both entertainment and it is protected speech. Now that tells me something about being a woman in this country.
>
> Andrea Dworkin, quoted in Edward de Grazia,
> *Girls Lean Back Everywhere: The Law of Obscenity and
> the Assault on Genius*

I open with this passage not simply to produce in advance the resistances, ambivalences, and concords that inevitably arise when someone speaks with passion and authority about sex and identity but, rather, to foreground here the centrality, to any public sphere politics of sexuality, of coming to terms with the conjunction of making love and making law, of fucking and talking, of acts and identities, of cameras and police, of pleasure in the text and patriarchal privilege, insofar as these couplings can be found in fantasies of citizenship and longings for freedom made in the name of national culture.

I'm going to tell you a story about this, a story about citizenship in the United States. It is about live sex acts, and also about a book called *Live Sex Acts*, and about a thing called national culture that, in reference to the United States, I mean to bring into

Reprinted by permission from *Feminist Studies*, 21/2 (Summer 1995), 379–404. Copyright © 1995 by Feminist Studies, Inc. c/o Department of Women's Studies, University of Maryland, College Park MD 20742. Thanks to Roger Rouse, Kim Scheppele, Michael Warner, and the great audiences at the University of Michigan, Rutgers, and Brown for much-needed conversation and challenge.

representation here—which is hard, because the modality of national culture in the United States I will describe exists mainly as a negative projection, an endangered species, the shadow of a fetish currently under a perceived attack by sex radicals, queers, pornographers, and pop music culture. Of course, national culture, an archive that perpetually seeks a future, is always a negative sign to be defined, even when it appears as a positive one with an essential character. Because the nation can only assure itself a past, the national culture industry that operates in the public sphere generates a mode of political discourse that, in the United States, seeks to trump all other explanations and images of collective sociality and power—just as the nation itself aspires to saturate the horizon of the modern political imagination in order proleptically to dominate the future. Above all, and for all the explicit information citizens receive about what is happening at the core of the nation and national society, the national culture industry in the United States also generates competing amnesias about the means by which the nation's hegemonic contradictions and contingencies are constructed, consented to, and displaced. The relation between knowledge and amnesia in this view is not a binary one, one of mutual negation. Rather, it remains always a point of contestation how thoroughly the forms of intelligibility that give citizens access to political culture are monuments to false consciousness, or the inevitable partial truths of publicly held information, or, as Michael Taussig says, the full 'coming together of reason and violence' that generates paradoxes of knowing and unknowing, such that constellations of ordinary pragmatic detail, good-enough comprehensions of national activity, and traumatized pseudoknowledges together can be said to constitute the ongoing lived relations among states, national ideology, and citizens.[1]

This essay began as a review of some recent feminist work on pornography.[2] In it I take no position on 'pornography', as such, but discuss it in terms of how, more broadly, the US citizen's vulnerability and aspiration to a nationally protected identity has been orchestrated through a variety of sexualizing media forms. In this regard the essay refocuses the discussion away from the domain of the politics of sexual difference and toward the conjunction of sexuality, mass culture, and mass nationality.

In particular, I am interested in tracing some meanings of privacy, a category of law and a condition of property that constitutes a boundary between proper and improper bodies, and a horizon of aspiration vital to the imagination of what counts as legitimate

US citizenship. Privacy here describes, simultaneously, a theoretical space imagined by US constitutional and statutory law; a scene of taxonomic violence that devolves privilege on certain actual spaces of practical life; a juridical substance that comes to be synonymous with secure domestic interiority; and a structure of protection and identity that sanctions, by analogy, other spaces that surround, secure, and frame the bodies whose acts, identities, identifications, and social value are the booty over which national culture wages its struggle to exist as a struggle to dominate sex.

Thus, this story will indeed contain graphic images, parental advisories, and magical thinking—that is to say, the usual dialectic between crassness and sublimity that has long dressed the ghosts of national culture in monumental forms and made it available for anxious citizens who need to invoke it on behalf of stabilizing one or another perceived social norm. This story has real and fictive characters, too—John Frohnmayer, Andrea Dworkin, Tipper Gore, and some fat, queer Nazis who try to join the military; but its main players are a little girl and an adult, both Americans. The little girl stands in this essay as a condensation of many citizenship fantasies. It is in her name as future citizen that state and federal governments have long policed morality around sex and other transgressive representations; the psychological and political vulnerability she represents has provided a model for other struggles to transform minority experience in the United States. And it is in her name that something other to her, called, let's say, 'adult culture', has been defined and privileged in many national domains. Although not without its contradictions: we have the 'adult' by whose name pornography is marked, as in 'adult books'—and the one who can, on the other hand, join with other adults to protect the still unhistorical little girl whose citizenship, if the adults act as good parents, might pass boringly from its minority to what has been called the 'zone of privacy' or national heterosexuality 'adult' Americans generally seek to inhabit.

'Zone of privacy' is a technical phrase, invented in a Supreme Court opinion of 1965. It was Justice William O. Douglass's opinion in *Griswold* v. *Connecticut* that designated for the first time the heterosexual act of intercourse in marital bedrooms as protected by a zone of privacy into which courts must not peer and with which they must not interfere. Justice Douglass's rezoning of the bedroom into a nationally protected space of privacy allowed married citizens of Connecticut for the first time to purchase birth control. It sought to make national a relation that it says precedes the Bill of Rights. It consolidated the kind of thinking that happened when the justices recently, in *Bowers* v. *Hardwick*, confirmed the irreducible heterosexuality of the national bedroom, as it established once again that homosexuality has no constitutionally supported privacy protections in the United States. It could have been otherwise. Writing a memo to be circulated among Supreme Court justices, Daniel Richman, a clerk for Thurgood Marshall, sought to instruct the Court about oral and anal sex. He wrote to the justices, in capital letters, 'THIS IS NOT A CASE ABOUT ONLY HOMOSEXUALS. ALL SORTS OF PEOPLE DO THIS KIND OF THING.'[3] He does not name the 'sorts' of people. But in almost referring to heterosexuality, that sacred national identity that happens in the neutral territory of national culture, Richman almost made the 'sex' of heterosexuality imaginable, corporeal, visible, public.

Thus, I mean to oppose a story about live sex acts to a story about 'dead citizenship'. Dead citizenship, which haunts the shadowland of national culture, takes place in a privacy zone and epitomizes an almost Edenic conjunction of act and identity, sacred and secular history. It involves a theory of national identity that equates identity with iconicity. It requires that I tell you a secret history of acts that are not experienced as acts, because they take place in the abstract idealized time and space of citizenship. I use the word 'dead', then, in the rhetorical sense designated by the phrase 'dead metaphor'. A metaphor is dead when, by repetition, the unlikeness risked in the analogy the metaphor makes becomes so conventionalized as to no longer seem figural, no longer open to history: the leg of a table is the most famous dead metaphor. In the fantasy life-world of national culture, citizens aspire to dead identities—constitutional personhood in its public sphere abstraction and suprahistoricity; reproductive heterosexuality in the zone of privacy. Identities not live, or in play; but dead, frozen, fixed, or at rest.

The fear of ripping away the privacy protections of heteronational culture has led to a national crisis over the political meanings of imaginable, live, and therefore transgressive sex acts, acts that take place in public either by virtue of a state optic or a subcultural style. By bringing more fully into relief the politics of securing the right to privacy in the construction of a sexuality that bears the definitional burden of national culture, I am in part telling a story about preserving a boundary between: what can be done and said in public, what can be done in private but not spoken of in public, and what can, patriotically speaking, neither be done nor legitimately spoken of at all, in the United States. Thus, there is nothing new about the new national anthem, 'Don't Ask, Don't Tell, Don't Pursue'. I am also telling a story about transformations of the body in mass national society and thinking about a structure of political feeling that characterizes the history of national sentimentality, in which, at moments of crisis, persons violate the zones of privacy that give them privilege and protection in order to fix something social that feels threatening: they practice politics, they generate publicity, they act in public, but in the name of privacy. I mean to bring into representation these forms of citizenship structured in dominance, in scenes where adults act on behalf of the little girl form that represents totemically and fetishistically the unhumiliated citizen.[4] She is the custodian of the promise of zones of privacy that national culture relies on for its magic and its reproduction.

LOOKING FOR LOVE IN ALL THE WRONG PLACES: LIVE SEX ACTS IN AMERICA

When John Frohnmayer made his pilgrimage to serve the National Endowment of the Arts (NEA) in Washington, DC, he was a 'babe in the woods' of politics who hoped to 'rekindl[e]' the 'free spirit' of a nation that he saw to be defiled by the televisually alienated forces of the public sphere in the United States. He initially imagined using the NEA to reproduce the nation through its localities—emphasizing not cities (which are, apparently, not localities) but the rural and provincial cultures whose neglected 'vitality' might help return the mass nation to a non-mass-mediated sense of tribal intimacy. Frohnmayer's autobiography, *Leaving Town Alive: Confessions of an Arts Warrior*, describes in great detail the deep roots of the nation in aesthetic genealogies of an organic citizenry. For example, he tells of the gospel roots of rap, the spirit of fiddling in an age of 'overamplified electronic music', Native American weaving, ballet, and other arts that make 'no mention of homosexuality, foul words, or nudity'[5]—which, according to this logic, become phenomena of cities and of mass culture.

But Frohnmayer's tenure at the NEA ran into the muck of the competition between a certain metropolitan and an uncertain national culture that finally drove him out of office. The cases of the X, Y, and Z portfolios of Robert Mapplethorpe, of the NEA Four, and of *Tongues Untied* are famous examples of how sex-radical performance aesthetics and visual cultures were inassimilable to the homophobic and mock-populist official national culture-making machine in Washington. But what got Frohnmayer fired was the NEA's support of a *literary* publication project in New York City that dragged the nation into the dirt, the waste, and the muck of sex and other gross particularities. This project, managed by a press called 'the portable lower east side', produced two texts in 1991: *Live Sex Acts* and *Queer City*. The Reverend Donald Wildmon made these texts available to every member of Congress, President George Bush, and Vice-President Dan Quayle. He also wrote a letter to them citing an excerpt from a poem as evidence for the virtually treasonous use of taxpayer money to support art that besmirched national culture. My first exhibit, or should I say, my first 'inhibit', is the poem 'Wild Thing', published in *Queer City*. 'Wild Thing', written by the poet 'Sapphire' (Ramona Lofton), performs in the fictive voice of one of the boys whose wilding expedition in 1989 resulted in the rape and beating of the woman called 'the Central Park jogger'.

> I remember when
> Christ sucked my dick
> behind the pulpit
> I was 6 years old
> he made me promise
> not to tell no one.[6]

I will return to this poem anon. But first, let me characterize these scandalous magazines. Frohnmayer describes *Queer City* accurately: 'Although some of the pieces were sexual in tone and content, they were clearly meant to be artful rather than prurient.'[7] *Queer City* is a collective work of local culture, positing New York as a vibrant site of global sexual identity, a multinational place where people come to traverse the streets, live the scene, have sex, write stories and poems about it, and take pictures of the people who live it with pleasure and impunity. It is an almost entirely apolitical book, except in the important sense that the title *Queer City* remaps New York by way of the spaces where queer sex takes place, such that sexual identities are generated in *public*, in a metropolitan public constituted by a culture of experience and a flourish of publicity.

In contrast, and although *Live Sex Acts* is equally situated in New York City, a marked majority of its texts explain sex in terms of the national context and the political public sphere; indeed, many of the essays in *Live Sex Acts* are explicit responses to the right-wing cultural agenda of the Reagan-Bush era. They demonstrate that it is not sexual identity as such that threatens America, which is liberal as long as sex aspires to iconicity or deadness, and suggest, rather, that the threat to national culture derives from what we might call sex acts on the live margin, sex acts that threaten because they do not aspire to the privacy protection of national culture, nor to the narrative containment of sex into one of the conventional romantic forms of modern consumer heterosexuality. This assertion of a sexual public sphere is also striking because *Live Sex Acts* closes by moving beyond a sexual performance ethic and toward other live margins. Two final segments, Krzysztof Wodiczko's 'Poliscar: A Homeless Vehicle' and a portfolio of poems by patients at Creedmoor Psychiatric Hospital, explicitly seek to redefine citizenship by naming who lives on the live margins, and how. They show how the waste products of America must generate a national public sphere and a civic voice. To do this, the live margin must find its own media. A radically redefined category of live sex acts here becomes a mass medium for addressing and redressing the national culture industry.

In any case, as Frohnmayer says, the scandal these two magazines created had nothing to do with what kinds of subversive effect their small circulation might conceivably have had or aspired to, with respect either to sexual convention or national identity. He describes the uproar as a scandal of reading. Donald Wildmon has spent much time in the last decade policing sexual subcultures by attempting to humiliate state and federal arts councils for using taxpayer money to support transgressions of norms a putative ordinary America holds sacred. To christen the national as a locale with discernible standards of propriety, he uses the logic of obscenity law, which since the 1970s has offered local zones the opportunity to specify local standards with respect to which federal law might determine the obscenity of a text.

Wildmon is unconcerned with the referential context of both the wild thing and the poem about it. He seeks to make irrelevant any full exploration of the wilding poem in terms of the juridical and popular ideology of live sex and national culture it both symptomatized and helped to consolidate. Many have noted how the serious discussion of this event in terms of the politics of public spaces, of housing projects, of city parks as homes and public property, of gender, of race, of classes and underclasses, of sexuality, of mass media, and of the law was deflected into a melodrama of the elite. But, already on record accusing the NEA of promoting 'blasphemy' *and* 'the homosexual lifestyle', Wildmon grasped the passage 'Christ sucked my dick' and brought its attention to Jesse Helms, who shortly thereafter got Frohnmayer, whom Pat Robertson had nicknamed 'Satan', fired.[8]

Frohnmayer claims to know nothing about homosexuality in the United States, and I believe he is right, although he knows something about homoeroticism. For example, in arguing against the Helms Amendment[9] he suggests the difficulty of telling 'whether homoeroticism differed from garden-variety eroticism, whether it applied to females as well as males, whether it would pass muster under the Fourteenth Amendment tests of rational classifications and equal protection, or whether it was illegal for two persons of the same gender to hold hands, kiss, or do something more in deep shadow'.[10] Of course we know there is no deep shadow for gay sex in America: deep shadow is the protected zone of heterosexuality, or dead citizenship, and meanwhile all queers have is that closet. But if Frohnmayer does not know sex law, he knows what art is and also knows that when the NEA funds works of art it effectively protects them from obscenity prosecution.[11] Thus, he legitimates this poem and *Queer City in toto* by reference to the standard of what art *attempts*. If the aspiration to art makes sexual representation protected by the national imprimatur, it is the content of 'Wild Thing' that secures the success of its aspiration.

These lines have been taken out of context and sensationalized. The poem, in its entirety, is emotional, intense and serious. . . . [It] deals with an actual event—the violent rape of a female jogger in Central Park— and must be read in its entirety in order to receive a fair appraisal. . . . It's not meant to make us feel good. It's not meant as an apology for a violent act. And it's certainly not meant to be sacrilegious, unless pedophilia is part of religious dogma. The poem is meant to make us think and to reflect on an incredibly brutal act in an allegedly civilized society.[12]

Again, there is much to say about wilding, the wild thing, the poem about it, the song it refers to, and the wild incitement to govern expression this unfinished event has generated, which results in the contest over national meaning and value. First of all, Wildmon reads the poem as a direct indictment of the church for its alleged implied support of homosexual child molestation. Frohnmayer contests this reading with one that focuses on the purported failure of the black family to guide youth toward disciplined obedience to patriarchal authority. In Frohnmayer's description, the fate of the white woman represents what will happen to America when undersocialized boys abused by life in the projects and failed by parents leave their degenerate natal locales. They will terrorize property, women, and the nation; they will be bad men.

Frohnmayer's version of the poem cuts out entirely the poet's image of the fun, the pleasure, indeed the death-driven *jouissance* of the wilding man, his relation to mass culture, to his own body, to his rage at white women and men, his pleasure in his mastery over language, and over the racist conventions he knows he inspires. Clearly that isn't the stuff of art or America. Most importantly, Frohnmayer also parentalizes the nation by locating the virtue of art in its disclosure that the source of sexual violence and social decay (the end of American civilization) is in absent fathers and failed mothers. He ventriloquizes the poet's ventriloquized poem about wayward youth to prophesy about the future of national culture, which is in danger of collective acts of wilding. This hybrid official image: of the nation as a vicious youth, and as a formerly innocent youth betrayed by bad parenting, and as a child who might be saved by good official parents, is at the heart of contemporary citizenship policy. Here is a story about the attempt to construct a national culture that resists an aesthetic of live sex in the name of youth, heterosexuality, and the national future.

WHAT 'ADULTS' DO TO 'LITTLE GIRLS': MINOR CITIZENS IN THE MODERN NATION

When Anthony Comstock made his pilgrimage to Washington in 1873 to show the Congress what kinds of literature, information, and advertisements about sex, contraception, and abortion were being distributed through the US mails, he initiated a process of nationalizing the discipline of sexual representation in the United States in the name of protecting national culture. Comstock installed this regime of anxiety and textual terror by invoking the image of youth and, in particular, the stipulated standard of the

285

little girl whose morals, mind, acts, body, and identity would certainly be corrupted by contact with adult immorality.[13] Until the 1957 *Roth* v. *United States* and the 1964 rulings on the novel *The Tropic of Cancer* and the film *Les Amants*, the Comstockian standard of the seducible little girl reigned prominently in court decisions about the obscenity of texts; indeed, as Edward de Grazia describes in *Girls Lean Back Everywhere: The Law of Obscenity and the Assault on Genius*, this putative little girl who might come into harmful contact with unsafe sexual knowledge and thus be induced by reading into performing harmful live sex acts (at least of interpretation) has been central to defining minor and full citizenship in the United States. She has come to represent the standard from which the privileged 'adult' culture of the nation has fallen. Protecting her, while privileging him, establishing therein the conditions of minor and full citizenship, has thus been a project of pornographic modernity in the United States.

To certify obscenity legally, a three-pronged standard must be met. The material must appeal to a prurient interest in sex, must be patently offensive to contemporary community standards, and must be 'utterly without redeeming social value'.[14] The Roth and Miller decisions nationalized obscenity law for the first time, thus defining the adult who consumes pornography as an American in the way that the Fourteenth Amendment enfranchised African-Americans as full citizens by locating primary citizenship in the nation and only secondarily in states. Speaking of pornography's consumers, Andrea Dworkin and Catharine MacKinnon put succinctly this conjuncture of what we might call pornographic personhood, an amalgam of nation, nurture, and sacred patriarchy: 'Pornography is their Dr. Spock, their Bible, their Constitution.'[15] De Grazia's history of American obscenity, along with his anthology *Censorship Landmarks*, reveals how the pressure to define obscenity has all along involved a struggle to define the relative power of national, state, and local cultures to control the contact the public might have with prurient materials. For example, in *Jacobellis* v. *Ohio*, the Ohio case concerning *Les Amants*, Justice Brennan argued: 'We recognize the legitimate and indeed exigent interest of States and localities throughout the Nation in preventing the dissemination of material deemed harmful to children. But that interest does not justify a total suppression of such material, the effect of which would be to reduce the adult population . . . to reading only what is fit for children.'[16] This tendency to nationalize the obscene, the child, and the adult has been checked by the 'community standards' doctrine embraced by Chief Justice Warren Burger in 1973. This doctrine empowers local police, judges, prosecutors, juries, and citizen interest groups to determine the standards of local morality from which the nation should protect them. The Burger court thus dissolved a major blockage to promoting a conservative cultural agenda, at least from the vantage-point of Supreme Court precedent; the constitutional protection of free speech against the 'chilling effect' of censorship, which sought to avert the terroristic effects of political repression on speech, could be avoided by localizing the relevant 'context' according to the most local community standards. Central to establishing and maintaining these standards is the figure of the vulnerable little girl, a figure for minors-in-general. The situation of protected minor citizenship is thus a privilege for protection from adult heterosexual exploitation that national culture confers on its youth, its little girls and boys; paradoxically, the aura of the little girl provides a rationale for protecting the heterosexual privacy zones of 'adult' national culture.

Sometimes, when the little girl, the child, or youth are invoked in discussions of pornography, obscenity, or the administration of morality in US mass culture, actually endangered living beings are being imagined. Frequently, however, we should understand that these disturbing figures are fetishes, effigies that condense, displace, and stand in for arguments about who 'the people' are, what they can bear, and when, if ever. The purpose of this excursus into the history of obscenity law has been to recast it within an assembly of parental gestures in which adult citizens are protected as children are protected from representations of violence and sex and violent sex, for fear that those representations are in effect understood as doctrine or as documentary fantasy. Even the most liberal obscenity law concedes that children must neither see nor hear immoral sex/text acts: they must neither know it or see it, at least until they reach that ever more unlikely moment of majority when they can consent freely to reading with a kind of full competence they must first be protected from having.

Nowhere is this infantilizing confluence of media, citizenship, and sex more apparent and symptomatically American than in the work of Andrea Dworkin, Catharine MacKinnon, and the 1986 report on obscenity popularly called the Meese Commission Report. Much has been written on the paradoxical effects of this collaboration between these radical feminists and the conservative cultural activity of the Republican-dominated State. Carole

Vance and Edward de Grazia give scathing, detailed accounts of the ideological excesses and incoherences of this collaboration, and MacKinnon and Dworkin write eloquently about why the sexual harms women experience must be mended by law.[17] I am not interested in adjudicating this debate here in its usual terms (civil rights/harm speech/antipatriarchal versus first amendment/free speech/sex radical)—but I mean to be entering it obliquely, by examining the logic of its citizenship politics. I am interested in how it has helped to consolidate an image of the citizen as a minor, female, youthful victim who requires civil protection by the state whose adult citizens, especially adult men, seem mobilized by a sexual- and capital-driven compulsion to foul their own national culture.

This story can be told in many ways. The first step of the argument by which pornography represents harm speech that fundamentally compromises women's citizenship in the United States establishes that pornography is a live sex act. It is live partly because, as the Milwaukee ordinance avows, 'Pornography is what pornography *does*.' There is a sense here, shared by many textual critics (not just of pornography), that texts are muscular active persons in some sense of the legal fiction that makes corporations into persons: texts can and do impose their will on consumers, innocent or consenting.[18] Second, this notion of textual activity, of the harm pornographic texts perform as a desired direct effect on their consumers, has become intensified and made more personal by the visual character of contemporary pornography.

The optical unconscious dominates the scene of citizenship and pornographic exploitation the Meese Commission conjures. I quote at length the opening to the chapter called 'The Use of Performers in Commercial Pornography'. This chapter opens with a passage from Andre Bazin's 'The Ontology of the Photographic Image': 'The objective nature of photography confers on it a quality of credibility absent from all other picture-making. . . . The photographic image is the object itself, the object freed from the conditions of time and space that govern it.' The text glosses this representation of the image:

The leap from 'picture making' to photography was . . . the single most important event in the history of pornography: images of the human body could be captured and preserved in exact, vivid detail. As with every other visible activity, sex could now, by the miraculous power of the camera, be 'freed from the conditions of time and space.' 'Sex' in the abstract, of course, remains invisible to the camera; it is particular acts of sex between individual people which photographs, films, and video tapes can record.

By equating the violence that photography performs on history and personhood with the citizenship harms of pornography, Dworkin and MacKinnon locate the solution to sexual violence in a return to the scene and the mode of production, and, indeed, MacKinnon sees herself as a materialist feminist for this reason. This view has effected a fundamental shift in the focus of assessments of pornography's effects. Although social scientists still try to measure whether seeing violence leads to violence, and how, the antipornography view also insists on engaging with the backstory of the porn, taking its effect on performers and on the businessmen who control the condition of the performers as an important measure of its meaning. Furthermore, as we shall see, the exploitation of the pornographic performer becomes the model for the exploitation and violence to all women inscribed in the circuit of pornography's circulation.

Unlike literature or drawing, sexually explicit photography cannot be made by one person. . . . No study of filmed pornography can thus be complete without careful attention to the circumstances under which individual people decide to appear in it, and the effects of that appearance on their lives. Nor is this an academic or trivial exercise. The evidence before us suggests that a substantial minority of women will at some time in their lives be asked to pose for or perform in sexually-explicit materials. It appears, too, that the proportion of women receiving such requests has increased steadily over the past several decades. If our society's appetite for sexually-explicit material continues to grow, or even if it remains at current levels, the decision whether to have sex in front of a camera will confront thousands of Americans.[19]

The ordinary woman and the pornographic model will experience second-class citizenship in US society, the argument goes, because sexualization constructs every woman as a potential performer of live sex acts that get photographed. Indeed, their story goes, even models in pornographic films insist that 'acting' in pornography is a fiction: it is sex work euphemized as acting; it is public euphemized as private and personal; it is coerced and exploitative, euphemized as consensual and part of a simple business exchange.

To find a precedent for protecting actors in pornography from experiencing in their jobs the unfreedom US women experience in everyday heterosexual life, the Meese Commission, MacKinnon, and Dworkin turn to the model of child pornography, both to psychologize the vulnerability of women and to justify the prosecution of all pornographers. 'Perhaps the single most common feature of models is their relative, and in the vast majority of cases, absolute youth.' By definition, pornographers are exploiting young girls when they pay women to perform sex acts in front of cameras. Exploiting women-as-young-girls, they are performing a class action against women's full citizenship in the American public sphere.

Pornographers promote an image of free consent because it is good for business. But most women in pornography are poor, were sexually abused as children, and have reached the end of this society's options for them, options that were biased against them as women in the first place. This alone does not make them coerced for purposes of the Ordinance; but the fact that some women may 'choose' pornography from a stacked deck of life pursuits (if you call a loaded choice a choice, like the 'choice' of those with brown skin to pick cabbages or the 'choice' of those with black skin to clean toilets) and the fact that some women in pornography say they made a free choice does not mean that women who are coerced into pornography are *not coerced*. Pimps roam bus stations to entrap young girls who left incestuous homes thinking nothing could be worse. . . . Young women are tricked or pressured into posing for boyfriends and told that the pictures are just 'for us', only to find themselves in this month's *Hustler*. . . . Women in pornography are bound, battered, tortured, harassed, raped, and sometimes killed. . . . Children are presented as adult women; adult women are presented as children, fusing the vulnerability of a child with the sluttish eagerness to be fucked said to be natural to the female of every age.[20]

Leo Bersani has argued that the big secret about sex is that most people don't like it, but also that the fundamental transgressiveness and irrationality of sex makes its enactment a crucial opportunity to resist the dead identities of the social.[21] We see in the antipornographic polemic of MacKinnon and Dworkin a fundamental agreement with Bersani's position: but, more dramatically, the little girl too sexualized to be a citizen has no privilege, no 'adult' advantages, that would allow her to shuttle between legitimated sociality and a sexual resistance to it. Rather, she is the opposite of 'someone who matters, someone with rights, a full human being, and a full citizen'.[22] The sentimental logic of this antipornography argument thus links women and children to the nation in a variety of ways. In terms of the public sphere where civil rights are experienced as a matter of everyday life, women are paradoxically both the bearers of the value of privacy and always exposed and available to be killed into identity, which is to say into photography, into a sexual optic, and into heterosexuality, but not the sacred kind. Thus, the cycle of pornography: it makes men child abusers who sentimentalize and degrade their objects; meanwhile, because young girls and women need to survive both materially and psychically in a culture of abuse, they become addicted to the stereotypical structure of sexual value and exploitation, forced to become either subjects in or to pornography. In this way the child's, the young girl's vulnerability is the scene merely covered over and displaced by the older women's pseudoautonomy; the young girl's minority is the true scene of arrested development of all US women's second-class citizenship. For this reason, this logic of infantile second-class citizenship has become both a moral dominant in the public sphere and a precedent in court prosecution of pornography.[23]

Court prosecution of pornography found its excuse to rescue adult women from pornographic performance by taking the image of the vulnerable child performer of sex acts as the auratic truth of the adult. The Supreme Court decision on *New York* v. *Ferber* in 1982 for the first time extended its analysis of such material to encompass the 'privacy interests' of the performers—in this case children. Filming children in the midst of explicit sexual activity not only harmed them because of the sexual abuse involved but also because 'the materials produced are a permanent record of the children's participation and the harm to the child is exacerbated by their circulation'. In addition, the continued existence of a market for such materials was bound to make it more likely that children would be abused in the future, thus justifying a ban on distribution.[24] We have seen this argument before—that child abuse begets itself, child porn begets both abuse and porn, and that these beget the damaged inner children of adult women, who therefore must be saved from the child pornography that is the truth of their submission to the sex apparatus that befouls the national culture whose privileges women have either no access to, or access to only by virtue of proximity to heterosexual genital intercourse. The stakes of this vision of juridical deliverance are therefore not just personal to some US women but reveal fundamental conditions of national identity for all women in the United States.

Even more striking is how vital a horizon of fantasy national culture remains, even to some radicals, in its promise of corporeal safety and the privacy of deep shadow. When Dworkin asserts that women's everyday experience of sexual degradation in the United States is both a condition of their second-class citizenship and the most fundamental betrayal of them all, she seeks to occupy the most politically privileged privacy protections of the very national sexuality whose toxic violence defines the lives of US women. Here America's promise to release its citizens from having a body to humiliate trumps the feminist or materialist visionary politics Dworkin might have espoused, politics that would continue to imagine a female body as a citizen's body that remains vulnerable because public and alive, engaged in the ongoing struggles of making history.

HOW TO RAISE PG KIDS IN AN X-RATED NATION

We have seen that in Washington the nationalist aspirations to iconicity of the high arts and the *ars erotica* play out a wish to dissolve the body. They reveal a desire for identity categories to be ontological; dead to history; not in any play or danger of representation, anxiety, improvisation, desire, or panic. This sentimentality suggests how fully the alarm generated around identity politics in the United States issues from a nostalgia or desire for a suprahistorical nationally-secured personhood that does not look to acts of history or to body for its identifications. Recently, the education of the American into these fantasy norms of citizenship has become an obsession about pedagogy. My third inhibit in this argument about how the moral domination of live sex works in contemporary US culture takes the form of a book report on Tipper Gore's *Raising PG Kids in an X-Rated Society*.[25]

It would be very easy to cite passages from this book in order to humiliate it. It is full of bad mixed metaphors, pseudoscience, and rickety thinking. But I want to take seriously its images of the citizen as a minor: the mirror that Gore looks into shows a terrible national present and foretells a frightening future for what she calls our national character. Her representation of the inner child of national culture repeats precisely the icon of feminized infantile vulnerability I have described as the scene of national anxiety in the previous two sections of this essay; she assumes as well the absolute value of the implicit, private, sacred, heterofamilial fetish of national culture. But my main interest is to trace the logic and social theory of citizen action that emerges here, which has become dominant in the contemporary US public sphere, for reasons I have tried to suggest. The book's very reference to 'PG kids' in its title suggests a theory of national personhood in which each person is an undeveloped film whose encounters with traumatic images and narratives might well make her or him a traumatized person who repeats the trauma the way a film repeats scenes. It suggests that a rating system for such persons might reveal their identities to each other and protect us all from the mere repetition of violence that is the social text of the United States, an X-rated place with X-rated adult citizens begetting a generation of monsters (someone might call it 'Generation X').

Raising PG Kids in an X-Rated Society opens like a slasher film, with a scene of Tipper Gore fleeing New York City to the 'familiarity, love, and comfort of home' in bucolic Washington, DC. Yet she finds that the sin of the big city has invaded Washington through the infectious circuits of mass culture. At home Gore faces what she has purchased for her 11-year-old daughter—a record, *Purple Rain*, which contains 'Darling Nikki', a song that glamorizes masturbation. With MTV, Gore realizes, Prince and his ilk make sexual trouble for her daughters: 'These images frightened my children; they frightened *me!*' Gore then sets out on a pilgrimage from her living-room, through Washington, to the nation, to defend youth from premature contact with sex. By 'sex' she means the practice of violent liveness the antipornography activists above employ, as portrayed here in lyrics, on album covers, in rock concerts, and on MTV. Meanwhile, what she means by youth is similarly elastic, as the vulnerable little girl citizen of US culture ranges in this book from age 1 to her early 20s, the time when, Gore admits, kids are finally competent to enter 'sexual relationships'.[26] However, she also uses the consumer bromide 'youth of all ages' to describe the ongoing surprise, hurt, humiliation, and upset even adults experience when having unwonted encounters with all kinds of 'excess', including sex, alcohol, drugs, suicide, and Satanism.

Under the pressure of this youth crisis, which also generalizes to all ages and is therefore in her view a crisis of national character and national culture, Gore joined with other concerned wives of men powerful in the US state apparatus to engender a counterpublic sphere—via the Parents Music Resource Center (PMRC) —whose purpose is to make the profit-driven, sexually suffused, popular music industry nationally accountable for terrorizing a generation of American youths through premature exposure to a world of live sex acts. Gore claims her arguments are anti-market but not anti-capitalist, anti-sex explicitness but not pro-censorship, 'pro-morality' but not anti-sex. She notes that there seems to be a lyric/narrative hierarchy in obscenity law. Although children are indeed not permitted access to adult films, books, and magazines, they are permitted access to equally explicit record covers, live performance rock concerts, and videos of songs, as well as lyrics that perform the same acts minors are not allowed to consume when they are not the market population designated by capitalists.

If no one under eighteen can buy *Penthouse* magazine, why should children be subjected to . . . hard-core porn in the local record shop? A recent album from the Dead Kennedys band contained a graphic poster of multiple erect penises penetrating vaginas. Where's the difference? In the hands of a few warped artists, their brand of rock music has become a Trojan Horse, rolling explicit sex and violence into our homes.[27]

In addition to pointing out the intemperance of the record industry and the artists who produce what she calls 'porn rock', and in addition to exposing the contradictions in the law's intention to protect children, two other issues dominate Gore's reading of the general crisis in national culture. They do not involve critiques of the immorality of capitalism and law. They involve the failure of American adults to be competent parents and a passionate argument, predictable but yet unfinished, to extend the model of infantile citizenship to nonminor US citizens through an image of the adult citizen as social parent. In particular, Gore depicts the devastating effects of adults' general refusal to acknowledge the specifically limited capacities of children, such that proper boundaries between children and adults are no longer being drawn. She also testifies to the failure of the family to compensate for the escalating norms of sexual and corporeal violence in everyday life, mass culture, and the public sphere at large.

Gore turns to social scientists and psychologists to mourn the loss of childhood in America—not only for latchkey children whose mothers work, not only broken families (that is, ones without fathers), but even in the 7 per cent of families with intact originary parents, stay-at-home mothers, and fully genetically related children, parents have begun to mistake the eloquence of children for 'mature reasoning powers and critical skills'. However, she argues that

anyone who attempts to debate the porn rock issue as if young people are in the same intellectual and emotional category as adults does them a terrible injustice. We need to let children be children. Children think differently from adults and process information according to their own stages of development.[28]

If the cognitive difference between children and adults were not enough to require special adult wisdom with respect to super-intending the lives of children, Gore goes on to show that the dissolution of the 'smiling nuclear family', increases in family violence, spouse abuse, and child abuse, and, most dramatically, the 'violent world' of life in the United States have resulted simul-taneously in the saturation of children's minds with scenes of ter-ror and the desensitization of their minds toward terror, indeed through its transformation into pleasure and entertainment. Gore argues that adults have ruined US society with their excesses and with their will to make public intimate and complicated relations, like sex, and with their negligent complacence about the violence, annihilation, exploitation, and neglect into which children are thrust daily. This sacrifice to the indulgences of American adult-hood is the distinguishing mark of the generation of children that currently exists. In contrast, Gore distinguishes (and, one must say, misremembers) her own generation, which we might call the generation of 1968, by its relation to two key texts: 'Twist and Shout' and 'I Love Lucy'.[29]

Thus, when Tipper Gore places the words 'Explicit Material—Parental Advisory' on the title-page of her book, we are to under-stand that her project is to train incompetent American adults to be parents, as a matter of civic and nationalist pedagogy. Although all Americans are youths in her view, in other words, incompet-ent to encounter live sex acts or any sex in public, she also des-perately tries to redefine 'adult' into a category of social decay more negative than any national category since the 'delinquent' of the 1950s. The new virtuous category of majority is 'parent'. The new activist citizenship Tipper Gore imagines to express the true morality of US national culture refuses the contradictions of traditional patriarchal privilege that both moralizes against and promotes the erotic terrorizing of women and children. (No sym-pathetic mention is made of the sexually terrorized Others on the live margins of national heterosexuality.) Gore advises parents in every chapter to think of parenting as a public profession, like being a lawyer or a politician; and she encourages what she calls 'parental solidarity' groups to take the private activity of nurtur-ing children away from mass media-induced but home-circulated materials that promote sex and violence. She imagines a nation controlled by a local, public, community matrix of parental public spheres. Above all, she characterizes this grass-roots model of citizenship on behalf of the 'rights' parents have to control what they and their children encounter as a model for national political agency itself. Here are the last words of the conclusion: 'It's not easy being a parent these days. It's even tougher being a kid. Perhaps together we can help our society grow up.'[30]

WILD THINGS

I was cruising, one early morning last spring, the Sunday morning talk shows: *Meet the Press, This Week with David Brinkley, Face the Nation*. But along the way I ran across a couple of video events that I have not yet recovered from seeing. The first was a Jerry Falwell commercial, played during the *Old Time Gospel Hour*. In it he offers us the opportunity to spend four dollars engaging in citizenship acts. We might call 1–900–3422 in support of 'the new homosexual rights agenda' soon, he said, to be signed into law by President Clinton. Or we might call 1–900–3401 to say that although we pray for the president, we do not support 'the new homosexual rights agenda', we do not want our 'children to grow up in an America where a new homosexual rights agenda' is law; he keeps repeating the phrase 'new homosexual rights agenda' and posts the phone numbers on the TV screen, the background for which is a purple, and not a lavender, map of mainland America. Next I flipped to C-Span, which happened—I say, as though it were random—to be showing a tape of a speech given by Major Melissa Wells-Petry, sponsored by the Christian Action Network, a speech shown at least once later the same day, which I taped and watched compulsively. Major Wells-Petry, a US military attorney, was giving a speech about why gays ought to be barred from the military. She described the vast incompatibility of the nation and the gay man; she knew the law, well, colloquially. Her reason for rejecting a gay presence in the military was that when someone says: 'I am a homosexual', there is 'data' to support that he is 'likely to engage in homosexual acts'. There is no possibility that a homosexual has an identity that is not evidenced in acts. She says the courts have proven that to be homosexual is to behave as a homosexual, just as a pilot can be said to be a pilot because he flies planes. I have no idea as to whether she was secretly thinking about the 'cruising' altitude of planes, or about the cliché that queers are light in the loafers. In any case, she also argues that gayness is only one of many behavioural identities the army bars from service, and she names two others: in an aside, she notes that fatness makes you unfit for service; more elaborately, she recounts a case where a Nazi walked into a recruiting station and asked to enlist but was barred from enlisting because being a Nazi makes you unfit to serve in the US military. I fell into a dream that day, about *Griswold* v. *Connecticut* and *Roe* v. *Wade*, two cases I was teaching the following week. These two cases are generally thought to be crucial to the struggle to gain sex equality in the United States. *Griswold* v. *Connecticut* made it possible for married couples to buy birth control; *Roe* v. *Wade* made it possible to abort some foetuses birth control didn't prevent from being conceived. But the language about heterosexuality and pregnancy these cases promoted did nothing to shake up the normative relations of sex and nationality in modern America. In my dream, I tried to explain to someone in a supermarket how the zone of privacy established for married sex acts in *Griswold* v. *Connecticut* even further enshrined heterosexual reproductive activity as the fundamental patriotic American fetish, so powerful it was entirely private; it was the only fixed sign in the national language. Indeed, I insisted on telling her, and with great painful prolixity, of Justice Harlan's opinion that the

right of privacy is not an absolute. Thus, I would not suggest that adultery, homosexuality, fornication and incest are immune from criminal enquiry, however privately practised. [But] . . . the intimacy of husband and wife is necessarily an essential and accepted feature of the institution of marriage, an institution which the State not only must allow, but which always and in every age it has fostered and protected.

Then, somehow bored in my own dream, I turned my back and looked out the window, where I saw a pregnant woman wandering naked in traffic. I watched her, transfixed, for the longest time. When I awoke, I asked myself, what is the wish of the dream? I didn't know, but what flashed up instead was a line from *Roe* v. *Wade*: 'The pregnant woman cannot be isolated in her privacy.'[31]

Let me review the argument: insofar as an American thinks that the sex she or he is having is an intimate, private thing constructed within a space governed by personal consent, she or he is having straight sex, straight sex authorized by national culture; she or he is practising national heterosexuality, which makes the sex act dead, in the sense I have described, using a kind of metaphor that foregrounds the ways hetero-familial American identity reigns as a sacred national fetish beyond the disturbances of history or representation, protected by a zone of privacy.

The privacy zone that projects national culture as a shadow effect of scandalous or potentially destabilizing acts of sexual alterity has a history, and I have tried to telegraph it here as a history of some live acts that counter an ideology of dead citizenship. Most importantly, until recently there has never in the United States been a public sphere organized around sex and sexuality—that is to say, a public sphere demarcated by what Geoff Eley has described as a political culture.[32] The prehistory of this moment must transform our accounts of the contemporary public sphere as well as of citizenship, nationality, acts, identities, sex, and so on. It might start with racial and gendered corporeal counterpolitics of the period after the Civil War, part of a general citizen reform movement, but also specifically around issues of property and reproduction, the two most sacrosanct areas the Constitution designates. Suffrage meant to bring these nineteenth-century primitivist categories into national modernity, and the history of national sentimentality this essay partly tells has to do with the public failure of suffrage to solve the relation between the body and the state in the United States, such that a tactical shuttling between assimilation and banishment remains central to the complicated histories of those sexed, racialized, female, underclassed subjects who can be seen animating the live margins of the US scene. In any case, as the Queer Nation motto 'We are everywhere, we want everything' suggests, the scandal of sexual subculture in the contemporary American context derives in part from its assertion of a non-infantilized political counter-public that refuses to tie itself to a dead identity; that sees sexuality as a set of acts and world-building activities whose implications are always radically TBA; that aspires to undermine the patriotic ethics in which it is deemed virtuous to aspire to live in abstract America, a place where bodies do not live historically, complexly, or incoherently, guided by a putatively rational, civilized standard. The basic sex-radical tactic has been to countercorporealize at every moment and so to de-elect the state and other social formations that have patriarchalized and parentalized national culture. This is not enough, as Michael Warner has argued.[33] But it is the beginning of a *movement*, and it's a live one.

This is to say that a radical social theory of sexual citizenship in the United States must not aspire to reoccupy the dead identities of privacy, or name the innocence of youth as the index of adult practice and knowledge, or nationalize sexuality or sex as the central mode of self-legitimation or public-identity making. In this way it can avoid repeating the utopian identification that infantile citizenship promises, which distracts everyone from turning to the nation form and thinking about its inexhaustible energy for harnessing capitalism to death through promises of eternal identity and images of live activity. It can then avoid repeating the struggle between crassness and sentimental sublimity that defines all of our bodies in the United States, all of our live sex if we're lucky enough to have it; our dead citizenship; and our potentially undead desires to form a live relation to power, nature, sensation, and history within or outside of the nation form as we know it. The risk is that peeling away the fantasies that both sustain and cover over the sexual bodies living the good life in the zone of privacy will also tear away some important protective coverings, like the fantasy of privacy itself, the way a Band-aid covering an unhealed wound will take away part of the wound and its bit of healing with it. But such violence and failure, such an opening of the wound to air, is a foundational condition for the next steps, which, after all, remain to be taken, seen, and critiqued, although not rated with an X, a PG, or a thumbs up—unless the thumb is related to something else, like a fist.

Notes

1. Michael Taussig has recently termed this saturation of the politics by the nation 'state fetishism'. This is a condition in which the state uses a sublime and magical official story of national identity to mask the nation's heterogeneity. See his '*Maleficium*: State Fetishism', in *The Nervous System* (New York: Routledge, 1992), 111–40, 223.

2. The original texts meant to be reviewed were Allison Assiter, *Pornography, Feminism, and the Individual* (London: Pluto Press, 1989); Gail Chester and Julienne Dickey, *Feminism and Censorship* (Blandford: Prism Press, 1988); Andrea Dworkin, *Pornography* (New York: E. P. Dutton, 1989); Susan Gubar and Joan Hoff, *For Adult Users Only* (Bloomington: Indiana University Press, 1989); Gordon Hawkins and Franklin E. Zimring, *Pornography in a Free Society* (New York: Cambridge University Press, 1988); Catherine Itzin, *Pornography: Women,*

Violence, and Civil Liberties (New York: Oxford University Press, 1991). I have also read more widely in the literature pro and con and assume the entire œuvre of Catharine MacKinnon in this essay as well.

Of these listed above, the British feminist texts (Assiter, Itzin, Chester, and Dickey) share with the work of MacKinnon and Dworkin a sense that issues of sexual difference cannot be solved by American-style liberal thinking about ontological selfhood but must address the ways the state and the nation frame the conditions of sex, sexual identity, and gender value. Of the American texts that do not take a clear pornography-is-patriarchy position, the most useful is *For Adult Users Only*, which rehearses and I think extends the feminist debate over the causes, effects, and possibilities pornography poses for US women. This essay takes no position on 'pornography' as such but places this discussion in a context of thinking about how the citizen's vulnerability and aspiration to a nationally protected identity has been orchestrated around a variety or constellation of sexualizing media forms ordinarily not included in this discussion. In this regard this article 'reviews' these texts by refocusing the discussion away from the domain of sexual difference and toward the conjunction of sexuality, mass culture, and mass nationality.

3. Daniel Richman, quoted in *New York Times* (25 May 1993), A8.
4. I take this way of thinking about the processes of making an institution appear hegemonic from Chandra Mohanty, who takes it from Dorothy Smith. See Chandra Mohanty's introduction, 'Cartographies of Struggle: Third World Women and the Politics of Feminism', in Chandra Talpade Mohanty, Ann Russo, and Lourdes Torres (eds.), *Third World Women and the Politics of Feminism* (Bloomington: Indiana University Press, 1991), 15–16; Dorothy Smith, *The Everyday World as Problematic: A Feminist Sociology* (Boston: Northeastern University Press, 1987), 108.
5. John Frohnmayer, *Leaving Town Alive: Confessions of an Arts Warrior* (Boston: Houghton Mifflin, 1993), 3, 337, 314, 202.
6. Ibid. 324.
7. Ibid. 326.
8. Ibid. 291, 324–25.
9. The 'Helms Amendment' was offered to the US Senate on 7 Oct. 1989. It reads: 'None of the funds authorized to be appropriated pursuant to this Act may be used to promote, discriminate, or produce materials that are obscene or that depict or describe, in a patently offensive way, sexual or excretory activities or organs, including but not limited to obscene depictions of sadomasochism, homoeroticism, the sexual exploitation of children, or individuals engaged in sexual intercourse.' See *Congressional Record*, 101st Congr., 1st Sess., 1989, 135, S12967.

10. Frohnmayer, 69.
11. Edward de Grazia, *Girls Lean Back Everywhere: The Law of Obscenity and the Assault on Genius* (New York: Random House, 1992), 637.
12. Frohnmayer, 326, 328–29.
13. De Grazia, *Girls Lean Back*, 4–5.
14. Ibid. 436–37. See also Edward de Grazia, *Gensorship Landmarks* (New York: R. R. Bowker, 1969).
15. Andrea Dworkin and Catharine A. MacKinnon, *Pornography and Civil Rights: A New Day for Women's Equality* (Minneapolis: Organizing against Pornography, 1988), 48.
16. *Jacobellis* v. *Ohio*, 378 US 184, 195 (1964); see also de Grazia, *Girls Lean Back*, 423–33. The case from which Justice Brennan quotes is *Butler* v. *Michigan*, 352 US 380, 383 (1957).
17. Carole S. Vance, 'The Pleasures of Looking: The Attorney General's Commission on Pornography versus Visual Images', in Carol Squiers (ed.), *The Critical Image* (Seattle: Bay Press, 1990), 38–58.
18. See Robin West, 'Pornography as a Legal Text', in *For Adult Users Only*, 108–30.
19. Attorney General's Commission on Pornography July 1986 Final Report vol. i, 839–40.
20. Dworkin and MacKinnon, *Pornography and Civil Rights*, 43, 45–6.
21. Leo Bersani, 'Is the Rectum a Grave?', *October*, 43 (Winter 1987): 197–222.
22. Dworkin and MacKinnon, *Pornography and Civil Rights*, 46.
23. There are many other domains where infantile citizenship animates adult conceptions of national culture. See Lauren Berlant, 'The Theory of Infantile Citizenship', *Public Culture*, 5 (Spring 1993): 395–410.
24. Attorney General's Commission on Pornography, i. 849.
25. Tipper Gore, *Raising PG Kids in an X-Rated Society* (Nashville: Abington Press, 1987).
26. Ibid. 17, 18, 41.
27. Ibid. 28.
28. Ibid. 39, 42.
29. Ibid. 43–48, 11.
30. Ibid. 167.
31. *Griswold* v. *Connecticut*, 381 US 479 (1965), *Roe* v. *Wade*, 410 US 113 (1973).
32. Geoffrey H. Eley, 'Nations, Publics, and Political Cultures: Placing Habermas in the Nineteenth Century', in Craig Calhoun (ed.), *Habermas and the Public Sphere* (Cambridge, Mass.: MIT Press, 1992), 289–339.
33. Michael Warner, 'The Mass Public and the Mass Subject', in *Habermas and the Public Sphere*, 399–400.

An Interview with Barbara Kruger

W. J. T. Mitchell

MITCHELL: Could we begin by discussing the problem of public art? When we spoke a few weeks ago, you expressed some uneasiness with the notion of public art, and I wonder if you could expand on that a bit.

KRUGER: Well, you yourself lodged it as the 'problem' of public art and I don't really find it problematic inasmuch as I really don't give it very much thought. I think on a broader level I could say that my 'problem' is with categorization and naming: how does one constitute art and how does one constitute a public? Sometimes I think that if architecture is a slab of meat, then so-called public art is a piece of garnish laying next to it. It has a kind of decorative function. Now I'm not saying that it always has to be that way—at all—and I think perhaps that many of my colleagues are working to change that now. But all too often, it seems the case.

MITCHELL: Do you think of your own art, insofar as it's engaged with the commercial public sphere—that is, with advertising, publicity, mass media, and other technologies for influencing a consumer public—that it is automatically a form of public art? Or does it stand in opposition to public art?

KRUGER: I have a question for you: what is a public sphere which is an uncommercial public sphere?

MITCHELL: I'm thinking of a utopian notion such as Habermas's idea of the liberal bourgeois sphere of the culture-debating public. You may recall how he opposes that to a culture-consuming public, which he thinks of as mainly consuming images and as

For examples of Barbara Kruger's work, including several of the images discussed in this interview please refer to *Love for Sale, The Words and Pictures of Barbara Kruger*, text by Kate Linker (New York, H. N. Abrams, 1990). This interview is reprinted from *Critical Inquiry*, 17/2 (Winter 1991), 434–48 by permission of the University of Chicago Press. Copyright © 1991 by The University of Chicago.

being spectatorial. He contrasts it with the culture-debating public, which he associates with the literary.

KRUGER: I live and speak through a body which is constructed by moments which are formed by the velocity of power and money. So I don't see this division between what is commercial and what is not commercial. I see rather a broad, non-ending flow of moments which are informed if not motored by exchange.

MITCHELL: But do you see yourself as 'going with the flow', as they used to say, or intervening in it?

KRUGER: Again, I think that the word *oppositional* becomes problematized because it's binary. It has to do with antis and pros, or whatever, and basically I feel that there are many of us who are working to make certain displacements, certain changes, who are invested in questions rather than the surety of knowledge. And I think that those are the ways that we displace that flow a little or redirect it.

MITCHELL: When someone feels like they're either intervening or redirecting a flow like the circulation of capital or publicity, I want to ask what they have to push off against that allows them to swim upstream or to make eddies against the current. I realize we're speaking very figuratively here, but you're awfully good with figures. Is it a sense of solidarity—you said others are also engaged in doing this sort of thing, trying to disrupt the flow, intervene in the circuits in some way? Is it the fact that there are others that gives you some way of having leverage?

KRUGER: Yes, in that one hopes to make a space for another kind of viewer. But I think that there are those of us who don't see ourselves as guardians of culture. We hope for a place which allows for differences and tolerances. What we are doing is trying to construct another kind of spectator who has not yet been seen or heard.

MITCHELL: You mean a kind of innocent spectator, who hasn't been seduced yet?

KRUGER: Oh, no, I didn't say anything about innocence.

MITCHELL: You said it was someone who hasn't been approached yet?

KRUGER: No, I said someone who in fact has not had control over the devices of their own representation. Now to me that doesn't have anything to do with innocence. I'm not talking about discourses of innocence or morality or anything like that. I'm just saying that we have always been represented rather than tried to represent ourselves.

MITCHELL: Would you say the issue, then, is empowerment rather than innocence?

KRUGER: Well, the question certainly is one of the constructions of power and how they work and what perpetuates them and what trips them. Sure. Absolutely.

MITCHELL: Let me ask you another question more specifically directed at some of your own work. I noticed that a couple of your pieces at least, I'm sure more than two, have in a somewhat technical sense been works of public art—that is, they were not only in a public space, but they had some kind of support from a public agency and public funding. The one I'm thinking of specifically is the 'We Don't Need Another Hero' billboard, which in one version—I think it may have been the Chicago version—it said 'A Foster and Kleiser Public Service Message' along the bottom of it. Did you have control over that text, or was that part of the billboard company's . . . ?

KRUGER: Of what text?

MITCHELL: The 'A Foster and Kleiser Public Service Message'.

KRUGER: Oh, no, they just had that on the billboard. That was in California. And I was so *happy* that it was there, because it in fact puts these words in the mouths of this corporate group which I think is great! To see that sort of enterprise saying 'we don't need another hero' is terrific! I wish that they would practise what they preach.

MITCHELL: Yes. 'This is a public service message. This is not something that comes from the art world.'

KRUGER: But it really isn't something that comes form the art world because I don't feel like I'm something that comes exclusively from the art world. And it basically is a line from a Tina Turner song from a Mad Max movie, and it's a plea to re-examine hierarchies, and I don't see it as coming from any vocational ghetto, one or the other.

MITCHELL: We started to talk last time about the Little Tokyo controversy which looks like a classic engagement in the public art battles of the eighties. It's recently been connected with previous controversies over unpopular works of public art. I wonder if you could say a little more about your point of view on that controversy, what you think it meant, and the way it has worked out for you.

KRUGER: I don't see it tied to any other so-called controversies around so-called public art because to me, the process was one of negotiation. I learned a lot from it, I really liked the people who I spoke to and spoke to me and we had a very generative exchange. I basically don't feel that I'm like some mediator between God and the public who comes into a space and has got an inspiration and that's it. To me, all my work comes out of the idea of a social relation. And I hope that all my work—regardless of where it's seen—is an extension of that relation.

MITCHELL: So you think that the process of social exchange, political negotiation, that went on around it is as much a part of the object as the thing on the wall?

KRUGER: Sure. Absolutely.

MITCHELL: Let me switch tracks a little bit and move over to the art world, a place you say you're not from, at least not exclusively.

KRUGER: Well, to say 'from' ... the only reason I said that is because you said that 'this message came from the art world'.

MITCHELL: Much of your work seems quite capable of leaving the art world if it ever felt it had to be there—that is, when I say 'the art world' I'm thinking of physical places like the gallery or museum. Your work seems in some sense independent of that, it makes its way in the larger sphere of publicity—billboards, bumper stickers, postcards, and posters—yet it also seems, to use a loaded word, 'destined' to return to the gallery and museum. What do you think is the effect of this kind of circuit, the circulation of your images—or anybody else's images—between the spaces of the art object and the spaces of publicity?

KRUGER: Well, I don't see them as separate spaces. I'm interested in pictures and words because they have specific powers to define who we are and who we aren't. And those pictures and words can function in as many places as possible.

MITCHELL: But do you think those spaces are undifferentiated or alike?

KRUGER: No, no, I think that they're different, that there are different contexts and that the contexts themselves create different meanings. I don't want to collapse the difference of those spaces *at all*, but it would be nice to occupy as many of them as possible.

MITCHELL: I agree. It seems to me that one of the interesting things about them is that as they move between these different places, it's as if they pick up momentum from one place that might be carried into another one, so that something that appears in the space of the postcard, or the shopping bag, or the poster, looks at first as if it belongs there but also doesn't belong there. Do you think that that kind of double take of the image belonging to its place but also looking like it came from somewhere else is . . . is that something you're trying to achieve?

KRUGER: Yeah, that could be good. Basically, the most important thing is that in order for these images and words to do their work they have to catch the eye of the spectator. And one does what one can to make that moment possible.

MITCHELL: Do you have any sense of how long you want to catch the spectator's eye? One thing that always strikes me about advertising is that there's a whole lot of imagery that's competing for attention. I suppose the measure of success is how it does in that competition and perhaps also how long the image stays with you, some kind of implantation in memory. Are those the sort of criteria that you're using? How do you decide when one of your images is successful?

KRUGER: Well, I really think the criteria change for different images, and certain images are successful in one site and not in another. For instance, there are pictures that I would choose to show in a more intimate gallery space that I wouldn't use as billboards, and . . . well the pictures that are on billboards usually work in both spaces, but I think it's important to realize who your audiences are. I also think that my work is a series of attempts, and some make it for some people and not for others.

MITCHELL: So your notion of success and failure is very much tied to the site, the audience, the particular context that it's addressed to.

KRUGER: Yeah, I don't think in those terms of 'success' and 'failure', as sort of chiselled somewhere in bronze or something. I think that there are some pieces which have really done their work and have pleased me and others, and that others have found totally ineffective.

MITCHELL: Can you exemplify that a bit for me? What works do you think of as most successful or least successful?

KRUGER: Oh, I can't say since the effectiveness of various works depends on the pleasures of various viewers, and I wouldn't want to make a declaration of 'successes'.

MITCHELL: What if I were to take a couple images that I think of as epitomizing what strikes me most and what at least I'm puzzled by or what doesn't arrest me, and try them on you?

KRUGER: Okay, but I should say, it's hard for me to talk about specific meanings in specific works because it creates a kind of closure that I'm really wary of. I like people to sort of generate their own meanings, too, and if I start naming, 'Well this is what I meant here and this is . . .', it's too tied to the conventions of a closed reading. But if you want to ask me some things in particular, I'll see how far I can go with it.

MITCHELL: Okay. This isn't so much a matter of meanings as a matter of affect.

KRUGER: Well, yeah, but what's one without the other?

MITCHELL: I don't know. These are the two images: one which I feel I don't understand yet, but it really strikes me and stays with me; and the other one . . . it isn't that it disappears for me, but I feel that perhaps I've exhausted it too quickly. The one that really strikes me and has kind of been haunting me for the last week is the last image in *Love for Sale*, 'Remember Me'. I told you I wasn't going to give you an interpretation, but for some reason that image just strikes me and remains deposited indelibly in my memory. Now the other one I was looking at was 'You Are Not Yourself', the shattered mirror with the logo 'You Are Not Yourself'. It's not that I forget the image but it's just that it somehow doesn't keep working. Partly, I guess, it's because I feel like the fragmentation of the image and the fragmentation of the words perhaps translate too easily for me, that there isn't enough resistance between word and image. Does any of this make sense to you?

KRUGER: Yeah, I just think that basically there are viewers for different images and certain viewers can decline that image. I've had much feedback on that second image. Not all of it, but a lot of it comes from women. It's a picture of a woman who's in front of the mirror. So, if in fact the so-called empathetic device in that piece is not sort of ringing your bell, I can certainly understand why. But it also doesn't mean that all identity is structured through gender, necessarily, I'm not saying that. But I'm saying that certain works speak more to certain people.

MITCHELL: Perhaps it's that identity for me isn't structured through a mirror. That that's just not my . . .

KRUGER: That's very interesting. What kind of enzyme are you lacking? That's terrific.

MITCHELL: I don't know. Could be that this is the missing gene.

KRUGER: Or some kind of weird Lacanian lapse and you missed the mirror stage.

MITCHELL: I passed right through it to something else.

KRUGER: I would venture to guess that many people heed their mirrors at least five times a day and that vigilance certainly can structure physical and psychic identity.

MITCHELL: One other image—and I apologize if this seems like a predictable question, but what the heck. The piece 'You Invest in the Divinity of the Masterpiece', the Michelangelo creation scene, I take it, is a satire on the ideology of artistic genius, particularly in the trinity of Father, Son, and Michelangelo, suggesting the patriarchal succession of genius. The piece is now the property of the Museum of Modern Art, and I guess this is a question also about places that works occupy and what happens in that place. Do you think in this case the piece is undermined by the place it occupies, or does it undermine the place?

KRUGER: Neither. I think the binary form of *either/or* is not a necessary handle.

MITCHELL: Then my question is, is there a third way of seeing this which is better than those two alternatives?

KRUGER: Oh, well there are thirds, fourths, and fifths for sure. I wouldn't be that deluded as to think that I'm going to undermine the power of the trustees of the Museum of Modern Art. I basically *knew* when that piece was sold that it was sold to MOMA and luckily the curator who was working there *knew* how much it meant to me, that that work, of the works that they were looking at, be the one that they should have. It seems to me that very seldom does one have a chance to address the power relations of an institution from within that institution in that way. Ironically, the second time was when I curated the show 'Picturing Greatness', also at MOMA. To me, life is far more complex than either being pure or co-opted. I don't think anyone exists outside the gravitational pull of power and exchange. I believe that we can be effective when we come to terms with concrete social realities rather than a deluded sense of utopianism. So I'm very *pleased* that the work is there, I'm very *pleased* that people come to museums, and I'm *convinced* that a lot of people, if not most people, who go to museums don't know why they're there, except this strange need to affiliate with what they think is high-class 'culcha'. I don't go to museums very much, but every time I go I remember the kind of staging-ground for power that they can be. I would be only too happy to—I'd love to—be in there to make other assertions and to plant some doubts and ask some questions. Absolutely.

MITCHELL: You said before that no one is completely outside the market, the circuit of exchange. On the other side, would you say that no one is completely inside of it?

KRUGER: No, I wouldn't say that. Again because I think that there are more than two ways to look at this, and it's not just the old 'in and out'. So, no I wouldn't say that. I'd say that all of us in some way—and this is not to collapse differences of nationhood and differences of culture—I definitely think that we are all touched by the constructions of exchange. Yeah, absolutely.

MITCHELL: But do you think we're determined by them? Completely?

KRUGER: To some degree, yes. I can't say what percentage, but of course, sure.

MITCHELL: Can I ask you some questions about pictures and words? I wanted to ask you first whether you have a sense of traditional functions or characteristic roles played by word and image that you are trying to work against. If you want I'll elaborate that, or I'll just stop and let you . . .

KRUGER: Okay, elaborate.

MITCHELL: Elaborate. Okay. Kate Linker, in her introduction to *Love for Sale*, says that your pictures entice and your words accost, and that seemed like a handy formula.

KRUGER: Sometimes it could be the opposite, too. There is no recipe. At times it is just as Kate has written it. Yes, that is very true. But I think it needn't always be that way.

MITCHELL: In your book, you also talked about one of the dialectics of your work being the attempt to bring together the ingratiation of wishful thinking with the criticality of knowing better. Do you think that those two functions—which seem dialectically related: one perhaps involved with the kind of thing that Linker means when she talks about 'enticement', that is ingratiation; the other one with criticality—that the composite form of word and image lends itself to the playing-off as contrary messages in that way?

KRUGER: I think it can, but I think that there are so many different kinds of playings-off. I think it's easy to be witty with pictures, and be seductive with pictures and words, and all that is very nice. But I think that it's important for me to somehow, through a collection of words and images, to somehow try to picture—or objectify, or visualize—how it might feel sometimes to be alive today. That's what my work, hopefully, is about, to some degree.

MITCHELL: Let me put the image-word relation in terms of gender, or ask you to do that. Do you have a sense of . . . here you have a semiotic opposition with word and image, and you're also very concerned with the general problem of difference and with the specific difference inscribed in gender. Could you say something about how word and image—how that difference— plays against gender difference?

KRUGER: Plays against gender difference?

MITCHELL: Or plays on it.

KRUGER: No, I don't think that there is a particular methodology that sort of operates across the board. No, not really. Do you want to maybe rephrase that?

MITCHELL: Well, for instance, one of the things I notice about your representations of women is that they often involve the text as a female speaker. It sounds as if the implied 'I' is female and the addressee is male. This looks to me like a deliberate going against the grain of certain traditional ways of organizing words and images. I don't need to tell you that little girls are brought up to think of themselves as things to be looked at. You can go back to the Old Testament to find sentiments like 'a silent woman is the gift of God'.

KRUGER: Oh, let me write that down.

MITCHELL: So, what I'm asking is, do you think that the media themselves come with traditional codes and associations?

KRUGER: I don't think that they're encoded in a *specific* way all the time. I think that frequently people think that there are conspiracies of admittance, and in fact it's not. It's just that people are socialized in cultures in specific ways, and they take that socialization into their lives, and into their jobs, and into their successes, and into their failures. Of course. So there have been stereotypes, and as Barthes said, the stereotype exists where the body is absent. When that embodiment—not just in a literal sense of embodiment—but when that which is embodied, or lives, is no longer there, there is a rampant sort of rushing-in of caricature and stereotype and repetition. Of course.

MITCHELL: Is part of the agenda of your images, then, to re-embody, or to restore the body to these stereotypes?

KRUGER: Yeah—and I hate to get to you on these words, but I wouldn't call it an agenda—but I would say that I am interested in sort of, in not just displacing and questioning stereotypes—of course I'm interested in that—but I also think that stereotype is a very powerful form and that stereotype sort of lives and grows off of that which was true, but since the body is absent, it can no longer be proven. It becomes a trace which cannot be removed. Stereotype functions like a stain. It becomes a memory of the body on a certain level, and it's very problematic. But I think that when we 'smash' those stereotypes, we have to make sure and think hard about what we're replacing them with and if they should be replaced.

MITCHELL: If stereotypes are stains, what is the bleach?

KRUGER: Well, I wouldn't say that there is a recipe, and I wouldn't say 'bleach'. Bleach is something which is so encoded in this racist culture that the notion of whitening as an antidote is something that should be avoided.

MITCHELL: So you just want to stop with the stain.

KRUGER: I don't want to get things whiter. If anything, I would hope when I say that basically to create new spectators with new meanings, I would hope to be speaking for spectators who are women, and hopefully colleagues of mine who are spectators and people of colour. Now that doesn't mean that women and people of colour can't create horrendous stereotypes also. Of course they can. But hopefully one who has had one's spirit tread upon can remember not to tread upon the spirit of others.

MITCHELL: Most of your work with the problem of difference has focused on gender. Are you interested in or working on problems with ethnicity, since that certainly involves a whole other problematic of embodiment?

KRUGER: Well, I think about that all the time. I think about it in terms of race, and culture. I think about it when I teach. I think about it in a series of posters that I do and of projects for public spaces, but I also—unlike a number of artists—feel very uncomfortable and do not want to speak for another. I basically feel that now is the time for people of colour to do work which represents their experience, and I support that, and have written about that work as a writer, but do not want to speak for others. I basically feel that right now people of colour can do a better job of representing themselves than white people can of representing them. It's about time.

MITCHELL: Let me just take one further step with the problem of word and image, and try to tie it back into the issue of public art. I'm interested in the combining of words and images in the art of publicity and in traditional public art, the old-fashioned monument. Let me just give you a little background on what I'm thinking here. The traditional public art, say, of the nineteenth century, is supposed to have been universally readable, or at least it's often invoked that way, as something that the whole public could relate to. Everybody knows what the Statue of Liberty was supposed to mean, what it 'says'. When modern works of public art are criticized, they're often characterized as 'unreadable' in contrast to traditional works which were supposedly universally popular. The modernist monument seems to be a kind of private symbol which has been inserted into the public space, as I think you said, the garnish next to the roast beef. So it looks as if modernism kept the monument in terms of its scale, and egotism, and its placement in a public site, but it eliminated the public access to meaning. This is all a kind of complicated preamble to asking whether it might be possible that word-image composite work—especially coming out of the sphere of advertising and commercial publicity—might make possible a new kind of public art. I know this is to bring you back to something you said you're not terribly in love with, or you have some problem with, the whole issue of public art. But, does this question make sense to you?

KRUGER: Yeah, I think that there is an accessibility to pictures and words that we have learned to read very fluently through advertising and through the technological development of photography and film and video. Obviously. But that's not the same as really making meanings, because film, and, well, television, really, and advertising—even though it wants to do the opposite —let's just talk about television—it's basically not about making meaning. It's about dissolving meaning. To reach out and touch a very relaxed, numbed-out, vegged-out viewer. Although we are always hearing about access to information, more cable stations than ever . . . . But it's not about the specificity of information, about notions of history, about how life was lived, or even how it's lived now. It's about another kind of space. It's about, as Baudrillard has said, 'the space of fascination', rather than the space of reading. 'Fascinating' in the way that Barthes says that stupidity is fascinating. It's this sort of incredible moment which sort of rivets us through its constancy, through its unreadability because it's not made to be read or seen, or really it's made to be seen but not watched. I think that we can use the fluency of that form and its ability to ingratiate, but perhaps also try to create meanings, too. Not just re-create the spectacle formally, but to take the formalities of the spectacle and put some meaning into it. Not just make a statement about the dispersion of meaning, but make it meaningful.

MITCHELL: That's what I was hoping you were going to say. My next question was whether you feel there's still some place for the unreadable image or object (which I've always thought of as one of the modernist canons: the idea that an image has mystery and aura and can't be deciphered).

KRUGER: But that's not what I'm saying. That is *not* what I'm saying.

MITCHELL: You're speaking of another kind of unreadability.

KRUGER: I'm not saying that something should be unreadable. I'm saying that it should be *readable*, but it should suggest different meanings or that it should give a meaning. I'm saying that what we have now is about meaninglessness, through its familiarity, accessibility, not through its obscurity. Whereas modernism, or what I take it to be (you've used the word), was meaningless to people because of its inaccessibility. What the media have done today is make a thing meaningless through its accessibility. And what I'm interested in is taking that accessibility and making meaning. I'm interested in dealing with complexity, yes. But not necessarily to the end of any romance with the obscure.

MITCHELL: There was one other question I wanted to ask you, and that's about interviews. The old idea about artists was that they weren't supposed to give interviews. The work was supposed to speak for itself. How do you feel about interviews?

KRUGER: I think that the work does speak for itself to some degree—absolutely. But I also feel that we're living in a time when an artist does not have to be interpreted by others. Artists can 'have' words. So it's not like I think I'm going to blow my cover if I open my mouth.

MITCHELL: Well, you certainly haven't blown your cover today.

12 Sex, Lies, and the Public Sphere: Reflections on the Confirmation of Clarence Thomas

Nancy Fraser

The making of mainstream public opinion is mainly a routinized affair, the business of pundits as opposed to lay citizens. Occasionally, however, something happens that explodes the circuits of professional opinion-making-as-usual and calls forth widespread and intense public debate. In such moments, something approximating mass participation crystallizes, and for a brief instant, at least, we sense the possibility of a robust political public sphere. Yet the experience is characteristically mixed. Intimations of democracy are laced with demagoguery and exclusion, which the bright light of hyperpublicity casts into sharp relief. These moments can accordingly have great diagnostic value. They make starkly visible the structures of inequality and practices of power that deform public-opinion-making in ordinary times, less obtrusively but more systematically.[1]

One such moment was the 1991 struggle over the confirmation of Clarence Thomas as an associate justice of the US Supreme Court. Combining flashes of democratic participation with practices of strategic containment, this struggle raised in a dramatic and pointed way key questions about the nature of contemporary publicity. It was not simply a battle for public opinion within an already constituted public sphere. What was at stake was, on the contrary, the very meaning and boundaries of publicity. The way the struggle unfolded, moreover, depended at every point on who had the power to draw the line between the public and the private. As a result, the 'Clarence Thomas affair' exposed crucial

First published in *Critical Inquiry*, 18 (Spring 1992), 595–612. This is a revised version which appeared as chapter 4 in Nancy Fraser, *Justice Interruptus: Rethinking Key Concepts of a Postsocialist Age* (Routledge, 1997). Copyright Routledge, Inc. (1997). Reprinted by permission.

obstacles to democratic publicity in our society. At the same time, it exposed the inadequacies of the classical liberal model of the public sphere, revealing that standard understandings of publicity are ideological.

WHOSE PRIVACY? WHICH PUBLICITY?

Recall the circumstances. Clarence Thomas, a black conservative, was nominated to the Supreme Court by George Bush in 1991. As former head of the federal Equal Employment Opportunity Commission, Thomas had presided over the transition to the 'post-civil-rights era', downsizing the agency's efforts to enforce laws outlawing discrimination. Predictably, his Supreme Court nomination was opposed in liberal, feminist, and civil-rights circles. Black organizations were divided, however, with many hesitating to take a stand against a man who was poised to become only the second African American on the Court in US history. During the regularly scheduled Senate Judiciary Committee confirmation hearings, Thomas played down his record, his 'race', and his constitutional and political views, stressing instead his humble origins and subsequent triumph over adversity. When these hearings were concluded and a Senate vote was set, he appeared certain to win confirmation—until he was publicly accused of sexually harassing a former EEOC subordinate.

Then, for several weeks, the country was riveted as the Judiciary Committee investigated the allegations by Anita F. Hill, a black female law professor who had served as Thomas's assistant at the Equal Employment Opportunity Commission in the 1980s. Hill charged that Thomas had repeatedly sexually harassed her at work during this period, pressuring her for dates despite her consistent refusals, graphically describing—over her repeated objections— pornographic films he had seen, and bragging to her about the size of his penis and his talents as a lover despite her requests that he stop. She filed no complaint at the time. The government agency that handles such complaints is the Equal Employment Opportunity Commission, then headed by Thomas, the very site where Hill claimed the harassment occurred. By the time her charges were publicly aired in 1991, the US Supreme Court had ruled that sexual harassment is a form of sex discrimination and is illegal under the US civil rights laws.

Thomas categorically denied Hill's charges. The cat, however, was out of the bag. Bowing to intense public pressure, the Senate delayed its scheduled confirmation vote to hold an unprecedented second round of televised Judiciary Committee hearings on the sexual-harassment accusations. Following these hearings, the Senate, by the narrowest margin ever in such votes, confirmed the appointment of Thomas to the Supreme Court.

Few dramas have so gripped the country as this one. Everywhere people put their ordinary activities aside to watch the hearings and to debate the issues. Everywhere, people argued passionately over whether Thomas or Hill was telling the truth. Radio talk shows were bombarded with callers, including women who claimed that they themselves had been sexually harassed in the past but until now had been too ashamed to tell anyone. The press was filled with opinion articles representing all sides of the issue. It was hard to find a corner of life where the talk was not about Clarence Thomas and Anita Hill.

In short, this was a rare moment in American life in which a lively contentious public sphere was in evidence. I mean a public sphere in Habermas's sense of an arena in which public opinion is constituted through discourse; where members of the public debate matters of common concern, seeking to persuade one another through giving reasons; and where the force of public opinion is brought to bear on government decision making.[2]

Indeed, the Clarence Thomas affair seems at first glance to provide a textbook example of the public sphere in action. The Senate Judiciary Committee hearings on Hill's accusations seemed to constitute an exercise in democratic publicity, as understood in the classical liberal model of the public sphere. The hearings opened to public scrutiny an aspect of government functioning, namely, the nomination and confirmation of a Supreme Court justice. They thus subjected a decision of state officials to the force of public opinion. Through the hearings, in fact, public opinion was constituted and brought to bear directly on the decision, affecting the process by which it was made as well as its substantive outcome. As a result, state officials were held accountable to the public by means of a discursive process of opinion and will formation.

On closer examination, however, these events belie the classical liberal model of the public sphere. That model treats the meaning and boundaries of publicity and privacy as simply given and self-evident. But the Thomas/Hill confrontation was largely a struggle over the meaning and boundaries of those categories. The antagonists vied over where precisely the line between the public and the private would be drawn. And the outcome depended on who had the power to enforce and defend that line.

Those issues underlay many of the questions that were explicitly debated: How should one view the initial public disclosure on 6 October 1991 of Hill's accusations, which had been communicated confidentially to Judiciary Committee staff? Was this a leak to the press aimed at torpedoing the Thomas nomination, hence an egregious breach of proper procedure and confidentiality? Or was it a heroic act of whistle-blowing that properly blew the lid off an outrageous cover-up? Was Hill's failure to go public with her accusations prior to 6 October grounds for doubting her account or was it consistent with her story? Should the behaviour Hill ascribed to Thomas be considered innocent camaraderie or abuse of power? Is such behaviour 'normal' or 'pathological'?

Moreover, do men and women have different views of these issues and are they positioned differently with respect to privacy and publicity? Did the efforts of Thomas's supporters to undermine the credibility of Hill constitute an unconscionable invasion of her privacy or a proper and vigorous exercise of public scrutiny? Were there significant differences in the ability of Thomas and Hill respectively to define and defend their privacy?

Was the subsequent injection of the issue of 'race' by Thomas a mere smokescreen or did the convening of an all-white public tribunal to adjudicate on television a dispute between two African Americans signal the existence of real racial-ethnic differences in relation to privacy and publicity? Is 'sexual harassment' a figment of the fevered imagination of puritanical, sexually repressed, elite white feminists or an instrument of gender, 'race', and class power? Does the vindication in this case of a black man's ability to defend his privacy against a white-dominated public represent an advance for his 'race' or a setback for black women?

Did the hearings themselves constitute a unseemly circus that degraded the democratic process or were they a rare exercise in democratic publicity, a 'national teach-in on sexual harassment'? Was the airing in public hearings of the charge of sexual harassment another sorry case of the American obsession with the private lives of public figures, an obsession that displaces real politics onto questions of 'character'? Or was it instead a historic breakthrough in an ongoing struggle to achieve a more equitable balance in the social relations of privacy and publicity?

Finally, is democratic publicity best understood as a check on the public power of the state or should it be understood more broadly as a check against illegitimate private power as well? And what is the relationship between various different publics that emerged here: for example, the official public sphere within the state (the hearings); the extragovernmental public sphere constituted by the mass media; various counter-publics associated with oppositional social movements like feminism and with ethnic enclaves like the African-American community (the feminist press, the black press); various secondary associations active in forming public opinion ('interest groups', lobbies); the ephemeral but intense constitution of informal public spheres at various sites in everyday life—at workplaces, restaurants, campuses, street corners, shopping centres, private homes, wherever people gathered to discuss the events? In each of those public arenas, whose words counted in the conflict of interpretations that determines the official public story of 'what really happened'? And why?

Underlying all these questions are two more general problems that are centred on power and inequality: Who has the power to decide where to draw the line between public and private? What structures of inequality underlie the hegemonic understandings of these categories as well as the struggles that contest them?

GENDER STRUGGLE

The first phase of the struggle was played out as a gender struggle, and it laid bare important gender asymmetries concerning privacy and publicity. These were not the familiar orthodoxies of an earlier stage of feminist theory, which protested women's alleged confinement to the private sphere and lack of public sphere participation. Rather, the asymmetries here concerned women's greater vulnerability to unwanted, intrusive publicity and lesser ability to define and defend their privacy.

These issues first emerged when the public-at-large learned of a struggle that had been waged behind closed doors for several weeks between Hill and members of the Senate Judiciary Committee over the handling of her accusations against Thomas. We learned that Hill had been approached by committee staff and asked to confirm a report that Thomas had harassed her; that she did so, but asked that the matter be pursued in a way that would protect her privacy by keeping her identity secret; that the committee had dropped the matter after only a very cursory investigation, although Hill had several times urged the committee to pursue it, finally agreeing that her name could be used; and that the committee had elected not to publicize the matter. A reporter broke the story, however.

In her first public news conference after her charges had been publicly reported, Hill put great stress on what she called her lack of 'control' over the routing, timing, and dissemination of her information. She was already having to defend herself against two apparently contradictory charges: first, that she had failed to make public her allegations in a timely fashion, as any bona fide victim of sexual harassment supposedly would have; but second, that in making these charges she was seeking publicity and self-aggrandisement. Hill sought to explain her actions, first, by insisting that 'control' over these disclosures 'never rested with me', and second, by acknowledging her difficulty in balancing her need for privacy against her duty to disclose information in response to the committee's inquiry.[3] As it turned out, she never succeeded in fully dispelling many Americans' doubts on these points.

For its part, the committee's decision not to publicize Hill's sexual harassment charges against Thomas represented an effort to delimit the scope of the first round of public hearings in September and to contain public debate about the nomination. Once the charges were made public, however, the committee lost control of the process. Instead, its members became embroiled in a public struggle with feminists who objected to the privatization of an important gender issue and accused the senators of 'sexism' and 'insensitivity'.

This gender struggle was widely reported in the media in counterpoint with a counterdiscourse of outrage over 'the leak'. These two themes of 'sexism in the Senate' and 'leaks' were for a time the two principal contenders in the battle for preeminence in interpreting the events, as a struggle was being waged over whether or not to delay the confirmation vote.[4] The vote *was* of course delayed, and feminists succeeded in broadening the space of the official national political public sphere to encompass, for the first time, the subject of sexual harassment.

Getting an issue on the public sphere agenda, however, does not guarantee success in controlling the discussion of it. Even as it was being decided that the vote on Thomas's nomination would be delayed and that public hearings on the sexual harassment charges would be held, there began a fierce back-stage contest to shape the public debate over the issues. While public debate focused on the question of the Senate's 'insensitivity', White House strategists worked behind the scenes to shape the focus of the hearings and the interpretation of events.

As it turned out, the administration plan to shape public debate and limit the scope of the hearings had three crucial features. First, the White House sought to construct the hearings as a 'he said, she said' affair by preventing or marginalizing any new allegations of sexual harassment by other victims. Second, it sought to rule off-limits any interrogation of what was defined as Thomas's private life, including what the *New York Times* called his 'well-documented taste for watching and discussing pornographic movies while he was at Yale Law School'.[5] Third, and last, it sought to exclude expert testimony about the nature of sexual harassment and the characteristic responses of victims, so that, in the words of one administration spin doctor, it could 'prevent this from turning into a referendum on 2000 years of male dominance and sexual harassment'.[6]

Together these three moves cast Thomas and Hill in very different relations to privacy and publicity. Thomas was enabled to declare key areas of his life 'private' and therefore off-limits. Hill, in contrast, was cast as someone whose motives and character would be subjects of intense scrutiny and intrusive speculation, since her credibility was to be evaluated in a conceptual vacuum. When the Senate Judiciary Committee adopted these ground rules for the hearings, it sealed in place a structural differential in relation to publicity and privacy that worked overwhelmingly to Thomas's advantage and to Hill's disadvantage.

Once these ground rules were in place, the administration concentrated on undermining Hill. It sought to ensure, as Republican Senator Alan K. Simpson presciently predicted in a speech on the Senate floor, that 'Anita Hill will be sucked right into the maw, the very thing she wanted to avoid most. She will be injured and destroyed and belittled and hounded and harassed, real harassment, different from the sexual kind.'[7]

Meanwhile, Thomas attempted to define and defend his privacy. His attempts had a certain ironic flavour, to be sure, given his insistence in the earlier, routine round of hearings on substituting his personal life story—or at least his version thereof—for discussion of his political, legal, and constitutional views. Having first tried to make his private character the public issue, he was nearly undone by the focus on his character when Hill's accusation was made public.

In the extraordinary, second round of hearings, Thomas responded to Hill's charges by trying to define what he thought was or should be his private life. He refused to accept questions that breached his privacy as he defined it. And he objected to 'reporters and interest groups . . . looking for dirt' as un-American and Kafkaesque.

I am not here . . . to put my private life on display for prurient interests or other reasons. I will not allow this committee or anyone else to probe into my private life . . . I will not provide the rope for my own lynching or for further humiliation. I am not going to engage in discussions nor will I submit to roving questions of what goes on in the most intimate parts of my private life, or the sanctity of my bedroom. These are the most intimate parts of my privacy, and they will remain just that, private.[8]

As it turned out, Thomas was relatively successful in enforcing his definitions of privacy and publicity. His questioners on the committee generally accepted his definition of privacy, and their questions did not trespass on that space as he had defined it. They didn't inquire into his sexual history or his fantasy life, and he was not in fact questioned about his practice of viewing and discussing pornographic films. On the one time when this subject was broached by Democratic Senator Patrick Leahy, at the session of 12 October 1991, Thomas successfully repulsed the inquiry:

SENATOR LEAHY: Did you ever have a discussion of pornographic films with . . . any other women [than Professor Hill]?
THOMAS: Senator, I will not get into any discussions that I might have about my personal life or my sex life with any person outside of the workplace.[9]

The question was not pursued. Later, after the Senate confirmed the nomination, Democratic members of the Judiciary Committee defended their failure to cross-examine Thomas vigorously by saying that he had put up a 'wall' and refused to answer questions about his private life.[10]

So successful, in fact, was Thomas in defending his privacy that while the country was awash in speculation concerning the character, motives, and psychology of Hill, there was no comparable speculation about him. No one wondered, it seemed, what sort of anxieties and hurts could lead a powerful and successful self-made black man from a very poor background to sexually harass a black female subordinate from a similar background.

Hill also sought to define and defend her privacy but was far less successful than Thomas. Although she sought to keep the focus on her complaint and on the evidence that corroborated it, the principal focus soon became *her* character. During the course of the struggle, it was variously suggested that Hill was a lesbian, a heterosexual erotomaniac, a delusional schizophrenic, a fantasist, a vengeful spurned woman, a perjurer, and a malleable tool of liberal interest groups. Not only the Republican hit men, Senators Arlen Specter, Orrin Hatch, and Alan Simpson, but even her female co-workers from the Equal Employment Opportunity Commission tarred her with many of the classical sexist stereotypes: 'stridently aggressive', 'arrogant', 'ambitious', 'hard', 'tough', 'scorned', 'opinionated'. Nor did any of the Democratic committee members succeed, or for that matter even try, to limit the scope of inquiry into her privacy.[11]

Hill's lesser success in drawing the line between public and private testifies to the gendered character of these categories and to the way their constitution reflects an asymmetry or hierarchy of power along gender lines. That asymmetry is reflected in the phenomenon of sexual harassment as well. Consider the following account by Hill in response to the questioning of Democratic Senator Howell Heflin, who first read portions of her own opening statement:

I sense[d] that my discomfort with [Thomas's] discussions [of pornography] only urged him on as though my reaction of feeling ill at ease and vulnerable was what he wanted.

Then, in response to Heflin's request for elaboration, Hill replied:

It was almost as though he wanted me at a disadvantage . . . so that I would have to concede to whatever his wishes were . . . I would be under his control. I think it was the fact that I had said no to him that caused him to want to do this.[12]

As Hill saw it, then, Thomas's behaviour had been an assertion (or reassertion) of power, aimed simultaneously at compensating himself and punishing her for rejection. She herself had lacked the power to define their interaction as professional, not sexual. He, in contrast, had had the power to inject what liberals consider private sexual elements into the public sphere of the workplace against her wishes and over her objections.

Given the gender differential in ability to define and protect one's privacy, we can understand some of the deeper issues at stake in Thomas's insistence on avoiding the 'humiliation' of a 'public probe' into his 'privacy'. This insistence can be understood in part as a defence of his masculinity. To be subject to having one's privacy publicly probed is to be feminized.

Women's difficulty in defining and defending their privacy was also attested by an extremely important absence from the hearings: the last-minute non-appearance of Angela Wright, a second black woman who claimed to have been sexually harassed by Thomas and whose scheduled testimony to that effect was to have been corroborated by yet another witness, Rose Jordain, in whom Wright had confided at the time. Given that disbelief of Hill was often rationalized by the assertion that there were no other complainants, the non-appearance of Wright was significant. We can speculate that had she testified and proved a credible witness, the momentum of the struggle might have shifted decisively. Why then did Angela Wright suddenly not appear? Both sides had reasons to privatize her story. Fearing that a second accusation would be extremely damaging, Thomas's supporters threatened to discredit Wright by introducing information concerning her personal history. Meanwhile, Hill's supporters may have feared that a woman described in the press as presenting 'a more complex picture than Professor Hill'[13] would appear to lack credibility and undermine Hill's as well. Thus, the silencing of a complainant who lacked Hill's respectability was a crucial and possibly even decisive factor in the dynamics and outcome of the struggle.

THE STRUGGLE OVER 'RACE'

During the first, gender-dominated phase of the struggle, the issue of 'race' was barely discussed, despite repeated but unelaborated references to the Senate as an all-white body.[14] The relative silence about 'race' was soon shattered, however, when Thomas himself broached the issue. Moving quickly to occupy an otherwise vacant discursive terrain, he and his supporters managed to establish a near-monopoly on 'race' talk, and the result proved disastrous for Hill.

Thomas declared that the hearings were a 'high-tech lynching' designed to stop 'uppity Blacks who in any way deign to think

for themselves'.[15] He also spoke repeatedly about his defenceless-
ness before charges that played into racial stereotypes of black men
as having large penises and unusual sexual prowess.[16] Here it is
important to note that by combining references to lynching with
references to stereotypes about black men's sexual prowess, Thomas
artfully conflated two stereotypes that, although related, are by no
means identical. The first is the stereotype of the black man as
sexual stud, highly desired by women and capable of providing
them great sexual pleasure. This was the figure that emerged from
Hill's testimony, according to which Thomas bragged about his
(hetero)sexual virtuosity. The second stereotype is that of the black
man as rapist, a lust-driven animal, whose sexuality is criminal
and out of control. There was no hint of that stereotype in Hill's
testimony.

It is possible that at an unconscious level there are affinities
between these two stereotypes, but they differ importantly in at
least one crucial respect. Although both have been embraced by
white racists, the first, but not the second, has also been embraced
by some black men.[17] Thus, while it may be inconceivable that
Thomas would have elected to affect the persona of the black man
as rapist, it is not inconceivable that he would have affected the
persona of the black male sexual stud. Yet by conflating these two
stereotypes, Thomas was able to suggest that Hill's reports of his
behaviour as a would-be stud were equivalent to southern white
racist fabrications of criminal sexuality and rape. This turned out
to be a rhetorical master-stroke. The Democrats on the committee were too cowed by Thomas's charge of racism to question the
nominee's logic. Many leading black liberals seemed caught off
guard and unable to respond effectively; most simply denied that
'race' had any relevance in the case at all.

The mainstream press contributed to the confusion. The *New
York Times*, for example, printed solemn quotations from Harvard
psychologist Alvin Poussaint about the effects of Hill's charges on
black men:

Black men will feel [her allegations] reinforce negative stereotypes
about them as sexual animals out of control. . . . It will increase their
level of tension and vulnerability around charges of this type. . . . There's
a high level of anger among black men . . . that black women will betray
them; that black women are given preference over them; that white men
will like to put black women in between them to use them. Black men
feel that white men are using this black woman to get another black
man.[18]

I have no way of knowing whether or to what extent Poussaint was accurately reporting the views and feelings of black men. What is clear, however, was the lack of any comparable discussion of the effects of the case on black women. In the absence of such discussion, moreover, the fears ascribed to black men seemed to acquire legitimacy. They were not contextualized or counterpointed by any other perspective. The press coverage of the racial dimensions of the struggle generally slighted black women. It focused chiefly on questions such as whether or not all black men would be tarred in the eyes of white America, and whether or not another black man would get a shot at a seat on the Supreme Court.

One of the most important features of the entire struggle was the absence from the hearings and from the mainstream public sphere debate of a black feminist analysis. No one who was in a position to be heard in the hearings or in the mass media spoke about the historic vulnerability of black women to sexual harassment in the United States, or about the use of racist-misogynist stereotypes to justify such abuse and to malign black women who protest.

The lone exception was Ellen Wells, a witness who corroborated Hill's version of events by testifying that Hill had told her that Thomas was harassing her at the time. In the course of her testimony, Wells explained why Hill might have none the less maintained contact with Thomas:

My mother told me, and I'm sure Anita's mother told her. When you leave, make sure you leave friends behind, because you don't know who you may need later on. And so you do at least want to be cordial. I know I get Christmas cards from people that I . . . quite frankly do not wish to [see]. And I also return their cards and will return their calls. And these are people who have insulted me and done things which have degraded me at times. But these are things you have to put up with. And being a black woman you know you have to put up with a lot. And so you grit your teeth and you do it.[19]

Wells's voice was, however, the exception that proved the rule. Absent from the mainstream public sphere was the sort of black feminist analysis that could have corroborated and contextualized Hill's experience. As a result, African-American women were in effect 'asked to choose . . . whether to stand against the indignities done to them as women, sometimes by men of their own race, or to remember that black men take enough of a beating from the white world and to hold their peace.'[20]

In other words, there was no widely disseminated perspective that persuasively integrated a critique of sexual harassment with a critique of racism. The struggle was cast as *either* a gender struggle *or* a 'race' struggle. It could not, apparently, be both at once.

The result was that it became difficult to see Anita Hill as a black woman. She became, in effect, functionally white. Certainly, Thomas's references to lynching had the effect of calling into question her blackness. The lynching story requires a white woman as 'victim' and pretext. To my knowledge, no black man has ever been lynched for the sexual exploitation of a black woman. Thomas's charge thus implied that Hill might not really be black. Perhaps because she was a tool of white interest groups. Or perhaps because she had internalized the uptight, puritanical sexual morality of elite white feminists and had mistaken Thomas's lower-class African-American courting style for abuse, a view propounded by Harvard sociologist Orlando Patterson in an op-ed piece in the *New York Times*.[21] Or perhaps most ingeniously of all because, like Adela Quested, the white female protagonist of E. M. Forster's *A Passage to India*, Hill was an erotomaniacal spinster who fantasized abuse at the hands of a dark-skinned man out of the depths of her experiences of rejection and sexual frustration. This view was apparently originated by a witness named John Doggett, who declared that Hill had once been obsessed with him. But it was more effectively —because less selfservingly—presented by Senator Orrin Hatch and other Thomas supporters.

Whichever of these scenarios one chose to believe, the net effect was the same: Hill became functionally white. She was treated, consequently, very differently from the way Angela Wright would probably have been treated had *she* testified. Wright might very well have been cast as Jezebel, opposite Hill's Adela Quested, in a bizarre melodramatic pastiche of traditional and non-traditional casting.

The 'whitening' of Anita Hill had much broader implications, however, since it cast black women who seek to defend themselves against abuse at the hands of black men as traitors or enemies of the 'race'. Consequently, when the struggle was cast exclusively as a racial struggle, the sole black protagonist became the black man. He was made to stand synechdochically for the entire 'race', and the black woman was erased from view.

The dynamics of black female erasure during the hearings did not pass uncontested by black feminists. In the heat of the struggle, a group called African American Women in Defense of

Ourselves formed, seeking to redress their erasure. Although the group developed a highly sophisticated analysis, it was unable to attract media coverage. Eventually, having raised sufficient funds to purchase space, it published a statement in the *New York Times* on 17 November 1991, a full month after Thomas was confirmed. Although this statement appeared too late to influence events, it is worth quoting at some length:

Many have erroneously portrayed the allegations against Clarence Thomas as an issue of either gender or race. As women of African descent, we understand sexual harassment as both. We further understand that Clarence Thomas outrageously manipulated the legacy of lynching in order to shelter himself from Anita Hill's allegations. To deflect attention away from the reality of sexual abuse in African American women's lives, he trivialized and misrepresented this painful part of African American people's history. This country, which has a long legacy of racism and sexism, has never taken the sexual abuse of Black women seriously. Throughout US history, Black women have been sexually stereotyped as immoral, insatiable, perverse; the initiators in all sexual contact— abusive or otherwise. The common assumption in legal proceedings as well as in the larger society has been that Black women cannot be raped or otherwise sexually abused. As Anita Hill's experience demonstrates, Black women who speak of these matters are not likely to be believed.

In 1991 we cannot tolerate this type of dismissal of any one Black woman's experience or this attack upon our collective character without protest, outrage, and resistance. . . . No one will speak for us but ourselves.[22]

What is so important about this statement is its rejection of the view, held by many supporters of Hill, that 'race' was simply irrelevant to this struggle, apart from Thomas's manipulation of it. Instead, the statement implies that the categories of privacy and publicity are not simply gendered categories; they are racialized categories as well. Historically, African Americans have been denied privacy in the sense of domesticity. As a result, black women have been highly vulnerable to sexual harassment at the hands of masters, overseers, bosses, and supervisors. At the same time, they have lacked the public standing to claim state protection against abuse, whether suffered at work or at home. Black men, meanwhile, have lacked the rights and prerogatives enjoyed by white men, including the right to exclude white men from 'their' women and the right to exclude the state from their 'private' sphere.

Perhaps, then, it is worth exploring the hypothesis that in making his case before the white tribunal, Thomas was trying to claim the same rights and immunities of masculinity that white men have historically enjoyed, especially the right to maintain open season on black women. Or perhaps he was not claiming *exactly* the same rights and immunities as white men. Perhaps he was not seeking these privileges *vis-à-vis* all women. After all, no white woman claimed to have been sexually harassed by him. Is that because in fact he never sexually harassed a white woman, although he married one? And if so, is *that* because he felt less of a sense of entitlement in his interactions with his white female subordinates at work? If so, then perhaps his references to lynching were not *merely* a smokescreen, as many liberals and feminists assumed. Perhaps they were also traces of the racialization of his masculinity. In any event, we need more work that theorizes the racial subtext of the categories of privacy and publicity and its intersection with the gender subtext.[23]

CLASS STRUGGLE?

Sexual harassment is not only a matter of gender and racial domination but one of status and class domination as well. The scene of harassment is the workplace or educational institution. The protagonists are superordinate bosses, supervisors, or teachers on the one hand and subordinate employees or students on the other. The effect of the practice is to maintain the class or status control of the former over the latter.[24] Sexual harassment, therefore, raises the classic issues of workers' power in the workplace and students' power in the school. It should be high on the agenda of every trade union, labour organization, and student association.

Yet the class and status dimensions of the struggle over Thomas's confirmation were not aired in the public sphere debates. No trade unionist or workers' or students' representative testified in the hearings. Nor did any publish an op-ed piece in the *New York Times*. In general, no one in a position to be widely heard articulated support for Hill grounded in class or status solidarity. No one foregrounded the accents of class to rally workers and students to her side.

The absence of a discourse of class conflict in the United States is no surprise. What is surprising perhaps was the deployment in the final phase of the struggle of a counterdiscourse of class resentment to mobilize support for Thomas. On the day before the

Senate confirmation vote, the *New York Times* printed an op-ed piece by someone purporting to be a friend of labour. Peggy Noonan, former speechwriter for Presidents Reagan and Bush, predicted victory for Thomas based on a 'class division' between the 'chattering classes' supporting Hill and the 'normal humans', who believed Thomas. She also glossed this as a division between the 'clever people who talk loudly in restaurants and those who seat them':

You could see it in the witnesses. For Anita Hill, the professional, move-ment-y, and intellectualish Susan Hoerchner, who spoke with a sincere, unmakedupped face of inherent power imbalances in the workplace. For Clarence Thomas, the straight-shooting Maybellined J. C. Alvarez, who once broke up a mugging because she hates bullies and who paid $900 she doesn't have to get there because she still hates 'em. . . . Ms Alvarez was the voice of the real, as opposed to the abstract America: she was like a person who if a boss ever sexually abused her would kick him in the gajoobies and haul him straight to court.[25]

Noonan appealed to the 'real American' workers (tough and macho, even if wearing eyeliner) to resist the effeminate (albeit makeup-free) intellectuals who impersonate them and feign concern for their interests, but whose American-ness is suspect (shades of com-munism). The scenario thus appeared to oppose 'the real worker', J. C. Alvarez, to 'the intellectual', Susan Hoerchner. Yet Alvarez here actually represented Thomas, the boss, while the aggrieved sub-ordinate, Hill, disappeared altogether. Moreover, by painting 'the worker' as a Maybellined tough guy, Noonan simultaneously updated and perpetuated masculinist stereotypes. The result was that it became hard to see most women, who do not repay sexual harass-ment with a kick to the groin, as workers.

Noonan's rhetoric mobilized class resentment in support of Thomas by 'disappearing' Hill as a worker. A similar tack was taken by Orlando Patterson, whose own *New York Times* op-ed piece appeared the following week in the guise of an analytical post mortem. Although Patterson acknowledged Hill's lower-class ori-gins, he none the less treated her as an instrument of 'elitist' forces. In his scenario she was a tool not simply of whites or of feminists but of *elite, upper-class* white feminists bent on using the law to impose a class-specific sexual morality on poor and working-class populations with different, less repressive norms. Workers were in effect called to defend their class culture—by siding with the boss against his assistant.[26]

Both Noonan and Patterson in effect bourgeoisified Hill, just as Thomas had earlier whitened her. Her actual social origins in rural poverty, which she had stressed in her opening statement to the committee, had by the end of the affair become so clouded by the rhetoric of class resentment that to many she was just another yuppie. The way, once again, was paved by Thomas. Very early on, even before the sexual harassment story broke, he staked out a strong claim to the discourse of impoverished origins. And as in the case of 'race', here too he retained a near-monopoly.

The 'class struggle' in this affair, then, was largely a matter of manipulating the signifiers of class to mobilize resentment in the interests of management. But was class not relevant in any other sense? Were there no class differences in the way Americans viewed these events and in the way they chose sides?

Some news reports following closely upon Thomas's confirmation portrayed white working-class women and women of colour of all classes as unsympathetic to Hill. For example, in an article titled 'Women See Hearing from a Perspective of Their Own Jobs', the *New York Times* reported that blue-collar women were put off by her soft-spokenness and what they construed as her inability to take care of herself. The story contrasted this 'blue-collar' view with the views of female 'lawyers, human service professionals, and politicians', who strongly sympathized with and believed Hill.[27] Despite the title of the article, the *Times* did not consider the possibility that these putative class differences could be rooted in different class work structures. It could be the case, for example, that working-class people who felt that Hill should simply have told Thomas off, quit, and found another job were not attuned to professional career structures, which require cultivation of one's reputation in the profession by means of networking and long-term maintenance of relationships.

There was another sense in which class affected this struggle, but it remained largely unspoken and implicit. Polls taken on the last night of the hearings showed that party affiliation was the most statistically significant factor distinguishing Thomas's supporters from Hill's.[28] This suggests that a large part of what was at stake in the confirmation struggles over this and other Republican Supreme Court nominees, that of Robert Bork, for example, was the continuation—or not—of the Reagan–Bush agenda, broadly conceived. For a moment, the question of sexual harassment became the condensation point for a host of anxieties, resentments, and hopes about who gets what and who deserves what in the United

States. In our current political culture, those anxieties, resentments, and hopes are often articulated in discourses of gender and 'race', but they are also necessarily about status and class. Noonan and Patterson notwithstanding, class remains the great unarticulated American secret. As such, it remains highly susceptible to manipulation and abuse.

MORALS OF THE STORY

The extraordinary struggle over Clarence Thomas's nomination proved the continuing importance of the public sphere in relation to state power. However, it also showed the need to revise the standard liberal view of the public sphere, which takes the categories of public and private as self-evident. This struggle showed, in contrast, that these categories are multivalent and contested. Not all understandings of them promote democracy. For example, male-supremacist constructions enshrine gender hierarchy by privatizing practices of domination like sexual harassment. They enforce men's privacy rights to harass women with impunity in part by smearing in public any woman who dares to protest. As Alan Simpson understood so well, women are effectively asked to choose between quiet abuse in private and noisy, discursive abuse in public.

However, the gendered character of the categories 'publicity' and 'privacy' cannot today be understood in terms of Victorian separate-spheres ideology, as some feminists have assumed. It is not the case now, and never was, that women are simply excluded from public life; nor that the private sphere is women's sphere and the public sphere is men's; nor that the feminist project is to collapse the boundaries between public and private. Rather, feminist analysis shows the political, ideological, gender-coded character of these categories. And the feminist project aims in part to overcome the gender hierarchy that gives men more power than women to draw the line between public and private.

Yet even that more complicated view is still too simple, because the categories of public and private also have a racial-ethnic dimension. The legacy of American slavery and racism has denied black women even the minimal protections from abuse that white women have occasionally managed to claim, even as their disadvantaged economic position has rendered them more vulnerable to sexual harassment. That same legacy has left black men without white men's privacy rights; and they have sometimes tried to claim those rights in ways that endanger black women. That suggests the need to develop an anti-racist project that does not succeed at black women's expense, one that simultaneously attacks the racial and gender hierarchy embedded in hegemonic understandings of privacy and publicity.

Recognizing how the categories of publicity and privacy have become coded by gender and 'race' points up several inadequacies of the liberal theory of the public sphere. For one thing, it is not adequate to analyze these categories as supports for and challenges to state power exclusively. Rather, we need also to understand the ways in which discursive privatization supports the 'private' power of bosses over workers, husbands over wives, and whites over blacks. Publicity, then, is not only a weapon against state tyranny, as its bourgeois originators and current Eastern European exponents assume. It is also potentially a weapon against the extra-state power of capital, employers, supervisors, husbands, and fathers, among others. There was no more dramatic proof of the emancipatory side of publicity in relation to private power than the way in which these events momentarily empowered many women to speak openly for the first time of heretofore privately suffered humiliations of sexual harassment.

Nevertheless, it is not correct to view publicity as always and unambiguously an instrument of empowerment and emancipation. For members of subordinate groups, it will always be a matter of balancing the potential political uses of publicity against the dangers of loss of privacy.

These events also show that even emancipatory uses of publicity cannot be understood simply in terms of making public what was previously private. They demonstrate that merely publicizing some action or practice is not always sufficient to discredit it. That is the case only when the view that the practice is wrong is already widely held and uncontroversial. When, in contrast, the practice is widely approved or contested, publicity means staging a discursive struggle over its interpretation. Certainly, a key feature of the Thomas/Hill confrontation was the wider struggle it sparked over the meaning and moral status of sexual harassment.

The way that struggle played out, moreover, reflected the then-current state of American political culture. The drama unfolded at a point at which a feminist vocabulary for naming and interpreting the behaviour ascribed to Thomas had already been created in the feminist counterpublic sphere and disseminated to a broader public. Not only was that vocabulary thus available and ready to hand, but it was also even encoded in the law. However, the feminist interpretation of sexual harassment was neither deeply rooted in the culture nor widely understood and accepted by the public at large. Consequently, it was contested and resisted throughout these dramatic events despite its official legal standing. In fact, it was precisely the disjuncture between the official legal acceptance of the feminist interpretation, on the one hand, and the widespread popular resistance to that interpretation, on the other, that helped determine the shape of the struggle. Much of the disbelief of Hill may well have been a disguised rejection of the feminist view of sexual harassment as a wrong, a rejection that could not easily be openly expressed and that was displaced onto doubts about Hill. Moreover, because the feminist understanding had legal legitimacy before it had widespread popular legitimacy, it could become a target for the expression of class, ethnic, and racial resentments. Although it is not the case, in other words, that the feminist perspective *is* elitist, white, upper-class, and so forth, it was vulnerable to being coded as such. Consequently, people with any number of a range of class, ethnic, or racial resentments, as well as those with gender resentments, could express them by disbelieving Hill.[29] And that may have tipped the balance in Thomas's favour.

Of course, Thomas's victory did not end the public-sphere struggle over sexual harassment. It merely sharpened and broadened the battle of interpretation. There are some grounds for thinking that the confirmation hearings really did function as a national teach-in. Polls taken a year after Thomas's confirmation showed a sharp decrease in the percentage of respondents who believed him and a corresponding increase in those who believed Hill. Those results suggest a genuine learning process. At the same time, however, the emergence of sexual harassment as an issue in the public sphere spurred antifeminists to develop counter-arguments and interpretations. In the period following this struggle, they sought to recast the matter as an issue of free speech, presenting women who object to harassment as infringing men's First Amendment rights.[30]

If one result of this struggle was increased consciousness-raising and increased contestation about sexual harassment, another was the fracturing of the myth of homogeneous 'communities'. 'The black community', for example, is now fractured into black feminists versus black conservatives versus black liberals versus various other strands of opinion that are less easy to fix with ideological labels. The same fracturing holds for 'the women's community'. This struggle showed that women don't necessarily side with women just because they are women. Rather, for what the polls taken at the hearing's close are worth (and it may not be much), they showed that a plurality of women in every age, income, and education group said they found Thomas more credible than Hill.[31] Perhaps these events should lead us to consider replacing the homogenizing, ideological category of 'community' with the potentially more critical category of 'public' in the sense of a discursive arena for staging conflicts.

This last point suggests that if these events expose some weaknesses in the liberal theory of the public sphere, they also point in the direction of a better theory. Such a theory would need to take as its starting point the multivalent, contested character of the categories of privacy and publicity with their gendered and racialized subtexts. It would have to acknowledge that in highly stratified late-capitalist societies, not everyone stands in the same relation to privacy and publicity; some have more power than others to draw and defend the line. Further, an adequate theory of the public sphere would need to theorize both the multiplicity of pubic spheres in contemporary late-capitalist societies and also the relations among them. It would need to distinguish, for example, official governmental public spheres, massmediated mainstream public spheres, counter-pubic spheres, and informal public spheres in everyday life. It would also need to show how some of these publics marginalize others. Such a theory would certainly help us better understand discursive struggles like the Thomas/Hill confrontation. Perhaps it could also help inspire us to imagine, and to fight for, a more egalitarian and democratic society.[32]

Notes

1. Research for this chapter was supported by the Newberry Library, the National Endowment for the Humanities, and the American Council of Learned Societies. I am grateful for helpful comments from and conversations with Laura Edwards, Jim Grossman, Miriam Hansen, and Eli Zaretsky. Susan Reverby generously shared ideas from her and Dorothy Helley's introduction to their jointly edited book, *Gendered Domains: Rethinking the Public and Private in Women's History* (Ithaca: Cornell University Press, 1992).
2. See Jürgen Habermas, *The Structural Transformation of the Public Sphere: An Inquiry into a Category of Bourgeois Society*, trans. Thomas

Burger with Frederick Lawrence (Cambridge, Mass.: MIT Press, 1989).

3. 'Excerpts of News Conference on Harassment Accusations against Thomas', *New York Times*, 8 Oct. 1991, p. A20.

4. Maureen Dowd, 'The Senate and Sexism', *New York Times*, 8 Oct. 1991, p. A1.

5. Maureen Dowd, 'Image More Than Reality Became Issue, Losers Say', *New York Times*, 16 Oct. 1991, p. A14. The mainstream press frequently referred to Thomas's alleged porn habit. See Michael Wines, 'Stark Conflict Marks Accounts Given by Thomas and Professor', *New York Times*, 10 Oct. 1991, p. A18, for an account by one of Thomas's fellow Yale Law School students.

6. 'Bush Emphasizes He Backs Thomas in Spite of Uproar', *New York Times*, 10 Oct. 1991, p. B14.

7. Alan K. Simpson, *Congressional Record: Senate*, 102d Cong. 1st sess., 1991, 137, pt. 143: 14546.

8. Clarence Thomas, 'Hearing of the Senate Judiciary Committee', 11 Oct. 1991, morning sess., in Nexus Library, FEDNWS file, Federal News Service.

9. 'Excerpts from Senate's Hearings on the Thomas Nomination', *New York Times*, 13 Oct. 1991, p. A30.

10. Quoted in Dowd, 'Image More Than Reality Became Issue, Losers Say'.

11. Maureen Dowd, 'Republicans Gain in Battle by Getting Nasty Quickly', *New York Times*, 15 Oct. 1991, p. A18.

12. 'Excerpts from Senate's Hearings on the Thomas Nomination', *New York Times*, 12 Oct. 1991, p. A14.

13. Peter Applebone, 'Common Threads between the 2 Accusing Thomas of Sexual Improprieties', *New York Times*, 12 Oct. 1991, p. A11.

14. See e.g. Anna Quindlen, 'Listen to Us', *New York Times*, 9 Oct. 1991, p. A25. These references rendered invisible the Asian Americans and Hispanic Americans in the Senate, thereby attesting to the American cultural tendency to binarize 'race' into the stark opposition of white versus black.

15. 'Thomas Rebuts Accuser: "I Deny Each and Every Accusation"', *New York Times*, 12 Oct. 1991, p. A1.

16. See Richard L. Berke, 'Thomas Backers Attack Hill: Judge, Vowing He Won't Quit, Says He Is Victim of Race Stigma', *New York Times*, 13 Oct. 1991, p. A1.

17. In a round-table discussion on a local Chicago television talk show, three black male journalists, Salim Muwakkil (*In These Times*), Ty Wansley (WVON radio), and Don Wycliff (*Chicago Tribune*), agreed with the suggestion of black political satirist Aaron Freeman (author of the play *Do the White Thing*) that many black men embrace the stereotype of the sexual stud.

18. Alvin Poussaint, quoted in Lena Williams, 'Blacks Say the Blood Spilled in the Thomas Case Stains All', *New York Times*, 14 Oct. 1991, p. A16.

19. Ellen Wells, quoted in 'Questions to Those Who Corroborated Hill's Account', *New York Times*, 14 Oct. 1991. p. A13.

20. Anna Quindlen, 'The Perfect Victim', *New York Times*, 16 Oct. 1991, p. A25.

21. See Orlando Patterson, 'Race, Gender, and Liberal Fallacies', *New York Times*, 20 Oct. 1991, p. E15.

22. 'African American Women in Defense of Ourselves', advertisement, *New York Times*, 17 Nov. 1991, p. A19.

23. A good beginning was made in two important articles that appeared shortly after the end of the struggle. See Nell Irvin Painter, 'Who Was Lynched?', *Nation*, 11 Nov. 1991, p. 577, and Rosemary L. Bray, 'Taking Sides Against Ourselves', *New York Times Magazine*, 17 Nov. 1991, pp. 56, 94–5, 101. The following year, a groundbreaking anthology appeared. See Toni Morrison, ed., *Race-ing Justice, Engendering Power: Essays on Anita Hill, Clarence Thomas, and the Construction of Social Reality* (New York: Pantheon, 1992).

24. There is in addition another variety of sexual harassment, in which male workers harass female co-workers who are not formally under their supervisory authority. This sort of harassment is frequent in situations when very small numbers of women enter heavily male-dominated and masculinized occupations such as construction, firefighting, and military service. Women in these fields are often subject to harassment from co-workers who are technically their peers in the occupational hierarchy—in the form, for example, of the display of pornography in the workplace, sexual taunts, non-cooperation or sabotage, and even having male co-workers urinate in front of them. This sort of 'horizontal' harassment differs significantly from the 'vertical' variety discussed in the present essay, which involves harassment of an occupational subordinate by a superordinate. 'Horizontal' harassment merits a different sort of analysis.

25. Peggy Noonan, 'A Bum Ride', *New York Times*, 15 Nov. 1991, p. A15.

26. Orlando Patterson, 'Race, Gender, and Liberal Fallacies', *New York Times*, 20 Oct. 1991, p. A15.

27. Felicity Barringer, 'Women See Hearing from a Perspective of Their Own Jobs', *New York Times*, Midwest edn., 18 Oct. 1991, pp. A1.

28. See Elizabeth Kolbert, 'Most in National Survey Say Judge Is the More Believable', *New York Times*, 15 Oct. 1991, pp. A1, A20.

29. Perhaps this helps explain the otherwise surprising fact, disclosed in polls, that large numbers of people who said they believed Hill none the less supported Thomas's confirmation, either minimizing the seriousness of her accusations, or judging her to be too prudish, or insisting that she should have handled the situation herself by simply telling him where to get off.

30. See Catharine MacKinnon, *Only Words* (Cambridge, Mass.: Harvard University Press, 1995).

31. See *New York Times*, 15 Oct. 1991, pp. A1, A10.

32. For an attempt to develop such a theory, see my 'Rethinking the Public Sphere: A Contribution to the Critique of Actually Existing Democracy', in *Justice Interruptus: Rethinking Key Concepts of a Post-socialist Age* (London: Routledge, 1997).

On Being the Object of Property

Patricia J. Williams

Reflections

For some time I have been writing about my great-great-grand-mother. I have considered the significance of her history and that of slavery from a variety of viewpoints on a variety of occasions: in every speech, in every conversation, even in my commercial transactions class. I have talked so much about her that I finally had to ask myself what it was I was looking for in this dogged pursuit of family history. Was I being merely indulgent, looking for roots in the pursuit of some genetic heraldry, seeking the inheritance of being special, different, unique in all that primo-geniture hath wrought?

I decided that my search was based in the utility of such a quest, not mere indulgence, but a recapturing of that which had escaped historical scrutiny, which had been overlooked and underseen. I, like so many blacks, have been trying to pin myself down in history, place myself in the stream of time as significant, evolved, present in the past, continuing into the future. To be without documentation is too unsustaining, too spontaneously ahistorical, too dangerously malleable in the hands of those who would rewrite not merely the past but my future as well. So I have been picking through the ruins for my roots.

What I know of my mother's side of the family begins with my great-great-grandmother. Her name was Sophie and she lived in Tennessee. In 1850, she was about 12 years old. I know that she was purchased when she was 11 by a white lawyer named Austin Miller and was immediately impregnated by him. She gave birth

From *Signs* 14/1 (1988), 5–24. Reprinted by permission of the University of Chicago Press. Copyright © 1988 by The University of Chicago.

to my great-grandmother Mary, who was taken away from her to be raised as a house servant.[1] I know nothing more of Sophie (she was, after all, a black single mother—in today's terms—suffering the anonymity of yet another statistical teenage pregnancy). While I don't remember what I was told about Austin Miller before I decided to go to law school, I do remember that just before my first day of class, my mother said, in a voice full of secretive reassurance, 'The Millers were lawyers, so you have it in your blood.'[2]

When my mother told me that I had nothing to fear in law school, that law was 'in my blood', she meant it in a very complex sense. First and foremost, she meant it defiantly; she meant that no one should make me feel inferior because someone else's father was a judge. She wanted me to reclaim that part of my heritage from which I had been disinherited, and she wanted me to use it as a source of strength and self-confidence. At the same time, she was asking me to claim a part of myself that was the dispossessor of another part of myself; she was asking me to deny that disenfranchised little black girl of myself that felt powerless, vulnerable, and, moreover, rightly felt so.

In somewhat the same vein, Mother was asking me not to look to her as a role model. She was devaluing that part of herself that was not Harvard and refocusing my vision to that part of herself that was hard-edged, proficient, and Western. She hid the lonely, black, defiled-female part of herself and pushed me forward as the projection of a competent self, a cool rather than despairing self, a masculine rather than a feminine self.

I took this secret of my blood into the Harvard milieu with both the pride and the shame with which my mother had passed it along to me. I found myself in the situation described by Marguerite Duras in her novel *The Lover*:

We're united in a fundamental shame at having to live. It's here we are at the heart of our common fate, the fact that [we] are our mother's children, the children of a candid creature murdered by society. We're on the side of society which has reduced her to despair. Because of what's been done to our mother, so amiable, so trusting, we hate life, we hate ourselves.[3]

Reclaiming that from which one has been disinherited is a good thing. Self-possession in the full sense of that expression is the companion to self-knowledge. Yet claiming for myself a heritage the weft of whose genesis is my own disinheritance is a profoundly troubling paradox.

PATRICIA J. WILLIAMS

Images

A friend of mine practises law in rural Florida. His office is in Belle Glade, an extremely depressed area where the sugar industry reigns supreme, where blacks live pretty much as they did in slavery times, in dormitories called slave ships. They are penniless and illiterate and have both a high birth rate and a high death rate.

My friend told me about a client of his, a 15-year-old young woman pregnant with her third child, who came seeking advice because her mother had advised a hysterectomy—not even a tubal ligation—as a means of birth control. The young woman's mother, in turn, had been advised of the propriety of such a course in her own case by a white doctor some years before. Listening to this, I was reminded of a case I worked on when I was working for the Western Center on Law and Poverty about eight years earlier. Ten black Hispanic women had been sterilized by the University of Southern California–Los Angeles County General Medical Center, allegedly without proper consent, and in most instances without even their knowledge.[4] Most of them found out what had been done to them upon inquiry, after a much-publicized news story in which an intern charged that the chief of obstetrics at the hospital pursued a policy of recommending Caesarian delivery and simultaneous sterilization for any pregnant woman with three or more children and who was on welfare. In the course of researching the appeal in that case, I remember learning that one-quarter of all Navajo women of childbearing age—literally all those of childbearing age ever admitted to a hospital—have been sterilized.[5]

As I reflected on all this, I realized that one of the things passed on from slavery, which continues in the oppression of people of colour, is a belief structure rooted in a concept of black (or brown, or red) anti-will, the antithetical embodiment of pure will. We live in a society in which the closest equivalent of nobility is the display of unremittingly controlled will-fulness. To be perceived as unremittingly will-less is to be imbued with an almost lethal trait.

Many scholars have explained this phenomenon in terms of total and infantilizing interdependency of dominant and oppressed.[6] Consider, for example, Mark Tushnet's distinction between slave law's totalistic view of personality and the bourgeois 'pure will' theory of personality:

Social relations in slave society rest upon the interaction of owner with slave; the owner, having total dominion over the slave. In contrast, bourgeois social relations rest upon the paradigmatic instance of market

340

relations, the purchase by a capitalist of a worker's labor power; that transaction implicates only a part of the worker's personality. Slave relations are total, engaging the master and slave in exchanges in which each must take account of the entire range of belief, feeling, and interest embodied by the other; bourgeois social relations are partial, requiring only that participants in a market evaluate their general productive characteristics without regard to aspects of personality unrelated to production.[7]

Although such an analysis is not objectionable in some general sense, the description of master–slave relations as 'total' is, to me, quite troubling. Such a choice of words reflects and accepts— at a very subtle level, perhaps—a historical rationalization that whites had to, could do, and did do everything for these simple, above-animal subhumans. It is a choice of vocabulary that fails to acknowledge blacks as having needs beyond those that even the most 'humane' or 'sentimental' white slavemaster could provide.[8] In trying to describe the provisional aspect of slave law, I would choose words that revealed its structure as rooted in a concept of, again, black anti-will, the polar opposite of pure will. I would characterize the treatment of blacks by whites in whites' law as defining blacks as those who had no will. I would characterize that treatment not as total interdependency, but as a relation in which partializing judgements, employing partializing standards of humanity, impose generalized inadequacy on a race: if pure will or total control equals the perfect white person, then impure will and total lack of control equals the perfect black man or woman. Therefore, to define slave law as comprehending a 'total' view of personality implicitly accepts that the provision of food, shelter, and clothing (again assuming the very best of circumstances) is the whole requirement of humanity. It assumes also either that psychic care was provided by slave owners (as though a slave or an owned psyche could ever be reconciled with mental health) or that psyche is not a significant part of a whole human.

Market theory indeed focuses attention away from the full range of human potential in its pursuit of a divinely willed, invisibly handed economic actor. Master-slave relations, however, focused attention away from the full range of black human potential in a somewhat different way: it pursued a vision of blacks as simpleminded, strong-bodied economic actants.[9] Thus, while blacks had an indisputable generative force in the market-place, their presence could not be called activity; they had no active role in the market. To say, therefore, that 'market relations disregard the peculiarities of individuals, whereas slave relations rest on the mutual recognition

341

of the humanity of master and slave'[10] (no matter how dialectical or abstracted a definition of humanity one adopts) is to posit an inaccurate equation: if 'disregard for the peculiarities of individuals' and 'mutual recognition of humanity' are polarized by a 'whereas', then somehow regard for peculiarities of individuals must equal recognition of humanity. In the context of slavery this equation mistakes whites' over-zealous and oppressive obsession with projected specific peculiarities of blacks for actual holistic regard for the individual. It overlooks the fact that most definitions of humanity require something beyond mere biological sustenance, some healthy measure of autonomy beyond that of which slavery could institutionally or otherwise conceive. Furthermore, it overlooks the fact that both slave and bourgeois systems regarded certain attributes as important and disregarded certain others, and that such regard and disregard can occur in the same glance, like the wearing of horseblinders to focus attention simultaneously toward and away from. The experiential blinders of market actor and slave are focused in different directions, yet the partializing ideologies of each makes the act of not seeing an unconscious, alienating component of seeing. Restoring a unified social vision will, I think, require broader and more scattered resolutions than the simple symmetry of ideological bipolarity.

Thus, it is important to undo whatever words obscure the fact that slave law was at least as fragmenting and fragmented as the bourgeois world-view—in a way that has persisted to this day, cutting across all ideological boundaries. As 'pure will' signifies the whole bourgeois personality in the bourgeois world-view, so wisdom, control, and aesthetic beauty signify the whole white personality in slave law. The former and the latter, the slavemaster and the burgermeister, are not so very different when expressed in those terms. The reconciling difference is that in slave law the emphasis is really on the inverse rationale: that irrationality, lack of control, and ugliness signify the whole slave personality. 'Total' interdependence is at best a polite way of rationalizing such personality-splintering; it creates a bizarre sort of yin–yang from the dross of an oppressive schizophrenia of biblical dimension. I would just call it schizophrenic, with all the baggage that that connotes. That is what sounds right to me. Truly total relationships (as opposed to totalitarianism) call up images of whole people dependent on whole people; an interdependence that is both providing and *laissez-faire* at the same time. Neither the historical inheritance of slave-law nor so-called bourgeois law meets that definition.

None of this, perhaps, is particularly new. Nevertheless, as precedent to anything I do as a lawyer, the greatest challenge is to allow the full truth of partializing social constructions to be felt for their overwhelming reality—reality that otherwise I might rationally try to avoid facing. In my search for roots, I must assume, not just as history but as an ongoing psychological force, that, in the eyes of white culture, irrationality, lack of control, and ugliness signify not just the whole slave personality, not just the whole black personality, but me.

Vision

Reflecting on my roots makes me think again and again of the young woman in Belle Glade, Florida. She told the story of her impending sterilization, according to my friend, while keeping her eyes on the ground at all times. My friend, who is white, asked why she wouldn't look up, speak with him eye to eye. The young woman answered that she didn't like white people seeing inside her.

My friend's story made me think of my own childhood and adolescence: my parents were always telling me to look up at the world; to look straight at people, particularly white people; not to let them stare me down; to hold my ground; to insist on the right to my presence no matter what. They told me that in this culture you have to look people in the eye because that's how you tell them you're their equal. My friend's story also reminded me how very difficult I had found that looking-back to be. What was hardest was not just that white people saw me, as my friend's client put it, but that they looked through me, that they treated me as though I were transparent.

By itself, seeing into me would be to see my substance, my anger, my vulnerability, and my wild raging despair—and that alone is hard enough to show, to share. But to uncover it and to have it devalued by ignore-ance, to hold it up bravely in the organ of my eyes and to have it greeted by an impassive stare that passes right through all that which is me, an impassive stare that moves on and attaches itself to my left earlobe or to the dust caught in the rusty vertical geysers of my wiry hair or to the breadth of my freckled brown nose—this is deeply humiliating. It re-wounds, relives the early childhood anguish of uncensored seeing, the fullness of vision that is the permanent turning-away point for most blacks.

The cold game of equality-staring makes me feel like a thin sheet of glass: white people see all the worlds beyond me but not me. They come trotting at me with force and speed; they do not see me. I could force my presence, the real me contained in those eyes, upon them, but I would be smashed in the process. If I deflect, if I move out of the way, they will never know I existed.

Marguerite Duras, again in *The Lover*, places the heroine in relation to her family. 'Every day we try to kill one another, to kill. Not only do we not talk to one another, we don't even look at one another. When you're being looked at you can't look. To look is to feel curious, to be interested, to lower yourself.'[11]

To look is also to make myself vulnerable; yet not to look is to neutralize the part of myself which is vulnerable. I look in order to see, and so I must look. Without that directness of vision, I am afraid I will will my own blindness, disinherit my own creativity, and sterilize my own perspective of its embattled, passionate insight.

ON ARDOUR

The Child

One Saturday afternoon not long ago, I sat among a litter of family photographs telling a South African friend about Marjorie, my godmother and my mother's cousin. She was given away by her light-skinned mother when she was only 6. She was given to my grandmother and my great-aunts to be raised among her darker-skinned cousins, for Marjorie was very dark indeed. Her mother left the family to 'pass', to marry a white man—Uncle Frederick, we called him with trepidatious presumption yet without his ever knowing of our existence—an heir to a meat-packing fortune. When Uncle Frederick died thirty years later and the fortune was lost, Marjorie's mother rejoined the race, as the royalty of resentful fascination—Lady Bountiful, my sister called her—to regale us with tales of gracious upper-class living.

My friend said that my story reminded him of a case in which a swarthy, crisp-haired child was born, in Durban, to white parents. The Afrikaaner government quickly intervened, removed the child from its birth home, and placed it to be raised with a 'more suitable', browner family.

When my friend and I had shared these stories, we grew embarrassed somehow, and our conversation trickled away into a discussion of *laissez-faire* economics and governmental interventionism.
Our words became a clear line, a railroad upon which all other
ideas and events were tied down and sacrificed.

The Market

As a teacher of commercial transactions, one of the things that
has always impressed me most about the law of contract is a certain deadening power it exercises by reducing the parties to the
passive. It constrains the lively involvement of its signatories by
positioning enforcement in such a way that parties find themselves
in a passive relationship to a document: it is the contract that gov-
erns, that 'does' everything, that absorbs all responsibility and
deflects all other recourse.

Contract law reduces life to fairy tale. The four corners of the
agreement become parent. Performance is the equivalent of obedience to the parent. Obedience is dutifully passive. Passivity is valued
as good, contract-socialized behaviour; activity is caged in retrospective hypotheses about states of mind at the magic moment
of contracting. Individuals are judged by the contract unfolding
rather than by the actors acting autonomously. Non-performance
is disobedience; disobedience is active; activity becomes evil in
contrast to the childlike passivity of contract conformity.

One of the most powerful examples of all this is the case of
Mary Beth Whitehead, mother of Sara—of so-called 'Baby M'.
Ms Whitehead became a vividly original actor *after* the creation of
her contract with William Stern; unfortunately for her, there can be
no greater civil sin. It was in this upside-down context, in the picar-
esque unboundedness of breachor, that her energetic grief became
hysteria and her passionate creativity was funnelled, whorled, and
reconstructed as highly impermissible. Mary Beth Whitehead thus
emerged as the evil stepsister who deserved nothing.

Some time ago, Charles Reich visited a class of mine.[12] He discussed with my students a proposal for a new form of bargain by
which emotional 'items'—such as praise, flattery, acting happy or
sad—might be contracted for explicitly. One student, not alone in
her sentiment, said, 'Oh, but then you'll just feel obligated'. Only
the week before, however (when we were discussing the contract
which posited that Ms Whitehead 'will not form or attempt to

form a parent–child relationship with any child or children'), this same student had insisted that Ms Whitehead must give up her child, because she had *said* she would: 'She was obligated!' I was confounded by the degree to which what the student took to be self-evident, inalienable gut reactions could be governed by illusions of passive conventionality and form.

It was that incident, moreover, that gave me insight into how Judge Harvey Sorkow, of New Jersey Superior Court, could conclude that the contract that purported to terminate Ms Whitehead's parental rights was 'not illusory'.[13] (As background, I should say that I think that, within the framework of contract law itself, the agreement between Ms Whitehead and Mr Stern was clearly illusory.[14] On the one hand, Judge Sorkow's opinion said that Ms Whitehead was seeking to avoid her *obligations*. In other words, giving up her child became an actual obligation. On the other hand, according to the logic of the judge, this was a service contract, not really a sale of a child; therefore delivering the child to the Sterns was an 'obligation' for which there was no consideration, for which Mr Stern was not paying her.)

Judge Sorkow's finding the contract 'not illusory' is suggestive not just of the doctrine by that name, but of illusion in general, and delusion, and the righteousness with which social constructions are conceived, acted on, and delivered up into the realm of the real as 'right', while all else is devoured from memory as 'wrong'. From this perspective, the rhetorical tricks by which Sara Whitehead became Melissa Stern seem very like the heavy-worded legalities by which my great-great-grandmother was pacified and parted from her child. In both situations, the real mother had no say, no power; her powerlessness was imposed by state law that made her and her child helpless in relation to the father. My great-great-grandmother's powerlessness came about as the result of a contract to which she was not a party; Mary Beth Whitehead's powerlessness came about as a result of a contract that she signed at a discrete point of time—yet which, over time, enslaved her. The contract-reality in both instances was no less than magic: it was illusion transformed into not-illusion. Furthermore, it masterfully disguised the brutality of enforced arrangements in which these women's autonomy, their flesh and their blood, were locked away in word vaults, without room to reconsider—*ever*.

In the months since Judge Sorkow's opinion, I have reflected on the similarities of fortune between my own social positioning and that of Sara Melissa Stern Whitehead. I have come to realize that an important part of the complex magic that Judge Sorkow wrote into his opinion was a supposition that it is 'natural' for people to want children 'like' themselves. What this reasoning raised for me was an issue of what, exactly, constituted this 'likeness'? (What would have happened, for example, if Ms Whitehead had turned out to have been the 'passed' descendant of my 'failed' godmother Marjorie's mother? What if the child she bore had turned out to be recessively and visibly black? Would the sperm of Mr Stern have been so powerful as to make this child 'his' with the exclusivity that Judge Sorkow originally assigned?) What constitutes, moreover, the collective understanding of 'un-likeness'?

These questions turn, perhaps, on not-so-subtle images of which mothers should be bearing which children. Is there not something unseemly, in our society, about the spectacle of a white woman mothering a black child? A white woman giving totally to a black child; a black child totally and demandingly dependent for everything, for sustenance itself, from a white woman. The image of a white woman suckling a black child; the image of a black child sucking for its life from the bosom of a white woman. The utter interdependence of such an image; the selflessness, the merging it implies; the giving up of boundary; the encompassing of other within self; the unbounded generosity, the interconnectedness of such an image. Such a picture says that there is no difference; it places the hope of continuous generation, of immortality of the white self in a little black face.

When Judge Sorkow declared that it was only to be expected that parents would want to breed children 'like' themselves, he simultaneously created a legal right to the same. With the creation of such a 'right', he encased the children conforming to 'likeliness' in protective custody, far from whole ranges of taboo. Taboo about touch and smell and intimacy and boundary. Taboo about ardour, possession, license, equivocation, equanimity, indifference, intolerance, rancour, dispossession, innocence, exile, and candour. Taboo about death. Taboos that amount to death. Death and sacredness, the valuing of body, of self, of other, of remains. The handling lovingly in life, as in life; the question of the intimacy versus the dispassion of death.

In effect, these taboos describe boundaries of valuation. Whether something is inside or outside the market-place of rights has always been a way of valuing it. When a valued object is located outside the market, it is generally understood to be too 'priceless' to be accommodated by ordinary exchange relationships; when, in contrast, the prize is located within the market-place, all objects outside become 'valueless'. Traditionally, the *Mona Lisa* and human life have been the sorts of subjects removed from the fungibility of commodification, as 'priceless'. Thus when black people were bought and sold as slaves, they were placed beyond the bounds of humanity. And thus, in the twistedness of our brave new world, when blacks have been thrust out of the market and it is white children who are bought and sold, black babies have become 'worthless' currency to adoption agents—'surplus' in the salvage heaps of Harlem hospitals.

The Imagination

Familiar though his name may be to us, the storyteller in his living immediacy is by no means a present force. He has already become something remote from us and something that is getting even more distant. . . . Less and less frequently do we encounter people with the ability to tell a tale properly. . . . It is as if something that seemed inalienable to us, the securest among our possessions, were taken from us: the ability to exchange experiences.[15]

My mother's cousin Marjorie was a storyteller. From time to time I would press her to tell me the details of her youth, and she would tell me instead about a child who wandered into a world of polar bears, who was prayed over by polar bears, and in the end eaten. The child's life was not in vain because the polar bears had been made holy by its suffering. The child had been a test, a message from god for polar bears. In the polar bear universe, she would tell me, the primary object of creation was polar bears, and the rest of the living world was fashioned to serve polar bears. The clouds took their shape from polar bears, trees were designed to give shelter and shade to polar bears, and humans were ideally designed to provide polar bears with meat.[16]

The truth, the truth, I would laughingly insist as we sat in her apartment eating canned fruit and heavy roasts, mashed potatoes, pickles and vanilla pudding, cocoa, Sprite, or tea. What about roots and all that, I coaxed. But the voracity of her amnesia would disclaim and disclaim and disclaim; and she would go on telling me about the polar bears until our plates were full of emptiness and I became large in the space which described her emptiness and I gave in to the emptiness of words.

ON LIFE AND DEATH

Sighing into Space

There are moments in my life when I feel as though a part of me is missing. There are days when I feel so invisible that I can't remember what day of the week it is, when I feel so manipulated that I can't remember my own name, when I feel so lost and angry that I can't speak a civil word to the people who love me best. Those are the times when I catch sight of my reflection in store windows and am surprised to see a whole person looking back. Those are the times when my skin becomes gummy as clay and my nose slides around on my face and my eyes drip down to my chin. I have to close my eyes at such times and remember myself, draw an internal picture that is smooth and whole; when all else fails, I reach for a mirror and stare myself down until the features reassemble themselves like lost sheep.

Two years ago, my godmother Marjorie suffered a massive stroke. As she lay dying, I would come to the hospital to give her her meals. My feeding her who had so often fed me became a complex ritual of mirroring and self-assembly. The physical act of holding the spoon to her lips was not only a rite of nurture and of sacrifice, it was the return of a gift. It was a quiet bowing to the passage of time and the doubling back of all things. The quiet woman who listened to my woes about work and school required now that I bend my head down close to her and listen for mouthed word fragments, sentence crumbs. I bent down to give meaning to her silence, her wandering search for words.

She would eat what I brought to the hospital with relish; she would reject what I brought with a turn of her head. I brought fruit and yogurt, ice cream and vegetable juice. Slowly, over time, she stopped swallowing. The mashed potatoes would sit in her mouth like cotton, the pudding would slip to her chin in slow sad streams. When she lost not only her speech but the power to ingest, they put a tube into her nose and down to her stomach, and I lost even that medium by which to communicate. No longer was there the odd but reassuring communion over taste. No longer was there some echo of comfort in being able to nurture one who nurtured me.

This increment of decay was like a little newborn death. With the tube, she stared up at me with imploring eyes, and I tried to guess what it was that she would like. I read to her aimlessly and in desperation. We entertained each other with the strange embarrassed flickering of our eyes. I told her stories to fill the emptiness, the loneliness, of the white-walled hospital room.

I told her stories about who I had become, about how I had grown up to know all about exchange systems, and theories of contract, and monetary fictions. I spun tales about blue-sky laws and promissory estoppel, the wispy-feathered complexity of undue influence and dark-hearted theories of unconscionability. I told her about market norms and gift economy and the thin razor's edge of the bartering ethic. Once upon a time, I rambled, some neighbours of mine included me in their circle of barter. They were in the habit of exchanging eggs and driving lessons, hand-knit sweaters and computer programming, plumbing and calligraphy. I accepted the generosity of their inclusion with gratitude. At first, I felt that, as a lawyer, I was worthless, that I had no barterable skills and nothing to contribute. What I came to realize with time, however, was that my value to the group was not calculated by the physical items I brought to it. These people included me because they wanted me to be part of their circle, they valued my participation apart from the material things I could offer. So I gave of myself to them, and they gave me fruit cakes and dandelion wine and smoked salmon, and in their giving, their goods became provisions. Cradled in this community whose currency was a relational ethic, my stock in myself soared. My value depended on the glorious intangibility, the eloquent invisibility of my just being *part* of the collective; and in direct response I grew spacious and happy and gentle.

My gentle godmother. The fragility of life; the cold mortuary shelf.

Dispassionate Deaths

The hospital in which my godmother died is now filled to capacity with AIDS patients. One in sixty-one babies born there, as in New York City generally, is infected with AIDS antibodies.[17] Almost all are black or Hispanic. In the Bronx, the rate is one in forty-three.[18] In Central Africa, experts estimate that, of children receiving transfusions for malaria-related anaemia, 'about 1000 may have been infected with the AIDS virus in each of the last five years'.[19] In Congo, 5 per cent of the entire population is infected.[20] The

New York Times reports that 'the profile of Congo's population seems to guarantee the continued spread of AIDS'.[21]

In the Congolese city of Pointe Noir, 'the annual budget of the sole public health hospital is estimated at about $200,000—roughly the amount of money spent in the United States to care for four AIDS patients'.[22]

The week in which my godmother died is littered with bad memories. In my journal, I made note of the following:

Good Friday: Phil Donahue has a special programme on AIDS. The segues are:

a. from Martha, who weeps at the prospect of not watching her children grow up

b. to Jim, who is not conscious enough to speak just now, who coughs convulsively, who recognizes no one in his family any more

c. to Hugh who, at 85 pounds, thinks he has five years but whose doctor says he has weeks

d. to an advertisement for denture polish ('If you love your Polident Green/then gimmeeya SMILE!')

e. and then one for a plastic surgery salon on Park Avenue ('The only thing that's expensive is our address')

f. and then one for what's coming up on the five o'clock news (Linda Lovelace, of *Deep Throat* fame, 'still recovering from a double mastectomy and complications from silicone injections' is being admitted to a New York hospital for a liver transplant)

g. and finally one for the miracle properties of all-purpose house cleaner ('Mr Clean/is the man/behind the shine/is it wet or is it dry?' I note that Mr Clean, with his gleaming bald head, puffy musculature and fever-bright eyes, looks like he is undergoing radiation therapy). Now back to our show.

h. 'We are back now with Martha' (who is crying harder than before, sobbing uncontrollably, each jerking inhalation a deep unearthly groan). Phil says, 'Oh honey, I hope we didn't make it worse for you.'

Easter Saturday: Over lunch, I watch another funeral. My office windows overlook a graveyard as crowded and still as a rush-hour freeway. As I savour pizza and milk, I notice that one of the mourners is wearing an outfit featured in the window of Bloomingdale's (59th Street store) only since last weekend. This thread of recognition jolts me, and I am drawn to her in sorrow; the details of my own shopping history flash before my eyes as I reflect upon the sober spree that brought her to the rim of this earthly chasm, her slim suede heels sinking into the soft silt of the graveside.

Resurrection Sunday: John D., the bookkeeper where I used to work, died, hit on the head by a stray but forcefully propelled hockey puck. I cried copiously at his memorial service, only to discover, later that afternoon when I saw a black-rimmed photograph, that I had been mourning the wrong person. I had cried because the man I *thought* had died is John D. the office messenger, a bitter unfriendly man who treats me with disdain; once I bought an old electric typewriter from him which never worked. Though he promised nothing, I have harboured deep dislike since then; death by hockey puck is only one of the fates I had imagined for him. I washed clean my guilt with buckets of tears at the news of what I thought was his demise.

The man who did die was small, shy, anonymously sweet-featured and innocent. In some odd way I was relieved; no seriously obligatory mourning to be done here. A quiet impassivity settled over me and I forgot my grief.

Holy Communion

A few months after my godmother died, my Great Aunt Jag passed away in Cambridge, at 96 the youngest and the last of her siblings, all of whom died at 97. She collapsed on her way home from the polling place, having gotten in her vote for 'yet another Kennedy'. Her wake was much like the last family gathering at which I had seen her, two Thanksgivings ago. She was a little hard of hearing then and she stayed on the outer edge of the conversation, brightly, loudly, and randomly asserting enjoyment of her meal. At the wake, cousins, nephews, daughters-in-law, first wives, second husbands, great-grand-nieces gathered round her casket and got acquainted all over again. It was pouring rain outside. The funeral home was dry and warm, faintly, spicily clean-smelling; the walls were solid, dark, respectable wood; the floors were cool stone tile. On the door of a room marked 'No Admittance' was a sign that reminded workers therein of the reverence with which each body was held by its family and prayed employees handle the remains with similar love and care. Aunt Jag wore yellow chiffon; everyone agreed that laying her out with her glasses on was a nice touch.

Afterward, we all went to Legal Seafoods, her favourite restaurant, and ate many of her favourite foods.

ON CANDOUR

Me

I have never been able to determine my horoscope with any degree of accuracy. Born at Boston's now-defunct Lying-In Hospital, I am a Virgo, despite a quite poetic soul. Knowledge of the *hour* of my birth, however, would determine not just my sun sign but my moons and all the more intimate specificities of my destiny. Once upon a time I sent for my birth certificate, which was retrieved from the oblivion of Massachusetts microfiche. Said document revealed that an infant named Patricia Joyce, born of parents named Williams, was delivered into the world 'coloured'. Since no one thought to put down the hour of my birth, I suppose that I will never know my true fate.

In the meantime, I read what text there is of me.

My name, Patricia, means patrician. Patricias are noble, lofty, elite, exclusively educated, and well-mannered despite themselves. I was on the cusp of being Pamela, but my parents knew that such a me would require lawns, estates, and hunting dogs too.

I am also a Williams. Of William, whoever he was: an anonymous white man who owned my father's people and from whom some escaped. That rupture is marked by the dark-mooned mystery of utter silence.

Williams is the second most common surname in the United States; Patricia is *the* most common prename among women born in 1951, the year of my birth.

Them

In the law, rights are islands of empowerment. To be un-righted is to be disempowered, and the line between rights and no rights is most often the line between dominators and oppressors. Rights contain images of power, and manipulating those images, either visually or linguistically, is central in the making and maintenance of rights. In principle, therefore, the more dizzyingly diverse the images that are propagated, the more empowered we will be as a society.

In reality, it was a lovely polar bear afternoon. The gentle force of the earth. A wide wilderness of islands. A conspiracy of polar bears lost in timeless forgetting. A gentleness of polar bears, a fruitfulness of polar bears, a silent black-eyed interest of polar bears, a bristled expectancy of polar bears. With the wisdom of innocence, a child threw stones at the polar bears. Hungry, they rose from their nests, inquisitive, dark-souled, patient with foreboding, fearful in tremendous awakening. The instinctual ferocity of the hunter reflected upon the hunted. Then, proud teeth and warrior claws took innocence for wilderness and raging insubstantiality for tender rabbit breath.

In the newspapers the next day, it was reported that two polar bears in the Brooklyn Zoo mauled to death an 11-year-old boy who had entered their cage to swim in the moat. The police were called and the bears were killed.[23]

In the public debate that ensued, many levels of meaning emerged. The rhetoric firmly established that the bears were innocent, naturally territorial, unfairly imprisoned, and guilty. The dead child (born into the urban jungle of a black, welfare mother and a Hispanic, alcoholic father who had died literally in the gutter only six weeks before) was held to a similarly stern standard. The police were captured, in a widely disseminated photograph,[24] shooting helplessly, desperately, into the cage, through three levels of bars, at a *pietà* of bears; since this image, conveying much pathos, came nevertheless not in time to save the child, it was generally felt that the bears had died in vain.[25]

In the egalitarianism of exile, pluralists rose up as of one body, with a call to buy more bears, control juvenile delinquency, eliminate all zoos, and confine future police.[26]

In the plenary session of the national meeting of the Law and Society Association, the keynote speaker unpacked the whole incident as a veritable laboratory of emergent rights discourse. Just seeing that these complex levels of meaning exist, she exulted, should advance rights discourse significantly.[27]

At the funeral of the child, the presiding priest pronounced the death of Juan Perez not in vain, since he was saved from growing into 'a lifetime of crime'. Juan's Hispanic-welfare-black-widow-of-an-alcoholic mother decided then and there to sue.

The Universe Between

How I ended up at Dartmouth College for the summer is too long a story to tell. Anyway, there I was, sharing the town of Hanover, New Hampshire, with about 200 pre-pubescent males enrolled in Dartmouth's summer basketball camp, an all-white, very expensive, affirmative action programme for the street-deprived.

One fragrant evening I was walking down East Wheelock Street when I encountered about 100 of these adolescents, fresh from the courts, wet, lanky, big-footed, with fuzzy yellow crew cuts, loping toward Thayer Hall and food. In platoons of twenty-five or so, they descended upon me, jostling me, smacking me, and pushing me from the sidewalk into the gutter. In a thoughtless instant, I snatched off my brown silk headrag, my flag of African femininity and propriety, my sign of meek and supplicatory place and presentation. I released the armoured rage of my short nappy hair (the scalp gleaming bare between the angry wire spikes) and hissed: 'Don't I exist for you?! See Me! And deflect, godammit!' (The quaint professionalism of my formal English never allowed the rage in my head to rise so high as to overflow the edges of my text.)

They gave me wide berth. They clearly had no idea, however, that I was talking to them or about them. They skirted me sheepishly, suddenly polite, because they did know, when a crazed black person comes crashing into one's field of vision, that it is impolite to laugh. I stood tall and spoke loudly into their ranks: 'I have my rights!' The Dartmouth Summer Basketball Camp raised its collective eyebrows and exhaled, with a certain tested nobility of exhaustion and solidarity.

I pursued my way, manumitted back into silence. I put distance between them and me, gave myself over to polar bear musings. I allowed myself to be watched over by bear spirits. Clean white wind and strong bear smells. The shadowed amnesia; the absence of being; the presence of polar bears. White wilderness of icy meat-eaters heavy with remembrance; leaden with undoing; shaggy with the effort of hunting for silence; frozen in a web of intention and intuition. A lunacy of polar bears. A history of polar bears. A pride of polar bears. A consistency of polar bears. In those meandering pastel polar bear moments, I found cool fragments of white-fur invisibility. Solid, black-gummed, intent, observant. Hungry and patient, impassive and exquisitely timed. The brilliant bursts of exclusive territoriality. A complexity of messages implied in our being.

Notes

1. For a more detailed account of the family history to this point, see Patricia Williams, 'Grandmother Sophie', *Harvard Blackletter*, 3 (1986): 79.
2. Patricia Williams, 'Alchemical Notes: Reconstructing Ideals from Deconstructed Rights', *Harvard Civil Rights–Civil Liberties Law Review*, 22 (1987): 418.
3. Marguerite Duras, *The Lover* (New York: Harper & Row, 1985), 55.
4. *Madrigal* v. *Quilligan*, US Court of Appeals, 9th Circuit, Docket no. 78–3187, Oct. 1979.

5. This was the testimony of one of the witnesses. It is hard to find official confirmation for this or any other sterilization statistic involving Native American women. Official statistics kept by the US Public Health Service, through the Centers for Disease Control in Atlanta, come from data gathered by the National Hospital Discharge Survey, which covers neither federal hospitals nor penitentiaries. Services to Native American women living on reservations are provided almost exclusively by federal hospitals. In addition, the US Public Health Service breaks down its information into only three categories: 'White', 'Black', and 'Other'. Nevertheless, in 1988 the Women of All Red Nations Collective of Minneapolis, Minnesota, distributed a fact sheet entitled 'Sterilization Studies of Native American Women' which claimed that as many as 50 per cent of all Native American women of childbearing age have been sterilized. According to 'Surgical Sterilization Surveillance: Tubal Sterilization and Hysterectomy in Women Aged 15–44, 1979–1980', issued by the Centers for Disease Control in 1983, 'In 1980, the tubal sterilization rate for black women . . . was 45 per cent greater than that for white women' (7). Furthermore, a study released in 1984 by the Division of Reproductive Health of the Center for Health Promotion and Education (one of the Centers for Disease Control) found that, as of 1982, 48.8 per cent of Puerto Rican women between the ages of 15 and 44 had been sterilized.

6. See, generally, Stanley Elkins, *Slavery* (New York: Grosset & Dunlap, 1963); Kenneth Stampp, *The Peculiar Institution* (New York: Vintage, 1956): Winthrop Jordan, *White Over Black* (Baltimore: Penguin, 1968).

7. Mark Tushnet, *The American Law of Slavery* (Princeton, NJ: Princeton University Press, 1981), 6. There is danger, in the analysis that follows, of appearing to 'pick' on Tushnet. That is not my intention, nor is it to impugn the body of his research, most of which I greatly admire. The choice of this passage for analysis has more to do with the randomness of my reading habits; the fact that he is one of the few legal writers to attempt, in the context of slavery, a juxtaposition of political theory with psychoanalytic theories of personality; and the fact that he is perceived to be of the political left, which simplifies my analysis in terms of its presumption of sympathy, i.e. that the constructions of thought revealed are socially derived and unconscious rather than idiosyncratic and intentional.

8. In another passage, Tushnet observes: 'The court thus demonstrated its appreciation of the ties of sentiment that slavery could generate between master and slave and simultaneously denied that those ties were relevant in the law' (67). What is noteworthy about the reference to 'sentiment' is that it assumes that the fact that emotions could grow up between slave and master is itself worth remarking: slightly surprising, slightly commendable for the court to note (i.e.

in its 'appreciation')—although 'simultaneously' with, and presumably in contradistinction to, the court's inability to take official cognizance of the fact. Yet, if one really looks at the ties that bound master and slave, one has to flesh out the description of master-slave with the ties of father-son, father-daughter, half-sister, half-brother, uncle, aunt, cousin, and a variety of de facto foster relationships. And if one starts to see those ties as more often than not intimate family ties, then the terminology 'appreciation of . . . sentiment . . . between master and slave' becomes a horrifying mockery of any true sense of family sentiment, which is utterly, utterly lacking. The court's 'appreciation', from this enhanced perspective, sounds blindly cruel, sarcastic at best. And to observe that courts suffused in such 'appreciation' could simultaneously deny its legal relevance seems not only a truism; it misses the point entirely.

9. 'Actants have a kind of phonemic, rather than a phonetic role: they operate on the level of function, rather than content. That is, an actant may embody itself in a particular character (termed an acteur) or it may reside in the function of more than one character in respect of their common role in the story's underlying "oppositional" structure. In short, the deep structure of the narrative generates and defines its actants at a level beyond that of the story's surface content' (Terence Hawkes, *Structuralism and Semiotics* (Berkeley, Calif.: University of California Press, 1977), 89).

10. Tushnet, *The American Law of Slavery*, 69.

11. Duras, *The Lover*, 54.

12. Charles Reich is author of *The Greening of America* (New York: Random House, 1970) and professor of law at the University of San Francisco Law School.

13. See, generally, In the Matter of Baby 'M', A Pseudonym for an Actual Person, Superior Court of New Jersey, Chancery Division, Docket no. FM–25314–86E, 31 Mar. 1987. This decision was appealed, and on 3 Feb. 1988 the New Jersey Supreme Court ruled that surrogate contracts were illegal and against public policy. In addition to the contract issue, however, the appellate court decided the custody issue in favour of the Sterns but granted visitation rights to Mary Beth Whitehead.

14. 'An illusory promise is an expression cloaked in promissory terms, but which, upon closer examination, reveals that the promisor has committed himself not at all' (J. Calamari and J. Perillo, *Contracts*, 3rd edn (St Paul: West Publishing, 1987), 228).

15. Walter Benjamin, 'The Storyteller', in Hannah Arendt (ed.), *Illuminations* (New York: Schocken, 1969), 83.

16. For an analysis of similar stories, see Richard Levins and Richard Lewontin, *The Dialectical Biologist* (Cambridge, Mass.: Harvard University Press, 1985), 66.

17. B. Lambert, 'Study Finds Antibodies for AIDS in 1 in 61 Babies in New York City', *New York Times* (13 Jan. 1988): s. A.
18. Ibid.
19. 'Study Traces AIDS in African Children', *New York Times* (22 Jan. 1988): s. A.
20. J. Brooke, 'New Surge of AIDS in Congo May Be an Omen for Africa', *New York Times* (22 Jan. 1988): s. A.
21. Ibid.
22. Ibid.
23. J. Barron, 'Polar Bears Kill a Child at Prospect Park Zoo', *New York Times* (20 May 1987): s. A.
24. *New York Post* (22 May 1987): 1.
25. J. Barron, 'Officials Weigh Tighter Security at Zoos in Parks', *New York Times* (22 May 1987): s. B.
26. Ibid.
27. Patricia Williams, 'The Meaning of Rights' (address to the annual meeting of the Law and Society Association, Washington, DC, 6 June 1987).

All Hyped Up and No Place to Go

**David Bell, Jon Binnie, Julia Cream, and
Gill Valentine**

PREFACE

The joint authoring of a paper can be a troublesome affair, neces-
sitating some kind of initial 'coming clean' with regard to what went
on behind the scenes; what is there between the lines. The four
of us are positioned personally and politically very differently and
have different levels of investment in the identities and controversies which we discuss here. Hence in the preparation and writing
of this paper we adopted different, often contradictory standpoints.
Rather than attempt to create an artificial coherent argument out
of our 'troubles', we have tried to let the conflicts we experienced
producing this paper—we might say our *differences*—show in order
to illustrate precisely the tensions that we feel exist within theories
of gender identities and the subversive potentials of 'transgressive'
performances of identity in space.

INTRODUCTION: DOING GENDER, MAKING SPACE

This paper is concerned with the intersection of 'sex', 'gender',
'identity', and 'space'; with their construction and performance,
their *constructedness* and their *performativity*. The notion that places
are socially constructed has become commonsense, almost banal.
At the same time, the language of social relations and of identity
is inherently spatial. We need no reminding that geographers are
beginning to wake up to the idea that space is gendered and that

Reprinted by permission from *Gender, Place and Culture*, 1/1 (1994), 31–47.
Copyright © Carfax Publishing Ltd (1994) 11 New Fetter Lane, London EC4P4EE.

space is sexed (e.g. Bondi, 1992a; McDowell, 1992). The reverse has also been shown: gender, sex and sexuality are all 'spaced' (e.g. Jackson, 1991; Bondi, 1992b; Colomina, 1992; Knopp, 1992).

Work on what we might call lesbian and gay spaces has made equally apparent this notion of a mutual relationship between space and identity. It has been shown that sexual identity impacts on the use and reading of space, and that the socially and culturally encoded character of space has bearing on the assuming and acting out of sexual identities (Knopp, 1990; Abbott, 1992; Adler and Brenner, 1992; Valentine, 1993). As Joseph Bristow (1989: 74) says: '[I]t is possible to be gay [only] in specific places and spaces'. Here we have to think about what 'being gay' and 'being straight' means. Does it mean adopting a life-style, putting on an identity, which marks the bearer as sexual? It is often said in treatises on postmodernism that individuals are now 'free' to (self-)consciously experiment with identity, having at their disposal a rich wardrobe from which to pick and choose. But the risks involved in such choices can be deadly serious.

Many strategies employed by sexual dissidents have been focused on what might be described as the 'queering' of space through its active appropriation, whether through the processes of gentrification creating a 'pink power base' (Knopp, 1987) or through the actions of groups such as ACT UP, Queer Nation, Homocult and OutRage!, who seek to reveal through dramatic interventions and wild graphic art the socially constructed nature of sexual identities and sexually identified spaces (Crimp and Rolston, 1990; Davis, 1992; Geltmaker, 1992; Homocult, 1992; Knopp, 1992). It has thus clearly been demonstrated that not all space is 'straight'. But implicit in this is the notion that if space is not made gay or lesbian, then it *must* be straight. Straight space thus becomes the underlying frame with which we work: the space that gays subvert and the place that lesbians cohabit. We need to understand the straightness of our streets as an artefact; to interrogate the presumed *authentic* heterosexual nature of everyday spaces.

Inspired by the work of Judith Butler, especially in her book *Gender Trouble: Feminism and the Subversion of Identity* (Butler, 1990), we here try to highlight the importance of the spatial specificity of the performance of gender identities. Employing Butler's notion that there is a potential for transgressive politics within the parodying of heterosexual constructs, we try to assess whether the parallel argument can be made for the production of spaces. We are therefore trying to do more than simply locate the performance of gender in space; we are suggesting that space itself can also be interrogated in a similar manner. While it may be uncontroversial to assert that space (whether heterosexual or homosexual) is produced, how often is it still assumed that the heterosexual space came first? However implicitly, public (straight) space remains the original: the real space which gay space/queer space copies or subverts. It is as though it was there first; not produced, not artificial, but simply *there*. We have focused on the production of space that may look heterosexual, but is not. This should complicate matters; should cause some trouble. We hope it will hinder any facile attempt to tack sexuality on to space without interrogating how sexual identities are performed.

Through the deployment of the 'gay skinhead' and the 'lipstick lesbian'[1] and the place they produce and occupy, we hope to illuminate the 'unnaturalness' of both heterosexual everyday space and the masculine and feminine heterosexual identities associated with them. The exposure of the fabrication of both seamless heterosexual identities and the straight spaces they occupy should shatter the illusion of their just *being*, of simply naturally occurring.

The notion that gender is not simply an aspect of what one is, but it is something that one *does*, and does recurrently, in interaction with others (West and Zimmerman, 1991), and in space, highlights the performative character of both gender and of place. Gender as performance is no longer restricted by sex, so that Butler (1990: 6) suggests that gender may not restrict masculine to man and the male, nor feminine and woman to female. Consequently, public heterosexual space may not be restricted to heterosexuality.

The subversive potential to disrupt what 'we take for granted, to undermine and destabilize what counts as "natural"' is currently most likely to be found within the politics of drag (Butler, 1990). If there is no 'real' or 'original' gender that drag subverts, no fixed gender that drag copies, then the meaning and interpretation of drag is open to change. There is, however, nothing inherently transgressive about drag. What counts as radical and liberatory is contingent on time and space. Drag may endorse misogyny and reinforce cultural stereotypes, denying that masculinity and femininity are historical not biological facts through virtue of men not being able to dress or 'pass' as well as 'real women'. Epstein and Straub (1991: 23) rightly caution against the temptation 'to reify ambiguity and to celebrate the disruption of binary opposition without asking concrete questions about how power is distributed through that disruption or ambiguity'.

Drag can, however, successfully parody the seriousness and essentialism of heterosexuality. Indeed, the mimicry of heterosexuality by gay men and lesbians has the potential to transform radically the stability of masculinity and femininity, undermining its claim to originality and naturalness. Heterosexuality is a performance, just as constructed as homosexuality, but is often presumed and privileged as the original.

The excessive performance of masculinity and femininity within homosexual frames exposes not only the fabricated nature of heterosexuality but also its claim to authenticity. The 'macho' man and the 'femme' woman are not tautologies, but work to disrupt conventional assumptions surrounding the straight mapping of man/masculine and woman/feminine within heterosexual and homosexual constructs. The gay skinhead, with his Doctor Marten boots, drainpipe jeans held up by braces, bomber jacket and shaven head; and the lipstick lesbian, with her make-up and high heels, have different historical legacies and have intervened in different debates, from neofascism to feminism, but what unites them is their parodying of heterosexuality.

These lesbians and gay men in heterosexual drag occupy the same everyday life spaces that heterosexuals do. The presence of gay skinheads and lipstick lesbians in heterosexual spaces represents a double-coding of that space: to those who do not 'know' or do not 'see' that the skinhead is a gay man, or that the women in short skirts and stilettos are lesbians; their identities are read as heterosexual without a second look or thought. It might be tempting to rely on an essentialist plea, that says sexual identity is to be privileged over and above the 'skinhead' or 'lipstick' style (in fact calling it a 'style' is demoting it, making it seem superficial). This is a rather obvious danger to succumb to, which must be countered by saying that all these identities are fictions, copies.

The hypermasculine gay man and the hyperfeminine lesbian therefore occupy the same everyday spaces as the heterosexual masculine man and feminine woman. They may pass as heterosexual, deriving the privileges of heterosexuality, but their presence may signify a different production of space. If, as Butler argues, the parodic repetition and mimicry of heterosexual identities robs heterosexuality of its claims to naturalness and originality, then is the unquestioned nature of straight space undermined and disrupted by a copying of that space—of gay space in straight drag?

The potential to subvert may, importantly, depend on the status of the viewer. To those 'in the know', to those who can 'see', such a presence clearly parodies the heterosexuality of those spaces, since the gay skinhead and the lipstick lesbian can 'pass' as heterosexual. If you are 'in' on the joke, if you are aware of the redefining of that public space, then you see the gay skinhead not as a threat, but as a visible presence, parodying the aggression and power of the racist white man. Not all gay men could, if desired, parody this image. Whom and how does the lipstick lesbian challenge? It may be empowering to know that you are having the last laugh on the straight men trying to chat you up, protected from homophobic violence by passing as heterosexual, but are you actively challenging patriarchy through the parody of heterosexuality? This is one point we have been unable to agree on.

The sexual landscape is indeed changing. But only some of us know it. Does that matter? Tyler (1991) asks: if gender is not fixed to a biologically sexed body, why are only the homosexuals read and defined as drag—why not heterosexuals as well? According to Butler, the answer is in the author's intentions. The important issue is found in the theory of production rather than reception or perception. Perhaps, then, we could begin to introduce notions of unhegemonic performance of heterosexual identities that self-consciously reproduce heterosexuality in a way that does not reinforce authenticity of identity or of space. Sometimes, however, one is ironic without having intended it; and sometimes, despite one's best intentions, no one gets the joke. As Smyth (1992: 45) points out, those pessimistic about the transgressiveness of queer have suggested that 'queer will simply engender a situation where people are being transgressive for transgression's sake'.

So, to illustrate this very dilemma, to contemplate transgression, subversion, in-jokes and sex in space, we want now to go on to explore the performance of the two identities we have referred to, since, as Bordo (1992: 170) claims, 'determining whether a particular act or stance is "resistant" or subversive requires examining its practical, historical, institutional reverberations'. The subsequent sections thus explore the gay skinhead and the lipstick lesbian, who are both capable of 'passing' for heterosexuals—so that the space they produce may be interpreted as straight—endorsing or challenging the notion that space is heterosexual, just by being. As the preface points out, the arguments expressed in each section should not be taken as representative of all four of our views.

SKIN FOR SKIN: THE HYPERMASCULINE GAY MAN

In the early 1990s the skinhead 'look' became fashionable in gay London. This hypermasculine style is increasingly seen as a British successor to the US clone of the 1970s. It is fast becoming one form of gay 'uniform'. This identity is reflected in space through the emergence of a British gay skinhead group, the establishment of new one-night clubs such as 'Club 4 Skins' (which advertises itself as being for 'Queer Skins with Attitude'), and the proliferation of skinheads at any number of gay clubs and bars in the capital. In addition, the skinhead look is becoming an increasingly important component of the 'queer scene' in the USA.

This growing spatial visibility is mirrored in the pages of British gay newspapers which increasingly contain contact advertisements for skins. One of these, *Boyz*, even has a separate 'Boots and Braces' section for skins in search of skins. And we have witnessed the re-publication of skinhead classics from the early 1970s such as Richard Allen's (1992) pulp fiction novels *Skinhead*, *Suedehead*, and *Skinhead Escapes*, and the publication of George Marshall's (1991) *Spirit of '69: A Skinhead Bible*. These 'popular' mass-produced books of the 1970s are now visible in specialist book shops.

With the adoption of this hypermasculine style comes 'attitude'. As an item in *Boyz* proclaims:

Gone are the days when being a skinhead meant that you were either a thug or a fascist. There's a growing skin community living down those notions, and a lot of them are gay. For real skinheads, it's much more than just shaving your head, it's a way of life where clothes, music and attitude are every bit as important as hair. For lots of others, it's a mixture. Rough sex is always more likely to come with rough looks. (Rosner, 1992: 8)

The London Skinhead: A British Contribution to Gay Iconography

The London Apprentice bar opened in the early 1980s, initially as an 'American-style cruise bar' whose clientele in those pre-AIDS days was the clone and leather man—images and icons which originated on the West Coast of the USA, in the Castro district of San Francisco, and the gay ghetto of West Hollywood in Los Angeles. But since the onset of the AIDS crisis gay identities and styles have been transformed out of all recognition. The American clone look of check shirts, Levi 501 jeans, boots, and clipped moustache is intimately associated with the 'Golden Age' of the pre-AIDS Castro. It was a highly sexually charged style which invited sex. The look emphasized the erogenous zones of mouth, crotch, feet, and above all the 'ass' (tight jeans). This particular parodying of masculinity was a form of drag which made these gay men highly visible to other clones. In addition it meant that these men could 'pass' for straight (at least until the straights learnt how to spot a clone), thereby avoiding 'queer-bashing'.

But in the wake of the AIDS crisis, there was a reaction against the clone look (Levine, 1992). In the minds of those men coming out in their early twenties, the clones were 'responsible' for bringing AIDS: clone equals AIDS. There was a marked shift away from any specific assertive masculine gay 'look'. Instead, the young pretty boy look came into vogue. The party was over; promiscuous and kinky sex became unfashionable as the dominant AIDS discourses only encouraged fear of sex among the young. Inadequate, poorly-informed and above all sex-negative messages were the hallmark of the British Health Education Authority responses to the AIDS crisis in these early years. Early safer sex information was replete with references to curtailing promiscuity and sleeping around, and cutting down the number of partners.

The specific late 1980s gay adoption of the hypermasculine skin-head identity can be seen as a counter-trend—a safer-sex London 'clone' with many of the similar characteristics of 1970s San Francisco—a commitment to lots of sex, as often as one can get it, street cruising, safer-sex 'parties'. Sex is 'in' again so long as it's safer sex. The skinhead is a safer-sex slut, living out Douglas Crimp's call for 'principled promiscuity' as a strategy of refusal in the age of AIDS (Smith, 1993). This identity is also a counter-trend in terms of changing relations between lesbians and gay men. Whilst the clone look is commonly associated with separatism, the gay skinhead can be seen as a progressive identity. Gay skinheads share 'queer' spaces with a rich tapestry of identities including lipstick lesbians.

The hypermasculine skinhead thus stands for a resexualization of the gay body, a body that is hungry and ready for sex. The look shares many factors in common with the earlier Castro clone. Most important is the ultra-tight-fitting Levi 501 jeans, which display the crotch and 'ass' (and which contrast sharply with the baggy 'Joe Bloggs' look of the United Kingdom's rave scene). The skinhead substitutes the Fred Perry for the clone's Lacoste; Ben Sherman shirts for ordinary check shirts; and the Doc Marten for work boots.[2] Where the clone had cropped hair plus a handlebar moustache, the skinhead makes an equally dramatic gesture with hair— the No. 1 crop or no hair at all. And just as the clone look ages well and thus can look as good on someone aged 40 as it does on someone aged 25, so the same can be said for the skinhead look, which has that same odd 'democratisation' of age differences, a factor which sets itself against other parts of the youth-oriented gay scene.

But the hypermasculine skinhead image has also become intimately tied to specific (safer) sexual practices involving non-penetration. These include body shaving, boot licking, wrestling, as well as SM (sado-masochism):

Lots of skins are into shaving more than just their heads. Being tied up and being shaved or tying someone up and shaving them is sexy and should be safe...As well as shaving, skinheads often like rough sex, watersports and discipline. (Rosner, 1992: 8)

For many of those resisting the dominant discourses around AIDS, their anger and defiance against AIDS hysteria and the government's inadequate response to it is reflected in their hypermasculine self-presentation and their attitudes in taking to the streets to raise the visibility of AIDS.

As Sontag (1983: 144) says: 'Camp contains an explicit commentary on feats of *survival* in a world dominated by the taste, interests, and definitions of others.' Hence the importance of camp, or style, is even greater now than it ever has been. 'It's being so camp as keeps us going' (Dyer, 1992: 135), thus all the greater the care and attention invested in dress, oppositional or otherwise; the lavish care and devotion in polishing Doc Martens and ironing that T-shirt prior to clubbing it.

SKINHEAD SEMIOTICS: THE DIFFERENCE THAT SPACE MAKES?

The *Guardian* (Wilson, 1992) recently featured the skinhead look in a full-page report on lesbian and gay fashion in the 1990s. The author of the article expressed his surprise at how an image which has in the past and present been considered a homophobic image has now become a gay icon. But the response to the author's bewilderment lies in the potentially transgressive powers of this hypermasculine identity, a fact the author unconsciously reflects in his comment that 'The question "Is s/he?" is harder to answer now than ever before, especially when seemingly anti-gay images are mirrored by certain gay groups' (Wilson, 1992: 27).

Like the clone, the skinhead look has the advantage of 'passing for straight' because it is a hypermasculine identity. It might therefore challenge the assumption that 'all straights are straight'. As Bristow (1989: 70–71) puts it:

Stylizing particular aspects of conventional masculine dress, [gay men] can adopt and subvert given identities, appearing like 'real men' and yet being the last thing a 'real man' would want to be mistaken for: gay ... This type of gay identity, therefore, consciously inhabits a publicly acceptable one which is, in fact, its enemy. It appears that the mocking laughter of parody—the framing and sending-up of given forms—is at work here.

Clearly, then, the last thing any straight person expects skinheads to do is to hold hands in public, or to gently kiss. When this happens, people notice. By behaving in this way the gay skinhead can disrupt or destabilize not only a masculine identity but heterosexual space. Can you ever be sure again that you can read the identity of others or the identity of a space? And if not, then how can others read you?

But for the gay skinhead the power of performing this identity lies not only in its disruptive or transgressive qualities but in its power to create space. For in 1990s London the skinhead look is not a closet style, but a visible or clearly delineated look that makes it easy for those 'in the know' to distinguish. This visibility means that through the mutually-constituting exchange of glances on the street, gay skinheads create a queer space in a heterosexual world, which is in itself empowering.

But this hypermasculine look is often criticised for parodying a fascist style. This criticism was repeated in an item on gay skinheads on British television's lesbian and gay programme *Out* (Channel 4, 29 July 1992). This feature, 'Skin Complex', included an interview with Nicky Crane, previously an active member of the neo-Nazi British Movement, who 'came out' as gay. The magazine *Gay Times* (Anono, 1992: 66) called 'Skin Complex' 'gimmicky and heavy-handed', stomping over the issue of gay skinhead culture 'with the journalistic equivalent of 28-hole DMs', while a letter to the magazine interestingly contrasted fascist 'boneheads' with 'true skinheads' who are anti-Nazi (Ansell, 1992: 27). In another review of the programme, the international anti-fascist magazine *Searchlight* described Nicky Crane as having been involved in racist attacks (Searchlight, 1992: 9). The *Searchlight* article then went on to challenge the adoption of a skinhead style by some gay men, highlighting critical comments made on the *Out* item by some black gay men:

It is impossible for a black person to know if someone dressed as a skinhead is a 'real' skinhead or not. Even if the person is only a 'style' skinhead, he is still wearing the uniform of the oppressor. (*Searchlight*, 1992: 9)

But these critics all fall into the same trap. For them heterosexual or 'real' skinheads are positioned against gay 'style' skinheads. But why privilege the fascist heterosexual skin as 'real' and the gay skinhead as 'bad copy'? Why privilege heterosexual space as 'real' and queer space as pretended, fake or copy?

This denial of the validity of the gay identity is made all the more absurd by Richard Smith's research, broadcast on the BBC's Radio 1, as part of a one-off programme called 'Pink Pop' (Smith, 1992). Smith states that the early skinhead was first a gay image—later appropriated by the far right. So the 'real' heterosexual skinhead is not so real after all. For the gay hypermasculine identity is not a copy of the original heterosexual fascist look, but a copy of a copy. And this is the very power of the performance of a hypermascu-line identity, for it exposes not only the constructedness of gay identities and gay spaces, but the constructedness of heterosexual identities and heterosexual spaces. Amongst all this destabilised uncertainty, what is left of the hegemonic world of heterosexual binary opposites?

Critics not only challenge the authenticity of the skinhead look but also the 'attitude' it embraces. *Searchlight* (again) states that the *Out* programme showed 'disturbing evidence that some gay skin-heads are attracted to "White Power" sadomasochistic sex games' (*Searchlight*, 1992: 9). Considering the media hysteria around Operation Spanner[3] (Binnie, 1992; Bell, 1993), this is a very dis-turbing comment. It reinforces the dominant discourses around consensual same-sex sado-masochism which seek to criminalise SM queers. It also implies that sado-masochism is off-limits to black people, yet black people can be (and are) sado-masochists too, and do engage sexually with white gay skinheads. Once again then, the hypermasculine gay skinhead exposes the error of judging this identity as a copy of an authentic original fascist identity and the constructedness and instability of heterosexual identities and notions of what constitutes sex. This illustrates the importance of the intentions of the author of the identity, rather than the perceptions of the viewer.

In November 1992 the Countdown on Spanner campaign took to the streets of London to demonstrate against the conviction of sixteen men for consensual same sex SM. Among those taking part were numerous gay skinheads, marching through the streets of central London in their Doc Martens and bomber jackets—marching for civil rights, for justice. It would be unfortunate to equate these people with neo-Nazi, homophobic, racist thugs in the former German Democratic Republic. Russell Square is not Rostock.[4] The queer march is not a march of fake fascists taking place in a straight space. It is a march of those performing an identity which transgresses heterosexual preconceptions of gay and straight identities, which disrupts straight space and creates queer space. If you accept this can you ever be sure again of what you see and what you think you know about gender identities and spatial identities?

LIPSTICK AND HEELS: THE HYPERFEMININE LESBIAN

The dyke event of the year in London in the winter of 1986/7 was a glamour ball, 'Come Dancing' at which women once seen in boots, denim and leather appeared in frocks, high heels, lipstick and *décolletage*—items they would not have even thought of wearing in the seventies. Now everything's changed. Tickets were like gold dust. (Wilson, 1990: 67)

The rise of the lipstick lesbian from the ashes of androgynous feminist politics has thrown into relief once again questions about the relationship between the notion of woman, femininity and sexual behaviour, in other words between sex, gender and desire. The problem of accounting for the feminine lesbian has always dogged those seeking to link lesbianism with masculine personality traits, but for us the lipstick lesbian also raises the issue of the stability not only of heterosexual identities but also of heterosexual spaces; because, like the Trojan horse, make-up, high heels and the other trappings of femininity are claimed to allow lesbians to infiltrate and destabilize apparently 'heterosexual' environments. However, in order to understand the potential significance of 'lipsticks', it is

necessary first to trace the changing relationship between lesbianism and femininity.

The Invert: The Masculine Woman

Romantic friendships between women in Western society can
be identified at least as early as the Renaissance period. In the
nineteenth-century USA the notion of romantic friendship between
young women was considered commonplace. Such relationships
were perceived as a dress rehearsal for marriage and womanhood
(Faderman, 1991, Moore, 1992). But by the latter half of the nineteenth and into the early twentieth century, the scientific obsession with taxonomy, classification and evolutionary theory led the
new science of sexology to identify and classify such 'homosexual'
behaviour as 'abnormal'. Medical models evoking motions of biological essentialism attributed same-sex love to hereditary weak
genes (Faderman, 1991).

These early sexologists believed women's romances were 'inextricably linked to . . . their masculine behaviour and conception of
themselves as male' (Faderman, 1991: 41). The notion of the congenital invert, the man trapped in a woman's body, was born. This
theory was illustrated in Radclyffe Hall's (1928) book *The Well of
Loneliness*, in which the heroine has slim hips and a boyish appearance, and excels at masculine activities such as fencing and riding.
In a society based on appearance, the self-styled 'Stephen' distinguished herself from 'real women' in public space through her dress
and appearance. As Benstock (1987: 48) states, mannish dress in
this period represented 'a public announcement of a commitment
to lesbian relationships . . . registered . . . in a code that specifically
denied an allegiance to womanhood . . . Cross dressing constituted
a simultaneous denial of the feminine and a taunting of male
authority.' Furthermore, as Wilson (1988: 4) argues, 'Stephen's
apparel almost is her sexuality, and her sexual attraction is mediated through her masculine garb and accessories.' Stephen is not
attracted to another 'masculine invert' but to a feminine or 'real'
woman (for to fall in love with another almost-man would be a
real perversion), only to lose her lover, Mary, to a 'real' man.

By differentiating in this way between 'men in women's bodies'
and 'real' women, sexologists were able to explain the impossible—
women's sexual desire for each other—for those trying to maintain
a natural or essential relationship between biological sex, gender
identity, and sexual desire. By separating lesbians into 'congenital

inverts' and 'real women', sexologists maintained the heterosexual dichotomy of masculine–active, feminine–passive and the correlation between gender identity and sexual desire. Masculine appearance and behaviour in a woman (the invert) had to equal a sexual desire for a feminine 'real woman'. Correspondingly the 'real woman' attracted to the invert was responding to her 'natural' desire for the masculine, albeit trapped in a female body. In this way, sexologists re-established the certainty of the masculine–feminine 'heterosexual' dichotomy out of the apparent confusion engendered by the emergence of gender identities and sexual desires which did not appear to map neatly on to the binary sexed bodies of man and woman. This allowed women who were 'inverts' to triumph over their bodies by giving them the licence to perform their 'true' (masculine) gender and sexual identity in public space through mannish dress and behaviour. Therefore the invert copied but did not transgress the heterosexual norm and so perpetuated the stability of heterosexual identities and spaces.

Faderman (1991) argues that many women identified with these theories because they internalised the definition of ambition, physically and strength as male; they saw themselves as having been born men trappped in women's bodies. She goes on to argue that sexologists for the first time gave lesbians an identity and a vocabulary to describe themselves. Consequently, once they knew they were not alone and had a dress code to identify themselves from heterosexuals, they could go out and look for each other. The coincidence of the spread of these congenital invert theories and slight gains in economic independence for women allowed female inverts to find each other in the 'sexual underworld' of large cities at the turn of the century, and so lesbian subcultures were born.

Butch–Femme: Heterosexual Imitation?

The two world wars triggered a growth in women's economic and social independence. Aided by this, by the early 1950s, significant numbers of lesbians were coming together and creating gay spaces in the bars which were developing in major cities. But with no other role models, lesbian relationships appeared to continue to mirror the masculine and feminine difference of the 1920s, a difference symbolically represented through dress. Faderman (1991) argues that these binary dress, role and behaviour codes, by now called 'butch–femme', were crucial to the survival of lesbian subcultural spaces because they were an indicator of membership at a time when undercover police were used to entrap women in gay bars. Only those who understood the roles and the rules really belonged in the space and hence the community.

Lesbian masculine and feminine identities were therefore created in the semi-public space of gay venues. The binary world of the butch–femme bar of the 1950s was a site of conformity, when new women on the 'scene' were expected to adopt one role or the other. These identities and spaces are often assumed to have been stable signifiers and hence butch–femme to be a copy of the masculine–feminine, dominant–subordinate polarity of a heterosexual original. But oral histories throw into question this assumption.

Nestle (1984: 232) claims that

Butch–femme relationships, as I experienced them, were complex erotic statements, not phoney heterosexual replicas. They were filled with deeply Lesbian language of stance, dress, gesture, loving, courage and autonomy. None of the butch women I was with . . . ever presented themselves to me as men; they did announce themselves as tabooed women who were willing to identify their passion of other women by wearing clothes that symbolized the taking of responsibility. Part of this responsibility was sexual expertise.

Nestle (1984: 1987) and Faderman (1991) both also suggest that women adopted different roles at different times in different spaces: 'In the late 1950s I walked the streets looking so butch that straight teenagers called me a bulldyke: however, when I went to the Sea Colony, a working class bar in Greenwich Village, looking for my friends and sometimes a lover, I was a femme' (Nestle, 1987: 100). 'Once I went to an LA bar to meet this butch, and I was dressed femme. But she wasn't there so I decided to go on to another bar. On my way in the car, I changed to butch. Butches had a lot more opportunities in the bars and I just wanted to meet another woman' (Faderman, 1991: 172).

Blackman and Perry (1990) also disputed the fact that power in butch–femme relationships inevitably mirrored the patriarchal power of the male in heterosexual relationships. They maintain power was more fluid: 'Butches are on display and are looked at by femmes; a reversal of expectation of where the dominant "male gaze" should reside. By catching the butch's eye, the femme takes the initiative and so makes herself vulnerable to the butch' (Blackman and Perry, 1990: 72). Martin (1992: 111) argues that such accounts suggest that butch–femme dress codes did not reflect complementary gender identities but were about 'the both public and private construction of sexual differences, not gender differences between women'. Whilst to those in the know, butch–femme style may have parodied masculinity and femininity, because hetero-sexuals were not aware of the complex meanings of these appar-ently heterosexual identities, butch–femme did not transgress the heterosexual norm nor disrupt heterosexual space. Rather, to out-siders it appeared to reinforce the spatial hegemony of heterosexu-ality, for paradoxically lesbian spaces were seen to have imported and therefore to mirror heterosexual socio-sexual relationships.

Lesbian Feminism: Femininity as Oppression

The re-emergence of the women's movement in the 1970s chal-lenged such representations of both femininity and masculinity in the lesbian community.

For 1970s 'new lesbians', the pre-feminist world and the conviction that lesbians were failed women was no longer tenable or tolerable. In place of the belief in a lesbian essence or fixed minority identity signified by an inversion of gender, long synonymous with the image of lesbianism in the popular imagination, they substituted the universal possibility of 'woman-identified' behaviour. (Stein, 1988: 37)

In particular, feminists began to argue that gender identities were socially constructed and reproduced to create and perpetuate male dominance or patriarchy. They claimed that femininity expressed in clothing such as skirts and high heels restricts women's move-ments, damages feet and spines, and hence, as Bartky (1990: 34) argues, these 'restrictions on feminine body comportment gener-ate a restricted spatiality in women as well, a sense that the body is positioned within invisible spatial barriers'. In addition, they argued that femininity expressed through make-up is fundamentally about a representation of female sexuality for the male gaze.

Femininity and its trappings thus came to represent to some feminists women's oppression. Feminism sought to separate fem-ininity from the woman or gender identity from the sexed body and return to the 'original, natural' woman underneath all that make-up. This was an ideology which had a profound impact on lesbian 'communities' of the 1970s and early 1980s.

Dress became identified as a potentially powerful transgression of gender identity and sexuality:

If so much depended on women's bodily appearance and presentation then avoiding objectifying fashions might not only have a symbolic effect

—it might also contribute towards actually changing something. Most importantly, refusing to wear objectifying clothing . . . would contribute toward women retrieving their own subjectivity. Rather than sell their bodies feminists would reclaim their bodies as their own; rather than dress for men, feminists would deliberately dress against male expectations. (Green, 1991: 78)

But what should a lesbian feminist look like in order to transgress her gender identity and sexuality and therefore heterosexual and patriarchal spaces?

Since feminism was, if not against men, certainly against patriarchy or male power, and since it aimed to celebrate womanliness, a masculine style of dress must be *faux pas* for a lesbian feminist. On the other hand a wholeheartedly feminine manner of dressing must also be viewed askance, since feminism offered a critique of fashion, perceiving it as part of the ideology that kept women in their place. (Wilson, 1988: 50–1)

The result was an androgynous or what Wilson claims has been called a 'diluted butch look': unshaven legs, short cropped hair, Doc Martens, and baggy clothing. Lesbian feminism therefore created a new distinction between the 'androgynous' 'woman-defined woman' and the feminine 'male-defined woman'.

This feminist ideology was maintained in those lesbian spaces which were influenced by feminism (and not all were) through rigid dress and behavioural codes. A lesbian identity was therefore no longer a fate of birth but a political choice which had more to do with anti-materialistic lifestyles and counterculture than sexual desire. The success of dress as a transgression of heterosexuality/ patriarchy and heteropatriarchal space is reflected in the fact that dungarees (overalls) and Doc Marten boots became for the popular press synonymous with feminism, and feminism with lesbianism—a success which can be measured in the strength of the popular press backlash against these forms of dress (Wilson, 1988; Young, 1990) and in the abusive and hostile reactions of men in public space to women dressing in this way.

However, it has been argued that 'simply avoiding the structure of the symbolism in a male defined fashion for women did not challenge it and that patriarchal constructions of gender were untouched' (Green, 1991: 76). The patriarchal backlash merely intensified against any perceived gender transgressions expressed in lesbian feminist style. Instead, radical feminism was criticised for its universalistic and essentialist approach to women in its attempt to discover a 'correct' or 'natural' womanness (Green, 1991).

The Lipstick Lesbian: Transgressive Identity or Glitter and Glamour?

The emergence of the lipstick lesbian in the clubs and bars of the late 1980s and early 1990s was, some claim, an attempt to re-engage with the feminine on new terms. This was not femininity imposed on women, but femininity defined and controlled by women.

To all intents and purposes, then, the lipstick lesbian mirrors the heterosexual woman through her adoption of feminine dress. The hyperfemininity of the lipstick lesbian has theoretically broken the last link in the chain which joined man/woman and masculine/feminine together as binary opposites in a heterosexual matrix. For whilst the notions of inverts–'real women' and butch–femme broke the assumption that gender identity (masculinity or femininity) necessarily mapped neatly on to binary sexed bodies (male, female), these notions still maintained the link between gender identity and sexual desire, because the masculine woman (invert/butch) still desired the 'feminine' real woman. The lipstick lesbian is the feminine desiring the feminine, breaking the last stable concept of heterosexuality. Whilst butch–femme seemed to outsiders to reinforce the validity of the heterosexual original, the lipstick lesbian, with her subtle mixing of heterosexual signifiers within a feminine disguise, reveals that the heterosexual 'original' was, as Butler (1990) argues, only an imitation after all.

It is therefore claimed by some that this fluid, experimental and mocking expression of femininity by lipstick lesbians in heterosexual spaces destabilizes the very original heterosexual it is supposed to copy more than the hostile and confrontational separatism embodied by androgynous dress such as Doc Martens and dungarees (overalls). The transgressive qualities of this straight drag are said to lie in the fact that the softening or feminising effect of embellishments such as lipstick and heels also have, as Brownmiller (1984) argues, a 'heterosexual effect'. Hence it is claimed that lipstick lesbian style undermines a heterosexual's ability to determine whether feminine women in everyday spaces are lesbian or heterosexual. In other words, the public performance of femininity is no longer restricted to heterosexual women. This is claimed to be transgressive and threatening to straight men and women because 'images of selves trouble as they cut into spheres where they don't "belong"' (Probyn, 1992: 505). 'Lipstick style' therefore has the potential to make heterosexual women question how their own appearance is read, to challenge how they see other women and hence to undermine the production of heterosexual space. Similarly, the disruption of space in this way means that heterosexual men may be unable to distinguish the object of their desire—heterosexual women—from the object of their derision—the demonized 'dungaree-wearing lesbian'.

But surely the lipstick lesbian only undermines the 'straight' landscape if heterosexuals are aware that she may be there? The irony of heterosexual hegemony is that its very dominance means that many heterosexuals are ignorant of the changing homosexual landscape and have the arrogance not to think twice about the identities of 'straight-acting' individuals. If lipstick lesbians are to achieve anything more than their own transgressive pleasure in secretly sending up the 'hets', it requires a wider articulation of hyperfemininity as a political strategy.

However, the irony of adopting hyperfemininity as a political strategy to try to destabilise gender and sexual identities is that its origins as a form of lesbian style lie not in a reaction against heterosexual hegemony but in a political backlash against the ideological rigidity of lesbian feminism and androgynous style. First, lipstick lesbianism represents a reclaiming of womanliness and the notion that a woman can be attractive *and* a dyke. Second, it is aesthetic: as Bartky (1990) has argued, many women embrace femininity with enthusiasm because a woman can be a sex object for herself, taking an erotic satisfaction in her own body. Third, it is a reclaiming of lesbian sex from lesbian-feminism which emphasised same-sex love as a political choice rather than an issue of desire. Fourthly, feminine styling, if not outright lipstick lesbianism, has been made possible by the emergence in the 1980s of a generation of successful women with sufficient income to indulge in feminine fashions and a need to maintain appearances at work.

Even if hyperfemininity can be turned from a lesbian style to a conscious political strategy aimed at destabilizing heterosexual spaces, it is doubtful how successful it can be because, whilst it may make heterosexual women uneasy about feminine identities and spaces, it does nothing to undermine patriarchy. While lipstick style may be intended for the female gaze, it is also subject to the male gaze. Can you, in a patriarchy, wear clothes predominantly defined in a particular way by that patriarchy and have them read in a way other than they were intended? It would appear not. Whilst heterosexual space remains patriarchal, men are unlikely to be deterred from making sexual advances to a woman because they are uncertain of her sexuality. The evidence of previous feminist research (e.g. Wise and Stanley, 1987) is that men harass women everywhere: in the street, in the pub, in the work place; regardless of whether the women welcome their attentions or make it obvious that they are lesbian or just plain disinterested. And men are more likely to respond to rejection from a lipstick lesbian with verbal or actual physical abuse than retreat in a state of destabilized uncertainty. In this case the most important aspect of the transgression is not the intention of the author, as Butler claims, but the perception of the viewer—the heterosexual male. The realisation that the hyperfeminine woman is a lesbian may be surprising and therefore disruptive but it does not undermine the power invested in patriarchy. Hence it does not rob heteropatriarchal space of its legitimacy and authenticity.

In fact, the lipstick lesbian as Smyth (1992: 46) argues is 'only shocking and transgressive to hard-line feminists', creating tensions about dress codes, transgression and the meaning of style in lesbian-defined spaces (Stein, 1988) rather than heterosexually constructed spaces. It may therefore be contributing to the disintegration of the lesbian feminist project (and spaces) rather than challenging heteropatriarchal power, whilst merely allowing some women to gain heterosexual privilege (and a bit of transgressive fun on the side) through their ability to 'pass' in a society which sets such great store by a feminine appearance.

COMING TOGETHER/COMING APART

Lesbian and gay male dress codes have set themselves a difficult task to rework gender definitions. At different periods these codes have oscillated between two approaches: at one time there has been a clear alignment with gender characteristics of the opposite sex; at another it seems more important to identify as a member of one's own sex, to be a womanly woman, or a manly man. For women, however, either solution may appear or be experienced as oppressive and constraining, yet the androgyny of the centre can end up seeming sexless and self-effacing. (Wilson, 1988: 52)

The aim of this paper was to try to examine some recent work on gender identities and performativity as they operate in space; and to do this by focusing on particular identities which, through their performance in space, played with and troubled notions of gender, sex, and desire as these are mapped out in 'heterosexual' spaces.

377

Butler (1990) has illustrated how the gay deployment of hetero-sexual identities serves to undermine the naturalness and original-ity of heterosexual identities, and to thus reveal these identities as performative. We wanted to examine whether this also applies to the production of spaces. Does the replication of heterosexual spaces by 'others' expose the inauthenticity and constructedness of these spaces? Is the originality of these spaces destabilised and denatur-alised through the performance of 'hyperheterosexual' identities —by the hypermasculine gay skinhead and the hyperfeminine lipstick lesbian? We thus chose to talk about these two identities because they parody heterosexual identities. They do this by chal-lenging popular assumptions about homosexuality: that the lesbian is butch or 'manly', and that the gay man is effeminate (Chesebro and Klenk, 1981; Humphries, 1985).

We asked ourselves a series of questions. Does the performance of gay skinhead and lipstick lesbian identities disrupt the 'hetero-sexuality' of 'straight space'? Does it make it, in Butler's (1990: 124) words, 'the site of parodic contest and display that robs com-pulsory heterosexuality [and here we would add *heterosexual space*] of its claims to naturalness and originality'? What is transgression? What is parody? Who wins, and who loses, when 'in jokes' get told?

Bordo's engaging and insightful review of Butler's work (1990) highlights some of the troubles she had with *Gender Trouble*, and these are shared by (some of) us. For instance, Bordo (1992: 171) points out that Butler fails to locate her body-in-drag transgres-sion in a cultural context, and perhaps more significantly in view of the gay skinhead and lipstick lesbian's drag act, she 'does not consider the possibly different responses of various "readers" (male/female, black/white, young/old, gay/straight, etc.) or the various anxieties that might complicate their readings'. In short, she says, 'when we attempt to give [Butler's] abstract text some "body", we immediately run into difficulties' (Bordo, 1992: 171). And this is exactly what we have found: sometimes irreconcilable difficulties and differences arise in trying to deploy the lipstick lesbian and gay skinhead identities as embodiments of Butler's theories. We remain unclear and unable to agree about what trouble such trans-gression causes, for whom, and where.

Our own positions in relation to gender and sexual identities are very different, and we have different levels of investment in different identities and 'communities'. Consequently, as the pro-cess of writing progressed, as we individually read and thought and wrote about—then collectively discussed—these notions, it became apparent that our own ideas could not be squeezed into any coherent argument. We, too, it seemed, are troubled by these notions. We have therefore presented our theorizing and our detailed 'case studies'—the gay skinhead and the lipstick lesbian—to illustrate a set of ideas and thoughts, sometimes overlapping, sometimes opposing.

Certainly we have been less accepting of the transgressive possibilities of gender performance than other writers. We have found profound differences between the identities that we have talked about. In particular, we disagree about whether the transgressive power of the gay skinhead and the lipstick lesbian lies in the author's intentions or the viewer's perceptions. Hence we have had many disagreements over issues of race and gender.

The question of *where* transgression occurs has been central to our thinking. We have argued that space is constructed as heterosexual—not prediscursively, or essentially, but *actively*, through the performance of a set of identities which employ the heterosexual matrix of sex, gender, and desire. We have examined gay skinheads and lipstick lesbians in those spaces; and questioned the parodying of identities: does this parody space—creating gay space in straight drag?

The case studies highlight the important difference between knowing and not knowing. What kinds of (gender) trouble are most troublesome, and to whom? Ultimately, then, through trying to theorise the performance of identities and spaces, and attempting to explore our theorising in the context of gay skinheads and lipstick lesbians, we have ended up creating trouble for ourselves. Thus we have presented different arguments, which we are not all agreed upon, around hypermasculine and hyperfeminine 'gay' identities and consequently, we can go no further. This article is therefore intentionally a non-linear, ambivalent, multipositional piece, which we can only hope provokes the same kinds of trouble in the readers as it has in the writers. Having got all hyped up, we've found ourselves no place to go but this.

POSTSCRIPT: WRITING TROUBLE

The referees suggested that we should come 'clean' about the disagreements and unresolved debates which occurred during the writing of this paper. We toyed with various strategies—such as four parallel columns with 'I/I/I/I' replacing the unified 'we' (see Pile and Rose, 1992), or presenting a transcribed conversation. In the end we settled for a vaguer kind of polyvocality. The construction of the paper has taken place over 9 months and has involved constant negotiation (and arguing), during which time both individual and collective views have changed to such an extent that it is no longer possible to attribute particular points to particular individuals. Moreover our viewpoints, like our identities, are constantly in a state of flux!!!

Who had the most, if any authority to talk about the gay skinhead and the lipstick lesbian was central to our deliberations in writing the paper. Whilst it is becoming accepted within some academic circles to talk about autobiography and self-reflexivity, we still feel uncertain about where the boundaries of respectable academic discourse lie and how far we can push them. Although we recognise the importance of issues of representation we have felt unable to make clear our own 'identities' (at the time of writing) even though we accept that this is problematic for the paper. The issue of academic boundaries was brought home to us when, contrary to standard working practices, secretaries in a departmental office refused to type this manuscript because they objected to its content. Their action was subsequently endorsed by the institution concerned.

Although this paper has focused on the lipstick lesbian and the gay skinhead, our original aim was to expose the constructedness and performance of (hetero)sexuality and (hetero)sexual spaces. The extent to which we have achieved this is open to debate. We do not want this to be read merely as a paper about gay skinheads and lipstick lesbians, because we feel the issues of performance and the production of space are relevant to heterosexuals as well as sexual dissidents. We hope that readers will therefore question the production of all identities and spaces, including their own.

Acknowledgements

We would like to express our thanks to Claire Dwyer, Nuala Johnson, Peter Jackson, Liz Bondi, and three anonymous referees for reading and commenting on earlier versions of this paper. We are also eternally grateful to Guy and Trevor from the Department of Geography at University College London for miraculously resurrecting this (unsaved) article from oblivion when the computer crashed! Gill Valentine would also like to acknowledge the support of the Economic and Social Research Council (R00023 3600).

Notes

1. Throughout this paper we have used terms such as 'lipstick lesbian', and 'gay skinhead', and 'heterosexual'. However we recognize that these identities are not uniform. Similarly, for the purposes of this paper *only* we have felt it necessary to adopt the false dichotomy of heterosexual/homosexual.
2. The labels are important: Ben Sherman, Fred Perry, Doctor Marten, Levi—even skinheads outside the UK (such as those in the USA, as part of the 'Queercore' scene) fetishize the same brands of clothes.
3. In December 1990 16 gay men were given prison sentences or fined for engaging in consensual sado-masochistic (SM) sex acts. This followed a police investigation, code-named Operation Spanner, prompted by the chance finding of a videotape of SM activities. A campaign, Countdown on Spanner, mobilised SMers of all sexualities to protest, the biggest single event being an 'SM Pride' march in 1992. The men had their convictions upheld by the Court of Appeal and the Law Lords, and are now taking the matter to the European Court of Human Rights (for details, see Bell, 1993).
4. Russell Square is a leafy square and the gay cruising area in Bloomsbury, central London. The Countdown on Spanner march passed through this square en route to the adjacent University of London Union . The town of Rostock in the new German 'Land' of Mecklenburg-Vorpommern was the site of prolonged violent far-right attacks on hostels housing immigrants during 1992.

References

Abbott, C. (1992), 'Regal Landscapes? A Geography of Queens!' dissertation, Anglia Polytechnic.

Adler, S., and Brenner, J. (1992), 'Gender and Space: Lesbians and Gay Men in the City', *International Journal of Urban and Regional Research*, 16: 24–34.

Allen, R. (1992), *The Complete Richard Allen*, i (Dunoon, Skinhead Times Press).

Anon. (1992), 'Tranquil Sensuality' (television reviews), *Gay Times* (Aug.): 66.

Ansell, D. (1992), 'Not All Skinheads are Fascist' (letter), *Gay Times* (Sept.): 27.

Bartky, S. L. (1990), *Femininity and Domination* (London, Routledge).

Bell, D. J. (1993), 'Citizenship and the Politics of Pleasure', paper presented at the Annual Conference of the Institute of British Geographers, Egham, Jan.

Benstock, S. (1987), *Women on the Left Bank: Paris 1900–1940* (London, Virago).

Binnie, J. (1992), 'An International Cock-tail Party: The Spatiality of Fetishism', paper presented at the Sexuality and Space Network conference 'Lesbian and Gay Geographies?', London, Sept.

Blackman, I., and Perry, K. (1990), 'Skirting the Issue: Lesbian Fashion for the 1990s', *Feminist Review*, 34: 67–78.

Bondi, L. (1992a), 'Gender Symbols and Urban Landscapes', *Progress in Human Geography*, 16: 157–70.

—— (1992b), 'Sexing the City', paper presented at the Annual Conference of the Association of American Geographers, San Diego, Apr.

Bordo, S. (1992), Review essay: 'Postmodern Subjects, Postmodern Bodies', *Feminist Studies*, 18: 159–75.

Bristow, J. (1989), 'Being Gay: Politics, Pleasure, Identity', *New Formations*, 9: 61–81.

Brownmiller, S. (1984), *Femininity* (London, Hamish Hamilton).

Butler, J. (1990), *Gender Trouble: Feminism and the Subversion of Identity* (London, Routledge).

Chesebro, J. W. and Klenk, K. L. (1981), 'Gay Masculinity in the Gay Disco', in J. W. Chesebro (ed.), *Gayspeak* (New York, Pilgrim Press).

Colomina, B. (ed.) (1992), *Sexuality and Space* (New York, Princeton Architectural Press).

Crimp, D., and Rolston, A. (1990), *AIDS Demo Graphics* (Seattle, Bay Press).

Davis, T. (1992), 'Where Should We Go from Here? Towards an Understanding of Gay and Lesbian Communities', paper presented at the 27th International Geographical Congress, Washington, DC, Aug.

Dyer, R. (1992), *Only Entertainment* (London, Routledge).

Epstein, J., and Straub, K. (1991), 'Introduction: The Guarded Body', in J. Epstein and K. Straub (eds.), *Body Guards: The Cultural Politics of Gender Ambiguity* (London, Routledge).

Faderman, L. (1991), *Odd Girls and Twilight Lovers: A History of Lesbian Life in Twentieth-Century America* (London, Penguin).

Geltmaker, T. (1992), 'The Queer Nation Acts Up: Health Care, Politics, and Sexual Diversity in the County of Angels', *Environment and Planning D: Society and Space*, 10: 609–50.

Green, S. (1991), 'Making Transgressions: The Use of Style in a Women-Only Community in London', *Cambridge Anthropology*, 15: 71–87.

Hall, R. (1928), *The Well of Loneliness* (London, Jonathan Cape).

Homocult (1992), *Queer with Class: The First Book of Homocult* (Manchester, Ms Ed [The Talking Lesbian] Promotions).

Humphries, M. (1985), 'Gay Machismo', in A. Metcalf and M. Humphries (eds.), *The Sexuality of Men* (London, Pluto Press).

Jackson, P. (1991), 'The Cultural Politics of Masculinity: Towards a Social Geography', *Transactions of the Institute of British Geographers*, n.s. 16: 199–213.

Knopp, L. (1987), 'Social Theory, Social Movements and Public Policy: Recent Accomplishments of the Gay and Lesbian Movements in Minneapolis, Minnesota', *International Journal of Urban and Regional Research*, 11: 243–261.

—— (1990), 'Social Consequences of Homosexuality', *Geographical Magazine* (May): 20–5.

—— (1992), 'Sexuality and the Spatial Dynamics of Late Capitalism', *Environment and Planning D: Society and Space*, 10: 651–69.

Levine, M. P. (1992), 'The Life and Death of Gay Clones', in G. Herdt (ed.), *Gay Culture in America: Essays from the Field* (Boston, Mass., Beacon Press).

Marshall, G. (1991), *Spirit of '69: A Skinhead Bible* (Dunoon, Skinhead Times Press).

Martin, B. (1992), 'Sexual Practice and Changing Lesbian Identities', in M. Barrett and A. Phillips (eds.), *Destabilizing Theory: Contemporary Feminist Debates* (Cambridge, Polity Press).

McDowell, L. (1992), 'Doing Gender: Feminism, Feminists and Research Methods in Human Geography', *Transactions of the Institute of British Geographers*, n.s. 17: 399–416.

Moore, L. (1992), 'Something More Tender than Friendship': Romantic Friendship in Early-Nineteenth-Century England', *Feminist Studies*, 18: 499–520.

Nestle, J. (1984), 'The fem question', in: C. S. Vance (ed.), *Pleasure and Danger: Exploring Female Sexuality* (Boston, Mass., Routledge and Kegan Paul).

—— (1987), *A Restricted Country: Essays and Short Stories* (London, Sheba Feminist Press).

Pile, S., and Rose, G. (1992), 'All or Nothing? Politics and Critique in the Modernism–Postmodernism Debate', *Environment and Planning D: Society and Space*, 10: 123–36.

Probyn, E. (1992), 'Technologising the Self: A Future Anterior for Cultural Studies', in L. Grossberg, C. Nelson, and P. Treichler (eds.), *Cultural Studies* (London, Routledge).

Rosner, T. (1992), 'Rough', *Boyz* (5 Dec.), 74: 8–9.

Searchlight (1992), 'Nicky Crane Comes Out of the Closet' (Sept.): 9.

Smith, N. (1993), 'Homeless/Global: Scaling Places', in J. Bird, B. Curtis, T. Putnam, G. Robertson, and L. Tickner (eds.), *Mapping the Futures: Local Cultures, Global Change* (London, Routledge).

Smith, R. (1992), *Pink Pop*. BBC Radio 1.

Smyth, C. (1992), *Lesbians Talk Queer Notions* (London, Scarlet Press).

Sontag, S. (1983), *A Susan Sontag Reader* (London, Penguin).

Stein, A. (1988), 'Style Wars and the New Lesbianism', *Out/Look*, 1: 32–42.

Tyler, C. A. (1991), 'Boys Will Be Girls: The Politics of Gay Drag', in D. Fuss (ed.), *Inside/Out: Lesbian Theories, Gay Theories* (London, Routledge).

Valentine, G. (1993), '(Hetero)sexing Space: Lesbian Perceptions and Experiences of Everyday Spaces', *Environment and Planning D: Society and Space*, 11: 395–413.

West, C., and Zimmerman, D. (1991), 'Doing Gender', in J. Lorber and S. Farrell (eds.), *The Social Construction of Gender* (London, Sage).

Wilson, A. (1992), 'The Love That Dare Dress How It Likes', *Guardian* (20 Apr.): 27.

Wilson, E. (1988), *Hallucinations: Life in the Post-modern City* (London, Radius).

—— (1990), 'Deviant Dress', *Feminist Review*, 35: 67–74.

Wise, S., and Stanley, L. (1987), *Georgie Porgie: Sexual Harassment in Everyday Life* (London, Pandora).

Young, A. (1990), *Femininity in Dissent* (London, Routledge).

15 Celebrity Material: Materialist Feminism and the Culture of Celebrity

Jennifer Wicke

A materialist feminism could be defined, provisionally, as a feminism that insists on examining the material conditions under which social arrangements, including those of gender hierarchy, develop. While fully acknowledging that the gender hierarchy pervasively maintains 'men on top', materialist feminism avoids seeing this as the effect of a singular, persistent patriarchy and instead gauges the web of social and psychic relations that make up a material, historical moment, when the women in question may be situated in a variety of positions that defy a horizontal reading. The women of the Bloomsbury Group, for example—Virginia Woolf, Vanessa Bell, Dora Carrington, and others—are materially constellated differently than nineteenth-century Flemish female coal miners, or Georges Sand, or the Saudi Arabian women who boldly staged a 'drive-in' a few years ago.

Generally speaking, feminists in the United States have demarcated two arenas for the meta-analysis of feminism over the last twenty years or so: the arena of academic feminism, and the grass-roots feminism of the 'movement', made manifest in protests, organizations, clinics, hot lines, and shelters. This division has become entrenched, as have the polarized debates that surround it: 'mere' academic feminism is said to be an ivory-tower phenomenon cut off from grass-roots political vigour, or parasitic on those roots; the flip side argues that, while movement or public feminism often stresses essentialism, this is a strategic essentialism that academic feminism, or theory, can back in practice before eventually 'sophisticating' it, in theory. An equally prevalent brand of feminist self-examination or self-critique is the often trenchant claim that academic feminism is too overwhelmingly white and middle-class to articulate a feminism that will engage women of colour and/or working-class and poor women in its goals—and that those goals may even be inimical to such groups. These debates have been necessary, powerful, and profoundly generative, but now are relatively sterile and repetitious. Moreover, they fail to take into account the most materially evident new circumstance grounding feminism: the appearance of the domain that I call 'celebrity feminism'.

Before describing that domain, it is crucial to examine some of the reasons why the academic feminism/movement feminism divide is no longer relevant or compelling. First things first: there is no movement feminism in the United States. The large demonstrations in support of *Roe* v. *Wade* and reproductive rights illustrate a strong consensus among diverse women and men, many of whom refer to themselves as feminists, but this consensus has not emerged from discernible political movements that are exclusively feminist. The proliferation of battered women's shelters (and their great importance), to take one perceived 'real-world' feminist phenomenon, has been primarily due to the efforts of self-described feminist lawyers, social workers, and legislators rather than to any crystallized movement politics. Organizations like NOW are essentially (and essential) lobbying groups, and Take Back the Night rallies are almost always university (academic) affairs. I intend no belittling of the serious and stunningly successful endeavours in which so many have engaged on behalf of women or in the name of feminism, but rather a description of the fragmentary coalitions and the often antithetical premisses of self-defined feminist organizations. Noting the absence of movement politics should not be construed as either criticism or exhortation, but simply as an observation that may help to explain the void that celebrity feminism partially fills. The recent decision by NOW of New Jersey to support Christine Whitman in the 1993 gubernatorial election caused defections aplenty among those who deemed Jim Florio the feminist candidate; the financial fund for women seeking public office, known by its acronym EMILY's List (Early Money Is Like Yeast—in other words, it raises the dough), hardly constitutes a movement, since the candidates it funds are united mainly by gender (although I write this as a contributor). To the extent that academic feminism has an opposite, it is not movement feminism *per se*, but the celebrity pronouncements made by and about women with high visibility in the various media.

Nor is academic feminism itself a coherent, consistent, or reified realm; however, it does exist, and not in an ivory-tower vacuum of its own making. While most strongly present in the academy, tautologically enough, academic feminism eddies 'out' of those groves in the form of applied academic expertise in legal, corporate, and medical settings, through publishing and its attendant publicity, as art-making and mass-cultural representation, in televised trials and newspaper opinion pieces, in the living arrangements and social mores that persist beyond college, and in academic conflicts over turf and clout that reorder economic and cultural priorities across the board. Since academic feminism is fractured and divergent, it cannot be said to constitute an intra-academic movement, despite what Rush Limbaugh may say about 'feminazis', or Camille Paglia about an academic feminist mafia. Its very splinterings generate the multiple guises it wears in, and for the, public.

Celebrity feminism, the mediated nimbus around academic feminism, is a new locus for feminist discourse, feminist politics, and feminist conflicts, both conflicts internal to feminism and feminism's many struggles with antifeminist forces. Consequently, any materialist feminism directed at understanding our current moment (or 'conjuncture', as we used to say) also needs to understand the material effects of a celebrity culture. Feminism does not stand outside that culture, either in a privileged autonomous space or on an exalted moral or political, or even theoretical, plane. Feminism is not exempt from celebrity material, and more and more, feminism is produced (or feminisms are produced) and received in the material zone of celebrity. What follows is not a warning, not a cautionary tale, not a death knell for feminism, but an analysis of the culture of celebrity as a mixed blessing for materialist feminism. To return to the socially grounded particularities of a materialist analysis is to see how profoundly necessary it is to investigate the mediation of celebrity feminism.

Let's begin with academic feminism's nagging hangnail, Camille Paglia. As a self-styled enforcer who lauds her own accomplishments and delights in exacerbating animus against the university in general and its regnant feminisms in particular, Professor Paglia is a creature of the very academic feminism she condemns. Having attained her celebrity status courtesy of the academy, her ostensible arch-enemy, Paglia feeds from the hand she bites. Her first book, *Sexual Personae*, was a crossover publishing success with its roots in the academy.[1] Applying a Harold Bloomian grid of entrenched sexual, and gender, difference to the whole world and its artefacts, Paglia constructed a mythopoesis based on biology. Following Freud's *Civilization and Its Discontents* rather rigidly, she agreed that women were oppositional to cultural creation and that only the rare natural sport, a woman like herself, would be capable of doing anything more than nurturing received ideas. The vast sweep of her Northrop Frye-like schema allowed her to give raves to Cleopatra, Elvis, Shelley, and Madonna alike; her hit list was a greatest-hits list. The enthusiasm was captivating, the biologism baffling and absurd, the readings grandiose and interesting, the overall scheme self-aggrandizing and haphazard, yet compelling. Most non-academics did not read the book all the way through, or even part way, but its vivid statement of immutable sexual difference and male superiority, coupled with an endearing Oedipal relation to Father Bloom and an aggressively Nietzschean sex/drugs/rock and roll motif, made it a 1980s trailblazer. Paglia's quarrels, unlike Nietzsche's or Elvis's, were not with the universe but with the academy. The academy had done her wrong, giving other people—especially other women—the jobs she wanted or felt to be her due. Still, the academy was the place to lodge the protest, or to point the gun. Overcompensating madly, Paglia contrasted her effulgent sexuality with the dowdiness of women she took to be feminists (many academics are dowdy, and I hold no brief for this form of academic mufti), declared her vicarious joy in walking on the wild side, and, like Bloom before her, made common cause with gay men on the grounds that their imaginations are uniquely unfettered by domesticity or thoughts of reproduction, in short, by women. *Sexual Personae* thus became empowering for gay male students who usually thought of themselves as feminist, as a result of its emphasis on the matchless creativity and aesthetic imagination of gay men throughout history, and was absorbed into academic debates about women's studies in relation to lesbian and gay studies, among other internecine conflicts.

The women whom Paglia exempted from the general cultural rule of stagnation were stars or celebrities, figures of glamour who incarnated sexual power, icons of beauty capable of stopping men, and women, stone cold with awe. The paeans to Dietrich, Garbo, and Monroe, among others, have a salutary Nietzschean bravura; female 'star power' is indubitably more than a peripheral effect of objectification by the dreaded 'male gaze', and insofar as Paglia elided the impasses of feminine lack and feminine abjection through sheer ignorance of Lacanian psychoanalysis and feminist film theory, she offered a productive appraisal of the material effects of stardom. Paglia is defiantly anti-materialist, however; hence her quasi-Jungian account of the mythopoetic resonance of female stars. The triumphal biologism notwithstanding, it is her embrace of celebrity culture in the form of movie stars, rock stars, and mythic females like Amelia Earhart (whom a recent biographer depicts as having been obsessed with her celebrity image in the press), regardless of the Dionysian superstructure she erects over it, that causes Paglia's anti-academic feminism to bleed into the celebrity zone, thereby securing a good deal of the material power of those feamle celebrities for herself, and, to be fair, for her ideas. Female stardom is a trans-historical attribute on Paglia's limited political horizon: efforts to unravel the mechanisms of star creation, the array of technological and media forces that construct male and female stars alike, veer for Paglia into the despised provenance of social constructionism. For her, nature alone seems to have bestowed the star wattage evident in the iconic presences she invokes and admires. In truth, a materialist reading of celebrity material is much needed. Paglia does not supply it, but the material constructions of celebrity culture are so powerful that an excess celebrity energy accrues to those who only stand and wait for stardom; in a highly materialist fashion, one can indeed hitch one's wagon to a star or stars as Paglia inadvertently did, glittering with such celebrity lustre in her trajectory from academia to the mainstream culture of celebrity feminism. Lauren Hutton became her best friend.

The sharply contradictory labels applied to Camille Paglia's work are a case in point of this pyrotechnical cultural arc. (There seems to be a momentary lull in her work now, so I address the recent past.) Her opinions are rarely cited in the press or the popular media without a ritualized tag preceding her name: 'the antifeminist Paglia', or, more often, 'the——feminist Paglia', with the blank filled in by any one of a spectrum of adjectives from 'ardent' to 'radical'. The dizzy indeterminacy of these tags speaks to the dual mechanism of celebrity formation: first, the leap into visibility itself, and second, the 'celebrified' discourse of feminism in our historical period. Paglia's work is targeted for this labelling partly because she deliberately provokes it, but also because celebrity feminism is an ineluctable media category today, and a woman with a profile in the public sphere will be assimilated to it. So, despite the many ironies inherent in Paglia's expressed outrage over those she calls academic feminists, the explicitness of her lesbo-phobia, and her indignation over date-rape definitions and sexual-harassment codes, she is indubitably a celebrity feminist.

As I am using (and coining) the term, 'celebrity feminism' does not refer to a celebrity image, or not to that image alone. To deploy the term 'celebrity feminist' as a prima facie insult, as a pejorative reference to a presumably all-too-public persona, whether Paglia's or anyone else's, or as a dismissive epithet or rejoinder, would be to miss the point and the politics. Celebrity discourse is a powerful political site, a current state of being, a predominantly social process: stigmatizing it or prematurely moralizing over it ignores its reality and its political potential. The celebrity mode involves more than imagery, but even that aspect should not be dismissed as 'mere' or 'empty' imagery, fraudulent 'hype', or manipulative, damaging illusion. It may be necessary to reiterate that there are no authentic images to compare with supposedly false ones, and that celebrity visibility *per se* should not be automatically associated with corruption or selling out—our mass-cultural tag sale took place long ago. The logic of celebrity construction is complex, rich, and historically specific. The jealousy that some might feel over another's fame, or greater celebrity quotient, isn't an issue here, although it obviously informs some of Paglia's remarks, such as the one quoted in *Vanity Fair*: 'Susan Sontag, that bitch—it's taken me thirty years to overtake her, but I finally have.' After siphoning off the personal lust for celebrity, which we might deplore at the individual level, what is left as celebrity feminism is a complicated social practice, one with unique relevance to feminism today. Otherwise, how could Paglia be so widely viewed as a feminist spokesperson or model, as an acerbic icon of 'radical feminism', at the same time as Catharine MacKinnon is stalking the celebrity stage?

The celebrity zone is the public sphere where feminism is negotiated, where it is now in most active cultural play. This zone lies on the border of academic feminism, adjacent to it, sometimes invading it, at other times being invaded by it (as for the martial metaphor, with its implication that there may be aggressive and conflictual facets of feminism, or rival feminist interests—there *are*). The celebrity zone is fed by streams flowing from civil society: congressional hearings, court TV, Hillary Clinton's health plan, the LA riots, controversial judicial or cabinet nominees, and so forth. Whoopi Goldberg, hosting the Academy Awards, is in the celebrity feminism zone, as is Lani Guinier, appearing on 'Larry King Live', as is Oprah Winfrey, with her media empire—the relative ease with which African-American culture, and African-

American feminism specifically, crosses over, into, and through the celebrity zone is a model for a general materialist-feminist articulation and a subject for further investigation. A zone is neither an absolute space nor a permanent terrain. One could call it a place for territorialization and deterritorialization (citing Deleuze and Guattari) or a mutable narrating zone (nodding to Edward Said) or a place for de Certeauvian tactics and counterstratagems. I would strongly differentiate it from the liberal space of consensus and conversation that Richard Rorty tries to map, but I would not accord it the immediate resistance potential that some celebrants of mass-cultural liberation might. Good things happen in the celebrity zone and bad things happen in that zone; it is critical to see, though, that feminism is neither confined to the academy, haunting it like a pale ghost, nor swallowed up by the maw of patriarchy, nor expressly practised only by selfless care-providers in the public sector. Our models of political theory and practice lead us to envision feminist theory as an academic venture darting into the cultural spheres of representation (whether books, films, historical events, etc.) to contest ideological mystification at the source. Things look different, though, if the celebrity sphere is not immediately vilified as a realm of ideological ruin or relegated to aberrant or merely 'popular' practices. Rather, we must recognize that the energies of the celebrity imaginary are fuelling feminist discourse and political activity as never before.

I have mentioned Paglia's wilful blindness to the socially constructed nature of celebrity, a blindness that is immensely useful to her in allowing the devotional energies of fandom to spill over into the usually more sober adjudications of literary criticism. Even if she conceded the historical and material specificity of stardom, though, she would still have a legitimate objection to social-constructionist feminism. Social-constructionist feminism overlaps with materialist feminism, but doesn't entirely subsume it. The reasons for this are multiple and, I admit, largely of my own devising here: since no single strand of feminism has doxological status, the interconnections among its strands can be woven at will. Social constructionism, with its insistence on femininity, or female 'identity', as a social production rather than an innate female essence, has so persuasively made its case that even non-materialist feminists feel constrained to adopt its language; one senses the strain in the discourse of former female-essentialist thinkers like Elaine Showalter, but one credits the effort. Materialist feminism by no means goes deeper than social constructionism, in any competitive sense, but it argues that material conditions of all sorts play a vital role in the social production of gender, and it assays the different ways by which women collaborate and participate in these productions. One caveat to a pure social-constructionist outlook for feminists comes from an unlikely source, the historian Perry Anderson, in his superb outline, *In the Tracks of Historical Materialism*. Anderson points to the potential losses of a material (as in bodily) framework not in order to reinstall some given female essence, and certainly not to reinvoke Freud's 'anatomy is destiny', but to emphasize the importance of the body and of sex—as opposed to gender—differences. Without some attention being paid to this grey area of blurred biology, it can be slightly too easy to finesse gender, or sex, altogether, as a performative category affording no material constraints of the body whatsoever. The delirious whirl of sexual orientations and performances aside, not to mention the natural occurrence of hermaphroditism, there are areas of material interest in the fact that women can bear children, metabolize alcohol differently, are more sensitive to serotonin's absence, exhibit disparate AIDS symptomatology, and so on. Materialist feminism, in my view at least, is less likely than social constructionism to be embarrassed by the occasional material importance of sex differences, while being equally vigilant against attempts to construe gender differences as 'natural' or 'biological'.

The problems entailed by pitting a social-constructionist feminism against essentialist feminism, with no mediating materialist terms, are starkly apparent in a review essay by Carol Gilligan, who is prominent among essentialist feminists for her notion of a distinctly female 'ethic of care' and her positing of different views of justice obtaining for men and women. Writing in the *London Review of Books*, she surveys new books by Susan Bordo and Teresa Brennan to excoriate the prevailing 'postmodern' feminist paradigm.

Feminism has much in common with Post-Structuralism—an insistence on context, on plurality and on the social construction of reality—and joins Post-Modernism in celebrating diversity, openness, fluidity and the irreverent transgressing of boundaries. It is disturbing, then, that both Post-Structuralists and Post-Modernists have tended to eclipse or appropriate the feminist project.[2]

Gilligan finds aid and comfort in Bordo's *Unbearable Weight: Feminism, Western Culture, and the Body*, where Bordo 'registers her dismay at the rapidity with which the toppling of the Timeless

Truths of Western culture has moved into a fragmentation of culture and led to what the writer bell hooks has called a "stylish nihilism".[3] Scepticism in the academy about gender, which Gilligan traces to the excessive influence of social constructionism and postmodernism, is related by Bordo to the preoccupation with women's losing weight, making their bodies and their bodily experiences less and less visible in the public domain. There is subtlety in Gilligan's oblique attack on the very academic-feminist theory that has condemned the essentialism of her view of a unique 'woman's voice', subtlety in that it is couched in praise for Bordo's reservations about such theory, although Gilligan seems to have modulated her own views somewhat. Still, she sees academic feminism as having acceded to the 'disappearing' of women through dieting and in social-constructionist thought about gender. Her positive response to the Lacanian feminist Teresa Brennan is a trifle surprising, then, but it is due to Brennan's insistence on the bodily in her *History After Lacan*.[4] Brennan suggests that materiality invests thought; like Bordo, she too would break down the mind/body dualism of Western thinking, although, in Brennan's argument, by questioning the autonomy of the ego or 'self'. Bordo is big on bodies, while Brennan is big on the embodiment of the mind, explaining transference and other psychoanalytic experiences as the result of thoughts being literally shared and transferred. Gilligan manoeuvres her way between these two positions so that she can offer an allegory about feminists poised on the brink of a precipice and liable to fall before they voice their truths because they fear being labelled 'essentialists'. She concludes the review with a coda of some interest to materialist feminisms:

Like 'slim,' the word 'too' functions powerfully in the psychic economy of many women, encapsulating the variety of injunctions against transgression: not to be too loud, too sexual, too angry, too sad, too serious, too selfish, too aggressive, too inquisitive, too much. Bordo asks the generally unspoken question: why do we become skeptical about gender while continuing to maintain race and class as fundamentally grounding? Possibly because gender is too embodied, too closely associated with women, too radical.[5]

Gilligan can have her cake and eat it, too, in this conclusion. Gender essentialists are the real radicals because they insist on dragging women's bodies out into view, while social constructionists or materialists are really doing the conservative work of concealment and silencing. Of course, Gilligan seems unaware that neither race nor class is accepted as a fundamental (in the sense of fixed or essential) grounding, but what is especially intriguing about the mixed message of her concluding coda is the academic *ressentiment* spilling over into the public sphere. The supposed 'invisibility' of gender in academic feminism is the scandal; Gilligan doesn't look for the other arenas, or zones, of feminist engagement. But her own visibility as a celebrity feminist is quite assured—there is no shortage of publicity for her findings and her school studies; not a week seems to go by without Gilligan's being quoted in a newspaper or on television about the way that girls suddenly lose confidence and hope at age 12. As a scholar and a reviewer, Gilligan ignores celebrity feminism in her review, as indeed she should. However, its absence also underscores the non-materialist foundation of Gilligan's feminism. The discursive features of her own work in the public celebrity zone are far from disembodied or silent. She is an active player, perhaps by default, in celebrity feminism.

Unbearable weight: to see celebrity feminism in the making, one need only observe the celebrity Susan Powter, whom I will go out on a limb to label a celebrity feminist. Powter enters the zone from a different angle from Paglia's or MacKinnon's or Gilligan's. A TV phenomenon who first came to public attention via the semi-despised genre of the infomercial, Powter is the housewife aiming to *Stop the Insanity*™—her credo for breaking out of the rut of desperate overweight, ill-health, low self-esteem, and depression, both emotional and economic. Her infomercial, an evangelistic performance, touts exercise, breathing, and healthy food in large amounts, rather than any special products or tools. With her closely shaved platinum-blond hair, her energetic and raucous persona, her entrepreneurial skills, and her stand-up comedian's patter, she commands her audiences to 'move, eat, breathe'. Powter's business is selling herself, but that self is a profound translation of feminism not usually seen on television, let alone in an infomercial. Powter gets her mostly middle-class, racially mixed audiences to accept and to model themselves on a woman who is proud of having danced topless in a Texas bar, who is Jewish, who had an abortion, who underwent a devastating divorce and now supports her ex-husband, who disdains twelve-step programmes and the current preoccupation with abuse and therapy. She doesn't call her performances feminist, but her book is larded with the term, and her insistence on independence and mobility for women who feel stuck in relationships with men or socially inadequate articulates a kind of feminism *sans* political movement that deserves to be taken seriously. Powter is ingratiating because of her humour, including her ability to laugh at herself—she never lords it over her portly audiences in a leotard like the pneumatic Jane Fonda, and she uses the confessional mode so beloved by television to praise people only for what they have accomplished, not for what they have suffered. Anger is acknowledged and channelled into movement, self-nurture, and fuel for change. 'Stop the insanity!' is a mantra on which Powter puts a progressive spin. She uses it to repudiate the oppression of expensive dieting programmes and the medical and psycho-therapeutic communities that depend on them, offering a populist, homegrown feminism for women who get together in front of the TV. She deploys it to ward off the self-hatred that being domestically isolated, fat, or weak and fatigued can cause. She directs it at the isolation and boredom of both suburbia and urban, working-class neighbourhoods, at the self-doubt of the only moderately educated, at the victimization of women whose churches preach submission to them. The contradiction at the heart of weight loss programmes is that one is enjoined to love oneself as is, but to get that ugly weight off as fast as possible. Powter tries to make both sides of the incompatible equation feminist by stressing the positive effects of doing things—including breathing—for oneself, while slyly deprecating her distinctly unglamorous, if slim, celebrity image. Weight loss is not the be-all and end-all; empowerment is—the empowerment of an unspecified futurity. In her book, Powter confesses to the usually taboo emotion of despair at being just a housewife, and to boredom and exhaustion with her children.[6] The tensions of being a 'woman' in conventional domestic terms are turned into the war-cry 'Stop the insanity!' by means of a subtle slippage into refusal: if being fat is the bodily trope for being a culturally defined 'woman', then being fit is not only the best, but for some women the only, revenge. Powter crows with wonder over her implausible success, over her very appearance on a stage: fit, remarkably vigorous, brassy, assertive, and in solidarity with strength, not weakness. The transactions she effects with the female and male members of her audience are decidedly feminist and completely celebrity-driven, her slimness anything but a retreat from gender visibility.

This is a far cry from the recent spectacle of Tammy Faye Baker, disgraced ex-wife of the televangelist, appearing tearfully on Sally Jessy Raphael's daytime show and intoning, to massive applause, 'I just love women—they do so much'. Masochistically identifying with the overworked females admiring her from afar, she made what seemed like a Cabbage Patch doll's appeal for 'female power'. The closest thing to this conception on the celebrity feminism circuit now is the academic feminist Naomi Wolf, accessing the zone through her best-sellers *The Beauty Myth* and the recent *Fire with Fire*, which have garnered her talk-show appearances ad infinitum.[7] Wolf is somewhat hard to take at face value (as it were) if you happened to have known her when she was a Yale undergraduate; the subtitle for her first book could have been that irritating Pantene advertising line, 'Don't hate me because I'm beautiful'. Wolf equated the depredations of the beauty industry with the Holocaust in one shallow comparison, and so indifferent was she to research and evidence that she was unaware of how much the 'beauty industry' had meant to women's financial and political independence. The savage swipes that Paglia took at her fellow celebrity feminists were illuminating and often well-deserved: Wolf has indeed battened on to a reductive and out-of-date cultural feminism in order to launch her celebrity career. Not surprisingly, she was heartily taken to task by the folks on 'Oprah', who rightly saw how ridiculous it was for an Ivy League-educated professional to tell them that lipstick was keeping them down. Wolf's facile assessment of the beauty industry and its crimes suffers from an inability to measure degrees: for her, having to spend time on grooming every morning is as serious as developing anorexia from looking at advertising images of women's bodies. These outrages stem from the influence of (guess what)—media images—precisely one of which Wolf desires to become and does become, through a spate of puritanical self-flagellation. There is nothing more dear to the American psyche than denouncing images and representations at the same time as one is fervently embracing them. The academic component to Wolf's feminism was her application of retrograde rhetorical readings—a 1960s 'femininitude', on the order of the similarly celebratory stage of 'negritude'—to the cosmetics industry.

In her new book, *Fire with Fire*, she makes a 180-degree turn, retaining only her celebrity orientation. Here she revels in a 'female power' only a jot more sophisticated than Tammy Faye's. Upper-middle-class women are great babes who have already achieved parity; now, all they need to do is stop cavilling and vote with their pocketbooks, preferably their Judith Lieber handbags. Feminist 'issues' are old-hat; let the anti-abortionist women on board, let a thousand flowers bloom. Electoral politics and the power brunch constitute politics *in toto.* Compared to Powter, Wolf dumbs down celebrity feminism and depoliticizes it. Where *The Beauty Myth* was meant to grab the brass ring of celebrity feminism, *Fire with Fire* is feminism as espoused by the celebrity. This is not always unbearable; when Barbra Streisand made her dignified comments about the relative absence of women in the higher echelons of the film industry during the 'year of the woman', referring also to her failure to be nominated for an Academy Award as director of the execrable *Prince of Tides*, she was cocooned in the celebrity's imperviousness, but she still made a point. Wolf's turn-on-a-dime feminism is a celebrity feminism for young, straight professionals, for a world perhaps where anyone can marry an editor at the *New Republic.* Less sarcastically, one could infer from the success of *Fire with Fire* that it is participating in a debate over identity politics, a debate mirroring the fractious tendencies of US politics as a whole. Wolf's premiss is that women do constitute a bona fide class; the differences among them in terms of income, education, race, ethnicity, age, and religion can be overcome by an emphasis on their shared condition of 'womanhood'. Of course, such significant differences cannot be so easily ironed out in practice, and failing to see this, Wolf perfectly articulates a feminism made for and by her own cohort. As *New York Magazine* headed its laudatory article on the new, improved Wolf: 'The Prophet of Power Feminism: Is Naomi Wolf the Gloria Steinem of her Generation?'

However problematic, some form of feminist discourse is occurring within Wolfian celebrity space. My tart criticisms are meant for the insufficiencies of her book and of her politics, not for celebrityhood itself, much as the Scavullo photograph of Wolf on her book jacket annoys me—such big hair! The celebrity zone of my analysis has nothing to do with role models or exemplary 'feminists', whoever they may be; instead, it is a space for registering and refracting the current material conditions under which feminism is partly practised. Even those who repudiate the public sphere of celebrity for its so-called faulty representations of women are not immune to its allure. Katha Pollitt titled her gender column in the 10 February issue of *The Nation* 'I'm for Tonya', then repeated this slogan as her first line. Pollitt is a well-known feminist writer and poet, a proponent of equality feminism with an emphasis on economic equality as determinate in the first and last instances. She has had some rather bruising battles with Carol Gilligan and others over the extent to which one needs to emphasize feminine specificity, and for my money she has come out far ahead by virtue of her suspicious interrogations of cultural feminism. So far, so good. Her 'Tonya' essay, however, succumbs to the celebritizing of individual women as stock characters in a feminist melodrama. Having read Tonya Harding and Nancy Kerrigan as polar-opposite Women Writ Large on the national screen, Pollitt pursues her equality feminism to a peculiar conclusion. Tonya is praised for her 'spunk', her bad-girl defiance, and her singleminded pursuit of her skating dream, as if Kerrigan did not share that ambition. Even if Harding did know about the violence planned and executed against Kerrigan, her demonic drive for the gold demonstrates the fraudulence of the American Dream. It may take just such a venial, maniacal energy to bring the big bucks rolling in; Tonya somehow intuits this, and her cynicism deserves our political support. Pollitt links her to the Menendez brothers and Lorena Bobbitt in a virtual police line-up of celebrities—latter-day Bonnies and/or Clydes who knew that you could never get justice in this society, so just took what they wanted when the taking was good. For me, the Menendez brothers are an absurd element in the hardscrabble life; perhaps Pollitt buys their childhood-sex-abuse narrative and, as a consequence, heroizes their parenticide as a justified revolt. It chills me to read her essay as the feminist commentary that Pollitt intends it to be, however, because of the implication that we *must* choose sides whenever a celebrity slugfest is presented as and for pseudo-feminist debate. 'I'm for Tonya'— excuse me? Which word in the title should be stressed—'I'm', 'for', or 'Tonya'? If the last, why and in what sense—in the way her fan club is 'for' her, or the way some of her relatives are 'for' her? Since Tonya Harding derived no tangible benefit from our taking sides with or against her, and now derives none at all after having admitted to knowledge of the crime (at least) and having been put on probation, Pollitt was merely making the scandal a feminist political litmus test, using the celebrity figures 'Nancy' and 'Tonya' as her litmus strips. To consider Tonya Harding guilty of criminal misbehaviour and small-mindedness is not to exalt Nancy Kerrigan for her porcelain-doll ice skating—which is pretty impressive nonetheless—nor to naively cling to a defunct American Dream, nor to be guilty of scorning a working-class feminist *manqué*.

The pressure to see our feminist choices that way, like the over-heated argument of Pollitt's sanctimonious column, derives from the passion with which feminist battles are fought in the celebrity domain, even when the celebrity talking heads, or stalking heads, don't really fit their assigned roles. Perhaps such pressure is inevitable in the relatively new galaxy of feminist stardom; in other words, writers like Katha Pollitt, who tread the cusp of academic feminism yet cross over into the media arena because they write for journals of public interest and opinion, cannot avoid injecting celebrity discourse into their analyses because it is so pervasive. Since our public sphere is best represented by television, maybe even the more sober political analysts find it hard to resist being hooked by the immediacy and narrativity of that sphere, becoming wise gals in spite of themselves.

I've made it evident that, for me, Pollitt made the wrong call because she thought she had to make a call in the first place and then twisted her feminist logic to suit the Manichean circumstances. The predicament is a perilous one, though, as celebrity-feminist discourse must often be superimposed upon less than fitting narratives. No more egregious example can be found than the notorious 'domestic dispute' between the Bobbitts, the 'malicious wounding' that so grievously wounded our national psyche. There is ample room for a feminist analysis of the incident, and for reactions to it; what is dangerous is being led to see the castration itself as a feminist parable. So imperceptible is the line between celebrity-feminist analysis and celebrity feminism that scores of commentators and advocacy groups fell over it (and off the cliff), conflating Lorena Bobbitt's act and her spousal battering with a feminist intervention that women's groups had to reckon with. Castration is hardly a progressive political programme to be advocated or excused, yet celebrity feminism backed mainstream groups into a corner and had them pondering Lorena's act as a feminist categorical imperative. *Pace* Gilligan, gender was not the sole relevant form of embodiment in the fracas. Meanwhile, materialist analyses of the media event went begging, as it was hardly an individual melodrama but a symptom of national anxiety over waning US power and global losses. Against the backdrop of the Nafta signing, the allegory of the Bobbitts was made more transparent as fear for the misplaced national phallus, cavalierly tossed into a ditch across the road from a 7–11 convenience store. The infamous cut-and-toss job gave new meaning to Ross Perot's immortal line: 'That sucking sound you hear is jobs.' John Bobbitt was a white Marine—one of the few, the proud—Lorena Bobbitt, a citizen of Colombia, supporting her husband as a manicurist while chafing under his mistreatment. Many women, if not the majority, had little trouble saying, 'I'm for Lorena', but 'Lorena, *c'est moi*' was hardly a feminist slogan, if an aggrieved female one. Materialist feminism's bafflement over how to participate in a stridently celebrity-feminist sphere was amply demonstrated by the materialist vacuum in the discussion that raged incessantly, and globally, over Bobbittry.

This case gives me a segue into a discussion of what a contemporary materialist-feminist politics might look like, or what it would need to entail, by means of swerving to a recent collection of essays, *Feminists Theorize the Political*, edited by Judith Butler and Joan W. Scott.[8] This swerve is more of an epistemological braking or a caesura in the argument over celebrity feminism and its analysis here. Butler and Scott's estimable volume contains salient and superb offerings from a range of pivotal feminist theorists across several disciplines—Gayatri Spivak, Donna Haraway, Rey Chow, Chantal Mouffe, Mary Poovey, Denise Riley, and many others, including the two editors. The book decisively enters the academic feminist debates over both politics and theory, and it represents an important consolidation of non-essentialist feminist theorization. I interpolate it into my configuration of the relations between academic feminism and the more nebulous entity, celebrity feminism, for several reasons. On the simplest level, the strength of the collection lies in its formidable academic-feminist profile; none of the contributors is a celebrity feminist, although several of them are academic celebrities. More crucially, the tenor of the volume, which amounts to an argument running through all the essays, is that feminism cannot be based on a presumed stable female identity, nor can feminist politics be articulated on the basis of women's interests as a unitary group. Taking up poststructuralist and postmodern cudgels, the various theorists theorize the political-*sans*-gender identity. Drucilla Cornell writes:

Very simply put, equality of well-being in the area of sex and sexuality can only be protected by equivalent rights which value our difference as sexuate beings while, at the same time, breaking down and delegitimizing—and I have suggested that deconstruction engages precisely this delegitimization—the imposed sexual choices of our current gender hierarchy.[9]

Mary Poovey begins her essay with a caveat:

I expect the controversy about this argument to center on my effort to bring poststructuralist assumptions about 'the death of man' to bear on the formulation of the abortion question, for, in practice, this conjunction calls into question the basic tenets of liberal individualism—choice, privacy, and rights.[10]

Chantal Mouffe's discussion of radical democracy and its political positionings questions the pertinence of sexual difference:

Feminism, for me, is the struggle for the equality of women. But this should not be understood as a struggle for realizing the equality of a definable empirical group with a common essence and identity, women, but rather as a struggle against the multiple forms in which the category 'woman' is constructed in subordination. However, we must be aware of the fact that those feminist goals can be constructed in many different ways, according to the multiplicity of discourses in which they can be framed: Marxist, liberal, conservative, radical-separatist, radical-democratic, and so on. There are, therefore, by necessity many feminisms and any attempt to find the 'true' form of feminist politics should be abandoned.[11]

Denise Riley reassesses the thought processes and intellectual sources involved in writing her 'Am I That Name?' by restating the importance of language and its contexts:

The question of the politics of identity could be rephrased as a question of rhetoric. Not so much of whether there was for a particular moment any truthful underlying rendition of 'women' or not, but of what the proliferations of addresses, descriptions, and attributions were doing.[12]

These are brilliant formulations extracted from compelling and thoughtful essays; materialist feminism, at least as I conceive it, would concur in every instance, and indeed, many of the authors cited above would define their own projects as those of materialist feminism. Their common insistence on contextual, mutable, and ultimately conflictual identifications of 'women', and on the inevitability of multiple feminisms in light of that lack of fixed or essential identity, is a given here. What is intriguing as the essays stand together under the rubric *Feminists Theorize the Political* is how intra-academic the political is conceived to be, even where specific struggles, such as abortion rights, are invoked. I hasten to add that this is not a limitation of the essays or of the volume as a whole—it would be the rankest anti-intellectualism to insist on a non-academic focus. Instead, I touch on the shared insularity only to indicate that the predominance of a celebrity sphere for politics eludes the collective exhortations of this book. The struggles to which Mouffe refers are now largely waged symbolically rather than in the type of political engagement summoned up by the word 'struggle'. The celebrity imaginary occupies a huge territory in the reconstitution of politics, and certainly in that of feminist

401

politics. One academic stance toward this is to assume that the analysis of popular culture is perforce political, an assumption that I would not share. In any event, this is not the feature of the political to which I am drawing attention as a relative lacuna in *Feminists Theorize the Political*: we don't really have the relative luxury of 'positionality', as our Foucauldian vocabularies would articulate it. Yes, women's subject positions as women are multiple, fluctuating, relational, and often not pertinent. However, we ignore the opportunity to articulate a position that can participate in celebrity-feminist discourse at our peril—materialist-feminist subject positions that don't materialize leave an opening for the likes of Camille Paglia or Catharine MacKinnon, for non- or antifeminist melodramas involving women given quite fixed subject positions as Women, or for liberal feminists like Anna Quindlen, who has access to the *New York Times* and to the best-seller fiction lists.

The feminists in Butler and Scott's collection theorize the political in relation to theory; the jockeying for subject positions in flux, the calls for a non-essentialist feminism, are mounted against the backdrop of a hermetically sealed academic-feminist argument. Not that the argument is not worth making—I have resoundingly agreed that it is. Essentialist or cultural feminism has achieved hegemony in many women's studies programmes, with a strong voice in official campus feminisms, in curricula, and in regulations, so the academic feminist argument against essentialism entails high stakes and genuine consequences. That argument doesn't necessarily help us to account for the extent to which the political and theoretical terrains are now marked by a celebrity corridor with heavy traffic in all directions. Much of the debate over essentialist versus social-constructionist feminism has become moot because the stratagem known as 'Let's pretend to be essentialist feminists when it is strategically necessary', a phrase usually attributed to Gayatri Spivak but perhaps just a generic example of her wisdom, recapitulates the academic feminism/feminist movement split. I hope I have been somewhat persuasive in questioning whether that split is still the most appropriate or relevant one to make. Moreover, the stratagems within theory tend to reinforce a pure (read: academic) theory versus a muddled (read: movement) practice 'out there'. Yes, this is a binarism, but that's not what is primarily wrong with the division. Leaving out the celebrity corridor entirely, this bifurcation prevents us from seeing how infused with celebrity theory has become, and how obsolescent movement politics seems in celebrity terms.

Two minor examples may help to illustrate these circumstances. One derives from the private, and public, life of Judith Butler herself, and I regret having to allude to an episode that both disturbs and annoys her. *Lingua Franca* magazine, which glides along the edge of the celebrity corridor but keeps its base within the academy, reported in a fall 1993 issue that a female undergraduate at the University of Iowa was desk-top publishing a fanzine called *JUDY!* containing spurious anecdotes of Butler's life and loves and shamelessly professing lustful devotion to its iconic star. Since *JUDY!* has an extremely small circulation, it would not have attracted notice if it had not been publicized by the academic organ of wider circulation, *Lingua Franca*. It was to this publicity that Butler vehemently objected in both a statement quoted in the article and a follow-up letter to the journal. In her letter, Butler referred to the article as

an appalling and tasteless piece of journalism. . . . By citing uncritically from the fanzine and protecting [its author] from publicity, *Lingua Franca* has effectively entered the homophobic reverie of the fanzine itself. . . . If the fanzine signals the eclipse of serious intellectual engagement with theoretical works by a thoroughly hallucinated speculation on the theorist's sexual practice, *Lingua Franca* reengages that anti-intellectual aggression whereby scholars are reduced to occasions for salacious conjecture. . . . I am poignantly reminded why it was I never subscribed to *Lingua Franca*, for it proves to have no more value than *Heterodoxy* or the *National Enquirer*.[13]

Butler had every right to her revulsion and her anger. Bracketing her emotions about the 'zine and the article on it, which was flippant and trivializing, it is still possible to discern some underlying assumptions in the rhetoric of her letter. One major assumption concerns the gulf between the academy, as a site of intellectual speculation or theory, and 'gutter journalism', as a site of gossip or publicity. Butler was not protesting too much in the sense suggested by the reporter, who thought she might be secretly pleased by the adulation. On another score, however, Butler may have protested too much in order to reinstate a barrier that no longer exists, if it ever did, as a rigid line between unsullied intellectual thought and the corruption of the market-place. The theorist of performativity should not be surprised when 'serious intellectual engagement' gives way to, or even includes, more hallucinatory thoughts or desires. The jejune author/publisher of *JUDY!* craves celebrity, not Butler's body, the very celebrity that is conjured by

Butler's own reliance on theatrical and performative metaphors for her descriptions of gender in flux. I must underscore that my response is not of the 'she asked for it' variety; what interests me here is the recourse to a pure academicism to protect theory from celebrity culture. The problem is that theory and theorists disport there, travelling that corridor in complex and contradictory ways. The academy, including empyrean intellectual thought, is permeable to celebrity, colonized by it and colonizers of it in return. (Henry Abelove told me that, as he left the movie theatre after seeing *The Crying Game*, he heard one young spectator say to another in admiration of the film: 'How Butlerian!' One presumes that this allusion to her work in relation to popular, or celebrity, culture would be preferable to Butler—even delightfully welcome, as few of us would mind becoming a salutary adjective.) The issue on which this example turns is serious, though: materialist feminism cannot afford to reject celebrity culture and its practices out of hand in defence of an (illusory) authentic or totally uncontaminated intellectual theorizing. Theory and practice alike get roughed up in the celebrity market, but those rough edges have valuable sticking-points. To convey the proper sense of this mediation-within-mediation-within-mediation that I'm suggesting here requires invoking the likes of Judy Tenuta's goddess religion, Judyism, or Jim Nabors as the character Gomer Pyle doing his spectacularly poor imitation of Cary Grant on the now-syndicated 'Andy Griffith Show': 'Judy, Judy, Judy!'

My second small example has to do with a flash-in-the-pan political group predicated on celebrity, but insufficiently theorized. The Woman's Action Coalition (WAC) was a group of women artists who spontaneously formed a collective to offer counter-representations of women during exceptionally dark days in the Reagan/Bush years. The momentum behind the coalition came partly from celebrity feminism, in that many of the women were and are heavies in the art world and brought some expertise to the production of representational images and spectacles that were designed to attract media attention from the get-go. This celebrity aspect alone was not fatal to the group; what proved to be its undoing, after a meteoric rise fuelled partly by the publicity that certain members of the group generated, was the reluctance to theorize the political, particularly what the 'woman' in WAC stood for. Meetings apparently began to founder on the question of whether women were a transparently obvious class of people, allied by their essential experience, or, well, not. Lacking this theorized political, the actions that the coalition wanted to undertake lost their air of predetermination. The multiple feminist political directions cited by Chantal Mouffe, as quoted earlier, were never acknowledged or even recognized, so the incompatibilities between a political feminism and a Helen Reddy-like 'We are woman, watch us roar' sloganeering emerged. The only materiality in WAC was the bodily materiality of 'woman'; the group's desire to stake a claim to some of the celebrity turf was ingenious and promising, but that turf itself never became politicized, or only insofar as existing images were deemed antifeminist. One initial action by WAC consisted of a brief takeover of Grand Central Station during the commuter rush hour to protest the non-payment of child support by millions of scofflaw dads. As the legal theorist Paulette Caudwell noted in a talk on the comparative incomes of men and women in the United States, with special reference to the black community, the insistence on child-support payments contributes to the state's unwillingness to mandate parity in women's wages and to keeping welfare payments artificially low for children.[14] So much for WAC's first public foray—but the posters and the drumming were impressive, if silly, on the evening news. Its failure to politicize celebrity, as well as to celebritize politics, caused the nascent group to founder in its early days. Mouffe is correct in saying that the impulse to identify a singularly 'true' feminist politics is destined to fail; another element in WAC's demise, though, had to do with its repudiating celebrity while eagerly seeking it.

I find it hard to formulate this gracefully, but the bedrock feminism now creating its consensus on the claim that images of women in our culture do nothing more than sell women a bill of goods is empty and unproductive. These criticisms of media images are as vacuous as the politics of critiquing 'television violence,' all the more so because those voicing their suspicions of media images are those who revel most fully in them. The aforementioned Catharine MacKinnon has developed a paradoxical relation to celebrity feminism, as she rapidly consolidates a celebrity identity while denouncing the mechanisms of celebrity representation as just so much pornography. MacKinnon's latest opus, *Only Words*, is a fiery legal tract that declares words to be deeds (in an uncanny echo of Dostoevsky's *Crime and Punishment*).[15] On this account, representations deemed pornographic are not protected as free speech because they are not speech but acts, outright injuries enacted on innocent female victims: 'Unwelcome sex talk is an unwelcome sex act. . . . To say it is to do it, and to do it is to say it.' Following MacKinnon's logic, the philosopher Carlin Romano wrote a review of her book in which he begins by presenting a mock internal debate over planning a rape of MacKinnon as a thought-experiment prelude to writing the review.[16] The brave review was received with unutterable—or utterable—outrage by MacKinnon and her publisher, Harvard University Press. One peculiar facet of the defence of MacKinnon following Romano's verbal 'rape' of her was the paternalism made manifest in assuming her to have suffered an 'injury' by being negatively reviewed. MacKinnon does not just bristle at bad reviews; she morally denounces all who dare to criticize her work, so she did indeed take Romano's words for the deed. Her reaction to the review of her book by the legal scholar Floyd Abrams in the *New York Review of Books* was one of nearly as much rage as Romano had provoked,[17] and the journal finally held a debate between the two, publishing the transcript in the *New York Times Magazine*. Now, set this rage at representation—whether verbal or imagistic—against MacKinnon's increasingly visible celebrity profile. Her photograph appeared on the cover of *New York Magazine*, lip-locked with her unlikely fiancé, Jeffrey Masson, in a glamour smooch. Masson raves about MacKinnon in the cover story, noting especially the hours spent in silence as she vicariously *thinks* the suffering of rape victims all over the world. Having replaced his adolescent guru with the Goddess Catharine, Masson worships at her shrine, polishing her celebrity image all the while for our delectation.

MacKinnon is set squarely in the celebrity zone and looks likely to stay there for the time being. Richard Rorty has praised her work on the grounds that feminism needs no theory, and indeed MacKinnon has none. Perhaps this is the philosopher's version of praise by Occam's razor—simplifying down to the nub, shaving off the false beard of representational theory. MacKinnon's response to pornography is not one whit more sophisticated than the famous *New Yorker* cartoon caption: 'I say it's spinach, and I say the hell with it.' Her antitheoretical virulence gives her credence with the dignified Rorty as a feminist populist, one who dares to call a spade a spade. The danger of MacKinnon's position, and it is astonishingly dangerous, is that it is celebrity worship disguised as a purgative hatred of celebrity culture. If any word or image can be a deed, then there is no possibility of contextualization, ambiguity, personal agency, or mediation. MacKinnon is famous for scorning representation, as well as the political theory of those who recognize representation as an inevitable element of human making. At another level, she scorns mediation, in all of its senses —including the media-mediated publicity she seeks for her feminist Ludditism. There is no celebrity corridor without media or mediation, and no mediation without celebrification. Representation is inherent to the media because media images are representations. There might well be people who could masturbate to MacKinnon's cover photo, unlikely as that may seem; recalling Bishop Berkeley's paradox about the tree falling in the forest, were that to happen, would MacKinnon ever know herself to be subjected to such an injurious deed? An animus against representation eventually seeps out to cover all its forms, including those that have yet to be enacted, let alone fantasized. The odd contradiction is that MacKinnon vilifies Romano and company simply for taking her seriously as a legal theorist, if a gravely misguided one. She scrutinizes only academic writing for signs of 'violence' against her very person, while courting the celebrity renown she receives via mass-market magazines and television shows. She refuses to grant other people the latitude she thus gives herself, to decree only certain manifestations pornographic, to decide what injures women and what just promotes feminism. But pornography is not some bizarre outpost of media culture, nor is all media culture pornographic; celebrity feminism in MacKinnon's case is fuelled by her simplistic reductionism, made perversely entertaining as she exhibits her keen interest in and profound exhibitionism regarding celebrity mechanisms. I would unequivocally say that this is bad celebrity feminism.

What would a materialist feminism look like in the face of the obduracy and the promise of all this celebrity material? For me, materialist feminism will take cognizance of celebrity feminism without anathematizing it, shunning it, denouncing it, or avoiding it, for the culture of celebrity is the material culture in which we have our being as feminists. Materialist feminism will have traffic with celebrity feminism. Here is the juncture where I can be most easily critiqued—many will say that celebrity culture does not exhibit a strong materialist presence (to say the least) because it ideologically opposes materialist expression *tout court*. But I would respectfully disagree: much of our best, and even most utopian, materialist thinking comes on the wings of celebrity material. The celebrity zone is there, and we all pay heed to it, intersecting as it does with academic-feminist quarrels and controversies, with public debates, politics, and representations. To borrow an apposite and memorable line from John Guillory, 'The best place to be a traffic cop is at an intersection.' Materialist feminism and materialist feminists need to perceive the intersection as it currently stands, and take out—or take off—the white gloves.

Notes

1. Camille Paglia, *Sexual Personae: Art and Decadence from Nefertiti to Emily Dickinson* (New Haven, Conn., 1990). See also her essays collected in *Sex, Art, and American Culture* (New York, 1992).
2. Carol Gilligan, 'The Dream of Everywhere', *London Review of Books*, 16 (10 Mar. 1994): 6–7.
3. Susan Bordo, *Unbearable Weight: Feminism, Western Culture, and the Body* (Berkeley, Calif., 1992), quoted in Gilligan, 'Dream of Everywhere', 6.
4. Teresa Brennan, *History After Lacan* (London, 1993).
5. Gilligan, 'Dream of Everywhere', 7.
6. Susan Powter, *Stop the Insanity!* (New York, 1993).
7. Naomi Wolf, *The Beauty Myth: How Images of Beauty Are Used Against Women* (New York, 1991); *Fire with Fire* (New York, 1994).
8. Judith Butler and Joan W. Scott (eds.), *Feminists Theorize the Political* (New York, 1992).
9. Drucilla Cornell, 'Gender, Sex, and Equivalent Rights', in Butler and Scott, *Feminists Theorize the Political*, 293.
10. Mary Poovey, 'The Abortion Question and the Death of Man', in Butler and Scott, *Feminists Theorize the Political*, 239.
11. Chantal Mouffe, 'Feminism, Citizenship, and Radical Democratic Politics', in Butler and Scott, *Feminists Theorize the Political*, 384.
12. Denise Riley, 'A Short History of Some Preoccupations', in Butler and Scott, *Feminists Theorize the Political*, 122.
13. Judith Butler, Letter to the Editor, *Lingua Franca*, 4 (Nov./Dec. 1993): 5.
14. Paulette Caudwell, 'Black Hair: Cornrows and Beards in the Legal Domain of Work', paper presented to the New York University Law School, Gender Advisory Group Symposium, Oct. 1992.
15. Catharine MacKinnon, *Only Words* (Cambridge, Mass., 1993).
16. Carlin Romano, 'Between the Motion and the Act', *The Nation* (15 Nov. 1993): 563–70.
17. *New York Review of Books*, 68 (8 Mar. 1994): 5–9.

16 Hillary's Husband Re-elected! The Clinton Marriage of Politics and Power

Erica Jong

Here we are, two minutes after the last American presidential election in the twentieth century, and Hillary Rodham Clinton is still the most problematic First Lady in American history—admired abroad, hated at home, mistrusted by women journalists even though this Administration has actually done much good for women. Suspected of being a megalomaniac, embroiled in document-losing, spy-hiring, the suicide of an aide conjectured to be her lover, and possible perjury; pilloried in the press and jeered at in political cartoons; distrusted even by her admirers—can't Hillary do anything right? Why does she get no credit for all the positive things she has done?

The old campaign button that trumpeted 'Elect Hillary's Husband in '92' showed a picture of Hillary, not Bill. Indeed, it's hard to remember it now. It's even hard to remember how Hillary flouted the rules decreed for political wives: the obligatory Stepford Wife impersonation, the fake flirtatious flattery that makes wives seem feminine and non-threatening; the willingness to pretend to be the power behind the throne; the diplomatic surrender to the role of First Lady.

The kaleidoscope of Hillary images and the frequently self-destructive behaviour of the First Lady are particularly regrettable because both the Clinton Administration and the Clinton marriage are historic. As a couple, the Clintons raise important issues about both electoral and sexual politics. It is clear that without HRC's participation, Bill Clinton would have gone right down the Gary Hart sewer. Because his wife stood by him in that first Barbara Walters interview in 1992, because he did not exactly deny 'causing pain' in the marriage while Hillary held his hand supportively, the first Clinton campaign was able to weather and rise above what

First printed in *The Nation*, 263/17 (November 25, 1996), 11–15. Copyright © Erica Jong (1996). Reprinted by permission.

had been killing sexual crises for other presidential candidates. Unlike France, America does not coddle public adulterers. Only 'the little woman' can save them. She forgives, we forgive.

In those days—the first Clinton campaign—we were still hearing a lot about getting two for the price of one. Elect one, get one free. Hillary was the freebie. Never before in American politics had any couple campaigned this way. The very American ideal of a 'power couple' who add up to more than the sum of their parts was put on the ballot in the 1992 election. America was enthusiastic about it then. Indeed, the Clinton candidacy looked bravely feminist compared with the fuddy-duddy aura of Bush and Mrs Bush. But misogyny was far from dead, as we were soon to see.

The subsequent assault on Hillary demonstrated the entrenched woman-hating both of the American press and the bigoted public it so badly serves. When William Safire of the *New York Times* called HRC 'a congenital liar', surely he was subjecting her to a different standard from the one to which he had held other First Ladies. Can anyone in the laser glare of the public eye be expected to be candid all the time? Did anyone ask Pat Nixon what she thought of her husband's destruction of evidence? Was Nancy Reagan interrogated about Irangate? Certainly not. But HRC's gene pool was impugned at the drop of a document. With the roasting of Hillary it became clear that when we wish women to fail, we decree for them endless and impossible ordeals, like those that were devised for witches by their inquisitors. If they drown, they are innocent; if they float, they are guilty. This has pretty much been the way America has gotten rid of its cleverest political women, from the feminists Victoria Woodhull and Emma Goldman to Eleanor Roosevelt and the unsuccessful vice-presidential candidate Geraldine Ferraro. And there is no doubt that many people still wish HRC to fail. Even now.

Clinton strategists—including the disgraced Dick Morris—kept Hillary out of the limelight for most of the campaign. She was only seen (but not heard) in proper 'helpmeet' photo-ops like the Atlanta Olympics, the Wyoming vacation, and the exotic ports of call she visited with First Daughter Chelsea. America preferred— 58 per cent of men told pollsters that their view of Hillary was unfavourable—the duplicitous Southern charms of Elizabeth Hanford Dole: a driven career woman with no children who claims she is 'pro-life', a chief Red Cross administrator who uses her powerful charity as a political tool of the Republican Party, a soft-spoken, flirtatious belle married to an old man, a saccharine public speaker who used the Republican convention in San Diego as an excuse to drown the delegates in treacle. Duplicity in women makes America comfortable; straightforwardness does not. There was even, I learned, heated debate in the White House about whether HRC should speak at the Democratic convention or remain out of sight and earshot. After Liddy Dole's San Diego seduction, it was decided that, however risky, Hillary *had* to speak. What a far cry from 1992, when Hillary was considered an asset! By the summer of 1996, she was a liability to be hidden. This is what four years of Hillary-hating had accomplished.

The deal of the Clinton marriage fascinates me and I suspect it fascinates a good portion of the electorate. It reflects our period better than any political marriage I can think of. Clearly Hillary figured out in law school that if the time was not yet ripe for a woman President, it was likely to be ripe for a guy as driven and smart and personable as Bill Clinton. And she could be his chief adviser, patron (she made the money—with no small help from his political position), and disciplinarian. However much she warmed to his Southern charm, no matter how much she loved him, his political ambition turned her on just as much.

Not that there is anything wrong with a marital deal. You might even say that the more things that bind a couple together, the better chance they have of staying together. But theirs is a radical deal for an American political marriage. HRC has never staked out highway beautification as her bailiwick (as did Lyndon Baines Johnson's wife, Lady Bird) or crusaded to put warning labels on rock albums (once the one-woman campaign of Second Lady Tipper Gore). On the contrary, she has claimed centre stage with top policy issues—however politically naïve she may have been.

This audacity dazzled at first. But then, why should a First Lady stick to so-called women's issues? Hillary was always policy-minded, always loath to be ghettoized ideologically. She was always far more serious than Bill, even in college and law school. He was a people pleaser. She was a woman who put intellect first, which meant automatically that many men—and women—would not be pleased by her. One of the reasons she hooked up with Bill was that he was the first man who seemed not to be afraid of her intellect but rather challenged and attracted by it. He was determined 'to get the smartest girl in the class', as an old Arkansas buddy of his told Roger Morris. He was sick of beauty queens. 'If it isn't

Hillary, it's nobody, he informed his mother, cautioning her to be nice to Hillary before he brought her to meet the family in 1972. Though he apparently had nostalgia—and a use—for those beauty queens after he and Hillary were married, at the time of their courtship Hillary's brains thrilled him more. She excited him. Maybe she still does. After all, many powerful men yearn for the sting of a dominatrix's whip now and then; it seems to be a sovereign tonic for hubris.

One of the difficulties of being a smart, driven woman is finding men who are turned on by brains. Hillary's initial attachment to Bill probably had a lot to do with the excitement of finding such a fearless man. Later, it seems, she had invested so much of herself in the marriage and in the daughter they shared that she wasn't willing to throw it all away even if faced with compulsive, repeated infidelities. The stresses on HRC have been extreme, and one must say that despite them she has proved an exemplary mother. She has protected Chelsea from the media, allowed her the space to grow into womanhood, put her education ahead of politics. As the mother of a teenage daughter, I honour HRC for what she has achieved.

Still, we have to look at the strangeness of the public image put forward by this revolutionary presidential couple. They were elected as a team but have absolutely refused to make the terms of their marriage public except to admit that he 'caused pain'. It is the inconsistency of this position that has accounted for a great deal of the trouble. If you vote for a couple, you feel entitled to know about the bonds that hold them together. But Hillary has insisted that those bonds are private. People resent her determination to have it both ways. But how on earth could the Clintons own up to the details of Bill's sex life? The fact that they have quashed the issue thus far is nothing short of a miracle.

The more you read about Bill Clinton, the more it seems evident that not only *were* there affairs but that he used his position as governor to facilitate them, using state troopers as beards and panderers, getting them to pick up frilly little gifts at Victoria's Secret. But I assume that his erotic life is no better and no worse than any other male politician's. I am, in general, so disillusioned with male politicians that I actually prefer Bill Clinton the womanizer to Bob Dole the deadbeat dad who dumped the first wife who nursed him through his famous war wounds. (Dole actually got his political cronies to arrange an 'emergency divorce' so he could jettison the old wife and family more cheaply.) Fucking is fucking, but failing to pay child support is a *real* crime. At least Bill Clinton didn't abandon his wife and child.

Hillary's history is full of paradoxes. A baby boomer who grew up in a straight-arrow Methodist Republican-registered family in a white, upwardly mobile suburb of Chicago, she became a left-leaning Democrat at Wellesley College. At Yale Law School she was studious, solitary, solemn, given to wearing flannel shirts and thick glasses, noted for her brilliance and hard work. Her mother, a closet Democrat, had compromised with her life and did not want Hillary to compromise—a familiar mother-daughter story. Her father was stern, unambiguously Republican, tight with money and difficult to please. Imagine a girl like that winning the good ol' boy who has been dating beauty queens! It gives you an idea of how much his 'locking in on her' (as one old friend put it) must have meant to her.

Hillary is an appealing figure to me because her life shows the strange compromises gifted women make. She had already changed her politics, drifted away from her parents' reactionary attitudes. What lay ahead were other complete makeovers—looks, name, ideals. Everything would have to change for the greater glory of Bill Clinton and the pillow power he bestowed. If she has often come across as angry and unsettled, as constantly remaking her image, it is because this is the truth. How could she not be angry? Like an ancient Chinese noblewoman with bound feet, she has had to deform even her anatomy to get where she needed to go. She hobbled her own fierce ambitions to transplant herself to Arkansas and defend his. She gave up her end-of-the-sixties indifference to female fashion, her passion for social justice and her native disgust with hypocrisy. Then, while he used her feminism as a shield to cover his philandering, he proceeded to make a mockery of everything she believed in.

Since Bill Clinton had always been clear about his ambition to be a top Arkansas politician and then President, his path never changed. Hers changed constantly—and with it her hair, her eyes, her weight, her name. At some point she must have had to decide that all those changes were worth it. How else can a smart woman justify such a metamorphosis? She had to recommit herself over and over to life with him. No wonder she demanded paybacks, such as running health care reform and his public life. She would have felt demolished otherwise. One sympathizes with her strength to make demands. But the power struggle of the marriage inevitably

413

influenced the power politics of the nation, and that is what is so radically new about the Clinton presidency.

George Bush used his first day in the presidency to congratulate 'right to life' marchers, even while insinuating that First Lady Barbara Bush did not agree with him. No such stand for Bill Clinton. He and Hillary were joined at the hip politically, however much stress their marriage might be under. Their presidency has redefined public and private. Both Clintons' policies are in lockstep, even though their marriage may be chronically on the rocks.

'We cared deeply about a lot of the same things,' Hillary told an interviewer for the campaign film *The Man From Hope* in 1992. This revealing quote, edited out of the final film, makes the deal of the marriage clear. 'Bill and I really are bound together in part because we believe we have an obligation to give something back and to be part of making life better for other people,' she went on (as quoted by Bob Woodward in *The Choice*). The tragedy of their story is that such idealism had to be replaced by a ruthless commitment to politics, and this deformation of principle came much harder to her than to him. Hillary's image problem has several root causes. One is undoubtedly the ineptness of her staff. Another is the undeniable fact that there is no way for a smart woman to be public without being seen as a treacherous Lady Macbeth figure or bitch goddess (our failing, more than Hillary's). But the deepest problem is that Hillary comes across on television as cold and too controlled because that is the truth. She has rejigged her image so often, retailored it so much to please the spin doctors, that it comes across as inauthentic. It is.

The truth is that Bill is what he is—warm, tear-jerkingly populist, dying to please, woo and pander. He's a born salesman, 'riding on a smile', in the immortal words of Arthur Miller. Hillary, meanwhile, is a brainy girl trying to look like an Arkansas beauty queen, a corporate lawyer trying to look like a happy housewife, a fierce feminist who has submerged her identity in her husband's ambitions. It doesn't add up—too many contradictions—which is why we don't believe it. The pearls and pink put on for the campaign—as well as the new, practised smiling—are not totally convincing either. We expect Lady Macbeth to reappear, rubbing the blood from her hands.

We should weep for Hillary Clinton rather than revile her. She is a perfect example of why life is so tough for brainy women. The deformations of her public image reveal the terrible contortions expected of American women. Look pretty but be (secretly) smart. Conform in public; cry in private. Make the money but don't seem to be aggressive. Swallow everything your husband asks you to swallow, but somehow keep your own identity. Hillary shows us just how impossible all these conflicting demands are to fulfill.

For Hillary and her generation, 'no single act came to symbolize so vividly her role and sacrifice as the surrender of her maiden name', as Roger Morris points out in *Partners in Power*. Refusing to be submerged in the identity of wife is a burning issue for our generation. A woman can give up on this outwardly and continue to seethe inwardly. As with so many other Hillary transformations, the stress shows. I'm glad it does. It shows that she still has her conscience intact, if not her soul. She is not the consummately smooth performer her husband is.

Besides the constant hair transformations, nothing has shown Hillary's discomfort with her role as much as her choice of Jean Houston and Mary Catherine Bateson as spiritual guides. For all the idiocies of the American press, which cheaply depicted Hillary's spiritual quests as 'séances', Houston and Bateson are serious figures. Bateson is a writer and anthropologist, who, like her mother, Margaret Mead, is fascinated with the changing roles of twentieth-century women. Like her father, the English-born anthropologist Gregory Bateson, she also has a deep interest in spirituality in the modern world. Houston is a respected spiritual teacher and author. It is to Hillary's credit that she sought guidance from such interesting women. It also shows her deep need for reassurance in the midst of the nonstop Hate Hillary campaign that has been the salient feature of her public life. As Bob Woodward suggests, 'Hillary's sessions with Houston reflected a serious inner turmoil that she had not resolved'.

Apparently, Houston encouraged Hillary to take heart from her role model, Eleanor Roosevelt, and to use the technique of imaginary conversations with a mentor to confront her own deep hurt about the attacks, jealousy, and misunderstanding she has encountered as First Lady. This is an ancient technique for building self-knowledge and resolve. It was used during the Italian Renaissance by Machiavelli. Nevertheless, Hillary has been ridiculed as the dupe of séance-mongers for her very human need to reach out for help. This is beyond unkind. It is cruel and unusual punishment. I would rather put my faith in leaders who acknowledge their human need for guidance than in those who will accept none. Hillary remains deeply troubled on many levels; I wish she could open herself to psychological help. But then, of course, she might have to leave Bill!

Hillary herself is in great speaking form these days: passionate, strong, determined. She has even learned to soften political discourse with smiles. Once again her hair has been redesigned, her jewellery is smaller and more 'feminine'—the safety of pearls—and some adviser has connived to dress her in pastels. You could say she's on the Dole. She has been Liddyized. She frequently says, 'My husband and I believe' or 'the President believes', and she allows no public space for those who would divide them. She is poised, cool, in control. The anger does not show. All that is missing is the sense of the real woman underneath the pretty makeup and softly tailored suit.

One wants to say Hillary is the hollow woman—but in fact the opposite is true. She is a seething mass of contradictions, so she dares let none of her feelings show. 'Relaxed' is not a word you would use about her even now. She gives off an aura of discipline and ferocious tenacity. It's impossible to glimpse the human being beneath the mask. Yet all those stories of her breaking down in tears or rage in private after this perfect composure in public seem wholly believable. She seems to be holding herself together with hairspray.

What is familiar about this picture? A woman is sacrificed to her husband's ambitions. Her personality is deformed. She takes almost all the flak in the press while he gets away with murder. You might almost say she is taking the punishment for him, and for all women who step outside the lines prescribed for paper-doll political wives—in fact, for all contemporary women. Hillary Rodham Clinton looks more to me like Joan of Arc every day. She is burned as a witch week in and week out so that her husband can rise in the polls. She is the scapegoat half of the Clinton duo, the rear end that gets whipped so the smiling Clinton head can triumph. She is Agamemnon's Iphigenia sacrificed for a propitious wind, Euripides' Alcestis going across the Styx instead of her husband.

And this is the way the Clinton presidential couple is conventional rather than revolutionary. Yes, they dared to present themselves as a team. But once again it's the female half that gets trashed while the male half is forgiven for all his transgressions and winds up being President. Bill Clinton owes Hillary. Big. The only difference between him and other guys is that he seems to know it. History has burdened Hillary Clinton with changing the way powerful women are perceived in our culture. But if she can see herself as part of a historical continuum, as a pathfinder opening the way for her daughter's generation, she may be able to rise above the pain of daily crucifixions in the media.

With a second Clinton Administration, HRC has the rare opportunity to triumph over her detractors. She has already fulfilled her wish to be an Eleanor Roosevelt for the end of the century. In many ways her mainstreaming of feminism has prepared us to accept a woman President in the twenty-first century. By acting as a lightning rod she has gotten us comfortable with women who talk back in public, don't hide their brains, don't hide their passionate mothering. HRC is the latest incarnation of Miss Liberty. I'm glad she's a survivor. Her survival means I can survive. If the next Clinton ticket is HRC and Al Gore, I intend to vote for them more happily than I voted for Bill Clinton on Tuesday.

Part IV. Public and Private Identity: Questions for a Feminist Public Sphere

17 Impartiality and the Civic Public: Some Implications of Feminist Critiques of Moral and Political Theory

Iris Marion Young

Many writers seeking emancipatory frameworks for challenging both liberal individualist political theory and the continuing encroachment of bureaucracy on everday life, claim to find a starting-point in unrealized ideals of modern political theory. John Keane, for example, suggests that recent political movements of women, oppressed sexual and ethnic minorities, environmentalists, and so on, return to the contract tradition of legitimacy against the legalistic authority of contemporary state and private bureaucracies. Like many others, Keane looks specifically to Rousseau's unrealized ideals of freedom and cooperative politics.

According to Rousseau, individualism could no longer be seen as consisting in emancipation through mere competitive opposition to others; its authentic and legitimate form could be constituted only through the communicative intersubjective enrichment of each bodily individual's qualities and achievements to the point of uniqueness and incomparability. Only through political life could the individual become this specific, irreplaceable individual 'called' or destined to realize its own incomparable capacities.[1]

There are plausible reasons for claiming that emancipatory politics should define itself as realizing the potential of modern political ideals that have been suppressed by capitalism and bureaucratic institutions. No contemporary emancipatory politics wishes to reject the rule of law as opposed to whim or custom, or fails to embrace a commitment to preserving and deepening civil liberties. A commitment to a democratic society, moreover, can plausibly look upon modern political theory and practice as beginning the democratization of political institutions which we can deepen and extend to economic and other nonlegislative and nongovernmental institutions.

Nevertheless, in this chapter I urge proponents of contemporary emancipatory politics to break with modernism rather than recover suppressed possibilities of modern political ideals. Whether we consider ourselves continuous or discontinuous with modern political theory and practice, of course, can only be a choice, more or less reasonable given certain presumptions and interests. Since political theory and practice from the eighteenth to the twentieth centuries is hardly a unity, making even the phrase 'modern political theory' problematic, contemporary political theory and practice both continues and breaks with aspects of the political past of the West. From the point of view of a feminist interest, nevertheless, emancipatory politics entails a rejection of modern traditions of moral and political life.

Feminists did not always think this, of course. Since Mary Wollstonecraft, generations of women and some men wove painstaking argument to demonstrate that excluding women from modern public and political life contradicts the liberal democratic promise of universal emancipation and equality. They identified the liberation of women with expanding civil and political rights to include women on the same terms as men, and with the entrance of women into the public life dominated by men on an equal basis with them.

After two centuries of faith that the ideal of equality and fraternity included women has still not brought emancipation for women, contemporary feminists have begun to question the faith itself.[2] Recent feminist analyses of modern political theory and practice increasingly argue that ideals of liberalism and contract theory, such as formal equality and universal rationality, are deeply marred by masculine biases about what it means to be human and the nature of society.[3] If modern culture in the West has been thoroughly male dominated, these analyses suggest, then there is little hope of laundering some of its ideals to make it possible to include women.

Women are by no means the only group, moreover, that has been excluded from the promise of modern liberalism and republicanism. Many non-white people of the world wonder at the hubris of a handful of western nations to have claimed liberation for humanity at the very same time that they enslaved or subjugated most of the rest of the world. Just as feminists see in male domination no mere aberration in modern politics, so many others have come to regard racism as endemic to modernity as well.[4]

In this chapter I draw out the consequences of two strands of recent feminist responses to modern moral and political theory and weave them together. Section I is inspired by Gilligan's critique of the assumption that a Kantian-like 'ethic of rights' describes the highest stage of moral development, for women as well as men.[5] Gilligan's work suggests that the deontological tradition of moral theory excludes and devalues women's specific, more particularist and affective experience of moral life. In her classification, however, Gilligan retains an opposition between universal and particular, justice and care, reason and affectivity, which I think her insights clearly challenge.

Thus in section I, I argue that an emancipatory ethics must develop a conception of normative reason that does not oppose reason to desire and affectivity. I pose this issue by questioning the deontological tradition's assumption of normative reason as impartial and universal. I argue that the ideal of impartiality expresses what Theodor Adorno calls a logic of identity that denies and represses difference. The will to unity expressed by this ideal of impartial and universal reason generates an oppressive opposition between reason and desire or affectivity.

In section II, I seek to connect this critique of the way modern normative reason generates opposition with feminist critiques of modern political theory, particularly as exhibited in Rousseau and Hegel. Their theories make the public realm of the state express the impartial and universal point of view of normative reason. Their expressions of this ideal of the civic public of citizenship rely on an opposition between public and private dimensions of human life, which corresponds to an opposition between reason, on the one hand, and the body, affectivity and desire on the other.

Feminists have shown that the theoretical and practical exclusion of women from the universalist public is no mere accident or aberration. The ideal of the civic public exhibits a will to unity, and necessitates the exclusion of aspects of human existence that threaten to disperse the brotherly unity of straight and upright forms, especially the exclusion of women. Since man as citizen expresses the universal and impartial point of view of reason, moreover, someone has to care for his particular desires and feelings. The analysis in section II suggests that an emancipatory conception of public life can best ensure the inclusion of all persons and groups

423

not by claiming a unified universality, but by explicitly promoting heterogeneity in public.

In section III, I suggest that Habermas's theory of communicative action offers the best direction for developing a conception of normative reason that does not seek the unity of a transcendent impartiality and thereby does not oppose reason to desire and affectivity. I argue, however, that despite the potential of his communicative ethics, Habermas remains too committed to the ideals of impartiality and universality. In his conception of communication, moreover, he reproduces the opposition between reason and affectivity that characterizes modern deontological reason.

Finally, in section IV, I sketch some directions for an alternative conception of public life. The feminist slogan 'The personal is political' suggests that no persons, actions, or attributes of persons should be excluded from public discussion and decision-making, although the self-determination of privacy must nevertheless remain. From new ideals of contemporary radical political movements in the US, I derive the image of a heterogeneous public with aesthetic and affective, as well as discursive, dimensions.

I. THE OPPOSITION BETWEEN REASON AND AFFECTIVITY

Modern ethics defines impartiality as the hallmark of moral reason. As a characteristic of reason, impartiality means something different from the pragmatic attitude of being fair, considering other people's needs and desires as well as one's own. Impartiality names a point of view of reason that stands apart from any interests and desires. Not to be partial means being able to see the whole, how all the particular perspectives and interests in a given moral situation relate to one another in a way that, because of its partiality, each perspective cannot see itself. The impartial moral reasoner thus stands outside of and above the situation about which he or she reasons, with no stake in it, or is supposed to adopt an attitude toward a situation as though he or she were outside and above it. For contemporary philosophy, calling into question the ideal of impartiality amounts to questioning the possibility of moral theory itself. I will argue, however, that the ideal of normative reason as standing at a point transcending all perspectives is both illusory and oppressive.

Both the utilitarian and deontological traditions of modern ethical theory stress the definition of moral reason as impartial.[6] Here I restrict my discussion to deontological reason for two reasons. Utilitarianism, unlike deontology, does not assume that there is a specifically normative reason. Utilitarianism defines reason in ethics in the same way as in any other activity: determining the most efficient means for achieving an end, in the case of ethics, the happiness of the greatest number. I am interested here in modern efforts to define a specifically normative reason. Second, I am interested in examining the way a commitment to impartiality results in an opposition between reason and desire, and this opposition is most apparent in deontological reason.

The ideal of an impartial normative reason continues to be asserted by philosophers as 'the moral point of view'. From the ideal observer to the original position to a spaceship on another planet,[7] moral and political philosophers begin reasoning from a point of view they claim as impartial. This point of view is usually a counterfactual construct, a situation of reasoning that removes people from their actual contexts of living moral decisions, to a situation in which they could not exist. As Michael Sandel argues, the ideal of impartiality requires constructing the ideal of a self abstracted from the context of any real persons: the deontological self is not committed to any particular ends, has no particular history, is a member of no communities, has no body.[8]

Why should normative rationality require the construction of a fictional self in a fictional situation of reasoning? Because this reason, like the scientific reason from which deontology claims to distinguish itself, is impelled by what Theodor Adorno calls the logic of identity.[9] In this logic of identity reason does not merely mean having reasons or an account, or intelligently reflecting on and considering a situation. For the logic of identity reason is *ratio*, the principled reduction of the objects of thought to a common measure, to universal laws.

The logic of identity consists in an unrelenting urge to think things together, in a unity, to formulate a representation of the whole, a totality. This desire itself is at least as old as Parmenides, and the logic of identity begins with the ancient philosophical notion of universals. Through the notion of an essence, thought brings concrete particulars into unity. As long as qualitative difference defines essence, however, the pure programme of identifying thought remains incomplete. Concrete particulars are brought into unity under the universal form, but the forms themselves cannot be reduced to unity.

The Cartesian ego founding modern philosophy realizes the total-izing project. This *cogito* itself expresses the idea of pure identity as the reflective self-presence of consciousness to itself. Launched from this point of transcendental subjectivity, thought now more boldly than ever seeks to comprehend all entities in unity with itself and in a unified system with each other.

But any conceptualization brings the impressions and flux of experience into an order that unifies and compares. It is not the unifying force of concepts *per se* that Adorno finds dangerous. The logic of identity goes beyond such an attempt to order and describe the particulars of experience. It constructs total systems that seek to engulf the alterity of things in the unity of thought. The problem with the logic of identity is that through it thought seeks to have everything under control, to eliminate all uncertainty and unpredictability, to idealize the bodily fact of sensuous immer-sion in a world that outruns the subject, to eliminate otherness. Deontological reason expresses this logic of identity by eliminat-ing otherness in at least two ways: the irreducible specificity of situ-ations and the difference among moral subjects.

Normative reason's requirement of impartiality entails a re-quirement of universality. The impartial reasoner treats all situ-ations according to the same rules, and the more rules can be reduced to the unity of one rule or principle, the more this impar-tiality and universality will be guaranteed. For Kantian morality, to test the rightness of a judgement the impartial reasoner need not look outside thought, but only seek the consistency and univer-salizability of a maxim. If reason knows the moral rules that apply universally to action and choice, then there will be no reason for one's feelings, interests, or inclinations to enter in the making of moral judgements. This deontological reason cannot eliminate the specificity and variability of concrete situations to which the rules must be applied; by insisting on the impartiality and uni-versality of moral reason, however, it renders itself unable ration-ally to understand and evaluate particular moral contexts in their particularity.[10]

The ideal of an impartial moral reason also seeks to eliminate otherness in the form of differentiated moral subject. Impartial reason must judge from a point of view outside of the particular perspectives of persons involved in interaction, able to totalize these perspectives into a whole, or general will. This is the point of view of a solitary, transcendent God.[11] The impartial subject need acknowledge no other subjects whose perspective should be taken into account and with whom discussion might occur.[12] Thus the claim to be impartial often results in authoritarianism. By asserting oneself as impartial, one claims authority to decide an issue, in place of those whose interests and desires are manifest. From this impartial point of view one need not consult with any other, because the impartial point of view already takes into account all possible perspectives.[13]

In modern moral discourse, being impartial means especially being dispassionate: being entirely unaffected by feelings in one's judgement. The idea of impartiality thus seeks to eliminate alterity in a different sense, in the sense of the sensuous, desiring and emotional experiences that tie me to the concreteness of things, which I apprehend in their particular relation to me. Why does the idea of impartiality require the separation of moral reason from desire, affectivity and a bodily sensuous relation with things, people and situations? Because only by expelling desire, affectivity and the body from reason can impartiality achieve its unity.

The logic of identity typically generates dichotomy instead of unity. The move to bring particulars under a universal category creates a distinction between inside and outside. Since each particular entity or situation has both similarities with and differences from other particular entities and situations, and they are neither completely identical or absolutely other, the urge to bring them into unity under a category or principle necessarily entails expelling some of the properties of the entities or situations. Because the totalizing movement always leaves a remainder, the project of reducing particulars to a unity must fail. Not satisfied then to admit defeat in the face of difference, the logic of identity shoves difference into dichotomous normative oppositions: essence–accident, good–bad, normal–deviant. The dichotomies are not symmetrical, however, but stand in a hierarchy; the first term designates the positive unity on the inside, the second, less valued term designates the leftover outside.[14]

For deontological reason, the movement of expulsion that generates dichotomy happens this way. As I have already discussed, the construct of an impartial point of view is arrived at by abstracting from the concrete particularity of the person in situation. This requires abstracting from the particularity of bodily being, its needs and inclinations, and from the feelings that attach to the experienced particularity of things and events. Normative reason is defined as impartial, and reason defines the unity of the moral subject, both in the sense of knowing the universal principles of morality and in the sense of what all moral subjects have in common in the same way. This reason thus stands opposed to desire and affectivity as what differentiates and particularizes persons. In the next section I will discuss a similar movement of the expulsion of persons from the civic public in order to maintain its unity.

Several problems follow from the expulsion of desire and feeling from moral reason. Because all feeling, inclinations, needs, desires become thereby equally irrational, they are all equally inferior.[15] By contrast, premodern moral philosophy sought standards for distinguishing among good and bad interests, noble and base sentiments. The point of ethics in Aristotle, for example, was precisely to distinguish good desires from bad, and to cultivate good desires. Contemporary moral intuitions, moreover, still distinguish good and bad feelings, rational and irrational desires. As Lawrence Blum argues, deontological reason's opposition of moral duty to feeling fails to recognize the role of sentiments of sympathy, compassion and concern in providing reasons for and motivating moral action.[16] Our experience of moral life teaches us, moreover, that without the impulse of deprivation or anger, for example, many moral choices would not be made.

Thus as a consequence of the opposition between reason and desire, moral decisions grounded in considerations of sympathy, caring and an assessment of differentiated need are defined as not rational, not 'objective', merely sentimental. To the degree that women exemplify or are identified with such styles of moral decision-making, then, women are excluded from moral rationality.[17] The moral rationality of any other groups whose experience or stereotypes associate them with desire, need and affectivity, moreover, is suspect.

By simply expelling desire, affectivity and need, finally deontological reason represses them, and sets morality in opposition to happiness. The function of duty is to master inner nature, not to form it in the best directions. Since all desiring is equally suspect, we have no way of distinguishing which desires are good and which bad, which will expand the person's capacities and relations with others, and which stunt the person and foster violence. In being excluded from understanding, all desiring, feeling, and needs become unconscious, but certainly do not thereby cease to motivate action and behaviour. Reason's task thereby is to control and censure desire.

428

II. THE UNITY OF THE CIVIC PUBLIC

The dichotomy between reason and desire appears in modern political theory in the distinction between the universal, public realm of sovereignty and the state, on the one hand, and the particular private realm of needs and desires, on the other. Modern normative political theory and political practice aim to embody impartiality in the public realm of the state. Like the impartiality of moral reason, this public realm of the state attains its generality by the exclusion of particularity, desire, feeling and those aspects of life associated with the body. In modern political theory and practice this public achieves a unity in particular by the exclusion of women and others associated with nature and the body.

As Richard Sennett and others have written, the developing urban centres of the eighteenth century engendered a unique public life.[18] As commerce increased and more people came into the city, the space of the city itself was changed to make for more openness, vast boulevards where people from different classes mingled in the same spaces.[19] As Habermas has argued, one of the functions of this public life of the mid-nineteenth century was to provide a critical space where people discussed and criticized the affairs of the state in a multiplicity of newspapers, coffee-houses and other forums.[20] While dominated by bourgeois men, public discussion in the coffee-houses admitted men of any class on equal terms.[21] Through the institution of the salons, moreover, as well as by attending the theatre and being members of reading societies, aristocratic and bourgeois women participated and sometimes took the lead in such public discussion.[22]

Public life in this period appears to have been wild, playful, and sexy. The theatre was a social centre, a forum where wit and satire criticized the state and predominant mores. This wild public to some degree mixed sexes and classes, mixed serious discourse with play, and mixed the aesthetic with the political. It did not survive republican philosophy. The idea of the universalist state that expresses an impartial point of view transcending any particular interests is in part a reaction to this differentiated public. The republicans grounded this universalist state in the idea of the civic public which political theory and practice institutionalized by the end of the eighteenth-century in Europe and the US to suppress the popular and linguistic heterogeneity of the urban public. This institutionalization reordered social life on a strict division of public and private.

Rousseau's political philosophy is the paradigm of this ideal of the civic public. He develops his conception of politics precisely in reaction to his experience of the urban public of the eighteenth century,[23] as well as in reaction to the premisses and conclusions of the atomistic and individualist theory of the state expressed by Hobbes. The civic public expresses the universal and impartial point of view of reason, standing opposed to and expelling desire, sentiment, and the particularity of needs and interests. From the premisses of individual desire and want we cannot arrive at a strong enough normative conception of social relations. The difference between atomistic egoism and civil society does not consist simply in the fact that the infinity of individual appetite has been curbed by laws enforced by threat of punishment. Rather, reason brings people together to recognize common interests and a general will.

The sovereign people embodies the universal point of view of the collective interest and equal citizenship. In the pursuit of their individual interests people have a particularist orientation. Normative reason reveals an impartial point of view, however, that all rational persons can adopt, which expresses a general will not reducible to an aggregate of particular interests. Participation in the general will as a citizen is an expression of human nobility and genuine freedom. Such rational commitment to collectivity is not compatible with personal satisfaction, however, and for Rousseau this is the tragedy of the human condition.[24]

Rousseau conceived that this public realm ought to be unified and homogeneous, and indeed suggested methods of fostering among citizens commitment to such unity through civic celebrations. While the purity, unity, and generality of this public realm require transcending and repressing the partiality and differentiation of need, desire, and affectivity, Rousseau hardly believed that human life can or should be without emotion and the satisfaction of need and desire. Man's particular nature as a feeling, needful being is enacted in the private realm of domestic life, over which women are the proper moral guardians.

Hegel's political philosophy developed this conception of the public realm of the state as expressing impartiality and universality as against the partiality and substance of desire. For Hegel, the liberal account of social relations as based on the liberty of self-defining individuals to pursue their own ends properly describes only one aspect of social life, the sphere of civil society. As a member of civil society, the person pursues private ends for himself and his family. These ends may conflict with those of others, but exchange transactions produce much harmony and satisfaction. Conceived as a member of the state, on the other hand, the person is not a locus of particular desire, but the bearer of universally articulated rights and responsibilities. The point of view of the state and law transcends all particular interests, to express the universal and rational spirit of humanity. State laws and action express the general will, the interests of the whole society. Since maintaining this universal point of view while engaged in the pursuit of one's own particular interests is difficult if not impossible, a class of persons is necessary whose sole job is to maintain the public good and the universal point of view of the state. For Hegel, these government officials are the universal class.[25]

Marx, of course, was the first to deny the state's claim to impartiality and universality. The split between the public realm of citizenship and the private realm of individual desire and greed leaves the competition and inequality of that private realm untouched. In capitalist society application of a principle of impartiality reproduces the position of the ruling class, because the interests of the substantially more powerful are considered in the same manner as those without power.[26] Despite this critique, as powerful as it ever was, Marx stops short of questioning the ideal of a public that expresses an impartial and universal normative perspective; he merely asserts that such a public is not realizable within capitalist society.

I think that recent feminist analyses of the dichotomy of public and private in modern political theory imply that the ideal of the civic public as impartial and universal is itself suspect. Modern political theorists and politicians proclaimed the impartiality and generality of the public and at the same time quite consciously found it fitting that some persons, namely women, non-whites, and sometimes those without property, be excluded from participation in that public. If this was not just a mistake, it suggests that the ideal of the civic public as expressing the general interest, the impartial point of view of reason, itself results in exclusion. By assuming that reason stands opposed to desire, affectivity, and the body, the civic public must exclude bodily and affective aspects of human existence. In practice this assumption forces a homogeneity of citizens upon the civic public. It excludes from the public those individuals and groups that do not fit the model of the rational citizen who can transcend body and sentiment. This exclusion is based on two tendencies that feminists stress: the opposition between reason and desire, and the association of these traits with kinds of persons.

In the social scheme expressed by Rousseau and Hegel, women must be excluded from the public realm of citizenship because they are the caretakers of affectivity, desire, and the body. Allowing appeals to desires and bodily needs to move public debates would undermine public deliberation by fragmenting its unity. Even within the domestic realm, moreover, women must be dominated. Their dangerous, heterogeneous sexuality must be kept chaste and confined to marriage. Enforcing chastity on women will keep each family a separated unity, preventing the chaos and blood-mingling that would be produced by illegitimate children. These chaste, enclosed women can then be the proper caretakers of men's desire, by tempering its potentially disruptive impulses through moral education. Men's desire for women itself threatens to shatter and disperse the universal rational realm of the public, as well as to disrupt the neat distinction between the public and private. As guardians of the private realm of need, desire, and affectivity, women must ensure that men's impulses do not remove them from the universality of reason. The moral neatness of the female-tended hearth, moreover, will temper the possessively individualistic impulses of the particularistic realm of business and commerce, which like sexuality constantly threatens to explode the unity of society under the umbrella of universal reason.[27]

The bourgeois world instituted a moral division of labour between reason and sentiment, identifying masculinity with reason and femininity with sentiment and desire.[28] As Linda Nicholson has argued, the modern sphere of family and personal life is as much a modern creation as the modern realm of state and law, and as part of the same process.[29] The impartiality and rationality of the state depend on containing need and desire in the private realm of the family.[30] While the realm of personal life and sentiment has been thoroughly devalued because it has been excluded from rationality, it has nevertheless been the focus of increasingly expanded commitment. Modernity developed a concept of 'inner nature' that needs nurturance, and within which is to be found the authenticity and individuality of the self, rather than in the conformity, regularity, and universality of the public. The civil public excludes sentiment and desire, then, partly in order to protect their 'natural' character.

Not only in Europe, but in the early decades of the US as well, the white male bourgeoisie conceived republican virtue as rational, restrained, and chaste, not yielding to passion, desire for luxury. The designers of the American Constitution specifically restricted the access of the labouring class to this rational public, because they feared disruption of commitment to the general interests. Some, like Jefferson, even feared developing an urban proletariat. These early American republicans were also quite explicit about the need for the homogeneity of citizens, which from the earliest days in the republic involved the relationship of the white republicans to the black and Native American people. These republican fathers, such as Jefferson, identified the red and black people in their territories with wild nature and passion, just as they feared that women outside the domestic realm were wanton and avaricious. They defined moral, civilized republican life in opposition to this backward-looking uncultivated desire they identified with women and non-whites.[31]

To summarize, the ideal of normative reason, moral sense, stands opposed to desire and affectivity. Impartial civilized reason characterizes the virtue of the republican man who rises above passion and desire. Instead of cutting bourgeois man entirely off from the body and affectivity, however, this culture of the rational public confines them to the domestic sphere which also confines women's passions and provides emotional solace to men and children. Indeed, within this domestic realm sentiments can flower, and each individual can recognize and affirm his particularity. Because virtues of impartiality and universality define the public realm, it precisely ought not to attend to our particularity. Modern normative reason and its political expression in the idea of the civic public, then, has unity and coherence by its expulsion and confinement of everything that would threaten to invade the polity with differentiation: the specificity of women's bodies and desire, the difference of race and culture, the variability or heterogeneity of the needs, goals, and desires of each individual, the ambiguity and changeability of feeling.

III. HABERMAS AS OPPOSING REASON AND AFFECTIVITY

I have argued that the modern conception of normative reason derived from the deontological tradition of moral and political theory aims for a unity that expels particularity and desire and sets feeling in opposition to reason. To express that impartiality and universality, a point of view of reasoning must be constructed that transcends all situation, context, and perspective. The identification of such a point of view with reason, however, devalues and represses the concrete needs, feelings, and interests persons have in their practical moral life, and thus imposes an impossible burden on reason itself. Deontological reason generates an opposition between normative reason on the one hand and desire and affectivity on the other. These latter cannot be entirely suppressed and reduced to the unity of impartial and universal reason, however. They sprout out again, menacing because they have been expelled from reason.

Because the ideal of impartiality is illusory, and because claims to assert normative reason as impartial and universal issue practically in the political exclusion of persons associated with affectivity and the body, we need a conception of normative reason that does not hold this ideal and does not oppose reason to affectivity and desire. I think that Habermas's idea of a communicative ethics provides the most promising starting-point for such an alternative conception of normative reason. Much about the way he formulates his theory of communicative action, however, retains several problems that characterize deontological reason.

In his theory of communicative action Habermas seeks to develop a conception of rationality with a pragmatic starting-point in the experience of discussion that aims to reach an understanding. Reason in such a model does not mean universal principles dominating particulars, but more concretely means giving reasons, adopting the practical stance of being reasonable, willing to talk and listen. Truth and rightness are not something known by intuition or through tests of consistency, but are only achieved from a process of discussion. This communicative ethics eliminates the authoritarian monologism of deontological reason. The dialogic model of reason supplants the transcendental ego, presiding at a height from which it can comprehend everything by reducing it to synthetic unity.

In the theory of communicative action Habermas also seeks directly to confront the tendency in modern philosophy to reduce reason to instrumental reason, a tendency that follows from its assumption of a solitary reasoning consciousness. He insists that normative, aesthetic, and expressive utterances can be just as rational as factual or strategic ones, but differ from the latter in the manner of evaluating their rationality. For all these reasons, Habermas's theory of communicative action has much more to offer a feminist ethics than does modern ethical and political theory. Habermas's communicative ethics remain inadequate, however, from the point of view of the critique of deontological reason I have made. For he retains a commitment to impartiality and reproduces in his theory of communication an opposition between reason and desire.

A dialogic conception of normative reason promises a critique and abandonment of the assumption that normative reason is impartial and universal. Precisely because there is no impartial point of view in which a subject stands detached and dispassionate to assess all perspectives, to arrive at an objective and complete understanding of an issue or experience, all perspectives and participants must contribute to its discussion. Thus dialogic reason ought to imply reason as contextualized, where answers are the outcome of a plurality of perspectives that cannot be reduced to unity. In discussion, speakers need not abandon their particular perspective nor bracket their motives and feelings. As long as the dialogue allows all perspectives to speak freely, and be heard and taken into account, the expression of need, motive, and feelings will not have merely private significance, and will not bias or distort the conclusions because they will interact with other needs, motives, and feelings.

Habermas himself reneges on this promise to define normative reason contextually and perspectivally, however, because he retains a commitment to the ideal of normative reason as expressing an impartial point of view. Rather than arbitrarily presuppose a transcendental ego as the impartial reasoner, as does the deontological tradition, he claims that an impartial point of view is actually presupposed by a normative discussion that seeks to reach agreement. A faith in the possibility of consensus is a condition of beginning dialogue, and the possibility of such consensus presupposes that people engage in discussion 'under conditions that neutralize all motives except that of cooperatively seeking truth'.[32] Habermas claims here theoretically to reconstruct a presumption of impartiality implicitly carried by any discussion of norms that aims to reach consensus. I take this to be a transcendental argument, inasmuch as he poses this abstraction from motives and desires as a condition of the possibility of consensus. Through this argument he reproduces the opposition between universal and particular, reason and desire characteristic of deontological reason. A more thoroughly pragmatic interpretation of dialogic reason would not have to suppose that participants must abstract from all motives in aiming to reach agreement.[33]

Communicative ethics also promises to break down the opposition between normative reason and desire that deontological reason generates. Individual needs, desires, and feelings can be rationally articulated and understood, no less than can facts about the world or norms.[34] A possible interpretation of communicative ethics, then, can be that normative claims are the outcome of the expression of needs, feelings, and desires which individuals claim to have met and recognized by others under conditions where all have an equal voice in the expression of their needs and desires. Habermas stops short of interpreting normative reason as the dialogue about meeting needs and recognizing feelings, however. As Seyla Benhabib argues, because Habermas retains a universalistic understanding of normative reason, he finds that norms must express shared interests.[35] In his scheme, discussion about individual need and feeling is separate from discussion about norms.

I suggest that Habermas implicitly reproduces an opposition between reason and desire and feeling in his conception of communication itself, moreover, because he devalues and ignores the expressive and bodily aspects of communication. The model of linguistic activity Habermas takes for his conception of communicative action is discourse, or argumentation. In argumentation we find the implicit rules underlying all linguistic action, whether teleological, normative, or dramaturgical. In discourse people make their shared activity the subject of discussion in order to come to agreement about it. People make assertions for which they claim validity, give reasons for their assertions, and require reasons of others. In the ideal model of discourse, no force compels agreement against that of the better argument. This model of the communication situation, which any attempts to reach understanding presupposes, defines the meaning of utterances: the meaning of an utterance consists in the reasons that can be offered for it. To understand the meaning of an utterance is to know the conditions of its validity.[36]

In Habermas's model of communication, understanding consists of participants in discussion understanding the same meaning by an utterance, which means that they agree that the utterance refers to something in the objective, social or subjective world. The actors:

seek consensus and measure it against truth, rightness and sincerity, that is, against the 'fit' or 'misfit' between the speech act, on the one hand, and the three worlds to which the actor takes up relations with his utterances, on the other.[37]

The term 'reaching understanding' means, at the minimum, that at least two speaking and acting subjects understand a linguistic expression in the same way ... In communicative action a speaker selects a comprehensible linguistic expression only in order to come to an understanding *with* a hearer *about* something and thereby to make *himself* understandable.[38]

Behind this apparently innocent way of talking about discourse lies the presumption of several unities: the unity of the speaking subject, that knows himself or herself and seeks faithfully to represent his or her feelings, the unity of subjects with one another that makes it possible for them to have the same meaning, and the unity, in the sense of fit or correspondence, between an utterance and the aspects of one or more of the 'worlds' to which it refers. By this manner of theorizing language Habermas exhibits the logic of identity I discussed in section I, or also what Derrida calls the metaphysics of presence.[39] This model of communication presumes implicitly that speakers can be present both to themselves and one another, and that signification consists in the re-presentation by a sign of objects. To be sure, Habermas denies a realist interpretation of the function of utterances; it is not as though there are worlds of things apart from situated human and social linguistic life. Nevertheless, he presumes that utterances can have a single meaning understood in the same way by speakers because they affirm that it expresses the same relation to a world. As writers such as Michael Ryan and Dominick LaCapra have argued, such a conception of meaning ignores the manner in which meaning arises from the unique relationship of utterances to one another, and thereby ignores the multiple meaning that any movement of signification expresses.[40]

I suggest, moreover, that this model of communication reproduces the opposition between reason and desire because, like modern normative reason, it expels and devalues difference: the concreteness of the body, the affective aspects of speech, the musical and figurative aspects of all utterances, which all contribute to the formation and understanding of their meaning. John Keane argues that Habermas's model of discourse abstracts from the specifically bodily aspects of speech—gesture, facial expression, tone of voice, rhythm. One can add to this that it also abstracts from the material aspects of written language, such as punctuation and sentence construction. This model of communication also abstracts from the rhetorical dimensions of communication, that is, the evocative terms, metaphors, dramatic elements of the speaking, by which a speaker addresses himself or herself to this particular audience.[41] When people converse in concrete speaking situations, when they give and receive reasons from one another with the aim of reaching understanding, gesture, facial expression, and tone of voice (or in writing, punctuation, sentence structure, etc.), as well as evocative metaphors and dramatic emphasis, are crucial aspects of their communication.

In the model of ideal discourse that Habermas holds, moreover, there appears to be no role for metaphor, jokes, irony, and other forms of communication that use surprise and duplicity. The model of communication Habermas operates with holds an implicit distinction between 'literal' and 'figurative' meaning, and between a meaning and its manner of expression. Implicitly this model of communication supposes a purity of the meaning of utterances by separating them from their expressive and metaphorical aspects. He considers irony, paradox, allusion, metaphor and so on, as derivative, even deceptive, modes of linguistic practice, thus assuming the rational literal meaning in opposition to these more playful, multiple, and affective modes of speaking.[42] In the practical context of communication, however, such ambiguous and playful forms of expression usually weave in and out of assertive modes, together providing the communicative act.

Julia Kristeva's conception of speech provides a more embodied alternative to that proposed by Habermas, which might better open a conception of communicative ethics. Any utterance has a dual movement, in her conception, which she refers to as the 'symbolic' and 'semiotic' moments. The symbolic names the referential function of the utterance, the way it situates the speaker in relation to a reality outside of him or her. The semiotic names the unconscious, bodily aspects of the utterance, such as rhythm, tone of voice, metaphor, word play, and gesture.[43] Different kinds of utterance have differing relations of the symbolic and the semiotic. Scientific language, for example, seeks to suppress the semiotic elements, while poetic language emphasizes them. No utterance is without the duality of a relation of the symbolic and semiotic, however, and it is through their relationship that meaning is generated.

This understanding of language bursts open the unity of the subject which Habermas presupposes, as the sender and receiver and negotiator of meaning. The subject is in process, positioned by the slipping and moving levels of signification, which is always in excess of what is grasped or understood discursively. The heterogeneous semiotic aspects of utterances influence both speakers and hearers in unconscious, bodily and affective ways that support and move the expressing and understanding of referential meaning. Kristeva is quite clear in rejecting an irrationalist conception that would hold that all utterances are equally sensible and simply reduces any speech to play. The point is not to reverse the privileging of reason over emotion and body that it excludes, but to expose the process of the generation of referential meaning from the supporting valences of semiotic relations.

Though absolutely necessary, the thetic [i.e. proposition or judgement] is not exclusive: the semiotic, which also precedes it, constantly tears it open, and this transgression brings about all the various transformations of the signifying practice that are called 'creation'. Whether in the realm of metalanguage (mathematics, for example) or literature, what remodels the symbolic order is always the influx of the semiotic.[44]

What difference does such a theory of language make for a conception of normative reason grounded in a theory of communicative action? As I understand the implications of Kristeva's approach to language, it entails that communication is not only motivated by the aim to reach consensus, a shared understanding of the world, but also and even more basically by a desire to love and be loved. Modulations of eros operate in the semiotic elements of communication, that put the subject's identity in question in relation to itself, its own past and imagination, and to others, in the heterogeneity of their identity. People do not merely hear, take in, and argue about the validity of utterances. Rather we are affected, in an immediate and felt fashion, by the other's expression and its manner of being addressed to us.

Habermas has a place in his model of communication for making feelings the subject of discourse. Such feeling discourse, however, is carefully marked off in his theory from factual or normative discourse. There is no place in his conception of linguistic interaction for the feeling that accompanies and motivates all utterances. In actual situations of discussion, tone of voice, facial expression, gesture, the use of irony, understatement, or hyperbole, all serve to carry with the propositional message of the utterance another level of expression relating the participants in terms of attraction or withdrawal, confrontation, or affirmation. Speakers not only say what they mean, but they say it excitedly, angrily, in a hurt or offended fashion, and so on, and such emotional qualities of communication contexts should not be thought of as non- or prelinguistic. Recognizing such an aspect of utterances, however, involves acknowledging the irreducible multiplicity and ambiguity of meaning. I am suggesting that only a conception of normative reason that includes these affective and bodily dimensions of meaning can be adequate for a feminist ethics.

IV. TOWARD A HETEROGENEOUS PUBLIC LIFE

I have argued that the distinction between public and private as it appears in modern political theory expresses a will for homogeneity that necessitates the exclusion of many persons and groups, particularly women and racialized groups culturally identified with the body, wildness, and irrationality. In conformity with the modern idea of normative reason, the idea of the public in modern political theory and practice designates a sphere of human existence in which citizens express their rationality and universality, abstracted from their particular situations and needs and opposed to feeling. This feminist critique of the exclusionary public does not imply, as Jean Elshtain suggests, a collapse of the distinction between public and private.[45] Indeed, I agree with the many writers, including Elshtain, Habermas, and Wolin, who claim that contemporary social life itself has collapsed the public and that emancipatory politics requires generating a renewed sense of public life. Examination of the exclusionary and homogeneous ideal of the public in modern political theory, however, shows that we cannot envision such renewal of public life as a recovery of Enlightenment ideals. Instead, we need to transform the distinction between public and private that does not correlate with an opposition between reason and affectivity and desire, or universal and particular.

The primary meaning of public is what is open and accessible. For democratic politics this means two things: there must be public spaces and public expression. A public space is any indoor or outdoor space to which any persons have access. Expression is public when third parties may witness it within institutions that give these others opportunity to respond to the expression and enter a discussion, and through media that allow anyone in principle to enter the discussion. Expression and discussion are political when they raise and address issues of the moral value or human desirability of an institution or practice whose decisions affect a large number of people. This concept of a public, which indeed is derived from aspects of modern urban experience, expresses a conception of social relations in principle not exclusionary.

The traditional notion of the private realm, as Hannah Arendt points out, is etymologically related to deprivation. The private, in her conception, is what should be hidden from view, or what cannot be brought to view. The private, in this traditional notion, is connected with shame and incompleteness, and as Arendt points out, implies excluding bodily and personally affective aspects of human life from the public.[46]

Instead of defining privacy as what the public excludes, privacy should be defined, as an aspect of liberal theory does, as that aspect of his or her life and activity that any individual has a right to exclude others from. I mean here to emphasize the direction of agency, as the individual withdrawing rather than being kept out. With the growth of both state and non-state bureaucracies, defence of privacy in this sense has become not merely a matter of keeping the state out of certain affairs, but asking for positive state action to ensure that the activities of non-state organizations, such as corporations, respect the claims of individuals to privacy.

The feminist slogan 'The personal is political' does not deny a distinction between public and private, but it does deny a social division between public and private spheres, with different kinds of institution, activity, and human attribute. Two principles follow from this slogan: (a) no social institutions or practices should be excluded a priori as being the proper subject for public discussion and expression; and (b) no persons, actions, or aspects of a person's life should be forced into privacy.

1. The contemporary women's movement has made public issues out of many practices claimed too trivial or private for public discussion: the meaning of pronouns, domestic violence against women, the practice of men's opening doors for women, the sexual assault on women and children, the sexual division of housework, and so on. Radical politics in contemporary life consists of taking many actions and activities deemed properly private, such as how individuals and enterprises invest their money, and making public issues out of them.

2. The second principle says that no person or aspects of persons should be forced into privacy. The modern conception of the public, I have argued, creates a conception of citizenship which excludes from public attention most particular aspects of a person. Public life is supposed to be 'blind' to sex, race, age, and so on, and all are supposed to enter the public and its discussion on identical terms. Such a conception of a public has resulted in the exclusion of persons and aspects of persons from public life.

Ours is still a society that forces persons or aspects of persons into privacy. Repression of homosexuality is perhaps the most striking example. In the US today most people seem to hold the liberal view that persons have a right to be gay as long as they remain private about their activities. Calling attention in public to the fact that one is gay, making public displays of gay affection, or even publicly asserting needs and rights for gay people provoke ridicule and fear in many people. Making a public issue out of heterosexuality, moreover, by suggesting that the dominance of heterosexual assumptions is one-dimensional and oppressive, can rarely get a public hearing even among feminists and radicals. In general, contemporary politics grants to all persons entrance into the public on condition that they do not claim special rights or needs, or call attention to their particular history or culture, and that they keep their passions private.

The new social movements of the 1960s, 1970s, and 1980s in the US have begun to create an image of a more differentiated public that directly confronts the allegedly impartial and universalist state. Movements of racially oppressed groups, including black, chicano, and American-Indian liberation, tend to reject the assimilationist ideal and assert the right to nurture and celebrate in public their distinctive cultures and forms of life, as well as asserting special claims of justice deriving from suppression or devaluation of their cultures, or compensating for the disadvantage in which the dominant society puts them. The women's movement too has claimed to develop and foster a distinctively women's culture, and has asserted that both women's specific bodily needs and women's situation in male-dominated society require attending in public to special needs and unique contributions of women. Movements of the disabled, the aged, and gay and lesbian liberation have all produced an image of public life in which persons stand forth in their difference, and make public claims to have specific needs met.

The street demonstrations that in recent years have included most of these groups, as well as traditional labour groups and advocates of environmentalism and nuclear disarmament, sometimes create heterogeneous publics of passion, play, and aesthetic interest. Such demonstrations always focus on issues they seek to promote for public discussion, and these issues are discussed: claims are made and supported. The style of politics of such events, however, has many less discursive elements: gaily decorated banners with ironic or funny slogans, guerrilla theatre or costumes serving to make political points, giant puppets standing for people or ideas towering over the crowd, chants, music, song, dancing. Liberating public expression means not only lifting formerly privatized issues into the open of public and rational discussion which considers the good of ends as well as means, but also affirming in the practice of such discussion the proper place of passion and play in public.

As the 1980s progressed, and the particular interests and experience expressed by these differing social movements matured in their confidence, coherence, and understanding of the world from the point of view of these interests, a new kind of public has become possible which might persist beyond a single demonstration. This public is expressed in the idea of a 'Rainbow Coalition'. Realized to some degree only for sporadic months during the 1983 Mel King campaign in Boston and the 1984 Jesse Jackson campaign in certain cities, this is an idea of a political public which goes beyond the ideal of civic friendship in which persons unite for a common purpose on terms of equality and mutual respect.[47] While it includes commitment to equality and mutual respect among participants, the idea of the Rainbow Coalition specifically preserves and institutionalizes in its form of organizational discussion the heterogeneous groups that make it up. In this way it is quite unlike the Enlightenment ideal of the civil public (which might have its practical analogue here in the idea of the 'united front'). As a general principle, this heterogeneous public asserts that the only way to ensure that public life will not exclude persons and groups which it has excluded in the past is to give specific recognition to the disadvantage of those groups and bring their specific histories into the public.[48]

I have been suggesting that the Enlightenment ideal of the civil public, where citizens meet in terms of equality and mutual respect, is too rounded and tame an ideal of public. This idea of equal citizenship attains unity because it excludes bodily and affective particularity, as well as the concrete histories of individuals that make groups unable to understand one another. Emancipatory politics should foster a conception of public which in principle excludes no persons, aspects of persons' lives, or topic of discussion, and which encourages aesthetic as well as discursive expression. In such a public, consensus and sharing may not always be the goal, but rather the recognition and appreciation of differences, in the context of confrontation with power.[49]

Notes

1. John Keane, 'Liberalism Under Siege: Power, Legitimation, and the Fate of Modern Contract Theory', in *Public Life in Late Capitalism* (Cambridge: Cambridge University Press, 1984), 253. Andrew Levine is another writer who finds in Rousseau an emancipatory alternative to liberalism. See 'Beyond Justice: Rousseau Against Rawls', *Journal of Chinese Philosophy*, 4 (1977), 123–42.

2. I develop the contrast between commitment to a feminist humanism, on the one hand, and reaction against belief in women's liberation as the attainment of equality with men in formerly male-dominated institutions in my paper, 'Humanism, Gynocentrism and Feminist Politics', in *Hypatia: A Journal of Feminist Philosophy*, 3, special issue of *Women's Studies International Forum*, 8(5) (1985).

3. The literature on these issues has become vast. My own understanding of them is derived from reading, among others, Susan Okin, *Women in Western Political Thought* (Princeton, NJ: Princeton University Press, 1978); Zillah Eisenstein, *The Radical Future of Liberal Feminism* (New York: Longman, 1979); Lynda Lange and Lorrenne Clark, *The Sexism of Social and Political Theory* (Toronto: University of Toronto Press, 1979); Jean Elshtain, *Public Man, Private Woman*, (Princeton, NJ: Princeton University Press, 1981); Alison Jaggar, *Human Nature and Feminist Politics* (Totowa, NJ: Rowman & Allenheld, 1983); Carole Pateman, 'Feminist Critiques of the Public/Private Dichotomy', in S. I. Benn and G. F. Gaus (eds.), *Public and Private in Social Life* (New York: St. Martin's Press, 1983), 281–303; Hannah Pitkin, *Fortune Is a Woman* (Berkeley: University of California Press, 1984); Nancy Hartsock, *Money, Sex and Power* (New York: Longman, 1983); Linda Nicholson, *Gender and History* (New York: Columbia University Press, 1986).

4. See Cornel West, *Prophesy Deliverance* (Philadelphia: Westminster Press, 1983); and 'The Genealogy of Racism: On the Underside of Discourse', *The Journal*, The Society for the Study of Black Philosophy, 1(1) (Winter–Spring 1984), 42–60.

5. Carol Gilligan, *In a Different Voice* (Harvard: Harvard University Press, 1982).

6. Bentham's utilitarianism, for example, assumes something like an 'ideal observer' that sees and calculates each individual happiness and weights them all in relation to one another, calculating the overall amount of utility. This stance of an impartial calculator is like that of the warden in the panoption that Foucault takes as expressive of modern normative reason. The moral observer towers over and is able to see all the individual persons in relation to each other, while remaining itself outside of their observations. See Foucault, *Discipline and Punish* (New York: Vintage, 1977).

7. Bruce Ackerman, *Social Justice in the Liberal State* (New Haven, Conn.: Yale University Press, 1980).

8. Michael J. Sandel, *Liberalism and the Limits of Justice* (Cambridge: Cambridge University Press, 1982); cf. Seyla Benhabib, 'The Generalized and the Concrete Other', ch. 4 of Benhabib and Drucilla Cornell (eds.), *Feminism as Critique* (University of Minnesota Press, 1987); see also Theodore Adorno, *Negative Dialectics* (New York: Continuum, 1973), 238–9.

9. Theodor Adorno, 'Introduction', in *Negative Dialectics*.

10. Roberto Unger identifies this problem of applying universals to particulars in modern normative theory. See *Knowledge and Politics* (New York: Free Press, 1974), 133–44.

11. Thomas A. Spragens, Jr, *The Irony of Liberal Reason* (Chicago: University of Chicago Press, 1981), 109.

12. Rawls's original position is intended to overcome his monologism of Kantian deontology. Since by definition in the original position everyone reasons from the same perspective, however, abstracted from all particularities of history, place and situation, the original position is monological in the same sense as Kantian reason. I have argued this in my article 'Toward a Critical Theory of Justice', *Social Theory and Practice*, 7(3) (Fall 1981), 279–301; see also Sandel, *Liberalism*, 59–64, and Benhabib, 'The Generalized and the Concrete Other'.

13. Adorno, *Negative Dialectics*, 242; 295.

14. I am relying on a reading of Jacques Derrida's *Of Grammatology* (Baltimore: Johns Hopkins University Press, 1976), in addition to Adorno's *Negative Dialectics*, for this account. Several writers have noted similarities between Adorno and Derrida in this regard. See Fred Dallmayr, *Twilight of Subjectivity: Contributions to a Post-Structuralist Theory of Politics* (Amherst: University of Massachusetts Press, 1981), 107–14, 127–36; and Michael Ryan, *Marxism and Domination* (Baltimore: Johns Hopkins University Press, 1982), 73–81.

15. T. A. Spragens, *The Irony of Liberal Reason*, 250–6.

16. Lawrence A. Blum, *Friendship, Altruism and Morality* (London: Routledge & Kegan Paul, 1980).

17. This is one of Gilligan's points in claiming there is a 'different voice' that has been suppressed; see Benhabib, 'The Generalized and the Concrete Other'; see also Lawrence Blum, 'Kant's and Hegel's Moral Rationalism: A Feminist Perspective', *Canadian Journal of Philosophy*, 12 (June 1982), 287–302.

18. Richard Sennett, *The Fall of Public Man* (New York: Random House, 1974).

19. See Marshall Berman, *All That Is Solid Melts into Air* (New York: Simon & Schuster, 1982).

20. Jürgen Habermas, 'The Public Sphere: An Encyclopedia Article', *New German Critique*, 1(3) (Fall 1974), 49–55.

21. Sennett, *The Fall of Public Man*, ch. 4.

22. See Joan Landes, 'Women and the Public Sphere: The Challenge of Feminist Discourse', paper presented as part of Bunting Institute Colloquium, Apr. 1983.

23. Charles Ellison, 'Rousseau's Critique of Codes of Speech and Dress in Urban Public Life: Implications for His Political Theory', MS, University of Cincinnati.

24. Judith Shklar, *Men and Citizens* (Cambridge: Cambridge University Press, 1969).

25. See Z. A. Pelczynski, 'The Hegelian Conception of the State', in Pelczynski (ed.), *Hegel's Political Philosophy: Problems and Perspectives* (Cambridge: Cambridge University Press, 1971), 1–29; and Anthony S. Walton, 'Public and Private Interests: Hegel on Civil Society and the State', in Benn and Gaus, *Public and Private in Social Life*, 249–66.

26. There are many texts in which Marx makes these sorts of claims, including 'On the Jewish Question' and 'Critique of the Gotha Programme'. For some discussion of these points, see Shlomo Avineri, *The Social and Political Thought of Karl Marx* (Cambridge: Cambridge University Press, 1968), 41–8.

27. For feminist analyses of Hegel, see works by Okin, Elshtain, Einstein, Lange, and Clark, cited in n. 3. See also Joel Schwartz, *The Sexual Politics of Jean-Jacques Rousseau* (Chicago: University of Chicago Press, 1984).

28. See Genevieve Lloyd, *The Man of Reason: 'Male' and 'Female' in Western Philosophy* (Minneapolis: University of Minnesota Press, 1984); Lynda Glennon, *Women and Dualism* (New York: Longman, 1979).

29. Nicholson, *Gender and History*.

30. Eisenstein claims that the modern state depends on the patriarchal family; see *The Radical Future*.

31. Ronald Takaki, *Iron Cages: Race and Culture in Nineteenth Century America* (New York: Knopf, 1979).

32. Jürgen Habermas, *The Theory of Communicative Action*, i: *Reason and the Rationalization of Society* (Boston: Beacon Press, 1983;

Cambridge: Polity Press, 19), 19. In the footnote to this passage Habermas explicity connects this presumption to the tradition of moral theory seeking to articulate the impartial 'moral point of view'.

33. Richard Bernstein suggests that Habermas vacillates between a transcendental and empirical interpretation of his project in many respects. See *Beyond Objectivism and Relativism* (Philadelphia: University of Pennsylvania Press, 1983), 182–96.

34. Habermas, *Theory of Communicative Action*, i: 91–3.

35. Seyla Benhabib, 'Communicative Ethics and Moral Autonomy', presented at American Philosophical Association, Dec. 1982.

36. Habermas, *Theory of Communicative Action*, i: 115, 285–300.

37. Ibid. 100.

38. Ibid. 307.

39. I am thinking here particularly of Derrida's discussion of Rousseau in *Of Grammatology*. I have dealt with these issues in much more detail in my paper 'The Ideal of Community and the Politics of Difference', unpublished.

40. For critiques of Habermas's assumptions about language from a Derridian point of view, which argue that he does not attend to the difference and spacing in signification that generates undecideability and ambiguity, see Michael Ryan, *Marxism and Deconstruction* (Baltimore: Johns Hopkins University Press, 1982); Dominick LaCapra, 'Habermas and the Grounding of Critical Theory', *History and Theory* (1977), pp. 237–64.

41. John Keane, 'Elements of a Socialist Theory of Public Life', in *Public Life*, 169–72.

42. Habermas, *Theory of Communicative Action*, i: 331.

43. Julia Kristeva, *Revolution in Poetic Language* (New York: Columbia University Press, 1984) 124–47.

44. Ibid. 291.

45. Elshtain, *Public Man*, pt. ii.

46. Hannah Arendt, *The Human Condition* (Chicago: University of Chicago Press, 1958).

47. See Drucilla Cornell, 'Toward A Modern/Postmodern Reconstruction of Ethics', *University of Pennsylvania Law Review*, 133(2) (1985), 291–380.

48. Thomas Bender promotes a conception of a heterogeneous public as important for an urban political history that would not be dominated by the perspective of the then and now privileged; 'The History of Culture and the Culture of Cities', paper presented at meeting of the International Association of Philosophy and Literature, New York City, May 1985.

49. I am grateful to David Alexander for all the time and thought he gave to this essay.

Wounded Attachments: Late Modern Oppositional Political Formations

Wendy Brown

> If something is to stay in the memory, it must be burned in:
> only that which never ceases to *hurt* stays in the memory.
>
> Friedrich Nietzsche

Taking enormous pleasure in the paradox, Jamaican-born cultural studies theorist Stuart Hall tells this story of the postwar, postcolonial 'breakup' of English identity:

> in the very moment when finally Britain convinced itself it had to decolonize, it had to get rid of them, we all came back home. As they hauled down the flag [in the colonies], we got on the banana boat and sailed right into London. . . . [T]hey had ruled the world for 300 years and, at last, when they had made up their minds to climb out of the role, at least the others ought to have stayed out there in the rim, behaved themselves, gone somewhere else, or found some other client state. But no, they had always said that this [London] was really home, the streets were paved with gold, and bloody hell, we just came to check out whether that was so or not.[1]

In Hall's mischievous account, the restructuring of collective 'First World' identity and democratic practices required by postcoloniality did not remain in the hinterlands but literally, restively, came home to roost. The historical 'others' of colonial identity, cast free in their own waters, sailed in to implode the centre of the postcolonial metropoles, came to trouble the last vestiges of centred European identity with its economic and political predicates. They came to make havoc in the master's house after the master relinquished his military-political but not his cultural and metaphysical holding as *the* metonymy of man.

Hall's narrative of the palace invasion by the newly released subjects might also be pressed into service as metaphor for another historical paradox of late twentieth-century collective and individual identity formation: in the very moment when modern liberal states fully realize their secularism (as Marx put it in 'The Jewish Question'), just as the mantle of abstract personhood is formally tendered to a whole panoply of those historically excluded from it by humanism's privileging of a single race, gender, and organization of sexuality, the marginalized reject the rubric of humanist inclusion and turn, at least in part, against its very premisses. Refusing to be neutralized, to render the differences inconsequential, to be depoliticized as 'lifestyles', 'diversity', or 'persons like any other', we have lately reformulated our historical exclusion as a matter of historically produced and politically rich *alterity*. Insisting that we are not merely positioned but fabricated by this history, we have at the same time insisted that our very production as marginal, deviant, or subhuman is itself constitutive of the centrality and legitimacy of the centre, is itself what paves the centre's streets with semiotic, political, and psychic gold. Just when polite liberal (not to mention, correct leftist) discourse ceased speaking of us as dykes, faggots, coloured girls, or natives, we began speaking of ourselves this way. Refusing the invitation to absorption, we insisted instead upon politicizing and working into cultural critique the very constructions that a liberalism increasingly exposed in its tacit operations of racial, sexual, and gender privilege was seeking to bring to a formal close.

These paradoxes of late modern liberalism and colonialism, of course, are not a matter of simple historical accident—indeed, they are both incomplete and mutually constitutive to a degree which belies the orderly chronological scheme Hall and I have imposed on them in order to render them pleasurable ironies. Moreover, the ironies do not come to an end with the Jamaican postcolonials sailing into London, nor with the historically marginalized constructing an oppositional political culture and critique out of their historical exclusion. Even as the margins assert themselves as margins, the denaturalizing assault they perform on coherent collective identity in the centre turns back on them to trouble their own. Even as it is being articulated, circulated, and, lately, institutionalized in a host of legal, political, and cultural practices, identity is unravelling—metaphysically, culturally, geopolitically and historically—as rapidly as it is being produced. The same vacillation can be seen in the naturalistic legitimating narratives of collective identity as nationalism. Imploded within by the insurrectionary knowledges and political claims of historically subordinated cultures, and assaulted from without by the spectacular hybridities and supranational articulations of late twentieth-century global capitalism as well as crises of global ecology—nation formation, loosened from what retrospectively appears as a historically fleeting attachment to states, is today fervently being asserted in politico-cultural claims ranging from Islamic to deaf, indigenous to Gypsy, Serbian to queer.

Despite certain convergences, articulations, and parallels between such culturally disparate political formations in the late twentieth century, I shall not be considering the problematic of politicized identity on a global scale. Indeed, this essay is, among other things, an argument for substantial historical, geopolitical, and cultural specificity in an exploration of the problematic of political identity. My focus in the following pages will be on selected contradictory operations of politicized identity *within* late modern democracy, considering politicized identity as both a production and contestation of the political terms of liberalism, disciplinary-bureaucratic regimes, certain forces of global capitalism, and the demographic flows of postcoloniality which together might be taken as constitutive of the contemporary North American political condition. In recent years, enough stalemated argument has transpired about the virtues and vices of something named identity politics to suggest the limited usefulness of a discussion of identity, either in terms of the timeless metaphysical or linguistic elements of its constitution or in terms of the ethical-political rubric of good and evil. Beginning instead with the premiss that the proliferation and politicization of identities in the United States is not a moral or even political choice but a complex historical production, a more interesting contribution from scholars might consist in elucidating something of the nature of this production, in order to locate within it both the openings and the perils for a radically democratic or counter-hegemonic political project.

Many have asked how, given what appear as the inherently totalizing and 'othering' characteristics of identity in/as language, identity can avoid reiterating such investments in its ostensibly emancipatory mode.[2] I want to ask a similar question, but in a historically specific cultural-political register, not because the linguistic frame is unimportant but because it is insufficient for discerning the character of contemporary politicized identity's problematic investments. Thus, the sets of questions framing the work of this essay are these. First, given the subjectivizing conditions of identity production in a late modern capitalist, liberal, and disciplinary-bureaucratic social order, how can reiteration of these production conditions be averted in identity's purportedly emancipatory project? In the specific context of contemporary liberal and bureaucratic disciplinary discourse, what kind of political recognition can identity-based claims seek—and what kind can they be counted on to want—that will not resubordinate the subject, itself historically subjugated through identity, through categories such as race or gender which emerged and circulated as terms of power to enact subordination? The question here is not *whether* denaturalizing political strategies subvert the subjugating force of naturalized identity formation, but *what kind* of politicization, produced out of and inserted into *what kind* of political context, might perform such subversion. Second, given the widely averred interest of politicized identity in achieving emancipatory political recognition in a posthumanist discourse, what are the logics of pain in the subject-formation processes of late modern society that might contain or subvert this aim? What are the particular constituents—specific to our time yet roughly generic for a diverse spectrum of identities —of identity's desire for recognition that seem as often to breed a politics of recrimination and rancour, of culturally dispersed paralysis and suffering, a tendency to reproach power rather than aspire to it, to disdain freedom rather than practise it? In short, where do the historically and culturally specific elements of politicized identity's investments in itself, and especially in its own history of suffering, come into conflict with the need to give up these investments, to engage in something of a Nietzschean 'forgetting' of this history, in the pursuit of an emancipatory democratic project?

I will approach these questions by first offering a highly select-ive account of the discursive historical context of identity politics' emergence in the United States, and then elaborating, through reconsideration of Nietzsche's genealogy of the logics of *ressenti-ment*, the wounded character of politicized identity's desire within this context. This is not an essay about the general worth or accomplishments of 'identity politics', nor is it a critique of that oppositional political formation. It is, rather, an exploration of the ways in which certain aspects of the specific genealogy of politicized identity are carried in the structure of its political demands, with consequences that include self-subversion.

451

The tension between particularistic 'I's' and a universal 'we' in liberalism is sustainable as long as the constituent terms of the 'I' remain unpoliticized, indeed, as long as the 'I' itself remains unpoliticized on one hand and the state (as the expression of the ideal of political universality) remains unpoliticized on the other. That is, the latent conflict in liberalism between universal representation and individualism remains latent, remains unpoliticized, as long as differential powers in civil society remain naturalized, as long as the 'I' remains politically unarticulated, as long as it is willing to have its freedom represented abstractly, in effect, to subordinate its 'I-ness' to the abstract 'we' represented by the universal community of the state. This subordination is achieved either by the 'I' abstracting from itself in its political representation, thus trivializing its 'difference' so as to remain part of the 'we' (as in homosexuals who are 'just like everyone else except for who we sleep with') or by accepting its construction as a supplement, complement, or partial outsider to the 'we' (as in the history of women being 'concluded by their husbands', to use Blackstone's phrase, or homosexuals who are just 'different', or Jews whose communal affiliations lie partly or wholly outside their national identity). The history of liberalism's management of its inherited and constructed 'others' could be read as a history of variations on and vacillations between these two strategies.

The abstract character of liberal political membership and the ideologically naturalized character of liberal individualism together work against politicized identity formation.[3] A formulation of the political state and of citizenship which, as Marx put it in 'The Jewish Question', abstracts from the substantive conditions of our lives, works to prevent recognition or articulation of differences *as* political—as effects of power—in their very construction and organization; they are at most the stuff of divergent political or economic *interests*.[4] Equally important, to the extent that political membership in the liberal state involves abstracting from one's social being, it involves abstracting not only from the contingent productions of one's life circumstances but from the *identificatory* processes constitutive of one's social construction and position. Whether read from the frontispiece of Hobbes' *Leviathan*, in which the many are made one through the unity of the sovereign, or from the formulations of tolerance codified by John Locke, John

Stuart Mill, and, more contemporaneously, George Kateb, in which the minimalist liberal state is cast as precisely what enables our politically unfettered individuality, we are invited to seek equal deference—equal blindness from—but not equalizing *recognition* from the state, liberalism's universal moment.[5] As Marx discerned in his critique of Hegel, the universality of the state is ideologically achieved by turning away from and thus depoliticizing, yet at the same time *presupposing*, our collective particulars, not by embracing them, let alone emancipating us from them.[6] In short, the 'political' in liberalism is precisely not a domain for social identification: expected to recognize our political selves in the state, we are not led to expect deep recognition there. Put slightly differently, in a smooth and legitimate liberal order, if the particularistic 'I' must remain unpoliticized, so also must the universalistic 'we' remain without specific content or aim, without a common good *other than* abstract universal representation or pluralism. The abstractness of the 'we' is precisely what insists upon, reiterates, and even enforces the depoliticized nature of the 'I'. In Ernesto Laclau's formulation, 'if democracy *is* possible, it is because the universal does not have any necessary body, any necessary content'.[7]

While this détente between universal and particular within liberalism is potted with volatile conceits, it is rather thoroughly unravelled by two features of late modernity, spurred by developments in what Marx and Foucault respectively reveal as liberalism's companion powers: capitalism and disciplinarity. On one side, the state loses even its guise of universality as it becomes ever more transparently invested in particular economic interests, political ends, and social formations—as it transmogrifies from a relatively minimalist, 'night watchman' state to a heavily bureaucratized, managerial, fiscally enormous, and highly interventionist welfare–warfare state, a transmogrification occasioned by the combined imperatives of capital and the auto-proliferating characteristics of bureaucracy.[8] On the other side, the liberal subject is increasingly disinterred from substantive nation-state identification, not only by the individuating effects of liberal discourse itself but through the social effects of late twentieth-century economic and political life: deterritorializing demographic flows; the disintegration from within and invasion from without of family and community as (relatively) autonomous sites of social production and identification; consumer capitalism's marketing discourse in which individual (and sub-individual) desires are produced, commodified, and mobilized as identities; and disciplinary productions of a fantastic array of behaviour-based identities ranging from recovering alcoholic professionals to unrepentant crack mothers. These disciplinary productions work to conjure and regulate subjects through classificatory schemes, naming and normalizing social behaviours as social positions. Operating through what Foucault calls 'an anatomy of detail', 'disciplinary power' produces social identities (available for politicization because they are deployed for purposes of political regulation) which cross-cut juridical identities based on abstract right. Thus, for example, the welfare state's production of welfare subjects—themselves subdivided through the socially regulated categories of motherhood, disability, race, age, and so forth—potentially produce political identity through these categories, produce identities *as* these categories.

In this story, the always imminent but increasingly politically manifest failure of liberal universalism to the universal—the transparent fiction of state universality—combines with the increasing individuation of social subjects through capitalist disinterments and disciplinary productions. Together, they breed the emergence of politicized identity, rooted in disciplinary productions but oriented by liberal discourse toward protest against exclusion from a discursive formation of universal justice. This production, however, is not linear or even, but highly contradictory: while the terms of liberalism are part of the ground of production of a politicized identity which reiterates yet exceeds these terms, liberal discourse itself also continuously recolonizes political identity *as* political interest—a conversion which recasts politicized identity's substantive and often deconstructive cultural claims and critiques as generic claims of particularism endemic to universalist political culture. Similarly, disciplinary power manages liberalism's production of politicized subjectivity by neutralizing identity through normalizing practices. As liberal discourse converts political identity into essentialized private interest, disciplinary power converts interest into normativized social identity manageable by regulatory regimes. Thus, disciplinary power politically neutralizes entitlement claims generated by liberal individuation, while liberalism politically neutralizes rights claims generated by disciplinary identities.

In addition to the formations of identity which may be the complex effects of disciplinary and liberal modalities of power, I want to suggest one other historical strand relevant to the production of politicized identity, this one hewn more specifically to developments in recent political culture. Although sanguine to varying degrees about the phenomenon they are describing, many on the European and North American Left have argued that identity politics emerges from the demise of class politics attendant upon post-Fordism or pursuant to May 1968. Without judging the precise relationship between the breakup of class politics and the proliferation of other sites of political identification, I want to refigure this claim by suggesting that what we have come to call identity politics is partly dependent upon the demise of a *critique* of capitalism and of bourgeois cultural and economic values.[9] In a reading which links the new identity claims to a certain relegitimation of capitalism, identity politics concerned with race, sexuality, and gender will appear not as a supplement to class politics, not as an expansion of Left categories of oppression and emancipation, not as an enriching complexification of progressive formulations of power and persons—*all of which they also are*—but as tethered to a formulation of justice which reinscribes a bourgeois (masculinist) ideal as its measure. If it is this ideal which signifies educational and vocational opportunity, upward mobility, relative protection against arbitrary violence, and reward in proportion to effort, and if it is this ideal against which many of the exclusions and privations of people of colour, gays and lesbians, and women are articulated, then the political purchase of contemporary American identity politics would seem to be achieved in part *through* a certain renaturalization of capitalism which can be said to have marked progressive discourse since the 1970s. What this also suggests is that identity politics may be partly configured by a peculiarly shaped and peculiarly disguised form of class resentment, a resentment which is displaced onto discourses of injustice other than class, but a resentment, like all resentments, which retains the real or imagined holdings of its reviled subject as objects of desire. In other words, the enunciation of politicized identities through race, gender, and sexuality may require—rather than incidentally produce—a limited identification through class, and may specifically abjure a critique of class power and class norms precisely insofar as these identities are established *vis-à-vis* a bourgeois norm of social acceptance, legal protection, and relative material comfort. Yet when not only economic stratification but other injuries to the human body and psyche enacted by capitalism—alienation, commodification, exploitation, displacement, disintegration of sustaining albeit contradictory social forms such as families and neighbourhoods—when these are discursively normalized and thus depoliticized, other markers of social difference may come to bear an inordinate weight, indeed, all the weight of the sufferings

455

produced by capitalism in addition to that attributable to the explicitly politicized marking.[10]

If there is one class which articulates and even politicizes itself in late modern US life, it is that which gives itself the name of the 'middle class'. But the foregoing suggests that this is not a reactionary identity in the sense, for example, that 'white' or 'straight' are in contemporary political discourse. Rather, it is an articulation by the figure of the class which represents, indeed depends upon, the naturalization rather than the politicization of capitalism, the denial of capitalism's power effects in ordering social life, and the representation of the ideal of capitalism to provide the good life for all. Poised between the rich and poor, feeling itself to be protected from the encroachments of neither, the phantasmatic middle class signifies the natural and the good between, on one side, the decadent or the corrupt and, on the other, the aberrant or the decaying. It is a conservative identity in the sense that it semiotically refers back to a phantasmatic past, an idyllic, unfettered, and uncorrupted historical moment (implicitly located around 1955) when life was good again—housing was affordable, men supported families on single incomes, drugs were confined to urban ghettos. But it is not a reactionary identity in the sense of reacting to an insurgent politicized identity from below: rather, it precisely embodies the ideal to which non-class identities refer for proof of their exclusion or injury: homosexuals who lack the protections of marriage, guarantees of child custody or job security, and freedom from harassment; single women who are strained and impoverished by trying to raise children and hold paid jobs simultaneously; people of colour disproportionately affected by unemployment, punishing urban housing costs, inadequate health care programmes, and disproportionately subjected to unwarranted harassment and violence, figured as criminals, ignored by cab drivers. The point is not that these privations are trivial but that, without recourse to the white, masculine, middle-class ideal, politicized identities would forfeit a good deal of their claims to injury and exclusion, their claims to the political significance of their difference. If they thus require this ideal for the potency and poignancy of their political claims, we might ask to what extent a critique of capitalism is foreclosed by the current configuration of oppositional politics, and not simply by the 'loss of the socialist alternative' or the ostensible 'triumph of liberalism' in the global order. In contrast with the Marxist critique of a social whole and Marxist vision of total transformation, to what extent do identity politics require a standard internal to existing society against which to pitch their claims, a standard which not only preserves capitalism from critique but sustains the invisibility and inarticulateness of class, not accidentally, but endemically? Could we have stumbled upon one reason why class is invariably named but rarely theorized or developed in the multiculturalist mantra, 'race, class, gender, sexuality'?

II

The story of the emergence of contemporary identity politics could be told in many other ways—as the development of 'new social antagonisms' rooted in consumer capitalism's commodification of all spheres of social life, as the relentless denaturalization of all social relations occasioned by the fabrications and border violations of postmodern technologies and cultural productions, as a form of political consciousness precipitated by the black civil rights movement in the United States.[11] I have told the story this way in order to emphasize the *discursive political context* of its emergence, its disciplinary, capitalist, and liberal parentage, and this in order to comprehend politicized identity's genealogical structure as consisting of and not only opposing these very modalities of political power. Indeed, if the ostensibly oppositional character of identity politics also renders it something of the 'illegitimate offspring' of liberal, capitalist, disciplinary discourses, its absent fathers are not, as Donna Haraway suggests, 'inessential', but installed in the very structure of *desire* fuelling identity-based political claims: the psyche of the bastard child is hardly independent of its family of origin.[12] And if we are interested in developing the contestatory, subversive, potentially transformative elements of identity-based political claims, we need to know the implications of the particular genealogy and production conditions of identity's desire for recognition. We need to be able to ask: given what produced it, given what shapes and suffuses it, what does politicized identity want?

We might profitably begin these investigations with a reflection on their curious elision by the philosopher who also frames them, Michel Foucault. For Foucault, the constraints of emancipatory politics in late modern democracy pertain both to the ubiquity and to the pervasiveness of power—the impossibility of eschewing power in human affairs—as well as to the ways in which subjects and practices are always at risk of being resubordinated through the discourses naming and politicizing them. Best known for his formulation of this dual problem in the domain of sexual liberation, Foucault offers a more generic theoretical account in his discussion of the disinterment of the 'insurrectionary knowledges', of marginalized populations and practices:

> Is the relation of forces today still such as to allow these disinterred knowledges some kind of autonomous life? Can they be isolated by these means from every subjugating relationship? What force do they have taken in themselves? . . . Is it not perhaps the case that these fragments of genealogies are no sooner brought to light, that the particular elements of the knowledge that one seeks to disinter are no sooner accredited and put into circulation, than they run the risk of re-codification, re-colonisation? In fact, those unitary discourses which first disqualified and then ignored them when they made their appearance, are it seems, quite ready now to annex them, to take them back within the fold of their own discourse and to invest them with everything this implies in terms of their effects of knowledge and power. And if we want to protect these only lately liberated fragments, are we not in danger of ourselves constructing, with our own hands, that unitary discourse . . . ?[13]

Foucault's caution about the annexing, colonizing effects of invariably unifying discourses is an important one. But the question of the emancipatory orientation of historically subordinated discourse is not limited to the risk of co-optation or resubordination by extant or newly formed unitary discourses—whether those of humanism on one side, or of cultural studies, multiculturalism, subaltern studies, and minority discourse on the other. Nor is it reducible to what has always struck me as an unexamined Frankfurt School strain in Foucault, the extent to which the Foucauldian subject, originally desirous of freedom, comes to will its own domination—or, in Foucault's rubric, becomes a good disciplinary subject. Rather, I think that for Foucault, insofar as power always produces resistance, even the disciplinary subject is perversely capable of resistance and, in practising it, practices freedom. Discernible here is the basis of a curious optimism, even volunteerism in Foucault, namely his oddly physicalist and insistently non-psychic account of power, practices, and subject-formation. His removal of the 'will to power' from Nietzsche's complex psychology of need, frustration, impotence, and compensatory deeds is what permits

Foucault to feature resistance as always possible and as equivalent to practising freedom. In an interview with Paul Rabinow, Foucault muses:

I do not think that it is possible to say that one thing is of the order of 'liberation' and another is of the order of 'oppression.' ... No matter how terrifying a given system may be, there always remain the possibilities of resistance, disobedience, and oppositional groupings.

On the other hand, I do not think that there is anything that is functionally ... absolutely liberating. Liberty is a *practice*. ... The liberty of men is never assured by the institutions and laws that are intended to guarantee them. ... Not because they are ambiguous, but simply because 'liberty' is what must be exercised. ... The guarantee of freedom is freedom.[14]

My quarrel here is not with Foucault's valuable insistence upon freedom as a practice, but with his distinct lack of attention to what might constitute, negate or redirect the desire for freedom.[15] Notwithstanding his critique of the repressive hypothesis and postulation of the subject as an effect of power, Foucault seems tacitly to assume the givenness and resilience of the desire for freedom, a givenness that arises consequent to his implicit conflation of the will to power in resistance with a will to freedom. Thus, Foucault's confidence about the possibilities of 'practising' or 'exercising' liberty resides in a quasi-empirical concern with the relative *capacity* or space for action in the context of certain regimes of domination. But whether or not resistance is possible is a different question from what its aim is, what it is for, and especially whether or not it resubjugates the resisting subject. Foucault's rejection of psychoanalysis and his arrested reading of Nietzsche (his utter eclipse of Nietzsche's diagnosis of the culture of modernity as the triumph of 'slave morality') combine to locate the problem of freedom for Foucault as one of domain and discourse, rather than the problem of 'will' that it is for Nietzsche. Indeed, what requires for its answer a profoundly more psychological Nietzsche than the one Foucault embraces is not a question about when or where the practice of freedom is possible but a question about *the direction of the will to power*, a will which potentially, but only potentially, animates a desire for freedom. Especially for the Nietzsche of *The Genealogy of Morals*, the modern subject does not simply cease to desire freedom, as is the case with Foucault's disciplinary subject, but, much more problematically, loathes freedom.[16] Let us now consider why.

459

III

Contemporary politicized identity contests the terms of liberal discourse insofar as it challenges liberalism's universal 'we' as a strategic fiction of historically hegemonic groups and asserts liberalism's 'I' as social—both relational and constructed by power—rather than contingent, private, or autarkic. Yet it reiterates the terms of liberal discourse insofar as it posits a sovereign and unified 'I' that is disenfranchised by an exclusive 'we'. Indeed, I have suggested that politicized identity emerges and obtains its unifying coherence through the politicization of *exclusion* from an ostensible universal, as a protest against exclusion, a protest premised on the fiction of an inclusive/universal community, a protest which reinstalls the humanist ideal—and a specific white, middle-class, masculinist expression of this ideal—insofar as it premises itself upon exclusion from it. Put the other way around, politicized identities generated out of liberal, disciplinary societies, insofar as they are premised on exclusion from a universal ideal, require that ideal, as well as their exclusion from it, for their own perpetuity as identities.[17]

Politicized identity is also potentially reiterative of regulatory, disciplinary society in its configuration of a disciplinary subject. It is both produced by and potentially accelerates the production of that aspect of disciplinary society which 'ceaselessly characterizes, classifies, and specializes', which works through 'surveillance, continuous registration, perpetual assessment, and classification', through a social machinery 'that is both immense and minute'.[18] A recent example from the world of local politics makes clear politicized identity's imbrication in disciplinary power, as well as the way in which, as Foucault reminds us, disciplinary power 'infiltrates' rather than replaces liberal juridical modalities.[19] Last year the city council of my town reviewed an ordinance, devised and promulgated by a broad coalition of identity-based political groups, which aimed to ban discrimination in employment, housing, and public accommodations on the basis of 'sexual orientation, transsexuality, age, height, weight, personal appearance, physical characteristics, race, color, creed, religion, national origin, ancestry, disability, marital status, sex or gender'.[20] Here is a perfect instance of the universal juridical ideal of liberalism and the normalizing principle of disciplinary regimes conjoined and taken up within the discourse of politicized identity. This ordinance—variously called the 'purple hair ordinance' or the 'ugly ordinance' by state and national news media—aims to count every difference as no difference, as part of the seamless whole, but also to count every potentially subversive rejection of culturally enforced norms as themselves normal, as normalizable, and as normativizable through law. Indeed, through the definitional, procedural, and remedial sections of this ordinance (for instance, 'sexual orientation shall mean known or assumed homosexuality, heterosexuality, or bisexuality') persons are reduced to observable social attributes and practices; these are defined empirically, positivistically, as if their existence were intrinsic and factual, rather than effects of discursive and institutional power; and these positivist definitions of persons as their attributes and practices are written into law, ensuring that persons describable according to them will now become regulated through them. Bentham could not have done it better. Indeed, here is a perfect instance of how the language of recognition becomes the language of unfreedom, how articulation in language, in the context of liberal and disciplinary discourse, becomes a vehicle of subordination through individualization, normalization, and regulation, even as it strives to produce visibility and acceptance. Here, also, is a perfect instance of the way in which differences that are the effects of social power are neutralized through their articulation as attributes and their circulation through liberal administrative discourse: What do we make of a document which renders as juridical equivalents the denial of employment to an African-American, an obese man, and a white, middle-class youth festooned with tattoos and fuchsia hair?

What I want to consider, though, is why this strikingly unemancipatory political project emerges from a potentially more radical critique of liberal juridical and disciplinary modalities of power. For this ordinance, I want to suggest, is not simply misguided in its complicity with the rationalizing and disciplinary elements of late modern culture; it is not simply naive with regard to the regulatory apparatus within which it operates. Rather, it is symptomatic of a feature of politicized identity's *desire* within liberal-bureaucratic regimes, its foreclosure of its own freedom, its impulse to inscribe in the law and in other political registers its historical and present pain rather than to conjure an imagined future of power to make itself. To see what this symptom is a symptom of, we need to return once more to a schematic consideration of liberalism, this time in order to read it through Nietzsche's account of the complex logics of *ressentiment*.

461

IV

Liberalism contains from its inception a generalized incitement to what Nietzsche terms *ressentiment,* the moralizing revenge of the powerless, 'the triumph of the weak as weak'.[21] This incitement to *ressentiment* inheres in two related constitutive paradoxes of liberalism: that between individual liberty and social egalitarianism, a paradox which produces failure turned to recrimination by the subordinated, and guilt turned to resentment by the 'successful'; and that between the individualism that legitimates liberalism and the cultural homogeneity required by its commitment to political universality, a paradox which stimulates the articulation of politically significant differences on the one hand and the suppression of them on the other, and which offers a form of articulation that presses against the limits of universalist discourse even while that which is being articulated seeks to be harboured within—included —in the terms of that universalism.

Premissing itself on the natural equality of human beings, liberalism makes a political promise of universal individual freedom, in order to arrive at social equality, or achieve a civilized retrieval of the equality postulated in the state of nature. It is the tension between the promises of individualistic liberty and the requisites of equality that yields *ressentiment* in one of two directions, depending on the way in which the paradox is brokered. A strong commitment to freedom vitiates the fulfilment of the equality promise and breeds *ressentiment* as welfare-state liberalism—attenuations of the unmitigated licence of the rich and powerful on behalf of the 'disadvantaged'. Conversely, a strong commitment to equality, requiring heavy state interventionism and economic redistribution, attenuates the commitment to freedom and breeds *ressentiment* expressed as conservative antistatism, racism, charges of reverse racism, and so forth.

However, it is not only the tension between freedom and equality but the presumption of the self-reliant and self-made capacities of liberal subjects, conjoined with their unavowed dependence on and construction by a variety of social relations and forces, which makes *all* liberal subjects, and not only markedly disenfranchised ones, vulnerable to *ressentiment*: it is their situatedness within power, their production by power, and liberal discourse's denial of this situatedness and production, which casts the liberal subject into failure, the failure to make itself in the context of a discourse in which its self-making is assumed, indeed, is its assumed nature. This failure, which Nietzsche calls suffering, must either find a reason within itself (which redoubles the failure) or a site of external blame upon which to avenge its hurt, and redistribute its pain. Here is Nietzsche's account of this moment in the production of *ressentiment*:

> For every sufferer instinctively seeks a cause for his suffering, more exactly, an agent; still more specifically a *guilty* agent who is susceptible to suffering—in short, some living thing upon which he can on some pretext or other, vent his affects, actually or in effigy.... This ... constitutes the actual physiological cause of *ressentiment*, vengefulness, and the like: a desire to deaden pain by means of affects ... to deaden, by means of a more violent emotion of any kind, a tormenting, secret pain that is becoming unendurable, and to drive it out of consciousness at least for the moment: for that one requires an affect, as savage an affect as possible, and, in order to excite that, any pretext at all.[22]

Ressentiment in this context is a triple achievement: it produces an affect (rage, righteousness) which overwhelms the hurt; it produces a culprit responsible for the hurt; and it produces a site of revenge to displace the hurt (a place to inflict hurt as the sufferer has been hurt). Together these operations both ameliorate (in Nietzsche's terms, 'anaesthetize') and externalize what is otherwise 'unendurable'.

Now, what I want to suggest is that in a culture already streaked with the pathos of *ressentiment* for these reasons, there are several characteristics of late modern post-industrial societies which accelerate and expand the conditions of its production. My listing will necessarily be highly schematic: first, the phenomenon William Connolly names 'increased global contingency' combines with the expanding pervasiveness and complexity of domination by capital and bureaucratic state and social networks to create an unparalleled individual powerlessness over the fate and direction of one's own life, intensifying the experiences of impotence, dependence, and gratitude inherent in liberal capitalist orders and constitutive of *ressentiment*.[23] Second, the steady desacralization of all regions of life—what Weber called disenchantment, what Nietzsche called the death of God—would seem to add yet another reversal to Nietzsche's genealogy of *ressentiment* as perpetually available to 'alternation of direction'. In Nietzsche's account, the ascetic priest deployed notions of 'guilt, sin, sinfulness, depravity and damnation' to 'direct the *ressentiment* of the less severely afflicted sternly back upon themselves . . . and in this way [exploited] the bad instincts of all sufferers for the purpose of self-discipline, self-surveillance, and self-overcoming'.[24] However, the desacralizing tendencies of late modernity undermine the efficacy of this deployment and turn suffering's need for exculpation back toward a site of external agency.[25] Third, the increased fragmentation, if not disintegration, of all forms of association until recently not organized by the commodities market—communities, churches, families—and the ubiquitousness of the classificatory, individuating schemes of disciplinary society, combine to produce an utterly *unrelieved* individual, one without insulation from the inevitable failure, entailed in liberalism's individualistic construction. In short, the characteristics of late modern secular society, in which individuals are buffeted and controlled by global configurations of disciplinary and capitalist power of extraordinary proportions, and are at the same time nakedly individuated, stripped of reprieve from relentless exposure and accountability for themselves, together add up to an incitement to *ressentiment* that might have stunned even the finest philosopher of its occasions and logics. Starkly accountable yet dramatically impotent, the late modern liberal subject quite literally seethes with *ressentiment*.

Enter politicized identity, now conceivable in part as both product of and 'reaction' to this condition, where 'reaction' acquires the meaning Nietzsche ascribed to it, namely as an effect of domination that reiterates impotence, a substitute for action, for power, for self-affirmation that reinscribes incapacity, powerlessness, and rejection. For Nietzsche, *ressentiment* itself is rooted in 'reaction'— the substitution of reasons, norms, and ethics for deeds—and suggests that not only moral systems but identities themselves take their bearings in this reaction. As Tracy Strong reads this element of Nietzsche's thought:

Identity . . . does not consist of an active component, but is reaction to something outside; action in itself, with its inevitable self-assertive qualities, must then become something evil, since it is identified with that against which one is reacting. The will to power of slave morality must constantly reassert that which gives definition to the slave: the pain he suffers by being in the world. Hence any attempt to escape that pain will merely result in the reaffirmation of painful structures.[26]

If *ressentiment*'s 'cause' is suffering, its 'creative deed' is the reworking of this pain into a negative form of action, the 'imaginary revenge' of what Nietzsche terms 'natures denied the true reaction, that of deeds'.[27] This revenge is achieved through the imposition of suffering 'on whatever does not feel wrath and displeasure as he does'[28] (accomplished especially through the production of guilt), through the establishment of suffering as the measure of social virtue, and through casting strength and good fortune ('privilege' as we say today) as self-recriminating, as its own indictment in a culture of suffering: 'it is disgraceful to be fortunate, there is too much misery.'[29]

But in its attempt to displace its suffering, identity structured by *ressentiment* at the same time becomes invested in its own subjection. This investment lies not only in its discovery of a site of blame for its hurt will, not only in its acquisition of recognition through its history of subjection (a recognition predicated on injury, now righteously revalued), but also in the satisfactions of revenge which ceaselessly re-enact even as they redistribute the injuries of marginalization and subordination in a liberal discursive order which alternately denies the very possibility of these things or blames those who experience them for their own condition. Identity politics structured by *ressentiment* reverses without subverting this blaming structure: it does not subject to critique the sovereign subject of accountability that liberal individualism presupposes, nor the economy of inclusion and exclusion that liberal universalism establishes. Thus, politicized identity which presents itself as a self-affirmation now appears as the opposite, as predicated on and requiring its sustained rejection by a 'hostile external world'.[30]

Insofar as what Nietzsche calls 'slave morality' produces identity in reaction to power, insofar as identity rooted in this reaction achieves its moral superiority by reproaching power and action themselves as evil, identity structured by this ethos becomes deeply invested in its own impotence, even while it seeks to assuage the pain of its powerlessness through its vengeful moralizing, through its wide distribution of suffering, through its reproach of power as such. Politicized identity, premissed on exclusion and fuelled by the humiliation and suffering imposed by its historically structured impotence in the context of a discourse of sovereign individuals, is as likely to seek generalized political paralysis, to feast on generalized political impotence, as it is to seek its own or collective liberation through empowerment. Indeed, it is more likely to punish and reproach—'punishment is what revenge calls itself; with a hypocritical lie it creates a good conscience for itself'— than to find venues of self-affirming action.[31]

But contemporary politicized identity's desire is not only shaped by the extent to which the sovereign will of the liberal subject, articulated ever more nakedly by disciplinary individuation and capitalist disinternments, is dominated by late twentieth-century configurations of political and economic powers. It is shaped as well by the contemporary problematic of history itself, by the late modern rupture of history as a narrative, history as ended because it has lost its end, a rupture which paradoxically produces an immeasurable heaviness to history. As the grim experience of reading *Discipline and Punish* makes clear, there is a sense in which the gravitational force of history is multiplied at precisely the moment that history's narrative coherence and objectivist foundation is refuted. As the problematic of power in history is resituated from subject positioning to subject construction, as power is seen to operate spatially, infiltrationally, 'microphysically', rather than only temporally—permeating every heretofore designated 'interior' *space* in social lives and individuals—as the erosion of historical metanarratives takes with them both laws of history and the futurity such laws purported to assure, as the presumed continuity of history is replaced with a sense of its violent, contingent, and ubiquitous *force*, history becomes that which has weight but no trajectory, mass but no coherence, force but no direction; it is war without ends or end. Thus, the extent to which 'dead generations weight like a nightmare on the brains of the living' is today unparalleled, even as history itself disintegrates as a coherent category or practice. We know ourselves to be saturated by history, we feel the extraordinary force of its determinations; we are also steeped in a discourse of its insignificance, and above all, we know that history will no longer (always already did not) act as our redeemer.

I raise the question of history because in thinking about late modern politicized identity's structuring by *ressentiment*, I have thus far focused on its foundation in the sufferings of a subordinated sovereign subject. But Nietzsche's account of the logic of *ressentiment* is also tethered to that feature of the will which is stricken by history, which rails against time itself, which cannot 'will backwards', which cannot exert its power over the past— either as a specific set of events or as time itself.

Willing liberates but what is it that puts even the liberator himself in fetters? 'It was'—that is the name of the will's gnashing of teeth and most secret melancholy. Powerless against what has been done, he is an angry spectator of all that is past. . . . He cannot break time and time's covetousness, that is the will's loneliest melancholy.[32]

Although Nietzsche appears here to be speaking of the will as such, Zarathustra's own relationship to the will as a 'redeemer of history' makes clear that this 'angry spectatorship' can, with great difficulty, be reworked as a perverse kind of mastery, a mastery that triumphs over the past by reducing its power, by remaking the present against the terms of the past—in short, by a project of self-transformation which arrays itself against its own genealogical consciousness. In contrast with the human ruin he sees everywhere around him—'fragments and limbs and dreadful accidents'—it is Zarathustra's own capacity to discern and to make a future which spares him from a rancorous sensibility, from crushing disappointment in the liberatory promise of his will:

The now and the past on earth—alas, my friends, that is what *I* find most unendurable; and I should not know how to live if I were not also a seer of that which must come. A seer, a willer, a creator, a future himself and a bridge to the future—and alas, also as it were, a cripple at this bridge: all this is Zarathustra.[33]

Nietzsche here discerns both the necessity and the near-impossibility—the extraordinary and fragile achievement—of formulating oneself as a creator of the future and a bridge to the future in order to appease the otherwise inevitable rancour of the will against time, in order to redeem the past by lifting the weight of it, by reducing the scope of its determinations. 'And how could I bear to be a man if man were not also a creator and guesser of riddles and redeemer of accidents?'[34]

Of course, Zarathustra's exceptionality in what he is willing to confront and bear, in his capacities to overcome in order to create, is Nietzsche's device for revealing us to ourselves. The ordinary will, steeped in the economy of slave morality, devises means 'to get rid of his melancholy and to mock his dungeon', means which reiterate the cause of the melancholy, which continually reinfect the narcissistic wound to its capaciousness inflicted by the past. 'Alas,' says Nietzsche, 'every prisoner becomes a fool; and the imprisoned will redeems himself foolishly.'[35] From this foolish redemption—foolish because it does not resolve the will's rancour but only makes a world in its image—is born the wrath of revenge:

'that which was' is the name of the stone [the will] cannot move. And so he moves stones out of wrath and displeasure, and he wreaks revenge on whatever does not feel wrath and displeasure, as he does. Thus the will, the liberator, took to hurting; and on all who can suffer he wreaks revenge for his inability to go backwards. This . . . is what *revenge* is: the will's ill will against time and its 'it was'.[36]

Revenge as a 'reaction', a substitute for the capacity to act, produces identity as both bound to the history which produced it and as a reproach to the present which embodies that history. The will that 'took to hurting' in its own impotence against its past becomes (in the form of an identity whose very existence is due to heightened consciousness of the immovability of its 'it was', its history of subordination) a will that makes not only a psychological but a political practice of revenge, a practice which reiterates the existence of an identity whose present past is one of insistently unredeemable injury. This past cannot be redeemed *unless* the identity ceases to be invested in it, and it cannot cease to be invested in it without giving up its identity as such, thus giving up its economy of avenging and at the same time perpetuating its hurt—'when he then stills the pain of the wound, he at the same time infects the wound . . .'[37]

In its emergence as a protest against marginalization or subordination, politicized identity thus becomes attached to its own exclusion, both because it is premissed on this exclusion for its very existence as identity, and because the formation of identity at the site of exclusion, as exclusion, augments or 'alters the direction of the suffering' entailed in subordination or marginalization, by finding a site of blame for it. But in so doing, it installs its pain over its unredeemed history in the very foundation of its political claim, in its demand for recognition as identity. In locating a site of blame for its powerlessness over its past, as a past of injury, a past as a hurt will, and locating a 'reason' for the 'unendurable pain' of social powerlessness in the present, it converts this reasoning into an ethicizing politics, a politics of recrimination that seeks to avenge the hurt even while it reaffirms it, discursively codifies it. Politicized identity thus enunciates itself, makes claims for itself, only by entrenching, restating, dramatizing, and inscribing its pain in politics, and can hold out no future—for itself or others—which triumphs over this pain. The loss of historical direction, and with it the loss of futurity characteristic of the late modern age, is thus homologically refigured in the structure of desire of the dominant political expression of the age—identity politics. In the same way, the generalized political impotence produced by the ubiquitous yet discontinuous networks of late modern political and economic power is reiterated in the investments of late modern democracy's primary oppositional political formations.

What might be entailed in transforming these investments in an effort to fashion a more radically democratic and emancipatory political culture? One avenue of exploration may lie in Nietzsche's counsel on the virtues of 'forgetting', for if identity structured in part by *ressentiment* resubjugates itself through its investment in its own pain, through its refusal to make itself in the present, memory is the house of this activity and this refusal. Yet erased histories and historical invisibility are themselves such integral elements of the pain inscribed in most subjugated identities that the counsel of forgetting, at least in its unreconstructed Nietzschean form, seems inappropriate, if not cruel.[38] Indeed, it is also possible that we have reached a pass where we ought to part with Nietzsche, whose skills as diagnostician usually reach the limits of their political efficacy in his privileging of individual character and capacity over the transformative possibilities of collective political invention, in his remove from the refigurative possibilities of political conversation or transformative cultural practices. For if I am right about the problematic of pain installed at the heart of many contemporary contradictory demands for political recognition, all that such pain may long for more than revenge is the chance to be heard into a certain reprieve, recognized into self-overcoming, incited into possibilities for triumphing over, and hence losing, itself. Our challenge, then, would be to configure a radically democratic political culture which can sustain such a project in its midst without being overtaken by it, a challenge which includes guarding against abetting the steady slide of political into therapeutic discourse, even as we acknowledge the elements of suffering and healing we might be negotiating.

What if it were possible to incite a slight shift in the character of political expression and political claims common to much politicized identity? What if we sought to supplant the language of 'I am'—with its defensive closure on identity, its insistence on the fixity of position, its equation of social with moral positioning—with the language of 'I want'? What if we were to rehabilitate the memory of desire within identificatory processes, the moment in desire—either 'to have' or 'to be'—prior to its wounding?[39] What if 'wanting to be' or 'wanting to have' were taken up as modes of political speech that could destabilize the formulation of identity as fixed position, as entrenchment by history, and as having necessary moral entailments, even as they affirm 'position' and 'history' as that which makes the speaking subject intelligible and locatable, as that which contributes to a hermeneutics for adjudicating desires? If every 'I am' is something of a resolution of desire into fixed and sovereign identity, then this project might involve not only learning to speak but to *read* 'I am' this way, as in motion, as temporal, as not-I, as deconstructable according to a genealogy of want rather than as fixed interests or experiences.[40] The subject understood as an effect of an (ongoing) genealogy of desire, including the social processes constitutive of, fulfilling, or frustrating desire, is in this way revealed as neither sovereign nor conclusive, even as it is affirmed as an 'I'. In short, if framed in the right political language, this deconstruction could be that which reopens a language and practice of futurity where Nietzsche saw it foreclosed by the logics of rancour and *ressentiment*.

Such a slight shift in the character of the political discourse of identity eschews the kinds of ahistorical or utopian turns against identity politics made by a nostalgic and broken humanist Left, as well as the reactionary and disingenuous assaults on politicized identity tendered by the Right. Rather than opposing or seeking to transcend identity investments, the replacement—even the admixture—of the language of 'being' with 'wanting' would seek to exploit politically a recovery of the more expansive moments in the genealogy of identity formation, a recovery of the moment prior to its own foreclosure against its want, prior to the point at which its sovereign subjectivity is established through such foreclosure and through eternal repetition of its pain. How might democratic discourse itself be invigorated by such a shift from ontological claims to these kinds of more expressly political ones, claims which, rather than dispensing blame for an unlivable present, inhabited the necessarily agonist theatre of discursively forging an alternative future?

Notes

1. 'The Local and the Global', in Anthony King (ed.), *Culture, Globalization, and the World System: Contemporary Conditions for the Representation of Identity* (Albany, NY: State University of New York Press, 1991), 24.
2. 'An identity is established in relation to a series of differences that have become socially recognized. These differences are essential to its being. If they did not coexist as differences, it would not exist in its distinctness and solidarity.... Identity requires difference in

order to be, and it converts difference into otherness in order to secure its own self-certainty.' William Connolly, *Identity/Difference: Democratic Negotiations of Political Paradox* (Ithaca, NY: Cornell University Press, 1991), 64.

I cite from Connolly rather than the more obvious Derrida because Connolly is exemplary of the effort *within* political theory to think about the political problem of identity working heuristically with its linguistic operation. I cite from Connolly, as well, because the present essay is in some ways an extension of a conversation begun at a 1991 American Political Science Association round-table discussion of his book. In that discussion, noting that Connolly identified late modernity as producing certain problems for identity but did not historicize politicized identity itself, I called for such an historicization. To the degree that the present essay is my own partial response to that call, it—as the notes make clear—is indebted to Connolly's book and that public occasion of its discussion.

A short list of others who have struggled to take politicized identity through and past the problem of political exclusion and political closure might include: Stuart Hall, Trinh T. Minh-ha, Homi Bhabha, Paul Gilroy, Aiwah Ong, Judith Butler, Gayatri Spivak, Anne Norton.

3. Locke's (1689) 'Letter Concerning Toleration' signals this development in intellectual history. The 300-year process of eliminating first the property qualification, and then race and gender qualifications in European and North American constitutional states heralds its formal political achievement.

4. 'On the Jewish Question', in R. Tucker (ed.), *The Marx–Engels Reader*, 2nd edn. (New York: Norton, 1974), 34.

5. John Locke, *Letter on Toleration*; John Stuart Mill, 'On Liberty'; George Kateb, 'Democratic Individuality and the Claims of Politics', *Political Theory* (Aug. 1984).

6. In 'On The Jewish Question', (see note 4 above) Marx argues, 'far from abolishing these *effective* differences [in civil society, the state] exists only so far as they are presupposed; it is conscious of being a political state and it manifests its universality only in *opposition* to these elements' (p. 33). See also Marx's *Critique of Hegel's Philosophy of Right*, ed. J. O'Malley (Cambridge: Cambridge University Press, 1970), 91, 116.

7. Ernesto Laclau, 'Universalism, Particularism and the Question of Identity', *Identity in Question*, ed. J. Rajchman Routledge 1995. Laclau is here concerned not with the state but with the possibility of retaining a 'universal' in social movement politics where a critique of bourgeois humanist universalism has become quite central. Interestingly, Laclau's effort to preserve a universalist political ideal from this challenge entails making this ideal even more abstract, pulling it further away from any specific configuration or purpose

than the distance ordinarily managed by liberal discourse. Laclau's aim in voiding the universal completely of body and content is only partly to permit it to be more completely embracing of all the particulars; it is also intended to recognize the *strategic* value of the discourse of universality, the extent to which 'different groups compete to give their particular aims a temporary function of universal representation'. But how, if universal discourse may always be revealed to have this strategic function, can it also be taken seriously as a substantive value of democracy?

8. Jürgen Habermas's *Legitimation Crisis*, trans. T. McCarthy (Boston: Beacon, 1975) and James O'Connor's *Fiscal Crisis of the State* (New York: St. Martin's Press, 1973) remain two of the most compelling narratives of this development. Also informing this claim are Max Weber's discussion of bureaucracy and rationalization in *Economy and Society* and Sheldon Wolin's discussion of the 'mega-state' in *The Presence of the Past*, as well as the researches of Claus Offe, Bob Jessop, and Fred Block.

9. To be fully persuasive, this claim would have to reckon with the ways in which the articulation of African-American, feminist, queer or Native American 'values' and cultural styles have figured centrally in many contemporary political projects. It would have to encounter the ways in which the critique of cultural assimilation which I alluded to in this essay has been a critical dimension of identity politics. Space prohibits such a reckoning, but I think its terms would be those of capitalism and style, economics and culture, counterhegemonic projects and the politics of resistance.

10. It is, of course, also the abstraction of politicized identity from political economy that produces the failure of politicized identities to encompass and unify their 'members'. Not only striated in a formal sense by class, but also divided by the extent to which the suffering entailed, for example, in gender and racial subordination can be substantially offset by economic privilege, insistent definitions of Black, or Queer, or Woman sustain the same kind of exclusions and policing previously enacted by the tacitly White, male, heterosexual figure of the 'working class'.

11. See Ernesto Laclau and Chantal Mouffe, *Hegemony and Socialist Strategy* (London: Verso, 1985), 161; Scott Lash and John Urry, *The End of Organized Capitalism* (Madison: University of Wisconsin, 1987), ch. 9; David Harvey, *The Condition of Postmodernity* (Oxford: Blackwell, 1989), ch. 26; Bernice Johnson Reagon, 'Coalition Politics: Turning the Century', in Barbara Smith (ed.), *Home Girls: A Black Feminist Anthology* (New York: Kitchen Table: Woman of Color Press, 1983), 362.

12. In 'A Manifesto for Cyborgs', in L. Nicholson (ed.), *Feminism/Postmodernism* (New York: Routledge, 1990), Donna Haraway writes:

'cyborgs are the illegitimate offspring of militarism and patriarchal capitalism, not to mention state socialism. But illegitimate offspring are often exceedingly unfaithful to their origins. Their fathers, after all, are inessential' (p. 193).

13. 'Two Lectures', in *Power/Knowledge*, ed. Colin Gordon (New York: Patheon, 1980), 86.

14. 'Space, Knowledge, and Power', interview with Paul Rabinow in *The Foucault Reader*, ed. Paul Rabinow (New York: Pantheon, 1984), 245.

15. John Rajchman insists that Foucault's philosophy *is* 'the endless question of freedom' (p. 124), but Rajchman, too, eschews the question of desire in his account of Foucault's freedom as the 'motor and principle of his skepticism: the endless questioning of constituted experience' (p. 7). *Michael Foucault: The Freedom of Philosophy* (New York: Columbia University Press, 1985).

16. 'This instinct for freedom forcibly made latent—this instinct for freedom pushed back and repressed, incarcerated within and finally able to discharge and vent itself only on itself'; Friedrich Nietzsche, *The Genealogy of Morals*, trans. W. Kaufmann and P. J. Hollindale (New York: Vintage, 1969), 87.

17. As Connolly argues, politicized identity also reiterates the structure of liberalism in its configuration of a sovereign, unified, accountable individual. Connolly urges, although it is not clear what would motivate identity's transformed orientation, a different configuration of identity—one which understood itself as contingent, relational, contestatory and social. See *Identity/Difference*, esp. 171–84.

18. Michel Foucault, *Discipline and Punish*, trans. A. Sheridan (New York: Vintage, 1979), 209, 212.

19. Ibid. 206.

20. From a draft of 'An Ordinance of the City of Santa Cruz Adding Chapter 9.83 to the Santa Cruz Municipal Code Pertaining to the Prohibition of Discrimination'.

21. A number of political theorists have advanced this argument. For a cogent account, see pp. 21–7 of Connolly, *Identity/Difference*.

22. Nietzsche, *Genealogy Morals*, 127.

23. Connolly, *Identity/Difference*, 24–26.

24. Ibid. 128.

25. A striking example of this is the way that contemporary natural disasters, such as the 1989 earthquake in California or the 1992 hurricane in Florida and Hawaii, produced popular and media discourses about relevant state and federal agencies (e.g., the Federal Emergency Management Agency (FEMA)), that come close to displacing onto the agencies themselves responsibility for the suffering of the victims.

26. Tracy Strong, *Friedrich Nietzsche and the Politics of Transfiguration*, expanded edn. (Berkeley: University of California, 1988), 242.

27. *Genealogy of Morals*, 36.
28. *Thus Spoke Zarathustra*, in *The Portable Nietzsche*, ed. W. Kaufmann (New York: Penguin, 1954), 252.
29. *Genealogy of Morals*, 123, 124.
30. Ibid. 34.
31. *Zarathustra*, 252.
32. Ibid. 251.
33. Ibid. 250–251.
34. Ibid. 251.
35. Ibid.
36. Ibid. 252.
37. *Genealogy of Morals*, 126. In what could easily characterize the rancorous quality of many contemporary institutions and gatherings—academic, political, cultural—in which politicized identity is strongly and permissibly at play, Nietzsche offers an elaborate account of this replacement of pain with a 'more violent emotion' which is the stock in trade of 'the suffering':

   'The suffering are one and all dreadfully eager and inventive in discovering occasions for painful affects; they enjoy being mistrustful and dwelling on nasty deeds and imaginary slights; they scour the entrails of their past and present for obscure and questionable occurrences that offer them the opportunity to revel in tormenting suspicions and to intoxicate themselves with the poison of their own malice: they tear open their oldest wounds, they bleed from long-healed scars, they make evil-doers out of their friends, wives, children, and whoever else stands closest to them. 'I suffer: someone must be to blame for it'—thus thinks every sickly sheep.' (*Genealogy of Morals*, 127)
38. This point has been made by many, but for a recent, quite powerful phenomenological exploration of the relationship between historical erasure and lived identity, see Patricia Williams, *The Alchemy of Race and Rights* (Cambridge, Mass.: Harvard University Press, 1991).
39. Jesse Jackson's 1988 'Keep Hope Alive' presidential campaign strikes me as having sought to configure the relationship between injury, identity, and desire in just this way and to have succeeded in forging a 'Rainbow Coalition' *because* of the idiom of futurity it employed—want, hope, desires, dreams—among those whose modality during the 1980s had often been rancorous.
40. In Trinh T. Minh-ha's formulation, 'to seek is to lose, for seeking presupposes a separation between the seeker and the sought, the continuing me and the changes it undergoes'. 'Not You/Like You: Post-Colonial Women and the Interlocking Questions of Identity and Difference', *Inscriptions*, 3–4 (1988): 72.

19 Dealing With Difference: A Politics of Ideas or a Politics of Presence?

Anne Phillips

In the post-communist world of the 1980s and 1990s, liberalism and liberal democracy have achieved an impressive ascendancy, and can more plausibly present themselves as the only legitimate bases for equality, justice or democracy. Critics, of course, remain, but the grounds of complaint have shifted considerably. For many years, the central arguments against liberalism fell into three broad categories: that the liberal emphasis on individual freedoms and rights reflected a self-protective and competitive egotism that refused any wider community; that the liberal focus on 'merely' political equalities ignored or even encouraged gross inequalities in social and economic life; and that the liberal consolidation of representative democracy reduced the importance of more active citizen participation. None of these complaints has disappeared, but each has been reformulated in terms of diversity and difference. Feminist theorists, in particular, have identified liberalism with an abstract individualism that ignores its own gendered content, and many have criticized the homogenizing ideals of equality that require us to be or become the same.[1] Accusations of gender-blindness and race- or ethnicity-blindness have added weight to older complaints that liberalism is blind to class. At a moment when most political theorists have situated themselves more firmly in the liberal tradition, liberalism is extensively criticized for erasing diversity and difference.

From the standpoint of that much-maligned visitor from Mars (whose technical brilliance in negotiating the journey always combines with an astonishing ignorance of political ideas) it might

Reprinted by permission from *Constellations*, 1/1 (1994), 74–91. Copyright © Blackwell Publishers Ltd (1994). The work for this article was made possible by a Social Science Research Fellowship from the Nuffield Foundation, 1992–3, and the first version was presented as 'Democracy and Difference: Changing Boundaries of the Political'. Annual Conference for the Study of Political Thought at Yale University, New Haven, Conn., Apr. 1993.

well appear that liberals never thought about difference. Left at such a level of generality, the accusation is distinctly odd, for notions of diversity and difference have been central to liberalism from its inception and to liberal democracy throughout its formation. What gave the original impetus to liberalism was the perception that neither nature nor tradition guaranteed political order, and that the very equality of what we now see as male subjects increased the potential diversity and conflict. Hence the search for a contractual basis for political authority that would bind these different individuals into a coherent whole; hence the concern with rights and autonomies that would allow them to pursue part of their lives under their own steam. In these and subsequent developments, difference remained politically significant and theoretically important: a driving force, indeed, in the separation between public and private affairs.

The defining characteristics of liberal democracy, as Robert Dahl among others has clarified,[2] are also grounded in the heterogeneity of the societies that gave it birth. It was the diversity of the citizenry, as much as its absolute size, that made the earlier (more consensual) practices of Athenian democracy so inappropriate to the modern world. Lacking any half-credible basis for seeing citizens as united in their goals, theorists of liberal democracy took issue with the homogenizing presumptions of a common good or common purpose, and made diversity a central organizing theme. John Stuart Mill's famous vacillations over democracy derived from a double sense of democracy as both impetus and threat to diversity: something that breaks the hold of any single notion of the good life, but can also encourage a deadening conformity. In more straightforwardly confident vein, Georg Kateb has presented constitutional and representative democracy as that system *par excellence* that encourages and disseminates diversity. The procedures of electoral competition do not merely chasten and circumscribe the powers of government. By promoting a more sceptical attitude towards the basis on which competing claims are resolved, they also cultivate 'a general tolerance of, and even affection for diversity: diversity in itself, and diversity as the source of regulated contest and competition.'[3]

Difference is not something we have only just noticed. What we can more usefully say is that difference has been perceived in an overly cerebral fashion as differences in opinions and beliefs, and that the resulting emphasis on what I will call a politics of ideas has proved inadequate to the problems of political exclusion. The diversity most liberals have in mind is a diversity of beliefs, opinions, preferences, and goals, all of which may stem from the variety of experience, but are considered as in principle detachable from this. Even the notion of interests, which seems most thoroughly grounded in differential material conditions, lends itself to at least semi-detachment. The preference for higher taxes on those with higher incomes may be stronger among those with little money, especially if they believe the proceeds will finance public provision of educational or health services that would be otherwise beyond their reach. But support for higher taxation and better public provision is not restricted to those who most directly benefit: political preferences are influenced by material circumstances without being reducible to these. The interests of pensioners or the long-term unemployed can then be championed by those who are neither retired nor out of work: the interests of geographical localities can be represented by people who no longer live in the area; the interests of mothers with young children can be represented by childless men.

One consequence for democracy is that what is to be represented then takes priority over who does the representation. Issues of political presence are largely discounted, for when difference is considered in terms of intellectual diversity, it does not much matter who represents the range of ideas. One person may easily stand in for another; there is no additional requirement for the representatives to 'mirror' the characteristics of the person or people represented. What concerns us in the choice of representative is a congruity of political beliefs and ideals, combined perhaps with a superior ability to articulate and register opinions. The quality of the democracy is guaranteed by the extension of suffrage to all adults, each of whom contributes his or her vote to the opinions that gain public weight. Stripped of any pre-democratic authority, the role of the politician is to carry a message. The messages will vary, but it hardly matters if the messengers are the same. (Those who believe that men have a monopoly on the political skills of articulating policies and ideas will not be surprised that most messengers are men.)

The notion of representation as primarily a matter of ideas has not, of course, gone unchallenged. In 1789, a group of French-women laid claim to a place in the Estates General in the following terms:

Just as a nobleman cannot represent a plebeian and the latter cannot represent a nobleman, so a man, no matter how honest he may be, cannot represent a woman. Between the representatives and the represented there must be an absolute identity of interests.[4]

Shared experience here takes precedence over shared ideas: more precisely, no amount of thought or sympathy, no matter how careful or honest, can jump the barriers of experience. This assertion came, however, at a very particular point in the development of democracy, when the challenge to privilege momentarily centred around questioning which 'estates' were entitled to representation. Subsequent notions of citizenship seemed to make this an anachronism, the last gasp of a feudal tradition. Hard fought extensions of suffrage combined with the evolution of political parties as the basic medium of representation to encourage an alternative notion of politics as a battleground for contested ideas.

The socialist tradition is of interest here, not only because it threw up a politics of pressing for the 'representation of labour' (which seems to echo the earlier idea of representing different estates) but because it has been persistently troubled by tensions between a politics of ideas and an alternative politics of presence. Those involved in socialist parties often argued fiercely over the relationship between intellectuals and the 'authentically' working class, some feeling that a socialist politics should privilege the voices and presence of workers, others that class identities should signify less than adherence to socialist ideas. In *What Is to Be Done*, Lenin offered one classic refutation of the politics of presence. Stressing the multiplicity of arenas within which the power of capital was exerted, he argued the limits of an experience confined to any one of these, and the overriding importance of strategic links between one set of struggles and another. This privileged the all-seeing intellectual (who might in principle originate from any class position or faction), the political activist who could look beyond each specific struggle or campaign to its wider connections and ramifications, and fit the various pieces of the jigsaw together. When socialist feminists challenged such views in the 1970s, one of the things they pointed out was that they denied legitimacy to women's self-understandings; another was that they presumed an objectivity on the part of these activists that raised them to a God-like level. As Sheila Rowbotham remarked in her critique of Leninist conceptions of the vanguard party, 'The Party is presented as soaring above all sectional concerns without providing any guarantees that this soaring will not be in fact an expression of the particular preoccupations of the group or groups with power within it'.[5] Part of what was at issue in the development of an autonomous women's movement was the arrogance of those who thought that ideas could be separated from presence.

In Hanna Pitkin's influential discussion of representation, she criticizes the mirror view as beginning and ending with who is present, setting to one side the far more important question of what the representatives actually do. 'Think of the legislature as a pictorial representation or a representative sample of the nation,' she argues, 'and you will almost inevitably concentrate on its composition rather than its activities.'[6] But looking back at her discussion from a distance of twenty-five years, what is notable is how she elides the mapping of ideas with the mapping of people, not really distinguishing between a representative sample that captures the range of ideas, the range of interests, or the range of socially significant groups. Her emphasis throughout is on the distinction between being and doing, and her arguments are directed as much against versions of proportional representation that would more adequately reflect the multiplicity of parties and opinion as against later preoccupations with representing excluded or marginalized groups. Questions of power and inequality do not figure largely in Pitkin's account. Such questions have become central to democratic debate today.

It is no part of my intention to disparage politics as a battleground for ideas. Much of the radicalizing impetus to democracy has centred around initiatives to make ideas more rather than less important, as in efforts to bind representatives more closely to the opinions they profess to hold, or in measures to reduce the backstage manipulations of pressure groups that disrupt the higher politics of ideas. But when the politics of ideas is taken in isolation from the politics of presence, it does not deal adequately with the experiences of those social groups who by virtue of their race or ethnicity or religion or gender have felt themselves excluded from the democratic process. Political exclusion is increasingly—I believe rightly—viewed in terms that can only be met by political presence, and much of this development has depended on a more complex understanding of the relationship between ideas and experience. The separation between who and what is to be represented, and the subordination of one to the other, relies on an understanding of ideas and interests as relatively unproblematic. It is as if the field of politics is already clearly demarcated, containing with it various clusters of preferences or ideas or concerns that exist independently of any process of formation. This is in stark contrast with the preoccupations that ran through the early years of the contemporary women's movement, when women talked of the difficulties in finding a voice, the way that dominant definitions of politics blocked out alternatives, or hegemonic culture controlled what could or could not be said. The emphasis then shifted from an objectively defined set of interests (that just needed more vigorous pursuit) to a more exploratory notion of possibilities so far silenced and ideas one had to struggle to express. In this later understanding of the processes that generate needs and concerns and ideas, it is harder to sustain the primacy of ideas over political presence. If it is simply a question of representing a given range of ideas and interests, it may not much matter who does the work of representation. But if the range of ideas has been curtailed by orthodoxies that rendered alternatives invisible, there will be no satisfactory solution short of changing the people who represent and develop the ideas.

The renewed concern over the relationship between ideas and experience also figures in recent arguments over the limits of tolerance in dealing with difference. The classically liberal treatment of difference allows for private spaces within which people can get on with their own chosen affairs and a public realm ordered around a set of minimum shared presumptions. But the relegation of difference to a private world of private variation has been experienced as an injunction to keep peculiarities a secret, and the shared presumptions that control the public world have proved less than even-handed in their treatment of different groups. The separation of church from state has long been considered the solution to the problems of religious difference, but it achieves this by requiring all religions to adopt a similarly self-denying ordinance that will limit the relevance of religious precepts to practices in the private sphere. This resolution is more amenable to some religions than to others; in particular, it is more acceptable to the heavily secularized forms of Christianity that became the norm in contemporary Europe. In similar vein, we might say that the relegation of homosexuality to a private affair between consenting adults helps reduce more overt forms of discrimination, but it achieves this at the expense of any more public disruption of a heterosexual norm. Private deviation is permitted, but not equal public worth.

Part of the dissatisfaction with liberalism's treatment of difference is the feeling that toleration is a poor substitute for recognition.[7] We only tolerate what we do not like or approve of (otherwise there is no need for toleration[8]), and yet where difference is bound up with identity, this is hard for the tolerated to accept. You can put up with people thinking you a harmless freak for your membership in the Flat Earth Society. You may even revel in people thinking you a dangerous lunatic for your belief in communist revolution. It is not so easy to live with mere tolerance of your perverted sexuality or your denial of femininity or your irrationally fundamentalist religion. Tolerance is perceived as non-egalitarian, resting in some way on a distinction between majority norms and minority deviance, and incorporating some implied preference for a particular way of life.[9] It is perhaps one of the tributes to democracy that people do not find tolerance satisfactory for long, and that the imperatives of democratic equality seem to press on further towards the recognition of equal worth. One reflection of this pressure has been the emerging school of thought that looks to 'democratic' rather than 'liberal' ways of dealing with diversity:[10] instead of treating difference as something that can flourish in the private domain, it turns to public manifestations in which differences can be confronted and (hopefully) resolved. Here, too, presence becomes crucial, for any public domain marked by the systematic absence of significant groups cannot even approach this resolution.

Once raised, the issues of presence are unlikely to go away: these are questions that must be addressed if democracies are to deliver on political equality. My concern in the rest of this paper is with what happens next, and in particular with the tensions that arise between ideas and political presence. In the caricatures of those most resistant to a politics of presence, it is frequently misrepresented as a kind of 'group-think': something that is necessarily separatist, necessarily corrosive of any wider community, and falsely presuming not only that one has to be a member of a particular group in order to understand or represent that group's interests, but that all members of the group in question will think along similar lines.[11] The caricature misses its mark. Faced, for example, with that 1789 claim that 'between the representatives and the represented there must be an absolute identity of interests', most contemporary theorists will shy away from the implications of an essential female subject, or an authentic black subject, that can be represented by any one of its kind. Far more dominant today is the notion of multiple identities or multiple 'subject positions', each of which is subject to political transformation and change. An attention to difference does not entail an essentialist understanding of identity, nor does it demand any wholesale rejection of the

481

politics of competing ideas. But then the very sophistication of contemporary theories of identity can paralyse development; the very distance people have travelled from the caricatures of their position can remove them from democracy as it currently exists. In both the theoretical and the movement-centred literature which I now go on to discuss, issues of difference have been construed within a robustly democratic future that bears little relationship to contemporary political life. One of the challenges of democracy is how to combine the insights from such discussion with prescriptions that can be made relevant to representative democracy as practised today.

DEMOCRACY AS PUBLIC CONTESTATION

Much of the contemporary literature on democracy and difference operates with notions of a more active and vigorous democracy that depends crucially on public debate. Rejecting both the false harmony that stamps out difference and the equally false essentialism that defines people through some single, authentic identity, many theorists look to a democracy which maximizes citizen participation, and requires us to engage and contest with one another. In a recent essay on feminism and democracy, Susan Mendus suggests that difference is the rationale for democracy, and that 'whereas traditional democratic theory tends to construe difference as an obstacle to the attainment of a truly democratic state, feminist theory should alert us to the possibility that difference is rather what necessitates the pursuit of democracy'.[12] In his work on multiculturalism, Charles Taylor calls for a politics of democratic empowerment as the way of dealing with demands for equal recognition without thereby entrenching people in fragmented identities.[13] In his discussion of the republican revival, Cass Sunstein argues for a deliberative democracy to which all citizens will have equal access, and where all perspectives can be equally addressed.[14]

All such arguments assume equality of access (without necessarily exploring the conditions that would deliver this result), and all differentiate themselves from merely majoritarian decision-making by anticipating some process of transformation and change. Where the classically liberal resolution of difference relies on a combination of private spaces and majority norms (these in turn established by majority vote), the democratic resolution of difference expects us to engage more directly with each other. We bring our differences to the public stage; we revise them through public debate. Major disagreements then surface between those who anticipate a full 'resolution' in some newly achieved public consensus, and those who see differences as contingent but never as 'difference' going away. The first position looks more utopian than the second, but both operate at a level of generality that barely touches on democracy as practised today.

Consider William Connolly's arguments in *Identity Difference*,[15] which are particularly interesting in that they say both what should happen and why it almost certainly won't. Here, a 'robust' politics of democratic engagement is presented as something that neither evades nor confirms difference: a politics that enables people to disturb settled conventions and expose settled identities. All identities are formed through difference—you know who you are through your difference from some other—and all identities are simultaneously threatened by the difference(s) of the other. There is always a danger that identities will be dogmatized into some naturalistic or unchanging essence, and always a danger that difference will generate destructive resentments and fears. What keeps these at bay is a politics of mutual challenge and disruption in which we are constantly reminded of the contingent nature of our identities. This politics depends in turn on the successful permeation of a 'culture of genealogy' which helps us to see our identities as ambiguous and contestable and contested. Democracy then appears as an exciting engagement with difference: the challenge of 'the other'; the disruption of certainties; the recognition of ambiguities within one's self as well as one's differences with others.

All this is tremendously refreshing, and in no way relies on a future transcendence of difference. But just at the point where he has achieved the philosophical resolution, Connolly backs off from claiming any immediate relevance for today. The confidence that enables people to dispense with settled identities or to accept the contingencies of fate may not be available to those suffering from economic inequality and political exclusion. Indeed, in an environment characterized by systematic inequality, the appeals to a robust democracy in which no one shelters behind accusations of the other could 'too readily be received as yet another attack on those already excluded from democratic politics'.[16]

One compelling attraction of democracy is that it enables anyone to engage in fundamental riddles of existence through participation in a public politics that periodically disturbs and denaturalizes elements governing the cultural unconscious. But these same characteristics can intensify the reactive demand to redogmatize conventional identities if a large minority of the society is already suffering under the severe burden of material deprivation and effective exclusion from the good life offered to a majority.[17]

Robust democracy then becomes possible only when economic inequalities are substantially reduced. My problem with this is not that it begs the question of how we might achieve such a precondition (we all have difficulties answering this) but that so much of what currently drives a politics of identity and difference is precisely the sense of deprivation and exclusion that Connolly sees as making such a politics so dangerous. Again, this is a point Connolly himself makes, noting that against the background of US neo-conservatism, any politics of identity and difference tends to fuel 'the energies of ressentiment and the dogmatization of identity'.[18] The philosophical resolution of democracy and difference remains largely that.[19]

DEMOCRACY INSIDE SOCIAL MOVEMENTS

The second context in which these discussions take place is as interventions into specific movements that have formed around the politics of race, gender, sexuality, and ethnicity. All these movements have involved a critique of the phoney essentialisms that disguised systematic difference and inequality; nearly all of them, however, have also generated their own essentialisms that at some point or other claimed a unified female or lesbian or black or some other experience. Thus feminists took issue with the gender amnesia that transformed man 'into a paradigm of humankind as such'[20] but, in the further explorations of sexual difference, they often insisted on a primary distinction between men and women that obscured further differences between women. Lesbian feminists took issue with the hegemonic controls of a heterosexual norm but, in the search for an affirming identity, they often constructed 'the' authentic lesbian who would not tolerate differences of sexual practice or political attitudes within the lesbian community.[21] Anti-racists took issue with the mythologies of nation that had rendered black people invisible but, in the subsequent racial dualism that focused so exclusively on differences between 'black' and 'white' that they tended to obscure the cultural and religious pluralism that characterizes many non-white minorities.[22]

The problems of essentialism have, as a consequence, figured largely in the internal politics and debates of these movements. Much contemporary attention is focused on the conditions that can articulate group difference without thereby 'disciplining' group members into a single authentic identity; in the process, many have suggested limits to the very notion of 'a' group. As Shane Phelan puts it in her discussion of lesbian feminism in the United States: 'Politics that ignores our identities, that makes them "private", is useless; but non-negotiable identities will enslave us whether they are imposed from within or without.'[23] Speaking from the British context, Stuart Hall has suggested that we should pay more attention to the ways in which black experience is a diaspora experience, one in which the constructions of history and politics and culture are therefore fundamental, and not to be captured through notions of an essential black subject.[24] He talks here of 'the end of innocence', 'the recognition of the extraordinary diversity of subject positions, social experiences and cultural identities which compose the category "black"',[25] and the impossibility of grounding the black subject or black experience in the essentialisms of nature or any other such guarantee.

These arguments cut across the balder distinction between ideas and presence, for what is being identified are differences in experiences and identities within what has hitherto been seen as an all-embracing category or group. It is not simply that 'black' people or women or lesbians will disagree among themselves as to the appropriate policies and ideas and goals (they will vote for different parties, for example), but that their very senses of what it means to be black or female or lesbian will necessarily vary. In the context of the political movements with which these arguments engage, there seem to be two important implications. One is that the diversity of 'subject positions' should be reflected within the organizational structures that define who does or doesn't get into the conversation. There should be no privileging of some voices as more authentic than others, and no coercive imposition of a supposedly unified point of view. The other implication, however, is that there is no way of knowing in advance whether this diversity has been successfully acknowledged. Any prior setting of the boundaries risks restoring some version of the authentic subject, for even if the boundaries are significantly pluralized, they still define in advance what are the appropriate or relevant differences. Thus Stuart Hall argues that it is no longer possible to represent 'the black subject' without reference to class, gender, sexuality, ethnicity. But if this were taken as a series of guidelines about the different characteristics that must be covered within the membership of some campaigning organization, that would hardly be doing justice to his critique.

This is a problem that in some way or another besets every radical initiative, whether it is a matter of deciding whom to invite to address a meeting, who is to join an editorial board, or which groups are to participate in a campaign. We have become sufficiently attuned to the politics of presence to distrust the notion that anyone can 'stand in' for anyone else, and sufficiently alert to the coercive powers of homogeneity to want to reflect diversity. But the critiques of essentialism deprive us of any simple mechanism for achieving the appropriate balance, and remind us that diversity is too great to be captured in any categorial list.

In the context of political movements, this is not such a serious difficulty. At their best, such movements already enjoy the kind of robust democracy that is proposed as an ideal for the polity as a whole: allowing for, indeed incapable of containing, the kind of contestation and mutual challenge that acknowledges difference and simultaneously disrupts it. The vehemence of debate indicates both a recurrent tendency towards essentialism and a continuous challenge to this: people are tough enough to resist prior classification and far too argumentative to accept someone else's definition of their selves. It is also worth noting that the fluidity of this politics lends itself more easily to a kind of learning through trial and error, for none of the consequences that people may derive from their current understandings of identity or difference is likely to be set in stone. The larger difficulties arise where we seek out more compromised intervention into democracies that are still pretty feeble.

POLITICAL PRESCRIPTIONS FOR THE POLITY AS A WHOLE

When we turn to the political prescriptions that might flow from a new understanding of democracy and difference, we are not dealing in far-off utopias: there is a range of policies already proposed or implemented, and change is neither distant nor unlikely.

The problem, rather, is that because such prescriptions operate in a half-way house of remedial reform, they are less able to resolve the contradictory pressures between the politics of ideas and the politics of presence. The kinds of mechanism I have in mind include the quota systems adopted by a number of European political parties to achieve gender parity in elected assemblies, the redrawing of boundaries around black-majority constituencies to raise the number of black politicians elected in the United States, and the longer-established power-sharing practices of those European consociational democracies that have distributed executive power and economic resources between different religious and linguistic groups. In each of these instances, the initiatives operate within the framework of an existing (not very robust) democracy. Tensions that might more readily resolve themselves in a future ferment of activity and deliberation become more acute in what everyone knows is a compromise situation.

All the more immediate proposals for reform insist on deliberate intervention as necessary to break the link between social structures of inequality or exclusion and the political reflection of these in levels of participation and influence. All of them also agree in looking to specifically *political* mechanisms—rather than, or sometimes as well as, longer term social transformation. They take issue therefore with the complacencies of a free market in politics, which sees political equality as sufficiently guaranteed by the procedures of one person one vote; they also challenge the more standard radical alternative, which has focused attention on prior economic or social change. Whatever their differences on other issues, the traditions of revolutionary Marxism and welfare state social reform have tended to agree on a broadly materialist analysis of the problems of political equality, seeing equal political access as something that depends on more fundamental changes in social, economic, and sometimes educational conditions. The current interest in achieving equal or proportionate presence reverses this, focusing instead on institutional mechanisms—its critics would say 'political fixes'—that can achieve more immediate change.

The roots of this reversal lie partly in frustration with what has proved an unbelievably slow process of structural transformation (*first* eliminate the sexual division of labour . . . the racial ordering of income and education and employment . . . the class patterning that decides children's futures—is it any wonder we search for short cuts?). But political frustration is not new, and people do not normally change direction just because things take so long. The additional impetus comes from the kind of arguments already outlined, which suggest that the range of political ideas and preferences is seriously constrained by the characteristics of the people who convey them. In a more traditional base–superstructure model, we were advised to concentrate first on generating the social conditions for equal citizenship, then to enjoy the political equalization that flows from this. Such an approach, however, treats policy choices as more straightforward than they are, and fails to observe the way that strategies devised for equality reflect the limits of those currently in power.[26] Where policy initiatives are worked out *for* rather than *with* a politically excluded constituency, they rarely engage all relevant concerns. Again, it is only if we consider the field of politics as already clearly demarcated, with all possible options already in play, that we can put much confidence in such an approach.

I do not discount the criticism that regards institutional mechanisms for achieving equal or proportionate presence as a species of diversionary 'political fixing', but we should not be required to choose between these and other urgent tasks of social and economic transformation. When political exclusion is such a marked feature of contemporary democratic life, it seems inappropriate to rely on distant prospects of a more robustly participatory democracy and/or structural changes in social and economic conditions. The very distance of such prospects puts a premium on political prescriptions that can be made relevant to representative democracy as currently practised, and most of these will involve some form of affirmative action that can guarantee more equal representation in existing decision-making assemblies. Any specifically political mechanism, however, risks imposing a rigid definition of the identities that have to be included or the interests so far left out. The more complex understanding of multiple identities that change both over time and according to context is a potential casualty here, as is the continuing importance we would all want to attach to political disagreement and debate.

If we consider, for example, the mechanisms that might be appropriate in contemporary Britain to redress racial exclusions, one immediate problem is the diversity of non-white experience, and the major disagreements that have surfaced between taking race or ethnicity or religion as the basis of social identity and political exclusion. When we take race as the central indicator, this encourages a dualism of 'black' or 'white', a division of the universe which is often said to be closer to the political perceptions of Afro-Caribbeans than to the self-definitions of the significantly more numerous Asians. Tariq Modood, indeed, has argued that 'the concept of Black is harmful to Asians and is a form of political identity that most Asians do not accept as their primary public identity'.[27] But if we take ethnicity or religion instead, these are felt to be too closely associated with a politics of multicultural-ism that has looked to the greater dissemination of knowledge about ethnic and religious minorities as the way of breaking down racial stereotypes, and has been thought insufficiently vigorous in its challenges to racism *per se*. Alternative ways of defining group identities or redressing group exclusions have become loaded with political significance, with an attention to cultural diversity being variously perceived as something that depoliticizes the anti-racist struggle or is a crucial correcive to the simplicities of racial dualism.[28]

What, in this context, is an appropriate mechanism for deal-ing with political exclusion? Can Asians be represented by Afro-Caribbeans, Hindus by Muslims, black women by black men? Or do these groups have nothing more in common than their joint experience of being excluded from power? In their recent book on *Racialized Boundaries*, Floya Anthias and Nira Yuval-Davies con-clude that 'the form of political representation which has grown out of identity politics and equal opportunities and which has attempted to represent social difference more genuinely, has cre-ated an impossible mission for itself',[29] and that what is a positive diversity of overlapping identities becomes dangerously constrained in efforts towards proportional representation. But does this mean that nothing can be done: that given the risks, on the one hand, of an imposed and misleading uniformity, and the absurdities, on the other, of an endless search for sufficiently pluralized categories, we have to abandon the quest for specifically political mechan-isms? Caucuses and quotas are the most obvious political mech-anisms for dealing with political exclusion, yet both of these depend on a prior categorization of the basis on which people have been excluded. Neither seems adequate to the complexity of political identities.

The politics that has developed in the United States around the strategy of black-majority, single-member constituencies might seem more straightforward, for it seems clear enough that it is race rather than ethnicity that has been at issue in the political exclusion of African-Americans, and racial bloc voting is plausibly described as 'the single most salient feature of contemporary political life'.[30] But even so, a political resolution that privileges race as the prime consideration can make it more difficult for people to articulate what are complex and multiple identities: can obscure tensions, for example, around gender and class, can block out major disagreements over policy preferences and political ideas. The implication that black representatives are representative merely by virtue of being black is inevitably problematic, even where 'blackness' is a less contested category.

Those who consider the problems of political equality as adequately dealt with by provision for the equal right to vote will be happy to rest their case there, but criticism of the strategy of black electoral success has not been confined to these quarters. Equally powerful criticism comes from those who regard proportionate presence as a necessary but insufficient condition, and are concerned that the focus on numbers alone can reduce political accountability, limit prospects for multiracial coalition, and undermine the urgency of policy debate.[31] There is, in other words, a strong sense of the tensions that can develop between a politics of presence and a politics of ideas. But instead of resolving this by opting for the second over the first, critics have looked to alternative patterns of representation that can make it possible to combine the two. Some of the most innovative work in this area comes from those pressing for a return to the more competitive politics of multimember constituencies but based on forms of proportional representation and cumulative voting that would maintain the scope for electing representatives from minority groups.[32] It is felt, in other words, that mechanisms *can* be devised which continue the gains in black political presence without forcing an either/or choice between the politics of presence and the politics of ideas.

European initiatives on gender parity can also be seen as successfully negotiating the competing demands of ideas and presence—and here we enter the realm of policies already in position rather than proposals in contested debate. The favoured strategy involves pressuring existing political parties to introduce a more balanced ticket of both women and men in their candidates for winnable seats, thus maintaining accountability through party policies and programmes while changing the gender composition of elected assemblies. Often enough the mechanism has been a straightforward quota, which has contributed to a remarkable increase in the numbers of women elected in the Nordic countries. Critics of such strategies usually rest their case on the paucity of 'experienced' women, the potential loss of 'good' men to politics, and the risk that the overall calibre of politicians (not too high in my opinion) will fall. They do not dwell particularly on the essentialist presumptions of a 'woman's perspective', or the dangerous potential for women pressing only narrowly sectional concerns. There are just too many women for them to be considered as a unified or sectional group, and they are spread across every class or ethnic or religious dimension and every conceivable political persuasion. When it is applied to women, the politics of presence does not seriously disrupt the politics of competing ideas; it is relatively easy to pursue both of these together.

Outside the more established democracies of Europe and the United States, the arguments often start from the opposite direction, a feeling that *who* is to be represented has so far taken precedence over *what*, and that what is missing is the higher politics of ideas. One might think, for example, of the abuse of kinship networks and ethnic solidarities by political elites in post-colonial Africa, many of whom evacuated the terrain of contested policies and ideals to cultivate a power base around exclusionary identities. When the colonial powers retreated from Africa, they left behind societies in which the state had become the main avenue for economic and social advancement, and where the politics of patronage was almost doomed to flourish. In this context, people lived under what seemed an absence of politics, with the contrast between a civilian or military regime seeming of far less consequence than whether you had access to any of the rulers. As ethnic connections emerged as one of the main routes of access, ethnic rivalries became literally deadly, even when the ethnicities in question were relatively recent creations.[33] It is against this background that African radicals and writers have so eloquently called for a politics based on vision and ideals.[34]

Through all these examples, the biggest mistake is to set up ideas as the opposite of political presence: to treat ideas as totally separate from the people who carry them, or worry exclusively about the people without giving a thought to their policies and ideas. It should be said, however, that this is not such a frequent mistake as the caricatures suggest, and that those exploring equal or proportionate presence rarely regard it as a substitute for the politics of competing ideas. If anything, the most acute criticisms of the politics of presence have come from those most committed to challenging political exclusions, and the debate has long shifted beyond its either/or axis. What is, perhaps, emerging is that

491

the more satisfactory ways of redressing group exclusion are those which are the less group-specific. This seems to be the case in relation to gender quotas, if only because the category of 'woman' is so inclusive of other kinds of difference and division that it leaves open the necessary space for a multiplicity of political identities. It also seems to be the case in the proposals that have developed around the implementation of the Voting Rights Act in the United States, which have moved away from the more tightly drawn voting districts that provide a 'safe seat' for minority representatives towards a larger geographical constituency that can no longer pretend to contain only one voice.

Such developments acknowledge the danger in pre-emptive classifications of people's political identities, and are well aware that essentialist definitions of the groups that have been excluded can work to reduce political accountability and debate. They none the less take issue with the more traditional treatment of diversity and difference as simply a matter of contested ideas. The overly cerebral understanding of difference has not engaged sufficiently with the problems of political presence, for it has encouraged an unacceptable level of complacency over the homogeneity of political elites. We can no longer pretend that the full range of ideas and preferences and alternatives has been adequately represented when those charged with the job of representation are all white or all male or all middle-class; or that democracies complete their task of political equality when they establish a free market in political ideas. One would not want to take up permanent residence in the half-way house of remedial reform, but mechanisms should be—and can be—devised that address the problems of group exclusion without fixing the boundaries of character of each group.

Notes

1. I summarize and discuss many of these arguments in *Engendering Democracy* (University Park: University of Pennsylvania State Press, 1991). See also Jane Flax, 'Beyond Equality: Gender, Justice and Difference', in G. Bock and S. James (eds.), *Beyond Equality and Difference* (London: Routledge, 1992).
2. Robert A. Dahl, *Democracy and Its Critics* (New Haven, Conn.: Yale University Press, 1989).
3. George Kateb, 'The Moral Distinctiveness of Representative Democracy', *Ethics*, 91/3 (1981): 361.

4. Cited by Silvia Vegetti Finzi, 'Female Identity Between Sexuality and Maternity', in Bock and James, *Beyond Equality and Difference*, 128.
5. Sheila Rowbotham, 'The Women's Movement and Organising for Socialism', in S. Rowbotham, L. Segal, and H. Wainwright, *Beyond the Fragments: Feminism and the Making of Socialism* (London: Newcastle Socialist Centre and Islington Community Press, 1979), 61.
6. Hanna F. Pitkin, *The Concept of Representation* (Berkeley: University of California Press, 1967), 226.
7. See Shane Phelan's discussion of the way that lesbian feminists in the US came to reject liberalism: *Identity Politics: Lesbian Feminism and the Limits of Community* (Philadelphia: Temple University Press, 1989).
8. See Susan Mendus, *Toleration and the Limits of Liberalism* (London: Macmillan, 1989).
9. I do not know if this is intrinsic to tolerance, but I suspect it is. If we could imagine a world in which difference were genuinely detached from power—in which there really were multiple differences and none carried more weight than any other—than I am not sure we would be talking of the need for toleration. See also Kirstie McClure, 'Difference, Diversity and the Limits of Toleration', *Political Theory*, 18/3 (1990).
10. I owe this formulation to Peter Jones's paper 'Groups, Beliefs and Identities', presented at the European Consortium for Political Research, Leiden, Apr. 1993.
11. All these points can be found in Cynthia V. Ward, 'The Limits of' "Liberal Republicanism": Why Group-Based Remedies and Republican Citizenship Don't Mix', *Columbia Law Review*, 91/3 (1991). In querying the notion that *only* the members of particular disadvantaged groups can understand or represent their interests, she might usefully turn this question round to ask whether such understanding or representation is possible without the presence of *any* members of the disadvantaged groups.
12. Susan Mendus, 'Losing the Faith: Feminism and Demcoracy', in John Dunn (ed.), *Democracy: The Unfinished Journey 508* BC *to* AD *1993* (Oxford: Oxford University Press, 1992), 216.
13. Charles Taylor, *The Ethics of Authenticity* (Cambridge, Mass.: Harvard University Press, 1992); Charles Taylor and Amy Gutmann, *Multiculturalism and The Politics of Recognition* (Cambridge, Mass.: Harvard University Press, 1992).
14. Cass Sunstein, 'Beyond the Republican Revival', *Yale Law Journal*, 97/8 (1988).
15. William Connolly, *Identity/Difference: Democratic Negotiations of Political Paradox* (Ithaca, NY: Cornell University Press, 1991).
16. Ibid. 197.
17. Ibid. 211.

18. Ibid. 213.

19. In a review of Connolly's book, Iris Young describes his prescriptions as 'therapies'. *Political Theory*, 20/3 (1992): 514.

20. Adriana Cavarero, 'Equality and Sexual Difference: Amnesia in Political Thought', in Bock and James, *Beyond Equality and Difference*, 36.

21. Phelan, *Identity Politics*. Phelan notes in particular the rows that broke out over sado-masochism, and whether this was an 'acceptable' part of lesbian identity.

22. See the essays in Tariq Modood, *Not Easy Being British: Colour, Culture and Citizenship* (Stoke-on-Trent: Runnymede Trust and Trentham Books, 1992). The largest non-white group in Britain is Asians of Indian origin, many of whom have felt that the racial dualism of anti-racist politics rendered them invisible.

23. Phelan, *Identity Politics*, 170.

24. Stuart Hall, 'New Ethnicities', in J. Donald and A. Rattansi (eds.), *'Race', Culture and Difference* (London: Sage and Open University Press, 1992).

25. Ibid. 254.

26. Obvious examples include the post-war preoccupation with full employment as a condition for equal citizenship, where full employment was either unthinkingly equated with full employment for men or else extended formally to include women without any serious consideration of the structural changes that would then become necessary to reorder the relationship between paid and unpaid work. Will Kymlicka provides a different example in his discussion of the Trudeau reforms, which set out to promote more equal citizenship in Canada but equated full and equal participation for the native Indian population with a colour-blind constitution that would dismantle the system of segregated reserves. Though widely applauded by the country's media and even opposition parties, the proposals had to be withdrawn in the face of almost unanimous opposition from the Indians themselves. Kymlicka, *Liberalism, Community and Culture* (Oxford: Clarendon Press, 1989).

27. Modood, *Not Easy Being British*, 29.

28. For an excellent overview of these debates, and an attempt to push beyond them, see the essays in Donald and Rattansi, *'Race', Culture and Difference*.

29. Floya Anthias and Nira Yuval-Davies, *Racialized Boundaries: Race, Nation, Gender, Colour and Class and the Anti-Racist Struggle* (London: Routledge, 1992), 192.

30. S. Issacharoff, 'Polarized Voting and the Political Process: The Transformation of Voting Rights Jurisprudence', *Michigan Law Review*, 90/7 (1992): 1855.

31. Bernard Grofman and Chandler Davidson (eds.), *Controversies in Minority Voting: The Voting Rights Act in Perspective* (Washington,

DC: Brookings Institution, 1992) provides a comprehensive range of the arguments that have developed around minority representation.

32. Lani Guinier, 'The Triumph of Tokenism: The Voting Rights Act and the Theory of Black Electoral Success', *Michigan Law Review*, 89/5 (1991); 'No Two Seats: The Elusive Quest for Political Equality', *Virginia Law Review*, 77/8 (1991). I discuss this material at greater length in 'Political Inclusion and Political Presence. Or, Why Does It Matter Who Our Representatives Are?', paper presented at the Joint Sessions of the European Consortium on Political Research, Leiden, 2–7 Apr. 1993.

33. Think here of the Nigerian civil war and the attempted secession of Biafra. The Ibo people who provided the ethnic basis for Biafra only came into substantial existence as a unified 'people' through this war.

34. See Chinua Achebe's novels and essays, esp. *The Anthills of the Savannah* and *The Trouble with Nigeria*.

Index